Arguing Across the Disciplines

Arguing Across the Disciplines

A Rhetoric and Reader

Stuart Hirschberg

Rutgers: The State University of New Jersey, Newark

Terry Hirschberg

New York San Francisco Boston
London Toronto Sydney Tokyo Singapore Madrid
Mexico City Munich Paris Cape Town Hong Kong Montreal

Acquisitions Editor: Lauren A. Finn
Marketing Manager: Sandra McGuire
Production Manager: Denise Phillip
Project Coordination, Text Design, and Electronic Page Makeup: Pre-Press Company, Inc.
Cover Designer/Manager: Wendy Ann Fredericks
Cover Photos: Clockwise from top right: David Harrigan/Super Stock; Ryoichi Utsami/Amana Images/Getty Images; and Christine Balderas/Stockphoto
Photo Researcher: Chrissy McIntyre
Senior Manufacturing Buyer: Alfred C. Dorsey
Printer and Binder: R. R. Donnelley & Sons
Cover Printer: Phoenix Color Corporation

For permission to use copyrighted material, grateful acknowledgment is made to the copyright holders on pp. 581–585, which are hereby made part of this copyright page.

Library of Congress Cataloging-in-Publication Data
Hirschberg, Stuart.
  Arguing across the disciplines : a rhetoric and reader / Stuart and Terry Hirschberg.
    p. cm.
  Includes bibliographical references and index.
  ISBN 0-321-41925-1
  1. English language--Rhetoric--Problems, exercises, etc. 2. Persuasion (Rhetoric)--Problems, exercises, etc. 3. College readers. I. Hirschberg, Terry. II. Title.

PE1431.H56 2007
808.0427--dc22

2006025767

Visit us at www.ablongman.com

ISBN 0-321-41925-1
1 2 3 4 5 6 7 8 9 10—DOC—09 08 07 06

For our oldest fan,
Bessie Marcus,
with many thanks.

Contents

3 Supporting Arguments 72

4 Arguing in the Disciplines 115

7   Writing and Refuting Arguments   223

PART :: 2   357

Liberal Arts

Rhetorical Contents

Contents by the Kind of Claim

Arguments That Make Value Judgments

Arguments That Propose Solutions

Contents by Theme and Subject

Knowledge of Animate and Inanimate Worlds

The Mind and the Spirit

The Arts of Civilization

Preface

Arguing Across the Disciplines is designed to meet the needs of instructors teaching composition courses whose focus is the critical reading and writing of arguments across the curriculum. Students are shown why argument is important for the papers they will be writing in various courses. They can also learn a valuable method of reasoning through which they can critically evaluate events and facts and communicate their opinions, value judgments, and solutions to problems.

As a Rhetoric

Chapters 1, 2, 3, 4, 5, and 6 introduce students to the skills of critical reading, note taking, and summarizing, and to the basic strategies of argument, in order to show them how to identify central ideas and techniques as a first step in understanding and analyzing arguments. The discussion, based on the Stephen Toulmin model of claim, warrant, backing, support, and qualifier, examines different kinds of arguments, explores basic argumentative strategies, and places particular emphasis on the importance of underlying assumptions, definition, and types of evidence in different disciplines. The uses (and abuses) of logic and language in argument are discussed in depth. Selections illustrating points in the discussion are on topics ranging from privacy in Japan, educating moviegoers, marketing toward children, angiosperms, black English, conditioning slaves, bystander noninvolvement, and salmon migration, to population overload, business ethics, hypocrisy, and unanimous juries.

Chapter 7 provides guidance in writing effective arguments and discusses the important points of developing invention strategies, arriving at a thesis, adapting arguments for different audiences, using an outline, and revising a rough draft. The important role of critical thinking in bridging the gap between analyzing someone else's argument and generating one's own ideas is examined in detail. Students are introduced to the criteria important in evaluating the arguments of others and are provided with a sample student evaluation of an argument as well as a sample student refutation of someone else's argument.

Chapter 8 presents the important criteria by which to evaluate the design of documents and images. Students are asked to consider the purpose and audience for visual texts and to think critically about the explicit and implicit agendas they communicate. This chapter also discusses the use of charts and graphs, and principles of Web page design.

Chapter 9 introduces students to the methods of inquiry used to generate an argument from sources. The process of writing an argument from sources is covered step by step, including the crucial aspects of finding a question to answer, evaluating source materials, formulating the working thesis, note-taking procedures, quoting, writing and revising a rough draft, and using the MLA, APA, and CSE styles of documentation.

Additional tables of contents by subject and theme, kinds of argumentative claims, and rhetorical modes are included to allow the text to accommodate a variety of teaching approaches.

As a Reader

Part II provides readings categorized by disciplines in the liberal arts, social sciences, and the sciences.

The spectrum of subjects and points of view represented in these selections and their varying lengths and levels of difficulty will accommodate a variety of teaching approaches. The annotated table of contents identifies the discipline and central idea of each selection. End-of-selection questions explore the substance of each reading and its argumentative strategies. These questions are intended to engage students' interest in the key issues in the text and to direct their attention to the ways in which authors adapt their arguments for specific audiences: the general public, colleagues, or professionals in a particular academic field of study.

Throughout the Rhetoric and the Reader there are images that are typical of those that students encounter in everyday life and in argumentive contexts (cartoons, graphics, photographs, paintings, line drawings, and advertisements). Important principles of argument are illustrated by clear and timely examples including short editorials, personal accounts, and, most frequently, essays written for academic audiences.

Supplements

INSTRUCTOR'S MANUAL

An accompanying Instructor's Manual provides (1) strategies for teaching argumentative writing and approaches for teaching each selection, (2) suggested answers to the end-of-selection questions, (3) sample syllabi, and (4) supplemental bibliographies, Web sites on the subjects and authors, and additional activities.

MYCOMPLAB (WWW.MYCOMPLAB.COM)

A dynamic and comprehensive site that will engage students as it helps them to learn, MyCompLab provides market-leading online resources for grammar, writing, and research—all in one easy-to-use place. Here are just some of the highlights:

WRITING RESOURCES Exchange (online peer review tool); Visual Analysis instruction and exercises; Video tutorials on stages of the writing process; Activities (100 activities, some video- and image-based); Model Documents.

RESEARCH RESOURCES Citation Diagnostics and Exercises (MLA and APA); ResearchNavigator (access to searchable databases of credible sources and access to Autocite, a bibliography-maker); Avoiding Plagiarism and Evaluating Sources tutorials; Video tutorials on stages of the research process.

GRAMMAR RESOURCES Diagnostics; Common Error video tutorials; Exercise-Zone (over 4,600 self-grading practice exercises, including sentence and paragraph editing); ESL ExerciseZone.

OTHER RESOURCES Students using MyCompLab receive complimentary access to **Longman's English Tutor Center**. Instructors who order a MyCompLab package for their course can receive a complimentary subscription to **MyDropBox**, a leading online plagiarism detection service.

MyCompLab is available in four versions: Website with Grade Tracker, Course-Compass, Blackboard, WebCT. *Please contact your local Allyn & Bacon/Longman representative for more information.*

Acknowledgments

We want to acknowledge our appreciation for the encouragement and enthusiasm of our editor, Lauren Finn, and our gratitude to all those teachers of composition who reviewed the manuscript and offered their thoughtful and constructive suggestions, including Robert A. Schwegler, University of Rhode Island; Patricia Webb, Arizona State University; Bob Broad, Illinois State University; Sarah Kretz

McDowell, Augustana College; Peggy Jolly, University of Alabama at Birmingham; Karla Kitalong, University of Central Florida; Peggy Woods, University of Massachusetts, Amherst; Roy Stamper, North Carolina State University; James Comas, University of Missouri; Barbara Van Voorden, University of Missouri, St. Louis; David Beach, George Mason University; Vicki Martineau, National University; Heidi Emmerling, University of California, Santa Barbara; and Donna Strickland, University of Missouri.

We are grateful to the able staff at Longman including the always patient Carmen O'Donnell. We especially thank Jenny Bevington for obtaining the text permissions, and for her kindness and wonderful sense of humor. We also thank Chrissy McIntyre for obtaining permissions for the images. We would indeed be remiss if we did not heartily thank Joe Opiela for his support in starting this project.

Arguing Across the Disciplines

PART :: 1

CHAPTER

1

READING AND RESPONDING TO ARGUMENTS

Whether our argument concerns public affairs or some other subject we must know some, if not all, of the facts about the subject on which we are to speak and argue. Otherwise, we can have no materials out of which to construct arguments.

—*Aristotle*, Rhetoric

OVERVIEW: This chapter will introduce you to the nature of argument, and the skills of critical reading, note taking, and summarizing, as well as present a sampling of arguments in the liberal arts, social sciences, and the sciences.

The Nature of Argument

Some of the most interesting and effective writing you will encounter takes the form of arguments that seek to persuade a specific audience of the validity of a proposition or claim through logical reasoning supported by facts, examples, data, or other kinds of evidence. Formal arguments differ from assertions based on likes and dislikes or personal opinion. Unlike questions of personal taste, arguments rest on evidence—whether in the form of facts, examples, the testimony of experts, or statistics—that can be brought forward to prove or disprove objectively the thesis in question.

Although the two are frequently confused, argumentation differs from persuasion. Argument is a form of discourse in which statements are offered in support of a claim or proposition. Argument is based on a rational appeal to the understanding and builds its case on a network of logical connections.

The term *argument* also refers to the practice of giving reasons to convince or persuade an audience to accept a claim or proposition. Argument is a form of advocacy and a process of reasoning designed to support a claim. Making an assertion, offering a hypothesis, presenting a claim, and putting forth a moral objection are all ways of arguing. Thus, the process of argument is valuable because it provides an arena for testing the validity, truth, or probability of specific ideas, propositions, and claims.

Whereas argument presents reasons and evidence to gain an audience's intellectual agreement with the validity of a proposition, persuasion also includes appeals to the emotional needs and values of an audience to move them to approve an action or to take an action that the writer recommends. In argument, the audience's agreement with the truth of the claim has more to do with the soundness of the evidence than with the audience's response to the speaker's character and personality. Because of this, arguments are usually addressed to a general, unspecified audience, whereas persuasion is usually keyed to the beliefs, prejudices, interests, values, and needs of a specific audience. For example, political speeches employing persuasive appeals are usually keyed to the specific needs of an immediate audience. Persuasion is influenced by the audience's sense of the speaker's character, presence, and reputation. The difference between argument and persuasion can be clearly seen by comparing the following two short paragraphs.

Kirkpatrick Sale cites the results of various studies as evidence to support his claim that smaller communities are more neighborly and healthier places in which to live:

> There is another way of coming at the question of the human limits of a community. Hans Blumenfeld, the urban planner, suggests starting with the idea of the size at which "every person knows every other person by face, by voice, and by name" and adds, "I would say that it begins to fade out in villages with much more than 500 or 600 population." Gordon Rattray Taylor, the British science writer, has estimated that there is a "natural social unit" for humans, defined by "the largest group in which every individual can form some personal estimate of the significance of a majority of the other individuals in the group, in relation to himself," and he holds that the maximum size of such a group, depending on geography and ease of contact, is about 1,200 people.
>
> —*Kirkpatrick Sale*, Human Scale

Henry Fairlie, on the other hand, claims that life in a small community is subject to intrusion and loss of privacy and characterizes the typical village shop as follows:

> But the village shop, as one knew it personally, and as one can read about it in fiction, was usually an unattractive place, and frequently a malignant one. The gossip which was exchanged was, as often as not, inaccurate and cruel. Although there were exceptions, one's main memory of the village shopkeeper, man and

wife, is of faces which were hard and sharp and mean, leaning forward to whisper in ears that were cocked and turned to hear all that they could of the misfortunes or the disgrace of a neighbour. Whisper! Whisper! Whisper! This has always been the chief commodity of the village shop. And not only whispers, because the village shopkeeper, informed or misinformed, could always apply sanctions against those to whom disgrace or misfortune was imputed.

—*Henry Fairlie*, The Spoiled Child of the Western World

Notice how Sale relies on evidence and the testimony of experts to support his claim that small communities promote peace, social harmony, trust, and well-being. The character of Sale as a person is less important than the facts he presents to support his thesis or claim.

By contrast, Fairlie's description of the stifling character of small-town life is communicated by picturesque language that is designed to appeal to the imagination and arouse the emotions of his audience against this life. The audience's sense of Fairlie as a person is important, since his own observations are presented as a source of evidence drawn from his past experiences. There is no objective evidence as such in this passage. Fairlie's ability to appeal to the emotions of his audience through skillful use of provocative language is the only evidence he presents. Yet, it would be difficult to say which of these two passages is more persuasive. The point here is that the difference between argument and persuasion is one of degree. Arguments tend to emphasize appeals to logic, whereas persuasion tries to sway an audience through a calculated manipulation of the audience's needs and values. Real-world arguments, however, should be a blend of the two.

Rhetoric and Persuasion

Rhetoric came into existence as a specific field of study in the early part of the fifth century BC in Sicily to enable ordinary citizens to make an effective case concerning why they should be entitled to recover property that had been seized by a dictatorial tyrant. The claimants had to present their case without supporting documentation and construct an argument solely on the basis of inference and probability. This emphasis on discovering, arranging, and presenting arguments to enhance the probability of a claim defines the distinctive nature of argumentative discourse from this beginning to the present day.

The term *rhetoric* has acquired negative connotations of language calculated to deceive; "mere rhetoric" is associated with stylistic flourishes devoid of content, or empty talk without action. It was not always thus. For Aristotle, rhetoric meant discovering all the available means of persuasion in any given situation where the truth could not be known for certain (Aristotle, *Rhetoric*, Book I, Chapter 1, lines 26–27). Aristotle, of course, excluded coercive or violent means and concerned himself solely with systematic and skillful efforts that one person could use to get another to think in a certain way.

Rhetoric in its original context referred to the process of seeking out the best arguments, arranging them in the most effective way, and presenting them in the manner best calculated to win agreement from a particular audience.

Rhetoric is concerned with those questions in the realm of the contingent where the truth is not able to be known (Aristotle, *Rhetoric*, Book I, Chapter 2, line 15). It is up to arguers on all sides of the issues to find the most effective means for persuading audiences to believe or at least consider the probable truth of their claims.

Normally, the kinds of questions dealt with are those that are open to different interpretations; rhetoric, therefore, is concerned with the methods or strategies arguers may use in seeking acceptance of their position from an audience. Aristotle said there are three means by which people could persuade each other to adopt a certain point of view or approve a course of action. Broadly stated, these three elements—which are all present in some degree in every successful instance of persuasion—he identified as (1) the appeal to the audience's reason (*logos*), (2) the appeal to the audience's emotions (*pathos*), and (3) the degree of confidence that the speaker's character or personality could inspire in the audience (*ethos*) (Aristotle, *Rhetoric*, Book I, Chapter 2, lines 1–4).

The most persuasive arguments appeal to the "whole person"—to the intellect, the conscience, and the emotions.

The goal of all three of these appeals is the same, although each takes a different approach to achieve the same end of persuading or increasing the credibility or probable truth of the claim. The appeal to the audience's reason (*logos*) is often associated with formal logic and the citation of relevant facts and objective evidence (statistics, case histories, surveys, facts, examples, precedents). Well-constructed arguments that genuinely appeal to reason are indeed persuasive. And even though Aristotle made the point that appeals to an audience's deepest desires, needs, and values need not be deceptive, arguers soon became aware that appeals to the emotions (*pathos*), such as fear, greed, love of comfort, or desire for status, could substitute for appeals to reason, especially in those cases where the persuader had little evidence or lacked the skill necessary to construct a logical argument. The third means Aristotle identified (*ethos*) depended on the degree to which the arguer could win the confidence of the audience. The credibility and persuasiveness of the arguer's claims would be in direct proportion to the audience's view of the speaker or writer as a person of good sense, good moral character, and good intentions (Aristotle, *Rhetoric*, Book I, Chapter 2, line 13).

It is in the context of these three methods that we will discuss arguments—what makes some persuasive, others ineffective, some legitimate, and others deceptive—and look at the separate elements that collectively constitute effective argumentation. Even though at points we may, for the sake of clarity, discuss elements of argumentation separately from elements of persuasion, the two are inextricably intertwined in any successful instance of persuasion.

The purpose, then, of argument is to persuade an audience to accept the validity or probability of an idea, proposition, or claim. Essentially, a claim is an assertion that would be met with skepticism if it were not supported with sound evidence and logical reasoning. Argument plays a key role for writers who use the forums provided by newspapers and popular magazines as well as the more specialized literary and scientific journals to persuade colleagues and the general public alike of the truth of their ideas, discoveries, viewpoints, and conclusions.

Critical Reading for Ideas and Organization

One of the most important skills to have in your repertoire is the ability to survey unfamiliar articles, essays, or excerpts and come away with an accurate understanding of what the author wanted to communicate and how the material is organized. On the first and in subsequent readings of any of the selections in this text, especially the longer ones, pay particular attention to the title, look for introductory and concluding paragraphs (with special emphasis on the author's statement or restatement of central ideas), identify the headings and subheadings (and determine the relationship between these and the title), and identify any unusual terms necessary to fully understand the author's concepts.

As you work your way through an essay, you might look for cues to enable you to recognize the main parts of the argument or help you perceive the overall organization of the article. Once you find the main thesis, underline it. Then work your way through fairly rapidly, identifying the main ideas and the sequence in which they are presented. As you identify an important idea, ask yourself how this idea relates to the thesis statement you underlined or to the idea expressed in the title.

Identifying a Thesis

Identifying a thesis involves discovering the idea that serves as the focus of the essay. The thesis is often stated in the form of a single sentence that asserts the author's response to an issue that others might respond to in different ways. For example, the opening paragraphs of "The Case for Torture" present Michael Levin's view that challenges conventional assumptions:

> It is generally assumed that torture is impermissible, a throwback to a more brutal age. Enlightened societies reject it outright and regimes suspected of using it risk the wrath of the United States.
>
> I believe this attitude is unwise. **There are situations in which torture is not merely permissible but morally mandatory.** Moreover, these situations are moving from the realm of the imagination to fact.

The thesis (in bold type) represents the writer's view of a subject or topic from a certain perspective. Here, Levin states a view that will serve as a focus for his essay on the permissibility of torture.

As we can see, the thesis identifies the specific issue and presents the writer's opinion on it. It also makes it easier for readers to follow the author's reasoning offered to support it. An effective thesis suggests a clear direction for the argument. Thus, Levin is obliged to present examples that substantiate his claim ("there are situations in which torture is not merely permissible but morally mandatory").

Writers often place the thesis in the first paragraph or group of paragraphs so that the readers will be able to perceive the relationship between supporting evidence and this main idea.

As you read, you might wish to underline the topic sentence or main idea of each paragraph or section (since key ideas are often developed over the course of several paragraphs). Jot it down in your own words in the margins, identify supporting statements and evidence (such as examples, statistics, and the testimony of authorities), and try to discover how the author organizes the material to support the development of important ideas. To identify supporting material, look for any ideas more specific than the main idea that is used to support it. Also look for instances where the author uses examples, descriptions, statistics, quotations from authorities, comparisons, or graphs to make the main idea clearer or prove it to be true.

Pay particular attention to important transitional words, phrases, or paragraphs to better see the relationships among major sections of the selection. Noticing how certain words or phrases act as transitions to link paragraphs or sections together will dramatically improve your reading comprehension. Also look for section summaries, where the author draws together several preceding ideas.

Writers use certain words to signal the starting point of an argument. If you detect any of the following terms, look for the main idea they introduce:

> since, because, for, as, follows from, as shown by, inasmuch as, otherwise, as indicated by, the reason is that, for the reason that, may be inferred from, may be derived from, may be deduced from, in view of the fact that

An especially important category of words is that which includes signals that the author will be stating a conclusion. Words and phrases to look for are these:

> therefore, hence, thus, so accordingly, in consequence, it follows that, we may infer, I conclude that, in conclusion, in summary, which shows that, which means that, and which entails, consequently, proves that, as a result, which implies that, which allows us to infer, points to the conclusion that

You may find it helpful to create a running dialogue with the author in the margins, posing and then trying to answer the basic questions *who, what, where, when, and why,* and to note observations on how the main idea of the article, essay, or book is related to the title. These notes can later be used to evaluate how effectively any specific section contributes to the overall line of thought.

Responding to What You Read

When reading an essay that seems to embody a certain value system, try to examine any assumptions or beliefs the writer expects the audience to share. How is this assumption related to the author's purpose? If you do not agree with these assumptions, has the writer provided sound reasons and evidence to persuade you to change your mind?

You might describe the author's tone or voice and try to assess how much it contributed to the essay. How effectively does the writer use authoritities, statistics, or examples to support the claim? Does the author identify the assumptions or values on which his or her views are based? Are they ones with which you would agree or disagree? To what extent does the author use the emotional connotations of language to try to persuade his or her reader? Do you see anything unworkable or disadvantageous about the solutions offered as an answer to the problem the essay addresses? All these and many other ways of analyzing someone else's essay can be used to create your own. Here are some specific guidelines to help you.

When evaluating an essay, consider what the author's purpose is in writing it. Was it to inform, explain, solve a problem, make a recommendation, amuse, enlighten, or achieve some combination of these goals? How is the tone or voice the author projects toward the reader related to his or her purpose in writing the essay?

You may find it helpful to write short summaries after each major section to determine whether you understand what the writer is trying to communicate. These summaries can then serve as a basis for an analysis of how successfully the author employs reasons, examples, statistics, and expert testimony to support and develop his or her main points.

For example, if the essay you are analyzing cites authorities to support a claim, assess whether the authorities bring the most timely opinions to bear on the subject, or display any obvious biases, and determine whether they are experts in that particular field. Watch for experts described as "often quoted" or "highly placed reliable sources" without accompanying names, credentials, or appropriate documentation. If the experts cited offer what purports to be a reliable interpretation of facts, consider whether the writer also quotes equally trustworthy experts who hold opposing views.

If statistics are cited to support a point, judge whether they derive from verifiable and trustworthy sources. Also, evaluate whether the author has interpreted them in ways that are beneficial to his or her case, whereas someone who held an opposing view could interpret them quite differently. If real-life examples are presented to support the author's opinions, determine whether they are representative or whether they are too atypical to be used as evidence. If the author relies on hypothetical examples or analogies to dramatize ideas that otherwise would be hard to grasp, judge whether these examples are too far-fetched to back up the claims being made. If the essay depends on the stipulated definition of a term that might be defined in different ways, check whether the author provides clear reasons to indicate why one definition rather than another is preferable.

As you list observations about the various elements of the article you are analyzing, take a closer look at the underlying assumptions and see whether you can locate and distinguish between those assumptions that are explicitly stated and those that are implicit. Once the author's assumptions are identified, you can compare them with your own beliefs about the subject, determine whether these assumptions are commonly held, and make a judgment as to their validity. Would you readily agree with these assumptions? If not, has the author provided sound reasons and supporting evidence to persuade you to change your mind?

MARKING AS YOU READ

The most effective way to think about what you read is to make notes as you read. Making notes as you read forces you to go slowly and think carefully about each sentence. This process is sometimes called annotating the text, and all you need is a pen or a pencil. There are as many styles of annotating as there are readers, and you will discover your own favorite technique once you have done it a few times. Some readers prefer to underline major points or statements and jot down their reaction to it in the margin. Others prefer to summarize each paragraph or section to help them follow the author's line of thinking. Other readers circle key words or phrases necessary to understand the main ideas. Feel free to use your notes as a kind of conversation with the text. Ask questions. Express doubts. Mark unfamiliar words or phrases to look up later. If the paragraphs are not already numbered, you might wish to number them as you go to help you keep track of your responses. Try to distinguish the main ideas from supporting points and examples. Most important, go slowly and think about what you are reading. Try to discover whether the author makes a credible case for the conclusions he or she reaches. One last point: Take a close look at the idea expressed in the title before *and* after you read the essay to see how it relates to the main idea.

DISTINGUISHING BETWEEN FACT AND OPINION

As you read, distinguish between statements of fact and statements of opinion. Statements of fact relate information that is widely accepted and objectively verifiable. Facts are not open for debate. They can be easily verified through observation or because they are presented in trustworthy reference books such as dictionaries and encyclopedias. Facts are not usually disputed since they can be established empirically or by a consensus of experts. Facts are used as evidence to support the claim made by the thesis.

By contrast, an opinion is a personal interpretation of data or a belief or feeling that however strongly presented should not be mistaken by the reader for objective evidence. For example, consider the following claim by Edward T. Hall in "Hidden Culture":

> Each culture and each country has its own language of space, which is just as unique as the spoken language, frequently more so. In England, for example, there are no offices for the members of Parliament. In the United States, our congressmen and senators proliferate their offices and their office buildings and simply would not tolerate a no-office situation.

The only statement that could be verified or refuted on the basis of objective data is "In England . . . there are no offices for the members of Parliament." All the other statements, *however persuasive they may seem*, are Hall's interpretations of a situation (multiple offices and office buildings for U.S. government officials) that might be interpreted quite differently by another observer. These statements should not be mistaken for statements of fact.

A reader who could not distinguish between facts and interpretations would be at a severe disadvantage in understanding Hall's essay. Part of the difficulty in separating fact from opinion stems from the difficulty of remaining objective about statements that match our own personal beliefs.

Take a few minutes to read and annotate the following essay. Feel free to "talk back" to the author. You can underline or circle key passages or key terms. You can make observations, raise questions, and express your reactions to what you read.

A Sample Essay for Student Annotation

Edward T. Hall

Hidden Culture

Edward T. Hall (b. 1914) anthropologist and author of The Silent Language *(1959),* The Hidden Dimension *(1966), and* Understanding Cultural Differences *(1990), has taught at Northwestern University, the University of Denver, Bennington College, the Washington School of Psychiatry, the Harvard Business School, and the Illinois Institute of Technology. Best known for his work in intercultural communication, Hall has been a consultant to business and to government agencies. The following selection is drawn from* Beyond Culture *(1981).*

Thinking Critically

As you read Hall's piece, observe how he takes an anthropological, or comparative cultural, approach to his own experiences to understand the hidden logic that governs behavior in Japan.

A few years ago, I became involved in a sequence of events in Japan that completely mystified me, and only later did I learn how an overt act seen from the vantage point of one's own culture can have an entirely different meaning when looked at in the context of the foreign culture. I had been staying at a hotel in downtown Tokyo that had European as well as Japanese-type rooms. The clientele included a few Europeans but was predominantly Japanese. I had been a guest for about ten days and was returning to my room in the middle of an afternoon. Asking for my key at the desk, I took the elevator to my floor. Entering the room, I immediately sensed that something was wrong. Out of place. Different. I was in the wrong room! Someone else's things were distributed around the head of the bed and the table. Somebody else's toilet articles (those of a Japanese male) were in the bathroom. My first thoughts were, "What if I am discovered here? How do I explain my presence to a Japanese who may not even speak English?"

I was close to panic as I realized how incredibly territorial we in the West are. I checked my key again. Yes, it really was mine. Clearly they had moved somebody else into my room. But where was my room now? And where were my belongings? Baffled and mystified, I took the elevator to the lobby. Why hadn't they told me at the desk, instead of letting me risk embarrassment and loss of face by being caught in somebody else's room? Why had they moved me in the first place? It was a nice room and, being sensitive to spaces and how they work, I was loath to give it up. After all, I had told them I would be in the hotel for almost a month. Why this business of moving me around like someone who has been squeezed in without a reservation? Nothing made sense.

At the desk I was told by the clerk, as he sucked in his breath in deference (and embarrassment?) that indeed they had moved me. My particular room had been reserved in advance by somebody else. I was given the key to my new room and discovered that all my personal effects were distributed around the new room almost as though I had done it myself. This produced a fleeting and strange feeling that maybe I wasn't myself. How could somebody else do all those hundred and one little things just the way I did?

Three days later, I was moved again, but this time I was prepared. There was no shock, just the simple realization that I had been moved and that it would now be doubly difficult for friends who had my old room number to reach me. *Tant pis*, I was in Japan. One thing did puzzle me. Earlier, when I had stayed at Frank Lloyd Wright's Imperial Hotel for several weeks, nothing like this had ever happened. What was different? What had changed? Eventually I got used to being moved and would even ask on my return each day whether I was still in the same room.

5 Later, at Hakone, a seaside resort where I was visiting with friends, the first thing that happened was that we were asked to disrobe. We were given *okatas*, and our clothes were taken from us by the maid. (For those who have not visited Japan, the okata is a cotton print kimono.) We later learned, when we ventured out in the streets, that it was possible to recognize other guests from our hotel because we had all been equipped with identical okatas. (Each hotel had its own characteristic, clearly recognizable pattern.) Also, I noted that it was polite to wave or nod to these strangers from the same hotel.

Following Hakone, we visited Kyoto, site of many famous temples and palaces, and the ancient capital of Japan.

There we were fortunate enough to stay in a wonderful little country inn on the side of a hill overlooking the town. Kyoto is much more traditional and less industrialized than Tokyo. After we had been there about a week and had thoroughly settled into our new Japanese surroundings, we returned one night to be met at the door by an apologetic manager who was stammering something. I knew immediately that we had been moved, so I said, "You had to move us. Please don't let this bother you, because we understand. Just show us to our new rooms and it will be all right." Our interpreter explained as we started to go through the door that we weren't in that hotel any longer but had been moved to *another* hotel. What a blow! Again, without warning. We wondered what the new hotel would be like, and with our descent into the town our hearts sank further. Finally, when we could descend no more, the taxi took off into a part of the city we hadn't seen before. No Europeans here! The streets got narrower and narrower until we turned into a side street that could barely accommodate the tiny Japanese taxi into which we were squeezed. Clearly this was a hotel of another class. I found that, by then, I was getting a little paranoid, which is easy enough to do in a foreign land, and said to myself, "They must think we are very low-status people indeed to treat us this way."

As it turned out, the neighborhood, in fact the whole district, showed us an entirely different side of life from what we had seen before, much more interesting and authentic. True, we did have some communication problems, because no one was used to dealing with foreigners, but few of them were serious.

Yet, the whole matter of being moved like a piece of derelict luggage puzzled me. In the United States, the person who gets moved is often the lowest-ranking individual. This principle applies to all organizations, including the Army. Whether you can be moved or not is a function of your status, your performance, and your value to the organization. To move someone without telling him is almost worse than an insult, because it means he is below the point at which feelings matter. In these circumstances, moves can be unsettling and damaging to the ego. In addition, moves themselves are often accompanied by great anxiety, whether an entire organization or a small part of an organization moves. What makes people anxious is that the move usually presages organizational changes that have been coordinated with the move. Naturally, everyone wants to see how he comes out vis-à-vis everyone else. I have seen important men refuse to move into an office that was six inches smaller than someone else's of the same rank. While I have heard some American executives say they wouldn't employ such a person, the fact is that in actual practice, unless there is some compensating feature, the significance of space as a communication is so powerful that no employee in his right mind would allow his boss to give him a spatial demotion—unless of course he had already reached his crest and was on the way down.

10   These spatial messages are not simply conventions in the United States—unless you consider the size of your salary check a mere convention, or where your name appears on the masthead of a journal. Ranking is seldom a matter that people take lightly, particularly in a highly mobile society like that in the

United States. Each culture and each country has its own language of space, which is just as unique as the spoken language, frequently more so. In England, for example, there are no offices for the members of Parliament. In the United States, our congressmen and senators proliferate their offices and their office buildings and simply would not tolerate a no-office situation. Constituents, associates, colleagues, and lobbyists would not respond properly. In England, status is internalized; it has its manifestations and markers—the upper-class received English accent, for example. We in the United States, a relatively new country, externalize status. The American in England has some trouble placing people in the social system, while the English can place each other quite accurately by reading ranking cues, but in general tend to look down on the importance that Americans attach to space. It is very easy and very natural to look at things from one's own point of view and to read an event as though it were the same all over the world.

I knew that my emotions on being moved out of my room in Tokyo were of the gut type and quite strong. There was nothing intellectual about my initial response. Although I am a professional observer of cultural patterns, I had no notion of the meaning attached to being moved from hotel to hotel in Kyoto. I was well aware of the strong significance of moving in my own culture, going back to the time when the new baby displaces older children, right up to the world of business, where a complex dance is performed every time the organization moves to new quarters.

What was happening to me in Japan as I rode up and down elevators with various keys gripped in my hand was that I was reacting with the cultural part of my brain—the old, mammalian brain. Although my new brain, my symbolic brain—the neocortex—was saying something else, my mammalian brain kept repeating, "You are being treated shabbily." My neocortex was trying to fathom what was happening. Needless to say, neither part of the brain had been programmed to provide me with the answer in Japanese culture. I did have to put up a strong fight with myself to keep from interpreting what was going on as though the Japanese were the same as I. This is the conventional and most common response and one that is often found even among anthropologists. Any time you hear someone say, "Why *they* are no different than the folks back home—they are just like I am," even though you may understand the reasons behind these remarks you also know that the speaker is living in a single-context world (his own) and is incapable of describing either his world or the foreign one.

The "they are just like the folks back home" syndrome is one of the most persistent and widely held misconceptions of the Western world, if not the whole world. There is very little any outsider can do about this, because it expresses views that are very close to the core of the personality. Simply talking about "cultural differences" and how we must respect them is a hollow cliché. And in fact, intellectualizing isn't much more helpful either, at least at first. The logic of the man who won't move into an office that is six inches smaller than his rival's is *cultural* logic; it works at a lower, more basic level in the brain, a part of the brain that synthesizes but does not verbalize. The response is a total response that is difficult to explain to someone who doesn't already understand, because it is so dependent on context for correct interpretation. To do so, one must explain the entire system; otherwise, the man's behavior makes little sense. He may even appear to be acting childishly—which he most definitely is not.

It was my preoccupation with my own cultural mold that explained why I was puzzled for years about the significance of being moved around in Japanese hotels. The answer finally came after further experiences in Japan and many discussions with Japanese friends. In Japan, one has to "belong" or he has no identity. When a man joins a company, he does just that—joins himself to the corporate body—and there is even a ceremony marking the occasion. Normally, he is hired for life, and the company plays a much more paternalistic role than in the United States. There are company songs, and the whole company meets frequently (usually at least once a week) for purposes of maintaining corporate identity and morale.

15   As a tourist (either European or Japanese) when you go on a tour, you *join* that tour and follow your guide everywhere as a group. She leads you with a little flag that she holds up for all to see. Such behavior strikes Americans as sheeplike; not so the Japanese. The reader may say that this pattern holds in Europe, because there people join Cook's tours and the American Express tours, which is true. Yet there is a big difference. I remember a very attractive young American woman who was traveling with the same group I was with in Japan. At first she was charmed and captivated, until she had spent several days visiting shrines and monuments. At this point, she observed that she could not take the regimentation of Japanese life. Clearly, she was picking up clues, such as the fact that our Japanese group, when it moved, marched in a phalanx rather than moving as a motley mob with stragglers. There was much more discipline in these sightseeing groups than the average Westerner is either used to or willing to accept.

It was my lack of understanding of the full impact of what it means to belong to a high-context culture that caused me to misread hotel behavior at Hakone. I should have known that I was in the grip of a pattern difference and that the significance of all guests being garbed in the same okata meant more than that an opportunistic management used the guests to advertise the hotel. The answer to my puzzle was revealed when a Japanese friend explained what it means to be a guest in a hotel. As soon as you register at the desk, you are no longer an outsider; instead, for the duration of your stay you are a member of a large, mobile family. *You belong.* The fact that I was moved was tangible evidence that I was being treated as a family member—a relationship in which one can afford to be "relaxed and informal and not stand on ceremony." This is a very highly prized state in Japan, which offsets the official properness that is so common in public. Instead of putting me down, they were treating me as a member of the family. Needless to say, the large, luxury hotels that cater to Americans, like Wright's Imperial Hotel, have discovered that Americans do tenaciously stand on ceremony and want to be treated as they are at home in the States. Americans don't like to be moved around; it makes them anxious. Therefore, the Japanese in these establishments have learned not to treat them as family members.

Keeping a Reading Journal

The most effective way to keep track of your thoughts and impressions and to review what you have learned is to start a reading journal. The comments you record in your journal may express your reflections, observations, questions, and reactions to the essays you read. Normally, your journal would not contain lecture notes from class. A reading journal will allow you to keep a record of your progress during the term and can also reflect insights you gain during class discussions, and questions you may want to ask, as well as unfamiliar words you intend to look up. Keeping a reading journal becomes a necessity if your composition course will require you to write a research paper that will be due at the end of the semester. Keep in mind that your journal is not something that will be corrected or graded, although some instructors may wish you to share your entries with the class.

TURNING ANNOTATIONS INTO JOURNAL ENTRIES

Although there is no set form for what a journal should look like, reading journals are most useful for converting your brief annotations into more complete entries that explore in-depth your reactions to what you have read. Interestingly, the process of turning your annotations into journal entries will often produce surprising insights that will give you a new perspective. For example, a student who annotated Edward T. Hall's "Hidden Cultures" converted them into the following journal entries:

- Hall's personal experiences in Japan made him realize that interpreting an action depends on what culture you're from.

- Hall assumes hotels should treat long-term guests with more respect than overnight guests. "Like someone who had been squeezed in without a reservation" shows Hall's feelings.

- What does having your clothes replaced with an *okata*—cotton robe—have to do with being moved from room to room in a hotel?

- The hotel in Hakone encourages guests—all wearing the same robes—to greet each other outside the hotel in a friendly, not formal, manner.

- Hall says that in America, size of office = personal value and salary. Hall compared how space works in the U.S. in order to understand Japanese attitudes towards space.

- Thesis—"culturally defined attitudes toward space are different for each culture." Proves this by showing how unimportant space is to members of Parliament in England when compared with the great importance office size is to U.S. congresspersons and senators.

- Hall is an anthropologist. He realizes his reactions are instinctual. Hall wants to refute the idea that people are the same all over the world. Says what culture you are from determines your attitudes and behavior.

- He learns from Japanese friends that workers are hired for life and view their companies as family. Would this be for me? In Japan, group identity is all-important.

- Hall describes two tour groups, one Japanese and one American, as an example of Japanese acceptance of regimentation, whereas Americans go off on their own.

- The answer to the mystery of why he was being moved: moving him meant he was accepted as a member of the hotel family. They were treating him informally, as if he were Japanese: a compliment not an insult. Informality is highly valued because the entire culture is based on the opposite—regimentation and conformity.

SUMMARIZING

Reading journals may also be used to record summaries of the essays you read. The value of summarizing is that it requires you to pay close attention to the reading in order to distinguish the main points from the supporting details.

Summarizing tests your understanding of the material by requiring you to restate, concisely, the author's main ideas in your own words. First, create a list composed of sentences that express in your own words the essential idea of each paragraph, or each group of related paragraphs. Your previous underlining of topic sentences, main ideas, and key terms (as part of the process of critical reading) will help you follow the author's line of thought. Next, whittle down this list still further by eliminating repetitive ideas. Then formulate a thesis statement that expresses the main idea behind the article. Start your summary with this thesis statement and combine your notes so that the summary flows together and reads easily.

Remember that summaries should be much shorter than the original text (whether the original is 1 page or 20 pages long) and should accurately reflect the central ideas of the article in as few words as possible. Try not to intrude your own opinions or critical evaluations into the summary. Besides requiring you to read the original piece more closely, summaries are necessary first steps in developing papers that synthesize materials from different sources. The test for a good summary, of course, is whether a person reading it without having read the original article would get an accurate, balanced, and complete account of the original material.

Writing an effective summary is easier if you first compose a rough summary, using no more than two complete sentences to summarize each of the paragraphs or group of paragraphs in the original article. A student's rough summary of Hall's essay might appear as follows. Numbers show which paragraphs are summarized from the article.

1–4 Hall describes how an event that occurred while he was staying in a Tokyo hotel (the management moved his belongings to another room) aroused his curiosity. When this happens again Hall begins to wonder why this did not occur during his stay at Frank Lloyd Wright's Imperial Hotel in Tokyo.

5 At another hotel in Hakone, Hall is given an *okata*, a kind of cotton robe, to wear instead of his clothes and is encouraged to greet other guests wearing the same *okata* when he sees them outside the hotel.

6–8 At a third hotel, a country inn near Kyoto, Hall is moved again, this time to a different hotel in what he perceives to be a less-desirable location. Hall is angry that the Japanese see him as someone who can be moved around without his permission. The hotel turns out to be much more authentic than tourist hotels.

9 Hall thinks he is being treated shabbily because in the United States, one's status is linked with control over personal space.

10–11 Hall realizes that he has been applying an American cultural perspective to these actions. He remembers that in England, members of Parliament have no formal offices, while congressmen and senators equate office size with power.

12–15 Hall concludes each culture is based on a "hidden" logic that applies only to that culture. He learns that in Japan self-esteem does not depend on control over personal space, but on being part of a group. For example, Japanese tourists move as a group and closely follow their guide, while American tourists refuse to accept such discipline.

16 Hall realizes that being moved to different rooms and hotels and being given an *okata* means that he has been accepted and his informal treatment is an honor not an insult.

Based on this list, a student's formulation of a thesis statement expressing the essential idea of Hall's essay appears this way:

Every society has a hidden culture that governs behavior that might seem inexplicable to an outsider.

The final summary should contain both this thesis and your restatement of the author's main ideas without adding any comments that express personal feelings or responses to the ideas presented. Keep in mind that the purpose of a summary or concise restatement of the author's ideas in your own words is to test your understanding of the material. The summary would normally be introduced by mentioning the author as well as the title of the article:

Edward T. Hall, writing in "Hidden Culture," believes every society has a hidden culture that governs behavior that might seem inexplicable to an outsider. In Japan, Hall's initial reactions of anger to being moved to another room in a hotel in Tokyo, having his clothes replaced by a cotton kimono or *okata* in Hakone, and being relocated to a different hotel in Kyoto led him to search for the reasons behind such seemingly bizarre events. Although control over space in America is related to status, Hall realizes that in other cultures, like England, where members of Parliament have no offices, this is not the case. Hall discovers that rather than being an insult, being treated informally meant he was considered to be a member of the hotel "family."

Although some features of the original essay might have been mentioned, such as the significance of office size in corporations in the United States, the student's summary of Hall's essay is still an effective one. The summary accurately and fairly expresses the main ideas in the original.

CHECKLIST FOR SUMMARIZING

■ Read the selection or passage, identifying key ideas and supporting evidence.

■ Do a quick reread of the material to discover the sections of the argument and to identify the governing ideas and important terms.

■ Draft a rough summary by writing one or two sentences for each stage of thought.

■ Write a thesis sentence that concisely encapsulates the main point.

■ Write a first draft by combining this thesis sentence with the most important ideas in your rough summary and significant details from the selection.

■ Revise your summary by comparing it with the original material to see if you covered all the important points.

■ Check your style to make sure your summary follows a logical sequence and fairly represents the original passage.

Using Your Reading Journal to Generate Ideas for Writing

You can use all the material in your reading journal (annotations converted to journal entries, reflections, observations, questions, rough and final summaries) to relate your own ideas to the ideas of the person who wrote the essay you are reading. Here are several different kinds of strategies you can use as you analyze an essay in order to generate material for your own:

1. What is missing in the essay? Information that is not mentioned is often just as significant as information the writer chose to include. First, you must have already summarized the main points in the article. Then, make up another list of points that are not discussed, that is, missing information that you would have expected an article of this kind to have covered or touched on. Write down the possible reasons why this missing material has been omitted, censored, or down-played. What possible purpose could the author have had? Look for vested interests or biases that could explain why information of a certain kind is missing.

2. You might analyze an essay in terms of what you already know and what you didn't know about the issue. To do this, simply make a list of what concepts were already familiar to you and a second list of information or concepts that were new to you. Then write down three to five questions you would like answered about this new information and make a list of possible sources you might consult.

3. You might consider whether the author presents a solution to a problem. List the short-term and long-term effects or consequences of the action the writer recommends. You might wish to evaluate the solution to see whether positive short-term benefits are offset by possible negative long-term consequences not mentioned by the author. This might provide you with a starting point for your own essay.

4. After clearly stating what the author's position on an issue is, try to imagine other people who would view the same issue from a different perspective. How would the concerns of these people be different from those of the writer? Try to think of as many different people, representing as many different perspectives, as you can. Now, try to think of a solution that would satisfy both the author and at least one other person who holds a different viewpoint. Try to imagine you are an arbitrator negotiating an agreement. How would your recommendation require both parties to compromise and reach an agreement?

A writer presenting an argument must keep an open mind, consider points of view other than his or her own, define or stipulate the meaning of key terms in the argument, and present a clear statement of the thesis. The writer must present the argument in logical order; cite the best and most relevant evidence, statistics, examples, and testimony available; state assumptions when necessary; draw conclusions that seem plausible and are consistent with the known facts; and effectively use rhetorical strategies to adapt the argument for a given audience.

Three Short Arguments for Critical Reading

Examine the following three arguments and notice how Roger Ebert ("Great Movies") focuses on questions of artistic interpretation, Eric Schlosser ("Kid Kustomers") addresses a social phenomenon, and Loren Eiseley ("How Flowers Changed the World") proposes a scientific theory. All three authors, although in very different fields, propose answers or solutions that have arisen from their inquiries. The conclusions they reached almost certainly were not their first ideas. They followed a trial-and-error process of defining the problem more clearly and matching various explanations to available evidence.

Roger Ebert

Great Movies

Roger Ebert (b. 1942) is widely known for his television program Ebert and Roeper *and for his columns on film for the* Chicago-Sun Times, *where he has been on the staff since 1967. He won a Pulitzer Prize in 1975 for film criticism and has written, among other books,* A Kiss Is Still a

Kiss *(1985),* Behind the Phantom's Mask *(1993), and* The Great Movies *(2002), from which the following selection is reprinted.*

Thinking Critically

As you read, try to identify the artistic criteria that underlie the eclectic list of films Ebert mentions in his essay.

Every other week I visit a film classic from the past and write about it. My "Great Movies" series began in the autumn of 1996 and now reaches a landmark of 100 titles with today's review of Federico Fellini's "8 1/2," which is, appropriately, a film about a film director. I love my job, and this is the part I love the most.

We have completed the first century of film. Too many moviegoers are stuck in the present and recent past. When people tell me that "Ferris Bueller's Day Off" or "Total Recall" are their favorite films, I wonder: Have they tasted the joys of Welles, Bunuel, Ford, Murnau, Keaton, Hitchcock, Wilder or Kurosawa? If they like Ferris Bueller, what would they think of Jacques Tati's "Mr. Hulot's Holiday," also about a strange day of misadventures? If they like "Total Recall," have they seen Fritz Lang's "Metropolis," also about an artificial city ruled by fear?

I ask not because I am a film snob. I like to sit in the dark and enjoy movies. I think of old films as a resource of treasures. Movies have been made for 100 years, in color and black and white, in sound and silence, in widescreen and the classic frame, in English and every other language. To limit yourself to popular hits and recent years is like being Ferris Bueller but staying home all day.

I believe we are born with our minds open to wonderful experiences, and only slowly learn to limit ourselves to narrow tastes. We are taught to lose our curiosity by the bludgeon-blows of mass marketing, which brainwash us to see "hits," and discourage exploration.

5   I know that many people dislike subtitled films, and that few people reading this article will have ever seen a film from Iran, for example. And yet a few weeks ago at my Overlooked Film Festival at the University of Illinois, the free kiddie matinee was "Children of Heaven," from Iran. It was a story about a boy who loses his sister's sneakers through no fault of his own, and is afraid to tell his parents. So he and his sister secretly share the same pair of shoes. Then he learns of a footrace where third prize is . . . a pair of sneakers.

"Anyone who can read at the third-grade level can read these subtitles," I told the audience of 1,000 kids and some parents. "If you can't, it's OK for your parents or older kids to read them aloud—just not too loudly."

The lights went down and the movie began. I expected a lot of reading aloud. There was none. Not all of the kids were old enough to read, but apparently they were picking up the story just by watching and using their intelligence. The audience was spellbound. No noise, restlessness, punching, kicking, running down the aisles. Just eyes lifted up to a fascinating story. Afterward, we asked kids up on the stage to ask questions or talk about the film. What they said indicated how involved they had become.

Kids. And yet most adults will not go to a movie from Iran, Japan, France or Brazil. They will, however, go to any movie that has been plugged with a $30 million ad campaign and sanctified as a "box-office winner." Yes, some of these big hits are good, and a few of them are great. But what happens between the time we are 8 and the time we are 20 that robs us of our curiosity? What turns movie lovers into consumers? What does it say about you if you only want to see what everybody else is seeing?

I don't know. What I do know is that if you love horror movies, your life as a filmgoer is not complete until you see "Nosferatu." I know that once you see Orson Welles appear in the doorway in "The Third Man," you will never forget his curious little smile. And that the life and death of the old man in "Ikiru" will be an inspiration every time you remember it.

10   I have not written any of the 100 Great Movies reviews from memory. Every film has been seen fresh, right before writing. When I'm at home, I often watch them on Sunday mornings. It's a form of prayer: The greatest films are meditations on why we are here. When I'm on the road, there's no telling where I'll see them. I saw "Written on the Wind" on a cold January night at the Everyman Cinema in Hampstead, north of London. I saw "Last Year at Marienbad" on a DVD on my PowerBook while at the Cannes Film Festival. I saw "2001: A Space Odyssey" in 70mm at Cyberfest, the celebration of HAL 9000's birthday, at the University of Illinois. I saw "Battleship Potemkin" projected on a sheet on the outside wall of the Vickers Theater in Three Oaks, Mich., while three young musicians played the score they had written for it. And Ozu's "Floating Weeds" at the Hawaii Film Festival, as part of a shot-by-shot seminar that took four days.

When people asked me where they should begin in looking at classic films, I never knew what to say. Now I can say, "Plunge into these Great Movies, and go where they lead you."

There's a next step. If you're really serious about the movies, get together with two or three friends who care as much as you do. Watch the film all the way through on video. Then start again at the top. Whenever anyone sees anything they want to comment on, freeze the frame. Talk about what you're looking at.

The story, the performances, the sets, the locations. The camera movement, the lighting, the composition, the special effects. The color, the shadows, the sound, the music. The themes, the tone, the mood, the style.

There are no right answers. The questions are the point. They make you an active movie watcher, not a passive one. You should not be a witness at a movie, but a collaborator. Directors cannot make the film without you. Together, you can accomplish amazing things. The more you learn, the quicker you'll know when the director is not doing his share of the job. That's the whole key to being a great moviegoer. There's nothing else to it.

ENGAGING the Text

1. How has Ebert's lifelong obsession with movies taught him to value out of the way foreign films and underappreciated classics?

2. What factors have made audiences into consumers rather than film lovers?

EVALUATING the Argument

1. How does Ebert's example about free kiddie matinee films illustrate his thesis that great movies stand on their own and audiences do not need to limit themselves to preapproved "hits"?

2. What means does Ebert use to offset potential criticism that he is an elitist "film snob"?

EXPLORING the Issue

1. Do you agree with Ebert's contention that mass marketing brainwashes us and causes us to lose our natural curiosity?

2. Have you ever sought out an unfamiliar foreign film or classic film instead of the "hyped" hit of the moment? What is your favorite film and why do you like it?

CONNECTING Different Perspectives

1. Would John M. Darley and Bibb Latané's hypothesis ("Why People Don't Help in a Crisis") explain why moviegoers accept the consensus of the crowd and don't think independently as Ebert recommends?

Eric Schlosser

Kid Kustomers

Eric Schlosser is a contributing editor of The Atlantic. *His articles on marijuana and the law (August and September 1994) won a National Magazine Award for reporting. He has appeared on* 60 Minutes. *In "Kid Kustomers" from* Fast Food Nation: the Dark Side of the All-American Meal *(2001), Schlosser reveals how advertisers are becoming more savvy in marketing their products toward children. His latest book is* Reefer Madness: Sex, Drugs, and Cheap Labor in the American Black Market *(2003).*

Thinking Critically

Notice the range of evidence that Schlosser uses to substantiate his analysis of how children have become the pawns of companies who use them to pester their parents into buying certain products.

Twenty-five years ago, only a handful of American companies directed their marketing at children—Disney, McDonald's, candy makers, toy makers, manufacturers of breakfast cereal. Today children are being targeted by phone companies, oil companies, and automobile companies as well as clothing stores and restaurant chains. The explosion in children's advertising occurred during the 1980s. Many working parents, feeling guilty about spending less time with their kids, started spending more money on them. One marketing expert has called the 1980s "the decade of the child consumer." After largely ignoring children for years, Madison Avenue began to scrutinize and pursue them. Major ad agencies now have children's divisions, and a variety of marketing firms focus solely on kids. These groups tend to have sweet-sounding names: Small Talk, Kid Connection, Kid2Kid, the Gepetto Group, Just Kids, Inc. At least three industry publications—*Youth Market Alert, Selling to Kids,* and *Marketing to Kids Report*—cover the latest ad campaigns and market research. The growth in children's advertising has been driven by efforts to increase not just current, but also future, consumption. Hoping that nostalgic childhood memories of a brand will lead to a lifetime of purchases, companies now plan "cradle-to-grave" advertising strategies. They have come to believe what Ray Kroc and Walt Disney realized long ago—a person's "brand loyalty" may begin as early as the age of two. Indeed, market research has found that children often recognize a brand logo before they can recognize their own name.

The discontinued Joe Camel ad campaign, which used a hip cartoon character to sell cigarettes, showed how easily children can be influenced by the right corporate mascot. A 1991 study published in the *Journal of the American Medical Association* found that nearly all of America's six-year-olds could identify Joe Camel, who was just as familiar to them as Mickey Mouse. Another study found that one-third of the cigarettes illegally sold to minors were Camels. More recently, a marketing firm conducted a survey in shopping malls across the country, asking children to describe their favorite TV ads. According to the CME KidCom Ad Traction Study II, released at the 1999 Kids' Marketing Conference in San Antonio, Texas, the Taco Bell commercials featuring a talking chihuahua were the most popular fast food ads. The kids in the survey also like Pepsi and Nike commercials, but their favorite television ad was for Budweiser.

The bulk of the advertising directed at children today has an immediate goal. "It's not just getting kids to whine," one marketer explained in *Selling to Kids*, "it's giving them a specific reason to ask for the product." Years ago sociologist Vance Packard described children as "surrogate salesmen" who had to persuade other people, usually their parents, to buy what they wanted. Marketers now use different terms to explain the intended response to their ads—such as "leverage," "the nudge factor," "pester power." The aim of most children's advertising is straightforward: Get kids to nag their parents and nag them well.

James U. McNeal, a professor of marketing at Texas A&M University, is considered America's leading authority on marketing to children. In his book *Kids As Customers* (1992), McNeal provides marketers with a thorough analysis of "children's requesting styles and appeals." He classifies juvenile nagging tactics into seven major categories. A *pleading* nag is one accompanied by repetitions of words like "please" or "mom, mom, mom." A *persistent* nag involves constant requests for the coveted product and may include the phrase "I'm gonna ask just one more time." *Forceful* nags are extremely pushy and may include subtle threats, like "Well, then, I'll go and ask Dad." *Demonstrative* nags are the most high-risk, often characterized by full-blown tantrums in public places, breath-holding, tears, a refusal to leave the store. *Sugar-coated* nags promise affection in return for a purchase and may rely on seemingly heartfelt declarations like "You're the best dad in the world." *Threatening* nags are youthful forms of blackmail, vows of eternal hatred and of running away if something isn't bought. *Pity* nags claim the child will be heartbroken, teased, or socially stunted if the parent refuses to buy a certain item. "All of these appeals and styles may be used in combination," McNeal's research has discovered, "but kids tend to stick to one or two of each that proved most effective . . . for their own parents."

5   McNeal never advocates turning children into screaming, breath-holding monsters. He has been studying "Kid Kustomers" for more than thirty years and believes in a more traditional marketing approach. "The key is getting

children to see a firm . . . in much the same way as [they see] mom or dad, grandma or grandpa," McNeal argues. "Likewise, if a company can ally itself with universal values such as patriotism, national defense, and good health, it is likely to nurture belief in it among children."

Before trying to affect children's behavior, advertisers have to learn about their tastes. Today's market researchers not only conduct surveys of children in shopping malls, they also organize focus groups for kids as young as two or three. They analyze children's artwork, hire children to run focus groups, stage slumber parties and then question children into the night. They send cultural anthropologists into homes, stores, fast food restaurants, and other places where kids like to gather, quietly and surreptitiously observing the behavior of prospective customers. They study the academic literature on child development, seeking insights from the work of theorists such as Erik Erikson and Jean Piaget. They study the fantasy lives of young children, they apply the findings in advertisements and product designs.

Dan S. Acuff—the president of Youth Market System Consulting and the author of *What Kids Buy and Why* (1997)—stresses the importance of dream research. Studies suggest that until the age of six, roughly 80 percent of children's dreams are about animals. Rounded, soft creatures like Barney, Disney's animated characters, and the Teletubbies therefore have an obvious appeal to young children. The Character Lab, a division of Youth Market System Consulting, uses a proprietary technique called Character Appeal Quadrant analysis to help companies develop new mascots. The technique purports to create imaginary characters who perfectly fit the targeted age group's level of cognitive and neurological development.

Children's clubs have for years been considered an effective means of targeting ads and collecting demographic information; the clubs appeal to a child's fundamental need for status and belonging. Disney's Mickey Mouse Club, formed in 1930, was one of the trailblazers. During the 1980s and 1990s, children's clubs proliferated, as corporations used them to solicit the names, addresses, zip codes, and personal comments of young customers. "Marketing messages sent through a club not only can be personalized," James McNeal advises, "they can be tailored for a certain age or geographical group." A well-designed and well-run children's club can be extremely good for business. According to one Burger King executive, the creation of a Burger King Kids Club in 1991 increased the sales of children's meals as much as 300 percent.

The Internet has become another powerful tool for assembling data about children. In 1998 a federal investigation of Web sites aimed at children found that 89 percent requested personal information from kids; only 1 percent required that children obtain parental approval before supplying the information.

A character on the McDonald's Web site told children that Ronald McDonald was "the ultimate authority in everything." The site encouraged kids to send Ronald an e-mail revealing their favorite menu item at McDonald's, their favorite book, their favorite sports team—and their name. Fast food Web sites no longer ask children to provide personal information without first gaining parental approval; to do so is now a violation of federal law, thanks to the Children's Online Privacy Protection Act, which took effect in April of 2000.

10   Despite the growing importance of the Internet, television remains the primary medium for children's advertising. The effects of these TV ads have long been a subject of controversy. In 1978, the Federal Trade Commission (FTC) tried to ban all television ads directed at children seven years old or younger. Many studies had found that young children often could not tell the difference between television programming and television advertising. They also could not comprehend the real purpose of commercials and trusted that advertising claims were true. Michael Pertschuk, the head of the FTC, argued that children need to be shielded from advertising that preys upon their immaturity. "They cannot protect themselves," he said, "against adults who exploit their present-mindedness."

The FTC's proposed ban was supported by the American Academy of Pediatrics, the National Congress of Parents and Teachers, the Consumers Union, and the Child Welfare League, among others. But it was attacked by the National Association of Broadcasters, the Toy Manufacturers of America, and the Association of National Advertisers. The industry groups lobbied Congress to prevent any restrictions on children's ads and sued in federal court to block Pertschuk from participating in future FTC meetings on the subject. In April of 1981, three months after the inauguration of President Ronald Reagan, an FTC staff report argued that a ban on ads aimed at children would be impractical, effectively killing the proposal. "We are delighted by the FTC's reasonable recommendation," said the head of the National Association of Broadcasters.

The Saturday-morning children's ads that caused angry debates twenty years ago now seem almost quaint. Far from being banned, TV advertising aimed at kids is now broadcast twenty-four hours a day, closed-captioned and in stereo. Nickelodeon, the Disney Channel, the Cartoon Network, and the other children's cable networks are now responsible for about 80 percent of all television viewing by kids. None of these networks existed before 1979. The typical American child now spends about twenty-one hours a week watching television—roughly one and a half months of TV every year. That does not include the time children spend in front of a screen watching videos, playing video games, or using the computer. Outside of school, the typical American child spends more time watching television than doing any other activity except sleeping. During the course of a year, he or she watches more than thirty thousand TV commercials. Even the nation's youngest children are watching a great deal of television. About one-quarter of American children between the ages of two and five have a TV in their room.

ENGAGING the Text

1. What factors led to an upsurge in advertising directed toward children in the 1980s?

2. How is pester power used to influence what parents buy?

EVALUATING the Argument

1. What sophisticated marketing techniques do advertisers use to identify what children will want in the products they pester their parents to buy for them?

2. How do marketeers use the Internet as well as television to reach their audience?

EXPLORING the Issue

1. To research children's advertising you might watch a Saturday morning cartoon show and note the connections between the characters and the products directly linked to them. Write a short essay summarizing your findings.

2. Study an ad in any medium specifically targeted at children and in a few paragraphs analyze the components (characters, music, storyline, images, colors) that contribute to its effectiveness.

CONNECTING Different Perspectives

1. Compare and contrast the marketing strategies directed toward children and adults in Schlosser's essay and in Robert F. Hartley's analysis in "The Edsel: Marketing, Planning and Research Gone Awry."

Loren Eiseley

How Flowers Changed the World

Loren Eiseley (1907–1977) was born in Lincoln, Nebraska, and received his Ph.D. from the University of Pennsylvania in 1937. His academic career encompassed the teaching of anthropology, sociology, and the history of science at the University of Kansas, Oberlin College, Columbia, Berkeley, Harvard, and the University of Pennsylvania. His abilities as a natural scientist were matched by an equal sensitivity to language: Darwin's Century *(1958) won the National Phi Beta Kappa Science Award and the Atheneum of Philadelphia Literature Award. Eiseley's writing displays imagination, a passionate concern for the environment, and scientific lucidity. His works include* The Immense Journey *(1957),* The Night Country *(1971), and* All the Strange Hours *(1975). In* "How Flowers Changed the World," *Eiseley reveals the causal relationship between the evolution of flowers and the subsequent development of warm-blooded mammals and human life on earth.*

Thinking Critically

Consider how readers without a scientific background can understand Eiseley's essay because of his skill in communicating his knowledge.

If it had been possible to observe the Earth from the far side of the solar system over the long course of geological epochs, the watchers might have been able to discern a subtle change in the light emanating from our planet. That world of long ago would, like the red deserts of Mars, have reflected light from vast drifts of stone and gravel, the sands of wandering wastes, the blackness of naked basalt, the yellow dust of endlessly moving storms. Only the ceaseless marching of the clouds and the intermittent flashes from the restless surface of the sea would have told a different story, but still essentially a barren one. Then, as the millennia rolled away and age followed age, a new and greener light would, by degrees, have come to twinkle across those endless miles.

This is the only difference those far watchers, by the use of subtle instruments, might have perceived in the whole history of the planet Earth, Yet that slowly growing green twinkle would have contained the epic march of life from the tidal oozes upward across the raw and unclothed continents. Out of the vast chemical bath of the sea—not from the deeps, but from the element-rich, light-exposed platforms of the continental shelves—wandering fingers of green had crept upward along the meanderings of river systems and fringed the gravels of forgotten lakes.

In those first ages plants clung of necessity to swamps and watercourses. Their reproductive processes demanded direct access to water. Beyond the primitive ferns and mosses that enclosed the borders of swamps and streams the rocks still lay vast and bare, the winds still swirled the dust of a naked planet. The grass cover that holds our world secure in place was still millions of years in the future. The green marchers had gained a soggy foothold upon the land but that was all. They did not reproduce by seeds but by microscopic swimming sperm that had to wriggle their way through water to fertilize the female cell. Such plants in their higher forms had clever adaptations for the use of rain water in their sexual phases, and survived with increasing success in a wet land environment. They now seem part of man's normal environment. The truth is, however, that there is nothing very "normal" about nature. Once upon a time there were no flowers at all.

A little while ago—about one hundred million years, as the geologist estimates time in the history of our four-billion-year-old planet—flowers were not to be found anywhere on the five continents. Wherever one might have looked, from the poles to the equator, one would have seen only the cold dark monotonous green of a world whose plant life possessed no other color.

5   Somewhere, just a short time before the close of the Age of Reptiles, there occurred a soundless, violent explosion. It lasted millions of years, but it was an explosion, nevertheless. It marked the emergence of the angiosperms—the flowering plants. Even the great evolutionist, Charles Darwin, called them "an abominable mystery," because they appeared so suddenly and spread so fast.

Flowers changed the face of the planet. Without them, the world we know—even man himself—would never have existed. Francis Thompson, the English poet, once wrote that one could not pluck a flower without troubling a star. Intuitively he had sensed like a naturalist the enormous interlinked complexity of life. Today we know that the appearance of the flowers contained also the equally mystifying emergence of man.

If we were to go back into the Age of Reptiles, its drowned swamps and birdless forest would reveal to us a warmer but, on the whole, a sleepier world than that of today. Here and there, it is true, the serpent heads of bottom-feeding dinosaurs might be upreared in suspicion of their huge flesh-eating compatriots. Tyrannosaurs, enormous bipedal caricatures of men, would stalk mindlessly across the sites of future cities and go their slow way down into the dark of geologic time.

In all that world of living things nothing saw save with the intense concentration of the hunt, nothing moved except with the grave sleepwalking intentness of the instinct-driven brain. Judged by modern standards, it was a world in slow motion, a cold-blooded world whose occupants were most active at noonday but torpid on chill nights, their brains damped by a slower metabolism than any known to even the most primitive of warm-blooded animals today.

A high metabolic rate and the maintenance of a constant body temperature are supreme achievements in the evolution of life. They enable an animal to escape, within broad limits, from the overheating or the chilling of its immediate surroundings, and at the same time to maintain a peak mental efficiency. Creatures without a high metabolic rate are slaves to weather. Insects in the first frosts of autumn all run down like little clocks. Yet if you pick one up and breathe warmly upon it, it will begin to move about once more.

10   In a sheltered spot such creatures may sleep away the winter, but they are hopelessly immobilized. Though a few warm-blooded mammals, such as the

woodchuck of our day, have evolved a way of reducing their metabolic rate in order to undergo winter hibernation, it is a survival mechanism with drawbacks, for it leaves the animal helplessly exposed if enemies discover him during his period of suspended animation. Thus bear or woodchuck, big animal or small, must seek, in this time of descending sleep, a safe refuge in some hidden den or burrow. Hibernation is, therefore, primarily a winter refuge of small, easily concealed animals rather than of large ones.

A high metabolic rate, however, means a heavy intake of energy in order to sustain body warmth and efficiency. It is for this reason that even some of these later warm-blooded mammals existing in our day have learned to descend into a slower, unconscious rate of living during the winter months when food may be difficult to obtain. On a slightly higher plane they are following the procedure of the cold-blooded frog sleeping in the mud at the bottom of a frozen pond.

The agile brain of the warm-blooded birds and mammals demands a high oxygen consumption and food in concentrated forms, or the creatures cannot long sustain themselves. It was the rise of flowering plants that provided that energy and changed the nature of the living world. Their appearance parallels in a quite surprising manner the rise of the birds and mammals.

Slowly, toward the dawn of the Age of Reptiles, something over two hundred and fifty million years ago, the little naked sperm cells wriggling their way through dew and raindrops had given way to a kind of pollen carried by the wind. Our present-day pine forests represents plants of a pollen-disseminating variety. Once fertilization was no longer dependent on exterior water, the march over drier regions could be extended. Instead of spores simple primitive seeds carrying some nourishment for the young plant had developed, but true flowers were still scores of millions of years away. After a long period of hesitant evolutionary groping, they exploded upon the world with truly revolutionary violence.

The event occurred in Cretaceous times in the close of the Age of Reptiles. Before the coming of the flowering plants our own ancestral stock, the warm-blooded mammals, consisted of a few mousy little creatures hidden in trees and underbrush. A few lizard-like birds with carnivorous teeth flapped awkwardly on ill-aimed flights among archaic shrubbery. None of these insignificant creatures gave evidence of any remarkable talents. The mammals in particular had been around for some millions of years, but had remained well lost in the shadow of the mighty reptiles. Truth to tell, man was still, like the genie in the bottle, encased in the body of a creature about the size of a rat.

15   As for the birds, their reptilian cousins the Pterodactyls, flew farther and better. There was just one thing about the birds that paralleled the physiology of the mammals. They, too, had evolved warm blood and its accompanying temperature control. Nevertheless, if one had been seen stripped of his feathers, he would still have seemed a slightly uncanny and unsightly lizard.

Neither the birds nor the mammals, however, were quite what they seemed. They were waiting for the Age of Flowers. They were waiting for what flowers, and with them the true encased seed, would bring. Fish-eating, gigantic leather-winged reptiles, twenty-eight feet from wing tip to wing tip, hovered over the coasts that one day would be swarming with gulls.

Inland the monotonous green of the pine and spruce forests with their primitive wooden cone flowers stretched everywhere. No grass hindered the fall of the naked seeds to earth. Great sequoias towered to the skies. The world of that time has a certain appeal but it is a giant's world, a world moving slowly like the reptiles who stalked magnificently among the boles of its trees.

The trees themselves are ancient, slow-growing and immense, like the red-wood groves that have survived to our day on the California coast. All is stiff, formal, upright and green, monotonously green. There is no grass as yet; there are no wide plains rolling in the sun, no tiny daisies dotting the meadows underfoot. There is little versatility about this scene; it is, in truth, a giant's world.

A few nights ago it was brought home vividly to me that the world has changed since that far epoch. I was awakened out of sleep by an unknown sound in my living room. Not a small sound—not a creaking timber or a mouse's scurry—but a sharp, rending explosion as though an unwary foot had been put down upon a wine glass. I had come instantly out of sleep and lay tense, unbreathing. I listened for another step. There was none.

20   Unable to stand the suspense any longer, I turned on the light and passed from room to room glancing uneasily behind chairs and into closets. Nothing seemed disturbed, and I stood puzzled in the center of the living room floor. Then a small button-shaped object upon the rug caught my eye. It was hard and polished and glistening. Scattered over the length of the room were several more shining up at me like wary little eyes. A pine cone that had been lying in a dish had been blown the length of the coffee table. The dish itself could hardly have been the source of the explosion. Beside it I found two ribbon-like strips of a velvety-green. I tried to place the two strips together to make a pod. They twisted resolutely away from each other and would no longer fit.

I relaxed in a chair, then, for I had reached a solution of the midnight disturbance. The twisted strips were wistaria pods that I had brought in a day or two previously and placed in the dish. They had chosen midnight to explode and distribute their multiplying fund of life down the length of the room. A plant, a fixed, rooted thing, immobilized in a single pod, had devised a way of propelling its offspring across open space. Immediately there passed before my eyes the million airy troopers of the milkweed pod and the clutching hooks of the sandburs. Seeds on the coyote's tail, seeds on the hunter's coat, thistledown mounting on the winds—all were somehow triumphing over life's limitations.

Yet the ability to do this had not been with them at the beginning. It was the product of endless effort and experiment.

The seeds on my carpet were not going to lie stiffly where they had dropped like their antiquated cousins, the naked seeds on the pine-cone scales. They were travelers. Struck by the thought, I went out next day and collected several other varieties. I line them up now in a row on my desk—so many little capsules of life, winged, hooked or spiked. Every one is an angiosperm, a product of the true flowering plants. Contained in these little boxes is the secret of that far-off Cretaceous explosion of a hundred million years ago that changed the face of the planet. And somewhere in here, I think, as I spoke seriously at one particularly resistant seedcase of a wild grass, was once man himself.

ENGAGING the Text

1. How did the appearance of flowers unchain creatures from their dependency on the climate and make possible the existence of mammalian life?

2. If flowering plants had not appeared, why would birds still be flying reptiles?

EVALUATING the Argument

1. How does Eiseley use the illustration of the exploding seed pod to support his hypothesis about the crucial role played by flowering plants or angiosperms?

2. What words and phrases does Eiseley use to explain the chain of causation in which the appearance of flowering plants made it possible for creatures to evolve with higher metabolic rates?

EXPLORING the Issue

1. Using Eiseley's essay as a model, discuss how any other seemingly unimportant plant, insect, or animal plays an indispensable role in nature.

2. What measures does Eiseley use to communicate his knowledge of complex biological processes so that readers without a scientific background could understand his ideas?

CONNECTING Different Perspectives

1. Explore the conflict between Charles Darwin's theory ("On the Origin of Species") and Eiseley's analysis of what Darwin had called the "abominable mystery" of the sudden appearance of flowering plants.

2 STRATEGIES FOR ARGUING

OVERVIEW: This chapter will introduce you to the different kinds of claims that arguments can make (factual, causal, value, and policy) and will acquaint you with the Stephen Toulmin model of argumentation based on identifying the claim, warrant, backing, support, and qualifier. We will also examine the importance of clearly defined terms in effective arguments.

Introduction to the Toulmin Model

What we usually call an *argument* is not the same thing as a formal written argument. Arguments in everyday life are usually spontaneous, often illogical, and usually not well thought through. Yet the goal of everyday debates is often the same as the most elegant, well-reasoned argument: persuasion of an audience to come around to your point of view. A well-reasoned argument not only makes a claim but presents reasons and evidence necessary to convince an audience that the claim is true.

Arguments arise in any situation where a wide range of responses is possible. The most obvious example might be a court of law. The prosecution and the defense each tell one side of the story or one version of events. The judge or jury, acting as an audience, then decides which version of the events seems more plausible. As with a formal argument, the legal system requires evidence to meet certain standards and draws a distinction between admissible and inadmissible evidence. Expert witnesses also play the same role in the court as they do in a written argument. The adversary nature of the legal system assumes, as does a formal argument, that any reason that survives all objections raised against it is a valid one. Many other professions besides the law, such as journalism, science, and business, also depend on the formulation of convincing arguments to win an audience's assent. What all arguments have in common is the need to persuade an audience by means of exact and careful reasoning that a specific claim or assertion is true.

One of the most innovative researchers in the field of argumentation theory is British logician and philosopher Stephen Toulmin. Toulmin devised a precise means of identifying the important features of arguments as they are engaged in by people in real life. His analysis of the ways in which people actually reason led him to formulate what has become the leading approach to informal logic, that is, logic as it appears in natural language rather than in the form of syllogisms (fully discussed in Chapter 5). His approach offers a useful method of analyzing an existing argument and/or planning one's own arguments.

The model Toulmin proposed to reflect the way people actually reasoned has six elements, each of which plays a distinctive role. Toulmin first introduced this model in 1958 in his book *The Uses of Argument* and later proposed an expanded scheme (with Richard Reike and Allan Janik) in 1979 in *An Introduction to Reasoning*. The advantage of Toulmin's method is that it charts the different parts of an argument that an audience must reconstruct and helps us develop a complete picture of the unstated implicit components of the argument. This allows us to be in a better position to identify both the strengths and the weaknesses of any argument. In Toulmin's model, a fully developed individual argument has six elements instead of the three components of the traditional syllogism. The three basic parts are the *claim* (equivalent to the conclusion of a syllogism), the *warrant* (similar to the major premise), and the *grounds* (similar to the minor premise).

Using the three elements of grounds, warrant, and claim, let's see how they would work in a hypothetical argument.

> You have just purchased a ticket to the Super Bowl from a scalper outside the stadium, and as you present it you are told that you cannot go in. You argue that you should be allowed to gain admission.
>
> The grounds of this argument would be the factual basis that you possess a ticket inscribed with the correct date, time, and place. The warrant is the unstated but clearly understood general rule that "all bearers of a Super Bowl admission ticket are normally entitled to be admitted." On the basis of these grounds, and this warrant, you claim that you are entitled to be admitted to the stadium.

Thus, the three basic elements to be considered in any argument include (1) the claim or proposition the audience is to consider, (2) the evidence, support, or grounds the writer will have to produce to back up the claim, and (3) the warrant, the underlying assumption, belief, or rule that spells out the relationship between the claim and the evidence offered to support it.

In addition to these three basic parts, Toulmin also identifies three elements that are not reflected in the traditional structure of deductive argument. They are the backing, the qualifier, and the rebuttal (see Figure 2.1). Each of these six elements serves a distinctive function in an argument. The term *grounds* refers to the facts that serve as the foundation or support offered as evidence. Grounds may take the form of statistics, observations, testimony, or other factual data that literally "ground" the argument in something real. Grounds answer the question in the mind of an audience, "What have you got to go on to support your claim?" The *claim*, in turn, is what the arguer wants the audience to believe or accept. The claim is the same as the conclusion or result of an argument. *Warrants* are the reasons for believing a claim or the principles or generalizations that serve as reasons for interpreting the data in support of the claim. Thus, the warrant is the principle or idea that provides the basis that literally "warrants" moving from the grounds to the claim. It answers the question in the minds of the audience, "How do you get from the evidence to the claim?" The *backing* provides support for the warrant, showing why the warrant is safe to rely on in this particular argument, or it provides reasons why the warrant is true or in force. *Qualifiers* are words or phrases such as "probably," "sometimes," "in most

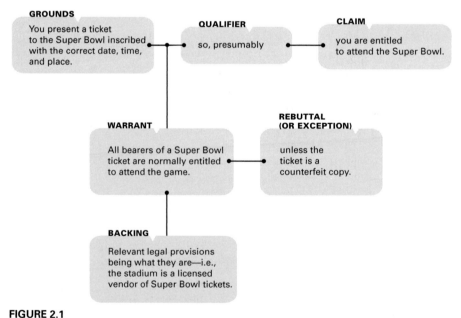

FIGURE 2.1
Six Elements to be Considered in an Argument, According to Toulmin.

cases," or "almost certainly" that express how reliable the speaker believes the claim to be. Qualifiers modulate the intensity of the claim. Toulmin's concept of *rebuttal*, like his analysis of other elements, is innovative and true to the ways in which people actually reason. The concept of rebuttal rests on the idea that the general rule or principle in the warrant may not always hold in every situation. The rebuttal identifies the circumstances or exceptions that might invalidate the claim in particular cases.

In the original example of being admitted to a Super Bowl game, the crucial role played by these additional three elements becomes clear. In diagram form, the argument might appear as shown in Figure 2.1.

Because warrants are often unstated, they frequently need to be spelled out explicitly. For example, a writer putting together a guidebook for travelers to Thailand would spell out rules and customs tourists would be wise to observe. She might warn tourists never to touch anyone—especially children—on the head, since Thais consider it to be the dwelling place of the soul. Other Thai customs based on assumptions every Thai knows, but the tourist might not, could, for example, necessitate explicitly warning the traveler never to cross the legs with one foot resting on the other knee. The feet are considered the lowliest part of the body and pointing at anyone with your foot, even if inadvertently, is taken as an insult. Other customs could be assumed to be more self-evident—such as showing disrespect to images or statues of Buddha—and the warrants for them would not have to be spelled out explicitly for those of other religions.

Thus, any argument recommending certain kinds of behavior in Thailand would have to make explicit the underlying warrant rather than taking it for granted that readers would connect the evidence to the claim in the same way as would the writer. A traveler would need to understand the rationale or underlying principles of Thai culture in order to know how to act correctly. The assumptions or rules about what constitutes proper behavior assures (or warrants) the claim or advice about what is considered correct behavior in different circumstances.

In our example, the writer might quote authorities, cite anecdotes of travelers' experiences, and appeal to the need of travelers not to embarrass themselves when traveling in other cultures. In other arguments, support can also take the form of specific facts, data, statistics, personal testimony, results of experiments or surveys, and appeals to the emotions, needs, and values of the audience. The character of the author of the guidebook would also support the claim insofar as the reader perceived him or her as a seasoned traveler, familiar with the values and customs of different cultures. Both the citation of evidence and the appeal to needs and values of an audience are valid means by which writers support claims.

Kinds of Claims

The proposition that we wish our audience to agree with or act on is called a claim. The claim is expressed as the thesis statement. Claims can be classified according to the kinds of questions that they answer.

I. **Factual Claim:** Prices of generic drugs are often well below those of leading brands.

Claims of fact seek to answer the question, what is the nature of [something]?

II. **Causal Claim:** Sex differences cause differences in mathematical ability.

Claims about cause or consequence try to answer the questions, what caused [something] to be the way it is? or what will happen as a result of [something]?

III. **Value Claim:** Affirmative action is morally justifiable.

Claims of value seek to answer the question, is [something] good or bad, right or wrong, moral or immoral, practical or impractical? These types of claims make value judgments.

IV. **Policy Claim:** Automobiles should not be allowed in Yellowstone National Park.

Claims about policy try to answer the question, what ought, should, or must we do about [something]? Claims of policy frequently appear as arguments that propose specific actions or policies as the best way to solve problems.

Claims may be phrased to suggest that there are certain kinds of conditions or limitations that prevent the claim from being advanced unconditionally. These qualifiers often take the form of adverbial phrases (*presumably, in all probability, apparently*) that indicate the provisional nature of the claim. In other cases, writers try to specify the sort of restrictions that limit the conditions under which the claim is true. For example, Dorothy Collier in "Where Is My Child?" concludes her argument with a policy recommendation that includes a qualification. Collier, as a mother who has given up her son for adoption, believes that the natural parents should have the right to learn the identity and whereabouts of their children even though they have given them up for adoption. She argues the case on the grounds that adopted children have the right to learn who their natural parents are. She is careful to phrase her policy claim so that the reader understands she would apply the same restrictions as now govern the disclosure of information to adopted children:

> The law applies only to the child [the Children Act signed into law Nov. 26, 1976 that permits adopted people to gain access to their own birth records and thus to find out who they are]. He has all the rights and all the initiatives. If my son, the child that I bore, is dead, I am denied even the right to know where his body lies. I cannot believe that that right should be abrogated by the stroke of the pen at the time when the mind has ceased to function. I believe firmly that, with the same safeguards as now apply to the children, the right to know, the right to acquire basic information, should be granted to the natural parents of adopted persons.

How Collier qualifies her claim can be seen in the following sentence (the qualifying phrase is emphasized):

> **Policy Claim:** I believe firmly that, **with the same safeguards as now apply to the children,** the right to know, the right to acquire basic information, should be granted to the natural parents of adopted persons.

Although we can more clearly see the distinctive qualities of each of these four types of claims (factual, causal, value, and policy) by discussing them separately, arguments frequently rely on more than just one type of claim. For example, Lori B. Andrews in "My Body, My Property" creates an argument that recommends changing the current system of voluntary donation of body parts (used in organ transplants) to permit the creation of a commercial market in organs and tissues (a claim about policy). In the course of her argument, Andrews defends the right of patients to sell their own body parts (a claim about value), defines the important difference between "regenerative" and "non-regenerative" organs and tissues (a claim about the nature of something), and discusses the benefits of such a market to donors, to recipients, and to society as a whole (a claim about consequences).

Moreover, each of these kinds of claims can be generated within the theoretical framework of different disciplines about the same subject. For example, the red-eyed tree frog lives in the tropical rain forests of Central America. As the subject of inquiry in the liberal arts, claims might be made about its unique coloration (predominantly neon green splashed with blue, yellow, and orange, and of course its distinguishing feature—bulging bright red eyes), and musical mating song. Social scientists might propose claims about its role in raising public awareness of the endangered rain forest because of its status as an indicator species susceptible to pollution, deforestation, and other changes in the environment. Biologists might generate hypotheses and make claims about the exact function of its red eyes and bright colors in startling and confusing predators.

The Goals of Claims

Different kinds of arguments seek to accomplish different objectives or goals. Generally speaking, four kinds of goals can be identified.

People can disagree about the essential nature of the subject under discussion, what it is similar to or dissimilar to, and how it should be defined. These are called *arguments of fact*. Even if people agree about the essential nature of X, they may disagree about what caused it or what effects it will cause in turn. These are *arguments of causation*. By the same token, even if all parties concerned agree what the nature of X is and what caused it and what the effects may be, they may disagree over whether it is good or bad or whether its effects are harmful or beneficial. These are *arguments about value*. The most complex form of argument, an argument about what should be done about X, is known as a *policy argument*. Policy arguments are complex because they may contain each of the preceding forms of argument.

For convenience, we will examine each of these four types of claims separately.

FACTUAL CLAIMS DEFINE AND DRAW DISTINCTIONS

Arguments that define and draw distinctions must identify the unique properties of the idea, term, or phenomenon being defined in a way that clearly distinguishes it from all others things with which it might be confused. Arguments that assert that a situation should be characterized in a certain way must identify the most important feature or crucial aspect of any situation, phenomenon, event, or idea.

Some arguments arise because of a lack of consensus about what commonly used terms actually mean. For example, in medicine, current technologies for prolonging life make it necessary to agree on what the terms *life* and *death* actually mean. Since machines can prevent cessation of respiration, the traditional definition of death—as occurring when respiration ceases and the heart stops beating—must be stipulated as occurring with *brain death*. In such cases, decisions as to when to terminate life support or to remove organs for transplantation will obviously depend on which definition is applied. Thus, an argument seeking to establish what is most essential about the subject will often depend on the definition of a key term or concept.

For example, an argument against deinstitutionalization of the mentally ill might begin with a factual claim intended to establish the essential nature of one particular kind of mental illness: "schizophrenia is a mental disorder." In this case, the factual claim could easily be verified by citing the official definition published in the reference manual of mental health professionals in the United States, the *Diagnostic and Statistical Manual of Mental Disorders*, 4th ed., 1994.

Questions for Discussion and Writing

1. Explain how each of the following statements might serve as a premise or line of reasoning for an argument about the nature of something, that is, an argument that expresses a factual claim.

    a. Americans are pragmatists. Pragmatists believe that whatever works must be right.

        —*William Schneider, "The New Shape of American Politics,"* The Atlantic Monthly

    b. Buddhism does not take its starting point on grand metaphysical questions like *who made the world?*; *what is the meaning of life?*; and *what happens to us after death?* It is not concerned with proving the existence of a God or gods. Rather its root focus is on the down-to-earth fact that all existence, including human existence, is imperfect in a very deep way. "Suffering I teach—and the way out of suffering," the Buddha declared.

        —*John Snelling*, The Buddhist Handbook

2. How does the following mini-argument define and draw distinctions about the nature of contemporary journalism?

THE IDIOT CULTURE

For more than fifteen years we have been moving away from real journalism toward the creation of a sleazoid infotainment culture . . . we are in the process of creating, in sum, what deserves to be called the idiot culture. Not an idiot *sub*culture, which every society has bubbling beneath the surface and which can provide harmless fun; but the culture itself.

I do not mean to attack popular culture. Good journalism *is* popular culture, but popular culture that stretches and informs its consumers rather than that which appeals to the ever descending lowest common denominator. If, by popular culture, we mean expressions of thought or feeling that require no work of those who consume them, then decent popular journalism is finished. What is happening today, unfortunately, is that the lowest form of popular culture—lack of information, misinformation, dis-information, and a contempt for the truth or the reality of most people's lives—has overrun real journalism.

—*Carl Bernstein, "The Idiot Culture,"* The New Republic

Evaluating the Reliability of Sources of Information

The persuasiveness of factual claims depends not only on specific reasons and evidence given to support the claim but also on the reliability of the source of the information. The reliability of an authority depends on how reliable this expert has been in the past and on his or her ability to make accurate observations and draw sound conclusions. Both the way information is selected and the way judgments are made should be free from bias. For this reason, it is important to be able to distinguish statements that you merely believe to be true from those that you know to be true. You might try to do this with the following two descriptions of the Suzuki Samurai truck when it was initially marketed. The first paragraph appears as the advertising copy in an issue of *Motor Trend*:

IT HAS FUN WRITTEN ALL OVER IT

- Take off your top with two piece removable hardtop.
- Haul your things around on a handy luggage rack.
- Fog lamps make great evening wear.
- Pull out of trouble with heavy duty compact winch.
- Protect your funmobile with durable brush guard.
- The Samurai logo. It has fun all over it.

The fun thing about a Suzuki Samurai (tm) is that you can give it a personality all your own. Genuine Suzuki accessories for America's favorite 4 × 4. We've got all kinds to choose from for the Suzuki look you want. Tops. Racks. Lamps. Western mirrors. Chrome bumpers. More. Make it sporty. Make it outdoorsy. Make it rugged. Make it yours. So go out and get a pure Suzuki. And make it your Suzuki.

The next series of paragraphs contain an evaluation of the same vehicle in *Consumer Reports*, a nonprofit magazine that accepts no advertising, and tests products and services and reports the findings:

Early this year a staff member was driving our new *Suzuki Samurai* slowly, in second gear, along a snow-covered dirt road leading to our auto test track when he felt the tires grab in a rut worn by earlier traffic. The driver turned the wheel to the right to steer clear. The front wheels pulled out of the rut and climbed approximately six inches up a ridge of plowed snow at the side of the road. Then, as the driver tried to straighten the wheels, the *Suzuki* flopped over on its side. The driver climbed out uninjured but with new respect for the laws of physics.

The Center for Auto Safety, a nonprofit consumer group, says it has received reports of 20 *Suzuki Samurai* rollover accidents resulting in 21 injuries and four deaths. It has also received reports of six rollovers in variants of the *Samurai*, such as the *Suzuki* SJ410, which is sold in Hawaii and the Virgin Islands; those resulted in seven injuries and one death. The National Highway Traffic Safety Administration has received 44 reports of *Samurai* rollovers, resulting in 16 deaths.

That's an ominous record of rollovers, considering that there are only 150,000 *Samurais* on U.S. roads so far and that many of them have been in use for less than a year.

In our judgment, the *Suzuki Samurai* is so likely to roll over during a maneuver that could be demanded of any car at any time that it is unfit for its intended use. We therefore judge it Not Acceptable.

In comparing these two accounts, we notice that the same vehicle is viewed very differently by the advertisers trying to sell their product and by the editors of *Consumer Reports*. As you can see, if we are to accurately evaluate the source of information, we must be aware of the vested interests of the people reporting the information. We must also understand how these interests or purposes may have influenced the way the information has been presented. The key questions to ask in determining reliability of sources of information are these:

1. How knowledgeable or experienced is the source?

2. What sort of a track record does the source of information have—that is, how reliable has this source been in the past?

3. Was the source able to make accurate observations in this particular case?

4. How could this information be objectively verified?

5. Do you have reason to believe that the information is incomplete or has been distorted by the self-interests of those relaying the information (due to the effects of income from advertising)?

A useful procedure by which to evaluate arguments is to: (a) draw up a list of all the factual statements made in the course of the article, (b) next to each statement, describe how this fact is verified, and (c) evaluate the reliability of the source.

CAUSAL CLAIMS IDENTIFY POSSIBLE CAUSES FOR A GIVEN EFFECT OR POSSIBLE EFFECTS FOR A GIVEN CAUSE

Claims about causation assert that two events do not merely appear together but are in fact causally connected. That is, the writer argues that one event is caused by another or will cause another to occur. Whatever form they take, causal arguments must demonstrate the means (sometimes called the *agency*) by which an effect could have been produced.

Causal arguments are necessary when an audience might doubt that something could have caused the effect in question and needs to be shown *how* it was possible for X to have caused Y. For example, a writer who claimed that "cancer is caused by industrial chemicals" would be obligated to show the means by which specific industrial chemicals could produce certain kinds of cancer.

Causal arguments also offer plausible explanations as to the cause or causes of a series of events or a trend. A trend is the prevailing tendency or general direction of a phenomenon that takes an irregular course, like the upward or downward trend of the stock market, or the growing tendency to ban smoking in public places.

A causal argument must present plausible grounds to support a claim as to why something happened or why something will happen. Writers may work backwards from a given effect and attempt to demonstrate what cause or chain of causes could have produced the observed effect, or show how further effects could follow from a known cause. To see how this works, let's examine the following news release (July 12, 2005) from the Insurance Institute for Highway Safety based on a study conducted in the Western Australian city of Perth:

> 1st Evidence of Effects of Cell Phone Use on Injury Crashes: Crash Risk Is Four Times Higher When Driver Is Using A Hand-Held Cell Phone.
>
> Common sense as well as experience tell us that handling and dialing cell phones while driving compromise safety, and evidence is accumulating that phone conversations also increase crash risk. New Institute research quantifies the added risk—drivers using phones are four times as likely to get into crashes serious enough to injure themselves. The increased risk was estimated by comparing phone use within 10 minutes before an actual crash occurred with use by the same driver during the prior week. Subjects were drivers treated in hospital emergency rooms for injuries suffered in crashes from April 2002 to July 2004. The study, "Role of cellular phone in motor vehicle crashes resulting in hospital attendance" by S. McEvoy et al., is published in the British Medical Journal, available at bmj.com.
>
> "The main finding of a fourfold increase in injury crash risk was consistent across groups of drivers," says Anne McCartt, Institute vice president for

research and an author of the study. "Male and female drivers experienced about the same increase in risk from using a phone. So did drivers older and younger than 30 and drivers using hand-held and hands-free phones."

Weather wasn't a factor in the crashes, almost 75 percent of which occurred in clear conditions.

Eighty-nine percent of the crashes involved other vehicles. More than half of the injured drivers reported that their crashes occurred within 10 minutes of the start of the trip.

To substantiate the claim that drivers using cell phones are four times as likely to get into a crash that can cause injuries serious enough to send them to the hospital, the researchers analyzed cell phone use by 456 drivers who were treated in an emergency room with mild to moderate injuries after a car accident. The causal relationship emerged when researchers compared cell phone use (based on interviews and phone company records) including calls and text messaging around the time of each crash with the person's phone activity while driving at the same time one day, three days, and one week before the accident. Use of the cell phone within ten minutes of the accident was associated with a fourfold increase in the likelihood of crashing. It is especially important that the Insurance Institute provided objective evidence for their claim since a call for reduced cell phone use would be so controversial. Moreover, most people would think that a hands-free phone would be less distracting and therefore safer, but the data suggested this was not the case.

The rhetorical strategies that come into play in causal analysis require the writer to describe the subject in question, identify and discuss probable causes, provide reasons and evidence to support the causal claim, and consider and reject alternative explanations. Some writers reverse the sequence so that their own argument for a probable cause follows a thorough evaluation and rejection of competing explanations.

One way to substantiate a causal claim entails citing statistical evidence showing that a correlation exists between an increase or decrease of the stipulated cause and a simultaneous change in the effect. For example, David Phillips at the University of California at San Diego wanted to know whether there was any relationship between stories about suicide and suicide statistics. Phillips found that:

> In the case of national stories, the rate jumped nationally. (Marilyn Monroe's death was followed by a temporary 12 percent increase in the national suicide rate.) Then Phillips repeated his experiment with traffic accidents. He took front-page suicide stories from the *Los Angeles Times* and the *San Francisco Chronicle* and matched them up with traffic fatalities from the state of California.

He found the same pattern. On the day after a highly publicized suicide, the number of fatalities from traffic accidents was, on average, 5.9 percent higher than expected. . . . and four days after, they rose 8.1 percent. (After ten days, the traffic fatality rate was back to normal.) Phillips concluded that one of the ways in which people commit suicide is by deliberately crashing their cars, and that these people were just as susceptible to the contagious effects of a highly publicized suicide as were people killing themselves by more conventional means.

—*Malcolm Gladwell*, The Tipping Point *(2002, pp. 222–23)*

We should keep in mind that simply because two things change at the same time does not mean that there is a causal correlation between them, that is, that the change in one has caused the change in the other.

Many studies in the social sciences investigate causal correlations. For example, the social psychologists John M. Darley and Bibb Latané, in "Why People Don't Help in a Crisis" in *Psychology Today*, designed experiments to identify what factors cause people, when part of a group, to be less likely to aid the same victims of street crime they would have helped on a one-to-one basis. Darley and Latané discovered a clear correlation between the numbers of people witnessing an emergency and the willingness of any one individual to come to the aid of the victim. Surprisingly, the more people in a group, the less likely any one person was to volunteer to help the victim. One such factor was peer pressure:

> A person trying to interpret a situation often looks at those around him to see how he should react. If everyone else is calm and indifferent, he will tend to remain so; if everyone else is reacting strongly, he is likely to become aroused. This tendency is not merely slavish conformity; ordinarily we derive much valuable information about new situations from how others around us behave. It's a rare traveler, who, in picking a roadside restaurant, chooses to stop at one where no other cars appear in the parking lot.

Darley and Latané's classic experiment disclosed a significant correlation between a measurable cause (number of bystanders) and an observable effect (willingness of any one individual to aid the victim). Causal analysis is an important tool used by researchers to discover the means by which social pressures control the behavior of people in groups. In this case, Darley and Latané's results challenged the traditional idea that apathy is the reason bystanders are unwilling to help victims of street crime.

Because of the complexity of causal relationships, writers must try to identify, as precisely as possible, the contributory factors in any causal sequence. The direct or immediate causes of the event are those most likely to have triggered the actual event, yet behind direct causes may lie indirect or remote causes that set the stage or create the framework in which the event could occur. Immediate or *precipitating* causes are those that can be identified as occuring just before the event, phenomenon, or trend. On the other hand, remote, indirect, or *background* causes occur in the past well before the actual event takes place.

For example, Aldous Huxley, political essayist and author of *Brave New World* (1932), distinguished between predisposing and triggering causes to explain why one segment of the German population was so easily swayed by Hitler's rhetoric:

> Hitler made his strongest appeal to those members of the lower middle class who had been ruined by the inflation of 1923, and then ruined all over again by the depression of 1929 and the following years. "The masses" of whom he speaks were these bewildered, frustrated and chronically anxious millions. To make them more masslike, more homogeneously subhuman, he assembled them, by the thousands and the tens of thousands, in vast halls and arenas, where individuals could lose their personal identity, even their elementary humanity, and be merged with the crowd.

In this passage from "Propaganda Under a Dictatorship" in *Brave New World Revisited* (1958), Huxley uses causal analysis to emphasize that the people most likely to yield to propaganda were those whose security had been destroyed by previous financial disasters. That is, previous cycles of financial instability (the disastrous inflation of 1923 and the depression of 1929) played a crucial role in predisposing the lower-middle classes, those whose security was most affected by the financial turmoil, to become receptive to Hitler's propaganda. Hitler, says Huxley, used techniques of propaganda—mass marches, repetition of slogans, scapegoating—to manipulate the segment of the population who were the least secure and most fearful.

Long-term, future effects are much more difficult to make a case for than are short-term, immediate effects. Determining with any degree of certainty that X caused Y is more complicated in situations where one cause may have produced multiple effects or the same effect could have been produced by multiple causes.

For example, David Hilfiker analyzes several causes that have, in his words, resulted in "private medicine's abandonment of the poor." As part of his analysis identifying the cause that, in his view, plays the dominant role, Hilfiker must consider and evaluate all possible causes as well:

> There are of course many complex factors that have precipitated private medicine's abandonment of the poor. The urbanization and anonymity of the poor,

the increasingly technological nature of medicine and the bureaucratic capriciousness of public medical assistance—all these serve to make private physicians feel less responsible for the medical needs of those who cannot afford the going rate.

But the cause that is probably most obvious to the lay public is singularly invisible to the medical community: Medicine is less and less rooted in service and more and more based in money. With many wonderful exceptions all over the country, American physicians as a whole have been turned away from the ideals of service by an idolatry of money. Physicians are too seldom servants and too often entrepreneurs. A profitable practice has become primary. The change has been so dramatic and so far-reaching that most of us do not even recognize that a transformation has taken place, that there might be an alternative. We simply take it for granted that economic factors will be primary even for the physician.

—*David Hilfiker, "A Doctor's View of Modern Medicine,"* The New York Times Magazine

In his article, Hilfiker draws on his own experience as a practicing physician to illustrate how a variety of pressures transformed him from a caring physician into a businessman concerned only with the efficient management of his office and medical practice. The fact that the average medical student can accrue enormous debt, the increasing cost of malpractice insurance, and the huge amounts of money necessary to set up and maintain an office are identified by Hilfiker as contributory causes in transforming the practice of medicine into just another profit-oriented business. Hilfiker then cites a range of effects (including the use of ever more costly "procedures," and the assembly-line approach of seeing 30 or more patients a day) that dramatically illustrate the negative consequences for patients when doctors become little more than businesspeople. How does the cartoon on p. 49 illustrate Hilfiker's thesis?

Causal arguments can get off the track when writers confuse sequence with causation. Events that merely follow each other in sequence should not be confused with true cause and effect. Simply because A preceeded B does not necessarily mean that A caused B. This confusion of antecedent or correlation with causation is called the *post hoc* fallacy, from the Latin *post hoc, ergo propter hoc* (literally, after this, therefore because of this).

Darrell Huff and Irving Geis provide an amusing example of one form the *post hoc* fallacy can take:

As an instance of the nonsense or spurious correlation that is a real statistical fact, someone has gleefully pointed to this: There is a close relationship between the salaries of Presbyterian ministers in Massachusetts and the price of rum in Havana.

FIGURE 2.2

> Which is the cause and which the effect? In other words, are the ministers benefiting from the rum trade or supporting it? All right. That's so farfetched that it is ridiculous at a glance. But watch out for other applications of *post hoc* logic that differ from this one only in being more subtle. In the case of the ministers and the rum it is easy to see that both figures are growing because of the influence of a third factor: the historic and world-wide rise in the price level of practically everything.
>
> —How To Lie with Statistics

The confusion here is based on the erroneous assumption that simply because two events occur in the same time period, there is also a cause-and-effect relationship. For example, a person who walked under a ladder and then, ten minutes later, tripped and fell, might attribute the fall to walking under the ladder. To avoid the *post hoc* fallacy, writers need to examine every cause and effect relationship carefully.

Writers should also be wary of attempting to oversimplify events that have complex causes. A common error is to mistake a necessary condition for a sufficient one. A *necessary* condition is one that must be present if the effect is to occur. For example, if electricity is considered a cause for light in an electric bulb, then without electricity, there can be no light. A *sufficient* condition is a condition in whose presence the effect will always occur. Using our example, a worn filament is a sufficient condition for the light to go out. But a worn filament is not a necessary condition; the light could also go out if the power lines were down because of a storm. To take another example, most people would agree that buying a lottery ticket is a necessary condition to winning a prize. That is, you cannot win without having bought a ticket. It is equally obvious that buying a lottery ticket, while necessary, does not of itself cause one to win the prize. By contrast, buying a lottery ticket with the correct numbers is a sufficient condition to cause one to win the prize—that is, it is a condition that will always ensure that the effect will occur.

Causes and effects can occur in connecting sequences of "chains of causation," where each effect itself becomes the cause of a further effect. Causal arguments must demonstrate how each cause produces an effect that then acts as a cause of a further effect. This type of causal argument often takes the form of a conditional prediction: If X happens then Y will occur.

For example, Joseph K. Skinner's argument in "Big Mac and the Tropical Forests" is developed around the conditional claim that (1) the destruction of tropical forests in Central and Latin America in order to raise cattle to produce cheap beef for fast-food chains could (2) accelerate the greenhouse effect by permitting rising levels of carbon dioxide to remain in the atmosphere and (3) thereby produce devasting changes in the world's weather systems. Because of the hypothetical nature of his thesis, Skinner is obligated to show how the world's weather system is much more vulnerable—and the consequences of the destruction of the tropical forests much more extreme—than people generally believe.

Questions for Discussion and Writing

1. In a few paragraphs, identify the causes you believe were responsible in your decision to attend your present college or university. Try to distinguish between long-term (predisposing) and short-term (triggering) causes for your decision. Can you discover any connecting sequences of causation that would constitute a chain of cause and effect. Be sure to state *how* the cause(s) you identify could have produced the end result.

2. Describe an invention (car, airplanes, air-conditioning, etc.) that changed history or an invention that does not yet exist that would make the world a better place. State *how* the effects you describe were or could be produced by the invention.

3. Analyze the following mini-argument on evolution. Sketch out or diagram, if you wish, the related sequences of cause and effect, chains of causation, and contributing causes identified by Gould in supporting his claim. How persuasive do you find his argument?

HUMAN LIFE IS AN ACCIDENT

The human species has inhabited this planet for only 250,000 years or so—roughly .0015 percent of the history of life, the last inch of the cosmic mile.

The world fared perfectly well without us for all but the last moment of earthly time—and this fact makes our appearance look more like an accidental afterthought than the culmination of a prefigured plan. Moreover, the pathways that have led to our evolution are quirky, improbable, unrepeatable and utterly unpredictable. Human evolution is not random; it makes sense and can be explained after the fact. But wind back life's tape to the dawn of time and let it play again—and you will never get humans the second time.

We are here because one odd group of fishes had a peculiar fin anatomy that could transform into legs for terrestrial creatures; because the earth never froze entirely during an ice age; because a small and tenuous species, arising in Africa a quarter of a million years ago, has managed, so far, to survive by hook and by crook. We may yearn for a "higher" answer—but none exists. This explanation, though superficially troubling, is not terrifying, is ultimately liberating and exhilarating. We cannot read the meaning of life passively in the facts of nature. We must construct these answers ourselves—from our own wisdom and ethical sense. There is no other way.

—*Stephen Jay Gould*, The Meaning of Life (*1991*)

4. From your personal experience and observation, does competition strengthen or undermine friendship? Make a plausible causal case to support your opinion.

VALUE CLAIMS MAKE VALUE JUDGMENTS

As distinct from arguments that debate matters of fact, value arguments apply ethical, moral, aesthetic, or utilitarian criteria to produce judgments that measure a subject against an ideal standard. For example, consider the following cases:

A sportswriter evaluates two teams and says that one has a better chance of winning the pennant because of better pitching.

A writer for *Consumer Reports* evaluates different brands of microwave ovens and selects the best.

A student writes an analysis arguing that the latest novel by a writer is his or her best work yet.

A critic writes a review evaluating a new restaurant, movie, or software program.

In all these cases, the writers are not merely expressing personal taste, but are making a reasoned judgment based on identifiable standards of value. Writers of value arguments must demonstrate that the standard being used as the yardstick is an appropriate one, and must provide a convincing argument of reasons and evidence in order to influence the readers' judgment and perception of the subject. For example, a writer who contended that "bilingual" education was or was not worthwhile, or that "euthanasia" was or was not immoral, would be obligated to present clearly the ideal standard against which the subject was being evaluated. Arguments that evaluate whether something is good or bad must provide (1) sufficient and verifiable evidence of a phenomenon and (2) an appropriate standard by which to measure value.

Writers frequently use comparison and contrast as a rhetorical strategy in organizing value arguments. Whether the comparison is between two books, two candidates, two kinds of automobiles, or any two subjects in the same class or category, evaluations are structured so that one choice is clearly seen as superior to the other when the two are directly compared. To get a more accurate idea of how writers use this strategy, consider the following argument by Jonathan Kozol in "The Human Cost of an Illiterate Society."

Kozol identifies the essential issue as the cost of illiteracy to a democratic society. His strategy in the entire essay contrasts the limitations that those who are illiterate must endure when compared with everyone else:

> Illiterates cannot read the menu in a restaurant. They cannot read the cost of items on the menu in the *window* of the restaurant before they enter. Illiterates cannot read the letters that their children bring home from their teachers.

Although Kozol's argument affirms a value with which few people would disagree, it is important to recognize that different people bring different value standards to bear within the same situation and therefore may produce very different value judgments. For example, a solution that might be perfectly acceptable on pragmatic or utilitarian grounds, might be unacceptable or even repugnant when judged by moral or aesthetic standards. For this reason, it is important for readers to identify the particular value system the writer is using as a criterion.

Value systems shape perceptions by influencing what people see, how they make sense out of what they see, and most important, how they interpret what they see. When people bring different value systems to the same situation, they perceive and understand the same events in radically different ways. Personal feelings, expectations, and interests strongly influence how people interpret events.

Michael Novak makes this point in his article "The Poor and Latin America":

> Latin Americans do not value the same moral qualities North Americans do. The two cultures see the world quite differently. . . . The "Catholic" aristocratic ethic of Latin America places more emphasis on luck, heroism, status, and *figura* than the relatively "Protestant" ethic of North America, which values diligence, regularity, and the responsible seizure of opportunity. Given two such different ways of looking at the world, intense love-hate relations are bound to develop.

As Novak's article illustrates, we should try to become aware of the extent to which value systems, our own and those of others, influence and shape our perceptions. This is crucial in arguments when we discover that our own perception differs drastically from that of others when we are seeing the same events. In these cases, we need to take a close look at the reasons and evidence that support our beliefs and decide whether the information on which these beliefs are based is reliable. This is one important function performed by value arguments: they challenge us to examine underlying assumptions that ordinarily remain unquestioned by forcing us to justify our view of the world.

Questions for Discussion and Writing

1. How might the following quotations serve as the basis for value arguments? In each case, state your own value judgment, summarize opposing views (if applicable), and show how your conclusion meets the appropriate criteria.

    a. "A bad peace is even worse than war."

    —Tacitus

    "The most disadvantageous peace is better than the most just war."

    —Erasmus

    b. "We are not the policeman of mankind. We are not able to run the world, and we shouldn't pretend that we can."

    —Walter Lippman

    "We have learned that we cannot live alone, at peace; that our own well being is dependent on the well-being of other nations, far away."

    —Franklin D. Roosevelt, Fourth Inaugural Address

c. "Group sex education amounts to a perversion of nature. It makes public and open that which is naturally private and intimate. Any teaching about sex in public setting violates privacy and intimacy. Sex education in the classroom is an insidious and unnatural invitation to sexual activity; it is erotic seduction; and it is even a form of child molestation, violating the natural latency and post-latency periods of child development, periods which are crucial for normal development of the whole person."

—*Randy Engel*, The New American

2. Extract the competing set of values in Figure 2.3. Rank each of these value criteria in order of their importance to you. Summarize the opposing views and either refute or accommodate each of the objections that might be raised to your value claim.

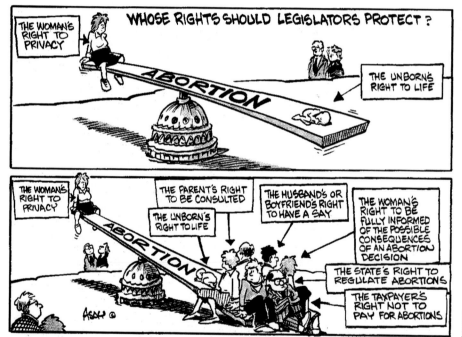

FIGURE 2.3

3. For each of the following situations, identify the criteria that you are applying, put them in order of importance to you, and show how your choice meets your criteria.

a. Evaluate the comparative benefits of Eastern forms of exercise such as tai chi or yoga with Western exercises such as aerobics or jogging. According to criteria that you stipulate, which is better and why?

b. Would you rather be popular with an entire group without forming a really close friendship or have one very close friend but not be popular with a group?

c. Would you prefer to have a short, exciting life in which you had unusual powers (you may choose any you wish) or a long uneventful life without those unusual powers?

POLICY CLAIMS MAKE RECOMMENDATIONS

In addition to arguments that characterize situations, make value judgments, or seek to establish causes or consequences, there are arguments that recommend policy changes. Many arguments in law and politics are of this kind, as are proposals in the fields of business, science, and technology.

A policy argument concerns itself first with establishing that a problem exists that is serious enough to need solving. The writer then analyzes the problem to discover the causes of the problem, puts forward a specific solution to the problem, and creates an argument that demonstrates that the proposed solution is workable (that is, can be implemented) and is superior to other proposed solutions.

An argument offering a proposed solution will often explore why there is a problem, investigate the circumstances that created it, describe who suffers because of the problem, and speculate about what will happen if the problem is not solved.

Frequently, the proposed solution is put in the form of a recommendation using the terms *should*, *ought*, or *must*. For example, Signified and Therese Engelmann, in their book *Give Your Child a Superior Mind*, argue that "parents *should* provide pre-school academic instruction for their children." Likewise, an advocate for teaching creationism in the public schools might phrase the recommendation thus: "public schools *ought* to give equal weight to the teaching of creationism and the theory of evolution in the classrooms." So, too, a staunch backer of drug testing might propose: "athletes competing in international sports events *must* be tested for steroids and other drugs."

Ideally, a policy argument should demonstrate that the way things are currently being done is producing negative consequences and that the recommended action or policy change would be capable of producing better results.

Besides meeting the specific requirements of the problem-solving situation, solutions must be feasible, effective, and attractive to the audience to whom they are proposed. The audience must feel that the writer understands both the problem's causes and its consequences, is familiar with the history of past efforts to deal with it, and is united with them in their desire to remedy the problem.

For example, notice how Richard N. Goodwin in "Money Has Corrupted the Legislative Process" establishes that a serious problem exists whose solution should be a matter of vital concern to his audience. He presents evidence to show that American government is being held hostage by special interest political action committee (PAC) groups. Implicit in Goodwin's article is the impression that he identifies with his reading public and is speaking out as any one of them might if he or she knew all the facts of the situation:

> Power of wealth has achieved dominion over the legislative process and, hence, the conduct of democratic government. . . .
>
> The principal instrument of this dominion is the political action committee, or PAC, which collects money from its members and gives it to the constitutional guardians of the public trust—members of Congress and aspirants to Congress.
>
> Most of these committees belong to economic interests that have an important stake in the actions of government—insurance companies, real-estate developers, chemical and drug companies, for example. In less than a decade they have become the single most important force in the contest for federal office. . . . PAC money is neither a "gift" nor a "contribution."
>
> It is an investment. The PACs expect recipients to give careful, and usually favorable, consideration to legislation that affects their economic well-being. Being experienced investors, they generally get what they expect. . . .
>
> The meaning of the PACs is clear. Congress is not *influenced* by special interests. Congress does not *represent* special interests. Congress is *owned* by special interests. Morally the system is bribery. It is not criminal only because those who make the laws are themselves accomplices. Government is for sale. But the bids are sealed, and the prices are very high. There is an easy way out: Eliminate PACs. We should place a rigorous ceiling on all congressional campaigns, allocate public funds to finance campaigns and require television stations—the most costly component of modern political campaigns—to give a specified amount of air time to candidates.
>
> *—Richard N. Goodwin, "Money Has Corrupted the*
> *Legislative Process," The Los Angeles Times*

As Goodwin's article illustrates, persuading readers to accept a recommendation means not only telling them what the best solution would be but also showing them through specific examples or hypothetical scenarios just how the solution would operate in practice. A writer who helps the reader visualize how the solution would work goes a long way toward refuting objections that the proposed solution might not be feasible, effective, or attractive; is too costly; or simply will not solve the problem. If possible, the writer should say who has the power to solve the problem.

It is important to keep in mind that because policy arguments are basically designed to motivate people to act or to approve of an action that has been taken, the writer must make every attempt to make the audience aware of just how serious the problem really is. It must be serious enough to warrant doing something about it. For this reason, writers often begin by pointing out the negative consequences of failing to solve the problem and also provide an account of past attempts to solve the same problem.

Next, writers propose a solution and evaluate it against alternative solutions, giving sound reasons for rejecting the alternative solutions. It is important that the writer be willing to admit honestly that difficulties could arise in carrying out his or her proposed solution and be willing to modify it in light of valid suggestions made by others.

Since policy arguments require not merely agreement, but action on the part of the audience, it is crucial for writers to try to anticipate how readers may react to the proposed solution. By putting yourself into the position of those you wish to persuade, you can generate a list of objections that might be made to your proposed solution. Would your critics reject your recommendation on any of the following grounds: your proposed action is too expensive, inefficient, unworkable, impractical, too disrupting to the status quo, or unacceptable on the grounds that it is morally offensive or aesthetically unappealing?

If substantial costs are involved, the writer should specify who will bear those costs and explain how the benefits achieved will outweigh the costs involved.

Equally important as any substantive concerns, writers of policy arguments would be wise to adopt an appropriate tone for their argument. Usually the purposes of a policy argument are best served if the writer presents him or herself as a reasonable person of good character who is well-informed on the issue in question and who is sensitive to the needs and concerns of the audience.

Questions for Discussion and Writing

1. Explain how each of the following examples might serve as a basis for a policy argument with which you might agree or disagree:

a.   It seems distressingly perverse that the very places where homeless people seek asylum, the shelters, are often, albeit by no means universally, the sites of greater risk than are the streets. Theft in shelters is rife: retention of personal belongings is accomplished by guile or domination, as even the best-staffed facilities can provide little real security. Shelter clients may fear their fellows—some recently released from jail, prison, or mental hospitals—who can be violent or exploitative; 34% of homeless people surveyed in Manhattan shelters and streets said they were afraid of being attacked in a shelter—a proportion similar to that of those who voiced fears of being attacked on the street.

—Pamela J. Fischer, Homelessness: A Prevention-Oriented Approach

b.   Professional sports management often means fan management, fan manipulation and exploitation of the fans' fantasies. Professional sports management has made viewing the game, in person or on television, less accessible, less affordable and less enjoyable. . . .

Professional sports management has successfully adjusted to the demands of TV by orchestrating what, when, and how we view professional sports. The marriage of sports management to television, players to agents and the games to show business are the result of economic decisions that have sidelined the fan, discarded him like a ticket stub after a home-game loss.

The scenario runs like this: Make the "product" so desirable that ticket prices are unattainable for the average family. Introduce mismanagement scenarios such as strikes, lockouts and collective bargaining. Demand higher TV rights fees, send players salaries up and increase the cost to the fans, regardless of the quality of the game. And when TV revenue decreases, make sure pay-per-view is forced down fans' throats so the bottom line remains intact.

That is what professional sports management has done. And the American sports fan is tired, disgusted, and wants a change.

—Nicholas F. Filla, The Sporting News, *July 13, 1992*

c.   There is a rule of evidence, used in all federal and state Courts in America, that defies logic, makes no sense whatsoever, and causes hundreds of serious miscarriages of justice each year. Its technical name is the Exclusionary Rule.

This pernicious rule prohibits the admission of evidence at trial if the evidence has been obtained by a policeman or other peace officer as a result of "unreasonable search and seizure" in violation of the Fourth Amendment to the U.S. Constitution. . . .

The Exclusionary Rule has created an upside-down system of criminal justice which diverts the focus of the criminal prosecution from the guilt or innocence of the defendant to a trial of the police! . . .

The Exclusionary Rule holds, in effect, that it is better for a murderer to go free than for the State to take advantage of any illegal conduct on the part of its officers.

—*L. Thaxton Hanson, "Protecting the Murderer"*

2. What problems confront students at your college or university (e.g., insufficient parking)? Which of these do you feel is most important and should be solved as soon as possible? Analyze the problem you consider most important in terms of the people who suffer because of it, the reasons why it exists, and the consequences of it failing to be solved. Speculate about why the problem has not been solved so far, and describe who (person, committee, or student body) has the power to solve it. Offer a proposed solution specifying the benefits, costs, and who will bear the costs. Why is your proposed solution better than alternative ones?

Definition

PURPOSES AND USES OF DEFINITION

Definition covers broad questions of what boundaries a writer chooses to draw around the issue, as well as specific meanings of key terms. Definition is the method of clarifying the meaning of words that are vague or ambiguous. These words may be important terms either in the claim of the argument or elsewhere in the essay. In other cases, you may wish to devote an entire essay to exploring all the connotations and denotations that have accrued to an unusual or controversial term or challenge preconceptions attached to a familar term.

In everday life, arguments on a whole range of issues are really arguments about how terms ought to be defined. There are several reasons why writers should clarify the basic nature of key terms on which an argument depends. First of all, as a practical matter the audience must understand what the writer means by certain unfamiliar terms crucial to the argument before they can even begin seriously considering the writer's thesis, or the evidence brought forward to support the claim. The writer must define ambiguous terms that might be mistaken to mean something other than what he or she intended. Otherwise audiences may bring their own assumptions, preconceptions, and associations to the meaning of the terms in question. Definition offers a writer a method by which to clarify the meaning of a term so that it will be free from extraneous associations and undesired connotations.

For example, an argument as to whether the government should censor pornographic materials would have to clarify exactly what is meant by such terms as *pornographic* or *obscene*. In *Roth v. U.S.* (1957), the United States Supreme Court defined "obscene and pornographic" material as material that is "patently offensive because it affronts contemporary community standards relating to the description or representation of sexual matters in a way that appeals only to 'prurient interests' and is without 'social value.'" Critics have responded that the Supreme Court's definition has itself raised questions about just how key terms such as *community, prurience*, and *social value*, in turn, ought to be defined. How is one really to gauge a community's standards—through a poll, or the testimony of leading citizens? And what type of "community" did the Supreme Court have in mind—a neighborhood, a town, a city, an entire county, a state, or region of the country? Moreover, might not an evaluation of what constitutes prurience be merely a matter of personal taste? And, how is one to identify characteristics that make it possible to say a work has or has not social value?

Likewise, an argument focusing on any of several issues surrounding organ transplantation would have to stipulate what is meant by the concept of death. A clear definition of death is important since developments in biomedical technology make it possible to sustain life by artificial means long after an individual would normally have died. The crux of the issue is that someone who would have been declared dead in the past might now be declared living. Traditionally, the courts would have relied on the definition of death as "the cessation of life; the ceasing to exist; defined by physicians as a total stoppage of the circulation of blood and a cessation of the animal and vital functions consequent thereon such as respiration, pulsation, etc." (*Black's Law Dictionary*, revised 4th ed.).

In other words, death was defined as occuring only when respiration and circulation of blood ceased. Machines, however, can sustain heartbeat and respiration indefinitely even in individuals who show no signs of brain activity. In "A Definition Of Irreversible Coma" (1968), Harvard Medical School proposed a new definition of death. This more accurate definition makes it possible to determine if and when respirators and other devices should be withdrawn, when a patient should be considered dead, and at what point still viable organs might be removed for transplantation.

Besides eliminating ambiguity and vagueness, or defining a term important to the development of the argument, definitions in argument can be used to influence the attitudes of an audience toward a particular issue. Definition becomes important in arguments where the ability to control the way a central term is perceived is equivalent to winning the argument. Definition of controversial terms not only defines the terms but effectively shapes how people will perceive the issue.

For example, during hearings by the Hawaiian State Legislature on a proposal to abolish the state's law against abortion, the following letter appeared in *The Honolulu Advertiser*:

> Dear Sir: You ask me how I stand on abortion. Let me answer forthrightly and without equivocation.
>
> If by abortion you mean the murdering of defenseless human beings; the denial of rights to the youngest of our citizens; the promotion of promiscuity among our shiftless and valueless youth and the rejection of Life, Liberty and the Pursuit of Happiness—then, Sir, be assured that I shall never waver in my opposition, so help me God. But, Sir, if by abortion you mean the granting of equal rights to all our citizens regardless of race, color or sex; the elimination of evil and vile institutions preying upon desperate and hopeless women; a chance for all our youth to be wanted and loved; and, above all, that God-given right for all citizens to act in accordance with the dictates of their own conscience— then, Sir, let me promise you as a patriot and a humanist that I shall never be persuaded to forego my pursuit of these most basic human rights. Thank you for asking my position on this most crucial issue and let me again assure of the steadfastness of my stand.
>
> Mahalo and Aloha Nui.

Definitions not only can change perceptions of an event by influencing the attitudes and emotions of an audience, but can affect the perception of facts as well.

For example, Dante Chinni in "One More Social Security Quibble: Who Is Middle Class?" calls into question conventional definitions of the "middle class":

> Everyone wants to believe they are middle class. For people on the bottom and the top of the wage scale the phrase connotes a certain Regular Joe cachet. But this eagerness to be part of the group has led the definition to be stretched like a bungee cord—used to defend/attack/describe everything from the Earned Income Tax Credit to the estate (death) tax.

The Drum Major Institute, a progressive think tank, has a website called www.themiddleclass.org that places the range for middle class at individuals making between $25,000 and $100,000 a year. Ah yes, there's a group of people bound to run into each other while house-hunting.

. . . It's nice that the definition of "middle class" is so elastic, but all that stretching has frayed it nearly to the point of being meaningless. A little more playing with it and it may snap.

—*Dante Chinni*, The Christian Science Monitor *2005*

Chinni argues that the available definition of "middle class" is not particularly accurate, but rather reflects a widespread need to identify oneself as a Regular Joe. Of course, a different definition of what constitutes "middle class" not only would alter an audience's perception but would change the facts in question and alter any conclusions that might be drawn. For example, in an election year both political parties might be expected to define "middle class" in a way that was favorable to their candidate. It is important for the writer to establish clearly a set of criteria and list distinctive characteristics of the term in question, especially if the writer's definition is really an argument for a different interpretation of the term.

Questions for Discussion and Writing

1. In what way did the meaning of the term "permission slip" become important as George Lakoff discusses it in "Framing 101: How to Take Back Public Discourse" in *Don't Think of an Elephant!* (2004)?

> Most of the United Nations consists of developing and underdeveloped countries. That means they are metaphorical children. Now let's go back to the State of the Union address. Should the United States have consulted the United Nations and gotten permission to invade Iraq? An adult does not "ask for a permission slip"! The phrase itself, *permission slip*, puts you back in grammar school or high school, where you need a permission slip from an adult to go to the bathroom. You do not need to ask for a permission slip if you are the teacher, if you are the principal, if you are the person in power, the moral authority. The others should be asking *you* for permission. That is what the *permission slip* phrase in the 2004 State of the Union address was about. Every conservative in the audience got it. They got it right away.
>
> Two powerful words: *permission slip*. What Bush did was evoke the adult-child metaphor for other nations. He said, "We're the adult." He was operating in the strict father worldview, and it did not have to be

explained. It is evoked automatically. This is what is done regularly by the conservatives.

METHODS OF DEFINING TERMS

Writers can use a variety of strategies either singly or in combination for defining terms. A description of eight of these strategies follows.

SYNONYMS   One of the simplest methods of defining words is to cite a synonym, that is, another word that has the same meaning. Thus, a writer who wanted to convey the meaning of *feast* might cite a synonym such as *banquet*. By the same token, a writer who wished to communicate the meaning of *labyrinth* could use the synonym *maze*. This method is efficient and workable but cannot always be used because many words have no exact synonyms.

For a more useful way of defining terms, we need to look at the method first discussed by Aristotle in the *Topica* (one of his treatises on logic) still in use today to define terms in dictionaries.

DICTIONARY OR LEXICAL   This method, sometimes called analytical definition, puts the thing to be defined into a *genus* or general class and then gives the *differentiae*, or distinguishing features that differentiate the subject being defined from all other things in its class with which it might be confused. For example, *teepee* is defined by *Webster's New Collegiate Dictionary* as "an American Indian skin-tent." The modifiers "American Indian" and "skin" are necessary to distinguish this particular type of tent from all other kinds of tent (e.g., a canvas Army tent) in the same general class. The terms used to define a word should be more specific, clear, and familiar than the actual term in question. Of course, there are many cases where a dictionary definition will not be adequate because the dictionary does not delve into specific criteria, characteristics, and qualities a writer might need to explore in the course of developing an argument. In these cases, the unabridged *Oxford English Dictionary* (*OED*) may prove useful because this voluminous work gives examples, in context, of how each word has been used down through the centuries.

ETYMOLOGICAL DEFINITION   Often a fascinating light is thrown on the meaning of words by studying their etymology, that is, by tracing a word to its origin and following its shift of meaning or acquisition of connotative meanings through the years. For example, William Safire, in *William Safire on Language* (1980), traces the derivation of the word *welfare*:

When words die, they deserve a decent burial, or at least a respectful obituary. One noun bit the dust recently, at least in government usage, and it is herein bid adieu. The noun is "welfare," as in "Department of Health, Education and Welfare." This fine old word was born before 1303, the offspring of the Middle English *wel*, meaning "wish" or "will," and *faren*, meaning "to go on a journey." In its youth, the word enjoyed a period on the stage: "Study for the people's welfare," Warwick advised Henry VI in Shakespeare's play. In middle age, the word was used in the same sense but with more of a governmental connotation, beginning in a 1904 *Century* magazine article about the "welfare manager . . . a recognized intermediary between employers and employees." About that time *The Westminster Gazette* was pinpointing its sociological birthplace: "The home of the 'welfare policy' is the city of Dayton, Ohio." According to the etymologist Sir Ernest Weekly, "*Welfare*, as in 'child welfare,' 'welfare center' and so forth, was first used in this sense in Ohio in 1904."

FIGURATIVE LANGUAGE—METAPHORS, SIMILES, AND ANALOGIES   Figurative language is used by writers who wish to define a term in order to persuade an audience to agree with their point of view. This form of definition uses metaphor, simile, and analogy to place a thing in its class and identify atypical properties.

For example, Len Deighton, in his book *Mexico Set*, writes: "In Mexico an air conditioner is called a politician because it makes a lot of noise but doesn't work very well."

In each of the following cases, consider how the writers use extended metaphors, similes, or analogies:

"Politics is the art of looking for trouble, finding it everywhere, diagnosing it incorrectly and applying the wrong remedies." (Groucho Marx)

"Money is like manure. If you spread it around, it does a lot of good, but if you pile it up in one place it stinks like hell." (Clint W. Murchison, Texas financier)

"Suicide is a permanent solution to a temporary problem." Phil Donahue (NBC, May 23, 1984)

"Golf is a good walk spoiled." (Mark Twain)

"An actor's a guy who, if you ain't talking about him, ain't listening." (Marlon Brando, *British Vogue*, August 1974)

STIPULATION   A stipulative definition proposes a meaning for a term that it did not have before being given it by the definition. In some cases, the writer introduces a brand-new term and stipulates that at least for the purposes of the argument, it is to carry a specific meaning. For example, Peter Singer (at Princeton University) coins the word *speciesism* by analogy with *racism* or *sexism*. This term characterizes an attitude that leads scientists involved in animal experimentation to rationalize their cruelty toward the animals used in their tests on the grounds that human beings, as the apex of all species, have every right to sacrifice other species to obtain information useful to humans. Singer feels that a new term is necessary to dramatize the low value industrial societies place on animal life. He stipulates the definition of speciesism to set the parameters of the debate in a way favorable to his viewpoint.

In still other cases, the writer stipulates an unconventional meaning for a traditional term to steer the argument in a direction favorable to his or her viewpoint.

For example, William F. Buckley's argument in *Execution Eve* against those "abolitionists" who favor eliminating capital punishment turns on his unconventional definition of the words *cruel and unusual* punishment. Buckley argues that capital punishment is by no means cruel and unusual (the Eighth Amendment to the U.S. Constitution expressly forbids "cruel and unusual" punishment) and goes on to stipulate his own definition for these terms. Buckley interprets the word *unusual* to mean simply *uncommon* or *infrequent*, in contrast to the framers of the Constitution, who used it to refer to bizarre methods of execution like death by public stoning, by the guillotine, and so on. Similarly, of the meaning of the word *cruel*, Buckley says:

> Capital punishment is cruel. That is a historical judgment. But the Constitution suggests that what must be proscribed as cruel is (a) a particularly painful way of inflicting death or (b) a particularly undeserved death: and the death penalty, as such, offends neither of these criteria and cannot therefore be regarded as objectively cruel.

While not everyone will be persuaded to accept Buckley's stipulated definitions of these words, we can see how he uses them to control and limit the argument.

NEGATION   Another useful strategy for defining a term is to specify what it is not. For example, Paul Theroux in *The Old Patagonian Express* provides this definition by negation of a *good flight*:

> You define a good flight by negatives: you didn't get hijacked, you didn't crash, you didn't throw up, you weren't late, you weren't nauseated by the food so you are grateful.

A negative definition does not release the writer from the responsibility of providing a positive definition of the term, but definition by negation is often a helpful first step in clearing away false assumptions. For example, Jesse Jackson uses both a negative definition and a figurative definition this way:

> America is not like a blanket—one piece of unbroken cloth, the same color, the same texture, the same size. America is more like a quilt—many patches, many pieces, many colors, many sizes, all woven and held together by a common thread.

EXAMPLE   Good examples are an essential part of effective writing. Nowhere is this more true than when a writer wishes to define an abstract term. Well-chosen examples are especially useful in clarifying the meaning of a term because they provide readers with a context in which to understand it. Examples may take the form of anecdotes, case histories, in-depth interviews, statistics, or even hypothetical cases that illuminate the meaning of the term in question. For instance, when Erwin Wickert in *The Middle Kingdom: Inside China Today* discusses contemporary Chinese culture, he offers clear-cut examples to illustrate the nature and meaning of *shame* in Chinese society, past and present:

> Thus the courts of ancient times did not so much punish a crime definable in terms of evidence as penalize the state of mind that led to its perpetration. Judicial verdicts and sentences are still coloured by this attitude. In the penal code of the *Qing* dynasty, which remained valid until the beginning of the twentieth century, forty lashes were prescribed as the punishment for "shameless conduct." Shameless conduct itself remained undefined because everyone knew what it was. We, on the other hand, live in a shameless society, where it would be difficult to reach a consensus about what is shameless and what is not.

The more abstract the concept the more important it is for the writer to provide a wide range of representative examples to clarify the meaning of the term in question. These examples may be drawn from personal observation, history, law, literature, or indeed any field as long as they are effective in clarifying the meaning of the term(s) to the audience. Down through the ages, the persuasive use of examples to define key terms can be seen in the writings and teachings of philosophers, poets, and preachers. For example, St. Paul (in I Corinthians, Chapter 13, *New Testament*) in his definition of the spiritual dimensions of love uses a range of examples, both real and hypothetical, along with synonyms and figurative language, to define a heightened state of being:

> And now I will show you the best way of all. I may speak in tongues of men or of angels, but if I am without love, I am a sounding gong or a clanging cymbal. I may

have the gift of prophecy, and know every hidden truth; I may have faith strong enough to move mountains; but if I have no love, I am nothing. I may dole out all I possess, or even give my body to be burnt, but if I have no love, I am none the better. Love is patient; love is kind and envies no one. Love is never boastful, nor conceited, nor rude; never selfish, not quick to take offence. Love keeps no score of wrongs; does not gloat over other men's sins, but delights in the truth.

There is nothing love cannot face; there is no limit to its faith, its hope, and its endurance. Love will never come to an end. Are these prophets? their work will be over. Are there tongues of ecstasy? they will cease. Is there knowledge. it will vanish away; for our knowledge and our prophecy alike are partial, and the partial vanishes when wholeness comes. When I was a child, my speech, my out-look, and my thoughts were all childish. When I grew up, I had finished with childish things. Now we see only puzzling reflections in a mirror, but then we shall see face to face. My knowledge now is partial; then it will be whole, like God's knowledge of me. In a word, there are three things that last for ever: faith, hope, and love; but the greatest of them all is love.

Without Paul's powerful examples, it would be rather difficult to see what he means by *love*. The examples broaden the range of associations and make the meaning of the term resonate through specific cases. Paul's definition of love suggests a spiritual depth and richness that goes far beyond what most people normally associate with the term.

Questions for Discussion and Writing

1. What method is being used in defining each of the following terms?

   a. *Free software*: The term *free software* is relatively new. However, free software itself is not. It is as old as computers themselves. Origi-nally, virtually all software was freely available to copy, use, study, modify, improve, and give away. Computer software was almost universally regarded as being akin to mathematics, i.e., something that anybody is permitted to use in any amount, with any desired modifications and for whatever purpose desired. Advances in mathematics cannot be copyrighted or patented, and they become immediately available for everyone to use for the advancement of civilization. Thus, there is no term *free mathematics*.

      —*"Free software definition" at http://www.bellevuelinux.org/free_software.html*

   b. *Workaholic*: While workaholics do work hard, not all hard workers are workaholics. I will use the word workaholics to describe those whose desire to work long and hard is intrinsic and whose work habits always exceed the prescriptions of the job they do and the expectations of the people for whom they work.

—*Marilyn Machlowitz*, Workaholics

c. *Bullshit*: For the essence of bullshit is not that it is *false* but that it is *phony*. In order to appreciate this distinction, one must recognize that a fake or a phony need not be in any respect (apart from authenticity itself) inferior to the real thing. What is not genuine need not also be defective in some other way. It may be, after all, an exact copy. What is wrong with a counterfeit is not what it is like, but how it was made. This points to a similar and fundamental aspect of the essential nature of bullshit: although it is produced without concern for the truth, it need not be false. The bullshitter is faking things. But this does not mean that he necessarily gets them wrong.

—*Harry G. Frankfurt*, On Bullshit

EXTENDED DEFINITION ESSAY An extended definition differs from other methods for defining terms because it is usually much longer and brings into play a greater variety of methods used. This type of definition expands on or uses any or all of the definition strategies previously discussed to clarify and define the basic nature of any idea, term, condition or phenomenon. The length can range from several paragraphs, to a complete essay or, conceivably, an entire book. In this sense, St. Paul's definition of love is an extended definition.

An extended definition can be developed into an entire essay when the writer delves more deeply into a concept by looking at its connotations, history, its defining criteria, and the variations in its meaning.

For example, James Baldwin in "If Black English Isn't a Language, Then Tell Me What Is" formulates an impassioned defense of the role played by black English as a "political instrument," "proof of power," and "the most vivid crucial key to identity." He relates the development of black English to the history and experience of blacks in the United States and uses a stipulated definition of *language* to develop his claim that black English is language, not merely a dialect. Baldwin does not suggest that black English be spoken instead of standard English but that it be accepted as a different but equal language.

Baldwin develops his claim by arguing that black English was created out of necessity as a form of communication between blacks who were brought from different tribes in Africa and did not speak the same language. This common language originated in the need to communicate with speed and accuracy the dangers they faced.

ST. PAUL DE VENCE, France—The argument concerning the use, or the status, or the reality of black English is rooted in American history and has absolutely nothing to do with the question the argument supposes itself to be posing. The argument has nothing to do with language itself but with the *role* of language. Language, incontestably, reveals the speaker. Language, also, far more dubiously, is meant to define the other—and, in this case, the other is refusing to be defined by a language that has never been able to recognize him.

People evolve a language in order to describe and thus control their circumstances, or in order not to be submerged by a reality that they cannot articulate. (And, if they cannot articulate it, they *are* submerged.) A Frenchman living in Paris speaks a subtly and crucially different language from that of the man living in Marseilles; neither sounds very much like a man living in Quebec, and they would all have great difficulty in apprehending what the man from Guadeloupe, or Martinique, is saying, to say nothing of the man from Senegal—although the "common" language of all these areas is French. But each has paid, and is paying, a different price for this "common" language, in which, as it turns out, they are not saying, and cannot be saying, the same things: They each have very different realities to articulate, or control.

What joins all languages, and all men, is the necessity to confront life, in order, not inconceivably, to outwit death: The price for this is the acceptance, and achievement, of one's temporal identity. So that, for example, though it is not taught in the schools (and this has the potential of becoming a political issue) the south of France still clings to its ancient and musical Provençal, which resists being described as a "dialect." And much of the tension in the Basque countries, and in Wales, is due to the Basque and Welsh determination not to allow their languages to be destroyed. This determination also feeds the flames in Ireland for among the many indignities the Irish have been forced to undergo at English hands is the English contempt for their language.

It goes without saying, then, that language is also a political instrument, means, and proof of power. It is the most vivid and crucial key to identity: it reveals the private identity, and connects one with, or divorces one from the larger, public, or communal identity. There have been, and are, times, and places, when to speak a certain language could be dangerous, even fatal. Or, one may speak the same language, but in such a way that one's antecedents are revealed, or (one hopes) hidden. This is true in France, and is absolutely true in England: The range (and reign) of accents on that damp little island make England coherent for the English and totally incomprehensible for everyone else. To open your mouth in England is (if I may use black English) to "put your business in the street": You have confessed your parents, your youth, your school, your salary, your self-esteem, and, alas, your future.

5   Now, I do not know what white Americans would sound like if there had never been any black people in the United States, but they would not sound the way they sound. *Jazz*, for example, is a very specific sexual term, as in *jazz me, baby*, but white people purified it into the Jazz Age. *Sock it to me*, which means, roughly, the same thing, has been adopted by Nathaniel Hawthorne's descendants with no qualms or hesitations at all, along with let *it all hang out* and *right on! Beat to his socks*, which was once the black's most total and despairing image of poverty, was transformed into a thing called the Beat Generation, which phenomenon was, largely, composed of *uptight*, middle-class white people, imitating poverty, trying to *get down*, to get *with it*, doing their *thing*, doing their despairing best to be *funky*, which we, the blacks, never dreamed of doing—we *were* funky, baby, like *funk* was going out of style.

Now, no one can eat his cake, and have it, too, and it is late in the day to attempt to penalize black people for having created a language that permits the nation its only glimpse of reality, a language without which the nation would be even more *whipped* than it is.

I say that this present skirmish is rooted in American history, and it is. Black English is the creation of the black diaspora. Blacks came to the United States chained to each other, but from different tribes: Neither could speak the other's language. If two black people, at that bitter hour of the world's history, had been able to speak to each other, the institution of chattel slavery could never have lasted as long as it did. Subsequently, the slave was given, under the eye, and the gun, of his master, Congo Square, and the Bible—or, in other words, and under these conditions, the slave began the formation of the black church, and it is within this unprecedented tabernacle that black English began to be formed. This was not, merely, as in the European example, the adoption of a foreign tongue, but an alchemy that transformed ancient elements into a new language: *A language comes into existence by means of brutal necessity, and the rules of the language are dictated by what the language must convey.*

There was a moment, in time, and in this place, when my brother, or my mother, or my father, or my sister, had to convey to me, for example, the danger in which I was standing from the white man standing just behind me, and to convey this with a speed, and in a language, that the white man could not possibly understand, and that, indeed, he cannot understand, until today. He cannot afford to understand it. This understanding would reveal to him too much about himself, and smash that mirror before which he has been frozen for so long.

Now, if this passion, this skill, this (to quote Toni Morrison) "sheer intelligence," this incredible music, the mighty achievement of having brought a people utterly unknown to, or despised by "history"—to have brought this people to their present, troubled, troubling, and unassailable and unanswerable place—if this absolutely unprecedented journey does not indicate that black English is a language, I am curious to know what definition of language is to be trusted.

10   A people at the center of the Western world, and in the midst of so hostile a population, has not endured and transcended by means of what is patronizingly called a "dialect." We, the blacks, are in trouble, certainly, but we are not doomed, and we are not inarticulate because we are not compelled to defend a morality that we know to be a lie.

The brutal truth is that the bulk of the white people in America never had any interest in educating black people, except as this could serve white purposes. It is not the black child's language that is in question, it is not his language that is despised: It is his experience. A child cannot be taught by anyone who despises him, and a child cannot afford to be fooled. A child cannot be taught by anyone whose demand, essentially, is that the child repudiate his experience, and all that gives him sustenance, and enter a limbo in which he will no longer be black, and in which he knows that he can never become white. Black people have lost too many black children that way.

And, after all, finally, in a country with standards so untrustworthy, a country that makes heroes of so many criminal mediocrities, a country unable to face why so many of the nonwhite are in prison, or on the needle, or standing, futureless, in the streets—it may very well be that both the child and his elder have concluded that they have nothing whatever to learn from the people of a country that has managed to learn so little.

Questions for Discussion and Writing

1. How does Baldwin use examples of the experience of those who still speak varieties of French, Basque, Welsh, and Irish (Gaelic) to stress the importance of political and cultural contexts on questions of group identity?

2. How might the same issue Baldwin discusses in his essay be treated by different disciplines? For example, what approach would a linguistics scholar take? How might a historian's account of the evolution of black English differ in method from that used by Baldwin?

3. In a short essay, explore Baldwin's assertion that black English has helped give American English a distinct identity. For example, what expressions has black English contributed to mainstream English?

3

SUPPORTING ARGUMENTS

OVERVIEW: This chapter will introduce you to the ways in which evidence can be used to support a claim, and the role that warrants (or assumptions) play in securing a convincing relationship between the claim and the evidence. We will also examine the steps that writers need to take to assure that their arguments are favorably received by their particular audiences.

Using Evidence

Every assertion or claim put forward in an argument should be supported by appropriate, authoritative, and timely evidence. Evidence can appear in a variety of forms including examples drawn from personal experience, hypothetical cases, analogies, the testimony of experts, and statistical data. Readers expect that evidence cited to substantiate or refute assertions will be sound, accurate, and relevant, and that conclusions will be drawn logically from this evidence. Readers also expect that a writer arguing in support of a proposition will acknowledge and answer objections put forth by the opposing side in addition to providing compelling evidence to support his or her own position.

TESTIMONY OF EXPERTS

The testimony of experts is an invaluable way of quickly demonstrating that the conclusions one has reached about a given issue are independently subscribed to by renowned authorities in the field. Writers rely on the opinion of authorities when their own ability to draw conclusions based on firsthand observations is limited. The authorities are presumed to have expertise based on many years of research and greater familiarity with the issues under investigation. The opinion of experts is no substitute for the process of reasoning by which you have arrived at your conclusion, but a well-known authority can add considerable weight to your opinion and a dimension of objective credibility to the argument.

When deciding whether to quote an authority consider the following guidelines:

1. The expert must be an authority in the field.

2. His or her testimony must be free from bias and result from free and open inquiry that is subject to public verification.

3. The opinion must be timely and not open to question on the grounds that it might have been true in the past, but is no longer relevant.

For example, Elizabeth W. and Robert A. Fernea, in "A Look Behind the Veil" (from *Human Nature*), cite the opinion of an expert on Islamic culture in their discussion of the changing attitudes toward wearing the veil in Mediterranean and Middle Eastern societies:

> The multiple meanings and uses of *purdah* and the veil do not explain how the pattern came to be so deeply embedded in Mediterranean society. Its origins lie somewhere in the basic Muslim attitudes about men's roles and women's roles. Women, according to Fatima Mernissi, a Moroccan sociologist, are seen by men in Islamic societies as in need of protection because they are unable to control their sexuality, are tempting to men, and hence are a danger to the social order. In other words, they need to be restrained and controlled so that society may function in an orderly way.

THREE FORMS EXPERT OPINION CAN TAKE   The opinion of experts offers an interpretation of a set of facts. The interpretation can take one of three forms: the expert (1) points out a causal connection, (2) offers a solution to a problem, or (3) makes a prediction about the future. Correspondingly, writers can use these "expert opinions" to support a causal claim (that is, to document the existence of causal correlation or connection), to support a proposed solution to a problem, or to authenticate the reliability of a prediction.

1. *Pointing Out a Causal Connection.* For example, a writer wishing to support a claim that where you live influences your chances of getting cancer might quote Samuel S. Epstein, a professor of occupational and

environmental medicine at the University of Illinois Medical Center, in "The Cancer-Producing Society":

A recent National Cancer Institute (NCI) atlas on cancer mortality rates, in different counties, has demonstrated marked geographical clustering of rates for various organs in the U.S. with populations in heavily industrialized areas. Such data suggest associations between cancer rates in the general community and the proximity of residence to certain industries.

The writer would probably mention Epstein's credentials and to further enhance the credibility of his source might cite the fact that Dr. Epstein's efforts were responsible for the enactment of legislation to control toxic substances.

2. *Offering a Solution to a Problem.* Besides citing experts to document the existence of causal connections, writers look to authorities for solutions to problems. For example, Bill McKibben, in "It's Easy Being Green" (from *Mother Jones*), cites an expert who offers answers to the energy-wasting practices so pervasive in American society:

In the words of Charles Komanoff, a New York energy analyst, "The choice is between love of oil and love of country," and at least "in the initial weeks after September 11, it seemed that Americans were awakening at last to the true cost of their addiction to oil." In an effort to take advantage of that political window, Komanoff published a booklet showing just how simple it would be to cut America's oil use by 5 or 10 percent—not over the years it will take for the new technologies to really kick in, but over the course of a few weeks and with only minor modifications to our way of life.

For instance, he calculated, we could save 7 percent of the gasoline we use simply by eliminating the one car trip in fourteen. The little bit of planning required to make sure you visit the grocery store three times a week instead of four would leave us with endlessly more oil than sucking dry the Arctic. Indeed, Americans are so energy-profligate that even minor switches save significant sums—if half the drivers in two-car households switched just a tenth of their travel to their more efficient vehicle, we'd instantly save 1 percent of our oil. Keep the damn Explorer; just leave it in the driveway once a week and drive the Camry.

Note how the expert opinion here takes the form of a solution offered to the problem of energy use.

3. *Making a Prediction.* A third form in which the testimony of authorities can be used to support a claim is as a prediction. For example, in *The*

World Is Flat (2005), Thomas L. Friedman foresees what will be an important aspect of our changing world:

> Clearly, it is now possible for more people than ever to collaborate and compete in real time with other people on more different kinds of work from more different corners of the planet and on a more equal footing than at any previous time in the history of the world—using computers, e-mail, networks, teleconferencing and dynamic new software. . . . that was what I discovered on my journey to India and beyond. And that is what this book is about. When you start to think of the world as flat, a lot of things make sense in ways that they did not before. But I was also excited personally, because what the flattening of the world means is that we are now connecting all the knowledge centers of the planet together into a single global network, which—if politics and terrorism do not get in the way—could usher in an amazing era of prosperity and innovation.

Keep in mind that the opinion of experts, however credible, is still only an interpretation of a set of facts. Other authorities might presumably reach diametrically opposite conclusions from the same evidence. This is why an argument should never be based on the opinion of experts alone. The writer should first create an independent, well-reasoned argument that can stand on its own and only then add the testimony of experts to strengthen the case.

EXAMPLES DRAWN FROM PERSONAL EXPERIENCES

Providing good examples is an essential part of effective argumentative writing. A single well-chosen example, or a range of illustrations, can provide clear cases that illustrate, document, and substantiate a writer's thesis. The report of a memorable incident, an account drawn from records, eyewitness reports, and a personal narrative account of a crucial incident, are all important ways examples can serve to document the authenticity of the writer's thesis.

For example, Donald A. Norman, in *Emotional Design: Why We Love (or Hate) Everyday Things*, draws on personal experience to underscore the issue that is at the heart of his book—the idea that we don't just use a product, we become emotionally involved with it:

> It was lunchtime. My friends and I were in downtown Chicago, and we decided to try Cafe des Architectes in the Sofitel Hotel. As we entered the bar area, a beautiful display greeted us: water bottles, the sort you can buy in a food market, set out as works of art. The entire rear wall of the bar was like an art gallery: frosted glass, subtly lit from behind, from floor to ceiling; shelves in front of the glass, each shelf dedicated to a different type of water. Blue, green, amber—all

the wonderful hues, the glass gracefully illuminating them from behind, shaping the play of color. Water bottles as art. I resolved to find out more about this phenomenon. How did the packaging of water become an art form?

"Walk down a grocery aisle in any town in the U.S., Canada, Europe, or Asia and there is a virtual tidal wave of bottled water brands," is how one web site that I consulted put it. Another web site emphasized the role of emotion: "package designers and brand manufacturers are looking beyond graphic elements or even the design as a whole to forge an emotional link between consumers and brands." The selling of premium bottled water in major cities of the world, where the tap water is perfectly healthful, has become a big business.

—*Donald A. Norman, "Three Levels of Design: Visceral, Behavioral, and Reflective"*

These observations serve to illustrate the thesis of Norman's book and provide a context for his discussion of why designers should consider the emotional impacts of objects in our everyday world and why they should be aesthetically pleasing.

One extremely effective way of substantiating a claim is by using a *case history*, that is, an in-depth account of the experience of one person that typifies the experience of many people in the same situation. The following account drawn from Michael Harrington's acclaimed sociological study *The Other America: Poverty in the United States* (1969) uses one woman's experiences to typify the plight of a whole class of older citizens:

Sometimes in the course of an official Government report, a human being will suddenly emerge from the shadows of statistics and analyses. This happened in a summary statement of the Senate Subcommittee on the Problems of the Aged and Aging in 1960. Louise W—comes to life: Louise W—, age 73, lives by herself in a single furnished room on the third floor of a rooming house located in a substandard section of the city. In this one room, she cooks, eats and sleeps. She shares a bathroom with other lodgers. Widowed at 64, she has few friends remaining from her younger years. Those who do remain do not live near her, and it is difficult for her to see them. She feels that the other older men and women living in the same rooming house are not good enough for her company (conversations with these persons reveal that they have the same attitude, too: their fellow inhabitants are not good enough for them either).

And so she stays confined to her one room and the bathroom shared by nine other people. When the weather is warm enough, she ventures down the long flight of stairs about once a week for a walk to the corner and back. Louise W—is symbolic of a growing and intense problem in American society.

The nation venerates youth, yet the proportion of the population over sixty-five years of age is increasing. For many of these older people, their declining years are without dignity.

The example of Louise W—serves as anecdotal proof that illustrates Harrington's claim that many of the elderly are among the most poverty-stricken people in the country. He shows, graphically and vividly, that many older people face a future very unlike the popular depiction of the "golden years."

Questions for Discussion and Writing

1. Create a one or two paragraph mini-argument drawing on personal experience or the experience of others (case history) that develops one or two of the following topics. (Support your claim with statements that refer to "a time when" or "a situation where.") Specify the audience to whom you would be making this argument; think of an audience (person or group) whose opinion you would want to change.

   - The transition from living at home to living in the dorm.
   - Friends who borrow money.
   - Long-distance relationships and high telephone bills.
   - Transportation issues (parking, bike lanes, etc.).
   - Coaches.
   - First apartments, landlords, roommates.
   - Having pets.
   - Budgeting finances.
   - The joys of cooking.
   - Bosses, supervisors.
   - Memorable dates, blind dates.
   - Clubs, study groups, ethnic or activity-related gatherings such as chorus.
   - The mall's effect on socializing.
   - Personal appearance, clothing, good- or bad-hair day.
   - Substance abuse.
   - Recreation, concerts, games, museums.
   - Dieting.
   - Internet pursuits, e-mail, blogging.
   - Sports or martial-arts training.
   - Culture clashes.

HYPOTHETICAL CASES (SCENARIOS AND "WHAT IF" SITUATIONS)

Not all examples need be real. In some types of causal arguments where no real and observable effects can be cited as examples, the writer is obliged to show how an effect that has never been observed is possible or could be produced. In these circumstances, hypothetical examples are useful in clarifying possible future consequences. For example, in "The Case for Torture" Michael Levin argues that in certain circumstances torture is "not merely permissible but morally mandatory." Levin uses a series of hypothetical examples to support this assertion. Levin's strategy is to begin with a very extreme hypothetical example of a terrorist who has "hidden an atomic bomb on Manhattan island" in order to compel the reader to examine his or her own assumptions as to whether or not torture is, if ever, permissible:

> Suppose a terrorist had hidden an atomic bomb on Manhattan Island which will detonate at noon on July 4 unless . . . (here follow the usual demands for money and release of his friends from jail). Suppose, further, that he is caught at 10 a.m. of the fateful day, but—preferring death to failure—won't disclose where the bomb is. What do we do? If we follow due process—wait for his lawyer, arraign him—millions of people will die. If the only way to save those lives is to subject the terrorist to the most excruciating possible pain, what grounds can there be for not doing so? I suggest there are none. In any case, I ask you to face the question with an open mind. Torturing the terrorist is unconstitutional? Probably. But millions of lives surely outweigh constitution-ality. Torture is barbaric? Mass murder is far more barbaric. Indeed, letting millions of innocents die in deference to one who flaunts his guilt is moral cowardice, an unwillingness to dirty one's hands. If you caught the terrorist, could you sleep nights knowing that millions died because you couldn't bring yourself to apply the electrodes?
>
> Once you concede that torture is justified in extreme cases, you have admit-ted that the decision to use torture is a matter of balancing innocent lives against the means needed to save them. You must now face more realistic cases involv-ing more modest numbers. Someone plants a bomb on a jumbo jet. He alone can disarm it, and his demands cannot be met (or if they can, we refuse to set a precedent by yielding to his threats). Surely we can, we must, do anything to the extortionist to save the passengers. How can we tell 300, or 100, or 10 people who never asked to be put in danger, "I'm sorry, you'll have to die in agony, we just couldn't bring ourselves to . . ."
>
> Here are the results of an informal poll about a third, hypothetical, case. Suppose a terrorist group kidnapped a newborn baby from a hospital. I asked four mothers if they would approve of torturing kidnappers if that were

necessary to get their own newborns back. All said yes, the most "liberal" adding that she would administer it herself.

—Michael Levin, "The Case for Torture," Newsweek (1982)

Levin's strategy is extremely effective. If a reader accepts the use of torture in some cases, then he or she would have to consider more seriously whether torture is appropriate in nonhypothetical cases in real life. If torture is acceptable: (1) to save the lives of millions of people from an atomic bomb hidden by terrorists, or (2) to save a few hundred people from a terrorist bomb on a jumbo jet, or (3) to save the life of one newborn child from kidnappers, then the reader must confront the question as to when torture is *not* appropriate. Levin imaginatively uses these scenarios to probe the issue and to compel his readers to seriously consider his claim that "the decision to use torture is a matter of balancing innocent lives against the means necessary to save them." Note how Levin uses results of an "informal poll" to suggest that even apart from extreme hypothetical cases, torture remains a viable option for those mothers whose children's lives are at stake. Levin's argumentative strategy is to work from extreme cases to more realistic ones, saying in effect, "If you agree with my first and second examples, then you must agree with my third." These invented episodes have the effect of provoking his audience to think beyond immediate responses and really consider whether or not torture is ever permissible.

ANALOGIES

Analogies are useful for bringing out convincing similarities among ideas, situations, and people in order to persuade an audience that if two things are similar in several observed respects, they may well be similar in other ways as well. The philosopher David Hume observed that "in reality all arguments from experience are founded on the similarity which we discover among natural objects, and by which we are induced to expect effects similar to those which we have found to follow from such objects." Analogy is effective as a rhetorical strategy in that it persuades an audience that if two subjects share a number of specific observable qualities, then they may probably share some unobserved qualities as well.

Analogies are an unparalleled means of clarifying complex ideas and abstract concepts. For example, the historian Arnold J. Toynbee employs an unusual analogy in "Challenge and Response" (from *A Study of History*) to illuminate his thesis that torpid societies become dynamic civilizations when their normal routine is challenged by an outside force. The crucial difference Toynbee discovered between primitive and higher cultures is that primitive societies remain static, whereas higher cultures respond creatively to challenge:

> Primitive societies as we know them by direct observation, may be likened to people lying torpid upon a ledge on a mountainside with a precipice below and a precipice above; civilizations may be likened to companions of these sleepers who have just risen to their feet and have started to climb up the face of the cliff above . . . we can observe that, for every single one now strenuously climbing, twice that number . . . have fallen back onto the ledge defeated.

Toynbee's analogy of cliff climbers and ledge sitters is meant to reflect the contrast between dynamic civilizations on one hand and stagnant cultures on the other. In his analogy, societies are represented by the dormant sleepers. The ledge below is the past they have risen above. The precipice above them is the next plateau they must reach to become flourishing civilizations. The analogy captures the readiness of some societies to risk a possible fall in order to leave the relative safety of the ledge and climb the precipice in search of the ledge above.

The preceding example illustrates one important aspect of creating effective analogies: every analogy is useful until the differences between the things being compared become greater than the similarities. Arguments based on analogy, however compelling, interesting, and imaginative the analogy might be, can only strive to demonstrate a high degree of probability, not absolute certainty. For this reason, the criteria for evaluating analogical arguments depend on comparing the number of respects in which the two subjects are said to be similar or analogous with the number of respects in which they are said to differ. A strong analogy is persuasive to the extent that the number of qualities shared by two subjects far outweighs the number of differences. Correspondingly, many points of difference between the two subjects greatly weaken the analogical argument by reducing the audience's perception that the two things are probably alike in many ways.

In the law, strong analogies serve as proof. When lawyers cite previously decided cases as legal precedents to argue that a case in question should be decided along the lines of the earlier cases, they are reasoning from strong analogies. For example, a lawyer might cite the *Miranda* case (Supreme Court decision, 1966) as a precedent in arguing that the defendant in the present case should not be tried because he was not advised of his rights (as the *Miranda* decision requires). The use of legal precedent in the courtroom is a form of reasoning from analogy. Lawyers may argue that the present case should be dismissed because a previous case was also dismissed on the same grounds.

Such straightforward reasoning assumes that enough similarities between two cases exist to support the claim that what was true of one case is also true of the other.

By contrast, weak or figurative analogies can clarify or illustrate a claim, but cannot serve as evidence to support it. For example, to discover if you can tell whether an analogy is strong enough to support a claim, consider the following argument by John Underwood:

> For if a drug test is an invasion of privacy, what is a blood test? A man's blood is certainly as private as his urine, and even if it might, in its course or of its type, communicate a deadly disease or produce a deformed child, the testing of it most assuredly requires an invasion. The common good, and every state in the union, nevertheless requires blood tests. Try to get a marriage license without one. Moreover, what is an eye test if not (by short extension of ACLU logic) an invasion of privacy? On the common sense basis that we already wreak havoc on our highways without allowing the physically disabled behind the wheels of our killer vehicles, the common good calls for eye tests. Try getting a driver's license without one.
>
> And what about the lie tests that are burgeoning in popularity as a means of screening security risks in both the government and private sectors? Is a lie test an invasion of privacy? Is a man's brain as sacred as his bladder, regardless of how much or little can be found in either? You betcha. What could be more intrusive than poking around in a man's thought processes. But we allow it. The common good demands it.
>
> —*John Underwood, "The Scourge of This Society Is Drug Abuse: Testing Is Clearly an Idea Whose Time Has Come,"* The Miami Herald

Underwood argues that drugs have caused such damage to society that civil-liberties groups are wrong to stand in the way of drug testing. He argues by analogy that just as eye tests, blood tests, and lie detector tests are widely accepted even though they invade privacy, so widespread drug testing should be instituted although admittedly it is also an invasion of privacy.

On first reading, Underwood's use of an analogy seems rooted in real similarities in comparable situations. The analogy, however, breaks down in some respects: the results of blood tests and eye tests are used to diagnose illness or cite deficiencies that can then be remedied. In other words, the results of these tests are used for the benefit of the person being tested. By contrast, a urinanalysis drug test has only one purpose: to identify a drug abuser to his or her employer or the government. The results are not used to benefit the person being tested and may even be used to the detriment of that person. In short, information derived from the test is used against the person being tested.

Lie detector tests seem to offer a closer analogy. Here, however, Underwood does not take into account the fact that the results from lie detector tests are not admissible as evidence in court. Thus, a crucial number of differences weaken his argument and greatly undercut the validity of his conclusion.

Questions for Discussion and Writing

1. Develop any of the following into a mini-argument in which you support a claim with either a hypothetical example or an analogy drawn from a precedent or a parallel instance. Evaluate your mini-argument for persuasiveness and credibility:

    a. Have you ever been romantically involved with someone from a different racial, religious, or political background? To what kinds of pressures from parents, relatives, and society were you subjected? What was the outcome of the relationship? What beliefs, views, or opinions did you evolve as a result?

    b. In your opinion, what pressures create difficulties in second marriages for the new spouse, children, and stepchildren in terms of fairness, financial equity, and other issues?

STATISTICS

Statistical evidence is among the most compelling kinds of proof a writer can offer to support a thesis. To be effective, statistical data should be drawn from recent data and be as up-to-date as possible. It is important that statistics come from reliable and verifiable sources such as the U.S. Bureau of Census, the Bureau of Labor, documented surveys conducted by well-established research centers or universities, or well-known polling organizations like those of Lou Harris and George Gallup. Statistical data are useful in many kinds of arguments because of the ease with which comparative differences can be evaluated in quantifiable form.

For example, Dennis Cauchon, in "Medical Miscalculation Creates Doctor Shortage" (from *USA Today*, 2005), cites available statistics to support his argument that contrary to what most people believe, the supply of physicians is shrinking:

> The United States dramatically expanded the number of doctors being trained in the 1960s and 1970s, creating two new physicians for every one that retired, says Richard Cooper, director of the Health Policy Institute at the Medical College of Wisconsin. But the production of new doctors has changed little since 1985. Today, new physicians roughly equal the number of doctors retiring. Within a decade, baby boom doctors licensed in the 1960s, 1970s and 1980s will retire in large numbers that will outstrip the 25,000 new doctors produced every

year, Cooper says. The effective number of physicians will fall even more, Cooper says, because doctors work shorter hours today. "The public expects good, innovative health care, but we're not producing enough physicians to provide it," says Cooper.

The portion of U.S. income spent on health care rose from 8.8% in 1980 to 15.4% in 2004 and will reach 18.7% in 2014, according to Medicare estimates. That means more doctors are needed, whether it's for hip replacements or prescribing new drugs. Demographic changes in the medical profession also contribute to the need for more physicians. Nearly half of new physicians are women, and studies show they work an average of 25% fewer hours than male physicians, Cooper says.

Physicians older than 55 work about 15% less than younger doctors. And medical residents have been limited to 80-hour weeks since 2003, ending decades of 100-plus-hour weeks. Most worrisome, the retirement of baby boom physicians means the number of doctors will start falling just as the first baby boomer turns 70 in 2016, says Ed Salsberg, a workforce specialist at the Association of American Medical Colleges.

It is important for Cauchon to establish that the supply of physicians is shrinking because the public is still under the illusion that there are and will be more than enough doctors. The way statistical evidence is used will depend on the nature of the claim. Evidence in the form of statistics may provide stronger support for a writer's claim than anecdotal cases or hypothetical examples.

Statistics are especially useful in arguments where writers use inductive reasoning (that is, drawing an inference from specific cases) to support a generalization extrapolated from a representative sampling of all the evidence that might be examined. As with other uses of evidence in inductive reasoning, writers must be careful not to draw conclusions, even from reliable objectively verifiable statistics, that go so far beyond what the available evidence warrants as to seem improbable. Perhaps the most famous illustration of unwarranted generalization from a relatively small sample was the erroneous prediction in the 1948 presidential election that the Republican governor of New York, Thomas E. Dewey, would definitely defeat the incumbent Democrat, Harry S. Truman. Unfortunately for the pollsters, the poll on which this prediction was made was drawn from an inadequate sample and did not represent the entire voting population.

Since any prediction based on polls is essentially an inference drawn from a number of individual cases, this claim or conclusion will become more probable as the size of the sample becomes greater. The claim, therefore, can be expressed in quantitative or statistical terms. For example, William J. Darby, in

"The Benefits of Drink" (from *Human Nature)*, cites a study of 120,000 patients that discovered that moderate drinkers were 30 percent less likely to have heart attacks than were teetotalers:

> A recent study by Arthur L. Klatsky and his colleagues at the Kaiser-Permanente Medical Center in Oakland, California, offers new evidence that moderate drinking may serve as a deterrent to heart attacks. They studied 464 patients who had been hospitalized with a first myocardial infarction (heart attack) and discovered that an unusually large proportion were teetotalers. Their curiosity aroused, Klatsky and his colleagues evaluated the medical histories of 120,000 patients and found that moderate alcohol users were 30 percent less likely to have heart attacks than were non-drinking patients or matched controls or so-called risk controls—people who suffer from diabetes, hypertension, obesity, high serum cholesterol, or who smoke. (All of these factors are associated with increased risk of heart attacks.)

Notice how the conclusion uses statistics to quantify the generalization about the mitigating effects of moderate drinking. In essence, the writer is saying, "Based on these 120,000 instances, I'm reasonably certain that similar results would be obtained in comparable studies on other groups of patients." Indeed, a follow-up study done by Klatsky in 1997 concluded that the data "robustly supports the inverse relations of alcohol use to CAD (coronary artery disease) risk."

THREE TYPES OF AVERAGES: THE ARITHMETIC MEAN, THE MEDIAN, AND THE MODE When a writer supports a claim by referring to the "average," he or she is purposely selecting a specific value to represent the qualities of a whole aggregate of things. But, it is important for the reader to realize that there is more than one type of average and to know the writer has used the right kind to support his or her claim. There are three main types of averages, called (1) the *mean,* (2) the *median,* and (3) the *mode.* Each has its own characteristics and the values they represent can, in different situations, be quite different from one another. The most commonly used kind of average is the *arithmetic mean*—or, as it is commonly called, the mean. To calculate it, you simply add up all the numerical values and divide by the total number. The resulting average is the arithmetic mean.

1. The *Arithmetic Mean.* One example of the mean might be in baseball, where a player's batting average shows statistically how often the batter has successfully hit the ball in comparison with the total number of times he has had at bat. While this kind of an average is useful

for giving a sense of where the "center of gravity" of any set (total number of times at bat, in this case) is located, the useful information drawn from it can be distorted by very large or very small instances averaged in with all the others. For example, a brokerage firm, in order to recruit account executive trainees, advertises that the average starting salary for new employees is $72,000 a year. Only later might a new account executive discover that the $72,000 was derived by averaging in the starting salary of $216,000 of a senior account executive with 10 years experience transferring in from another firm along with the $36,000 starting salary of four new account executive trainees. Here, the average of $72,000 is reached by adding $216,000 + 4 × $36,000 (equalling $360,000) divided by the five new employees.

2. The *Median.* Other ways of measuring the average would have provided prospective employees with a much more realistic figure of what starting salary they could expect. One of these more accurate kinds of averages is the median. The median is usually the central value in a set of values. The median also establishes a dividing line that separates higher from lower values in a set of numbers. In the preceding case, the median starting salary would be $36,000 (while the average or mean was $72,000). As the following list shows, the median establishes a dividing line with two salaries above and two salaries below:

$216,000
$36,000
$36,000 (the median)
$36,000
$36,000

3. The *Mode.* Another way of arriving at an average that is useful for interpretative purposes is called the mode. The mode is the value that occurs most frequently in any series of numbers. In the preceding case, more new employees (four out of five) start at $36,000 a year than any other amount; hence, $36,000 is the modal income. In this case, the median and the mode are both more reliable indicators for a prospective new employee than the more commonly relied on average arithmetical mean. This case illustrates how important it is for readers to understand what kind of average writers are using to substantiate a claim. Keep in mind that the three uses of the word *average* in the preceding example all draw different conclusions from exactly the same information. The median is a much more representative measure

than the mean or average because in any example, extremely high or extremely low readings on the scale will distort the average but not the median.

USING CHARTS AND GRAPHS   Evidence drawn from statistical data can be expressed and presented in charts, graphs, or percentages. The reader should determine whether conclusions drawn from statistics are consistent with other evidence in the argument.

Statistical information can be represented in a variety of graphic forms. For example, Figure 3.1 shows how the statistical breakdown of the answer to the question "who are the hungry?" is represented in a *pie chart* in *Scientific American*, 2005.

Statistical information can also appear in a *bar chart*. Figure 3.2 shows how past, current, and future assessments of daily caloric intake in various countries is shown in a special issue of *Scientific American*, 2005.

The context in which statistics are presented is important. For example, the National Safety Council urges people to buckle up their seat belts by announcing "80% of all fatal accidents occur 5 miles from home." Reading this, you're liable to have the mistaken impression that the area surrounding your house is more dangerous than other areas where you drive. What this public-service announcement neglects to add is that 80 percent of *all* driving is done within 5 miles of where you live, which explains why 80 percent of all accidents, fatal and otherwise, occur in this area. The statistics themselves are true but a proper context for evaluating what they mean has been omitted.

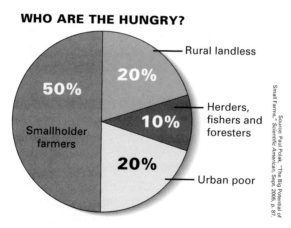

WHO ARE THE HUNGRY?

50% Smallholder farmers

20% Rural landless

10% Herders, fishers and foresters

20% Urban poor

Source: Paul Polak, "The Big Potential of Small Farms," *Scientific American*, Sept. 2005, p. 87.

FIGURE 3.1
■ Distribution of hunger in the world.

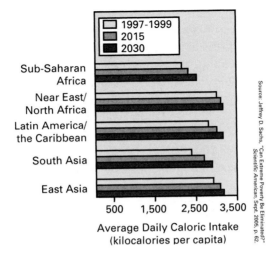

Source: Jeffrey D. Sachs, "Can Extreme Poverty Be Eliminated?" *Scientific American*, Sept. 2005, p. 62.

FIGURE 3.2

■ Average daily caloric intake.

To evaluate the validity of a survey, readers should be aware of the size of the sample used to compile the data, and the methods used to assure a fair cross section of the population under study. Opinion can be manipulated through seemingly impressive statistics where the sampling procedure used is subtly biased to support a preconceived opinion. For example, someone who reads that "nine out of ten dentists who recommend chewing gum, recommend XYZ gum" will probably overlook the key phrase "who recommend chewing gum." The statistics themselves might be true, but the sample has been skewed to survey only those dentists who recommend chewing gum—an atypical and miniscule subgroup of all dentists.

The most reliable technique for avoiding an error in sampling is to make sure the poll or study surveys a representative cross section of all those who might be polled. To ensure fairness, the sample must be random so that even if every individual cannot be polled, each member of the population has exactly the same chance of being included in the sample as any other.

This type of sampling procedure relies on probability principles. It is implemented by dividing the population into separate categories or *strata*. People interviewed are selected solely on a chance basis within each stratified category (for example, people who live in a certain part of town or earn a certain amount of money or have reached a certain level of education). The theory behind probability sampling is really quite straightforward. If one had a large barrel containing 10,000 marbles, half of which were red and half of which were blue, and wished to draw a probability sample of 200 marbles, one might draw the first marble while blindfolded to make sure that the marbles all stood an equal chance of being drawn. The barrel would be shaken after each trial to ensure that in subsequent drawings all the marbles still had an equal chance of being selected. The law of probability states that if this procedure were repeated an infinite number of times, the 200 marbles selected would be fairly close to a 50–50 division with approximately 100 of them being red and 100 of them being blue. The next most likely combination would be either 99 red and 101 blue or 99 blue and 101 red. The next most likely combination after that would be 98 red and 102 blue or 98 blue and 102 red, and so on. The most unlikely combination would produce 200 marbles that were either all red or all blue.

For the same reason, if each member of a population being surveyed has an equal chance of being selected, probability theory states that the sample will wind up being sufficiently representative to provide an accurate index of the whole population. In practice, the expense of surveying a large number of people means that the size of the sample is frequently less than might be optimally desirable since the larger the sample the smaller the sampling error that can be expected. *Sampling error* refers to the degree to which the results in the sample can be expected to differ from what the results would be if everyone in the population had been selected. It is expressed in terms of a range of percentage points above and below a reported percentage. For example, a survey based on 1,000 interviews might show that a candidate for governor might expect to be supported by 50 percent of the population. The margin of sampling error might be reported as plus or minus 4 percent. This means that if everyone in the population had been interviewed rather than only 1,000, the actual results might see the candidate supported by as few as 46 percent of the people or as many as 54 percent. If the election were really close, a completely different outcome could be possible within the sampling error.

Thus, statistics play an important role in arguments in which claims must be substantiated by reference to several cases where it would be impractical to test a whole population. At the same time, readers of arguments must be aware of the dangers of accepting statistics at face value without understanding both the procedures and the motives of those who gathered and interpreted the data.

Questions for Discussion and Writing

1. Critically evaluate each of the following mini-arguments in terms of the credibility of the experts cited, the kind of testimony offered, and the quality and methodology of the statistical evidence presented.

    a. According to a CDC epidemiologist, Tom Verstraeten, who had analysed the agency's massive data base containing the medical records of 100,000 children, a mercury-based preservative in the vaccines—thimerosal—appeared to be responsible for a dramatic increase in autism and a host of other neurological disorders in children. "I was actually stunned by what I saw," Verstraeten told those assembled at Simpsonwood [a conference convened by the Center for Disease Control and Prevention], citing the staggering number of earlier studies that indicate a link between thimerosal and speech delays, attention-deficit disorder, hyperactivity and autism. Since 1991, when the CDC and the FDA had recommended that three additional vaccines laced with the preservative be given to extremely young infants—in one case, within hours of birth—the estimated number of cases of autism had increased fifteen fold, from one in every 25,000 children to one in every 166 children.

Even for scientists and doctors accustomed to confronting issues of life and death, the findings were frightening. "You can play with this all you want," Dr. Bill Weil, a consultant for the American Academy of Pediatrics, told the group. The results "are statistically significant."

—*Robert F. Kennedy, Jr.* "*Deadly Immunity,*" Rolling Stone *(2005)*

b.   All that fall, the words "Morgenthau," "Von Bernstorff," "Bryce," "Armenian," "atrocities," "Germany," "Turks," "horrors," "refugees" made up the *New York Times* headlines. And these words were supplemented by numbers. What did it mean to a popular audience in 1915 to read the numbers of Armenian dead? The numbers brought home to Americans the urgency of the need to practice the Golden Rule. NINE THOUSAND ARMENIANS MASSACRED AND THROWN INTO TIGRIS (August 4, 1915); 600,000 STARVING ON ROAD (August 27, 1915); 1,500,000 ARMENIANS STARVE (September 5, 1915); 500,000 ARMENIANS SAID TO HAVE PERISHED (September 24, 1915); 800,000 ARMENIANS COUNTED DESTROYED; 10,000 DROWNED AT ONCE (October 7, 1915). Such death tolls for the mass killing of innocent people were without precedent in the history of the print media.

—*Peter Balakian,* The Burning Tigris: The Armenian Genocide and America's Response *(2004)*

Understanding Warrants

In everyday speech, a "warranted" or "unwarranted" conclusion refers to the fact that some ways of connecting claims with supporting evidence are legitimate whereas others are not. For this reason, a third important element, in addition to the claim and the support, in understanding arguments is the warrant.

The warrant is the reason or justification that links together the evidence offered and the conclusion drawn from that evidence. What Stephen Toulmin refers to as the warrant is what Aristotle referred to as the major premise in an argument: the overall justification for drawing a particular conclusion from the evidence offered to back up the claim. Sometimes the idea that justifies drawing the conclusion is assumed by the arguer and is not explicitly stated. When this happens it is often more helpful to think of the warrant as the underlying assumption that serves as the unexpressed major premise in an argument.

For example, if the arguer claimed that the United States no longer has the highest standard of living and has been surpassed by other countries including Sweden, Switzerland, and Denmark, the first thing we would want to know is the kind of evidence that would support this conclusion. If the arguer then brought forward comparative statistics measuring gross national product (GNP), infant mortality rate, and international rankings of students graduating from the educational systems of those countries, we might be more inclined to accept the claim (or conclusion). But, most important, we would have to accept the unexpressed warrant (or unstated major premise) that this kind of data or evidence (comparative statistics on economic output, quality of health care, and education) can logically justify drawing a particular conclusion. Within an argument, all claims are connected to evidence, examples, or other grounds by these stated or unstated assumptions.

For an argument to be persuasive, both the writer and the audience must have the same understanding of the logical justification or connection for drawing a particular conclusion from the data or evidence offered. If the audience did not believe that the GNP, infant mortality rate, international ranking of students, and so forth were reliable criteria to measure a country's standard of living, they could not accept the conclusions drawn from this data.

All claims are based on warrants or underlying assumptions. For an argument to be effective, the writer and the audience should share the same underlying assumptions or beliefs regarding the issue. Moreover, the audience must agree with, or at least let pass unchallenged the idea that a particular kind of evidence can be used in a specific way to support the claim. The warrant actually functions to guarantee the relationship between the claim and the support. Warrants guarantee (the ancient form of the word *guarantee* is *warrant*) that the evidence offered can really be used to support the claim in the way the writer says it does.

Questions for Discussion and Writing

1. For each of the following mini-arguments, identify the reasons why a particular conclusion can be drawn from a particular set of grounds, data, or

support. What logical justification does the arguer have in drawing conclusions from the data? How does the strength of the claim (or conclusion) vary according to the strength of the justification?

a. The fathers of this nation never dreamed that separation of church and state meant that God should be separated from government. The government buildings in Washington bear ample testimony to the belief that faith in God is the basis for establishing laws and running the affairs of a nation. For example, the Ten Commandments hang over the head of the chief justice of the Supreme Court. In the rotunda, the words "in God we trust" are engraved, and on the Library of Congress we have "the heavens declare the glory of God and the firmament showeth his handiwork." The Washington monument and other governmental buildings contain phrases of Scripture.

— *Erwin J. Lutzer,* Exploding the Myths That Could Destroy America

b. Though the educational establishment would rather die than admit it, multiculturalism is a desperate—and surely self-defeating— strategy for coping with the educational deficiencies, and associated social pathologies, of young blacks. Did these black students and their problems not exist, we would hear little of multiculturalism. There is no evidence that a substantial number of Hispanic parents would like their children to know more about Simon Bolivar and less about George Washington, or that Oriental parents feel that their children are being educationally deprived because their textbooks teach them more about ancient Greece than about ancient China.

— *Irving Kristol, "The Tragedy of Multiculturalism,"* The Wall Street Journal

UNDERLYING ASSUMPTIONS

Warrants provide a means of testing how the facts (in the form of statistics, real or hypothetical examples, expert opinion, and so on) are connected to a particular claim. If the support offered to prove the claim is relevant, then the warrant (in the form of a statute, precedent, rule, or principle) authorizes the writer to move from the evidence to the conclusion.

Warrants can take a variety of forms in different fields. In the law, warrants take the form of legal principles, statutes, licenses, or permits. The idea underlying a warrant survives today in the familiar term *arrest warrant*. In the natural and physical sciences, warrants take the form of scientific laws, formulas, and methods of calculation. In all these fields, warrants reflect acceptable methods of relating the evidence to the claim or chief assertion.

For example, in the law, the warrant is an explicit statute laying out the specific circumstances under which someone can be found guilty of an offense. The warrant permits the judge or the court to conclude that a particular defendant is guilty of an offense, if supporting evidence has been submitted and verified.

In other fields, like natural sciences and mathematics, warrants may take the form of relevant formulas that are used to confirm or reject a hypothesis or claim on the basis of evidence produced by experimentation and research. Within these fields, warrants appear as commonly accepted principles or "laws." For example, Boyle's law in thermodynamics states that at relatively low pressures the pressure of an ideal gas kept at constant temperature varies inversely with the volume of the gas. Likewise, Einstein's discovery of the relationship between mass and energy is contained in the famous equation or law $E = MC^2$.

In medicine, warrants derive more from principles generalized from the practioner's past experience than from formulas as such. A doctor making a diagnosis of a 7-year-old patient's illness might discover an unusual rash of raised, circular, small red spots and measure an elevated temperature (see Figure 3.3). On the basis of principles generalized from past experience, the doctor concludes that the patient has probably caught measles. To see how the warrant serves as a kind of rule dictating how the evidence (rash, elevated temperature) should be related to the particular claim (the patient has caught measles), examine the following analysis of the reasoning underlying the doctor's diagnosis:

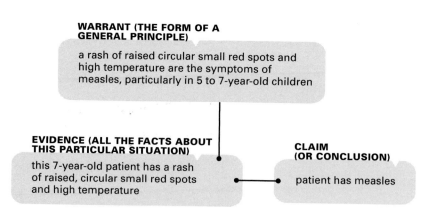

WARRANT (THE FORM OF A GENERAL PRINCIPLE)

a rash of raised circular small red spots and high temperature are the symptoms of measles, particularly in 5 to 7-year-old children

EVIDENCE (ALL THE FACTS ABOUT THIS PARTICULAR SITUATION)

this 7-year-old patient has a rash of raised, circular small red spots and high temperature

CLAIM (OR CONCLUSION)

patient has measles

FIGURE 3.3

A Toulmin diagram of a physician's diagnostis.

The warrant here is drawn from general principles of the kind that might be familiar to the doctor from past experience and from information provided by a medical textbook.

Warrants can be either explicit or implicit; that is, they can take the form of set rules or simply be assumptions and beliefs that both the writer and the audience share. Whereas warrants take the form of broad generalizations, rules of thumb, or general principles that could apply to various circumstances, claims, and support apply to specific events and circumstances. In the law or the sciences, warrants are generalizations based on extensive experience and data. Outside these formal fields of study, in everyday conversation, warrants take the form of beliefs, assumptions, or rule-of-thumb generalizations.

As with all other generalizations, warrants must ultimately rest on relevant facts and evidence. If the warrant or underlying assumption in an argument is challenged, the writer may have to produce some of the primary information or backing on which the warrant itself is based.

This body of information supplies the *backing*, or justification for the warrant. The strength and credibility of the warrant therefore depends on the strength and credibility of the backing, or the information used to back it up. For example, an argument that examined the relationship between risk of injury and vehicle size might rest on the assumption (or warrant or major premise) that driver risk increased as a car's size and weight decreased irrespective of other factors such as air bags, safety belts, or kind of crash. If this assumption were challenged, the arguer would have to show how the warrant was justified by a credible and persuasive series of studies of driver fatalities in lighter as compared to heavier cars. These studies would serve as the backing for the warrant. This is important because people often bring different assumptions to the same situation without realizing it.

For example, David R. Counts, an anthropologist who conducted research in New Guinea, discovered that in the village where he lived in Papua, food was given as a gift or shared as part of the social system and could not be bought with money. In the following episode, he describes how he became aware that he "read" the same situation in an entirely different way than did people in the village because of their different underlying cultural assumptions:

> We had established a pattern with respect to the gifts of food. When a donor appeared at our veranda we would offer our thanks and talk with them for a few minutes (usually about our children, who seemed to hold a real fascination for the villagers and for whom most of the gifts were intended) and then we would inquire whether they could use some tobacco. It was almost never refused, though occasionally a small bottle of kerosene, a box of matches, some laundry

soap, a cup of rice, or a tin of meat would be requested instead of (or even in addition to) the tobacco. Everyone, even Kolia, seemed to think this arrangement had worked out well.

Now, what must be kept in mind is that while we were following their rules—or seemed to be—we were *really still buying food*. In fact we kept a running account of what came in and what we "paid" for it. Tobacco as a currency got a little complicated, but since the exchange rate was one stick to one shilling, it was not too much trouble as long as everyone was happy, and meanwhile we could account for the expenditure of "informant fees" and "household expenses." Another thing to keep in mind is that not only did we continue to think in terms of our buying the food that was brought, we thought of them as *selling* it. While it is true they never quoted us a price, they also never asked us if we needed or wanted whatever they had brought. It seemed clear to us that when an adult needed a stick of tobacco, or a child wanted some chewing gum (we had enormous quantities of small packets of Wrigley's for just such eventualities) they would find something surplus to their needs and bring it along to our "store" and get what they wanted.

—From *"Too Many Bananas, Not Enough Pineapples, and No Watermelon at All: Three Object Lessons in Living with Reciprocity,"* The Humbled Anthropologist *(1990)*

We can understand how this principle of reciprocity baffled Counts and his family because he considered that he was actually "paying" for the goods that the villagers considered "gifts."

Identifying underlying beliefs is essential because many writers erroneously take it for granted that they and the audience share a common point of view. An audience that notices that they and the writer do not share the same assumptions might require the author to back up the warrant, since from the audience's point of view, the warrant might be questionable.

Assumptions in an argument often remain implicit when the writer feels that the audience shares his or her underlying beliefs. If the audience already agrees with these beliefs, the writer can feel comfortable in bringing forth reasons to support the claim. The contrary is true in those arguments where the writer feels the audience may not share his or her basic values. In these cases, an assumption that might prove controversial may need to be stated explicitly and defended at the outset. The writer must win a hearing for the assumption on which the argument is based before going on to present evidence that specifically bears on the question or exact point that is the subject of the argument.

Not all warrants will be explicitly stated in the course of an argument. Sometimes the writer will not explicitly state the warrant because the writer feels that both she or he and the audience share a common perspective on the issue. In effect, the writer is depending on the audience to mentally supply the implicit warrant to connect the evidence with the claim. This is especially true when writers argue before partisan audiences who already share the same beliefs and can be depended on to bring the same set of assumptions or warrants to the situation. For example, a lottery equipment manufacturer arguing for a national lottery before fellow manufacturers of lottery ticket–printing equipment will not have to state or defend the assumption that a national lottery will mean more business for lottery equipment manufacturers. His or her audience can be depended on to interpret any evidence the manufacturer presents in the light of this implicit warrant.

In other cases, the warrants will not be explictly stated because the writer does not want the audience to be aware that they disagree on underlying assumptions.

Questions for Discussion and Writing

1. For each of the following, state the implied assumption/warrant/premise and decide whether it is likely to be accepted by the audience for whom it was written. Why or why not? How do these warrants justify accepting the arguer's descriptions and interpretations of problems? What commonly held beliefs do these warrants reflect? How might the same data be made more acceptable for the different specified audience by reliance on a different set of assumptions?

   a. The original audience for this argument was composed of ecologists. How could you reinterpret the same grounds (evidence, reasons) for an audience of real-estate developers or mining company executives?

   If you have ever spent time with American Indians, you have noticed that their resistance to resource development is expressed as an effort to protect "Mother Earth." It is not only American Indians who use the phrase. So do Aborigines of the Australian desert, natives of the Pacific islands, Indians of the Ecuadorian jungles, Inuit from Arctic Canada; in fact, I have yet to find a native group that does not speak of the planet as "mother." And they all mean it literally. Plants, animals, all life as we know it is nurtured at her breast. We have germinated within her, we are part of her, we burst into life from her, and we dissolve back into her to become new life.

   Every culture that maintains the attitude about Mother Earth also has restrictions against any individual owning land, or mining it or selling it. Such ideas were unthinkable to native people until they met the invading Western cultures.

   —*Jerry Mander, "Mother Earth," Absence of the Sacred (1992)*

b. The original audience for this argument was for the educated general reader and, more specifically, other urban planners and economists. How could you reinterpret the same evidence and reasons for students who wish to attend your college or university?

> Credentialing, not educating, has become the primary business of North American universities. This is not in the interest of employers in the long run. But in the short run, it is beneficial for corporations' departments of human resources, the current name for personnel departments. People with the task of selecting successful job applicants want them to have desirable qualities such as persistence, ambition, and ability to cooperate and conform, to be a "team player." At a minimum, achieving a four-year university or college degree, no matter in what subject, seems to promise these traits.
>
> — *Jane Jacobs*, Dark Age Ahead *(2004)*

EVALUATING TYPES OF WARRANTS

Before you can evaluate the effectiveness of any particular warrant, you need to be able to identify all the warrants in any argument and to make explicit those that lie hidden beneath the surface. Writers must inquire (1) whether the warrant expresses a reliable generalization and (2) whether this generalization authorizes the connection between the facts and the conclusion in this particular case.

Evaluating how warrants work in a given argument means discovering whether the writer has used the correct kind of warrant to connect the evidence to the claim or has connected the evidence to the claim in the correct way. The first point has to do with the relevance of the evidence. The second concerns the quality of the writer's reasoning or use of logic.

A listing of the six main kinds of warrants writers use in creating arguments follows. The particular kind of warrant selected depends on the nature of the argument, the type of claim (of fact, causation, value or policy), and the specific audience addressed or the context in which the argument is formulated.

TYPES OF WARRANTS

GENERALIZATION WARRANT   A generalization warrant authorizes the movement from a number of specific examples offered as evidence to a generalization offered as a conclusion. The generalization warrant asserts that what is true of a sample is probably true of a group as a whole. The examples used must meet the test of being sufficiently representative, properly selected, and timely.

For example Sigmund Freud, in his classic essay "Typical Dreams" (from *Basic Writings of Sigmund Freud*), brings forward a whole range of examples from the dreams of children that illustrate one common theme—the death or disappearance of brothers or sisters. From these numerous case histories, Freud generalizes that children's dreams often reveal sibling rivalry, albeit in a disguised form. Freud's claim of the existence of sibling rivalry is an inference that should be verifiable as well in dreams of children whom Freud has not observed.

Looked at in terms of claim, support, and warrant, the argument appears this way:

Claim: The dreams of children featuring the death or disappearance of brothers or sisters reveal sibling rivalry in disguised form.

Support: Numerous case histories in which Freud observed sibling rivalry in children who had these kinds of dreams.

Generalization Warrant: Observations based on several case histories can be generalized to be true in as yet unobserved cases.

Everyday reasoning closely resembles arguments from generalizations, as do arguments whose claims are based on polls or surveys. For example, the Harris survey and the Gallup Opinion Poll generalizes from results drawn from a sample cross section of 1,200 to 1,500 adults to infer what is true of the entire population. If the sample, by a margin of 80 percent to 20 percent, holds the view that "American business is not paying its fair share of taxes," Gallup or Harris will predict that this opinion would also be true in the same proportion if every adult in the United States were polled.

CAUSE-AND-EFFECT WARRANT   Reasoning from cause assumes that one event can produce another. Causal generalization stipulates that if a particular cause is observed, a particular effect can be expected to follow. Conversely, the causal warrant may state that if a certain effect is observed, a particular cause may be assumed to have preceded it. Causal warrants may extend to chains of causation as well as multiple causes or multiple effects. For example, Wilson Bryan Key, a professor of communications, wanted to discover why many viewers of William Friedkin's movie *The Exorcist* became fearful, angry, and physically sick after seeing the film. As reported in his book *Media Sexploitation*, Key discovered that Friedkin had accompanied the images on the screen with a sound track in which sounds of squealing pigs and the buzzing of infuriated bees were recorded at a level below the audience's conscious awareness. Key argues that this subliminal use of sound, though not consciously perceived, created an undertone of fear that amplified the frightening nature of the images on the screen. He interviewed theater staff who heard the sound track before they actually viewed the film and discovered that they often experienced the same reactions of hysteria and anxiety as did members of the audience who saw *and* heard the movie. In outline form, Key's causal argument might look like this (notice that the warrant acts as the cause, while the claim expresses the effect):

Claim: The anxiety of audiences watching *The Exorcist* was, in part, an unconscious reaction to the sounds of squealing pigs and infuriated bees interwoven into the sound track at a subliminal level.

Support: Theater staff who heard only the sound track of the movie experienced reactions of hysteria and anxiety. Friedkin admitted that he interwove sounds of pigs and bees in a way that coordinated with the visual images.

Casual Warrant: Even if the sounds were not consciously perceived, people instinctively fear the sounds of squealing pigs and infuriated bees.

SIGN WARRANT   Arguments based on sign warrants point to a particular sign to support a claim that a certain event, condition, or situation exists. For example, a doctor may be reasoning from sign when he or she cites certain observable characteristics to justify the diagnosis that a patient may be suffering from a particular disease. Anne Wilson Schaef uses the same reasoning process in *When Society Becomes an Addict*:

> An addiction is any process over which we are powerless. It takes control of us, causing us to do and think things that are inconsistent with our personal values and leading us to become progressively more compulsive and obsessive. A sure sign of an addiction is the sudden need to deceive ourselves and others—to lie, deny, and cover up. An addiction is anything we feel *tempted* to lie about.

Although one could certainly dispute her definition of addiction, Schaef clearly reasons from signs (need to lie, deny, and cover up) to support a claim about the presence of the phenomenon (addiction) to which the sign refers.

The philosopher C. S. Peirce defines *sign* this way: "A sign is something which stands to somebody for something else, in some respect or capacity." We reason from sign anytime we drive down the highway, see a sign indicating a winding road, and slow down. The sign serves as a reliable indicator that a condition (a winding road) is or will be present. We do the same thing when we check our wallet before entering a restaurant in front of which we see a long green awning and a door attendant. The fancy facade is a usually reliable indicator that the restaurant is expensive.

In law, the concept of circumstantial evidence is based on the idea of reasoning from sign. A case may be constructed on a network of circumstantial facts based on the assumption or warrant that the defendant exhibits all the signs—which have been reliable indicators in past cases—of having committed the crime. In economics, economists look for signs of health or weakness in the nation's economy. These financial indicators (balance of trade, housing starts, unemployment figures, etc.) are believed to indicate the presence of a corresponding economic condition.

In "Why Do We Smoke, Drink and Use Dangerous Drugs?" Jared Diamond draws on the research of Israeli biologist Amotz Zahabi about the role of costly or self-destructive signals in animal behavior to answer the question posed in the title:

> A gazelle's signal to a lion that it sees approaching consists of a peculiar behavior termed "stotting." Instead of running away as fast as possible, the gazelle runs slowly while repeatedly jumping high into the air with stiff-legged leaps. Why on earth should the gazelle indulge in this seemingly self-destructive display, which wastes time and energy and gives the lion a chance to catch up? Or think of the males of many animal species that sport large structures, such as a peacock's tail or a bird of paradise's plumes, that make movement difficult. Males of many more species have bright colors, loud songs, or conspicuous displays that attract predators. Why should a male advertise such an impediment, and why should a female like it? These paradoxes remain an important unsolved problem in animal behavior today.
>
> Zahavi's theory goes to the heart of this paradox. According to his theory, those deleterious structures and behaviors constitute valid indicators that the signaling animal is being honest in its claim of superiority, precisely *because* those traits themselves impose handicaps. A signal that entails no cost lends itself to cheating, since even a slow or inferior animal can afford to give the signal. Only costly or deleterious signals are guarantees of honesty. For example, a slow gazelle that stotted at an approaching lion would seal its fate, whereas a fast gazelle could still outrun the lion after stotting. By stotting, the gazelle boasts to the lion, "I'm so fast that I can escape you even after giving you this head start." The lion thereby has grounds for believing in the gazelle's honesty, and both the lion and the gazelle profit by not wasting time and energy on a chase whose outcome is certain.

Diamond concludes that such seemingly self-destructive behavior in animals actually enhances the chances of survival whereas high-risk behaviors among humans are without benefit. Reduced to its essentials, Diamond's argument might look like this:

Claim: "By stotting, the gazelle boasts to the lion, 'I'm so fast that I can escape you even after giving you this head start.' "

Support: "A gazelle's signal to a lion that it sees approaching consists of a peculiar behavior termed 'stotting.' "

Sign Warrant: "Only costly or deleterious signals are guarantees of honesty."

Much of advertising attempts to appropriate this form of reasoning to persuade potential customers to purchase a product. Advertisers are very clever in using warrants from sign in persuading audiences that purchasing, wearing, or using a particular product will enable the purchaser to partake of the reality (such as wealth, beauty, health) of which the sign is an indicator. For example, an ad for expensive crystal glasses directed toward prospective brides might show a diamond ring and a wedding veil alongside the glasses. The ring and the veil are signs standing for marriage. The technique of advertising is based, in large part, on correlating attainable tangible objects with difficult-to-obtain feelings, moods, attitudes, and conditions. The advertiser can depend on the consumers reasoning from sign that the purchase of the attainable will be accompanied by the difficult to obtain. For example, an ad for an expensive watch might show it on a night table alongside a gold money clip holding a stack of thousand-dollar bills. Reasoning from sign, the consumer might conclude that the purchase of this watch (as a sign of the possessions of a wealthy person) would somehow enable him or her to possess other items associated with wealth.

ANALOGY WARRANT   Reasoning from analogy assumes that there are sufficient similarities between two things to warrant the claim that what is true of one can reasonably be expected to be true of the other. Anytime we look forward to reading a new novel by an author whose previous books we read and enjoyed, or seeing a new movie by a favorite director, we are reasoning by analogy. We infer that the new book or movie will resemble the works we previously enjoyed.

It is important that shared characteristics be directly relevant to the claim and that no important differences exist that would undermine or weaken the analogy. For example, if a car manufacturer issues a recall of a certain model because a structural weakness in the frame has led rear bumpers to fall off, then it can reasonably be assumed that other cars of the same make and model are likely to develop the same problem. This would hold true despite differences in appearance or options. Since structural weakness in one model can reasonably be expected to be true of other cars in the line, the shared characteristics are directly relevant to the claim.

The more the analogy departs from the literally shared resemblances, the less useful it will be in supporting a claim. This is not to say that such analogies cannot be extraordinarily helpful in describing or explaining some point, but

these analogies, sometimes called *figurative analogies*, cannot actually serve to warrant a claim. For example, Martin J. Rees and Joseph Silk, in "The Origin of Galaxies" (from *Scientific American*), formulated a figurative analogy to describe the phenomenon of an expanding universe:

> Perhaps the most startling discovery made in astronomy this century is that the universe is populated by billions of galaxies and that they are systematically receding from one another, like raisins in an expanding pudding.

The authors are not suggesting that the universe *is* an expanding pudding with raisins, but are simply using a figurative analogy to describe and explain an otherwise hard-to-grasp concept. It is important for any reader of an argument using analogies to evaluate just how the analogy is being used. The question to ask is, does the analogy simply describe or explain something or does it actually support an inference and thereby warrant the claim?

Consider how Bill Gates uses an analogy warrant in "The Next Revolution" from *The Road Ahead* to argue against the metaphor commonly used to describe the Internet:

> In the United States, the connecting of all these computers has been compared to another massive project: the gridding of the country with interstate highways, which began during the Eisenhower era. This is why the new network was dubbed the "information superhighway." The highway metaphor isn't quite right, though. The phrase suggests landscape and geography, a distance between points, and embodies the implication that you have to travel to get from one place to another. In fact, one of the most remarkable aspects of this new communications technology is that it will eliminate distance. It won't matter if someone you're contacting is in the next room or on another continent, because this highly mediated network will be unconstrained by miles and kilometers.
>
> A different metaphor that I think comes closer to describing a lot of the activities that will take place is that of the ultimate market. Markets from trading floors to malls are fundamental to human society, and I believe this new one will eventually be the world's central department store. It will be where we social animals will sell, trade, invest, haggle, pick stuff up, argue, meet new people, and hang out. Think of the hustle and bustle of the New York Stock Exchange or a farmers' market or of a bookstore full of people looking for fascinating stories and information. All manner of human activity takes place, from billion-dollar deals to flirtations.

In schematic form, the argument would appear this way:

Claim: The Internet should be more accurately characterized as the "ultimate market" rather than an "information superhighway."

Support: Markets, like the Internet, are places where "we social animals will sell, trade, invest, haggle, pick stuff up, argue, meet new people, and hang out."

Analogy Warrant: Unlike the metaphor of a superhighway, which "suggests landscape and geography," the analogy of the Internet as "the ultimate market" more accurately describes how people will actually use it.

Gates's argument depends on the analogy warrant or assumption that the Internet is analogous to a global farmer's market. For him, similarities between the two are more significant than the obvious differences. An opponent might assert that the dissimilarities between the two make any attempt to compare them unwarranted.

AUTHORITY WARRANT   Reasoning from authority presumes that the authority cited is in fact qualified to express an expert opinion on the subject of the claim. If the authority were to be challenged, the writer would have to supply backing for the warrant in the form of credentials and expertise that would qualify the authority in the particular circumstances.

In evaluating an argument based on authority, determine whether the writer clearly connects the claim and the authority's area of expertise. Also, try to determine whether the authority is acknowledged as such by other experts in the field. As an illustration, consider how Kurt Vonnegut, Jr., in "How to Write with Style," uses the words of widely respected sources to support his claim that the best writing is simple:

> As for your use of language: Remember that two great masters of language, William Shakespeare and James Joyce, wrote sentences which were almost childlike when their subjects were most profound. "To be or not to be?" asks Shakespeare's Hamlet. The longest word is three letters long. Joyce, when he was frisky, could put together a sentence as intricate and glittering as a necklace for Cleopatra, but my favorite sentence in his short story "Eveline" is this one: "She was tired." At that point in the story, no other words could break the heart of the reader as those three words do.
>
> Simplicity of language is not only reputable, but perhaps even sacred. The Bible opens with a sentence well within the writing skills of a lively fourteen-year-old: "In the beginning God created the heaven and the earth."

Vonnegut's point is that writers need not use obscure words and complicated language to be effective. To support his claim that simple language is the most effective, he cites the words of William Shakespeare, James Joyce, and the Bible because each of these is an acknowledged authority in matters of style, and

can be expected to persuade the reader to accept his claim. The three elements function as follows:

Claim: Simple language is the most effective.

Support: William Shakespeare, James Joyce, and the Bible express the most profound ideas in the simplest language.

Authority Warrant: The simple language used by great writers and a foremost religious work should serve as an example because of the stature of these sources.

Also, notice how Vonnegut structures the argument to end with the ultimate source on style, the Bible.

VALUE WARRANT Value warrants are moral or ethical principles or beliefs that the writer hopes will be shared by the audience. It is especially important that the value the warrant expresses be relevant to the claim and be a belief that the intended audience will perceive as important. Value warrants are frequently unexpressed in arguments and readers must make every effort to make explicit the value, principle, or belief that the writer may have taken for granted. Value warrants function exactly as any other kind of warrant to guarantee a connection between the claim and the evidence. Value warrants frequently embody ethical principles that designate certain kinds of actions as right or wrong, acceptable or unacceptable; or express the standards by which some actions should be considered good or bad, preferable or objectionable. In some cases, these value warrants will express societal consensus about the ethical propriety of certain kinds of actions. In other cases, they may express a personal, rather than universal, moral value.

In the following paragraphs from "Abolish the Insanity Defense?—Not Yet," *Rutgers Law Review* John Monahan uses a value warrant to explain how the insanity defense is based on an underlying belief that people who are incapable of knowing the meaning or consequences of their actions should not be punished:

> The existing Anglo-American system of criminal justice is based on a model of man as a responsible agent with a free will. The insanity defense is closely tied to this model. Oversimplifying somewhat, "the defense of insanity rests upon the assumption that insanity negates free will, and the law does not punish people who lack the capacity for choice."
>
> If an individual has a complete inability to know the nature and quality of the act he has committed, that is, if he is insane by M'Naghten standards, then, it is argued, he is incapable of forming the cognitive or mental component

(intent, recklessness, etc.) which is part of the definition of much serious crime. Since the insane person is held to be incapable of forming normal cognition, and since cognitive ability is part of the definition of crime, he has a complete defense to much criminal prosecution.

Split into the three elements, Monahan's case would appear thus:

Claim: Defendants who because of insanity are not consciously aware of the meaning of their acts should not be found guilty.

Support: A defendant is shown to be insane by M'Naghten standards.

Value Warrant: The law does not punish people who lack the capacity for choice.

This argument is unusual in that it rests on a basic assumption on which the entire system of criminal law is built, but it reaches a conclusion with which increasing numbers of people disagree. Some states have abolished the use of an insanity defense (upheld by the Supreme Court in 1994); others have amended their laws to include standards of "diminished capacity" or "guilty but mentally ill." When reading any argument based on a value warrant, try to identify any assumptions or unexamined beliefs that the writer expects the audience to share. Ask yourself how this assumption supports the author's purpose. Then compare this assumption (you may need to state it explicitly if the author does not) with your own beliefs on the issue, and decide whether the warrant, in fact, (1) is reliable and (2) actually applies to the particular case.

Questions for Discussion and Writing

1. Develop a short argument on one or two of the following issues. For each mini-argument you construct, identify the kind of warrant or rationale your argument relies on to justify acceptance of the interpretation, conclusion, claim, or recommendation you make. If you feel the warrant or assumption might be challenged by an audience, supply the appropriate backing to let your audience see how you reached the decision to use the warrant you did. The warrants can include:

    Generalization

    Drawing a causal relationship

    Sign warrant (or reasoning from circumstantial evidence)

    Drawing analogies

Believing an authority

Applying an ethical or moral principle

a. Lawyers are expected to provide free (*pro bono*) legal services at some time in their careers. Physicians should or should not have the same obligation to provide free medical care at some time in their careers to those who cannot afford it.

b. What actions and reactions of your own or of someone you know can serve as reliable indicators of being in love?

c. Do you consider having children important in your future? From instances you have observed, are people with children happier than those without them?

d. Should juveniles be treated differently from adult offenders? Why or why not? How might a researcher use statistics illustrating the relationship between lenient or harsh sentencing of juveniles and the percentage of those juveniles who subsequently commit worse crimes?

e. In any one day, you encounter a variety of claims that reach you through the media, reading material, classrooms, and conversations. These claims take a variety of forms that may include commercials, religious services, lectures, movie or concert reviews, and so on. Evaluate the strength of any claim in relationship to who makes it.

f. What influence, if any, has any major religious text (Bible, Koran, etc.) had on shaping your ideals and attitudes toward life?

Considering the Audience

Most of the things people write are written with the expectation that someone will read what they have written. Since each audience has its own characteristic concerns and values, writers must be acutely sensitive to the audience's special needs. Without knowing what was important to an audience, it would be difficult for writers to assess what kinds of arguments, evidence, and supporting material a particular audience would be likely to find convincing.

Writers should try to identify who the audience is or is likely to be by creating an audience profile. For example, how might the audience, from its point of view, define the issue at the center of the argument? If the audience sees the issue differently, is there anything the writer can do to take this into account while characterizing the problem or issue? The key question is, how can the writer create a common meeting ground?

Matching the argument to the audience is largely a matter of figuring out what particular argumentative strategy would work best with a particular audience. In a typical persuasion situation, the writer is trying to influence readers who have not made up their minds on the topic and can be presumed to have open minds or at least to be neutral on the issue.

In this situation, the writer can announce the thesis of the argument at the outset and then present reasons and evidence in a straightforward way. The writer is obliged to present, directly and without apology, the most timely, up-to-date, and relevant information and the most cogent arguments he or she can muster.

In other situations, the writer attempts to persuade an audience that has already formed strong opinions and beliefs. Clearly, different tactics are required. For example, the writer might wish to present both sides of the argument before announcing the thesis. Or, he or she might consider using deductive reasoning as a rhetorical strategy to win the audience's agreement to certain *premises* and then show how the conclusion must necessarily follow.

For many writers, a reasonable goal is not so much to change the readers' minds as to persuade them to give the writer's opposing point of view a fair hearing. The writer's goal is to get the audience to see the issue from a point of view or perspective different from their customary one.

There are several ways to enhance the probability that the writer's argument will address the readers' special concerns. But before this can happen, the writer must be able to define the issue in a way that will appeal to the audience's needs and values. At the very least, the writer must recognize and acknowledge the legitimacy of the audience's feelings on the issue. It is naive to assume that an audience will be persuaded by an argument, however well-written or well-supported, that fails to take into account psychological factors that can prevent each side from "hearing" the other.

THE ROGERIAN METHOD

One of the most useful attempts to study the factors that block communication was made by the psychologist Carl R. Rogers in "Communication: Its Blocking and Its Facilitation." He points out that people on both sides of an argument characteristically tend to dig in their heels and simply seek to justify their own opinion.

A variety of psychological reasons explains this intransigent mind-set. First of all, people tend to identify with their positions on issues and are not able to separate themselves from their opinions. This automatic preference for one's own opinions makes it impossible to allow oneself to even consider another point of view. Because people identify with their opinions, they feel the need to defend their positions no matter how weak because in essence they are defending themselves against what they perceive to be a personal attack.

This basic frame of mind brings with it the tendency to rationalize. Rationalization is a self-deceptive form of reasoning in which evidence is distorted to fit a previously formed opinion. By contrast, authentic reasoning relies on logic and evidence to reveal a conclusion that may or may not agree with the preconceived opinion. Rogers has studied how the need to defend one's personal values and self-image shuts out potentially useful ideas. To get beyond these limitations Rogers recommends the following exercise:

> The next time you get into an argument with your wife, or your friend, or with a small group of friends, just stop the discussion for a moment and for an experiment, institute this rule. "Each person can speak up for himself only *after* he has first restated the ideas and feelings of the previous speaker accurately, and to that speaker's satisfaction." You see what this would mean. It would simply mean that before presenting your own point of view it would be necessary for you to really achieve the other speaker's frame of reference—to understand his thoughts and feelings so well that you could summarize them for him. . . . Once you have been able to see the other's point of view, your own comments will have to be drastically revised. You will also find the emotion going out of the discussion, the differences being reduced, and those differences which remain being of a rational and understandable sort.

This intriguing method of introducing some psychological perspective makes it more likely that the writer will be able to define the issue at the center of the argument in terms that reflect the values and beliefs of the audience. That is, by being able to summarize impartially an opponent's viewpoint on an issue, in language that the opponent would consider a fair restatement of the issue, the writer immeasurably increases the chances of reaching a middle ground. As Rogers observes:

> Real communication occurs and this evaluative tendency is avoided when we listen with understanding. What does that mean? It means *to see the expressed idea and attitude from the other person's point of view, to sense how it feels to him, to achieve his frame of reference in regard to the thing he is talking about.*

Also, having a sense of the audience's values will allow the writer to allude to common experiences related to the issue. A knowledge of the readers' special concerns can suggest the kinds of hypothetical scenarios the writer might introduce to persuade the audience. In any case, it is important that writers make every attempt to adapt the argument to the needs and values of their particular audience. It is also crucial to set realistic persuasion goals in the context of the particular situation.

If the argument is well-formulated, with effective examples, evidence, and cogent reasons, most audiences will want to try out the new viewpoint, even if it means suspending their own views on the subject in the meantime. They will try on for size the writer's perspective simply to have the experience of seeing things from a different angle.

Questions for Discussion and Writing

1. Rephrase the following mini-arguments in your own words stating the issue impartially using nonconnotative language that the writer might consider a fair summary of his or her argument. Did you find it was easier to rephrase and summarize an argument with which you agreed than one with which you disagreed? What extra steps did you have to take to arrive at an impartial summary?

    a. It is getting harder and harder to follow an American discussion. We used to chide worrywarts with: "suppose one thing, suppose another, suppose a jackass was your brother." Now, however, supposition is the handmaiden of political correctness. I often run into this because of my penchant for voicing unthinkable opinions. "I'm sick of women," and my opponent retorts, "suppose you substituted *blacks* for *women* in that sentence?" It goes on. "Bugger the spotted owls." Suppose you substituted Jews for owls? "Brand criminals on the forehead." Suppose you substituted *gays* for *criminals*? This is not sensitivity but rhetorical tumult.

    —*Florence King, "The Misanthrope's Corner,"* National Review

    b. Rich people are pompous. Rich people are deluded. Rich people have to tell you every moment of their lives how rich they are. Rich people are stingy, coldhearted, mean, cowardly, immoral, furtive, dishonest, arrogant, petty, backbiting, ruthless, and pointless.

    Well, maybe some of them are okay. The ones who came by their money inadvertently by doing something they really like, and some lost souls who inherited money and give it to weird performance artists can possibly be allowed to live. But mainly they're a scourge.

And here's the thing: It's not their fault. Rich people would be perfectly fine if we would all just stop sucking up to them.

We're all so busy trying to pry a little loose change out of them, trying to get them to buy this painting, that car, this precious little Ming vase. They start really thinking that maybe they are just too fabulous. And the more money they make, the more Porsches they buy the more people seem to adore them! Rich people desperately want to believe their own press, they need so severely to think they are one of the chosen. This is what turns them into monsters.

—*Cynthia Heimel, "Rich People: Blow Me,"* Get Your Tongue Out of
My Mouth. I'm Kissing You Goodbye

2. Speculate for any of the preceding mini-arguments on who the audience might be. Create a brief audience profile as to political leanings, economic class, level of education, gender or ethnicity (if relevant), and profession. What can you assume they know or care about? What might their attitude be toward the issue? What common assumptions or values might the audience share with the arguer? What kind of desired effect is the argument designed to produce on this specified audience according to your profile of their characteristics and values?

THE TOULMIN MODEL

BACKING Sometimes merely considering the argument as it appears to an audience will not be sufficient. It is at this point that the concept of *backing* becomes important. An audience may not be satisfied that the warrant used to connect the evidence or grounds to the claim is an appropriate one to apply to the present case. Backing supplies additional evidence necessary to support the warrant, and it provides the assurance that the assumptions used in formulating the argument really rest on solid and trustworthy grounds. Of course, not all arguments will require the writer to produce the broader foundation of backing. Only when readers can be presumed to view the claims of an argument with doubt or skepticism need backing be produced. For example, you and a friend might be arguing over whether a particular tennis player would win Wimbledon. You might claim that player X was a sure bet to win Wimbledon this year and back up your claim with statistics about the relative strengths of this year's crop of tournament players. You might even state your warrant in the form of an assumption that "only a tennis player who had a strong serve-and-volley game has a real chance to take the Wimbledon title."

At this point, your skeptical friend might question the validity of your assumption. You would then have to produce the backing on which your warrant rests to clarify your claim and answer your friend's doubts. In this case, backing might take the form of an analysis of the serve-and-volley game of past winners of Wimbledon. Thus, warrants or assumptions that are not accepted by your audience at face value must be supported to clarify and substantiate the underlying structure of your claim.

Backing is required so often that it should be considered a basic part of any argument, satisfying the doubts of an audience that wants to know that the writer can, if challenged, provide further support.

QUALIFIERS   Another way writers take audiences into account is by using what are called *qualifiers*. Realistically, no claim is ever presented in a vacuum. The qualifier represents the writer's assessment of the relative strength or weakness of the claim. Qualifiers express limitations that may have to be attached to a claim in order to pass the scrutiny of a particular audience. Frequently qualifiers take the form of phrases such as *in all probability*, *very likely*, *presumably*, or *very possibly*.

For example, let's say you're having a discussion with a friend about computer software and you want to recommend the use of a new spreadsheet program. Rather than making your recommendation in an unqualified way without conditions or restrictions, you phrase your recommendation so as to indicate the kind of strength you wish to be attributed to your claim. To do this you need to include a qualifying word or phrase such as "program X, *as far as I can tell*, will make the job much easier." In this way, arguers take their audiences into account by modifying a claim to include a restriction whose effect is to enhance the persuasiveness of the message.

REBUTTALS OR EXCEPTIONS   While the addition of *backing* and *qualifiers* to the basic structure of claim-support-warrant goes a long way to adapting an argument to cope with the contrary beliefs, expectations, or skepticism of an audience, writers are aware that one further element is required to create a persuasive case. This element, called the *rebuttal* or *exception*, arises from the writer's responsibility in confronting special circumstances or extraordinary instances that challenge the claim being made. Inserting the rebuttal or exception into the structure of the argument enhances the persuasiveness of the claim by honestly recognizing that there may be some particularly exceptional circumstances under which the claim could not be directly supported by the grounds. For example, a typical use of the rebuttal or exception is in the form of warnings printed by pharmaceutical companies regarding contraindications or situations where an otherwise safe-to-prescribe drug should not be used. This type of argument might appear as follows:

Grounds: This patient is on a weight control program.

Backing: Clinical experience shows that—

Warrant: As part of a weight control program, D-amphetamine may be prescribed.

Qualifier: It appears very likely that—

Claim: This patient needs D-amphetamine as part of a weight control program.

Rebuttal or Exception: Unless that patient has a history of heart disease, high blood pressure, thyroid disease or glaucoma, or is allergic to any amphetamine or has a history of abusing amphetamine medications, or is pregnant (because of possible links to birth defects).

To illustrate how backing, qualifiers, and rebuttals work in a real situation, consider the following speech given by Bruce Springsteen at the induction of Roy Orbison into the Rock and Roll Hall of Fame:

In 1970, I rode for 15 hours in the back of a U-Haul truck to open for Roy Orbison at the Nashville Music Fair. It was a summer night and I was 20 years old and he came out in dark glasses, a dark suit and he played some dark music.

In '74, just prior to going in the studio to make *Born To Run*, I was looking at Duane Eddy for his guitar sound and I was listening to a collection of Phil Spector records and I was listening to Roy Orbison's *All-Time Greatest Hits*. I'd lay in bed at night with just the lights of my stereo on and I'd hear *Cryin'*, *Love Hurts*, *Runnin' Scared*, *Only The Lonely* and *It's Over* fillin' my room. Some rock 'n' roll reinforces friendship and community, but for me, Roy's ballads were always best when you were alone and in the dark. Roy scrapped the idea that you need verse-chorus-verse-chorus-bridge-verse-chorus to have a hit.

His arrangements were complex and operatic, they had rhythm and movement and they addressed the underside of pop romance. They were scary. His voice was unearthly.

He had the ability, like all great rock 'n' rollers, to sound like he'd dropped in from another planet and yet get the stuff that was right to the heart of what you were livin' in today, and that was how he opened up your vision. He made a little town in New Jersey feel as big as the sound of his records.

I always remember layin' in bed and right at the end of *It's Over*, when he hits that note where it sounds like the world's going to end, I'd be laying there promising myself that I was never going to go outside again and never going to talk to another woman. Right about that time my needle would slip back to the first cut and I'd hear . . . [the opening riff to] Pretty Woman/I don't believe you/You're not the truth/No one could look as good as you. And that was when I understood.

I carry his records with me when I go on tour today, and I'll always remember what he means to me and what he meant to me when I was young and afraid to love. In '75, when I went into the studio to make *Born To Run*, I wanted to make a record with words like Bob Dylan that sounded like Phil Spector, but most of all I wanted to sing like Roy Orbison. Now everybody knows that nobody sings like Roy Orbison.

— *Bruce Springsteen*, Roy Orbison in Dreams

The heart of the speech is really an argument. The claim appears in this sentence:

Some rock 'n' roll reinforces friendship and community, but for me, Roy's ballads were always best when you were alone and in the dark.

In diagram form (Figure 3.4) the relationship of the parts of Springsteen's speech might appear as follows:

Notice how Springsteen *qualifies* his assertion with the words "for me"; includes an *exception* ("some rock 'n' roll reinforces friendship and community"); and adds *backing* (in the form of his personal recollections) to support his *warrant* for members of the audience who might feel differently about what constitutes a great rock 'n' roll ballad.

Questions for Discussion and Writing

1. Select one of the following issues and write a short essay that expresses and supports your opinion and takes opposing views into account. Before you write, consider what kinds of information you would need and what specific audience you would wish to persuade. As you draft your argument consider whether you need to qualify your claim, present exceptions or provide backing for assumptions.

    If you and some other members of your class have written arguments taking opposing views on the same issue, you might try the following exercise:

    ■ Form groups that identify the key interest of each perspective.

    ■ Drawing on the Rogerian approach, summarize the positions involved as a first step toward mediating the conflict (the class may wish to appoint a student to act as a mediator posing questions to each of the opposing parties).

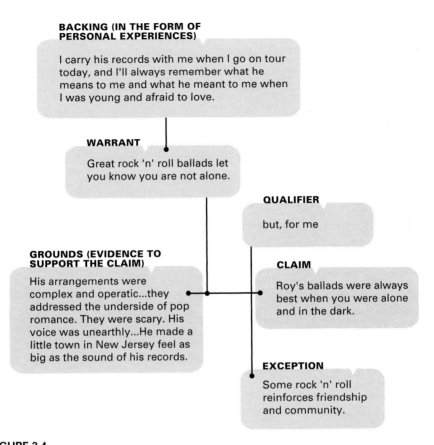

FIGURE 3.4
■ The Relationship of the Parts of Springsteen's Speech.

- ■ Try to come to a compromise that takes into consideration the interests of all parties involved.
- ■ As a class write a collaborative statement that takes all sides into account.

1. Should schools be given the task of offering explicit sex education for children? In your opinion, at what age should this be started, if at all? When children are 6, 8, 10, or some other age? Identify the assumptions underlying your opinion.

2. Should people who smoke cigarettes have to pay for their own health insurance? Why or why not?

3. Should religious institutions be required to pay taxes?

4. Should advertising on television directed at children be restricted?

5. Is the United States solving its immigration problem?

6. Is there a date rape crisis on college campuses?

7. Do student athletes receive a genuine academic education?

8. Should intelligent design be taught along with evolution in public schools?

9. Does prolonged exposure to violent video games make children more aggressive and violent?

10. Should profiling be allowed to combat terrorism?

11. Should the federal government fund stem cell research?

12. Is the United States ready for a recurrence of a 1918-style flu pandemic?

13. Should the laws be changed to permit same-sex marriage?

14. Is global warming a real threat?

15. What explains the recent upsurge in rates of autism?

16. Will outsourcing jobs and services ultimately be beneficial to America?

17. How would you characterize the impact of blogging and/or iPods on personal communications?

CHAPTER 4

ARGUING IN THE DISCIPLINES

OVERVIEW: This chapter will introduce you to the conventions and assumptions that govern the kinds of issues and methods of inquiry that characterize the different disciplines across the curriculum.

Writers and researchers in all academic disciplines often are compelled to convince others (colleagues, fellow researchers, or the general public) of the validity of their ideas and discoveries. Discussion and debate accompany the development of central ideas, concepts, and laws in all fields of study. Writers in the liberal arts, the social sciences, and the sciences use strategies of argument to support new interpretations of known facts or establish plausible cases for new hypotheses.

Although arguments explore important issues and espouse specific theories, the forms in which they appear vary according to the style and format of the individual discipline. Evidence in different disciplines can appear in a variety of formats, including the interpretation of statistics, laws, precedents, or the citation of authorities. The means used to construct arguments depends on the audience within the discipline being addressed, the nature of the thesis being proposed, and the accepted methodology for that particular discipline.

Like general arguments, the structure of arguments within the disciplines requires (1) a clear statement of a proposition or claim, (2) grounds that are relevant to the claim and sufficient to support it, and (3) a warrant based on solid backing that guarantees the appropriateness and applicability of the grounds in supporting the claim. So, too, appropriate qualifiers or possible exceptions to the claim must be stated as part of the argument.

Inquiry in the Liberal Arts, Social Sciences, and Sciences

Each of the three broad areas in the curriculum—liberal arts, social sciences, and sciences—seeks different kinds of knowledge and, therefore, has a different method of inquiry. That is to say, each area stipulates what kinds of problems or issues it considers worth addressing.

In the liberal arts, critics evaluate and interpret works of art; review music, dance, drama, and the film; and write literary analyses. Philosophers probe the moral and ethical implications of people's actions, and advocate specific ways of meeting the ethical challenges posed by new technologies. Historians interpret political, military, and constitutional events; analyze their causes; and theorize about how the past has influenced the present. Historians study primary sources in an effort to create a coherent story as to what happened, when it happened, who was responsible and in what order events occurred. They must piece together fragments of information and make inferences that separate what is true from fictionalized versions.

Social scientists collect and analyze data about patterns and motivation of the behavior of people in groups. The results of the experiments that apply hypotheses from social theory to the real world are presented in statistical form.

Lawyers and constitutional scholars argue for specific ways of applying legal and constitutional theory to everyday problems. Economists debate issues related to changes wrought by technology, distribution of income, unemployment, and commerce. Political scientists look into how effectively governments initiate and manage social change, and ask basic questions about the limits of governmental intrusion into individual rights. Sociologists analyze statistics and trends to evaluate how successfully institutions accommodate social change.

In the sciences, biologists, as well as biochemists, zoologists, botanists, and other natural scientists, propose theories to explain the interdependence of living things and their natural environment. Psychologists champion hypotheses based on physiological, experimental, social, and clinical research to explain various aspects of human behavior. Physicists, as well as mathematicians, astronomers, engineers, and computer scientists, put forward and defend hypotheses about the basic laws underlying the manifestations of the physical world, from the microscopic to the cosmic.

The broad areas of the curriculum function as specific audiences. Each discipline has its own needs, aims, interests, and expectations and sets its own standards about what constitutes acceptable reasoning.

The kinds of knowledge sought and the procedures used by the social sciences are quite different from those of the liberal arts. These disciplines have, to a large extent, adapted the techniques and objectives of the physical and natural sciences to study how human beings interact within the context of social, political, business, legal, psychological, and cultural relationships.

The types of information sought and the methods employed within the domain of the sciences aim at providing an accurate, systematic, and comprehensive account of the world around us as well as a framework within which new hypotheses can be put forward and evaluated.

We can appreciate the relevance of claims only in the context of the requirements of the larger fields within which the claims are advanced. That is, there are certain defining features and distinctive goals of each discipline that determine which items, data, or evidence will be seen as relevant to the claim. Training in different fields consists in learning what kinds of evidence are accepted as appropriate in supporting claims within that particular field. (The following discussions applying the Toulmin model to a range of disciplines have been adapted from Stephen Toulmin, Richard Rieke, and Allan Janik, *An Introduction to Reasoning* [1984]. Future in-text citations refer to this source; page numbers are given in parentheses.)

Different fields have different concepts of what constitutes evidence to be introduced to support a claim. Grounds, evidence, and data that are appropriate in a legal argument will be of a different kind and will be judged differently than evidence in a scientific argument or in an argument in the arts. As in general arguments, warrants in the disciplines are statements, formulas, and rules that authorize the way evidence (all data: pertinent information, all that is known about a situation, the known variables, and so on) can be interpreted so as to justify the conclusion reached or the claim being made.

In fields such as natural and physical sciences, computer science, engineering, and mathematics, warrants most frequently take the form of exact formulas used to convert raw data (in the form of known variables) into a significant conclusion (50). In mathematics, for example, the circumference of a circle can be discovered by applying a relevant formula, 2π. For example, if the radius is measured at 3 feet, you would apply the formula multiplying 2 times pi times the radius to discover the value of the circumference. Of course, many more complex formulas govern other applied and theoretical sciences. These warrants are known, reliable, and exact, and can be depended on.

By contrast, the law, assuming there is no disagreement about what the facts of the situation are, applies warrants in the form of relevant statute or precedents to discover whether one has or has not violated the law in a given situation (51).

Loose Parts by Dave Blazek

Hodgkiss quieted the crowd with his
mathematical proof that there is, indeed,
no business like show business.

FIGURE 4.1

How does this cartoon illustrate different methods of proof used in different disciplines?

As in general arguments, warrants are backed up in different ways. In science, the backing is the theoretical and experimental basis on which the warrant relies for its authority. In law, all the legal history of a particular statute would constitute the backing (whereas the warrant would be the statute that is appropriate to apply in that particular case).

In medicine, the backing for a diagnosis would be all the research that the physician might consult to make sure that the diagnosis was based on a generalization (the warrant) that provided the most accurate interpretation of the facts (symptoms, results of laboratory work, past medical history, etc.) of a particular case (53). Backing in all disciplines always refers to the underlying body of research in that specific field that justifies using a particular warrant (67).

Professional training is designed to familiarize students with concepts of evidence, and with how the methodology of any particular field is related to its larger purposes or goals. Apprenticeship in various disciplines involves the process of discovering what warrants are appropriate to apply in different circumstances. In many fields, warrants do not take the form of exact formulas or statutes, but rather are general principles, capable of being learned only through years of experience in that field. For example, in medicine, a skillful diagnostician draws on years of accumulated experience as well as information learned in medical school.

The way a veterinarian reaches a conclusion is characteristic of medical diagnoses. For example, James Herriot in *All Creatures Great and Small* diagnoses the true causes of a cow's sudden illness:

> I have a vivid recollection of a summer evening when I had to carry out a rumenotomy on a cow. As a rule, I was inclined to play for time when I suspected a foreign body—there were so many other conditions with similar symptoms that I was never in a hurry to make a hole in the animal's side. But this time diagnosis was easy; the sudden fall in milk yield, loss of cudding; grunting, and the rigid sunken-eyed appearance of the cow. And to clinch it the farmer told me he had been repairing a hen house in the cow pasture—nailing up loose boards. I knew where one of the nails had gone.

In reaching his conclusion, Herriot is able to relate the meaning of the signs of illness the cow displays to general principles drawn from his experience and presumably from veterinary textbooks. In effect, he says, these kinds of symptoms can mean the cow has ingested a foreign body like a nail, and in this particular case, there is a good chance that is what happened. Therefore, he concludes that a rumenotomy, or surgical incision into the cow's stomach to remove a foreign body, should be performed.

Broken down into the separate elements in the argument, Herriot's line of thought appears as follows:

Grounds: Sudden fall in milk yield, loss of cudding, grunting, rigid sunken-eyed appearance, nails used to repair loose boards in a hen house in the cow pasture.

Warrant: A cow that swallows a foreign body like a nail can be expected to display characteristic symptoms of sudden fall in milk yield, and so forth.

Claim (Expressed as a Diagnosis): The cow needs a rumenotomy to remove the foreign body.

Qualifier or Exception: Unless it can be established that the cow definitely did not swallow one of the loose nails.

Because the purposes or goals of different disciplines are different, each field brings different perspectives to bear even when the same subject is viewed. By examining how various disciplines look at what appears to be the same thing, we can see how the same phenonenon becomes, in effect, a different object of inquiry according to the conceptual framework within which it is investigated. For example, a psychiatrist, Judith L. Rapoport, has looked at the life and music of the early twentieth-century French composer, Erik Satie, in *The Boy Who Couldn't Stop Washing*, as part of her study of obsessive-compulsive disorder (OCD). Those suffering from OCD are compelled to repeat certain acts over and over again—washing, counting, checking, or other more elaborate rituals:

> Although he lived alone in Paris and at times in great poverty, he dressed fastidiously and his personal trappings were typical of OCD. No one was allowed to enter his room during his life. When he died, his wardrobe was found to contain a dozen identical new suits, shirts, collars, hats, walking sticks, and a cigar box was found with several thousand pieces of paper with the same symbols and inscriptions. All of them for some unknown reason, about Charlemagne. Satie's OCD may have also influenced his music, although this is less clear. Satie's "trinitarian obsession" as musicologists refer to it was manifested in his works which were frequently conceived in groups of three. Within his music, Satie wrote he intended to present different views on a theme. Almost always, three were offered, the three *Gymnopedies* the best known.

By contrast, Joseph Machlis, a musicologist, in the *Introduction to Contemporary Music* views Satie and the same work *Gymnopedies* within the completely different conceptual framework of his discipline. For example:

> Satie is best known to the public for his early piano pieces: the *Sarabandes* (1887), *Gymnopedies* (1887) and *Gnossiennes* (1890). Each set contains three dance pieces in the composer's characteristic manner. These works anticipate certain procedures that later became associated with Debussy, notably the unconventional handling of unresolved chords of the ninth, the modal idiom, and the movement of the harmony in parallel block-like formations.
>
> This music has a grave simplicity. It displays certain hallmarks of Satie's style: short symmetrical phrases repeated over and over; an airy medodic line, with an easy swing; limpid harmony, whose modal character is brought into focus at the cadences; lightness of texture and establishment at the outset of a rhythmic pattern that persists throughout.

Professionals in other disciplines have also studied Satie from their perspective including his association with innovative movements in the world of art—cubism, dadaism, and surrealism.

Arguing in the Arts

The essential nature of the arts is to provide insight into the human condition, that is, to communicate what being human actually means and how humanity appears at different times under different social conditions. The ultimate criterion by which works of art (both creative and interpretive) are judged is how well this is done without falsifying or distorting the human condition. This primary concern with the often inexpressible qualitative sense of the human experience defines both the kinds of problems as well as the methods used to address them within the arts.

For the artist, the question is how well the techniques of the craft have been used to bring the audience into direct contact with internal real-life experiences each artist tries to express. Thus, arguments at this level are often technical over the best means of achieving a desired effect (352). We can see this at work in Tom Wolfe's "Why Aren't They Writing the Great American Novel Anymore?" where Wolfe analyzes how dissatisfaction with traditional techniques led innovative journalists to incorporate many of the narrative techniques of fiction—scene-by-scene construction; personal viewpoint; details of furnishings, clothes, and social status; eccentric punctuation; slang and the vernaculars of different subcultures—to enhance their ability to report on human experience. In schematic form, Wolfe's argument appears as follows:

> **Grounds:** You, as a nonfiction writer, want to achieve the effects of immediacy, concrete reality, emotional involvement, and a gripping or absorbing quality.
>
> **Backing:** The technical experiments and innovations of Fielding, Smollett, Balzac, Dickens, and Gogol have established that:
>
> **Warrant:** In the genre of fiction writing an effective way of introducing realism is to introduce (1) scene-by-scene construction, (2) realistic dialogue, (3) third-person point of view, and (4) a record of people's everyday gestures, habits, manners, customs, and other details symbolic of the entire pattern of behavior through which people express their position in the world.
>
> **Claim:** You, as a nonfiction writer, should try to use all the techniques of novelists to obtain the effects of immediacy, concrete reality, emotional involvement, and a gripping or absorbing quality.

The audiences for whom the arts are created judge an artist's work from a different perspective (353). For the audience, the key question is how effectively the artist's work succeeds in deepening, enriching, or extending the sense of being human and conveying insight into human nature. As representative of and mediator for the audience's reactions, the critic or reviewer evaluates the work of art or the artist's performance. For example, in "The Boo Taboo" the acerbic theater critic John Simon offered this evaluation of Richard Tucker's performance in the opera *Carmen*:

> The most illuminating occurrence for me was a recent Saturday matinee at the Met. It was Barrault's wretched staging of *Carmen*, with Richard Tucker as Don Jose. Now Tucker had once been in possession of a good, strong voice; but he had never been a genuine artist with a sense of shading, expressive range, a feeling for the emotional depth of the part or the language in which he was singing. By this time, with even his basic organ gone, Tucker is long overdue for retirement. In this Don Jose, Tucker's voice was as off as it had been for years, his phrasing as unlovely as it had always been. Visually, he was a geriatric travesty; histrionically, even by the shockingly low standards of operatic acting, a farce. Even his French was, let us say, hyper-Tourelian. After he got through mangling the Flower Song, and after the orchestra was through as well, I added to the general applause three loud *phooeys*—a *phooey* cuts through applause better than a boo or hiss.

When each of the elements in Simon's critique is identified, the outline of his argument appears this way:

Grounds: Tucker's basic singing voice although once good and strong was gone. His phrasing was unlovely; visually, he was a geriatric travesty; his acting fell below even the "shockingly low standards of operatic acting." His French was not authentic. He mangled the "Flower Song" from *Carmen*.

Backing: Viewers, listeners, and critics of operatic performances have generally agreed that:

Warrant: Good operatic singing requires a strong voice, a sense of shading, and expressive range, a feeling for the emotional depth of the part and the language in which the performer is singing, appropriate visual appearance, and competent acting ability.

Claim: Richard Tucker should not be performing since he can no longer meet the standards required for professional operatic singing.

Qualifier or Exception: Despite the fact that there was general applause for Tucker's performance.

The broadest perspectives are brought to bear by academic disciplines in the liberal arts that interpret the meaning of an individual work as it relates to other works of that type and to the historical context in which it was produced (354). For example, the art historian Alan Wallach views particular paintings by William L. Haney and Jan van Eyck as they relate to larger social and cultural contexts. Open-endedness of interpretive issues and problems are characteristic of the humanities and liberal arts. That is, although arguments take the form of interpretations (however well-supported and effective the arguments may be), they do not foreclose the possibility of new, different, and equally convincing interpretations in the future. Reduced to its essentials, Wallach's argument in "William L. Haney and Jan van Eyck" appears like this:

> **Grounds:** In Haney's *The Root of It All*, the gold ring of the American Stock Exchange is drastically foreshortened and made to resemble a casino gambling table. Haney further complicates things by placing near the front of the gold ring an anamorphic image of a black man's severed head. . . . Another composite technique Haney shares with van Eyck is a picture within a picture. Van Eyck's *Giovanni Arnolfini and His Bride* contains a convex mirror at the rear of the marriage chamber which reflects in extraordinary detail the couple and the otherwise invisible witnesses to the scene. In *A Present Tense of Extinct Too*, Haney's painting of a CBS sound stage, five television monitors play a similar role, commenting on the picture and augmenting its meaning with images of the Vietnam War, a 19th-century buffalo hunt, a mushroom cloud, and so on.

> **Warrant:** Artists, even those who live centuries apart, belonging to different worlds and different social conditions, often use the same techniques to express artistic judgments about the societies in which they live.

> **Claim:** Both Haney and van Eyck solved problems of showing how spirituality was ruthlessly subordinated to materialism by (1) creating the illusion of unified compositions that break down upon closer inspection, (2) using architecture surrounding figures to bring together seemingly unrelated scenes, (3) using the technique of painting a picture within a picture, and (4) employing submerged symbolism to comment on the materialism of their respective societies.

How does the convex mirror in Jan van Eyck's *The Arnolfini Marriage* (1434), on the next page, illustrate the artist's unique approach? Can you see the reflection of van Eyck's image and another figure who may have been the official witness to the ceremony?

Arguing in Ethics

Originally a branch of philosophy, the field of ethics as a discipline in its own right has grown increasingly important as society has become more specialized and technological. As people are more locked into specialized roles and see things only from narrow viewpoints, an ethical view is required as a counterbalance so that they can evaluate the consequences of their actions in relation to society as a whole.

Ethics, as a field, tries to mediate claims between traditional professional or societal demands and those larger overriding human concerns by providing a systematic procedure that makes it possible to discover which course of action, among many choices, is preferable. Because ethical dilemmas involve a choice of actions, the ability to create hypothetical or "what if" situations is invaluable, as it allows one to construct different scenarios in which the effects of different kinds of choices can be dramatized. A consideration of ethical choices should always involve understanding the consequences of choices for all those who will be affected.

Ethics is concerned with questions of what should be done because it seeks to investigate what kinds of actions are acceptable or unacceptable, right or wrong, good or bad, when judged according to a specified moral or ethical criterion. Thus, typical arguments require the writer to apply a general ethical principle in the form of a warrant to discover whether an action that has already happened or is being considered is good or bad, desirable or regrettable, and is to be chosen or avoided (402–3).

We can see how this works by examining the argument made by Terence Cardinal Cooke in an address delivered to the First Annual American Health Congress. Cooke argues that doctors, nurses, and other health care professionals need to think about their professional obligations in light of equally compelling ethical and moral considerations. The occasion prompting Cooke's speech was the imminent passage of a "death with dignity" bill in the state legislature that would require health care professionals to take an active role in disconnecting life-support systems of terminally ill patients (without any immediate family with whom to confer) whose life, in the opinion of three physicans, was meaningless.

This is a typical ethical argument in that Cooke is addressing a conflict between a role health care professionals would be obligated to play and equally compelling moral considerations. Cooke argues that medical professionals should not be put in a situation where they are able to "play God" and decide when a patient's life is or is not meaningful.

The ethical principle Cooke applies as a warrant is based on the assumption that life is a God-given gift and that no human being has the right to take the life of another regardless of the circumstances. Represented in outline form, Cooke's argument appears thus:

Grounds: Allowing "death with dignity" would become an accepted part of health care professionals' duties because the bill under consideration by the state legislature stated that any disabled person with no immediate family, and for whom, in the opinion of three physicians, the prolongation of life would be meaningless, could be granted "death with dignity."

Warrant: Permitting a patient's life to be terminated on the grounds that it is meaningless is against the law of God and should be justly labeled as "murdering a human being."

Claim: Health care professionals should not be party to a practice labeled "death with dignity" because it is against the law of God and constitutes murder.

Arguing in History

History explains how the present has been affected by the past and provides a clear account of the conditions in which societies have lived. Historical research brings to life important military, social, economic, and political events from the past. To create a persuasive reconstruction of past events, historians need to examine a wide range of records (private journals, letters, newspaper accounts, photographs if available, and other primary documents from the period under study), as well as secondary documents (such as interpretations of the same events by other historians). In seeking to delineate a plausible explanation for past events, historians may also draw on the information and research methods of political science (which studies how governments manage their affairs), sociology (which investigates the relationships between individuals and institutions in society), anthropology and archaeology (which reconstruct past cultures and inquire into why they have different customs and patterns of development), and psychology (which studies human behavior). Historians may also use statistical and computer analyses to form a more accurate picture of past events.

The methods of inquiry used in history attempt to provide a clear picture of who, what, where, when, and how events took place. Some historians go beyond these basic issues and offer interpretations as to why the events took place. Arguments in history often take the form of revising older interpretations or taking into account new information that forces a reevaluation of previously held beliefs. For example, in *The Peculiar Institution: Slavery in the Ante-Bellum South* (1956), Kenneth M. Stampp, an American historian, has investigated the relationship between the southern plantation system and slavery. In contrast to previous historians, such as Ulrich B. Phillips, who claimed in *American Negro Slavery* (1918) that slavery was part of the social structure of the plantation system, Stampp asserted that a shortage of labor and a desire to increase profits were the real reasons behind the phenomenon of slave labor.

In "To Make Them Stand in Fear" from his 1956 work, Stampp uses a variety of source documents, including recorded testimony of slave owners in Mississippi, South Carolina, North Carolina, and Virginia, as well as quotations from the actual manuals written to advise plantation owners on the management of slaves, to support his analysis of conditioning procedures used to instill fear and dependency in newly arrived blacks. In outline form, Stampp's argument appears as follows:

Grounds: The manual *Discourses on the Management of Slaves* provided specific instructions on all phases of the "programming process." Stampp identifies five separate steps: (1) establishing strict discipline modeled on army regulations, (2) implanting in the bondsman a consciousness of inferiority, (3) instilling a sense of awe at the master's enormous power, (4) persuading the bondsman to value the success of the master's enterprise, and (5) creating a habit of perfect dependence.

Warrant: The study of original source documents provides valuable new information with which to reevaluate and revise previously held interpretations of events in history. (The warrant expresses the methodology underlying the concept of historical revisionism practiced by Stampp.)

Claim: Contrary to historical interpretations that view slavery as an integral component of the plantation system, original source documents reveal a calculated effort on the part of slave owners to transform newly arrived blacks into slaves who would be psychologically conditioned to believe that what was good for the plantation owners was good for them as well.

Arguing in the Social Sciences

The social sciences are often referred to as the behavioral sciences because they focus on what can be observed objectively about human beings—their actions or behavior. These disciplines seek to discover causal connections (sometimes expressed as statistical laws) that have both descriptive and predictive value and that can be confirmed or refuted by data from subsequent research.

The social sciences have adapted in some measure both the techniques and the objectives of the physical and natural sciences in order to study how human beings interact in the context of social, political, business, legal, psychological, and cultural relationships.

To ensure an objectivity comparable to that of the physical and natural sciences, social science researchers rely on statistical surveys, questionnaires, and other data-gathering techniques. Social scientists draw on a whole range of theoretical models to explain human behavior and explore how individual behavior may be conditioned by expectations of the surrounding culture. The range of theories available often raises the question as to which theoretical model should be applied to explain the data in question. Social scientists strive to achieve results in quantifiable and repeatable form so that other researchers can repeat and thereby confirm the validity of the results of their experiments.

The ways in which social sciences have adapted methodology from the natural and physical sciences can be seen in the procedures social scientists use for gathering evidence through observation and controlled experiments. First and foremost, social sciences (including sociology, psychology, anthropology, archaeology, education, economics, political science, business and management, and so forth) emphasize the importance of systematic and objective observation of events and people recorded in concrete language, without interposing any personal opinion as to motives. Events and human behavior must be recorded as objectively as possible so other social scientists can verify the observations and authenticate the findings. Of course, some social sciences such as archaeology have to gather information after the event has taken place and must gather data in the form of artifacts and records.

To look at this methodology more closely, we might examine its use in sociology, a discipline that is concerned with the observation, description, and explanation of the behavior of people in groups. Sociologists investigate institutions within society, their origins, their capacity for accommodating social change, and the mechanisms within them that influence the behavior of individuals.

Questions to be answered or problems to be solved are expressed in the form of hypotheses whose validity can be measured by empirical means. For example, in a classic experiment John Darley and Bibb Latané used small groups of people to test their "diffusion of responsibility" theory to answer the question of why people don't help in a crisis. By varying the number of people who thought others also were aware of a crisis, Darley and Latané demonstrated in quantifiable form a plausible mechanism to explain the real causes of seeming apathy in bystanders.

Since it would be impractical for social scientists to test everyone in a particular population in order to gather evidence, researchers test a sample or small group of people from a specific population. Darley and Latané's research took the typical form of an experimental study in which they manipulated one variable (the number of people in the group in a room filling with smoke) and observed the effect on a second variable (the likelihood that any of the subjects would report the smoke to an external authority).

The professional journal in which the results of their study appeared is an appropriate forum within which arguments can be tested and evaluated. By studying the methodology of this experiment, other researchers could set up comparable experiments to test for themselves the validity of Darley and

Latané's conclusions. The authors explain the design of the experiment, the hypothesis being tested, and the results in a brief abstract that precedes their article "Group Inhibition of Bystander Intervention in Emergencies":

> Male undergraduates found themselves in a smoke-filling room, either alone, with 2 non-reacting others, or in groups of 3. Ss [subjects] were less likely to report the smoke when in the presence of passive others (10%) or in groups of 3 (38% of groups) than when alone (75%). These results seemed to have been mediated by the way Ss interpreted the ambiguous situation; seeing other people remaining passive led Ss to decide the smoke was not dangerous.

In outline form, Darley and Latané's argument appears as follows:

Grounds: Male undergraduates found themselves in a smoke-filling room, either alone, with two nonreacting others, or in groups of three. Ss (subjects) were less likely to report the smoke when in the presence of passive others (10 percent) or in groups of three (38 percent of groups) than when alone (75 percent).

Backing: Prior research by social psychologists (Darley and Latané, Latané and D. C. Glass, S. Schacter, E. Goffman, R. Brown) makes it probable that the diffusion-of-responsibility model determines how people in groups react to a crisis.

Warrant: The diffusion-of-responsibility hypothesis states that if an individual is alone when an emergency occurs, he or she feels solely responsible. When others are present, individuals feel that their own responsibility for taking action is lessened, making them less likely to help.

Claim: The behavior of the people in the situation is explained by the diffusion-of-responsibility model. As Darley and Latané conclude, "seeing other people remaining passive led Ss to decide the smoke was not dangerous."

Arguing in the Law

Features of legal arguments are determined by the purpose of the law, that is, to provide protection for individuals in society and for society as a whole. Accordingly, legal decisions have to do with protecting life and liberty, property, and public order and with providing systematic guidelines in ensuring the performance of contractual relationships (281).

The law provides a procedure for reaching decisions that are binding on all parties. Beyond this goal, the law strives to make decisions that are consistent with previous statutes, codes, and precedents, and with what society considers to be fair, equitable, and just (284). As with other arguments, the process of legal reasoning depends on the interplay between evidence or grounds and claims and warrants to produce the legal decision expressed as a claim.

In court, legal reasoning makes use of an adversarial procedure whereby two opposing parties present the strongest case they can assemble for their proposed claims. Each party tells its story or version of the truth, and the court (judge or jury) decides which version is more credible (284). The court chooses between the two opposing versions rather than working out a negotiated settlement that would be acceptable to both parties. The adversary character of legal reasoning can be seen in other legal forums where arguments are heard such as congressional hearings where individuals provide competing versions of the facts.

The examination of evidence is at the center of legal reasoning. Evidence is entered in the form of exhibits. Letters, documents, contracts, tape recordings, videotapes, and a wide range of physical evidence are then evaluated to see whose claim they best support (302).

Evidence or grounds can also take the form of testimony of witnesses to be tested by cross-examination, or the expert opinion of authorities, which is also subjected to cross-examination. Cross-examination is an important feature of legal reasoning, as are rules governing what evidence the jury will or will not be allowed to hear (302). For example, evidence cannot be admitted from certain kinds of protected relationships (doctor-patient, lawyer-client, priest-parishioner, husband-wife). In other cases, the court must rule whether particular circumstantial or hearsay evidence is admissible.

As with other types of arguments, a range of warrants specific to the law authorizes a connection between the claim and the evidence (304). Some warrants justify the use of expert testimony (for example, taking the form of an assumption that the testimony of a person with extensive experience and expertise in a particular field can be taken as authoritative). Other legal warrants justify the use of circumstantial, physical evidence to reach a conclusion. Still others take the form of particular cases to be used as precedents in reaching a decision on a current case (307).

Whereas regular legal arguments simply apply rules and precedents, some arguments challenge the very procedures or rules used in arriving at judgments. (308).

To see how rule-setting decisions become precedents that lawyers can use in ordinary legal arguments, we might examine the legal reasoning underlying the historic 1954 Supreme Court ruling on segregation in public schools (*Brown v. Board of Education of Topeka*). The decision was written by Earl Warren, then

Chief Justice of the Supreme Court. In outline form, Warren's decision on behalf of the Court appears this way:

Grounds: Warren cites the results of psychological studies showing that segregated schools instill a sense of inferiority, retard mental development, and deprive the children of minority groups of equal educational opportunities.

Warrant: A crucial clause in the Fourteenth Amendment, namely, "no state shall . . . deny to any person within its jurisdiction the equal protection of the laws," empowers the court to evaluate how well states manage the important function of education for citizens.

Claim: Warren concluded that "in the field of public education the doctrine of 'separate but equal' has no place." The Court ruled that separate educational facilities are inherently unequal and found that segregation in the public schools deprives children of minorities of the educational opportunities they should rightfully enjoy under the Fourteenth Amendment.

An argument like this, which challenges the very interpretation of what the law is, is obviously of a different order than an argument that simply applies accepted rules or methodology. This Supreme Court decision served as a catalyst for the civil rights movement, and permanently altered existing social attitudes toward the acceptability of racial discrimination.

Arguing in Business

Every phase of business production—finance, research and development, purchasing, marketing, and organizational development—entails a variety of decisions. Business in the present context refers to the part of the economy that provides goods and services for society.

Arguments in business differ from arguments advanced by scientists, historians, literary critics, ethicists, and so forth, in several important respects. Because the goal of business is to make a profit, arguments tend to focus on questions of tactics or strategy in accomplishing this purpose.

In contrast to law, where arguments take place in an adversary framework, business and management decisions require all the parties involved to arrive at a consensus or practical compromise (370). Furthermore, most business decisions have to be made within a certain time. Not to decide within the time available is equivalent to not making the decision at all. Moreover, business decisions sometimes have to be made despite the fact that circumstances are not completely understood or information is incomplete. In this respect, business decisions are unlike those arguments advanced by historians and scientists where time constraints play almost no part and where the emphasis is on taking as much time as is necessary to understand circumstances as fully as possible (371).

The forums within which business arguments take place include board room conferences, stockholder meetings, consultations between managers, and any other administrative setting where management must explain the basis of its decision to others both inside and outside the company—that is, to employees, stockholders, and government officials (370).

Claims in business take the form of policy recommendations. These proposals may concern actions that should be taken to introduce a new product or service, decisions as to whether to invest in a new plant, and proposals covering a wide range of issues (383). For example, should the company branch out, change its pricing strategies? How should it best respond to the marketing strategies of the competition? What use should be made of market research data in order to market a product more effectively? Most business arguments are utilitarian, short- or medium-term proposals, and are concerned with questions of strategies and tactics rather than discussions of ultimate goals and purposes.

Grounds or support in business arguments consist of all the information on which claims can be based (383–84). This includes economic information and data gleaned from market research, as well as relevant government regulations. Information used to support claims frequently appears as a detailed breakdown of all types of expenses (administrative, market research, and costs of development). Business today also avails itself of a whole range of systematized information in the form of databases.

The manipulation of information in business uses a problem-solving model that defines the nature of the problem, uses a variety of search techniques (brainstorming, breaking it into subproblems, and so forth), and generates a list of alternative solutions. The most feasible solution is presented as a proposal or claim. Solutions are evaluated in terms of what constitutes the best match of the company's resources and proven competence consistent with government regulations and expectations of society.

Most business warrants relate directly to the underlying purpose of business itself; that is, whatever promises to produce a greater profit consistent with the proven methods should be selected from any field of alternatives (385–86). Likewise, whatever promises to lessen the cost of operation in producing a product or service, or promises to promote the more efficient functioning of the company should be chosen from any field of various alternatives.

We can see these basic elements operating in a typical situation where a municipality has entered into a long-term agreement to have trash collected by a private contractor. Town officials must now decide whether to sell their own equipment (trucks, shovels, plows) that the municipality no longer needs for the present and probably will not need for some years in the future.

Arguments in favor of selling the equipment emphasize the cost of maintaining and repairing it and the revenue its sale could generate. Arguments against selling the equipment refer to the experience of other municipalities that, having sold their trucks and so on, were at the mercy of the contractor when the agreement came up for renegotiation. Ultimately, the municipality officials decided not to sell in order to avoid a situation where they would be dependent on private contractors who would know they would be forced to pay because they could not provide the service themselves. In outline form, the argument appears as follows:

> **Grounds:** The projected cost of maintaining the equipment, the revenue its sale would generate, and the projected costs of hiring and keeping a private contractor to collect the trash.
>
> **Backing:** Precedents are provided by other municipalities that initially entered into long-term service contracts because of low prices, sold their equipment, and subsequently were at the mercy of contractors who raised their prices dramatically when the service agreement came up for renewal.
>
> **Warrant:** In the short term the sale would produce apparent savings, but in the long term it might prove very costly. In weighing two alternatives, long-term disadvantages outweigh short-term advantages.
>
> **Claim:** The municipality should keep its equipment (trucks, plows, etc.) rather than put it up for sale.
>
> **Qualifier or Exceptions:** Unless unforeseen costs in maintanence and storage become excessive.

Arguing in the Sciences

The types of information sought and the methods employed within the domain of the sciences aim at providing an accurate, systematic, and comprehensive account of the world around us as well as a framework within which new hypotheses can be put forward and evaluated (315).

The forums in which argumentation takes place in the sciences include professional meetings, refereed journals, and conferences. These public forums guarantee that all ideas will be tested to determine their underlying validity.

Scientists, even those on the losing side of an argument, have a common interest in gaining a more accurate picture of the natural world, its origin, makeup, and functioning (317). Thus, the putting forth and disputing of claims is not an end in itself as it is in the law, but a means to clarify and improve a picture of the world.

The way science solves problems and generates new knowledge can be seen by examining procedures used by the biologists Arthur D. Hasler and James A. Larsen in "The Homing Salmon." Their experiments solved the mystery of how salmon could find their way back to the exact streams where they were born, even from distances as great as 900 miles, by pinpointing the role played by the salmon's olfactory sense.

Well-documented observations based on the recovery of tagged salmon in the streams where they were originally born had established that the homing instinct was a scientific problem worth investigating. For scientists, observation plays a crucial role in identifying mysterious phenomena or anomalies (319). How salmon remember their birthplace and find their way back to the stream in which they were born, sometimes from great distances, is an enigma that has fascinated naturalists for many years.

Once observations show the existence of a problem needing explanation, scientists formulate a tentative explanation or hypothesis to account for this otherwise inexplicable event.

Scientists then design specific experiments to measure in objective and quantifiable form whether the hypothesis provides an adequate explanation of the phenomenon. A scientific hypothesis, if true, should have both descriptive and predictive value. That is, it must accurately predict that in particular circumstances (which other scientists can duplicate) certain kinds of measurable effects can be observed. These effects should confirm the truth of the hypothesis.

For this reason, the design of the experiment is the essential feature of scientific research. The experiment should make it possible to isolate, control, and measure the role played by one key variable. In Hasler and Larsen's experiment, half of a group of salmon were marked and deprived of their olfactory sense and the other half were used as a control group. When all the salmon were released downstream, it was determined that the control group correctly returned as usual to the original stream, whereas the "odor-blinded" fish migrated in random fashion "picking the wrong stream as often as the right one."

The way in which evidence or grounds, warrants, and claims play a part in scientific problem solving as a method of inquiring into the truth (as opposed to advocating a position, as in the law) can be seen in the following outline:

Grounds:

> We took water from two creeks in Wisconsin and investigated whether fish could learn to discriminate between them. Our subjects, first minnows, then salmon, were indeed able to detect a difference. If, however, we destroyed a fish's nose tissue, it was no longer able to distinguish between the two water samples. Chemical analysis indicated that the only major difference between the two waters lay in the organic material. By testing the fish with various fractions of the water, separated by distillation, we confirmed that the identifying material was some volatile organic substance. The idea that fish are guided by odors in their migrations was further supported by a field test. From each of the two different branches of the Issaquah River in the state of Washington, we took a number of sexually ripe silver salmon which had come home to spawn. We then plugged with cotton the noses of half the fish in each group and placed all the salmon in the river below the fork to make the upstream run again. Most of the fish with unplugged noses swam back to the stream they had selected the first time. But the 'odor-blinded' fish migrated back in random fashion, picking the wrong stream as often as the right one.

Backing: The experience of scientists in developing systematic procedures for testing hypotheses that claim to account for otherwise inexplicable phenomena.

Warrant: The established procedures of scientific research state that the results of an experiment designed in such a way as to make it possible to isolate, control, and measure the role played by one key variable can be reliably depended on to explain and predict a previously inexplicable phenomenon.

Claim: (takes the form of a clear-cut working hypothesis for investigating the mystery of the homing salmon):

> We can suppose that every little stream has its own characteristic odor, which stays the same year after year; that young salmon become conditioned to this odor before they go to sea; that they remember the odor as they grow to maturity, and that they are able to find it and follow it to its source when they come back upstream to spawn.

Sometimes the anomalies observed and theories formulated to explain them are in such conflict with existing paradigms or agreed-upon scientific laws that they demand the establishment of new theoretical models to guide further research

(328–29). Charles Darwin's observations (*On The Origin of Species by Means of Natural Selection*, 1859) in the Galapagos Islands of adaptive mutations in finches, tortoises, and other species, ultimately led him to formulate a theory of evolution.

In outline form, Darwin's argument appears as follows:

Grounds: On journeys to the Galapagos Islands (over a period of some five years) Darwin observed different kinds of finches on different islands, with different bill structures suited to the kind of food available on individual islands (on some islands, finches ate insects and on others they ate seeds). Darwin thought that variations among individual representatives of a species make some better equipped to survive than others in a particular environment. These qualities are selected, passed on to their descendants, and over the passage of time, these changes are sufficient to result in a complete change of species. Darwin termed this evolutionary adaptive mechanism "natural selection" and thereby explained how new varieties of species continued to develop—a phenomenon previous scientific studies could not explain.

Warrant: A new theory that explains phenomena that are not explicable by previous theories should supercede previous explanations.

Claim: Darwin's theory of "natural selection" deserves to supercede previous scientific explanations.

Thus, Darwin advanced science by challenging existing theories and replacing them with a new theoretical model.

Three Short Arguments for Analysis

Kenneth M. Stampp

To Make Them Stand in Fear

Kenneth M. Stampp (b. 1912) earned a Ph.D. from the University of Wisconsin in 1942. Stampp was Morrison Professor of American History at the University of California at Berkeley and Harmsworth Professor of American History at Oxford University. His works include And the War Came *(1950) and* The Peculiar Institution: Slavery in the Ante-Bellum South *(1956) from which the following essay is drawn. His latest book is* The United States and National Self-Determination: Two Traditions *(1991).*

Thinking Critically

Consider what you know about various techniques of behavioral conditioning and the goals they seek to accomplish.

A wise master did not take seriously the belief that Negroes were natural-born slaves. He knew better. He knew that Negroes freshly imported from Africa had to be broken to bondage; that each succeeding generation had to be carefully trained. This was no easy task, for the bondsman rarely submitted willingly. Moreover, he rarely submitted completely. In most cases there was no end to the need for control—at least not until old age reduced the slave to a condition of helplessness.

Masters revealed the qualities they sought to develop in slaves when they singled out certain ones for special commendation. A small Mississippi planter mourned the death of his "faithful and dearly beloved servant" Jack: "Since I have owned him he has been true to me in all respects. He was an obedient trusty servant. . . . I never knew him to steal nor lie and he ever set a moral and industrious example to those around him. . . . I shall ever cherish his memory." A Louisiana sugar planter lost a "very valuable Boy" through an accident: "His life was a very great one. I have always found him willing and obedient and never knew him to fail to do anything he was put to do." These were "ideal" slaves, the models slaveholders had in mind as they trained and governed their workers.

How might this ideal be approached? The first step, advised those who wrote discourses on the management of slaves, was to establish and maintain strict discipline. An Arkansas master suggested the adoption of the "Army Regulations as to the discipline in Forts." "They must obey at all times, and under all circumstances, cheerfully and with alacrity," affirmed a Virginia slaveholder. "It greatly impairs the happiness of a negro, to be allowed to cultivate an insubordinate temper. Unconditional submission is the only footing upon which slavery should be placed. It is precisely similar to the attitude of a minor to his parent, or a soldier to his general." A South Carolinian limned a perfect relationship between a slave and his master: "that the slave should know that his master is to govern absolutely, and he is to obey implicitly. That he is never for a moment to exercise either his will or judgment in opposition to a positive order."

The second step was to implant in the bondsmen themselves a consciousness of personal inferiority. They had "to know and keep their places," to "feel the difference between master and slave," to understand that bondage was their natural status. They had to feel that African ancestry tainted them, that their color was a badge of degradation. In the country they were to show respect for even their master's nonslaveholding neighbors; in the towns they were to give way on the streets to the most wretched white man. The line between the races must never be crossed, for familiarity caused slaves to forget their lowly station and to become "impudent."

5   Frederick Douglass explained that a slave might commit the offense of impudence in various ways: "in the tone of an answer; in answering at all; in not answering; in the expression of countenance; in the motion of the head; in the gait, manner and bearing of the slave." Any of these acts, in some subtle way, might indicate the absence of proper subordination. "In a well regulated community," wrote a Texan, "a negro takes off his hat in addressing a white man. . . . Where this is not enforced, we may always look for impudent and rebellious negroes."

The third step in the training of slaves was to awe them with a sense of their master's enormous power. The only principle upon which slavery could be maintained, reported a group of Charlestonians, was the "principle of fear." In his defense of slavery James H. Hammond admitted that this, unfortunately, was true but put the responsibility upon the abolitionists. Antislavery agitation had forced masters to strengthen their authority: "We have to rely more and more on the power of fear. . . . We are determined to continue masters, and to do so we have to draw the reign tighter and tighter day by day to be assured that we hold them in complete check." A North Carolina mistress, after subduing a troublesome domestic, realized that it was essential "to make them stand in fear"!

In this the slaveholders had considerable success. Frederick Douglass believed that most slaves stood "in awe" of white men; few could free themselves altogether from the notion that their masters were "invested with a sort of sacredness." Olmsted saw a small white girl stop a slave on the road and boldly order him to return to his plantation. The slave fearfully obeyed her command. A visitor in Mississippi claimed that a master, armed only with a whip or cane, could throw himself among a score of bondsmen and cause them to "flee with terror." He accomplished this by the "peculiar tone of authority" with which he spoke. "Fear, awe, and obedience . . . are interwoven into the very nature of the slave."

The fourth step was to persuade the bondsmen to take an interest in the master's enterprise and to accept his standards of good conduct. A South Carolina planter explained: "The master should make it his business to show his slaves, that the advancement of his individual interest, is at the same time an advancement of theirs. Once they feel this, it will require but little compulsion to make them act as it becomes them." Though slaveholders induced only a few chattels to respond to this appeal, these few were useful examples for others.

The final step was to impress Negroes with their helplessness, to create in them "a habit of perfect dependence" upon their masters. Many believed it dangerous to train slaves to be skilled artisans in the towns, because they tended to become self-reliant. Some thought it equally dangerous to hire them to factory owners. In the Richmond tobacco factories they were alarmingly independent and "insolent." A Virginian was dismayed to find that his bondsmen, while working at an iron furnace, "got a habit of roaming about and *taking care of themselves.*" Permitting them to hire their own time produced even worse results. "No higher evidence can be furnished of its baneful effects," wrote a Charlestonian, "than the unwillingness it produces in the slave, to return to the regular life and domestic control of the master."

10   A spirit of independence was less likely to develop among slaves kept on the land, where most of them became accustomed to having their master provide their basic needs, and where they might be taught that they were unfit to look out for themselves. Slaves then directed their energies to the attainment of mere "temporary ease and enjoyment." "Their masters," Olmsted believed, "calculated on it in them—do not wish to cure it—and by constant practice encourage it."

Here, then, was the way to produce the perfect slave: accustom him to rigid discipline, demand from him unconditional submission, impress upon him his innate inferiority, develop in him a paralyzing fear of white men, train him to adopt the master's code of good behavior, and instill in him a sense of complete dependence. This, at least, was the goal.

But the goal was seldom reached. Every master knew that the average slave was only an imperfect copy of the model. He knew that some bondsmen yielded only to superior power—and yielded reluctantly. This complicated his problem of control.

ENGAGING the Text

1. Stampp demonstrates that the process of conditioning newly arrived blacks depended on instilling a set of psychological controls. What are these, and what were they designed to achieve?

2. As Stampp describes it, slaveholders were fearful of allowing slaves to be trained as independent workers. In a paragraph or two, discuss the reasons for this.

EVALUATING the Argument

1. How does Stampp's division of the conditioning process into a number of distinct steps help his readers to grasp his thesis and understand his analysis?

2. The manuals Stampp uses to illustrate his analysis describe the goal to be achieved and the methods for achieving it as an ideal. Is it plausible that the methods described here could have produced the required results? Why or why not?

EXPLORING the Issue

1. How does Stampp's use of source documents, including extensive quotations from discourses on the management of slaves, typify the methods historians use to reconstruct and interpret past events?

2. How does the historian's analysis of past events resemble, yet differ from, the analysis of current political or social events by news commentators?

CONNECTING Different Perspectives

1. How would Stampp's research have been made more difficult if Fred Kaplan's scenario in "The End of History" had been in effect?

John M. Darley and Bibb Latané

Why People Don't Help in a Crisis

John M. Darley (b. 1938) received a Ph.D. from Harvard in 1965. Since 1972 he has been professor of psychology at Princeton University where the focus of his research concerns the principles of moral judgment in children and adults. With Bibb Latané, Darley has coauthored The Unresponsive Bystander: Why Doesn't He Help? *(1970) and* Help in a Crisis: Bystander Response to an Emergency *(1976). Bibb Latané (b. 1937) received a Ph.D. from the University of Minnesota (1963) and was a professor of psychology at the University of North Carolina–Chapel Hill. This essay, drawn from their prize-winning research, describes an ingenious experiment designed to identify the causes of noninvolvement in bystanders who witness street crimes.*

Thinking Critically

What factors determine if a bystander is willing to help a victim of street crime?

Kitty Genovese is set upon by a maniac as she returns home from work at 3 A.M. Thirty-eight of her neighbors in Kew Gardens, N.Y., come to their windows when she cries out in terror; not one comes to her assistance, even though her assailant takes half an hour to murder her. No one so much as calls the police. She dies.

Andrew Mormille is stabbed in the head and neck as he rides in a New York City subway train. Eleven other riders flee to another car as the 17-year-old boy bleeds to death; not one comes to his assistance, even though his attackers have left the car. He dies.

Eleanor Bradley trips and breaks her leg while shopping on New York City's Fifth Avenue. Dazed and in shock, she calls for help, but the hurrying stream of people simply parts and flows past. Finally, after 40 minutes, a taxi driver stops and helps her to a doctor.

How can so many people watch another human being in distress and do nothing? Why don't they help?

5 Since we started research on bystander responses to emergencies, we have heard many explanations for the lack of intervention in such cases. "The megalopolis in which we live makes closeness difficult and leads to the alienation of the individual from the group," says the psychoanalyst. "This sort of disaster," says the sociologist, "shakes the sense of safety and sureness of the individuals involved and causes psychological withdrawal." "Apathy," says others. "Indifference."

All of these analyses share one characteristic: they set the indifferent witness apart from the rest of us. Certainly not one of us who reads about these incidents in horror is apathetic, alienated or depersonalized. Certainly these terrifying cases have no personal implications for us. We needn't feel guilty, or re-examine ourselves, or anything like that. Or should we?

If we look closely at the behavior of witnesses to these incidents, the people involved begin to seem a little less inhuman and a lot more like the rest of us. They were not indifferent. The 38 witnesses of Kitty Genovese's murder, for example, did not merely look at the scene once and then ignore it. They continued to stare out of their windows, caught, fascinated, distressed, unwilling to act but unable to turn away.

Why, then, didn't they act?

There are three things the bystander must do if he is to intervene in an emergency: *notice* that something is happening; *interpret* that event as an emergency; and decide that he has *personal responsibility* for intervention. As we shall show, the presence of other bystanders may at each stage inhibit his action.

The Unseeing Eye

10 Suppose that a man has a heart attack. He clutches his chest, staggers to the nearest building and slumps sitting to the sidewalk. Will a passerby come to his assistance? First, the bystander has to notice that something is happening. He must tear himself away from his private thoughts and pay attention. But Americans consider it bad manners to look closely at other people in public. We are taught to respect the privacy of others, and when among strangers we close our ears and avoid staring. In a crowd, then, each person is less likely to notice a potential emergency than when alone.

Experimental evidence corroborates this. We asked college students to an interview about their reactions to urban living. As the students waited to see the interviewer, either by themselves or with two other students, they filled out a questionnaire. Solitary students often glanced idly about while filling out their questionnaires; those in groups kept their eyes on their own papers.

As part of the study, we staged an emergency: smoke was released into the waiting room through a vent. Two thirds of the subjects who were alone noticed the smoke immediately, but only 25 percent of those waiting in groups saw it as quickly. Although eventually all the subjects did become aware of the smoke—when the atmosphere grew so smoky as to make them cough and rub their eyes—this study indicates that the more people present, the slower an individual may be to perceive an emergency and the more likely he is not to see it at all.

Seeing Is Not Necessarily Believing

Once an event is noticed, an onlooker must decide if it is truly an emergency. Emergencies are not always clearly labeled as such; "smoke" pouring into a waiting room may be caused by fire, or it may merely indicate a leak in a steam pipe. Screams in the street may signal an assault or a family quarrel. A man lying in a doorway may be having a coronary—or he may simply be sleeping off a drunk.

A person trying to interpret a situation often looks at those around him to see how he should react. If everyone else is calm and indifferent, he will tend to remain so; if everyone else is reacting strongly, he is likely to become aroused. This tendency is not merely slavish conformity; ordinarily we derive much valuable information about new situations from how others around us behave. It's a rare traveler who, in picking a roadside restaurant, chooses to stop at one where no other cars appear in the parking lot.

15   But occasionally the reactions of others provide false information. The studied nonchalance of patients in a dentist's waiting room is a poor indication of their inner anxiety. It is considered embarrassing to "lose your cool" in public. In a potentially acute situation, then, everyone present will appear more unconcerned than he is in fact. A crowd can thus force inaction on its members by implying, through its passivity, that an event is not an emergency. Any individual in such a crowd fears that he may appear a fool if he behaves as though it were.

To determine how the presence of other people affects a person's interpretation of an emergency, Latané and Judith Rodin set up another experiment. Subjects were paid $2 to participate in a survey of game and puzzle preferences conducted at Columbia University by the Consumer Testing Bureau. An attractive young market researcher met them at the door and took them to the testing room, where they were given questionnaires to fill out. Before leaving, she told them that she would be working next door in her office, which was separated from the room by a folding room-divider. She then entered her office, where she shuffled papers, opened drawers and made enough noise to remind the subjects of her presence. After four minutes she turned on a high-fidelity tape recorder.

On it, the subjects heard the researcher climb up on a chair, perhaps to reach for a stack of papers on the bookcase. They heard a loud crash and a scream as the chair collapsed and she fell, and they heard her moan, "Oh, my foot . . . I . . . I . . . can't move it. Oh, I . . . can't get this . . . thing . . . off me." Her cries gradually got more subdued and controlled.

Twenty-six people were alone in the waiting room when the "accident" occurred. Seventy percent of them offered to help the victim. Many pushed back the divider to offer their assistance; others called out to offer their help.

20   Among those waiting in pairs, only 20 percent—8 out of 40—offered to help. The other 32 remained unresponsive. In defining the situation as a non-emergency, they explained to themselves why the other member of the pair did not leave the room; they also removed any reason for action themselves. Whatever had happened, it was believed to be not serious. "A mild sprain," some said. "I didn't want to embarrass her." In a "real" emergency, they assured us, they would be among the first to help.

The Lonely Crowd

Even if a person defines an event as an emergency, the presence of other bystanders may still make him less likely to intervene. He feels that his responsibility is diffused and diluted. Thus, if your car breaks down on a busy highway, hundreds of drivers whiz by without anyone's stopping to help—but if you are stuck on a nearly deserted country road, whoever passes you first is likely to stop.

To test this diffusion-of-responsibility theory, we simulated an emergency in which people overheard a victim calling for help. Some thought they were the only person to hear the cries; the rest believed that others heard them, too. As with the witnesses to Kitty Genovese's murder, the subjects could not *see* one another or know what others were doing. The kind of direct group inhibition found in the other two studies could not operate.

For the simulation, we recruited 72 students at New York University to participate in what was referred to as a "group discussion" of personal problems in an urban university. Each student was put in an individual room equipped with a set of headphones and a microphone. It was explained that this precaution had been taken because participants might feel embarrassed about discussing their problems publicly. Also, the experimenter said that he would not listen to the initial discussion, but would only ask for reactions later. Each person was to talk in turn.

The first to talk reported that he found it difficult to adjust to New York and his studies. Then, hesitantly and with obvious embarrassment, he mentioned that he was prone to nervous seizures when he was under stress. Other students then talked about their own problems in turn. The number of people in the "discussion" varied. But whatever the apparent size of the group—two, three or six people—only the subject was actually present; the others, as well as the instructions and the speeches of the victim-to-be, were present only on a pre-recorded tape.

25   When it was the first person's turn to talk again, he launched into the following performance, becoming louder and having increasing speech difficulties: "I can see a lot of er of er how other people's problems are similar to mine because er I mean er they're not er e-easy to handle sometimes and er I er um I think I I need er if if could er er somebody er er er give me give me a little er give me a little help here because er I er *uh* I've got a a one of the er seiz-er er things coming *on* and and er uh uh (choking sounds) . . ."

Eighty-five percent of the people who believed themselves to be alone with the victim came out of their room to help. Sixty-two percent of the people who believed there was *one* other bystander did so. Of those who believed there were four other bystanders, only 31 percent reported the fit. The responsibility-diluting effect of other people was so strong that single individuals were more than twice as likely to report the emergency as those who thought other people also knew about it.

The Lesson Learned

People who failed to report the emergency showed few signs of the apathy and indifference thought to characterize "unresponsive bystanders." When the experimenter entered the room to end the situation, the subject often asked if the victim was "all right." Many of them showed physical signs of nervousness; they often had trembling hands and sweating palms. If anything, they seemed more emotionally aroused than did those who reported the emergency. Their emotional behavior was a sign of their continuing conflict concerning whether to respond or not.

Thus, the stereotype of the unconcerned, depersonalized *homo urbanus*,[1] blandly watching the misfortunes of others, proves inaccurate. Instead, we find that a bystander to an emergency is an anguished individual in genuine doubt, wanting to do the right thing but compelled to make complex decisions under pressure of stress and fear. His reactions are shaped by the actions of others—and all too frequently by their inaction.

[1]City dweller.

And we are that bystander. Caught up by the apparent indifference of others, we may pass by an emergency without helping or even realizing that help is needed. Once we are aware of the influence of those around us, however, we can resist it. We can choose to see distress and step forward to relieve it.

ENGAGING the Text

1. What experiment did Darley and Latané design to investigate why bystanders were unwilling in some situations to help victims of street crime?

2. How did the results challenge the conventional idea that apathy explained why people would not come to the aid of victims? What factors actually determine whether a bystander is willing to help a victim?

EVALUATING the Argument

1. How was Darley and Latané's experiment designed to isolate the key variable that came into play when social pressures altered the behavior of individual bystanders when they were in a group?

2. What evidence did Darley and Latané present to disprove the conventional idea that bystanders who failed to help others are merely apathetic?

EXPLORING the Issue

1. To what extent was deception involved in creating this experiment? In a short essay, address the ethical issues of manipulating subjects in order to obtain data.

2. Have you ever had an experience where you could observe the relationship between the number of people in a group who witness a crime and the willingness of any one person to do something about it? Do your experiences confirm Darley and Latané's findings?

CONNECTING Different Perspectives

1. Apply Darley and Latané's findings to Philip G. Zimbardo's study "The Stanford Prison Experiment" in terms of the results obtained and the insights into peer pressure and social roles.

Arthur D. Hasler and James A. Larsen

The Homing Salmon

Arthur D. Hasler (1908–2001) earned a Ph.D. in zoology from the University of Wisconsin in 1937. He served as president of the American Society of Zoologists. His pioneering studies into the migration of fish and the study of freshwater habitats shed light on the crucial role played by the sense of smell in orienting fishes in parent streams. In 2004, the Madison campus of the University of Wisconsin dedicated the Arthur D. Hasler Laboratory of Limnology.

James A. Larsen (b. 1921) earned a Ph.D. in ecology in 1968 and has distinguished himself as a botanist studying bioclimatology in the Arctic. The classic experiment "The Homing Salmon" (the results of which appeared in Scientific American, *June 1955) describes an ingenious experiment that solved the riddle of how the adult Chinook salmon finds it way back to the stream where it was born, 900 miles away.*

Thinking Critically

What mechanisms might be responsible for the patterns of migration in different species?

A learned naturalist once remarked that among the many riddles of nature, not the least mysterious is the migration of fishes. The homing of salmon is a particularly dramatic example. The Chinook salmon of the U.S. Northwest is born in a small stream, migrates downriver to the Pacific Ocean as a young smolt and, after living in the sea for as long as five years, swims back unerringly to the stream of its birth to spawn. Its determination to return to its birthplace is legendary. No one who has seen a 100-pound Chinook salmon fling itself into the air again and again until it is exhausted in a vain effort to surmount a waterfall can fail to marvel at the strength of the instinct that draws the salmon upriver to the stream where it was born.

How do salmon remember their birthplace, and how do they find their way back, sometimes from 800 or 900 miles away? This enigma, which has fascinated naturalists for many years, is the subject of the research to be reported here. The question has an economic as well as a scientific interest, because new dams which stand in the salmon's way have cut heavily into salmon fishing along the Pacific Coast. Before long nearly every stream of any appreciable size in the West will be blocked by dams. It is true that the dams have fish lifts and ladders designed to help salmon to hurdle them. Unfortunately, and for reasons which are different for nearly every dam so far designed, salmon are lost in tremendous numbers.

There are six common species of salmon. One, called the Atlantic salmon, is of the same genus as the steelhead trout. These two fish go to sea and come back upstream to spawn year after year. The other five salmon species, all on the Pacific Coast, are the Chinook (also called the king salmon), the sockeye, the silver, the humpback and the chum. The Pacific salmon home only once: after spawning they die.

A young salmon first sees the light of day when it hatches and wriggles up through the pebbles of the stream where the egg was laid and fertilized. For a few weeks the fingerling feeds on insects and small aquatic animals. Then it answers its first migratory call and swims downstream to the sea. It must survive many hazards to mature: an estimated 15 percent of the young salmon are lost at every large dam, such as Bonneville, on the downstream strip; others die in polluted streams; many are swallowed up by bigger fish in the ocean. When, after several years in the sea, the salmon is ready to spawn, it responds to the second great migratory call. It finds the mouth of the river by which it entered the ocean and then swims steadily upstream, unerringly choosing the correct turn at each tributary fork, until it arrives at the stream, where it was hatched. Generation after generation, families of salmon return to the same rivulet so consistently that populations in streams not far apart follow distinctly separate lines of evolution.

5   The homing behavior of the salmon has been convincingly documented by many studies since the turn of the century. One of the most elaborate was made by Andrew L. Pritchard, Wilbert A. Clemens and Russell E. Foerster in Canada. They marked 469,326 young sockeye salmon born in a tributary of the Fraser River, and they recovered nearly 11,000 of these in the same parent stream after the fishes' migration to the ocean and back. What is more, not one of the marked fish was ever found to have strayed to another stream. This remarkable demonstration of the salmon's precision in homing has presented an exciting challenge to investigators.

At the Wisconsin Lake Laboratory during the past decade we have been studying the sense of smell in fish, beginning with minnows and going on to salmon. Our findings suggest that the salmon identifies the stream of its birth by odor and literally smells its way home from the sea.

Fish have an extremely sensitive sense of smell. This has often been observed by students of fish behavior. Karl von Frisch showed that odors from the injured skin of a fish produce a fright reaction among its schoolmates. He once noticed that when a bird dropped an injured fish in the water, the school of fish from which it had been seized quickly dispersed and later avoided the area. It is well known that sharks and tuna are drawn to a vessel by the odor of bait in the water. Indeed, the time-honored custom of spitting on bait may be founded on something more than superstition; laboratory studies have proved that human saliva is quite stimulating to the taste buds of a bullhead. The sense of taste of course is closely allied to the sense of smell. The bullhead has taste buds all over the surface of its body; they are especially numerous on its whiskers. It will quickly grab a piece of meat that touches any part of its skin. But it becomes insensitive to taste and will not respond in this way if a nerve serving the skin buds is cut.

The smelling organs of fish have evolved in a great variety of forms. In the bony fishes the nose pits have two separate openings. The fish takes water into the front opening as it swims or breathes (sometimes assisting the intake with cilia), and then the water passes out through the second opening, which may be opened and closed rhythmically by the fish's breathing. Any odorous substances in the water stimulate the nasal receptors chemically, perhaps by an effect on enzyme reactions, and the resulting electrical impulses are relayed to the central nervous system by the olfactory nerve.

The human nose, and that of other land vertebrates, can smell a substance only if it is volatile and soluble in fat solvents. But in the final analysis smell is always aquatic, for a substance is not smelled until it passes into solution in the mucous film of the nasal passages. For fishes, of course, the odors are already in solution in their watery environment. Like any other animal, they can follow an odor to its source, as a hunting dog follows the scent of an animal. The quality or effect of a scent changes as the concentration changes; everyone knows that an odor may be pleasant at one concentration and unpleasant at another.

10   When we began our experiments, we first undertook to find out whether fish could distinguish the odors of different water plants. We used a special aquarium with jets which could inject odors into the water. For responding to one odor (by moving toward the jet), the fish were rewarded with food; for responding to another odor, they were punished with a mild electric shock. After the fish were trained to make choices between odors, they were tested on dilute rinses from 14 different aquatic plants. They proved able to distinguish the odors of all these plants from one another.

Plants must play an important role in the life of many freshwater fish. Their odors may guide fish to feeding grounds when visibility is poor, as in muddy water or at night, and they may hold young fish from straying from protective cover. Odors may also warn fish away from poisons. In fact, we discovered that fish could be put to use to assay industrial pollutants: our trained minnows were able to detect phenol, a common pollutant, at concentrations far below those detectable by man.

All this suggested a clear-cut working hypothesis for investigating the mystery of the homing of salmon. We can suppose that every little stream has its own characteristic odor, which stays the same year after year; that young salmon become conditioned to this odor before they go to sea; that they remember the odor as they grow to maturity, and that they are able to find it and follow it to its source when they come back upstream to spawn.

Plainly there are quite a few ifs in this theory. The first one we tested was the question: Does each stream have its own odor? We took water from two creeks in Wisconsin and investigated whether fish could learn to discriminate between them. Our subjects, first minnows and then salmon, were indeed able to detect a difference. If, however, we destroyed a fish's nose tissue, it was no longer able to distinguish between the two water samples.

Chemical analysis indicated that the only major difference between the two waters lay in the organic material. By testing the fish with various fractions of the water separated by distillation, we confirmed that the identifying material was some volatile organic substance.

15 The idea that fish are guided by odors in their migrations was further supported by a field test. From each of two different branches of the Issaquah River in the State of Washington we took a number of sexually ripe silver salmon which had come home to spawn. We then plugged with cotton the noses of half the fish in each group and placed all the salmon in the river below the fork to make the upstream run again. Most of the fish with unplugged noses swam back to the stream they had selected the first time. But the "odor-blinded" fish migrated back in random fashion, picking the wrong stream as often as the right one.

In 1949 eggs from salmon of the Horsefly River in British Columbia were hatched and reared in a hatchery in a tributary called the Little Horsefly. Then they were flown a considerable distance and released in the main Horsefly River, from which they migrated to the sea. Three years later 13 of them had returned to their rearing place in the Little Horsefly, according to the report of the Canadian experimenters.

In our own laboratory experiments we tested the memory of fish for odors and found that they retained the ability to differentiate between odors for a long period after their training. Young fish remembered odors better than the old. That animals "remember" conditioning to which they have been exposed in their youth, and act accordingly, has been demonstrated in other fields. For instance, there is a fly which normally lays its eggs on the larvae of the flour moth, where the fly larvae then hatch and develop. But if larvae of this fly are raised on another host, the beeswax moth, when the flies mature they will seek out beeswax moth larvae on which to lay their eggs, in preference to the traditional host.

With respect to the homing of salmon we have shown, then, that different streams have different odors, that salmon respond to these odors and that they remember odors to which they have been conditioned. The next question is: Is a salmon's homeward migration guided solely by its sense of smell? If we could decoy homing salmon to a stream other than their birthplace, by means of an odor to which they were conditioned artificially, we might have not only a solution to the riddle that has puzzled scientists but also a practical means of saving the salmon—guiding them to breeding streams not obstructed by dams.

We set out to find a suitable substance to which salmon could be conditioned. A student, W. J. Wisby, and I [Arthur Hasler] designed an apparatus to test the reactions of salmon to various organic odors. It consists of a compartment from which radiate four runways, each with several steps which the fish must jump to climb the runway. Water cascades down each of the arms. An odorous substance is introduced into one of the arms, and its effect on the fish is judged by whether the odor appears to attract fish into that arm, to repel them or to be indifferent to them.

20   We needed a substance which initially would not be either attractive or repellent to salmon but to which they could be conditioned so that it would attract them. After testing several score organic odors, we found that dilute solutions of morpholine neither attracted nor repelled salmon but were detectable by them in extremely low concentrations—as low as one part per million. It appears that morpholine fits the requirements for the substance needed: it is soluble in water; it is detectable in extremely low concentrations; it is chemically stable under stream conditions. It is neither an attractant nor a repellent to unconditioned salmon, and would have meaning only to those conditioned to it.

Federal collaborators of ours are now conducting field tests on the Pacific Coast to learn whether salmon fry and fingerlings which have been conditioned to morpholine can be decoyed to a stream other than that of their birth when they return from the sea to spawn. Unfortunately this type of experiment may not be decisive. If the salmon are not decoyed to the new stream, it may simply mean that they cannot be drawn by a single substance but will react only to a combination of subtle odors in their parent stream. Perhaps adding morpholine to the water is like adding the whistle of a freight train to the quiet strains of a violin, cello and flute. The salmon may still seek out the subtle harmonies of an odor combination to which they have been reacting by instinct for centuries. But there is still hope that they may respond to the call of the whistle.

ENGAGING the Text

1. How was Hasler and Larsen's experiment designed to test their hypothesis as to how salmon were able to return to their exact birthplace over 900 miles away?

2. How did Hasler and Larsen's experiment disclose that the salmon's homeward migration is guided solely by its memory of the odors of the parent stream in which it was spawned?

EVALUATING the Argument

1. What technical terms do the authors define to help their readers understand the process they are investigating?

2. How might the organization of Hasler and Larsen's research, in which they list assumptions they wish to test, reports of past research, alternate

theories, and a model designed to test key variables in a form that can be duplicated, illustrate the scientific method?

EXPLORING the Issue

1. Since the salmon reproduces only once in its lifetime, why would the results of Hasler and Larsen's research be important in deciding where to place dams in the tributaries of streams?

2. What mechanisms have scientists identified to explain migratory patterns or the homing instinct in other species?

CONNECTING Different Perspectives

1. What insight is offered into the relationship between adaptive instinct and survival in "The Homing Salmon" and in Robert Sapolsky's "Bugs in the Brain"?

5 REASONING IN INDUCTIVE AND DEDUCTIVE ARGUMENTS

OVERVIEW: Arguments that ring true are usually based on clear reasoning. The following discussion spells out the distinctive features of correct reasoning and shows some signs by which you can recognize arguments based on faulty logic. Traditionally, the study of logic has centered on two methods of reasoning, induction and deduction, and the analyses of fallacies that short-circuit the rules of logic.

Methods of Reasoning

INDUCTIVE REASONING

Reasoning that moves from the observation of specific cases to the formulation of a hypothesis is called inductive reasoning (from the Latin *in ducere*, "to lead toward"). Inductive reasoning depends on drawing inferences from particular cases to support a generalization or claim about what is true of all these kinds of cases (including those that have not been observed).

Many inferences we draw every day follow this pattern. For example, if three friends tell you independently of each other that a particular movie is worth seeing, you infer that the movie in question is probably good. Or, if you bought two pairs of the same brand of shoes on two separate occasions, and found them to be comfortable, you might reasonably infer that a third pair of the same brand would prove equally satisfactory. Drawing inferences about a movie you have not yet seen or shoes you have not yet bought typically involves what is called an *inductive leap*. Thus, inductive reasoning strives toward a high degree of probability rather than absolute certainty.

The ability to generalize is a fundamental reasoning skill based on discerning common qualities shared by groups of things. For example, consider this traditional form of inductive reasoning:

Luis is human and mortal.

John is human and mortal.

Marsha is human and mortal.
Therefore it is reasonable to infer that all human beings are mortal.
Since it would be impossible to observe every human being in the world, the inductively reached conclusion can only suggest what is probably true (even if the conclusion in this particular case seems certain). Inductive reasoning extrapolates that all human beings are mortal based on the three particular cases that have actually been observed.

Because inductive reasoning generalizes from specific cases, the conclusion will be stronger in proportion to the number of relevant examples the writer can cite to support it. Arguments based on atypical or sparse examples are less convincing than those based on conclusions drawn from a greater number of representative examples.

Conclusions reached by inductive reasoning can be stated only in terms of relative certainty because it is unlikely that all instances in a particular class of things can ever be observed. A generalization based on the observation of any phenomenon, from a virus to a spiral nebulae, does not rule out the chance that new observations made in the future will require the formulation of totally new hypotheses.

Writers use inductive reasoning to draw inferences from evidence in order to convince an audience to accept a claim. Evidence may take the form of historical documents, laboratory experiments, data from surveys, the results of reports, personal observations, and the testimony of authorities. When our ability to draw conclusions based on firsthand observations is limited, we frequently rely on the opinion of authorities whose field of expertise includes a greater depth of knowledge about the instances, examples, or case histories under investigation.

Writers draw on specific cases and a wide range of empirical evidence to form a generalization that asserts that what is true of specific instances is also true of the whole. As an argumentative strategy, the more different kinds of evidence are used as the basis of an inductive generalization, the stronger the argument will be. An argument that generalizes from a variety of sources, including personal experience, observation, the results of experiments, statistics, and historical research, will provide stronger support for a generalization from an audience's point of view than an argument that generalizes from fewer kinds of evidence.

Because inductive reasoning makes predictions or draws inferences about an entire class of things, writers must be careful not to draw conclusions from so limited a sample that these conclusions extend far beyond what the available evidence warrants and thus seem improbable.

The process of forming a generalization always involves making this inductive leap. Inductive arguments therefore aim at establishing a sense of high probability rather than certainty. There are three main kinds of inductive reasoning: causal generalization, sampling, and analogy. They vary according to their ability to persuade audiences to accept the likelihood of the connection made in the claim. We will examine these forms from the strongest to the weakest.

BY MEANS OF CAUSAL GENERALIZATION, SAMPLING, AND ANALOGY

CAUSAL GENERALIZATION   Inductive reasoning can take the form of a causal argument that makes a claim about cause and effect, or correlation. The argument is inductive because it still requires an inference to explain the connections between events.

Causal analysis attempts to persuade an audience that one event caused another. Like other kinds of inductive reasoning, causal analysis aims at establishing probability rather than certainty. Writers may work backward from a given effect and seek to discover what might have caused it or work forward and predict what further effects will flow from the known cause. Argument based on causal analysis must identify as precisely as possible the contributory factors in any causal chain of events. The direct or immediate causes of the event are those that are likely to have triggered the actual event. Yet, behind the direct causes may lie indirect or remote causes that set the stage or create the framework in which the event could occur.

It often helps to distinguish between several meanings of the word *cause*. First, the concept of cause may refer to a *necessary condition* that must be present if a specific effect is to occur. For example, buying a lottery ticket is a necessary condition for winning the lottery. Yet, a necessary condition does not by itself guarantee the effect will occur. For the effect to be produced, there must be a *sufficient condition*, that is, a condition in whose presence the effect will always occur. If, for example, you bought a lottery ticket with the winning numbers, that alone would be a sufficient condition to ensure the effect (winning the lottery).

A claim that one event could have caused another is expressed as a generalization. This generalization either explains why an event has happened or predicts why it will happen in the future. For example, William Bryant Logan, an arborist, in *OAK: The Frame of Civilization* asserts that the decline of hand-crafted oak barrels can be traced to three sources:

> Hand and machine coopering survived side-by-side up until the rapid decline of the craft between the two world wars.
>
> Three things killed coopering: bottles, aluminum, and forklifts. Bottles for both wine and beer were rare before the eighteenth century. As they became more common, the demand for casks slackened. Beer and ale do not actually react with the oak—or if they do, the beer sours—so the loss of the cask was no great matter. As to wine, though it acquired a great deal of its character through the interaction with the tannins in the oak, it could still be aged in oak and then shipped and sold in bottles. The rise of aluminum casks in the twentieth century further reduced the need for coopers. Aluminum barrels were tougher and longer lasting than wooden barrels, and they imparted no flavor at all to their contents. Bulk shipment in long, cylindrical metal containers further reduced the need for casks.
>
> But forklifts were the worst, because they removed the very need for barrels. The great thing about casks was that they could be rolled. In order to get the roll, however, you had to sacrifice some product space. With a machine to move the containers, it was actually a disadvantage to make them rollable. Why not use that little bit of extra space for product? So the rectilinear container won, and the barrel died. Only for aging wine and spirits does it survive, because there is no substitute for the flavor that oak imparts to fermented and distilled products.

Notice how Logan's claim requires him to demonstrate how the causes he identifies are capable of producing this result. Readers might wonder whether there are causes of equal or greater importance that Logan omits.

Questions for Discussion and Writing

1. In a short essay, present a plausible account that might persuade an audience to accept your explantion for the causes or consequences of a single or repeated event, puzzling phenomenon, or social trend. Try to take into account alternative hypotheses, and suggest reasons why these other explanations should not be seen as credible.

   a. It may come as no surprise that Americans spend less time reading than most people from other countries, but a recent study's results, released in June 2005 from market research organization NOP World (www.nopworld.com), prove that we aren't the biggest couch potatoes, either. NOP World interviewed more than 30,000 people in 30 countries to discover that consumers in Thailand watch the most TV, those from Argentina are the most likely to rock out to the radio, and Taiwanese spend the most time in front of their computers. In America, we have a long way to go before we can rival the bookworms in India, but reading this magazine is a step in the right direction.

—September 2005/celifestyles.com

b. It's true, you *can* go home again—if you're a 20-something, that is. Members of that age group are having a hard time finding jobs or their bliss, so boomerang kids are moving back in with Mom and Dad. Big time. In fact, 65% of recent college grads said that's where *they're* headed.

—"Money Trendlets," Reader's Digest *(August 2005)*

2. Does the following "Cathy" cartoon offer a reasonable generalization that can be inferred from the data supplied? Why or why not? What other causal influences might have played a role in producing the effect she cites?

FIGURE 5.1

3. How might any of the following questions be developed by showing causal relationships?

   a. What are some of the consequences of the rise of Islamic fundamentalism in the Middle East?

   b. From a historical perspective, what accounts for the enormous popularity of country music?

   c. What accounts for the unusual number of major hurricanes that have occurred in the United States in the last few years?

SAMPLING   Sampling arguments draw inductive inferences or generalizations from specific instances that realistically can never exhaust all the samples from the pool of instances. Sampling must always involve an extrapolation or inductive leap from the unknown to the highly probable. For example, a poll can never ask every single individual in a population about his or her opinion but must project the results from a representative sample.

Inductive generalizations depend on a process known as sampling, based on the selection of a sample drawn from a group. The sample must be drawn so as accurately to represent the composition and makeup of the entire group from which it is taken. All other things being equal, the larger the sample, the more probable it is that important characteristics in the larger population will be represented. For example, if the subject of a study were a small town with a population of 10,000, the sample should not be less than 200 townspeople lest the sample not be broad enough to be significant. Furthermore, because the townspeople that constitute the whole population can be categorized into different subgroups or strata, a reliable sampling must reflect that stratification. No survey of townspeople should fail to take into account small, but important segments of different racial, cultural, or ethnic groups. The sample procedure should be random to ensure that a true cross section of townspeople are selected to represent the entire group about which the generalization or prediction is made. Just how this works can be seen on election nights, right after the polls have closed, when commentators report that "on the basis of a very small percentage of the vote" in sample precincts, candidate X or Y is declared the winner. More often than not these predictions turn out to be correct because the sample precincts accurately represent the district, state, or region as a whole.

The samples (1) must be randomly selected, (2) must be broad enough to be significant, and (3) must accurately reflect the general population from which it is taken. Evidence presented to support an inductive generalization must be clearly relevant to the conclusion drawn, objectively presented, and supported strongly enough to withstand challenges from opposing evidence. This last point is crucial since writers of arguments must always assume that evidence can be brought forward to challenge their conclusions.

Questions for Discussion and Writing

1. How does the following example illustrate the way conclusions are drawn using sampling procedures?

> In the case of the [Internet dating] ads, how forthright (and honest) are people when it comes to sharing their personal information? . . . Two economists and a psychologist recently banded together to address these questions. Ali Hortacsu, Gunter J. Hitsch, and Dan Ariely analyzed the data from one of the mainstream dating sites, focusing on roughly 30,000 users, half in Boston and half in San Diego. Fifty-seven percent of the users were men, and the median age range for all users was twenty-six to thirty-five. Although they represented an adequate racial mix to reach some conclusions about race, they were predominantly white.
>
> They were also a lot richer, taller, skinnier, and better-looking than average. More than 4 percent of the online daters claimed to earn more than 200,000 a year, whereas fewer than 1 percent of typical Internet users actually earn that much, suggesting that three of the four big earners were exaggerating. Male and female users typically reported that they are about an inch taller than the national average. As for weight . . . the women typically said they weighed about twenty pounds less than the national average.
>
> —*Steven D. Levitt and Stephen J. Dubner,* Freakonomics *(2005, pp. 80–81)*

2. What might an archaeologist in the year 2025 conclude about the civilization in which you are living now based on a survey of the contents of your most cluttered desk or dresser drawer? Sketch out the likely hypotheses as to the ritual or functional purposes of any three items he or she has found. Explain the pattern of reasoning that would lead to inferences drawn from these three items.

ANALOGY   The weakest kind of inductive argument requiring the greatest inductive leap is based on analogy or precedent. Here, the argument must persuade the audience that what is true for A is also true for B because of similarities the arguer claims exist between A and B.

Arguments from analogy rely on inductive reasoning to suggest that things or events that are alike in some ways are probably similar in other ways as well.

The use of analogy in argument differs from the purely illustrative use of analogy to clarify subjects that otherwise might prove to be hard to visualize or be difficult to understand.

A writer uses analogy for argumentative (rather than descriptive or illustrative) purposes to show how evidence serves to support a particular conclusion. An instance of arguing by analogy can be observed in Abraham Lincoln's famous rebuttal silencing the critics who condemned his administration for dragging its heels in settling the Civil War. Notice how Lincoln structures the analogy to bring out similarities between his own situation and the one faced by Blondin (the famous tightrope walker who crossed Niagara Falls three separate times—in 1855, in 1859, and again in 1860):

> Gentlemen, I want you to suppose a case for a moment. Suppose that all the property you were worth was in gold, and you had put it in the hands of Blondin, the famous rope-walker, to carry across the Niagara Falls on a tight rope. Would you shake the rope while he was passing over it, or keep shouting to him, "Blondin, stoop a little more! Go a little faster!"? No, I am sure you would not. You would hold your breath as well as your tongue, and keep your hand off until he was safely over. Now, the Government is in the same situation. It is carrying an immense weight across a stormy ocean. Untold treasures are in its hands. It is doing the best it can. Don't badger it! Just keep still, and it will get you safely over.

Lincoln asserts that none of the spectators would have dreamed of distracting Blondin while he was attempting to cross the falls. Nor would anyone in the audience have dared to "shake the rope" while Blondin was crossing the falls, especially since Lincoln has stipulated that Blondin is carrying "all the property you were worth . . . in gold." Next, Lincoln points out the similarities between Blondin's situation and the government's own precarious circumstances. Lincoln says that the government, too, is walking a tightrope bearing the burden of trying to resolve the Civil War. Lincoln concludes that "it [his administration] is doing the best it can." The inductive inference based on the number of ways in which the two situations are analogous is quite clear: critics should refrain from "shaking the rope" and let Lincoln strive to settle the war as he sees fit. Doubtless Lincoln did not depend on this analogy alone to make the case against interference; most likely he supported the same conclusion with other evidence (reports from generals in the field, attempts at behind-the-scenes negotiations, etc.). Although some analogical arguments are better than others, it is important to remember that like other forms of inductive reasoning, the conclusions are probable, not certain.

Questions for Discussion and Writing

1. Evaluate the strengths of analogies in the following mini-arguments. Are the analogies literal (drawn from the same class of subjects) or figurative (drawn between different classes of things). Do similarities outweigh dissimilarities? If the analogy is weak, how might it be strengthened?

   a. Alison Lurie, "The Language of Clothes"

   For thousands of years human beings have communicated with one another first in the language of dress. Long before I am near enough to talk to you on the street, in a meeting, or at a party, you announce your sex, age and class to me through what you are wearing—and very possibily give me important information (or misinformation) as to your occupation, origin, personality, opinions, tastes, sexual desires and current mood. I may not be able to put what I observe into words, but I register the information unconsciously; and you simultaneously do the same for me. By the time we meet and converse we have already spoken to each other in an older and more universal language.

   b. John McMurty, "Kill 'Em! Crush 'Em! Eat 'Em Raw!"

   The family resemblance between football and war is, indeed, striking. Their languages are similar: "field general," "long bomb," "blitz," "take a shot," "front line," "pursuit," "good hit," "the draft," and so on. Their principles and practices are alike: mass hysteria, the art of intimidation, absolute command and total obedience, territorial aggression, censorship, inflated insignia and propaganda, blackboard maneuvers and strategies, drills, uniforms, formations, marching bands and training camps. And the virtues they celebrate are almost identical: hyper-aggressiveness, coolness under fire and suicidal bravery. . . .

DEDUCTIVE REASONING

Whereas inductive reasoning at best can only establish a sense of high probability, deductive reasoning can offer audiences a sense of certainty. This difference in effects on audiences is due to the differences between the two forms in their methods of drawing conclusions. Inductive reasoning always requires an inductive leap or inference of some kind whether based on an analogy, sampling procedures, or causal argument. The generalization that is reached by inductive reasoning can never be proved to be absolutely certain. By contrast, deductive reasoning begins from a generalization that is widely agreed upon and then applies this axiom, or *major premise*, to a specific case to draw a valid conclusion about the particular case. If the premises are taken to be true, the conclusion must invariably also be certain. Looked at in this way, deductive reasoning is a method of reasoning that complements inductive reasoning. Rather than moving from the evidence provided by specific cases to a conclusion, deduction allows us to infer the validity of a particular case from generalizations or *premises*. The generalization "therefore it is reasonable to infer that all human beings are mortal" can be used deductively to predict that all as yet unobserved human beings will also be mortal. The classic form illustrating the relationship between the *premises* and the conclusion is known as a *syllogism*:

> **Major Premise:** All human beings are mortal.
>
> **Minor Premise:** John is a human being.
>
> **Conclusion:** Therefore, John is mortal.

Notice how deductive reasoning applies a general statement to a particular case to draw a logical conclusion (whereas inductive reasoning uses individual cases, facts, and examples to create a hypothesis or generalization). The statements on which deductive reasoning is based appear as categorical propositions or *laws*. If inferences from the original statements or premises are drawn correctly according to the rules of logic, then the conclusion is valid.

In contrast to inductive reasoning (which draws inferences or generalizes from specific cases), deductive reasoning (from the Latin, *de ducere*, "to lead from") draws inferences from statements called premises that are assumed to be true or "self-evident." Conclusions drawn via deductive reasoning are both logically necessary and certain (in contrast to the merely probable conclusions reached via inductive reasoning).

Deductive logic assumes that the truth of the premises is sufficient to establish the truth of the conclusion. No external evidence is required beyond the statements from which the conclusion is drawn. This conclusion is logically certain or valid because it follows necessarily from the premises. The term *validity* here refers only to the way in which the conclusion is drawn. If either the major or the minor premise is not true, then the conclusion, although logically valid, will be not be true either.

It is frequently overlooked that many of the self-evident truths taken as premises in deductive reasoning are generalizations that have been previously established by inductive reasoning from empirical evidence and observation. **The process of inductive reasoning supplies the generalizations that appear as the starting point or major premise in deductive reasoning.**

To see how this works, examine the following passage from Arthur Conan Doyle's story "The Red-Headed League" (1892), one of the innumerable exploits of his legendary character, Sherlock Holmes:

> "How, in the name of good fortune, did you know all that, Mr. Holmes?" he asked.
>
> "How did you know, for example, that I did manual labor? It's true as gospel, for I began as a ship's carpenter."
>
> "Your hands, my dear sir. Your right hand is quite a size larger than your left. You have worked with it and the muscles are more developed."

Diagrammed in the form of a syllogism, Holmes's reasoning might appear thus:

Major Premise: All men in whom at least one hand has more developed muscles do manual labor.

Minor Premise: This man's right hand is a size larger than his left and the muscles are much more developed.

Conclusion: Therefore, this man has done manual labor.

This deductive syllogism comprises a major premise that generalizes about an entire group or class, a minor premise that identifies the individual as a member of that class, and a conclusion expressing the inference that what is true of all manual laborers must be true of the man Holmes has encountered.

The major premise is a generalization reached by Holmes inductively; after all, Holmes had observed many instances where the hand muscles of manual laborers were much more highly developed than the average person's. The minor premise places this particular man in the general category of all those whose hands exhibit signs of unusual muscular development. The conclusion Holmes draws is valid in its reasoning; that is, his process of reasoning from the premises to the conclusion is correct. However, if one or both of the premises were false, the argument would be untrue even though the process of reasoning is correct and the conclusion is validly drawn.

For example, Holmes's major premise might be untrue; perhaps there are men whose right hands are more muscular than their left who do not do manual labor. For instance, squash or tennis might produce unusual muscular development of the one hand used to grip the racquet. His minor premise could also have been untrue. For example, the "manual laborer" might have actually been Moriarty, Holmes's arch nemesis in disguise, wearing a prosthetic device to lead Holmes to his erroneous conclusion.

Since major premises are often assumed to express self-evident truths, value arguments use deductive reasoning. In these arguments, the major premise states an absolute moral or ethical obligation. The minor premise specifies an instance or individual that falls within the scope of this obligation. The conclusion connects the general obligation to the individual case.

For example, the following syllogism illustrates how an absolute moral obligation can be applied to a specific case to produce a value judgment:

Major Premise: The physician's duty—to which he or she is bound by the oath of Hippocrates—is to prevent or at least minimize harm to his or her patient.

Minor Premise: In this case, giving the patient information X will do greater harm to the patient on balance than withholding the information will.

Conclusion: Therefore, in this case, it is the physician's duty to withhold information X from the patient.

—*adapted from Allen E. Buchanan, "Medical Paternalism"*

This example illustrates that deductive reasoning is useful in developing an argument leading to a conclusion that might be disputed if it were presented as a starting point. This application of deductive reasoning allows the writer to build an argument step-by-step that will lead an audience to consider the possibility of a claim they might have rejected initially. In this case, the claim is that in certain circumstances, physicians are justified in withholding information from patients even if it means deceiving them.

The syllogisms we have been discussing are known as *categorical* syllogisms because the major premise sets up classes or categories ("all men" in the Sherlock Holmes syllogism, and "all physicans"). The minor premise identifies an individual or instance as part of that class, and the conclusion affirms that the specific case shares characteristics with the general class.

Except for the ever-logical Mr. Data, most people do not think in the form of syllogisms. In deductive arguments expressed in ordinary language (not syllogisms), one premise is usually implicit and understood rather than actually stated. Occasionally, the conclusion is implied rather than being explicitly stated. The result is called an *enthymeme*.

More typically, an enthymeme takes for granted the warrant or unexpressed major *premise*. For example, Charles de Gaulle was quoted as saying "how can you be expected to govern a country that has 246 kinds of cheese?" De Gaulle takes for granted the unexpressed major premise that might be stated thus: any country whose citizens have hundreds of preferences in cheese is unlikely to unite behind one political leader.

It is often helpful to make the unexpressed major premise explicit in order to evaluate the soundness of different parts of the argument. For example, suppose you and a friend were driving past a factory and your friend said, "Look at the picket line over there; there must be a strike at the factory." The unexpressed major premise here would be that picket lines are present only at strikes. The premise expresses a sign warrant: a picket line indicates the presence of a strike.

As we have seen, deductive reasoning is useful as a rhetorical strategy in situations when an audience might reject a conclusion if it were stated at the outset. A writer who can get an audience to agree with the assumptions on which the argument is based stands a better chance of getting them to agree with the conclusion if he or she can show how this conclusion follows logically from the premises.

Questions for Discussion and Writing

1. Locate the major premise, minor premise, and conclusion in the following mini-argument. Would you disagree with the major premise but have to accept the conclusion as valid?

   a. If suicide is a right, then it is one that has remained undiscovered throughout the ages by the great thinkers in law, ethics, philosophy, and theology. It appears nowhere in the Bible or the Koran or the Talmud. Committing suicide wasn't a "right" 1,000 years ago, and it isn't one now. That's why most societies—including our own—have passed laws against it.

      —Washington Times

2. Make explicit and state the implicit or unstated major premise in the following enthymeme. How might this unstated assumption connect the arguer to the audience in terms of the values and beliefs they share?

   a. I am a Born Again Christian. I believe marijuana should be legalized, and I have Scripture to back me up.

      —*Kat Marco, St. Petersburg, Florida, reported in* Parade Magazine

3. Write a short deductive argument expanding the lines of reasoning laid out in the following mini-argument.

   a. The traditional school calendar was not designed to be an educational calendar. It has no particular instructional benefit. It was designed solely to support the 19th-century agricultural economy. Change is long overdue.

      —*Charles Ballinger,* USA Today

4. Create a deductive argument drawing on either or both of the following responses to a telephone poll of 1,000 Americans (Yankelovich, reported in *Time*) on the subject of organ transplants.

a. Is it ethical to ask a child under the age of 18 to give up a kidney for transplant to a relative? Yes 45% No 42%

b. Is it morally acceptable for parents to conceive a child in order to obtain an organ or tissue to save the life of another one of their children? Yes 47% No 37%

Logical Fallacies

In addition to analyzing the way conclusions are reached, whether inductively or deductively, you need to consider the soundness of the reasoning. Among the dozens of different kinds of logical fallacies, here are some of the most common.

FALLACIES THAT RESULT WHEN NO REAL EVIDENCE IS PRESENTED TO SUPPORT THE CLAIM

BEGGING THE QUESTION   This is an argument that offers as proof the claim that the argument itself exists to prove; also known as *circular reasoning*. For example:

How do you know God exists?

It says so in the Bible.

How do you know the Bible is a reliable source?

Because the Bible is the divinely inspired word of God.

FALLACIES THAT RESULT WHEN THE EVIDENCE IS NOT RELEVANT TO THE CLAIM

RED HERRING   Irrelevant evidence intended to divert attention from the real issue is known as a red herring. For example: Commentator Rush Limbaugh's response to news that dolphins may be almost as intelligent as humans:

Could somebody please show me one hospital built by a dolphin? Could somebody show me one highway built by a dolphin? Could somebody show me one automobile invented by a dolphin?

NON SEQUITUR   A non sequitur (meaning "it does not follow") is a statement that does not logically follow from a preceding one. For example: Lawrence P. Goldman, chief executive of the NJPAC as reported in *The Newark Star Ledger* (June 14, 2005) commented "We're not going to let a developer put up an ugly building—there has to be shops and galleries, and cafes, because that's in our DNA."

STRAW MAN The use of an easily refuted objection to divert attention from the real issue is called a straw man. For example: Richard Nixon's "Checkers" speech (September 23, 1952) in which he concluded that "the kids like all kids, love the dog and I just want to say this, right now, that regardless of what they say about it, we're going to keep it," as if accepting the gift of a dog was equal to the serious charge against him of using a political fund for his own personal use.

INAPPROPRIATE USE OF AUTHORITIES A baseball player might be credible on baseball-related subjects yet his endorsement of, say, snow tires projects him as an authority in an area unrelated to his expertise.

AD HOMINEM Ad hominem comes from the Latin, "to the man," and is an attack on the person rather than the issue. For example: Senator X is divorced so how can we listen to his pleas for federal funding for homeless shelters.

THE BANDWAGON ARGUMENT An example of the bandwagon argument is: "Five out of six people use brand X, so you should too."

FALLACY OF THE UNDISTRIBUTED MIDDLE A conclusion is reached that draws a wider inference than is warranted by stated facts. For example: "Socrates is a mammal, giraffes are mammals, so Socrates is a giraffe."

APPEAL TO PITY Also called "special pleading," the appeal to pity happens when the arguer seeks to settle a factual matter by using irrelevant appeals to sentiment. For example: The defendant on trial for murdering his parents pleads that the court should show mercy because he is now an orphan.

APPEAL TO FORCE Also known as "scare tactics," the appeal to force seeks to intimidate an audience to compel acceptance of a claim. For example: ads that try to scare consumers into using products to avoid (unpopularity such as those for mouthwash or deodorant).

FALLACIES THAT RESULT WHEN INSUFFICIENT EVIDENCE IS OFFERED TO SUPPORT A CLAIM

HASTY OR SWEEPING GENERALIZATION This is a conclusion based on too little evidence that is not representative of all possible cases. For example: "I once got a loaf of moldy bread from that store, and so I will never buy bread there again." An unreasonable and irrational form of inaccurate generalizing is stereotyping.

FALLACIES THAT RESULT FROM UNWARRANTED ASSUMPTIONS

OVERSIMPLIFICATION   When writers assume that complex events can be explained by pointing to one single cause, they are using oversimplification. For example: The claim "sugar-laden junk food makes children hyperactive" ignores the role played by metabolism and heredity.

COMPLEX QUESTIONS   Also known as "loaded" questions, complex questions make the unwarranted assumption that another unasked question has been answered positively. For example: "Where did you put the DVDs you took from me?"

FALSE DILEMMA   A false dilemma (either/or) assumes that an issue has only two sides. For example: "What's to be done about illegal immigration from Mexico? Either we build a wall along the border or the economies of California and Texas will collapse."

FAULTY CAUSE-EFFECT RELATIONSHIPS

  a.   Overlooking a common cause results from the failure to recognize that two seemingly related events may both be effects of a third common cause.

  b.   *Post Hoc Ergo Propter Hoc* ("after this, therefore because of this") argues that because B follows A, A must have caused B to occur. For example: Roger Blough, former president of U.S. Steel Corporation, once observed that "steel prices cause inflation like wet sidewalks cause rain."

SLIPPERY SLOPE   This results when writers assume that accepting X automatically entails accepting Y. For example: In 1901, Henry T. Finck (writing in *The Independent*) forecast dire consequences if women were given the vote: "Doctors tell us . . . that thousands of children would be harmed or killed before birth by the injurious effect of untimely political excitement on their mothers."

FALSE ANALOGY   The false analogy is based on the assumption that two things that are similar in one way must be similar in many ways. For example: Producers hope that sequels of hit movies and spin-offs of popular television shows will be as successful as the originals.

A Sample Inductive Argument For Analysis

Garrett Hardin

Lifeboat Ethics: The Case Against Helping The Poor

Garrett Hardin (1915–2003) was born in Dallas, Texas, and received a Ph.D. from Stanford University in 1941. He was professor of human ecology at the University of California at Santa Barbara until 1978. He was the author of many books including Ostrich Factor: Our Population Myopia *(1998) and over two hundred articles. The following selection first appeared in* Psychology Today *(September 1974) and formulates an ingenious analogy that compares an affluent country to a lifeboat already full of people. Outside the lifeboat are the poor and needy who desperately wish to get in. Hardin claims that an ill-considered ethic of sharing will lead to the swamping of the lifeboat unless its occupants maintain a margin of safety by keeping people out.*

Thinking Critically

What would be an appropriate metaphor to characterize the ability of a society to support itself and immigrants?

Environmentalists use the metaphor of the earth as a "spaceship" in trying to persuade countries, industries and people to stop wasting and polluting our natural resources. Since we all share life on this planet, they argue, no single person or institution has the right to destroy, waste or use more than a fair share of its resources.

But does everyone on earth have an equal right to an equal share of its resources? The spaceship metaphor can be dangerous when used by misguided idealists to justify suicidal policies for sharing our resources through uncontrolled immigration and foreign aid. In their enthusiastic but unrealistic generosity, they confuse the ethics of a spaceship with those of a lifeboat.

A true spaceship would have to be under the control of a captain, since no ship could possibly survive if its course were determined by committee. Spaceship Earth certainly has no captain; the United Nations is merely a toothless tiger, with little power to enforce any policy upon its bickering members.

If we divide the world crudely into rich nations and poor nations, two thirds of them are desperately poor, and only one third comparatively rich, with the United States the wealthiest of all. Metaphorically each nation can be seen as a lifeboat full of comparatively rich people. In the ocean outside each lifeboat swim the poor of the world, who would like to get in, or at least to share some of the wealth. What should the lifeboat passengers do?

5   First, we must recognize the limited capacity of any lifeboat. For example, a nation's land has a limited capacity to support a population and as the current energy crisis has shown us, in some ways we have already exceeded the carrying capacity of our land.

Adrift in a Moral Sea

So here we sit, say fifty people in our lifeboat. To be generous, let us assume it has room for ten more, making a total capacity of sixty. Suppose the fifty of us in the lifeboat see 100 others swimming in the water outside, begging for admission to our boat or for handouts. We have several options: We may be tempted to try to live by the Christian ideal of being "our brother's keeper," or by the Marxist ideal of "to each according to his needs." Since the needs of all in the water are the same, and since they can all be seen as "our brothers," we could take them all into our boat, making a total of 150 in a boat designed for sixty. The boat swamps, everyone drowns. Complete justice, complete catastrophe.

Since the boat has an unused excess capacity of ten more passengers, we could admit just ten more to it. But which ten do we let in? How do we choose? Do we pick the best ten, the neediest ten, "first come, first served"? And what do we say to the ninety we exclude? If we do let an extra ten into our lifeboat, we will have lost our "safety factor," an engineering principle of critical importance. For example, if we don't leave room for excess capacity as a safety factor in our country's agriculture, a new plant disease or a bad change in the weather could have disastrous consequences.

Suppose we decide to preserve our small safety factor and admit no more to the lifeboat. Our survival is then possible, although we shall have to be constantly on guard against boarding parties.

While this last solution clearly offers the only means of our survival, it is morally abhorrent to many people. Some say they feel guilty about their good luck. My reply is simple: "Get out and yield your place to others." This may solve the problem of the guilt-ridden person's conscience, but it does not change the ethics of the lifeboat. The needy person to whom the guilt-ridden person yields his place will not himself feel guilty about his good luck. If he did, he would not climb aboard. The net result of conscience-stricken people giving up their unjustly held seats is the elimination of that sort of conscience from the lifeboat.

10   This is the basic metaphor within which we must work out our solutions. Let us now enrich the image, step by step, with substantive additions from the real world, a world that must solve real and pressing problems of overpopulation and hunger.

The harsh ethics of the lifeboat become even harsher when we consider the reproductive differences between the rich nations and the poor nations.

The people inside the lifeboats are doubling in numbers every eighty-seven years; those swimming around outside are doubling, on the average, every thirty-five years, more than twice as fast as the rich. And since the world's resources are dwindling, the difference in prosperity between the rich and the poor can only increase.

As of 1973, the U.S had a population of 210 million people, who were increasing by 0.8 percent per year. Outside our lifeboat, let us imagine another 210 million people (say the combined populations of Colombia, Ecuador, Venezuela, Morocco, Pakistan, Thailand and the Philippines), who are increasing at a rate of 3.3 percent per year. Put differently, the doubling time for this aggregate population is twenty-one years, compared to eighty-seven years for the U.S.

Multiplying the Rich and the Poor

Now suppose the U.S. agreed to pool its resources with those seven countries, with everyone receiving an equal share. Initially the ratio of Americans to non-Americans in this model would be one-to-one. But consider what the ratio would be after eighty-seven years, by which time the Americans would have doubled to a population of 420 million. By then, doubling every twenty-one years, the other group would have swollen to 354 billion. Each American would have to share the available resource with more than eight people.

But, one could argue, this discussion assumes that current population trends will continue, and they may not. Quite so. Most likely the rate of population increase will decline much faster in the U.S. than it will in the other countries, and there does not seem to be much we can do about it. In sharing with "each according to his needs," we must recognize that needs are determined by population size, which is determined by the rate of reproduction, which at present is regarded as a sovereign right of every nation, poor or not. This being so, the philanthropic load created by the sharing ethic of the spaceship can only increase.

The Tragedy of the Commons

15 The fundamental error of spaceship ethics, and the sharing it requires, is that it leads to what I call "the tragedy of the commons." Under a system of private property, the men who own property recognize their responsibility to care for it, for if they don't they will eventually suffer. A farmer, for instance, will allow no more cattle in a pasture than its carrying capacity justifies. If he overloads it, erosion sets in, weeds take over, and he loses the use of the pasture.

If a pasture becomes a commons open to all, the right of each to use it may not be matched by a corresponding responsibility to protect it. Asking everyone to use it with discretion will hardly do, for the considerate herdsman who refrains from overloading the commons suffers more than a selfish one who says his needs are greater. If everyone would restrain himself, all would be well; but it takes only one less than everyone to ruin a system of voluntary restraint. In a crowded world of less than perfect human beings, mutual ruin is inevitable if there are no controls. This is the tragedy of the commons.

One of the major tasks of education today should be the creation of such an acute awareness of the dangers of the commons that people will recognize its many varieties. For example, the air and water have become polluted because they are treated as commons. Further growth in the population or per-capita conversion of natural resources into pollutants will only make the problem worse. The same holds true for the fish of the oceans. Fishing fleets have nearly disappeared in many parts of the world, technological improvements in the art of fishing are hastening the day of complete ruin. Only the replacement of the system of the commons with a responsible system of control will save the land, air, water and oceanic fisheries.

The World Food Bank

In recent years there has been a push to create a new commons called a World Food Bank, an international depository of food reserves to which nations would contribute according to their abilities and from which they would draw according to their needs. This humanitarian proposal has received support from many liberal international groups, and from such prominent citizens as Margaret Mead, U.N. Secretary General Kurt Waldheim, and Senators Edward Kennedy and George McGovern.

A world food bank appeals powerfully to our humanitarian impulses. But before we rush ahead with such a plan, let us recognize where the greatest political push comes from, lest we be disillusioned later. Our experience with the "Food for Peace program," or Public Law 480, gives us the answer. This program moved billions of dollars' worth of U.S. surplus grain to food-short, population-long countries during the past two decades. But when P.L. 480 first became law, a headline in the business magazine *Forbes* revealed the real power behind it: "Feeding the World's Hungry Millions: How It Will Mean Billions for U.S. Business."

20   And indeed it did. In the years 1960 to 1970, U.S. taxpayers spent a total of $7.9 billion on the Food for Peace program. Between 1948 and 1970, they also paid an additional $50 billion for other economic-aid programs, some of which went for food and food-producing machinery and technology. Though all U.S. taxpayers were forced to contribute to the cost of P.L. 480, certain special interest groups gained handsomely under the program. Farmers did not have to

contribute the grain; the Government, or rather the taxpayers, bought it from them at full market prices. The increased demand raised prices of farm products generally. The manufacturers of farm machinery, fertilizers and pesticides benefited by the farmers' extra efforts to grow more food. Grain elevators profited from storing the surplus until it could be shipped. Railroads made money hauling it to ports, and shipping lines profited from carrying it overseas. The implementation of P.L. 480 required the creation of a vast Government bureaucracy, which then acquired its own vested interest in continuing the program regardless of its merits.

Extracting Dollars

Those who proposed and defended the Food for Peace program in public rarely mentioned its importance to any of these special interests. The public emphasis was always on its humanitarian effects. The combination of silent selfish interests and highly vocal humanitarian apologists made a powerful and successful lobby for extracting money from taxpayers. We can expect the same lobby to push now for the creation of a World Food Bank.

However great the potential benefit to selfish interests, it should not be a decisive argument against a truly humanitarian program. We must ask if such a program would actually do more good than harm, not only momentarily but also in the long run. Those who propose the food bank usually refer to a current "emergency" or "crisis" in terms of world food supply. But what is an emergency? Although they may be infrequent and sudden, everyone knows that emergencies will occur from time to time. A well-run family, company, organization or country prepares for the likelihood of accidents and emergencies. It expects them, it budgets for them, it saves for them.

Learning the Hard Way

What happens if some organizations or countries budget for accidents and others do not? If each country is solely responsible for its own well-being, poorly managed ones will suffer. But they can learn from experience. They may mend their ways, and learn to budget for infrequent but certain emergencies. For example, the weather varies from year to year, and periodic crop failures are certain. A wise and competent government saves out of the production of the good years in anticipation of bad years to come. Joseph taught this policy to Pharaoh in Egypt more than 2,000 years ago. Yet the great majority of the governments in the world today do not follow such a policy. They lack either the wisdom or the competence, or both. Should those nations that do manage to put something aside be forced to come to the rescue each time an emergency occurs among the poor nations?

But it isn't their fault!" some kindhearted liberals argue. "How can we blame the poor people who are caught in an emergency? Why must they suffer for the sins of their governments?" The concept of blame is simply not relevant here. The real question is, what are the operational consequences of establishing a world food bank? If it is open to every country every time a need develops, slovenly rulers will not be motivated to take Joseph's advice. Someone will always come to their aid. Some countries will deposit food in the world food bank, and others will withdraw it. There will be almost no overlap. As a result of such solutions to food shortage emergencies, the poor countries will not learn to mend their ways, and will suffer progressively greater emergencies as their populations grow.

Population Control the Crude Way

25 On the average, poor countries undergo a 2.5 percent increase in population each year; rich countries, about 0.8 percent. Only rich countries have anything in the way of food reserves set aside, and even they do not have as much as they should. Poor countries have none. If poor countries received no food from the outside, the rate of their population growth would be periodically checked by crop failures and famines. But if they can always draw on a world food bank in time of need, their populations can grow unchecked, and so will the "need" for aid. In the short run, a world food bank may diminish that need, but in the long run it actually increases the need without limit.

Without some system of worldwide food sharing, the proportion of people in the rich and poor nations might eventually stabilize. The overpopulated poor countries would decrease in numbers, while the rich countries that had room for more people would increase. But with a well-meaning system of sharing, such as a world food bank, the growth differential between the rich and the poor countries will not only persist, it will increase. Because of the higher rate of population growth in the poor countries of the world, 88 percent of today's children are born poor, and only 12 percent rich. Year by year the ratio becomes worse, as the fast-reproducing poor outnumber the slow-reproducing rich.

A world food bank is thus a commons in disguise. People will have more motivation to draw from it than to add to any common store. The less provident and less able will multiply at the expense of the abler and more provident, bringing eventual ruin upon all who share in the commons. Besides, any system of "sharing" that amounts to foreign aid from the rich nations to the poor nations will carry the taint of charity, which will contribute little to the world peace so devoutly desired by those who support the idea of a world food bank.

As past U.S. foreign-aid programs have amply and depressingly demonstrated, international charity frequently inspires mistrust and antagonism rather than gratitude on the part of the recipient nation.

Chinese Fish and Miracle Rice

The modern approach to foreign aid stresses the export of technology and advice, rather than money and food. As an ancient Chinese proverb goes: "Give a man a fish and he will eat for a day; teach him how to fish and he will eat for the rest of his days." Acting on this advice, the Rockefeller and Ford Foundations have financed a number of programs for improving agriculture in the hungry nations. Known as the "Green Revolution," these programs have led to the development of "miracle rice" and "miracle wheat," new strains that offer bigger harvests and greater resistance to crop damage. Norman Borlaug, the Nobel Prize–winning agronomist who, supported by the Rockefeller Foundation, developed "miracle wheat," is one of the most prominent advocates of a world food bank.

30   Whether or not the Green Revolution can increase food production as much as its champions claim is a debatable but possibly irrelevant point. Those who support this well-intended humanitarian effort should first consider some of the fundamentals of human ecology. Ironically, one man who did was the late Alan Gregg, a vice president of the Rockefeller Foundation. Two decades ago he expressed strong doubts about the wisdom of such attempts to increase food production. He likened the growth and spread of humanity over the surface of the earth to the spread of cancer in the human body, remarking that "cancerous growths demand food; but, as far as I know, they have never been cured by getting it."

Overloading the Environment

Every human born constitutes a draft on all aspects of the environment: food, air, water, forests, beaches, wildlife, scenery and solitude. Food can, perhaps, be significantly increased to meet a growing demand. But what about clean beaches, unspoiled forests and solitude? If we satisfy a growing population's need for food, we necessarily decrease its per-capita supply of the other resources needed by men.

India, for example, now has a population of 600 million, which increases by 15 million each year. This population already puts a huge load on a relatively impoverished environment. The country's forests are now only a small fraction of what they were three centuries ago, and floods and erosion continually destroy the insufficient farmland that remains. Every one of the 15 million new lives added to India's population puts an additional burden on the environment, and increases the economic and social costs of crowding. However humanitarian our intent, every Indian life saved through medical or nutritional assistance from abroad diminishes the quality of life for those who remain, and for subsequent generations. If rich countries make it possible, through foreign aid, for 600 million Indians to swell to 1.2 billion in a mere twenty-eight years, as their current growth rate threatens, will future generations of Indians thank us for hastening the destruction of their environment? Will our good intentions be sufficient excuse for the consequences of our actions?

My final example of a commons in action is one for which the public has the least desire for rational discussion—immigration. Anyone who publicly questions the wisdom of current U.S. immigration policy is promptly charged with bigotry, prejudice, ethnocentrism, chauvinism, isolationism or selfishness. Rather than encounter such accusations, one would rather talk about other matters, leaving immigration policy to wallow in the crosscurrents of special interests that take no account of the good of the whole, or the interest of posterity.

Perhaps we still feel guilty about things we said in the past. Two generations ago the popular press frequently referred to Dagos, Wops, Polacks, Chinks and Krauts, in articles about how America was being "overrun" by foreigners of supposedly inferior genetic stock. But because the implied inferiority of foreigners was used than as justification for keeping them out, people now assume that restrictive policies could only be based on such misguided notions. There are no other grounds.

A Nation of Immigrants

35 Just consider the numbers involved. Our Government acknowledges a net inflow of 400,000 immigrants a year. While we have no hard data on the extent of illegal entries, educated guesses put the figure at about 600,000 a year. Since the natural increase (excess of births over deaths) of the resident population now runs about 1.7 million per year, the yearly gain from immigration amounts to at least 19 percent of the total annual increase, and may be as much as 37 percent if we include the estimate for illegal immigrants. Considering the growing use of birth-control devices, the potential effect of educational campaigns by such organizations as Planned Parenthood Federation of America and Zero Population Growth, and the influence of inflation and the housing shortage, the fertility rate of American women may decline so much that immigration could account for all the yearly increase in population. Should we not at least ask if that is what we want?

For the sake of those who worry about whether the "quality" of the average immigrant compares favorably with the quality of the average resident, let us assume that immigrants and native born citizens are of exactly equal quality, however one defines that term. We will focus here only on quantity; and since our conclusions will depend on nothing else, all charges of bigotry and chauvinism become irrelevant.

Immigration vs. Food Supply

World food banks *move food to the people*, hastening the exhaustion of the environment of the poor countries. Unrestricted immigration, on the other hand, *moves people to the food*, thus speeding up the destruction of the environment of the rich countries. We can easily understand why poor people should want to make this latter transfer, but why should rich hosts encourage it?

As in the case of foreign-aid programs, immigration receives support from selfish interests and humanitarian impulses. The primary selfish interest in unimpeded immigration is the desire of employers for cheap labor, particularly in industries and trades that offer degrading work. In the past, one wave of foreigners after another was brought into the U.S. to work at wretched jobs for wretched wages. In recent years, the Cubans, Puerto Ricans and Mexicans have had this dubious honor. The interests of the employers of cheap labor mesh well with the guilty silence of the country's liberal intelligentsia. White Anglo-Saxon Protestants are particularly reluctant to call for a closing of the doors to immigration for fear of being called bigots.

But not all countries have such reluctant leadership. Most educated Hawaiians, for example, are keenly aware of the limits of their environment, particularly in terms of population growth. There is only so much room on the islands, and the islanders know it. To Hawaiians, immigrants from the other forty-nine states present as great a threat as those from other nations. At a recent meeting of Hawaiian government officials in Honolulu, I had the ironic delight of hearing a speaker, who like most of his audience was of Japanese ancestry, ask how the country might practically and constitutionally close its doors to further immigration. One member of the audience countered: "How can we shut the doors now? We have many friends and relatives in Japan that we'd like to bring here some day so that they can enjoy Hawaii too." The Japanese-American speaker smiled sympathetically and answered: "Yes, but we have children now, and someday we'll have grandchildren too. We can bring more people here from Japan only by giving away some of the land that we hope to pass on to our grandchildren some day. What right do we have to do that?"

40   At this point, I can hear U.S. liberals asking: "How can you justify slamming the door once you're inside? You say that immigrants should be kept out. But aren't we all immigrants, or the descendants of immigrants? If we insist on staying, must we not admit all others?" Our craving for intellectual order leads us to seek and prefer symmetrical rules and morals: a single rule for me and

everybody else; the same rule yesterday, today, and tomorrow. Justice, we feel, should not change with time and place.

We Americans of non-Indian ancestry can look upon ourselves as the descendants of thieves who are guilty morally, if not legally, of stealing this land from its Indian owners. Should we then give back the land to the now living American descendants of those Indians? However morally or logically sound this proposal may be, I, for one, am unwilling to live by it and I know no one else who is. Besides, the logical consequence would be absurd. Suppose that, intoxicated with a sense of pure justice, we should decide to turn our land over to the Indians. Since all our wealth has also been derived from the land, wouldn't we be morally obliged to give that back to the Indians too?

Pure Justice vs. Reality

Clearly, the concept of pure justice produces an infinite regression to absurdity. Centuries ago, wise men invented statutes of limitations to justify the rejection of such pure justice, in the interest of preventing continual disorder. The law zealously defends property rights, but only relatively recent property rights. Drawing a line after an arbitrary time has elapsed may be unjust, but the alternatives are worse.

We are all descendants of thieves, and the world's resources are inequitably distributed. But we must begin the journey to tomorrow from the point where we are today. We cannot remake the past. We cannot safely divide the wealth equitably among all peoples so long as people reproduce at different rates. To do so would guarantee that our grandchildren, and everyone else's grandchildren, would have only a ruined world to inhabit.

To be generous with one's own possessions is quite different from being generous with those of posterity. We should call this point to the attention of those who, from a commendable love of justice and equality, would institute a system of the commons, either in the form of a world food bank, or of unrestricted immigration. We must convince them if we wish to save at least some parts of the world from environmental ruin.

45   Without a true world government to control reproduction and the use of available resources, the sharing ethic of the spaceship is impossible. For the foreseeable future, our survival demands that we govern our actions by the ethics of a lifeboat, harsh though they may be. Posterity will be satisfied with nothing less.

ENGAGING the Text

1. What extended analogy does Hardin use as a graphic illustration of his thesis?

2. What does Hardin mean by the expression the "tragedy of the commons"?

EVALUATING the Argument

1. Evaluate Hardin's assumption that an obligation to future generations should override our desire to help starving masses in the present.

2. How fairly does Hardin state arguments that opponents might raise against his position and what reasons and evidence does he give for rejecting these arguments?

EXPLORING the Issue

1. Write an essay directed at your classmates that responds to Hardin's argument. You might formulate your essay as a letter to the editor of your campus newspaper.

2. To put Hardin's scenario into terms of a personal moral choice, consider the following dilemma: would you be willing to add five years to your life even though it meant taking five years away from the life of someone you didn't know? How would your decision change if you knew the person?

CONNECTING Different Perspectives

1. How might Philip Wheelwright's "The Meaning of Ethics" be applied to Hardin's scenario?

A Sample Deductive Argument For Analysis

Milton Friedman

The Social Responsibility of Business Is to Increase Its Profits

Milton Friedman (b. 1912) won the Nobel Prize for Economics in 1976. Since 1977 he has been a Senior Research Fellow at the Hoover Institution, Stanford University. His extensive publications include A Monetary History of the United States *(1963) and* Monetary Trends in the United States and the United Kingdom *(1982). He and his wife published* Milton and Rose D. Friedman, Two Lucky People: Memoirs *(1998). A recent work is a 2005 reprint of* The Optimum Quantity of Money *first published in 1969. The following article originally appeared in the* New York Times Magazine *(September 13, 1970) and remains a classic exposition of conservative free-market theory.*

Thinking Critically

Does business owe anything to the society that enables it to derive profits?

When I hear businessmen speak eloquently about the "social responsibilities of business in a free-enterprise system," I am reminded of the wonderful line about the Frenchman who discovered at the age of 70 that he had been speaking prose all his life. The businessmen believe that they are defending free enterprise when they declaim that business is not concerned "merely" with profit but also with promoting desirable "social ends; that business has a social conscience" and takes seriously its responsibilities for providing employment, eliminating discrimination, avoiding pollution and whatever else may be the catchwords of the contemporary crop of reformers. In fact they are—or would be if they or anyone else took them seriously—preaching pure and unadulterated socialism. Businessmen who talk this way are unwitting puppets of the intellectual forces that have been undermining the basis of a free society these past decades.

The discussions of the "social responsibilities of business" are notable for their analytical looseness and lack of rigor. What does it mean to say that "business" has responsibilities? Only people can have responsibilities. A corporation is an artificial person and in this sense may have artificial responsibilities, but "business" as a whole cannot be said to have responsibilities, even in this vague sense. The first step toward clarity in examining the doctrine of the social responsibility of business is to ask precisely what it implies for whom.

Presumably, the individuals who are to be responsible are businessmen, which means individual proprietors or corporate executives. Most of the discussion of social responsibility is directed at corporations, so in what follows I shall mostly neglect the individual proprietor and speak of corporate executives.

In a free-enterprise, private-property system, a corporate executive is an employee of the owners of the business. He has direct responsibility to his employers. That responsibility is to conduct the business in accordance with their desires, which generally will be to make as much money as possible while conforming to the basic rules of the society, both those embodied in law and those embodied in ethical custom. Of course, in some cases his employers may have a different objective. A group of persons might establish a corporation for an eleemosynary purpose—for example, a hospital or a school. The manager of such a corporation will not have money profit as his objective but the rendering of certain services.

5   In either case, the key point is that, in his capacity as a corporate executive, the manager is the agent of the individuals who own the corporation or establish the eleemosynary institution, and his primary responsibility is to them.

Needless to say, this does not mean that it is easy to judge how well he is performing his task. But at least the criterion of performance is straightforward, and the persons among whom a voluntary contractual arrangement exists are clearly defined.

Of course, the corporate executive is also a person in his own right. As a person, he may have many other responsibilities that he recognizes or assumes voluntarily—to his family, his conscience, his feelings of charity, his church, his clubs, his city, his country. He may feel impelled by these responsibilities to devote part of his income to causes he regards as worthy, to refuse to work for particular corporations, even to leave his job, for example, to join his country's armed forces. If we wish, we may refer to some of these responsibilities as "social responsibilities." But in these respects he is acting as a principal, not an agent; he is spending his own money or time or energy, not the money of his employers or the time or energy he has contracted to devote to their purposes. If these are "social responsibilities," they are the social responsibilities of individuals, not of business.

What does it mean to say that the corporate executive has a "social responsibility" in his capacity as businessman? If this statement is not pure rhetoric, it must mean that he is to act in some way that is not in the interest of his employers. For example, that he is to refrain from increasing the price of the product in order to contribute to the social objective of preventing inflation, even though a price increase would be in the best interests of the corporation. Or that he is to make expenditures on reducing pollution beyond the amount that is in the best interests of the corporation or that is required by law in order to contribute to the social objective of improving the environment. Or that, at the expense of corporate profits, he is to hire "hard-core" unemployed instead of better-qualified available workmen to contribute to the social objective of reducing poverty.

In each of these cases, the corporate executive would be spending someone else's money for a general social interest. Insofar as his actions in accord with his "social responsibility" reduce returns to stockholders, he is spending their money. Insofar as his actions raise the price to customers, he is spending the customers' money. Insofar as his actions lower the wages of some employees, he is spending their money.

10   The stockholders or the customers or the employees could separately spend their own money on the particular action if they wished to do so. The executive is exercising a distinct "social responsibility," rather than serving as an agent of the stockholders or the customers or the employees, only if he spends the money in a different way than they would have spent it.

But if he does this, he is in effect imposing taxes, on the one hand, and deciding how the tax proceeds shall be spent, on the other.

This process raises political questions on two levels: principle and consequences. On the level of political principle, the imposition of taxes and the expenditure of tax proceeds are governmental functions. We have established elaborate constitutional, parliamentary and judicial provisions to control these functions, to assure that taxes are imposed so far as possible in accordance with the preferences and desires of the public—after all, "taxation without representation" was one of the battle cries of the American Revolution. We have a system of checks and balances to separate the legislative function of imposing taxes and enacting expenditures from the executive function of collecting taxes and administering expenditure programs and from the judicial function of mediating disputes and interpreting the law.

Here the businessman—self-selected or appointed directly or indirectly by stockholders—is to be simultaneously legislator, executive and jurist. He is to decide whom to tax by how much and for what purpose, and he is to spend the proceeds—all this guided only by general exhortations from on high to restrain inflation, improve the environment, fight poverty and so on and on.

The whole justification for permitting the corporate executive to be selected by the stockholders is that the executive is an agent serving the interests of his principal. This justification disappears when the corporate executive imposes taxes and spends the proceeds for "social" purposes. He becomes in effect a public employee, a civil servant, even though he remains in name an employee of a private enterprise. On grounds of political principle, it is intolerable that such civil servants—insofar as their actions in the name of social responsibility are real and not just window-dressing—should be selected as they are now. If they are to be civil servants, then they must be selected through a political process. If they are to impose taxes and make expenditures to foster "social" objectives, then political machinery must be set up to guide the assessment of taxes and to determine through a political process the objectives to be served.

15   This is the basic reason why the doctrine of "social responsibility" involves the acceptance of the socialist view that political mechanisms, not market mechanisms, are the appropriate way to determine the allocation of scarce resources to alternative uses.

On the grounds of consequences, can the corporate executive in fact discharge his alleged "social responsibilities"? On the one hand, suppose he could get away with spending the stockholders' or customers' or employees' money. How is he to know how to spend it? He is told that he must contribute to fighting inflation. How is he to know what action of his will contribute to that end? He is presumably an expert in running his company—in producing a product or selling it or financing it. But nothing about his selection makes him an expert on inflation. Will his holding down the price of his product reduce inflationary pressure? Or, by leaving more spending power in the hands of his customers, simply divert it elsewhere? Or, by forcing him to produce less because of the lower price, will it simply contribute to shortages? Even if he could answer these questions, how much cost is he justified in imposing on his stockholders, customers and employes for this social purpose? What is the appropriate share and what is the appropriate share of others?

And, whether he wants to or not, can he get away with spending his stockholders', customers' or employees' money? Will not the stockholders fire him? (Either the present ones or those who take over when his actions in the name of social responsibility have reduced the corporation's profits and the price of its stock.) His customers and his employees can desert him for other producers and employers less scrupulous in exercising their social responsibilities.

This facet of "social responsibility" doctrine is brought into sharp relief when the doctrine is used to justify wage restraint by trade unions. The conflict of interest is naked and clear when union officials are asked to subordinate the interest of their members to some more general social purpose. If the union officials try to enforce wage restraint, the consequence is likely to be wildcat strikes, rank-and-file revolts and the emergence of strong competitors for their jobs. We thus have the ironic phenomenon that union leaders—at least in the U.S.—have objected to Government interference with the market far more consistently and courageously than have business leaders.

The difficulty of exercising "social responsibility" illustrates, of course, the great virtue of private competitive enterprise—it forces people to be responsible for their own actions and makes it difficult for them to "exploit" other people for either selfish or unselfish purposes. They can do good—but only at their own expense.

20   Many a reader who has followed the argument this far may be tempted to remonstrate that it is all well and good to speak of government's having the responsibility to impose taxes and determine expenditures for such "social" purposes as controlling pollution or training the hard-core unemployed, but that the problems are too urgent to wait on the slow course of political processes, that the exercise of social responsibility by businessmen is a quicker and surer way to solve pressing current problems.

Aside from the question of fact—I share Adam Smith's skepticism about the benefits that can be expected from "those who affected to trade for the public good"—this argument must be rejected on grounds of principle. What it amounts to is an assertion that those who favor the taxes and expenditures in question have failed to persuade a majority of their fellow citizens to be of like mind and that they are seeking to attain by undemocratic procedures what they cannot attain by democratic procedures. In a free society, it is hard for "good" people to do "good," but that is a small price to pay for making it hard for "evil" people to do "evil," especially since one man's good is another's evil.

I have, for simplicity, concentrated on the special case of the corporate executive, except only for the brief digression on trade unions. But precisely the same argument applies to the newer phenomenon of calling upon stockholders to require corporations to exercise social responsibility (the recent G.M. crusade, for example). In most of these cases, what is in effect involved is some stockholders trying to get other stockholders (or customers or employees) to contribute against their will to "social" causes favored by the activists. Insofar as they succeed, they are again imposing taxes and spending the proceeds.

The situation of the individual proprietor is somewhat different. If he acts to reduce the returns of his enterprise in order to exercise his "social responsibility," he is spending his own money, not someone else's. If he wishes to spend his money on such purposes, that is his right, and I cannot see that there is any objection to his doing so. In the process, he, too, may impose costs on employees and customers. However, because he is far less likely than a large corporation or union to have monopolistic power, any such side effects will tend to be minor.

Of course, in practice the doctrine of social responsibility is frequently a cloak for actions that are justified on other grounds rather than a reason for those actions.

25   To illustrate, it may well be in the long-run interest of a corporation that is a major employer in a small community to devote resources to providing amenities to that community or to improving its government. That may make it easier to attract desirable employees, it may reduce the wage bill or lesson losses from pilferage and sabotage or have other worthwhile effects. Or it may be that, given the laws about the deductibility of corporate charitable contributions, the stockholders can contribute more to charities they favor by having the corporation make the gift than by doing it themselves, since they can in that way contribute an amount that would otherwise have been paid as corporate taxes.

In each of these—and many similar—cases, there is a strong temptation to rationalize these actions as an exercise of "social responsibility." In the present climate of opinion, with its widespread aversion to "capitalism," "profits," the "soulless corporation" and so on, this is one way for a corporation to generate goodwill as a by-product of expenditures that are entirely justified in its own self-interest.

It would be inconsistent of me to call on corporate executives to refrain from this hypocritical window-dressing because it harms the foundations of a free society. That would be to call on them to exercise a "social responsibility"! If our institutions, and the attitudes of the public make it in their self-interest to cloak their actions in this way, I cannot summon much indignation to denounce them. At the same time, I can express admiration for those individual proprietors or owners of closely held corporations or stockholders of more broadly held corporations who disdain such tactics as approaching fraud.

Whether blameworthy or not, the use of the cloak of social responsibility, and the nonsense spoken in its name by influential and prestigious businessmen, does clearly harm the foundations of a free society. I have been impressed time and again by the schizophrenic character of many businessmen. They are capable of being extremely far-sighted and clearheaded in matters that are internal to their businesses. They are incredibly short-sighted and muddle-headed in matters that are outside their businesses but affect the possible survival of business in general. This short-sightedness is strikingly exemplified in the calls from many businessmen for wage and price guidelines or controls or incomes policies. There is nothing that could do more in a brief period to destroy a market system and replace it by a centrally controlled system than effective governmental control of prices and wages.

The short-sightedness is also exemplified in speeches by businessmen on social responsibility. This may gain them kudos in the short run. But it helps to strengthen the already too prevalent view that the pursuit of profits is wicked and immoral and must be curbed and controlled by external forces. Once this view is adopted, the external forces that curb the market will not be the social consciences, however highly developed, of the pontificating executives; it will be the iron fist of Government bureaucrats. Here, as with price and wage controls, businessmen seem to me to reveal a suicidal impulse.

30   The political principle that underlies the market mechanisms is unanimity. In an ideal free market resting on private property, no individual can coerce any other, all cooperation is voluntary, all parties to such cooperation benefit or they need not participate. There are no "social" values, no "social" responsibilities in any sense other than the shared values and responsibilities of individuals. Society is a collection of individuals and of the various groups they voluntarily form.

The political principle that underlies the political mechanism is conformity. The individual must serve a more general social interest—whether that be determined by a church or a dictator or a majority. The individual may have a vote and a say in what is to be done, but if he is overruled, he must conform. It is appropriate for some to require others to contribute to a general social purpose whether they wish to or not.

Unfortunately, unanimity is not always feasible. There are some respects in which conformity appears unavoidable, so I do not see how one can avoid the use of the political mechanism altogether.

But the doctrine of "social responsibility" taken seriously would extend the scope of the political mechanism to every human activity. It does not differ in philosophy from the most explicitly collectivist doctrine. It differs only by professing to believe that collectivist ends can be attained without collectivist means. That is why, in my book "Capitalism and Freedom," I have called it a "fundamentally subversive doctrine" in a free society, and have said that in such a society, "there is one and only one social responsibility of business—to use its resources and engage in activities designed to increase its profits so long as it stays within the rules of the game, which is to say, engages in open and free competition without deception or fraud."

ENGAGING the Text

1. How does Friedman's argument depend on the premises or assumptions that: (a) CEOs are employees of owners of the firm and hence cannot spend shareholders money on social programs, and (b) although individuals may voluntarily dedicate time, effort, or money to social programs, they have no right to divert resources belonging to the business to fulfill social responsibilities?

2. How does Friedman use the phrase "taxation without representation" (one of the causes of the American Revolution) to support his view that imposing government regulations to use profits for social purposes is a form of socialism? Instead, where should these profits go?

EVALUATING the Argument

1. What purpose does Friedman's discussion of wildcat strikes by trade unions have in his overall argument?

2. Evaluate Friedman's claim that feeling guilt over social inequities is in business terms a "suicidal impulse."

EXPLORING the Issue

1. What firms have defied Friedman's worst-case scenarios and allocated business profits for social purposes without suffering in the competive marketplace?

2. As a research project, trace the link between Adam Smith's doctrine of *laissez-faire* capitalism and Friedman's views. In your opinion, is it in society's best interest for government to leave business alone? Why or why not?

CONNECTING Different Perspectives

1. Does Joseph K. Skinner's (see "Big Mac and the Tropical Forests") analysis of the environmental effects of deforestation challenge the assumptions underlying Friedman's argument?

6 THE ROLE OF LANGUAGE IN ARGUMENT

OVERVIEW: The words a writer uses play a vital role in making any argument more effective for a given audience. By adapting the style of the argument to a particular audience, writers can increase their chances of not only getting a fair hearing for their case but also convincing the audience to share their outlook. For some audiences, tone, style, and syntax that are colloquial may work best. For others, a more formal, literary style may be more appropriate. Of all the stylistic means a writer can use to develop an argument, three areas deserve a close look: (1) tone (including irony and satire), (2) persuasive techniques (including the rhetoric of advertising) and (3) propaganda techniques (including doublespeak, downplaying, and intensifying). Tone reveals a writer's attitude toward the subject, persuasive techniques include every means a writer uses to encourage an audience to share this viewpoint, and propaganda techniques identify the ethical standards implicit in any act of persuasion.

Tone

Tone is a vital element in the audience's perception of the author. In *Rhetoric*, Aristotle discussed how an audience's confidence in the character and credibility of the writer or speaker was a key element in persuading its members to accept a claim. He emphasized that the audience would most likely reach their estimate of the writer or speaker's character not so much from what they already knew about the writer, which might be very little, but from the speech itself. This is why the question of tone is crucial. Aristotle believed that credibility was created by the audience's perception of the writer or speaker as a person of good sense, moral integrity, and good intentions. Good sense might be shown by the writer's knowledge of the subject, adherence to the principles of correct reasoning, and judgment in organizing a persuasive case. The more intangible qualities of character might be gauged from the writer's respect for commonly accepted values and unwillingness to use deceptive reasoning simply to win a point.

The most appropriate tone is usually a reasonable one. A reasonable tone shows that the writer cares about the subject under discussion and is sensitive to the needs and concerns of the audience.

Tone is produced by the combined effect of word choice, sentence structure, and the writer's success in adapting her or his particular "voice" to suit the subject, the audience, and the occasion. Choosing between a casual or formal tone might be compared with choosing between wearing jeans or a tuxedo to a party. Most likely, the choice of clothes would fall somewhere in the middle. So, too, the most useful tone is neither undisciplined, nor formal and pretentious, but one that creates an impression of a reasonable person calmly discussing issues in a natural voice.

When we try to identify and analyze the tone of a work, we are seeking to hear the "voice" of the author in order to understand how he or she intended the work to be perceived. Tone indicates the author's attitude toward both the subject and the audience. Tone is a projection of the writer's self. The entire essay or argument creates an impression of the writer as a certain kind of person. It is important for writers to know what image of themselves they are projecting in their writing. Writers should consciously decide on what kind of style and tone best suits the audience, the occasion, and the specific subject matter of the argument. Although a casual tone might be suitable for a conversation between friends, the same tone would be inappropriate for an argument designed to convince an audience to accept the validity of a claim.

For example, consider the tone of George F. Will's comment in his essay "Government, Economy Linked":

> The government in its wisdom considers ice a "food product." This means that Antarctica is one of the world's foremost food producers.

Will's point is that the government has inappropriately included ice in its classification of "food products." His purpose in writing is to persuade his audience to protest this senseless bureaucratic categorization. That much is obvious. What is less obvious, but is just as important is the tone of Will's comment. His tone reveals a well-developed sarcastic sense of humor, a dry wit, common sense, and a readiness to spot bureaucratic absurdities. Beyond this, we can sense Will's basic conservative position that big government should not wield too much power.

Of all the characteristics of tone, the first and most important to audiences is clarity. Write so that nothing you put down can be misunderstood. Use a natural rather than an artifical vocabulary. Adopt a tone that reinforces what you want your audience to think and feel about the issue. Keep in mind that insight, wit, and sensitivity are always appreciated.

Certain kinds of tone are more difficult for apprentice writers to manage successfully. A writer who is flippant will run the risk of not having the argument taken seriously by the audience. Arrogance, belligerence, and anger are usually inappropriate in argumentative essays. Even if you are indignant and outraged, make sure you have evidence to back up your emotional stance or else you will appear self-righteous and pompous. By the same token, steer away from special pleading, sentimentality, and an apologetic "poor me" tone—you want the audience to agree with your views, not to feel sorry for you. Keep out buzzwords or question-begging epithets ("bleeding heart liberal" or "mindless fundamentalist") that some writers use as shortcuts to establish identification with readers instead of arguing logically and backing up their position with facts and evidence.

IRONY

In arguments, writers can use irony to invite the reader to share their response to the subject. Irony results from a clash between appearance and reality, expectation and outcome, or when there is a discrepancy between the literal meaning of words and the intent. Writers adopt this strategy to draw the audience's attention to a gap between the ideal and the real, and most often, between the way things are and the way the writer thinks things ought to be. In *verbal irony*, the intended meaning of a statement or work is different from (often the opposite of) what the statement or work literally says. *Understatement*, in which an opinion is expressed less emphatically than it might be, is a form of verbal irony, often used for humorous or cutting effect. *Situational irony* refers to an occurrence that is contrary to what is expected or intended. For example, how does the following cartoon by Don Wright use different kinds of irony to encourage the reader to share his attitude on the issue of death with dignity (Figure 6.1)?

Sometimes it is difficult to pick up the fact that not everything a writer says is intended to be taken literally. Authors will occasionally say the opposite of what they mean to catch the attention of the reader. Often, the first response to an ironic statement or idea is "can the writer really be serious?" If that is your response to an argument, look for clues meant to signal you that the writer

FIGURE 6.1

means the opposite of what is being said. Irony draws the reader into a kind of secret collaboration with the author in a way that very few other rhetorical strategies can accomplish. One clear signal the author is being ironic is a noticeable disparity between the tone and the subject.

For example, in Jonathan Swift's "A Modest Proposal" (1729) the tone in which the narrator speaks is reasonable, matter-of-fact, and totally at odds with his recommendation that Ireland solve its overpopulation problem by encouraging poor people to sell their babies as food to the wealthy:

> I shall now therefore humbly propose my own thoughts, which I hope will not be liable to the least objection.
>
> I have been assured by a very knowing American of my acquaintance in London, that a young healthy child well nursed is at a year old a most delicious, nourishing, and wholesome food, whether stewed, roasted, baked, or boiled, and I make no doubt that it will equally serve in a fricassee, or a ragout.
>
> I do therefore humbly offer it to public consideration, that of the hundred and twenty thousand children already computed, twenty thousand may be reserved for breed, whereof only one fourth part to be males, which is more than we allow to sheep, black-cattle, or swine, and my reason is that these children are seldom the fruits of marriage, a circumstance not much regarded by our savages, therefore one male will be sufficient to serve four females. That the

remaining hundred thousand may at a year old be offered in sale to the persons of quality, and fortune, through the kingdom, always advising the mother to let them suck plentifully in the last month, so as to render them plump, and fat for a good table. A child will make two dishes at an entertainment for friends, and when the family dines alone, the fore or hind quarter will make a reasonable dish, and seasoned with a little pepper or salt will be very good boiled on the fourth day, especially in winter.

I have reckoned upon a medium [average], that a child just born will weigh 12 pounds, and in a solar year if tolerably nursed increaseth to 28 pounds.

I grant this food will be somewhat dear, and therefore very proper for land-lords, who, as they have already devoured most of the parents, seem to have the best title to the children.

You may have noticed the practical, down-to-earth, and understated voice with which the narrator enumerates the financial and culinary advantages of his pro-posed "solution." The discrepancy between his matter-of-fact tone and the out-rageous content is a clear signal that the writer means the exact opposite of what is being said. If you missed Swift's signals, you might even think he was being serious!

SATIRE

Laughing at someone else is an excellent way of learning how to laugh at oneself; and questioning what seem to be the absurd beliefs of another group is a good way of recognizing the potential absurdity of many of one's own cherished beliefs.

—*Gore Vidal, U.S. novelist and critic (b. 1925) "Satire in the 1950s,"* Nation *(April 26, 1958)*

Satire is an enduring form of argument that uses parody and caricature to poke fun at a subject, idea, or person. Satirists ridicule both people and social institu-tions, often in an effort to bring about social reform. Exaggeration, wit, sarcasm, and irony are frequent devices used by satirists.

Satire has run along two channels beginning with the Roman poets Horace (65 BC–8 BC) and Juvenal (AD 55–AD 135). Horatian satire is mild, amused, and sophisticated and uses laughter to correct the follies and abuses it uncovers. Juvenalian satire is vitriolic and indignant and from his works we can deduce that he disliked almost everything in his era. He scorned the decadent life of the wealthy and fashionable and lashed fools as well as philosophers in his quotable epigrams.

As we have seen in "A Modest Proposal," the satirist can create a "mask" or *persona* in order to shock or horrify the audience into a new awareness about an established institution or custom. Swift creates the *persona* of a reasonable, seemingly well-intentioned bureaucrat who proposes, in an off-hand way, that Ireland solve its economic problems by slaughtering and exporting 1-year-old children as foodstuffs. To mistake the voice as that of Swift's would be to miss the ironic contrast between what is said and what is meant. As with other works, the writer must be in full control of the material no matter how strongly he or she feels personally.

Enduring satirical works include Aristophanes' *The Birds* (414 BC), Samuel Johnson's *Rasselas* (1759), Voltaire's *Candide* (1759), Swift's *Gulliver's Travels* (1726), Mark Twain's *A Connecticut Yankee in King Arthur's Court* (1889), and Joseph Heller's *Catch 22* (1961). These works assail folly, greed, corruption, pride, self-righteous complacency, hypocrisy, and other permanent targets of the satirists' pen.

Questions for Discussion and Writing

1. How does George Carlin in the following example use irony and satire to get his points across? What taken-for-granted cultural value does he mock?

> So now you got a houseful of stuff. And, even though you might like your house, you gotta move. Gotta get a bigger house. Why? Too much stuff! And that means you gotta move all your stuff. Or maybe, put some of your stuff in storage. Storage! Imagine that. There's a whole industry based on keepin' an eye on other people's stuff.
>
> Or maybe you could sell some of your stuff. Have a yard sale, have a garage sale! Some people drive around all weekend just lookin' for garage sales. They don't have enough of their own stuff, they wanna buy other people's stuff.
>
> Or you could take your stuff to the swap meet, the flea market, the rummage sale, or the auction. There's a lotta ways to get rid of stuff. You can even give your stuff away. The Salvation Army and Goodwill will actually come to your house and pick up your stuff and give it to people who don't have much stuff. It's part of what economists call the Redistribution of Stuff.
>
> OK, enough about your stuff. Let's talk about other people's stuff. Have you ever noticed when you visit someone else's house, you never quite feel at home? You know why? No room for your stuff! Somebody *else's* stuff is all over the place. And what crummy stuff it is! "God! Where'd they get *this* stuff?"
>
> And you know how sometimes when you're visiting someone, you un-expectedly have to stay overnight? It gets real late, and you decide to stay over? So they put you in a bedroom they don't use too often . . . because

Grandma died in it eleven years ago! And they haven't moved any of her stuff? Not even the vaporizer?

Or whatever room they put you in, there's usually a dresser or a nightstand, and there's never any room on it for your stuff. Someone else's shit is on the dresser! Have you noticed that their stuff is shit, and your shit is stuff? "Get this shit off of here, so I can put my stuff down!" Crap is also a form of stuff. Crap is the stuff that belongs to the person you just broke up with. "When are you comin' over here to pick up the rest of your crap?"

—*George Carlin, "A Place for Your Stuff,"* Braindroppings *(1997)*

2.   What current social issue is satirized on Jibjab.com?

....

An Essay for Analysis

Mark Twain

The Lowest Animal

Mark Twain (1835–1910), the pseudonym of Samuel Langhorn Clemens, was brought up in Hannibal, Missouri. After serving as a printer's apprentice, Twain became a steamboat pilot on the Mississippi (1857–1861), adopting his pen name from the leadsman's call ("mark twain" means "by the mark two fathoms") sounding the river in shallow places. In 1865, in the New York Saturday Press, *Twain published "Jim Smiley and His Jumping Frog," which then became the title story of* The Celebrated Jumping Frog of Calaveras County and Other Sketches *(1867). His reputation as a humorist was enhanced by* Innocents Abroad *(1869), a comic account of his travels through France, Italy, and Palestine, and by* Roughing It *(1872), a spoof of his mining adventures. His acknowledged masterpieces are* The Adventures of Tom Sawyer *(1876) and its sequel,* The Adventures of Huckleberry Finn *(1885), works of great comic power and social insight. Twain's later works, including* The Man That Corrupted Hadleyburg *(1900), a fable about greed, and* The Mysterious Stranger *(1916), published six years after Twain's death, assail hypocrisy as endemic to the human condition. "The Lowest Animal" (1906) shows Twain at his most iconoclastic, formulating a scathing comparison between man and the so-called lower animals.*

Thinking Critically

Consider the methods and objectives of satire.

I have been studying the traits and dispositions of the "lower animals" (so-called), and contrasting them with the traits and dispositions of man. I find the result humiliating to me. For it obliges me to renounce my allegiance to the Darwinian theory of the Ascent of Man from the Lower Animals; since it now seems plain to me that that theory ought to be vacated in favor of a new and truer one, this new and truer one to be named the Descent of Man from the Higher Animals.

In proceeding toward this unpleasant conclusion I have not guessed or speculated or conjectured, but have used what is commonly called the scientific method. That is to say, I have subjected every postulate that presented itself to the crucial test of actual experiment, and have adopted it or rejected it according to the result. Thus I verified and established each step of my course in its turn before advancing to the next. These experiments were made in the London Zoological Gardens, and covered many months of painstaking and fatiguing work.

Before particularizing any of the experiments, I wish to state one or two things which seem to more properly belong in this place than further along. This in the interest of clearness. The massed experiments established to my satisfaction certain generalizations, to wit:

1. That the human race is of one distinct species. It exhibits slight variations—in color, stature, mental caliber, and so on—due to climate, environment, and so forth; but it is a species by itself, and not to be confounded with any other.

2. That the quadrupeds are a distinct family, also. This family exhibits variations—in color, size, food preferences and so on; but it is a family by itself.

3. That the other families—the birds, the fishes, the insects, the reptiles, etc.—are more or less distinct, also. They are in the procession. They are links in the chain which stretches down from the higher animals to man at the bottom.

Some of my experiments were quite curious. In the course of my reading I had come across a case where, many years ago, some hunters on our Great Plains organized a buffalo hunt for the entertainment of an English earl—that, and to provide some fresh meat for his larder. They had charming sport. They killed seventy-two of those great animals; and ate part of one of them and left the seventy-one to rot. In order to determine the difference between an anaconda and an earl—if any—I caused seven young calves to be turned into the anaconda's cage. The grateful reptile immediately crushed one of them and swallowed it, then lay back satisfied. It showed no further interest in the calves, and no disposition to harm them. I tried this experiment with other anacondas; always with the same result. The fact stood proven that the difference between an earl and an anaconda is that the earl is cruel and the anaconda isn't; and that the earl wantonly destroys what he has no use for, but the anaconda doesn't. This seemed to suggest that the anaconda was not descended from the earl. It also seemed to suggest that the earl was descended from the anaconda, and had lost a good deal in the transition.

I was aware that many men who have accumulated more millions of money than they can ever use have shown a rabid hunger for more, and have not scrupled to cheat the ignorant and the helpless out of their poor servings in order to partially appease that appetite. I furnished a hundred different kinds of wild and tame animals the opportunity to accumulate vast stores of food, but none of them would do it. The squirrels and bees and certain birds made accumulations, but stopped when they had gathered a winter's supply, and could not be persuaded to add to it either honestly or by chicane. In order to bolster up a tottering reputation the ant pretended to store up supplies, but I was not deceived. I know the ant. These experiments convinced me that there is this difference between man and the higher animals: he is avaricious and miserly, they are not.

5   In the course of my experiments I convinced myself that among the animals man is the only one that harbors insults and injuries, broods over them, waits till a chance offers, then takes revenge. The passion of revenge is unknown to the higher animals.

Roosters keep harems, but it is by consent of their concubines; therefore no wrong is done. Men keep harems, but it is by brute force, privileged by atrocious laws which the other sex is allowed no hand in making. In this matter man occupies a far lower place than the rooster.

Cats are loose in their morals, but not consciously so. Man, in his descent from the cat, has brought the cat's looseness with him but has left the unconsciousness behind—the saving grace which excuses the cat. The cat is innocent, man is not.

Indecency, vulgarity, obscenity—these are strictly confined to man; he invented them. Among the higher animals there is no trace of them. They hide nothing; they are not ashamed. Man, with his soiled mind, covers himself. He will not even enter a drawing room with his breast and back naked, so alive are he and his mates to indecent suggestion. Man is "The Animal that Laughs." But so does the monkey, as Mr. Darwin pointed out; and so does the Australian bird that is called the laughing jackass. No—Man is the Animal that Blushes. He is the only one that does it—or has occasion to.

At the head of this article we see how "three monks were burnt to death" a few days ago, and a prior "put to death with atrocious cruelty." Do we inquire into the details? No; or we should find out that the prior was subjected to unprintable multilations. Man—when he is a North American Indian—gouges out his prisoner's eyes; when he is King John, with a nephew to render untroublesome, he uses a red-hot iron; when he is a religious zealot dealing with heretics in the Middle Ages, he skins his captive alive and scatters salt on his back; in the first Richard's time he shuts up a multitude of Jew families in a tower and sets fire to it; in Columbus's time he captures a family of Spanish Jews and—but *that* is not printable; in our day in England a man is fined ten shillings for beating his mother nearly to death with a chair, and another man is fined forty shillings for having four pheasant eggs in his possession without being able to satisfactorily explain how he got them. Of all the animals, man is the only one that is cruel. He is the only one that inflicts pain for the pleasure of doing it. It is a trait that is not known to the higher animals. The cat plays with the frightened mouse; but she has this excuse, that she does not know that the mouse is suffering. The cat is moderate—unhumanly moderate: she only scares the mouse, she does not hurt it; she doesn't dig out its eyes, or tear off its skin, or drive splinters under its nails—man-fashion; when she is done playing with it she makes a sudden meal of it and puts it out of its trouble. Man is the Cruel Animal. He is alone in that distinction.

10   The higher animals engage in individual fights, but never in organized masses. Man is the only animal that deals in that atrocity of atrocities, War. He is the only one that gathers his brethren about him and goes forth in cold blood and with calm pulse to exterminate his kind. He is the only animal that for sordid wages will march out, as the Hessians[1] did in our Revolution, and as the boyish Prince Napoleon did in the Zulu war, and help to slaughter strangers of his own species who have done him no harm and with whom he has no quarrel.

Man is the only animal that robs his helpless fellow of his country—takes possession of it and drives him out of it or destroys him. Man has done this in all the ages. There is not an acre of ground on the globe that is in possession of its rightful owner, or that has not been taken away from owner after owner, cycle after cycle, by force and bloodshed.

Man is the only Slave. And he is the only animal who enslaves. He has always been a slave in one form or another, and has always held other slaves in bondage under him in one way or another. In our day he is always some man's slave for wages, and does that man's work; and this slave has other slaves under him for minor wages, and they do *his* work. The higher animals are the only ones who exclusively do their own work and provide their own living.

Man is the only Patriot. He sets himself apart in his own country, under his own flag, and sneers at the other nations, and keeps multitudinous uniformed

---

[1] Hessians: the German auxillary soldiers brought over by the British to fight the Americans during the Revolutionary War.

assassins on hand at heavy expense to grab slices of other people's countries, and keep *them* from grabbing slices of *his*. And in the intervals between campaigns he washes the blood off his hands and works for "the universal brotherhood of man"—with his mouth.

Man is the Religious Animal. He is the only Religious Animal. He is the only animal that has the True Religion—several of them. He is the only animal that loves his neighbor as himself, and cuts his throat if his theology isn't straight. He has made a graveyard of the globe in trying his honest best to smooth his brother's path to happiness and heaven. He was at it in the time of the Caesars, he was at it in Mahomet's time, he was at it in the time of the Inquisition, he was at it in France a couple of centuries, he was at it in England in Mary's day, he has been at it ever since he first saw the light, he is at it today in Crete—as per the telegrams quoted above—he will be at it somewhere else tomorrow. The higher animals have no religion. And we are told that they are going to be left out, in the Hereafter. I wonder why? It seems questionable taste.

15   Man is the Reasoning Animal. Such is the claim. I think it is open to dispute. Indeed, my experiments have proven to me that he is the Unreasoning Animal. Note his history, as sketched above. It seems plain to me that whatever he is he is *not* a reasoning animal. His record is the fantastic record of a maniac. I consider that the strongest count against his intelligence is the fact that with that record back of him he blandly sets himself up as the head animal of the lot: whereas by his own standards he is the bottom one.

In truth, man is incurably foolish. Simple things which the other animals easily learn, he is incapable of learning. Among my experiments was this. In an hour I taught a cat and a dog to be friends. I put them in a cage. In another hour I taught them to be friends with a rabbit. In the course of two days I was able to add a fox, a goose, a squirrel and some doves. Finally a monkey. They lived together in peace; even affectionately.

Next, in another cage I confined an Irish Catholic from Tipperary, and as soon as he seemed tame I added a Scotch Presbyterian from Aberdeen. Next a Turk from Constantinople; a Greek Christian from Crete; an Armenian; a Methodist from the wilds of Arkansas; a Buddhist from China; a Brahman from Benares. Finally, a Salvation Army Colonel from Wapping. Then I stayed away two whole days. When I came back to note result, the cage of Higher Animals was all right, but in the other there was but a chaos of gory odds and ends of turbans and fezzes and plaids and bones and flesh—not a specimen left alive. These Reasoning Animals had disagreed on a theological detail and carried the matter to a Higher Court.

One is obliged to concede that in true loftiness of character, Man cannot claim to approach even the meanest of the Higher Animals. It is plain that he is constitutionally incapable of approaching that altitude; that he is constitutionally afflicted with a Defect which must make such approach forever impossible, for it is manifest that this defect is permanent in him, indestructible, ineradicable.

I find this Defect to be *the Moral Sense*. He is the only animal that has it. It is the secret of his degradation. It is the quality *which enables him to do wrong*. It has no other office. It is incapable of performing any other function. It could never have been intended to perform any other. Without it, man could do no wrong. He would rise at once to the level of the Higher Animals.

20   Since the Moral Sense has but the one office, the one capacity—to enable man to do wrong—it is plainly without value to him. It is as valueless to him as is disease. In fact, it manifestly is a disease. *Rabies* is bad, but it is not so bad as this disease. Rabies enables a man to do a thing which he could not do when in a healthy state: kill his neighbor with a poisonous bite. No one is the better man for having rabies. The Moral Sense enables a man to do wrong. It enables him to do wrong in a thousand ways. Rabies is an innocent disease, compared to the Moral Sense. No one, then, can be the better man for having the Moral Sense. What, now, do we find the Primal Curse to have been? Plainly what it was in the beginning: the infliction upon man of the Moral Sense: the ability to distinguish good from evil; and with it, necessarily, the ability to *do* evil; for there can be no evil act without the presence of consciousness of it in the doer of it.

And so I find that we have descended and degenerated, from some far ancestor—some microscopic atom wandering at its pleasure between the mighty horizons of a drop of water perchance—insect by insect, animal by animal, reptile by reptile, down the long highway of smirchless innocence, till we have reached the bottom stage of development—namable as the Human Being. Below us—nothing. Nothing but the Frenchman.

ENGAGING the Text

1. Why does Twain believe that the "Moral Sense" would more appropriately be called a defect rather than a virtue?

2. What do Twain's experiments reveal about the effects of this human attribute?

EVALUATING the Argument

1. Why does Twain choose a point-by-point rather than a subject-by-subject method for the organization of his essay? How does this make his analysis more effective?

2. What specific words and phrases express Twain's attitude? For example, why is the title significant?

EXPLORING the Issue

1. In what way does Twain satirize and misrepresent Darwin's theory? To what extent does the mock-scientific format of the essay parody not only Darwin's conclusions, but the scientific method itself?

2. What contemporary social satirist uses parody in much the same way as Twain (for example, Jon Stewart, George Carlin, Ellen Degeneres, Gary Trudeau, Chris Rock)?

CONNECTING Different Perspectives

1. Compare Twain's "experiment" with Philip G. Zimbardo's (see "The Stanford Prison Experiment") in terms of what they reveal about human nature.

Language and Persuasion

Man does not live by words alone, despite the fact that sometimes he has to eat them.

— Adlai Stevenson

LANGUAGE SHAPES THOUGHT

Language clearly has an influence on our beliefs and actions. Those who have an interest in persuading us to believe or buy something are quite skillful in using language to persuade. Thus, if we are more aware of how others, including politicians and advertisers, use language to manipulate our behavior, the less likely it becomes that we can be deceived into acting against our own best interests.

EMOTIONALLY CHARGED LANGUAGE

Emotionally charged language is a principal means by which language affects perceptions. Basically, emotive language is designed to elicit certain feelings in an audience.

For example, imagine you saw your 3-year old child playing next to the stove, in danger of tipping over a pan of boiling water. Consider how different your reactions would sound using nonemotive language and emotive language to express your concern:

Please get away from the stove. It is dangerous to play near the stove when something is cooking. You might get burned.

My God, you're going to get burned! Get away from there!

Or consider the difference in impact of a factual and an emotive account of the same event:

Rutgers wins over Syracuse.

Rutgers clobbers Syracuse.

The sports page abounds with accounts of one team *shooting down*, *jolting*, *blasting*, *mauling*, *bombing*, or *outslugging* another team. Sportswriters purposely choose verbs that will produce the most dramatic effect, such as "the Devils submerge the Penguins." The feelings evoked in the readers are as important as the scores of the games.

CONNOTATIONS OF WORDS

The connotations of words are often far more persuasive than their explicit or primary meanings. For example, *home* connotes qualities of security, comfort, affection, and caring, which ultimately are far more persuasive in influencing perception than the simple denotative meaning of the word.

In the hands of a skilled writer, connotations can be used to arouse positive or negative emotions toward the subject. For example, think of the different feelings you would have about the following subjects depending on which words the writer used:

Youthful offender instead of juvenile delinquent

Perspire instead of sweat

Sanitation engineers instead of garbage collectors

Pass away instead of die

Full-figured instead of fat

Celebrities often change their names to avoid negative connotations or to elicit positive associations from audiences. To see how this works, compare the person's real name with his or her stage name:

Sean Combs	Diddy
Marion Morrison	John Wayne
Steveland Judkins Morris	Stevie Wonder
Marvin Lee Aday	Meat Loaf

Reginald Kenneth Dwight	Elton John
David Robert Jones	David Bowie
Demetria Gene Guynes	Demi Moore
Marshall Bruce Mathers III	Eminem

So, too, advertisers spend considerable time, money, and effort in formulating brand names for products that are designed to trigger favorable connotations. The fashion and cosmetics industries take great care in naming their products. Plain brown carpeting might be marketed as Coffee Buff, Berber Beige, or Plantation Amber. Likewise, red lipstick might be marketed under the brand names Red, Hot and Blue, Fire and Ice, or Roseberry. In automotive advertising, car names play an important role in manipulating the emotions of the car-buying public. To appeal to the need for status, cars are named Regal, Le Baron, and Grand. To conjure up places where the wealthy congregate, cars are named Riviera, Monte Carlo, and Fifth Avenue. To evoke feelings of freedom, uninhibited expression, and power, cars take on real and mythological animal names such as Mustang, Cougar, Firebird, and Thunderbird.

Sometimes, brand names can take on unintended negative connotations, especially when product names are translated into other languages to be marketed in other countries. Occasionally, the original English name takes on entirely different connotations in a different culture. For example, in "What's in a Name?" David A. Ricks points out that Ford's Pinto was introduced in Brazil under its English name. After Ford discovered that Pinto in Portuguese slang meant "a small male appendage," the company changed the car's name to Corcel (*horse* in Portuguese). In another case, a foreign company introduced its chocolate concoction with the unappetizing English name of Zit. To avoid such negative connotations, companies often conduct extensive research to produce names like Kodak and Exxon that can be pronounced but have no specific meanings in any language.

EUPHEMISMS

Euphemism comes from Greek ("to speak well of" or "to use words of good omen"). Originally these words were used to placate the gods.

Euphemistic language is used to smooth things over, present activities in a more favorable light, and make things seem better than they are. More commonly, euphemisms are used to avoid taboo subjects. For example, in ancient Greece, baby boys were encouraged to call their genitals their "kokko," their "laloo," or their "lizard." Roman nannies taught little girls to call their genitals their "piggy." In the nineteenth century, Victorians used a wide range of euphemisms to avoid explicit references to sex, birth, and bodily functions. Trousers were called "unmentionables," sexual organs became "private parts," and the birth of a baby became the arrival of "the little stranger" or "the patter of tiny feet."

Today, poverty has replaced sex and bodily functions as a taboo subject. The use of euphemisms to disguise reality is the basis of this observation:

> I used to think I was poor. Then they told me I wasn't poor, I was needy. They told me it was self-defeating to think of myself as needy, I was deprived. Then they told me underprivileged was overused. I was disadvantaged. I still don't have a dime. But I have a great vocabulary.
>
> —*Jules Feiffer, quoted in* Safire's Political Dictionary

A principal subject of euphemisms is death, whose implacable reality has been skirted by such phrases as the following: to go to a better place, cash in one's chips, to croak, go to the hereafter, meet the grim reaper, bite the dust, pass out of the picture, slip away.

In fact, the systematic use of language to mask the reality of death has been the subject of satiric novels like Evelyn Waugh's *The Loved One* and exposés like Jessica Mitford's *The American Way of Death*. In this profession, the word *coffin* has long since been displaced by the term *casket,* a shroud is called a "slumber robe," and the room in which the dead body is viewed is called the "slumber room" or the "reposing room."

In all these cases, euphemisms are designed to foster favorable perceptions, or at least neutralize unfavorable ones.

Questions for Discussion and Writing

1. Why are disabilities and impairments called challenges?

2. What are the connotations of the following terms, and how are they intended to alter perceptions? politically correct, new right, liberal, pro-life, pro-choice, neocon

3. How are the connotations of key terms in the following intended to influence the audience's responses?

> Jones is now ready for casketing (this is the present participle of the verb "to casket"). In this operation his right shoulder should be depressed slightly "to turn the body a bit to the right and soften the appearance of lying flat on the back." Positioning the hands is a matter of importance and special rubber positioning blocks may be used. The hands should be cupped for a more life like, relaxed appearance. Proper placement of the body requires a delicate sense of balance. It should lie as high as possible

in the casket, yet not so high that the lid, when lowered, will hit the nose. On the other hand, we are cautioned, placing the body too low "creates the impression that the body is in a box." Jones is next wheeled into the appointed slumber room where a few last touches may be added—his favorite pipe placed in his hand or, if he was a great reader, a book propped into position. (In the case of Little Master Jones a Teddy bear may be clutched.)

— *Jessica Mitford, "Mortuary Solaces,"* American Way of Death *(1963)*

4. Decipher the stated versus the implied meaning of the language of a classified ad for an apartment, (e.g., cozy = small), job, or car, or a personal ad.

SLANTING

Information that is edited to reflect a particular point of view is referred to as being *slanted*. Slanting can take the form of selecting facts to purposely mislead, quoting out of context, or presenting facts in a biased way. We might easily accept these biased characterizations without thinking them through. For example, *question-begging epithets* like *flaming liberal* or *arch conservative* attempt to slip value judgments past the reader disguised as objective descriptions.

Slanting can also result from apparently innocuous word choices, or use of quotation marks around a word or exclamation points that draw special attention!!!

People employ a subtle form of slanting when they use words like *nothing but, only, just, mere, little more than, nothing more than*, or some other disparaging qualifier. For example, "her speech was *mere* rhetoric," "he is *only* an adolescent," "she's *just* a freshman," or "she's *little more than* a secretary."

LABELS THAT STEREOTYPE

How a person or event is labeled influences the readers' or listeners' perception of what is being described. Labels can be damaging because they classify people in ways that stereotype or stigmatize. The label creates a stereotyped picture that portrays the person only in terms of a single trait. Perhaps the most dangerous thing about stereotypes is that they create a mind-set that makes it impossible to accept people as they really are. Stereotypes distort our perception and make it impossible to acknowledge experiences that conflict with the stereotypes. Research shows that if your expectations about members of an entire group are shaped by a stereotyped view, you are more likely to disregard contradictory evidence in order to avoid giving up the stereotype.

Labels act as filters to screen out everything that does not confirm the stereotype. For example, let's say you were asked to complete any of the following statements:

1. Southerners are . . . Easterners are . . .

2. Texans are . . . Hairdressers are . . .

3. Rock stars are . . . Football players are . . .

Each completed statement reveals one of your attitudes or beliefs. If you were then asked to write down whatever experiences you have had that justify or explain this attitude, you might discover that your ideas are based much more on portrayals and labels conveyed by the media than on your own personal experiences.

One of the most interesting studies of how proper names (literally, how we are labeled) evoke stereotypes that operate without our being aware of them was conducted by Gordon W. Allport in *The Nature of Prejudice:*

Thirty photographs of college girls were shown on a screen to 150 students. The subjects rated the girls on a scale from one to five for *beauty, intelligence, character, ambition, general likability.* Two months later the same subjects were asked to rate the same photographs and fifteen additional ones (introduced to complicate the memory factor). This time five of the original photographs were given Jewish surnames (Cohen, Kantor, etc.), five Italian (Valenti, etc.), and five Irish (O'Brien, etc.); and the remaining girls were given names chosen from the signers of the Declaration of Independence and from the Social Register (Davis, Adams, Clark, etc.).

When Jewish names were attached to photographs there occurred the following changes in ratings:

decrease in liking

decrease in character

decrease in beauty

increase in intelligence

increase in ambition

For those photographs given Italian names there occurred:

decrease in liking

decrease in character

decrease in beauty

decrease in intelligence

Thus a mere proper name leads to prejudgments of personal attributes.

The unconscious assumptions triggered by students' names meant that each person was no longer perceived as being a complete human being. The label set up expectations that would block any conflicting new information and make it probable that only information that could be interpreted to support the preconception would be believed. It is for these reasons that all labels designed to persuade us must be carefully identified and analyzed.

SEXIST, RACIST, AND AGIST LANGUAGE

One form discriminatory labeling takes is sexist language, that is, any language that expresses a stereotyped attitude that presumes the inherent superiority of one sex over the other. As with other kinds of labeling, people placed in the devalued categories are, by definition, stigmatized and treated as less than fully human. Although linguistic reforms have been successful in reducing sexist language, even a cursory examination of slang, metaphors, definitions, and other usages, reveals underlying attitudes about what it means to be man or woman in contemporary society. Alleen Pace Nilsen, a sociolinguist, has studied these patterns:

> Going back to what I learned from my dictionary cards, I was surprised to realize how many pairs of words we have in which the feminine words has acquired sexual connotations while the masculine word retains a serious businesslike aura. For example, a *callboy* is the person who calls actors when it is time for them to go on a stage, but a *callgirl* is a prostitute. Compare *sir* and *madam*. *Sir* is a term of respect, while *madam* has acquired the specialized meaning of a brothel manager. Something similar has happened to *master* and *mistress*. Would you rather have a painting by an old *master* or an old *mistress*?
>
> —*"Sexism in English: A 1990's Update"*

Researchers have studied how language can be used to demean women, but we must admit that sexist language cuts both ways and can be used to dehumanize and stereotype men as well. For example, Eugene R. August in "Real Men Don't, or Anti Male Bias in English," has studied how terms used to label social outcasts (such as nerd, dork, jerk) are applied almost exclusively to males. Moreover, "nearly all the words for law-breakers suggest males rather than females to most students. These words include *murderer, swindler, crook, criminal, burglar, thief*, . . . and *terrorist*."

According to Robin Lakoff in "Language and Woman's Place," the origin of these gender stereotypes begins with the very different ways in which boys and girls are socialized and the very different expectations for each sex that are reflected in their typical speech patterns: "If a little girl 'talks rough' like a boy, she will normally be ostracized, scolded, or made fun of." Lakoff concludes that this style of deference by women and assertion by men leads to lifelong inequity between the sexes.

The prospect of changing attitudes by changing language (or reflecting changed attitudes in new terminology) has resulted in the *The Government's Dictionary of Occupational Titles* replacing potentially discriminatory job titles with sex-neutral terms. For example, *telephone linemen* has been replaced by *telephone line installers*, *firemen* are now listed as *firefighters*, *airline stewardesses* are now *flight attendants*, and *policewoman* has become simply *police officer*.

Historically, stigmatization always precedes disenfranchisement. Haig A. Bosmajian in "Defining the American Indian" reminds us that:

> One of the first important acts of an oppressor is to redefine the oppressed victims he intends to jail or eradicate so that they will be looked upon as creatures warranting suppression and in some cases separation and annihilation.

Agist stereotypes, that is, the negative labels used to refer to old age, are as destructive as racist or sexist language. Referring to elderly women as *biddy* or *hag* or to elderly men as *codger, coot, geezer,* or *fogey* fosters a conception of the elderly as senile, incapable of learning new things, and antiquated. These labels promote a notion of the elderly that makes it difficult for the young and middle-aged to identify with them as human beings. Agist language encourages discriminatory reactions toward the elderly and reinforces a negative self-image among older people. The mechanisms involved are identical to those of racism (based on differences in skin color) or sexism (based on differences in gender). As in these cases, the use of dehumanizing language paves the way for discounting the elderly and treating them as second-class citizens. This issue has been studied by Frank Nuessel in "Old Age Needs a New Name but Don't Look for It in Websters," who concludes that "in this regard the extensive, perjorative, and agist vocabulary of the English language constitutes a verbal record of this society's fear of getting old."

Questions for Discussion and Writing

1. Formulate three short descriptions using neutral, negative, or positive adjectives for the postal service, the National Rifle Association, the American Civil Liberties Union, or any other defined association or organization.

2. Analyze any portion of a speech by a public official to see whether it reveals the presence of slanting, labeling, stereotyping, or guilt or virtue by association.

WORDS THAT CREATE IMAGES

The ability to create compelling images in picturesque language is an important element in communicating a writer's thoughts, feelings, and experiences. For example, consider how picturesque terms are often used by wine experts to describe different kinds of wines. A wine might be said to be *robust* or *mellow* or *round*; a beaujolais might be described as "witty" or "an amusing little wine."

The way a writer chooses to describe something expresses an opinion that is capable of persuading an audience. In the following descriptions of New Orleans each writer selects details that reinforce the dominant impression he has of the city, organizes these details in terms of his main impression, and creates a vivid word picture that allows the reader to see the city as he does. The first account relies on an objective description using denotative language:

> Here one finds the narrow streets with overhanging balconies, the beautiful wrought-iron and cast-iron railings, the great barred doors and tropical courtyards. Many of these fine houses are more than a century and a quarter old, and they stand today as monuments to their forgotten architects. For it must be remembered that New Orleans was a Latin city already a century old before it became a part of the United States; and it was as unlike the American cities along the Atlantic seaboard as though Louisiana were on another continent.
>
> — *Federal Writer's Project, "New Orleans: A City Guide" (1938)*

Contrast this with the following subjective description using connotative language:

> I alight at Esplanade in a smell of roasting coffee and creosote and walk up Royal Street. The lower Quarter is the best part. The ironwork on the balconies sags like rotten lace. Little French cottages hide behind high walls. Through deep sweating carriageways one catches glimpses of courtyards gone to jungle.
>
> — *Walker Percy, "The Moviegoer" (1961)*

In contrast to the description provided by the Federal Writer's Project, Walker Percy's account of New Orleans relies on words whose emotive effect is enhanced by his skillful use of picturesque language. The fact that Percy does not make a formal claim does not lessen the impact of this description. The word picture itself expresses his opinion. Or, consider how Fred Allen's opinion of

Hollywood is strengthened by the unusual image he creates: "You can take all the sincerity in Hollywood, place it in the navel of a fruit fly, and still have room enough for three caraway seeds and a producer's heart."

Creating a vivid picture or image in an audience's mind requires writers to use metaphors and similes (and other figures of speech). Imagery works by evoking a vivid picture in the audience's imagination. A simile compares one object or experience to another using *like* or *as*. For example, if you wrote that "on a trip home the train was crowded and the passengers were packed in like sardines," your audience would be expected to understand the idea rather than literally assume you were accompanied by sardines in the train. A metaphor applies a word or phrase to an object it does not literally denote in order to suggest the comparison. Thus, if you looked into the crowded train and yelled "Hey, you sardines," most people on the train would know what you meant.

To be effective, metaphors must look at things in a fresh light to let the reader see a familiar subject in a new way. As George Orwell observed in "Politics and the English Language," "The sole aim of a metaphor is to call up a visual image." When they are first conceived, metaphors can call up pictures in the mind, but worn-out metaphors lack the power to summon these images. What is meant by an effective metaphor can be illustrated by two short descriptions drawn from Henry Allen's "The Corps." In describing the Marine Corps drill instructors, Allen notes "the wry ferocity drill instructors cultivate, the squinted eyes and the mouth about as generous as a snapping turtle's, and the jut-jawed arrogance of their back-of-the throat voices."

Of one particularly feared drill instructor, Allen writes, "He is seething, he is rabid, he is wound up tight as a golf ball, with more adrenalin surging through his hypothalmus than any cornered slum rat. . . ." And, of the new recruits, Allen comments "fat and forlorn, they look like 60 sex perverts trapped by a lynch mob."

Questions for Discussion and Writing

1. How might you complete any of the following, using positive or negative analogies to persuade an audience of the benefits or disadvantages of the proposed action? Develop the thought as an extended simile that expresses your feelings. Add the phrase "is like" after each of the topics you choose.

   a. Screening roommates

   b. Making up your own personal ad to meet someone to date or a classified ad to sell something

   c. Sleep deprivation

    d.   Living together before marriage

    e.   Writing your résumé

    f.   Being interviewed for a job

    g.   Having your best friend get married

2.   Try your hand at composing a personal ad for yourself. What aspects of your personality would the ad emphasize? You might consider switching among class members and then trying to guess who wrote which ad.

SLANG

"I have seen the future and it is slang."

—Eric Overmeyer On the Verge

A particularly vivid, playful, and ephemeral form of picturesque language is called *slang*. Slang does not take itself seriously, and expresses itself in down-to-earth, direct idioms. Many slang expressions use picturesque language metaphorically. For example, consider the range of terms used to describe drinking too much:

bombed, blotto, zonked, plastered, tanked, juiced, hung over, tight, tipsy, smashed

How slang is created can be seen in the origin of the the term *hype* (hyping a movie, product, book). The term originated as a turn-of-the-century abbreviation for a hypodermic needle. *Hype* gradually lost its connection with an actual hypodermic needle but retained the idea of injecting or infusing. Today, it refers to artificially stimulated public relations phenomena designed to generate publicity and sales.

CLICHÉS

Words that, through overuse lose their power to evoke concrete images become clichés. A cliché is a trite, time-worn expression or outworn phrase that has become commonplace or lost its freshness. Initially, each of the following descriptions of mental deficiency probably seemed quite inventive the first time it was used:

not playing with a full deck, out to lunch, not the sharpest tool in the shed

The fact that these clichés are used so much has made them predictable. Metaphors that are no longer relevant, stereotyped expressions, and overused idioms no longer have the ability to conjure up an image in the hearer's mind. They have been used so often that they become a ready-made way of substituting a phrase to avoid thinking, as in the following list of clichés about money:

> as sound as a dollar, it's money in the bank, a penny for your thoughts, put your two cents in, as good as gold

Some clichés depend on effects of alliteration and rhyming to produce sets of words that are easy to remember: bag and baggage, wishy washy, safe and sound, high and dry, fair and square, and wear and tear. Other clichés use two words where one would be sufficient: ways and means, null and void. Still other clichés are really overused similes:

> clean as a whistle, cool as a cucumber, fit as a fiddle, flat as a pancake, free as a bird, fresh as a daisy, light as a feather, quiet as a mouse, slippery as an eel

An even greater sin than using stale metaphors is using them incorrectly, as John Simon complained of the film critic, Rex Reed:

> Reed's brain is incapable of grasping how metaphors work. In perusing some of Reed's pieces in *Vogue* I came upon some truly remarkable formulations. For example: "the note of reigning terror is struck in the first scene (a dull woman's body is being examined by a Fascist doctor)." A dull corpse? How many witty ones has Reed known? But a corpse so dull as to strike a note of terror? That *is* dull, even for a corpse.
>
> —*John Simon, "Why Reed Can't Write"*

ABSTRACT AND CONCRETE LANGUAGE

Abstract and concrete language plays a crucial role in argument. Concrete words refer to actual things, instances, or experiences. By contrast, writers need abstractions to generalize about experience and discuss qualities or characteristics apart from specific objects or to sum up the qualities of whole classes of things. For example, we have been using the term *warrant* to refer to the rules or principles that allow conclusions to be connected to evidence. The term is used to convey an abstract idea. Yet, the term *warrant* originally referred to a literal document (as in arrest *warrant* or search *warrant*) that gave the possessor authority to take an action. In this book, the term *warrant* preserves the essential idea—of justifying an action (in argument, drawing a conclusion) by referring to a particular principle that authorizes connecting evidence to a claim.

Without being able to call on abstractions with which to generalize we would find ourselves in a situation similar to the one described by Jonathan Swift in Book III ("Voyage to Laputa") of *Gulliver's Travels* (1727). There, Gulliver, on a visit to a "school of languages," learns of a "Scheme for Entirely Abolishing All Words Whatsoever." The rationale behind this unlikely enterprise is that "since words are only names for things, it would be more convenient for all men to carry about them, such things as were necessary to express the particular business they are to discourse on." Thus, instead of speaking, citizens would carry sacks filled with the physical objects about which they wished to converse, and a "conversation" would appear as follows:

> If a man's business be very great and of various kinds, he must be obliged in proportion to carry a greater bundle of Things upon his back unless he can afford one or two strong servants to attend him. I have often beheld two of those sages almost sinking under the weight of their packs like peddlars among us who when they meet in the streets would lay down their loads, open their sacks and hold conversation for an hour together, then put up their implements, help each other to resume their burdens and take their leave.

This amusing caricature of a conversation without speech dramatizes the disadvantages of being unable to use abstractions to symbolize qualities or express ideas.

Arguments are frequently misunderstood because key terms evoke entirely different specifics (or referents) for the writer than they do for the audience. The chances for communicating improve if the writer attempts to discover what the key terms in the argument actually mean to the audience. Although it would be quite literally impossible to think without being able to generalize, it is clear that any argument requires a balance between the use of abstract terms to make generalizations and concrete or literal terms to provide supporting details and evidence.

Concrete terms provide specific details that allow the writer to focus the audience's attention on all the particulars of the case on which generalizations are based. Without a specific frame of reference and supporting details, examples, and anecdotes, abstract terms can be used to conceal rather than to reveal and clarify. A historian, Arthur Schlesinger Jr., observed that the use of abstractions in politics has long been a problem:

> So words, divorced from objects, became instruments less of communication than of deception. Unscrupulous orators stood abstractions on their head and transmuted them into their opposites, aiming to please one faction by the sound

and the contending faction by the meaning. They did not always succeed. "The word *liberty* in the mouth of Webster," Emerson wrote with contempt after the Compromise of 1850, "sounds like the word *love* in the mouth of a courtezan." Watching Henry Kissinger babbling about his honor at his famous Salzburg press conference, one was irresistibly reminded of another of Emerson's nonchalant observations: "The louder he talked of his honor, the faster we counted our spoons."

— *Arthur Schlesinger Jr., "Politics and the American Language"*

JARGON

An important kind of language often encountered in arguments within specialized fields is jargon. Basically, jargon is the specialized language of a trade, field, or profession. It provides a shorthand way of quickly communicating a lot of information. For example, in publishing, horror stories combined with romantic melodrama are called "creepy weepys," and historical romances filled with sex and violence to stimulate sales are known as "bodice rippers." In police work, officers refer to confiscated drug money as "dead presidents."

The word *jargon* comes from the fifteenth-century French term *jargoun*, (twittering or gibberish). In its original context, *jargoun* referred to the secret language criminals used to communicate with each other without being understood by the authorities.

Each academic discipline has its own specialized language used by insiders to facilitate communication. For example, financial services use the term "big bang" to mark the launch of a major project, and anyone getting a home mortgage discovers that the term "closing costs" means the fees and expenses owed to the lender. Applicants to law school may receive a "hold letter" that informs them that they are still under consideration. In writers' jargon the phrase "on spec" means submitting a manuscript without an invitation to do so. Some terms that have an ordinary meaning acquire a specialized significance when used within a particular profession. For example, in lumberjack jargon the term "barber chair" refers to a tree that splits upward along the grain as it falls. Other terms make sense only in the context of a particular field. For example, in baseball a count of three balls and two strikes is referred to as a "full count" and in computer jargon the term "blog" refers to a Web log, or publicly accessible personal journal that is usually updated daily.

One of the drawbacks of jargon is that it can be used to prevent outsiders from understanding the inner workings of a particular trade or profession and to justify exorbitant costs. For example, in exposés of procurement costs of the military, a thirteen cent ordinary steel nut is described as a "hexiform rotatable surface compression unit" and costs $2,043 for one (cited in William Lutz's *Doublespeak*).

THE ETHICAL DIMENSION OF PERSUASION

As we will see in our examination of the methods advertisers use to influence consumers (chapter 8), ethical questions are implicit in every act of persuasion. For example, what are we to make of a persuader whose objectives in seeking to influence an audience may be praiseworthy but who consciously makes use of distorted facts or seeks to manipulate an audience by playing on their known attitudes, values, and beliefs? Is success in persuasion the only criterion or should we hold would-be persuaders accountable to some ethical standards of responsibility about the means they use to achieve specific ends? Perhaps the most essential quality in determining whether any act of persuasion is an ethical one depends on the writer maintaining an open dialogue with different perspectives that might be advanced on a particular issue. By contrast, any act of persuasion that intentionally seeks to avoid self-criticism or challenges from competing perspectives will come across as insincere, dogmatic, deceptive, and defensive. The desire to shut down debate or control an audience's capacity to respond to the argument might well be considered unethical. The consequence of this attitude may be observed in the arguer's use of fraudulent evidence, illogical reasoning, emotionally laden irrelevant appeals, simplistic representation of the issue, or the pretense of expertise. Standards to apply when judging the ethical dimension in any act of persuasion require us to consider whether any element of coercion, deception, or manipulation is present. This becomes especially true when we look at the relationship between propaganda as a form of mass persuasion and the rhetorical means used to influence large groups of people.

PROPAGANDA: THE LANGUAGE OF DOUBLESPEAK

Ultimately, it is the intention with which words are used that determines whether any of the techniques already discussed, such as slanting, labeling, and emotionally loaded language, pose a political danger. Of themselves, strategies of persuasion are neither good nor bad; it is the purpose for which they are employed that make them unethical and offensive. For this reason, the misuse of techniques of rhetorical persuasion have been decried throughout the ages. Aldous Huxley in "Propaganda Under a Dictatorship" discussed how the manipulation of language through propaganda techniques in Nazi Germany conditioned thoughts and behavior. Some of the key techniques identified by Huxley included the use of slogans, unqualified assertions, and sweeping generalizations. Huxley notes that

Hitler had said "all effective propaganda must be confined to a few bare necessities and then must be expressed in a few stereotyped formulas. . . . Only constant repetition will finally succeed in imprinting an idea upon the memory of a crowd." Hitler knew that any lie can seem to be the truth if it is repeated often enough. Repeated exposure encourages a sense of acceptance and familiarity with the slogan. Hitler's use of propaganda required that all statements be made without qualification.

George Orwell commented frequently on the dangers posed by political propaganda. In his novel *1984*, he coined the term *doublespeak* to show how political language could be used to deceive, beg the question, and avoid responsibility.

Doublespeak can take forms that can range from the innocuous, such as Lt. Colonel Oliver North's intention to give "a non-visual slide show" (cited in *Quarterly Review of Doublespeak*), to the deceptive and dangerous, such as the Pentagon's reference to the neutron bomb as "an efficient nuclear weapon that eliminates an enemy with a minimum degree of damage to friendly territory." Or consider a statement by the U.S. Army that "we do not call it 'killing,' we call it 'servicing the target.' " In each of these cases, language is used against itself to distort and manipulate rather than to communicate.

INTENSIFYING AND DOWNPLAYING: STRATEGIES FOR PERSUASION

One of the most valuable ways of analyzing forms of public persuasion was suggested by Hugh Rank ("Teaching About Public Persuasion: Rationale and a Schema"). Rank observed that all acts of public persuasion are variations of what he terms *intensifying* and *downplaying*.

Persuaders use intensifying and downplaying in the following ways: (1) to intensify, focus on, or draw attention to anything that would strengthen their case; (2) to intensify, focus on, or draw attention to anything that would weaken their opponent's arguments; (3) to downplay, dismiss, or divert attention from any weak points that would make their case look bad; and (4) to downplay, dismiss, or divert attention from anything that would make their opponent's case look good.

What is meant by intensifying and downplaying can be seen by comparing the words a country uses to refer to actions of the enemy (by intensifying) with those words it uses to describe its own identical activities (by downplaying):

INTENSIFYING	DOWNPLAYING
Bombing	Air Support
Spying	Intelligence Gathering
Invasion	Pacification

Infiltration	Reinforcement
Retreat	Strategic Withdrawal

The calculated manipulation and conditioning of thought and behavior by propaganda experts is now a fact of everyday life. Professional persuaders have an unequal advantage over those whom they seek to influence and persuade. By contrast, the average citizen has never received any training in critically examining the various techniques professional persuaders use.

The three basic techniques of intensification are (1) repetition, (2) association, and (3) composition.

REPETITION   Slogans, unqualified assertions, and sweeping generalizations seem more true if they are constantly repeated. Much of commercial advertising is built on the repetition of slogans, product logos, and brand names. Political campaigns rely on repetition of candidates' names and messages over the airwaves, on the Internet, and on posters and bumper stickers.

ASSOCIATION   Intensifying by association is a technique that is also known as virtue (or guilt) by association. This strategy depends on linking an idea, person, or product with something already loved or admired (or hated and despised) by the intended audience. That is, an idea, person, or product is put into a context that already has an emotional significance for the intended audience. Once market researchers discover the needs and values of a target audience, political campaigns and advertising for commercial products can exploit the audience's needs by linking their idea, candidate, or product to values already known to appeal to the audience. Much of advertising exploits this technique of correlating feelings and emotions with purchasable objects.

COMPOSITION   A message gains intensity when it is arranged in a clearly perceivable pattern. Arranging the message can rely on the traditional rhetorical patterns (comparison and contrast, cause and effect, process analysis, classification, analogy, narration, description, and exemplification) as well as inductive or deductive logic or any other distinctive way of grouping the elements of the message.

The three basic techniques of downplaying are (1) omission, (2) diversion, and (3) confusion.

OMISSION   If persuaders wish to downplay, or divert attention away from, an issue that is felt to be potentially damaging to their purposes, they can use the opposite of each of the intensifying techniques. If repetition is an effective way to intensify, persuaders can downplay by omitting, biasing, or slanting. Omissions can range from euphemisms that downplay serious issues to acts of overt censorship.

DIVERSION   Just as persuaders intensify by associating, they can downplay by diverting attention through an emphasis on unimportant or unrelated side issues. Many of these tactics (discussed in the section on Logical Fallacies) include the *red herring, nonsequitur, straw man, argumentum ad hominem, argumentum ad populum, argumentum ad misericordiam* (or *appeal to pity*), *argumentum ad baculum* (or *appeal to force*), *circular reasoning* (or *begging the question*), and *appeal to ignorance*. All these techniques are used to divert or distract attention from the main issues to peripheral or entirely unrelated issues.

CONFUSION   Just as a message gains intensity when it is well-structured and coherent, so persuaders can downplay by using a variety of techniques designed to obscure or cloud the points at issue. These techniques include the calculated use of faulty logic, including the *fallacy of complex question, false dilemma, false cause, post hoc, slippery slope*, and *faulty analogy*. Downplaying via confusion also results from the use of ambiguous terms or phrases as in the fallacies of *equivocation* and *accent*, as well as the use of bureaucratese, medicalese, legalese, pentagonese, and all other jargons used to obscure the real issues.

We should realize that all these strategies of intensifying and downplaying can take place *simultaneously* during any attempt to persuade.

To see how this works in practice, we can apply the "intensifying/downplaying" schema to "The Case of the Non-Unanimous Jury" by Charles Sevilla and "Justice Can Be Served Despite Dissenting Votes" by Robert E. Jones (reprinted later in this chapter). The point at issue is whether unanimous juries are necessary to the process of reaching fair verdicts. Sevilla *intensifies the virtues of his argument* by using the movie *Twelve Angry Men* to dramatically illustrate how the need for a unanimous verdict compels juries to review facts and evidence carefully. Sevilla uses this classic movie to illustrate his claim that the current system offers a better chance for a correct result by offering dissenters the opportunity to argue points in testimony that other jurors may have missed.

At the same time, Sevilla *intensifies negative aspects of his opponent's* (Jones's) *argument* by arguing that despite the current system, innocent people are still convicted; therefore, eliminating the requirement for unanimous verdicts (as Jones recommends) would lead to more mistaken convictions. Sevilla also claims that removing the need for dissenting jurors to justify their decisions would compromise a crucial element of our justice system. Simultaneously, Sevilla *downplays points on which his case might be vulnerable* by claiming that hung juries are statistically such a small fraction of all cases that they do not warrant changing the system and losing the benefits of a unanimous verdict. At the same time, he concedes that the requirements for unanimity can lead to inconclusive results but asserts that no verdict is better than an erroneous one. Last, he *downplays what might be seen as a positive point for the other side* by suggesting that if Jones is so interested in saving money, trials might be done away with altogether (*reductio ad absurdum*).

By contrast, Jones, arguing the opposite position, *intensifies the virtues of his own argument* by citing his own twenty years' experience as a trial judge overseeing civil cases where verdicts were reached by ten out of twelve jurors, and not one person convicted by a nonunanimous jury was later found to be innocent. Jones also aids his case by presenting an accurate summary of Sevilla's argument thereby enhancing his credibility as a thoughtful and objective person taking the opponent's position into account. Jones *intensifies weak points of Sevilla's argument* by asserting that trials may be aborted by one or two kook jurors whose irrationality does not blossom until after the jury is locked up for deliberations.

At the same time, Jones *downplays points on which he might be vulnerable* by failing to mention that the mock trials set up to compare unanimous with nonunanimous verdicts were not designed to test for the blossoming of kook jurors. Last, he *downplays what might be seen as good points of his opponent's argument* by arguing that Henry Fonda notwithstanding, it is improbable that one juror could convince eleven others, as is depicted in *Twelve Angry Men*. Jones also *downplays or undercuts his opponent's claim* that hung juries are infrequent by citing research and mock trials to prove that hung juries happen often enough to justify judicial reform.

Questions for Discussion and Writing

1. Locate coverage of a recent event in the school or a local newspaper and analyze how the event was depicted. What features were ignored, and what features were focused on and intensified? To what extent were differences in reporting due to a different agenda on the part of the reporter or the audience for whom the report was written?

2. Analyze the effect of a photograph in a newspaper or magazine that played an important role in shaping public response toward a natural disaster, war, or famine.

Two Short Arguments for Analysis

Charles Sevilla

The Case of the Non-Unanimous Jury

Charles Sevilla is a former Chief Deputy Public Defender for the state of California who now practices trial law in San Diego. Sevilla believes the number of cases reaching trial that result in hung juries is so small that it doesn't warrant losing the benefits of a unanimous verdict. The article first appeared in the January 23, 1983, issue of the Los Angeles Times.

Thinking Critically

Consider why the jury system lends itself to dramatic treatment in films and television programs.

One of Henry Fonda's most memorable roles was as one of *Twelve Angry Men* selected to determine the fate of a young Puerto Rican accused of murdering his father. They were angry because the majority's quest for a speedy verdict of guilty was frustrated by Fonda's lone vote for acquittal. Without unanimity, a verdict could not be returned, and the other jurors, anxious to get home to dinner or out to a ballgame, were furious.

In real life, the lone dissenting juror on a first ballot almost always succumbs to the pressure and joins ranks to return a verdict. Fonda's character was different. He convinced the others to pause long enough to discuss the evidence and hear him out. After all, he said, the defendant, a slum youth, had been ignored most of his life. The jury owed him some time for a just verdict.

In the next 90 tension-filled minutes Fonda argued the importance of subtle points of testimony that the others had missed; he proved that the murder weapon, a knife, was not as distinctive as the prosecutor had insisted; he pointed out lapses in the defense attorney's presentation, all the while importuning the others to reach a verdict through reason rather than emotion. One by one, the others came around to join him, the last capitulating only when his underlying motivation was revealed—the defendant reminded him of his wayward son.

Hollywood melodrama though it was, the film's depiction of a jury struggling to do its duty is a rare illustration of unanimity's function in the difficult job of jury decisionmaking.

5   Perhaps nothing epitomizes the concept of American liberty as well as the right to a trial by a jury. The jury is one of a handful of institutions that allow individual citizens, not government, to make important societal decisions. A crucial component of the jury trial is the rule that verdicts be unanimous.

It has always been the rule in federal criminal trials, in the overwhelming majority of states.

Critics of the right to a unanimous verdict in serious criminal cases see it as a costly medieval relic. Los Angeles new district attorney, Robert Philobosian, is the latest to join the chorus. He wants the verdict requirement shrunk from 12 jurors to 10 (in all but capital cases) so that one or two people will not be able to force a retrial.

Hung Juries

The costs of hung juries do not warrant losing the benefits of the unanimous verdict. Statistically, jury trials play a minor role in the criminal-justice system. The vast majority of defendants plead guilty and have no trial. In 1981, only about 7 percent of accused felons had jury trials. The incidence of hung juries is thus but a fraction of the already small fraction of cases that go to trial.

Some money undoubtedly could be saved by such a reform. Even more could be saved by abolishing jury trials altogether.

That juries occasionally are deadlocked does not demonstrate a flaw in our criminal-justice system. Our concept of justice does not require juries to decide every case. Hung juries usually occur when the case is close—that is, when neither side has presented convincing evidence. Further, juries that wind up deadlocked with one or two members in dissent usually start with a more substantial minority of four or five which indicates that the evidence is not clear-cut.

10   Even though the requirement of unanimity may lead to an inconclusive result from time to time, no verdict is better than a wrong one. Despite the protection of unanimous verdicts, we still manage to convict some innocent people each year. Eliminating the unanimity requirement would only increase the opportunity for mistakes. Unanimity guarantees give-and-take among jurors and filters out the biases of individuals. It makes the ultimate decision truly reflective of the community. Most important, it provides a better chance that the result will be correct by affording a counterbalance to the state's inherent advantages, such as the jurors' subconscious presumption that a defendant who is on trial must be guilty.

Consider what would have happened if the decision in *Twelve Angry Men* could have been made by 10 jurors instead of 12. After the first ballot, the 11 who voted "guilty" could have put an end to the deliberations, without having to listen to Fonda.

What could be more fundamental to justice than verdicts that can be trusted and respected? If even one juror has doubts, that is enough to undermine society's confidence that a proper verdict has been reached.

ENGAGING the Text

1. Why does Sevilla believe that even though "juries occasionally are deadlocked," this "does not demonstrate a flaw in our criminal-justice system"?

2. Why does Sevilla believe that keeping the existing system, which requires all twelve jurors to agree on a verdict, is superior to adopting a system that would allow a verdict to be reached if only ten of the twelve jurors agreed?

EVALUATING the Argument

1. How does Sevilla use the classic film *Twelve Angry Men* to illustrate his thesis? What events occur in this film that underscore his central point? How does his use of a worst-case scenario in the next-to-last paragraph dramatize what the consequences would be if the proposed reforms were enacted?

2. How does Sevilla use statistical evidence about the percentage of hung juries to support his argument? How does this portion of his argument depend on the tactic of *reductio ad absurdum* or extrapolating the opposite view to an illogical extreme in order to refute it?

EXPLORING the Issue

1. In an essay, evaluate the assumptions underlying Sevilla's argument. Points to consider include: (a) whether lone dissenting jurors should have the opportunity to argue subtle points in testimony that other jurors may have missed, (b) whether one juror's doubt is sufficient to raise the question of whether a proper verdict has been reached, and (c) whether the current requirement of unanimity encourages dissenting jurors to support their opinions and disclose possible biases or prejudices that may have influenced their reasoning. If dissenting jurors did not have to justify their decisions, would the justice system suffer as Sevilla claims?

2. What famous cases or verdicts (such as the eleven-to-one May 3, 2006 decision to imprison for life rather than execute the convicted terrorist Zacharias Moussaoui) illustrate the virtues or defects of the present system?

CONNECTING Different Perspectives

1. Look at Sevilla's proposal through Jean-Paul Sartre's framework in "Existentialism" in terms of each individual being expected to take responsibility.

Robert E. Jones

Justice Can Be Served Despite Dissenting Votes

Robert E. Jones has served as a criminal-felony trial judge for over twenty years on the Oregon Supreme Cout. Jones draws on his extensive experience on the bench to argue that the present system ought to be reformed to include nonunanimous verdicts where only ten out of the twelve jurors have to agree. This article originally appeared in the January 23, 1983, issue of the Los Angeles Times.

Thinking Critically

Do you think that the jury system is fair as it stands?

After sitting for 20 years as a criminal-felony trial judge in Oregon, where jurors in all but first-degree murder cases are allowed to return a verdict if 10 out of 12 agree, I believe that such a system delivers fair, if not perfect justice to both the state and the defendant. In my experience, no one who was convicted by a nonunanimous jury later was shown to have been innocent.

While unanimous verdicts are still required in federal trials, the U.S. Supreme Court ruled in 1972 that the Constitution does not require them in state trials.

Those who are opposed to allowing nonunanimous verdicts in criminal trials base their arguments on several assumptions: that the views of the minority will be given less consideration and that there will be less opportunity for persuasion, that jurors will be less inclined to engage in "earnest and robust argument" to quote the late U.S. Supreme Court Justice William O. Douglas; that there will be a less thorough examination of the facts; that jurors will not be as likely to review as much of the testimony or adhere as carefully to the judge's instructions and that the deliberations will be shorter, thereby making it easier to jump to conclusions.

Unfortunately for those who make such arguments, there is no scientific evidence to support those claims.

5   Many people cite the example of *Twelve Angry Men*, in which Henry Fonda played a holdout juror who managed to bring around 11 bigoted or misguided jurors to a verdict for the defense. I doubt that this occurs very often in real life, but stranger things have happened.

The main argument for nonunanimous verdicts is that no matter how carefully the jury is picked, a trial in which a unanimous verdict is required may be aborted by one or two kook jurors whose irrationality does not blossom until after the jury is locked up for deliberations. I think this is a pretty convincing claim.

You have to wonder about the mentality or motives of certain jurors when you see cases, usually involving hardened criminals, in which the prosecution's witnesses remain unimpeached, the defense offers nothing and still the jury returns a guilty verdict of 11–1 or 10–2.

Experiment

In 1976, Alice Padawer-Singer and Allen Barton of Columbia University's Bureau of Applied Social Research set up an experiment with actual jurors participating in mock trials under different rules in order to compare unanimous and nonunanimous verdicts. The 23 12-member juries that were required to reach unanimous decisions returned 10 not-guilty and eight guilty verdicts with five winding up deadlocked. Of the 23 panels that were not required to reach unanimity, nine returned not-guilty verdicts, nine guilty and five deadlocked. The average deliberation time for reaching a verdict was 178 minutes for the unanimous juries and 160 minutes for the nonunanimous.

From a statistical standpoint the differences between the two groups were insignificant. In short, the study did not prove that one system was better than the other. They were indistinguishable.

10 Last year I took a random sample of 164 felony cases tried before 12-person nonunanimous juries in Portland and found that 155 had resulted in verdicts— 128 convictions and 27 acquittals. Of the convictions, 52 were unanimous, 35 were reached on a vote of 11–1 and 41 were 10–2. Of the acquittals, 9 were unanimous and 18 were split. Of those 18, seven were 11–1 and 11 were 10–2. Nine juries were deadlocked.

Chief Justice James Burns of the U.S. District Court in Oregon has had the rare opportunity to view both verdict systems in operation, first on our state court and then for the last decade on the federal trial court where unanimous verdicts are required. When I asked him to compare the two, his conclusion surprised me.

"I don't think it makes a bit of difference," he said. "A good or bad case will be spotted by either type of jury. The only difference seems to be that unanimous juries deliberate several minutes or sometimes several hours longer." He said that hung juries were rare—occurring only in about one out of 200 trials— something I have also observed in the Oregon state courts.

In sum, I believe that nonunanimous jury verdicts have no harmful consequences for our criminal-justice system. And, since such verdicts speed the jury-selection process and protect the system from irrational jurors, they provide a model that other states should follow.

ENGAGING the Text

1. Why does Jones believe, based on his personal experience as a criminal-felony trial judge, that nonunanimous jury verdicts are not incompatible with justice?

2. How does Jones draw on mock trials set up to compare unanimous with nonunanimous jury verdicts to dispute the claim that "a trial in which a unanimous verdict is required may be aborted by one or two kook jurors whose irrationality does not blossom until after the jury is locked up for deliberations"?

EVALUATING the Argument

1. How does Jones use the testimony of Chief Justice James Burns to support his claim?

2. Evaluate the design of the experiment conducted by Alice Padawer-Singer and Allen Barton in terms of how adequately it could test for the occasional irrational kook juror.

EXPLORING the Issue

1. If you were a defendent on trial for murder or any other capital crime, which jury system—unanimous or nonunanimous—would you want to judge your guilt or innocence? Discuss your reasons in an essay citing relevant arguments from either Charles Sevilla's or Jones's essays.

2. Evaluate Jones's summary of the opposing viewpoint by comparing it with the reasons Charles Sevilla presents to support his thesis. Does Jones fairly restate Sevilla's argument and its underlying assumptions?

CONNECTING Different Perspectives

1. Is Jones's rationale (that compensates for the possibility of a kook juror blossoming after deliberations have begun) consistent with Philip G. Zimbardo's findings in "The Stanford Prison Experiment"?

CHAPTER 7

WRITING AND REFUTING ARGUMENTS

OVERVIEW: This chapter provides guidance in writing effective arguments and discusses the important points of invention strategies, arriving at a thesis, adapting arguments for different audiences, using an outline, and revising a rough draft. You will be introduced to the criteria that are important in evaluating the arguments of others and writing both a critique and a refutation, illustrated by two sample student essays.

The process of writing an argumentative essay is similar to writing other kinds of essays, in that it requires you to find a subject, define your approach to the topic, establish a thesis sentence, decide on your purpose, identify your audience, plan your essay (with or without an informal outline) write a rough draft, and revise, edit, and proofread to produce a final paper.

Prewriting

The issue you choose to write about must be genuinely debatable. Rule out arguments over facts that could be settled by looking in a reference book. Also eliminate questions of personal taste. What you are looking for is an issue about which knowledgeable people disagree. The assumption is that if people who know a lot about the issue disagree, then the facts of the situation can be interpreted in different ways, and therefore that issue would make a good subject to explore in your essay.

SELECTING AN ISSUE

To get started, you might begin by listing possible topics you already know about.

Next, consider whether the issue requires research just to find out what is entailed.

To discover whether you have found a genuinely debatable topic, consider whether the same facts are open to more than one interpretation.

Genuinely debatable topics are found when people bring two competing sets of values to the same situation, perhaps without even being aware of it. Thus, a tradition of the Christmas season may have been a manger scene in front of the town hall, yet groups have protested that having such a scene on a municipally owned piece of property violates the First Amendment's "establishment clause" separating church and state. This is an emotional issue precisely because people bring competing sets of values to bear on the same set of circumstances.

Even if you are not assigned a specific subject, topics that can become sources of good arguments are all around you. All that is required is that you discover a situation that is subject to more than one interpretation and where it is probable that neither side has a lock on the truth. For example, you read about a case where strict Christian Scientists would not permit doctors to give a blood transfusion to their severely injured child. The hospital appealed to a judge, who allowed the transfusion despite the parents' religious convictions. Who made the correct decision in this case? Do you think the court was warranted in overstepping the parents' wishes?

TOPICS FOR POSSIBLE PAPERS IN THE LIBERAL ARTS, SOCIAL SCIENCES, AND SCIENCES

Any of these topics can be framed according to the academic discipline in which you are interested. For example, the topic of meditation might be framed by different disciplines, that is:

a. History would study into the tradition of meditation in different cultures through the ages.

b. Sociology would inquire into the group dynamics of meditation classes.

c. Medicine would investigate into the measurable physiological benefits in those who practice meditation on a regular basis.

1. Arguments in the Liberal arts—arguments that offer interpretations:

   ▪ Is morality absolute or relative to the social and cultural customs and mores of a particular culture?

   ▪ By what standards would you decide that unsigned paintings in an exhibition would display talent or the lack of it? Make the case for the values you would apply.

- What criteria would you apply to judge if a poem you had written was a "good" poem?
- Is it immoral to keep animals in zoos for our entertainment and edification?
- What lessons does history have to teach us about what could happen to individual rights and freedoms if genetic information is readily available to employers, insurers, schools, courts, politicians, the military, and others who make far-reaching decisions?
- Write a review of a recent movie, television program, play, concert, or book, clearly stating your criteria, and compare it to the judgments made by other reviewers.
- What characteristics define any popular form of entertainment such as westerns, detective stories, soap operas, and science fiction?
- In what contemporary works of literature are the issues of economic necessity and class differences explored most effectively?
- What current works of literature present significant insights into the relationships between men and women?
- What contemporary works of literature have contributed to your understanding how gender, class, and ethnicity have shaped the identity of any ethnic group in the United States?
- Can science coexist with faith?

2. Arguments in the social sciences—arguments that correlate behavior of individuals and groups:

- What are the social consequences of the presence of "gangs" in any major city?
- Are privately operated prisons a good idea?
- Is advertising fundamentally deceptive? Does it create insecurity in order to sell goods? Does it perpetuate stereotypes? Is it a harmful or harmless addition to our lives?
- What are the consequences of control of the media by a few giant corporations?
- Should campus newspapers publish or suppress false or misleading advertising (for example, for a book or speaker denying the Holocaust)?
- Are media portrayals of women and/or minorities still limited and stereotyped?

- Should bilingual education programs be eliminated? Does the evidence support the benefits of bilingual education?
- What might be the consequence of Asian-Americans being stereotyped as a "model minority"?
- Should parents have the right to review or approve course materials used in public schools?
- Should gays and lesbians have the right to marry and to adopt children?
- Under what conditions should physicians be allowed to assist terminally ill patients commit suicide?
- Should the United States adopt a national health care program?
- Is there a case to be made for arranged marriages?
- Should American sports teams such as the Atlanta Braves, Washington Redskins, Cleveland Indians, Florida State Seminoles, and Kansas City Chiefs take into account the concern for stereotyping expressed by Native Americans?
- Why don't 18-year-olds vote as often as other age groups do?
- Should limits be placed on the awards paid out as a result of malpractice suits?

3. Arguments in the sciences—arguments that identify and explain anomolies, and explore research questions about nature and the universe:

- How credible are theories of global warming?
- Should immunization against childhood diseases be mandatory for all children?
- The evidence for extrasensory perception is far from conclusive.
- Is there a connection linking intelligence to birth order?
- Is the evidence provided by accounts of people who have survived near-death experiences conclusive?
- What practices of the cosmetic surgery industry do you consider the most controversial?
- Should the U.S. Food and Drug Administration (FDA) suspend rules requiring extensive testing of new drugs to provide seriously ill people with immediate access to the most promising drugs and treatment?
- What direction should the exploration of space take? What considerations ought to guide this exploration?

- Are prices for pharmaceuticals unconscionably high? Are price controls justified to ensure access to essential medications (by the poor, AIDS victims, etc.)?

- Is there a case to be made that organically grown foods are better than foods that are commercially processed?

- What novels or films (for example, *Blade Runner* directed by Ridley Scott, *Jurassic Park* directed by Steven Spielberg) probe contemporary fears, anxieties, and concerns about the impact of scientific discoveries?

Invention Strategies

After selecting the issue that is most interesting to you from your list, excluding those that are too broad, are matters of fact, or are simple disagreements over personal preferences, consider whether this issue can be investigated within the amount of time you have to write about it and within the number of pages you have been assigned.

At this point, you might wish to consider any or all of the following invention strategies that have proved useful to many writers in discovering their particular aspect of a topic and how best to approach it in developing an essay. The basic invention strategies we will discuss include:

Freewriting

Five W's

Discovering different perspectives

Mapping

Writing a dialogue

FREEWRITING

Freewriting is a technique for setting down whatever occurs to you on the topic within a few minutes to a half hour. There are no restrictions whatsoever on what can or cannot be put down. Freewriting serves a sound psychological purpose. It lets you find out what you already know about the issue without imposing any editorial constraints on your thought processes. Simply free-associate everything you think of that has to do with this issue. Write without stopping to edit or correct.

For example, let's say that in your social psychology class, you read an account of the Kitty Genovese case (in which a young woman was stabbed to death while her neighbors watched and did not call the police) and have decided to try to focus on the components of the case to discover a genuinely debatable topic.

Your freewriting might appear thus:

> Why would thirty eight people ignore a woman's cries for help, maybe afraid to get involved, what were they thinking, hassles with the police, legal proceedings, open court and criminal would get off and come back and kill them, what did they say to themselves, why did they do nothing, isn't plausible that all thirty eight were apathetic, maybe each thought another called police, rationalize not doing anything wonder if the number of people has anything to do with the decision, how aware were these people of each other.

Questions for Discussion and Writing

1. To generate your own ideas for freewriting, use the following starters as lead-ins:

   My pet peeve is . . .

   I wish I could talk my (mother, father, brother, sister, boyfriend, girlfriend, professor) into . . .

   The last argument I had with someone was about . . .

   Current rules at my college require . . .; I believe they should be changed in the following way . . .

THE FIVE W's

Next, you might wish to ask and answer questions journalists often use to define what can be known about the subject.

WHO is involved in this situation?

WHAT is at stake? What action or outcome is hanging in the balance?

WHEN did the action take place?

WHERE did the action take place?

WHY is what happened an important issue?

In the Genovese case, your answers might be:

Who: Thirty eight people, Kitty Genovese, the murderer.

What: Kitty Genovese is attacked as she returns home from work at 3 A.M. Thirty eight of her neighbors in Kew Gardens, New York come to their windows when she cries out in terror. Not one comes to her assistance even though her assailant takes approximately half an hour to murder her. The murderer is twice frightened away and returns. No one so much as calls the police. She dies.

When: 1968.

Where: Apartment building in Kew Gardens, Queens, New York.

Why: Why did none of the thirty eight people help the woman or call the police at any time during the thirty five minutes? Why did the witnesses continue to look out of their windows at the scene only to ignore what was happening?

Use the five W's to analyze different elements connected with the personal experiences you have had with a particular issue. In answering "why" tell how your experience has influenced the opinions you now hold (for example, sexual harrassment, drug testing, etc.).

DISCOVERING DIFFERENT PERSPECTIVES

You can also explore your topic from different angles. This invention strategy will help you generate and develop material for your essay by looking at an issue from several perspectives. It requires you to take the topic and write for a few minutes from each of the following perspectives:

1. What is the issue connected to or related to? What does this issue bring to mind? What common elements does this situation share with other situations I am familar with?

2. What is the issue similar to or different from? What distinguishes this situation from other situations that at first glance might look very similar?

3. Analyze the different elements involved. Break the topics into its component parts. How might the same event appear through the eyes of each of the people involved? How do they relate to each other?

4. Define the issue. The purpose of defining is to try to arrive at a working definition of the topic. What are the distinctive elements in this particular situation that give it its unique quality or meaning? Try to isolate the

most important qualities of the issue and discuss what they mean. Write for a few minutes.

MAPPING

This technique allows you to visually perceive the relationship between important ideas. Begin by writing down the word or phrase that contains a key idea or represents a starting point, draw a circle around it, and when you think of related ideas, topics, or details that are connected to it, jot them down nearby and draw lines as a way of representing the connections between related ideas. When you group ideas in this way, you discover a map, or cluster, of ideas and patterns that will help you decide which ideas are central and which are subordinate. This strategy can help you narrow your topic and see details and examples that you can use to support your thesis (see Figure 7.1 below).

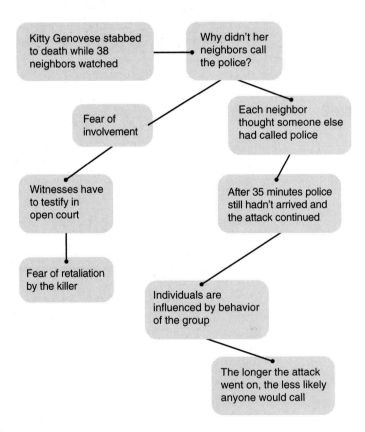

FIGURE 7.1

Computer software is also available that will allow you to organize topics and ideas into idea trees. These clusters are connected (as in Figure 7.1) to visually display the levels and relationships between ideas that a linear outline would not. But, unlike a text-based map, these software programs allow you to use icons, symbols, sounds, colors, and pictures in addition to text that can be easily modified while you are brainstorming your topic.

WRITING A DIALOGUE

Writing a dialogue is another invention strategy useful in discovering what is at stake in the issue.

To construct the dialogue, simply begin by making an assertion that expresses your view on any aspect of the issue. Then put yourself in the position of someone who had an opposing viewpoint. Next, put down what you would reply. Then challenge that view by putting yourself in the frame of mind of your opponent, who views the issue from a totally different angle or perspective. You will know you are on the right track when the dialogue assumes a momentum of its own. If you get stuck, ask yourself a question, taking the part of your opponent.

Arriving at a Thesis: Claims of Fact, Causation, Value, and Policy

It may take several tries to arrive at a clear and supportable thesis statement. Arriving at a thesis involves discovering an idea you think is important enough to serve as the focus of your essay. The thesis is stated in the form of a single sentence that asserts your personal response to an issue that others might respond to in different ways. If, for example, the issue were euthanasia, your response might be that "mercy killing, in some circumstances, is not only morally permissible but a humane course of action." Or, you might wish to assert the contrary, that "mercy killing, under any circumstances, is not morally permissible."

The thesis usually is not the first thought that springs to mind on an issue; it should not be an automatic response but rather an idea you have carefully considered. The thesis is an idea that you have arrived at by thinking through an issue or problem until you feel you have come up with an opinion capable of being substantiated with good reasons. Of course, only when you get into the actual process of writing the essay will you discover whether you have enough good reasons and supporting evidence to persuade your audience to agree with your thesis.

The thesis statement should be phrased as an assertion that makes a claim of fact (what is it?), value (is it good or bad?), causation (what caused it?), or policy (what should be done about it?). For example, the thesis statement "mercy killing, under any circumstances, is not morally permissible" expresses a value judgment that requires the writer to persuade the audience to agree with a set of moral criteria and then to judge the phenomenon of mercy killing accordingly.

Obviously, it is helpful to figure out what kind of question your thesis, and consequently your entire essay, will answer, since the methods by which your essay will be developed are keyed to the specific goal you have in mind. The kind of evidence you use and how you develop your argument will, of course, depend on your specific thesis, but here are some examples of different kinds of thesis statements along with possible ways of developing them.

1. A thesis statement that makes a *factual claim*: The material you have gathered in the prewriting and invention stages can be invaluable in helping you focus on what people argue about when they argue about that issue. When people disagree over (1) what happened, (2) what the nature of the event is, or (3) how to define a phenomenon, your argument can best be developed as a claim of fact. Your essay will explain your particular interpretation of the facts and offer evidence to support your interpretation about the nature of X. You may wish to develop your argument through comparisons or analogies that make it easy for your audience to grasp the basic nature of your subject. The first thing to do is phrase your claim as a thesis statement. For example:

> The evidence provided by the accounts of people who have survived near-death experiences is compelling but hardly conclusive proof of some form of life after death.

To develop a factual claim like this you would need to add several "because" clauses that express your own reasons for holding this view. Support for your claim might be in the form of evaluations of available accounts, anecdotal personal experience if appropriate, or theories advanced by scientists and theologians.

2. A thesis statement that makes a *causal claim*:

> Deinstitutionalization programs by the nation's hospitals is the major cause of the hundreds of thousands of homeless people wandering the streets of our major cities.

Notice how the thesis statement implies how the paper should be organized. The author would need to show what the hospital policy was before, why it was changed, and exactly what effects the change produced. It is important not to assume that your thesis statement is permanent. In this case, the writer discovered midway into the process of writing the essay that a big part of the homeless population in our big cities were the unemployed, those displaced by natural disasters, and all those who simply could not afford the price of housing. This meant that the thesis would have to be modified, restated, or perhaps even scrapped entirely.

3. A thesis statement that makes a *value claim*: Do the notes and observations from the prewriting and invention exercises suggest that when people disagree it is because they hold completely incompatible or conflicting beliefs that stem from different sets of values? If so, your essay will require that you decide which side, if any, you agree with or offer you the chance to explore the issue without trying to prove that either side is right or wrong. For example, you may assert:

> It is wrong for Hollywood stars to be treated preferentially by being allowed to work off drug sentences in community service whereas ordinary people convicted of the same crimes have to serve jail time.

Notice how this value claim could be organized around a comparison showing how Hollywood stars are treated in contrast to how ordinary people are treated who have committed the same drug-related crimes.

4. A thesis statement that makes a *policy claim*: Let's say that your prewriting observations reflected your concern with the conflict over government subsidies for tobacco companies. At the core of the argument, people disagree about the double standard of requiring health warnings while giving money to the same companies about whose products the public is being warned. You decide that instead of continuing this policy the government should simply cut off the subsidies. You might phrase your claim as follows:

> Since the federal government already requires health warnings on every pack of cigarettes, and forbids advertising of cigarettes on radio and television, tax money should not be used to subsidize tobacco growers.

When you have added "because" clauses to this claim, it will require you to support your recommendation with credible statistics, evaluations of the impact on public health, and projections as to the kinds of effects a change in government policy would produce.

A good thesis statement is like a schematic blueprint of a building that shows what the building will look like before money, effort, and time are spent on its construction. By the same token, it makes more sense to put in extra time in drafting your thesis statement than to spend extra time later extensively rewriting your entire essay, hoping that some central point or thesis will emerge.

The thesis should express the idea that you would want your audience to reach after they had read through your entire essay. Place the thesis statement in the first paragraph or group of paragraphs so that your readers will be able to evaluate each of the reasons you present to support your thesis and be better able to perceive the relationship between these reasons and the main idea of your argument.

Questions for Discussion and Writing

1. When people argue about one of the following issues, what do they disagree about?

    a. Behavior modification for stopping smoking, obesity, drinking

    b. The right-to-die issue: a dilemma for religion, law, and medicine

    c. The increase/decrease in the crime rate

    d. Psychotherapists on the radio and television: helpful or harmful?

    e. Rights of smokers versus rights of nonsmokers

    f. The FDA's drug approval procedure: careful or just bureaucratic?

    g. Socialized medicine: will it work in the United States?

    h. Should children be prosecuted as adults for serious crimes?

    i. Funeral practices: costs and methods

    j. Global warming: does it exist and if so, what are its effects?

2. Develop a workable thesis on one of the above topics or one of your own choosing. Follow this claim with several "because" clauses that express your own reasons. If you and some of your classmates have written arguments taking opposing views on the same issue, prepare a summary of your position. You might also wish to write summaries of the opposing position to see how well you understood what the other side was saying.

3. If you have trouble finding an issue about which people disagree, you might consider one of the following. To develop each claim, follow it with several "because" clauses that express your own reasons. What would an essay written along these lines need to show? How should it be organized? Think of an audience (person or group) whose opinion you would want to change.

    a. Factual arguments about the nature of things or how something should be defined:

        ▪ How have views on marriage changed over the past fifty years?

        ▪ Which professions continue to attract almost all men and which almost all women? Is there any evidence of a change?

    b. Arguments over causation:

        ▪ Can humor teach as well as entertain?

- How has the use of photography affected the perceptions of war, famine, and natural disasters?
- Why don't 18-year-olds vote as often as other age groups vote?

c. Value arguments:

- Is it morally wrong to use human fetal tissue for medical research?
- Is advertising fundamentally deceptive?
- Is surrogate mothering a form of exploitation?

d. Policy arguments over what should be done:

- Should children with disabilities be mainstreamed into regular classrooms?
- How early should the topic of AIDS be addressed in public schools?
- Is there a case to be made for arranged marriages?
- What endangered plant or animal species should be protected?
- Should profiling be allowed to combat terrorism?

Making Up an Outline: Supporting Your Claim

If you have a workable thesis that expresses the conclusion you would want your audience to reach, consider whether it is capable of being adequately supported with evidence in the form of examples, statistics, or expert testimony. An easy way to do this, and at the same time to see what the structure of the paper you intend to write will look like, is to draw up an outline before writing the rough draft. For example, an outline of a student paper on drug use, with the kinds of evidence brought in to support each idea, can appear as follows:

I. Current theories explaining widespread drug use.

—supported by evidence in the form of expert opinions by a psychologist and a sociologist

II. Increasing drug use in the success-oriented areas of sports, finance, and entertainment.

—supported by evidence of personal testimony, sports medicine experts, interviews, and surveys

III. Unsuccessful efforts of the government to stop the drug epidemic.

—supported by statistics, reports by government agencies, testimony of psychologists and lawyers, and court cases

IV. The crucial role of education in preventing drug abuse.

—supported by government-supplied statistics

Even an informal outline, as long as it sets the boundaries for different sections of your paper, will prove invaluable as a blueprint in pointing out structural weaknesses in the organization of your essay. The outline might reveal that two short partially developed sections in the argument might be better joined together as one complete, fully developed section. Likewise, your outline may disclose an overly long section that might be more effective if it were split into two or more shorter paragraphs. Check your outline to make sure your essay has covered all the important points necessary to the development of your argument.

Writing the Introduction

The function of the initial paragraph or introduction is to engage the reader in the central issue and to present your claim regarding the question at hand. If you intend to disagree with widely held views or if the nature of the issue is complex or unfamiliar to your readers, you might use the first few paragraphs to briefly summarize relevant background information before explicitly stating your thesis.

Sometimes writers find it helpful to compose the introduction first, informing readers in a straightforward way of the topic and the thesis the paper will cover. But at other times the introduction just isn't evident when they begin to write, so they proceed to subsequent paragraphs and return to the introduction later, when they have a clearer idea of the focus of the paper.

Introductions can take many forms other than a straightforward statement of the issue. They can include:

- a provocative question that challenges readers to reexamine their beliefs on a subject,

- a dramatic or amusing story or anecdote,

- a relevant quotation,

- a brief overview about the historical context,

- a striking statistic,

- a brief description of both sides of a debate, or

- a description of a central person, place, or event.

In all of these cases, the introductory paragraph should either include or relate to your thesis. Persuasive essays (ones that are arguing for a particular point) often include the thesis at the start. In contrast, analytical essays (ones that are exploring a question) may lead up to the thesis in the concluding paragraphs.

Even though your introductory paragraph is the most logical place to state your thesis, you can also put the central assertion of your essay in the title.

Lance Morrow does this in the title of his essay "Imprisoning Time in a Rectangle." The title immediately alerts the reader to Morrow's thesis that photojournalists, through pictures, influence our perception of historical events. Titles do not necessarily have to contain the writer's thesis but should refer to the subject of the essay. For example, one would surmise that Philip Wheelwright's article "The Meaning of Ethics" addresses the moral dilemas in daily life.

Writing the Middle of the Essay According to the Type of Argument

The choices open to the writer in organizing an argumentative essay depend on the nature of the thesis, the kind of claim on which the thesis is based, and most important, the anticipated attitude of the audience toward this claim. The traditional argumentative essay has three parts: the introduction, the middle, or body, and the conclusion. If the audience is inclined to agree with the writer's basic assumptions, the essay can be organized deductively, with the thesis declared at the outset; if the audience is neutral or not inclined to agree with the author's thesis, an inductive pattern of organization that arrives at the thesis after the preliminary exploration would be most effective.

This basic format can be easily modified to accommodate different kinds of arguments. For example, if the argument makes a value judgment, the introduction can describe the subject to be evaluated, provide background discussion, discuss the criteria being applied, and present the writer's opinion on the issue. In some cases, the writer may have to stipulate a meaning for key terms (such as *euthanasia*) that appear in the claim.

The middle portion of the essay presents reasons that support the value judgment with persuasive evidence that backs up the reasons. Often an evaluation essay or value argument relies on comparison to establish that something is either good or bad compared with something else. The middle portion may also contain a critical analysis of opposing value judgments along with reasons why the writer's value judgment should be accepted as more compelling.

The conclusion should allude to reasons developed within the essay and end on a note of commonality by emphasizing the concerns, values, and beliefs shared with the audience.

If the argument focuses on a causal claim, the introduction must first describe the phenomenon and demonstrate its importance for the audience by using statistics, authoritative testimony, or illustrative examples.

Keep in mind that audiences are most skeptical about "how" A could have caused B. Your argument will need to demonstrate in a persuasive way why it is likely that A could have caused or will cause B.

The main portion of the essay identifies the probable causes of a single event or chain of events, distinguishing immediate causes from those that are remote. Like other forms of argument, a causal claim requires the writer to consider alternative causes and give sound reasons for rejecting them.

The conclusion follows the pattern of other kinds of arguments. The writer concludes the essay by restating important points and by emphasizing how they support the thesis. The conclusion should convey a feeling of closure on the issue.

For policy arguments, a different plan of organization is required. Policy arguments are usually arranged in a problem-solution format that concludes with an appeal for action. Although the basic plan can be as simple as demonstrating the existence of a problem, proposing a solution, and providing reasons supported by evidence for accepting the solution, a fully developed policy argument should delve into a whole range of related issues. The statement of the problem must show that the problem exists, and is serious enough to need solving, by documenting negative effects the problem is causing. In some cases, the writer might discuss the consequences of failing to solve the problem. Next, the writer must identify the cause of the problem, determine who or what has caused it, and provide a history of the problem, including a discussion of past efforts to solve it.

The writer is obliged not only to present reasons showing why the solution is practical but also to present and refute counterobjections that may be made to the proposed solution.

The conclusion should stress that the solution is the best, most feasible alternative. It may also make an appeal to the audience to act on the writer's recommendation.

Writing the Conclusion

In general, the conclusion brings together all the lines of reasoning developed in the body of the essay. Your readers should feel that you fulfilled the obligation you incurred when you presented your thesis. You can achieve this sense of clo-sure in several ways, including:

- summarizing the points made in the paper as they relate to the thesis,

- referring to points presented in the opening paragraph or introduction,

- challenging the reader to think further about the issue, or

- providing a personal response.

The conclusion can echo the ideas in the opening paragraph. For instance, here are the introduction and the conclusion of an argument "Why We Live in the Musical Past" by Edward Rothstein, a music critic, which explains why music written in the nineteenth century appeals so greatly to modern audiences:

Introduction:
We are living in a most peculiar musical age. Musical life is booming, audiences are growing, seasons are expanding, conservatories are turning out virtuosos. In New York, well over a *hundred* concerts are given every week. There is an extra-ordinary bustle and whirl in the music world and its accompanying business. But in the midst of all that activity, there is a certain stillness, and an immoveable center. For our musical life is based upon repetition.

Conclusion (note how this final paragraph recaps the opening):
So our repetitions of 19th-century repertory have a darker, more disturbing side. On a vast scale, we mythologize the 19th-century. We anxiously savor mu-sic at its most heroic moment, before it went awry with the beginnings of mod-ernism. We attempt, perhaps, to "restore an earlier state of things." We define what music should be by repeating the works of a single European century. Like myths, these works give our origins; like fairy tales, they offer us promises. But there is something in the present that they miss; they do not show us the future.

Another strategy writers use is to end on a note of reaffirmation and challenge. Edward Abbey does this in "The Right to Arms" by arguing that countries where citizens are prohibited from owning guns are, for the most part, oppressive police states:

If guns are outlawed, only the government will have guns. Only the police, the secret police, the military. The hired servants of our rulers. Only the government—and a few outlaws. I intend to be among the outlaws.

Still another way to conclude an argumentative essay is with irony or a striking paradox. For example, C. R. Creekmore in "Cities Won't Drive You Crazy" argues that contrary to popular belief, cities are far better places in which to live than rural areas:

> It is a power that gives them the means of meeting the city on its own fierce terms of constant stress. And it is profoundly the case that your true [urbanite] rejoices in stress; the crowds, the dirt, the stench, the noise. Instead of depressing him, they urge him onto an unexpected "high," a state of euphoria in which the loftiest of ambitions seems readily attainable.

The most traditional kind of ending is one that sums up the points raised in the argument and brings the essay to a focused conclusion. We can see this in the archaeologist Sir Leonard Woolley's last paragraph of "The Flood" in which he describes the conclusions he reached in ascertaining the true nature of the biblical flood:

> Noah's Flood was not a universal deluge; it was a vast flood in the valley of the Rivers Tigris and Euphrates. It drowned the whole of the habitable land between the eastern and the western deserts; for the people who lived there that was all the world. It wiped out the villages and exterminated their inhabitants, and although some of the towns set upon mounds survived, it was but a scanty and dispirited remnant of the nation that watch the waters recede at last. No wonder that they saw in this disaster the gods' punishment of a sinful generation and described it as such in a great religious poem; and if, as may well have been the case, one household managed to escape by boat from the drowned lowlands, the head of that house would naturally be made the hero of the saga.

Audience

The specific audience for whom you are writing your argumentative essay determines, to some extent, what reasons you present to support your claim.

Unless you have inquired into what beliefs and attitudes your audience already holds, you won't be able to determine the best way to present your argument. Try to estimate how much the audience knows about the issue in question. If they are unfamiliar with the issue, you might provide a brief summary of background information, to give them a more complete context in which to appreciate why this particular issue is an important one. If your audience already knows something about the issue, how do they feel about it?

To understand what writers do to increase the chances that an argument will be accepted by the audience for whom it is intended, we might use a simple analogy: Writing an argumentative essay is rather like cooking and serving a meal. Just as the process of writing an essay moves through the stages of prewriting, writing, and revising, the process of preparing a meal moves through the stages of planning the meal, cooking the food, and serving it in an appetizing way.

Audience considerations play an important part in both processes. Both processes require the writer or chef to look at actions performed in the present with reference to what will be required in the future. The writer uses a variety of invention strategies to generate a thesis while looking at the thesis from the perspective of how well it will serve as a focus for a rough draft. The writer also evaluates the thesis in light of the purpose of the whole essay and the particular audience for whom it is intended. Only by looking to the end point of what can be accomplished by addressing this particular audience can the writer avoid formulating an unrealistic thesis. So, too, the chef looks ahead to the particular audience during the planning stages. Who the audience is and what the occasion is will alter the decision of what to cook. Without these considerations, the chef might begin to prepare a rib roast for vegetarians.

Writing the first draft involves combining the thesis, an outline of the organization of the paper, and any notes generated in the prewriting stage while keeping in mind the particular needs, values, and concerns of the audience for whom the argument is being written. The order in which the writer raises points, the kinds of examples a particular audience would find effective, and questions of tone can be correctly gauged only by keeping in mind potential audience reactions.

The next stage, revising, encompasses everything that must be done in terms of transforming the essay to make it easier to understand: revising ambiguous words or unclear phrases and garbled sentences, checking to see that the essay has an attention-getting introduction and an effective conclusion, and adding transition sentences to help the audience see the relationship between sections of the argument.

The most important shift in perspective relates to seeing what is being prepared from the potential audience's point of view. In our analogy, the chef's attitude toward the food changes so that he or she no longer sees only the ingredients being transformed into this or that kind of a dish but now perceives the task as one of making the food acceptable to others in terms of their needs and expectations. So, too, the writer must be able to look at the work as it is being written from the perspective of those who will read and "digest" it.

To put this into practice, try to create an audience "inventory" by answering each of the following questions:

What do I know about the audience's background?

What are they already likely to know about the issue?

Based on what they know, what explanations, definitions of terms, and descriptions of unfamilar processes would they need to know to better understand the issue?

How might the audience be expected to feel about the issue?

What might be the audience's misconceptions about the issue that I could clarify?

By studying the list of responses to these questions, you will have a clearer sense of which of the following approaches might be the most persuasive for your specific audience.

You might wish to write what is called a traditional argumentative essay that presents your views on the issue, provides a background to set the issue in context, briefly summarizes opposing views, and offers counterarguments for each opposing reason. This is fine for audiences that are neutral or even predisposed to agree with you, but for audiences who might disagree with you, a different kind of an approach is necessary. You risk antagonizing these negative audiences if you use the traditional approach. For this reason, your essay must take a more conciliatory approach by pointing out areas of agreement between you and those opposed to your views by stating the opponent's views fairly, by conceding good points to the opposition, and, most important, by basing your argument on those values both you and your audience might share.

Questions for Discussion and Writing

1. To put these principles into practice, select one of the following topics and decide what kind of claim (fact, cause, value, policy) would be the most appropriate on which to base your argument. Suggest an organizational plan that might be well suited to develop an argument on this topic for neutral, positive, or negative audiences. Should your argument be shaped inductively to work up to the thesis or deductively to explore implications drawn from the thesis? For any topic you choose, try to create a scene or story designed to establish an emotional bond with the audience at the outset. What would your title be? How would you wish to change your audience's perception of the topic?

   a. Should public high schools distribute condoms?

   b. Should the embryo/fetus be accorded civil rights?

   c. Does the Patriot Act overstep civil rights?

   d. Is pornography harmful to women?

    e.   Will blogging ultimately lead to an increase in prosecution of illegal activities that would have gone unreported?

2. After developing an essay based on any topic identified in this chapter, exchange it with other students in the class. Write a short evaluation of the most effective and least effective features of the essay you are evaluating. How well did the writer connect or fail to connect with the audience? How effective were the writer's strategies in getting the audience to see his or her point of view?

Writing the First Draft

As you begin your first draft you might find the following suggestions useful:

1. Give yourself enough time to write the rough draft so that you'll have time to look it over and make necessary changes.

2. If you are not sure about spelling, punctuation, or a question of grammar, simply make a note and come back to it later.

3. Don't erase or delete what you write. Instead, cross it out lightly on the printout so that you can still use it later if you want to.

4. Keep in mind that this draft is temporary and discardable, and that for once neatness does *not* count.

5. Don't get hung up on how to open or close your argument. Just concentrate on stating your thesis and laying out the points and evidence that support it.

6. If you lose the thread of your argument, take some time off and come back to it later. If this doesn't work, go back to notes you accumulated during the prewriting and invention stages and try to find another aspect to the topic that might prove more productive.

    The rough draft is the place to go through the progression of reasons and supporting evidence that your readers will need to come to the conclusion you stated at the outset as your thesis. Since the purpose of the argument is to win people over to your side, it is important to look at your rough draft from the audience's point of view.

    Whereas the introduction or opening paragraphs state the nature of the problem and may briefly touch on opposing arguments, the body of the essay creates a structure of assertions or claims backed up by evidence in the form of examples, statistics, or the testimony of experts. The exact order in which you acknowledge and respond to counterarguments, will, of course, depend on the kind of argument you are presenting.

When you suspect that your audience does not share your viewpoint, your argument should be presented in the spirit of a mutual search for the best reasons to support your claim rather than in a spirit of trouncing the opposition. Your goal should be to present your argument as an open-minded inquiry, expressed in a reasonable tone, for people who may not share your views initially, but who you assume will be fair enough to acknowledge any good reasons brought forward to support your argument.

Conclude your essay with the strongest and most persuasive reasons for your point of view.

With audiences who agree with you or who are neutral on the issue, begin the main part of your essay with the strongest reasons you have in order to reinforce the audience's attitudes and win their assent.

Revising and Rewriting Your Essay

Although revision is often discussed as if it were something you do after writing your essay, it is actually part of the continuous editing process that goes on as you write your paper.

Read your essay aloud so that you can hear how your writing sounds. You may hear inconsistencies in grammatical structure or usage, and you may spot repetitive words or phrases that escaped your notice. Another helpful strategy is to ask for the reactions of others—your friends, teachers, and classmates. Many campuses have writing centers or tutoring services that provide reviewers.

RECONSIDERING THE WHOLE   Here are some questions for you or your reviewer to use in assessing the overall structure of your paper:

1. Does the paper's introduction capture the reader's interest and introduce the thesis?

2. At what points might the reader need more examples to clarify an idea? Which assumptions need to be supported with more evidence? Have you taken into account how someone who holds an opposing view might regard your analysis? What new information could you add to be more persuasive?

3. Are the issues raised in the best possible order? Would some other arrangement more effectively communicate the relationships implicit in the thesis?

4. Do transitions effectively signal connections between paragraphs and ideas? You might need to write sentences to guide your readers smoothly from one idea or section to the next.

RECONSIDERING PARAGRAPHS   Once you are satisfied with the overall organization of your ideas, consider what might be clarified within paragraphs.

- Does each paragraph have a topic sentence that is related to the paper's thesis?

- Do other sentences in the paragraph explain the idea in the topic sentence or present evidence to support it?

- If the sentences were in a different order, would the explanation be clearer?

- Are there assertions that need to be supported by examples or quotations?

- Are there any short paragraphs that can be consolidated under a more general idea?

- Are there very long paragraphs that can be divided?

RECONSIDERING SENTENCES   After you are satisfied with the overall organization of your paper and the coherence of the paragraphs, it is time to turn your attention to matters of grammar, usage, punctuation, and style.

Look for verbs in the passive voice that might be recast in the active voice. Find the verb, ask who is the doer of the action, and rewrite the sentence in the basic subject-verb-object pattern.

Consider how you might improve your choice of words. Choose words that express your ideas clearly, simply, and concretely. Be on the lookout for (1) mixed metaphors, (2) abstract jargon (if technical terms are necessary, define them the first time you use them), (3) clichés, and (4) roundabout phrases whose idea could be expressed in a single word.

REVISING THE TITLE   As you read through your rough draft, you may think of a different title that would better reflect a change in emphasis in your paper or more accurately express the idea in the thesis. Titles are a concise means of focusing the reader's attention on the main idea of the essay.

PROOFREADING   Proofreading means focusing on spelling, punctuation, repeated words, spacing, margins, and anything else that would impair the look of the final paper. Most people find it easier and more accurate to proofread on paper than onscreen, and many people also find it helpful to proofread aloud.

If you habitually misspell certain words, make a list of them and consult it when you proofread. Do not rely on your computer's spell-checking program to catch all spelling errors because it cannot tell when you have typed the wrong word, such as *a* for *as* or *won* for *own*.

Make sure you have properly documented the source of every quotation, paraphrase, and summary. Compare your in-text citations with your list of works cited, and compare that list with your record of the sources to make sure you did not change any words or punctuation.

Check the formatting of your paper. Most English instructors require papers to be formatted in Modern Language Association (MLA) style, but teachers in other classes may require American Psychological Association (APA) style, *Chicago Manual of Style* (CMS) style, or Council of Science Editors (CSE) style. Here, however, are some universal formatting points to check during proofreading:

- one-inch margins on the top, bottom, and sides of each page

- page number and running head on each page (you can use the "header" function for this)

- half an inch indentation of the first line of each paragraph

- double-spaced text in a standard 12-point font (do not put extra double spaces between paragraphs)

- works cited (or references) on a separate page at the end of the paper (for citation guidelines in MLA style, see "Documenting Sources in MLA Style" in the next chapter)

- your name, the title of the paper, the name of your school or the course, and the date on the title page (if one is required by your instructor) or on the first page of the essay

Analyzing Someone Else's Argument

GAIN AN OVERVIEW

An overview of the text will help you identify the topic and assess what you might learn from the piece before you start reading through it. You can get an overview by reading

- the title,

- any internal headings, and

- the opening and closing paragraphs.

In addition, some articles in the sciences and social sciences are preceded by abstracts that summarize the entire piece, and readings in anthologies are sometimes preceded by headnotes that include facts about the author or the selection. After you have identified the topic and the scope of the article, ask yourself what you already know about the subject (for example, stem cell research, stereotyping) as a way of creating a frame of reference from which to understand the selection.

READ THE TEXT FOR BASIC MEANING AND ORGANIZATION

After you have considered all these elements, read the text to understand its literal meaning and to identify its *thesis* (that is, the central or controlling idea). Look for the sequence of ideas and internal organizations. Pay attention to your reactions, and note any questions you have. As you identify the various elements, also note them in the margin (see the sample annotated essay, below).

The organization of a piece of writing usually reflects its purpose. For example, if its purpose is to suggest how a problem might be resolved, you might reasonably expect the writer to describe the problem, explore its possible causes, and propose a solution. Or if the purpose is to persuade the audience that a particular thesis or opinion is valid, the piece is likely to use a series of examples based on research, observation, or personal experience. Other kinds of organizational strategies include chronological or spatial descriptions, comparison and contrast of two things, and process explanations.

REREAD THE TEXT AND ANALYZE THE RHETORICAL SITUATION

After you have read the text once to understand its literal meaning and basic structure, read it a second time to analyze how it develops and supports the central ideal. Consider its *rhetorical situation* (the context for its writing) by assessing the following elements:

1. The *author*. What are the author's credentials for writing about the subject? Are they based on personal experience or professional expertise? What is the author's **attitude**—that is, his or her emotional stance—toward the topic? What is the **tone** of the piece; that is, what sense do you get of the writer's personality and his or her attitude toward the subject? How are word choice and sentence structure used to convey this tone?

2. The *audience*. Who was the original **audience**—the intended readers—for the piece? What kind of language does the author use? Is it formal?

informal? technical? What **assumptions** (beliefs) does the author expect the audience to share? What level of education or previous knowledge about the subject does the author assume the audience has?

3. The *purpose*. What does the writer hope to accomplish—that is, what
   is the writer's **purpose?** Is he or she writing to explain something, to
   convey information, to persuade an audience, to express feelings, or to
   entertain? Most writing has more than one purpose, but one usually
   predominates. For example, in the sample annotated essay that follows, Judith Ortiz Cofer is explaining the various myths about Latinas,
   but she does so by expressing her feelings about her experiences with
   those myths.

4. The *occasion*. What prompted the writer to create this piece—that is,
   what was the **occasion** for its writing? What was happening at the time
   the piece was written? Where did it originally appear? For example,
   was it first published in an academic journal or in a popular magazine?
   (For a selection in an anthology, you can often find this information in
   the headnote or in the list of permissions, usually in the back of the
   book.)

5. The *topic*. What do you, the reader, know about the **topic**—that is, the
   subject of the piece? What opinions do you already have about it? What
   assumptions are you making about it, especially if it is an unfamiliar
   topic? Do you expect to be bored or interested? Do you expect that you
   will understand the essay easily or that you will have to work at it?

HOW TO ANALYZE AN ARGUMENT

Some pieces of writing specifically attempt to change the readers' thinking or to
get them to take a new course of action. The basic structure of an *argument* is
(1) the statement of an opinion and (2) the presentation of one or more reasons
to support that opinion. To analyze an argument, you must consider not only
the elements of the rhetorical situation listed above but also how the argument
anticipates readers' reactions and what kinds of support it uses.

DOES THE ARGUMENT ACKNOWLEDGE OTHER POINTS OF VIEW?

Arguments are more persuasive when they try to take into account readers'
prior knowledge, beliefs, and values and their probable reactions to the argument. Sometimes writers try to establish common ground with readers, presenting the argument in the spirit of a mutual search for the best information to

support the claim. Sometimes they try to anticipate readers' objections by objectively summarizing their positions while pointing out weaknesses in the opposing viewpoints. Writers who seek to identify the likely causes or probable consequences of something should be sure to consider alternative explanations. If the argument suggests a course of action, it should be objective about other solutions to the problem.

TEXT ANNOTATIONS

As you read and reread a text to grasp its meaning and to understand its rhetorical context, you should make notes about what you discover and any questions you have. Those notes can go right on the pages of the text, or in a reading journal. Later, you can draw on them when you write a paper about the text.

Annotations create a dialogue between you and the writer. By asking questions and making observations about meaning and structure in the margins, you can better understand what you are reading. Here are some suggestions for annotating a text:

- Write your own responses to the author's ideas in the margin. Use the margin to create a conversation with the author. Ask questions. Agree or disagree with points the author makes.

- Identify central ideas expressed in the title, the headings (if there are any), and the introductory and concluding paragraphs.

- When you locate the thesis (the central claim or assertion that the text develops), underline it. If the thesis is not stated in so many words, compose an explicit version and write it at the top or bottom of the first or last page (see the sample annotated essay that follows for an example). Sometimes writers place the thesis in the first paragraph to help readers perceive the relationship between the supporting evidence and this main idea. At other times, in essays that are exploring an idea rather than arguing a point, the thesis may not become clear until the end of the piece.

- Identify examples, statistics, quotations from authorities, comparisons, visual features (such as charts, graphs, and tables), and other evidence that supports or clarifies the primary assertions.

- Look up unfamiliar words, and write their definitions in the margin.

- Note transitional words and phrases that show relationships between ideas. These *transitions* may express chronological relationships (*now, when, before, after*) or casual relationships (*because, therefore*), or they may signal additional information (*furthermore, moreover*) or qualifying information (*although, however*).

You can see how this process works in the sample annotation of Judith Ortiz Cofer's essay "The Myth of the Latin Woman: I Just Met a Girl Named María" that follows:

Sample Annotated Essay

Judith Ortiz Cofer

The Myth of the Latin Woman: I Just Met a Girl Named María

On a bus trip to London from Oxford University where I was earning some graduate credits one summer, a young man, obviously fresh from a pub, spotted me and as if struck by inspiration went down on his knees in the aisle. With both hands over his heart he broke into an Irish tenor's rendition of "María" from *West Side Story*. My politely amused fellow passengers gave his *lovely* voice the round of *gentle* applause it deserved. Though I was not quite as amused, I managed my version of an English smile: no show of teeth, no extreme contortions of the facial muscles—I was at this time of my life practicing reserve and cool. Oh, that British control, how I coveted it. But María had followed me to London, reminding me of a prime fact of my life: *you can leave the Island, master the English language, and travel as far as you can, but if you are a Latina, especially one like me who so obviously belongs to Rita Moreno's gene pool, the Island travels with you.*

> *What is "the myth"? Is it defined?*

> *Sarcasm?*

> *Example supporting thesis*

> *Thesis?*

This is sometimes a very good thing—it may win you that extra minute of someone's attention. But with some people, the same things can make *you* an island—not so much a tropical paradise as an Alcatraz, a place nobody wants to visit. As a Puerto Rican girl growing up in the United States and wanting like most children to "belong," I resented *the stereotype that my Hispanic appearance called forth from many people I met.*

> *Metaphor with two contrasting meanings*

> *Part of thesis?*

= miniature
model of
something

= grocery store

What's the
author's
attitude to
these
contrasts?

= Puerto Rican
neighborhood

Mainstream =
positive models

= houses

= young
woman

Personal
experience
with
stereotype

Why weren't
teachers
models?

Our family lived in a large urban center in New Jersey during the sixties, where life was designed as a microcosm of my parents' casas on the island. We spoke in Spanish, we ate Puerto Rican food bought at the bodega, and we practiced strict Catholicism complete with Saturday confession and Sunday mass at a church where our parents were accommodated into a one-hour Spanish mass slot, performed by a Chinese priest trained as a missionary for Latin America.

As a girl I was kept under strict surveillance, since virtue and modesty were, by cultural equation, the same as family honor. As a teenager I was instructed on how to behave as a proper señorita. But it was a conflicting message girls got, since the Puerto Rican mothers also encouraged their daughters to look and act like women and to dress in clothes our Anglo friends and their mothers found too "mature" for our age. It was, and is, cultural, yet I often felt humiliated when I appeared at an American friend's party wearing a dress more suitable to a semiformal than to a playroom birthday celebration. At Puerto Rican festivities, neither the music nor the colors we wore could be too loud. I still experience a vague sense of letdown when I'm invited to a "party" and it turns out to be a marathon conversation in hushed tones rather than a fiesta with salsa, laughter, and dancing—the kind of celebration I remember from my childhood.

I remember Career Day in our high school, when teachers told us to come dressed as if for a job interview. It quickly became obvious that to the barrio girls, "dressing up" sometimes meant wearing ornate jewelry and clothing that would be more appropriate (by mainstream standards) for the company Christmas party than as daily office attire. That morning I had agonized in front of my closet, trying to figure out what a "career girl" would wear because, essentially, except for Marlo Thomas on TV, *I had no models on which to base my decision.* I knew how to dress for school: at the Catholic school I attended we all wore uniforms; I knew how to dress for Sunday mass, and I knew what dresses to wear for parties at my relatives' homes. Though I do not recall the precise details of my Career Day outfit, it must have been a composite of the above choices. But I remember a comment my friend (an Italian-American) made in later years that coalesced my impressions of that day. She said that at the business school she was attending the Puerto Rican girls always stood out for wearing "everything at once." She meant, of course, too much jewelry, too many accessories. On that day at school, we were simply made the *negative models* by the nuns who were themselves not credible fashion experts to any of us. But it was painfully obvious to me that to the others, in their tailored skirts and silk blouses, we must have seemed "hopeless" and "vulgar." Though I now know that *most adolescents feel out of step much of the time*, I also know that for the Puerto Rican girls of my generation that sense was intensified. The way our teachers and classmates looked at us that day in school was just a taste of the culture clash that awaited us in the real world, where prospective employers and men on the street would often misinterpret our tight skirts and jingling bracelets as a come-on.

Mixed cultural signals have perpetuated certain stereotypes—for example, that of the Hispanic woman as the "Hot Tamale" or sexual firebrand. It is a one-dimensional view that the media have found easy to promote. In their special vocabulary, advertisers have designated "sizzling" and "smoldering" as the adjectives of choice for describing not only the foods but also the women of Latin America. From conversations in my house I recall hearing about the harassment that Puerto Rican women endured in factories where the "boss men" talked to them as if sexual innuendo was all they understood and, worse, often gave them the choice of submitting to advances or being fired.

It is custom, however, not chromosomes, that leads us to choose scarlet over pale pink. As young girls, we were influenced in our decisions about clothes and colors by the women—older sisters and mothers who had grown up on a tropical island where the natural environment was a riot of primary colors, where showing your skin was one way to keep cool as well as to look sexy. Most important of all, on the island, women perhaps felt freer

---

Margin notes (left):

Puerto Rican women = negative models for Anglo students

"Text" of Puerto Rican style misunderstood by Anglos

Puerto Rican women = positive models for Puerto Rican girls

Margin notes (right):

A universal experience—so true!

Examples of other myths of Latinas used by media

= culture, not biology

Compare to "tropical paradise" in para. 2

to dress and move more provocatively, since, in most cases, they were protected by the traditions, mores, and laws of a Spanish/Catholic system of morality and machismo whose main rule was: *You may look at my sister, but if you touch her I will kill you.* The extended family and church structure could provide a young woman with a circle of safety in her small pueblo on the island; if a man "wronged" a girl, everyone would close in to save her family honor.

= village

Contrast "small pueblo" to "large urban center in New Jersey" in para. 3 and men on the street at end of para. 5

This is what I have gleaned from my discussions as an adult with older Puerto Rican women. They have told me about dressing in their best party clothes on Saturday nights and going to the town's plaza to promenade with their girlfriends in front of the boys they liked. The males were thus given an opportunity to admire the women and to express their admiration in the form of *piropos*: erotically charged street poems they composed on the spot. I have been subjected to a few piropos while visiting the Island, and they can be outrageous, although custom dictates that they must never cross into obscenity. This ritual, as I understand it, also entails a show of studied indifference on the woman's part; if she is "decent," she must not acknowledge the man's impassioned words. So I do understand how things can be lost in translation. *When a Puerto Rican girl dressed in her idea of what is attractive meets a man from the mainstream culture who has been trained to react to certain types of clothing as a sexual signal, a clash is likely to take place.* The line I first heard based on the aspect of the myth happened when the boy who took me to my first formal dance leaned over to plant a sloppy overeager kiss painfully on my mouth, and when I didn't respond with sufficient passion said in a resentful tone: "I thought you Latin girls were supposed to mature early"—my first instance of being thought of as a fruit or vegetable—I was supposed to *ripen*, not just grow into womanhood like other girls.

Reason why she knows about life on the island

Compare to "English smile" in para. 1

A more specific way to describe thesis?

Personal experience supporting thesis

Was she angry? embarrassed?

Stereotype makes "other" different from mainstream

It is surprising to some of my professional friends that some people, including those who should know better, still put others "in their place." Though rarer, these incidents are still commonplace in my life. It happened to me most recently during a stay at a very classy metropolitan hotel favored by young professional couples for their weddings. Late one evening after the theater, as I walked toward my room with my colleague (a woman with whom I was coordinating an arts program), a middle-aged man in a tuxedo, a young girl in satin and lace on his arm, stepped directly into our path. With his champagne glass extended toward me, he exclaimed, "Evita!"

Our way blocked, my companion and I listened as the man half-recited, half-bellowed "Don't Cry for Me, Argentina." When he finished, the young girl said: "How about a round of applause for my daddy?" We complied, hoping this would bring the silly spectacle to a close. I was becoming aware that our little group was attracting the attention of the other guests. "Daddy" must have perceived this too, and he once more barred the way as we tried to walk past him. He began to shout-sing a ditty to the tune of "La Bamba"—except the lyrics were about a girl named María whose exploits all rhymed with her name and gonorrhea. The girl kept saying "Oh, Daddy" and looking at me with pleading eyes. She wanted me to laugh along with the others. My companion and I stood silently waiting for the man to end his offensive song. When he finished, I looked not at him but at his daughter. I advised her calmly never to ask her father what he had done in the army. Then I walked between them and to my room. My friend complimented me on my cool handling of the situation. I confessed to her that I really had wanted to push the jerk into the swimming pool. I knew that this same man—probably a corporate executive, well educated, even worldly by most standards— would not have been likely to regale a white woman with a dirty song in public. He would perhaps have checked his impulse by assuming that she could be somebody's wife or mother, or at least *somebody* who might take offense. But to him, I was just an Evita or a María: *merely a character in his cartoon-populated universe.*

Because of my education and my proficiency with the English language, I have acquired many mechanisms

Margin notes:

Personal experience supporting thesis

Musical and movie about wife of former Argentinian president

Why did girl say this?

Popular song of the '50s

Why did girl want Cofer to laugh?

What did she mean by this?

Is this true? Or would he be obnoxious to any woman?

Good way to express what a stereotype is

Para. 13 is example of one mechanism

for dealing with the anger I experience. This was not true for my parents, nor is it true for the many Latin women working at menial jobs who must put up with stereotypes about our ethnic group such as: "They make good domestics." This is another facet of the *myth of the Latin woman* in the United States. Its origin is simple to deduce. Work as domestics, waitressing, and factory jobs are all that's available to women with little English and few skills. The myth of the Hispanic menial has been sustained by the same media phenomenon that made "Mammy" from *Gone with the Wind* America's idea of the black woman for generations; María, the housemaid or counter girl, is now indelibly etched into the national psyche. The big and the little screens have presented us with the picture of the funny Hispanic maid, mispronouncing words and cooking up a spicy storm in a shiny California kitchen.

This media-engendered image of the Latina in the United States has been documented by feminist Hispanic scholars, who claim that such portrayals are partially responsible for the denial of opportunities for upward mobility among Latinas in the professions. I have a Chicana friend working on a Ph.D. in philosophy at a major university. She says her doctor still shakes his head in puzzled amazement at all the "big words" she uses. Since I do not wear my diplomas around my neck for all to see, I too have on occasion been sent to that "kitchen," where some think I obviously belong.

One such incident that has stayed with me, though I recognize it as a minor offense, happened on the day of my first public poetry reading. It took place in Miami in a boat-restaurant where we were having lunch before the event. I was nervous and excited as I walked in with my notebook in my hand. An older woman motioned me to her table. Thinking (foolish me) that she wanted me to autograph a copy of my brand new slender volume of verse, I went over. She ordered a cup of coffee from me, assuming that I was the waitress. Easy enough to mistake my poems for menus, I suppose. I know that it wasn't an intentional act of cruelty, yet of all the good things that

Marginal annotations:

- This is the title
- Stereotype of Latinas compared to black women
- Role of media again
- Scholarly research to support thesis
- Sounds angry
- Personal experience that supports thesis

happened that day, I remember that scene most clearly, because it reminded me of *what I had to overcome before anyone would take me seriously*. In retrospect I understand that my anger gave my reading fire, that I have almost always taken doubts in my abilities as a challenge—and that the result is, most times, a feeling of satisfaction at having won a convert when I see the cold, appraising eyes warm to my words, the body language change, the smile that indicates that I have opened some avenue for communication. That day I read to that woman and her lowered eyes told me that she was embarrassed at her little faux pas, and when I willed her to look up at me, it was my victory, and she graciously allowed me to punish her with my full attention. We shook hands at the end of the reading, and I never saw her again. She has probably forgotten the whole thing but maybe not.

> Consequence of the myth

> interesting choice of words

Yet I am one of the lucky ones. My parents made it possible for me to acquire a stronger footing in the mainstream culture by giving me the chance at an education. And books and art have saved me from the harsher forms of ethnic and racial prejudice that many of my Hispanic *compañeras* have had to endure. I travel a lot around the United States, reading from my books of poetry and my novel, and the reception I most often receive is one of positive interest by people who want to know more about my culture. There are, however, thousands of Latinas without the privilege of an education or the entrée into society that I have. *For them life is a struggle against the misconceptions perpetuated by the myth of the Latina as whore, domestic, or criminal.* We cannot change this by legislating the way people look at us. The transformation, as I see it, has to occur at a much more individual level. My personal goal in my public life is to try to replace the old pervasive stereotypes and myths about Latinas with a much more interesting set of realities. Every time I give a reading, I hope the stories I tell, the dreams and fears I examine in my work, can *achieve some universal truth which will get my audience past the particulars of my skin color, my accent, or my clothes.*

> Why doesn't she give any examples of harsher forms of prejudice?

> = women friends

> Thesis?

> Call for change

> Goal = to overcome stereotype through art

Thesis: Women who appear Latina because of their skin color, accent, or clothes have to struggle "against the misconceptions perpetuated by the myth of the Latina as whore, domestic, or criminal.

I once wrote a poem in which I called us Latinas "God's brown daughters." This poem is really a prayer of sorts, offered upward, but also, through the human-to-human channel of art, outward. It is a prayer for *communication, and for respect*. In it, Latin women pray "in Spanish to an Anglo God / with a Jewish heritage," and they are "fervently hoping / that if not omnipotent, / at least He be bilingual."

Is poem example of her goal in para. 14?

Identifying Your Thesis

As you explore and narrow your topic with the invention strategies discussed previously, you may also discover a thesis for your paper (although you may decide to alter it as you continue writing). In an analytical essay, a thesis is a sentence or two that identifies the paper's topic and the author's opinion about it or approach to it; the thesis can also indicate the author's purpose and establish the tone. It may take several tries to come up with a workable thesis, but once it is formulated, you can use it as a way to test the relevance and effectiveness of the evidence and conclusion.

The thesis is a type of contract or promise; it tells readers what to expect. For example, consider this thesis statement that a student composed for a rough draft of her paper about the reading that was annotated earlier:

In "The Myth of the Latin Woman: I Just Met a Girl Named María," Judith Ortiz Cofer refutes the "María" stereotype by creating an impression of herself as an articulate and accomplished Latina.

This example of a trial thesis (which may be revised as the paper takes shape) contains the title of the original essay, the author's name, and the student's main assertion, stated as a single sentence. This thesis obligates the student to

1. define the "María" stereotype and explain why Cofer finds it demeaning,

2. show specifically how Cofer creates "an impression of herself as an articulate and accomplished Latina," and

3. show how Cofer uses stylistic techniques to persuade her audience.

Each of these three ideas can then be developed in paragraphs or sections of the paper. You can create an informal outline to explore the insights expressed in your thesis. An informal outline can help you identify the key ideas you will develop in each section and the kind of evidence that will support these ideas.

An analytical essay does not have to take apart every single aspect of the original essay. You need to be selective and discuss only those elements that support your thesis, or main assertion. After formulating a thesis that expresses your evaluation of the text, you need to be able to refer to specific passages in the text to support your thesis. You do this by summarizing (discussed in Chapter 1), paraphrasing, and quoting these passages as evidence to support your analysis.

SAMPLE SUMMARY

In "The Myth of the Latin Woman: I Just Met a Girl Named María," Judith Ortiz Cofer relates how, although she is highly educated and is an acclaimed writer, she is still treated according to the stereotypes of Latinas. Cofer, who is Puerto Rican, describes how her Hispanic appearance provokes inappropriate responses from people who should know better and would never treat a white woman as a "hot tamale" or assume she was a menial worker. She attributes these misunderstandings between cultures to the different codes that govern behavior and clothing in Puerto Rico and on the U.S. mainland and to media stereotyping of minorities.

Providing Evidence by Paraphrasing or Quoting

PARAPHRASES Paraphrasing is the restatement of an author's ideas in your own words. Unlike summaries, which aim to be concise, paraphrases attempt to convey the complexity of the original text and are often similar in length to it. Paraphrasing is something of an art because it involves re-presenting in your own words the meaning of a passage written by someone else.

First of all, your paraphrase must be different enough from the original so that it does not lead you to commit plagiarism, or to use someone else's words as if they were your own.

Not only do you need to make the paraphrase sufficiently different from the text, but you must also make sure that you do not project your own biases into the paraphrase. A thesaurus can sometimes prove useful when you are paraphrasing, but you must check the dictionary definition of the synonym you intend to use in case there is a subtle difference in meaning. For example, if you substitute the word *aroma* for the word *odor*, you might create a positive **connotation** (an associative meaning) that is not in the original.

QUOTATIONS Quotations are useful when you wish to support, illustrate, or document important points by citing the opinion of experts or authorities who either support or challenge your position. Direct quotations are preferable to paraphrases when the original passage is especially important, vivid, or memorable. Quotations let your readers hear the author's voice. Be careful, though, not to overuse quotations; your paper needs to be primarily in your own words. It should not be simply a patchwork of stitched-together quotations.

Brief quotations (no more than four lines) are normally run into the text and enclosed in double quotation marks (" "). Include the author's name with the quotations, either in your text (as in the following example) or in a parenthetical reference. Parenthetical citations for page numbers follow the closing quotation marks but precede the punctuation mark at the end of the sentence:

> As Cofer writes, "It is custom, however, not chromosomes, that leads us to choose scarlet over pale pink" (252).

Longer quotations (more than four lines) are separated from the text, indented one inch from the left margin, and reproduced without quotation marks. These block quotations are introduced with a colon (:) if they follow a grammatically complete introductory clause. Parenthetical citations of page numbers follow the quotation's final mark of punctuation. Use longer quotations for complex or especially vivid passages, but don't use too many. Here is an example of a long quotation:

> In her essay, "The Myth of the Latin Woman: I Just Met a Girl Named María," Judith Ortiz Cofer analyzes the role culture plays in stereotyping and concludes:
>
>> It is custom, however, not chromosomes, that leads us to choose scarlet over pale pink. As young girls, it was our mothers who influenced our decisions about clothes and colors—mothers who had grown up on a tropical island where the natural environment was a riot of primary colors, where showing your skin was one way to keep cool as well as to look sexy (252).

If you quote more than one paragraph, the first line of the second subsequent paragraphs should be indented an additional quarter-inch or three spaces.

Quotations must be accurate. If you need to omit part of a passage to integrate it into your text, you must replace the omitted segment with an ellipsis mark, or three spaced periods, as in the following example:

> As Cofer says, "It is custom, . . . not chromosomes, that leads us to choose scarlet over pale pink."

The ellipsis (. . .) indicates that a word or words have been omitted.

When you add words to a quotation to clarify it, use square brackets around the words you have added, as in the following example that shows the translation of a foreign word:

> Cofer says, "Our life was designed by my parents as a microcosm of their *casas* [homes] on the island."

When you wish to emphasize a word or phrase in a quotation, you may italicize or underline it, but you must indicate that you have done so by adding the phrase "emphasis added" in parentheses after the closing quotation mark. Here is an example:

> Cofer says that "it is *custom*, however, not chromosomes, that leads us to choose scarlet over pale pink" (emphasis added).

Whenever you quote, summarize, or paraphrase material from a source, you must identify the source. If you do not, you are committing plagiarism, that is, appropriating the language and ideas of another person or representing them as your own. Source documentation also shows readers the scope of your research and enables them to refer to the original materials if they wish.

Writing from a Single Source: Sample Student Essay

As you read through the following essay, which analyzes Judith Ortiz Cofer's essay presented earlier, note how quotations, paraphrases, and summaries are used as evidence of the thesis statement. Note also its organization into a discussion of the content of Cofer's essay and then of its style.

Clark 1

The title refers to the thesis statement.

Examining the Latina Stereotype

In the musical *West Side Story*, the beautiful and innocent Maria, newly arrived from Puerto Rico, falls tragically in love with the leader of an Anglo gang. The play is filled with memorable songs,

The introduction gives the background for Cofer's title.

but the characters, including Maria and her friend, the Puerto Rican "spitfire" Anita, are familiar stereotypes of Latinas. In "The Myth of the Latin Woman: I Just Met a Girl Named María," Judith Ortiz Cofer refutes these stereotypes by contrasting them with the realities of her life as an articulate and accomplished individual.

Thesis statement

Clark 2

A Puerto Rican writer of some renown, Cofer is offended when strangers make unwarranted assumptions about her. She confesses that since childhood she has been troubled by these cross-cultural misperceptions:

> You can leave the Island, master the English language, and travel as far as you can, but if you are a Latina, especially one like me who so obviously belongs to Rita Moreno's gene pool, the Island travels with you.

Quotations for four lines indented one inch.

Cofer uses personal experiences to show how she has learned to cope with these misperceptions about her. As a Puerto Rican growing up in the United States, she was caught between her parents' Puerto Rican culture and the values of her Anglo schoolmates. When Cofer was young, Puerto Rican mothers encouraged their daughters to dress and act like women. So on her high school's Career Day, she and her Puerto Rican friends wore their mothers' flashy jewelry and clothing, which their teachers and Anglo classmates, who were attired in tailored skirts and silk blouses, ridiculed.

Paragraph answers an alternative viewpoint.

Some people might disagree with Cofer's blaming cross-cultural misunderstandings and feel that she was old enough and had lived on the mainland long enough to know what clothes were appropriate. But Cofer was raised in a Puerto Rican community in New Jersey and had never been out in the world. Given her background, it was natural for her to interpret the meaning of "dressing up" in an entirely different way than her Anglo classmates and teachers. She explains that "it is custom, . . . not chromosomes, that leads us to choose scarlet over pale pink."

Ellipsis mark shows omission of word or words from source.

Years later, when Cofer was in graduate school at Oxford, she was unexpectedly treated as a Latina stereotype. On a bus trip to

Clark 3

London, a drunken young passenger knelt before her and serenaded her with "Maria" from *West Side Story*; imagine a total stranger coming up and singing, "Maria—I just kissed a girl named Maria/ And suddenly I found how wonderful a sound can be." Although her fellow passengers were "politely amused," Cofer struggled to hide her anger with her version of "an English smile"—a response that recalls the "studied indifference" of the young women subjected to off-color *piropos* on Saturday nights in the plaza of her mother's village in Puerto Rico.

In addition to the assumption that Latinas are sexually available, there is a second damaging aspect of the stereotype: that all Latinas are uneducated, socially inferior, and suited only for menial work. Cofer likens the stereotype of the funny Hispanic maid "cooking up a spicy storm in a shiny California kitchen" to the "Mammy" stereotype of black women, which allows them to be treated in ways that would be unthinkable if they were white.

Transitional sentence signals two-part structure of discussion of stereotype.

As an example, Cofer describes an event that happened before her first public poetry reading. Upon arriving at the restaurant, Cofer was called over to a table by an older woman. Nervous and excited, Cofer walked over, expecting to autograph a copy of her newly published volume of poems. However, when she reached the table, the woman, who had assumed that she was the waitress, ordered a cup of coffee. Cofer expresses her anger with irony: "Easy enough to mistake my poems for menus, I suppose."

Transitional sentence signals switch from discussion of content to analysis of style.

The language and the organization of the essay are carefully crafted, demonstrating that Cofer is indeed an accomplished and articulate writer. In the introductory paragraphs, she uses two

Clark 4

contrasting metaphors of an island to express what it feels like to be stereotyped. In the first paragraph, "the Island" is Puerto Rico, the vividly colored "tropical paradise" that is the homeland of her parents. But in the second paragraph the island becomes gray and barren, "an Alcatraz, a place nobody wants to visit"—a metaphor for her feeling of isolation in mainland Anglo culture.

Cofer's essay has a loosely chronological structure—a series of episodes that trace the development of her reactions to cultural stereotyping from childhood to adulthood. As a child, Cofer felt humiliated and "out of step" when she was dressed "wrong" for a birthday party or a Career Day.

To help the reader understand the difference between Puerto Rican and Anglo customs, Cofer inserts into the chronological series her mother's description of Saturday nights on the town plaza when she was young. There, the flirtations between boys and girls had clear boundaries, and the fundamental rule, says Cofer, was "You may look at my sister, but if you touch her I will kill you." To illustrate the lack of such boundaries on the mainland, Cofer describes her date's mistaken assumptions and unwanted kiss at her first formal dance.

As she gained more experience and more confidence as well as professional success, Cofer's reaction changed to anger at disrespectual behavior that diminished her as a person. When she was accosted in a hotel lobby by a tuxedoed guest singing an off-color version of "La Bamba," she waited in silence until he was finished and then insulted him indirectly but sharply by cautioning his daughter never to ask him what he had done in the army. Later

Clark 5

Cofer told her friend that she had really wanted "to push the jerk into the swimming pool."

In the last episode of the essay, when she was mistaken for a waitress rather than a poet, Cofer also responded with anger, gazing intently at the offending woman throughout her poetry reading— a tactic that Cofer describes as "punish [ing] her with my full attention."

Cofer's adolescent feelings of embarrassment have changed into regarding stereotyped assumptions as challenges to open some avenue for "communication." Her goal, she says, is to use her art "to try to replace the old pervasive stereotype. . .with a much more interesting set of realities."

Conclusion refers back to thesis statement

Cofer concludes her essay with an example of that art: lines from a poem about Latinas that she calls "a prayer for communication, and for respect." Her Latin women praying "in Spanish to an Anglo god / with a Jewish heritage / . . . fervently hoping / that if not omnipotent, / at least He be bilingual" are one of the realities behind the stereotype of Maria.

Refuting Arguments

An important aspect of writing arguments depends on the ability to refute opposing views. In fact, some arguments are entirely refutations of the opposition's argument.

An analysis of someone else's argument, like any argument of your own, must center on a thesis or central assertion. When you evaluate another's argument, the thesis will be your overall assessment of how convincingly the author has succeeded in bringing forward good reasons and persuasive evidence to justify the conclusions reached. Your thesis should not express your opinion of the issue, but rather should be an objective evaluation of the skill with which the author uses different strategies of argumentation to present his or her case.

ANALYZING AN ARGUMENT AND INVENTING YOUR OWN

If you have never gone through the process of analyzing someone else's argument before creating your own, you might find it difficult to know what to look for. Fortunately, there are several strategies you can use both for analyzing someone else's argument and for inventing material for your own. For example, you might analyze someone else's argument to determine the author's purpose and how well he or she accomplished it. You might describe the author's tone or voice and try to assess how much it contributed. How effectively does the writer use authorities, statistics, or examples to support the claim? Does the author identify the assumptions or warrants on which the argument is based, and are they ones with which you agree or disagree? To what extent does the author use the emotional connotations of language to try to persuade his or her audience? Do you see anything unworkable or disadvantageous about the solutions offered as an answer to the problem the essay addresses? All these and many other ways of analyzing someone else's argument can be used to create your own case. The entire range of strategies has come to be known collectively as *critical thinking*, which differs from taking things for granted or taking things at face value.

Critical thinking involves becoming aware of the reasoning processes other people use and that you yourself use in thinking about experiences. The central element in critical thinking is the ability to evaluate information critically. This means you must be able to identify the main idea underlying someone else's argument, locate the reasons and evidence that support the idea, express the idea in your own words, and evaluate how well (in terms of formal strategies of argument) the author makes his or her case. You must also be able to see the relationship between the main idea and other things that you already know.

You think critically when you change your views about something from what you first thought. Critical thinking not only involves being willing to change your views when the evidence warrants it, but encompasses being able to see how the same phenomenon can be viewed very differently by people with different perspectives. For example, you might have seen a movie and not liked it initially and then seen it later on television and found it more enjoyable. By the same token, a first reaction of not liking someone you met might have been an automatic response. On reflection, you might have changed your attitude later.

In a different context, thinking critically means being open to new perspectives that add something to your understanding. First, of course, you must be aware of the angle from which you view events and your own preconceptions, expectations, and biases. Critical thinking makes it possible to generate ideas when you take the trouble to review what you think you already know. You may often discover that you have been passively taking in information and making other people's beliefs your own without exploring or testing them. If someone else's argument makes you rethink things and examine your reasons for holding beliefs, you will discover material enough for more essays than you will ever have time to write. In this sense, critical thinking means becoming aware of how you react to an issue. Of course, you must be honest enough to modify your views, if the evidence warrants it, as you go about the process of examining, questioning, and inquiring into the issue at stake in someone else's argument.

The process of evaluating someone else's argument requires you to systematically assess the quality of the argument in terms of its strength and persuasiveness. Draw from your annotations and notes based on your observations of the effectiveness of each part of the argument. You must be able to identify the writer's *claim*, thesis, or proposition and discover where the writer chooses to place the thesis. Does the placement of the thesis suggest that the writer is addressing an audience that is neutral, inclined to agree, or opposed to the thesis? You should also be able to locate any *grounds* the writer presents in the form of data, examples, statistics, testimony, or other kinds of evidence. Try to make explicit the underlying assumptions, or *warrants*, that justify drawing specific conclusions from the evidence presented. Does the writer need to support these assumptions with *backing* that explains why a particular warrant is appropriate? To what extent might the prospective audience find the writer's reasons persuasive because they share the same values? To what extent and how fairly does the writer summarize opposing views? Does the argument provide clear rebuttals to counterarguments or concede good points to the opposition? What kind of impression does the writer create for him or herself in terms of persona, image, and *ethos*? What use does the writer make of connotations, metaphors, images, and appeals to *pathos* and the audience's emotions?

A signal that the writer is relying more on implicit assumptions than on evidence, statistics, expert testimony, logic, and sound reasoning is the frequent use of words whose emotional connotations are meant to prejudice the reader into automatically agreeing with the author's viewpoint. When you come across one of these loaded terms or phrases, or question-begging epithets, ask yourself whether you agree with the writer's characterizations. Are the assumptions underlying these characterizations supported independently by real reasons and examples elsewhere in the article? When looking for a conclusion, try to identify pivotal terms (*because, likewise, consequently*) that indicate the writer is bringing together various elements of the argument to support an inference or generalization. Is the conclusion warranted by the preceding facts and reasons?

The arguments you are evaluating may not appear legitimate, may contain flawed reasoning, may be impractical, or otherwise may pose unrealistic or unworkable alternatives. To refute these kinds of arguments look carefully to see whether the claim is based on implausible warrants or assumptions, whether the proposed solutions would produce disadvantageous effects, whether the evidence cited to support the claim is irrelevant or insufficient, or whether the logic underlying the reasoning is faulty (For a discussion of the most common logical fallacies, see Chapter 5). Bring the same standards to bear on an argument you are evaluating that you would on an argument you were writing.

Another element of critical thinking requires you to relate your own ideas to those of the person who wrote the argument you are reading. You can use this to generate material for your own essay if you can evaluate your own attitudes at the same time you evaluate someone else's argument. The more you are challenged or even threatened by what the person says, the greater your opportunity to use the conflict, tension, or discomfort being produced to look at your own values and beliefs.

Does the writer you are analyzing make assumptions about human nature, society, religion, or culture that are different from your own? In what way do they differ? Keep in mind that you wouldn't even be aware you had these assumptions if you weren't analyzing why someone else's assumptions are making you uncomfortable. Essentially, this is how the analytical process can be used as an opportunity for critical thinking. The extent to which the argument you are reading forces you to question your own highly personal beliefs and values, or provides you with new perspectives you can use to change your own point of view, depends solely on how you react. The encounter with someone who makes a compelling case for something you do not believe can be unsettling because it forces you to examine the reasons underlying your own beliefs. The point is that you can use any discomfort creatively as an opportunity to engage the issue.

To do this, of course, you must be able to (1) identify the basic issues at stake, (2) summarize the main points of the arguments, and (3) understand why the writer used particular kinds of evidence to support this specific viewpoint. Most important, use the occasion of analyzing someone else's argument as an opportunity to critically examine your own beliefs. Read critically and try to be aware of your own attitudes as they emerge while you are responding to someone else's argument.

An Argument with a Student's Refutation

The following argument, "The Business World as a Hunting Ground," is a chapter from Esther Vilar's *The Manipulated Man*. It is followed by student Helene Santos's refutation.

Esther Vilar

The Business World as a Hunting Ground

Esther Vilar was born of German parents in 1935 in Buenos Aires. She received an M.D. from the University of Buenos Aires and practiced as a physician in Munich before beginning a career as a freelance writer. Her works include The Manipulated Man *(1972, reprinted 1998) in which the following chapter first appeared, which aroused a public furor. She has also written a play* Speer *that was first staged in 1999,* The Mathematics of Nina Gluckstein *(1999), and the 2007 work* The Polygamous Sex. *She divides her time between London and Barcelona.*

Thinking Critically

Do the goals of men and women differ in the workplace?

There are many women who take their place in the working world of today. Secretaries and shop assistants, factory workers and stewardesses—not to mention those countless hearty young women who populate the colleges and universities in ever-increasing numbers. One might even get the impression that woman's nature had undergone a radical change in the last twenty years. Today's young women appear to be less unfair than their mothers. They seem to have decided—perhaps out of pity for their victims—not to exploit men any more, but to become, in truth, their partners.

The impression is deceptive. The only truly important act in any woman's life is the selection of the right partner. In any other choice she can afford to make a mistake. Consequently, she will look for a man where he works or studies and where she can best observe and judge the necessary masculine qualities she values. Offices, factories, colleges, and universities are, to her, nothing but gigantic marriage markets.

The particular field chosen by any young woman as a hunting ground will depend to a large extent on the level of income of the man who has previously been her slave, in other words, her father. The daughters of men in the upper income brackets will choose colleges or universities. These offer the best chances of capturing a man who will earn enough to maintain the standards she has already acquired. Besides, a period of study for form's sake is much more convenient than a temporary employment. Girls from less-well-off homes will have to go into factories, shops, offices, or hospitals for a time—but again with the same purpose in mind. None of them intend to stay in these jobs for long. They will continue only until marriage—or, in cases of hardship, till pregnancy. This offers woman one important advantage: any woman who marries nowadays has given up her studies or her job "for the sake of the man of her choice"—and "sacrifices" of this nature create obligations.

Therefore, when women work and study, it merely serves to falsify statistics and furthermore to enslave men more hopelessly than ever, because education and the professions mean something very different when applied to women as opposed to men.

5   When a man works it is a matter of life and death, and, as a rule, the first years of his life are decisive. Any man of twenty-five who is not well on his way up the ladder can be considered, to all intents and purposes, a hopeless case. At this stage, all his faculties are being developed, and the fight with his competitors is a fight to the death. Behind a mask of business friendship, he is constantly on the watch for any sign of superiority in one of his associates, and he will note its appearance with anxiety. If this same associate shows signs of weakness or indecision, it must be taken advantage of at once. Yet man is only a tiny cog in a gigantic business machine, he himself being in effect exploited at every turn. When he drives others, he drives himself most of all. His orders are really orders from above, passed on by him. If the men at the top occasionally take time to praise him, it is not in order to make him happy: it is only to spur him on, to stimulate him to greater effort. For man, who was brought up to be proud and honorable, every working day is merely an endless series of humiliations. He shows enthusiasm for products he finds useless, he laughs at jokes he finds tasteless, he expresses opinions which are not his own. Not for a moment is he allowed to forget that the merest oversight may mean demotion, that one slip of the tongue may spell the end of his career.

Yet woman, who is the prime cause of all these struggles, and under whose very eyes these fights take place, just stands aside and watches. Going to work means to her flirting and dates, teasing and banter, with the odd bit of "labor" done for the sake of appearances—work for which, as a rule, she has no responsibility. She knows that she is only marking time, and even if she does have to go on working for one reason or another, at least she has had years of pleasant dreams. She watches men's battles from a safe distance, occasionally applauding one of the contestants, encouraging or scolding, and while she makes their coffee, opens their mail, or listens to their telephone conversations, she is cold-bloodedly taking her pick. The moment she has found "Mr. Right," she retires gracefully, leaving the field open to her successors.

The same applies to university education. American colleges admit more and more women, but the percentage who actually complete their courses is less than before the Second World War. They sit happily in lectures designing their spring wardrobe and between classes flirt with the boys. With their scarlet nails carefully protected by transparent rubber gloves, they play around with corpses in the dissecting rooms, while their male colleagues realize their whole future is at stake. If a woman leaves the university with an engagement ring on her finger, she has earned her degree; man has hardly begun when he obtains his diploma.

Degrees are, after all, easy to come by—you have only to memorize. How many examiners can tell the difference between real knowledge and bluff? Man, however, has to *understand* his subject as well. His later success will depend on whether his knowledge is well-founded; his later prestige will be built on this, and often other people's lives are dependent on it.

None of these battles exists for woman. If she breaks off her studies and marries a university lecturer, she has achieved the same level as he has without exerting herself. As the wife of a factory owner she is treated with greater respect than he is (and not as somebody who at best would be employable on the assembly line in the same factory). As a wife she always has the same standard of living and social prestige and has to do nothing to maintain them—as he does. For this reason the quickest way to succeed is always to marry a successful man. She does not win him by her industry, ambition, or perseverance—but simply through an attractive appearance.

We have already seen what demands the well-trained man makes on a woman's appearance. The best women trainers—without the least effort—catch the most successful fighters among men. The so-called "beautiful" women are usually those who have had an easy life from their childhood days and therefore have less reason than others to develop their intellectual gifts (intelligence is developed only through competition); it follows as a logical consequence that very successful men usually have abysmally stupid wives (unless, of course, one considers woman's skill at transforming herself into bait for man a feat of intelligence).

10　　It has almost become a commonplace that a really successful man, be he a company director, financier, shipping magnate, or orchestra conductor, will, when he reaches the zenith of his career, marry a beautiful model—usually his second or third wife. Men who have inherited money often take such a super-girl as their first wife—although she will be exchanged over the years for another. Yet, as a rule, models are women of little education who have not even finished school and who have nothing to do until they marry but look beautiful and pose becomingly in front of a camera. But they are "beautiful"—and that makes them potentially rich.

As soon as a woman has caught her man, she "gives up her career for love"—or, at least, that is what she will tell him. After all, he could hardly be flattered by the thought that she had been saved in the nick of time from having to sweat her way through examinations. He would much rather get drunk on the idea of the love "that knows no compromise," which this woman pretends to feel for him. Who knows, he thinks, she might have become a famous surgeon (celebrated prima ballerina, brilliant journalist), and she has given it all up for him. He would never believe that she preferred to be the wife of a famous surgeon, to have his income and prestige without having either the work or the responsibility. Therefore, he resolves to make her life at his side as comfortable as possible to compensate for her great sacrifice.

A small percentage (ten to twenty percent) of women students in industrial countries of the West do, in fact, obtain their degrees before they get married. Despite occasional exceptions, they are, as a rule, less attractive and have failed to catch a suitable provider while still in school. But then, this degree will automatically raise their market value, for there are certain types of men who feel bolstered if their wife has a degree—providing they have one themselves. It is clear evidence of his own cleverness if such a highly educated woman is interested in him. If by chance this female mastermind happens to be sexy, he will be beside himself with joy.

But not for long. Even women doctors, women sociologists, and women lawyers "sacrifice" their careers for their men, or at least set them aside. They withdraw into suburban ranch houses, have children, plant flower beds, and fill their homes with the usual trash. Within a few years these new entertainments obliterate the small amount of "expert knowledge," learned by rote, of course, and they become exactly like their female neighbors.

ENGAGING the Text

1. What misconception does Vilar intend to correct in her essay?

2. What is Vilar's overall assessment of what motivates women to pursue an education or to find employment? What ultimate fate awaits women who are successful in their quest?

EVALUATING the Argument

1. How is Vilar's argument constructed on a set of radically different assumptions governing the reality of men's lives as those compared with women? How does the fact that Vilar is a physician make these assumptions more or less credible?

2. To what extent does Vilar rely on evidence that can be measured and to what extent does she rely on highly charged emotional characterizations of women?

EXPLORING the Issue

1. In your opinion, were Vilar's assumptions about what motivates women to advance their education or have a career ever true and if so, are they true today?

2. Write a short essay agreeing or disagreeing with Vilar in which you fairly state her position and analyze the reasons and evidence she presents to support her claim.

272 CHAPTER 7 WRITING AND REFUTING ARGUMENTS

CONNECTING Different Perspectives

1. In what way is the shopping mall as described by Richard Keller Simon in "The Shopping Mall and the Formal Garden" designed to reinforce the values that dominate women's lives (as Vilar claims)?

A Student's Refutation of Vilar's Essay

Helene Santos

Are Men Really the Slaves of Women?

In "The Business World as a Hunting Ground," Vilar substitutes catchy phrases for evidence to develop her argument that women seek an education or employment to find husbands. Vilar claims that women seek education or employment to reach this objective because "offices, factories, colleges and universities are, to her, nothing but gigantic marriage markets."

Vilar says that women have to do nothing other than marry someone who will support them for the rest of their lives. Vilar claims that "as soon as a woman has caught her man she 'gives up her career for love'—or, at least that is what she will tell him." Upon hearing this, the husband, in Vilar's view, is so flattered and guilt-ridden that "he resolves to make her life at his side as comfortable as possible to compensate for her great sacrifice."

Vilar fails to provide objective evidence such as surveys, interviews, or case histories, to support her thesis that women have no goals other than finding "Mr. Right." For example, Vilar presents no documentation to support her claim that the percentage of women who graduated from American colleges are "less than before the Second World War." The reader has to depend on Vilar's interpretation because she doesn't give any statistics. She bases her argument on erroneous assumptions and unexamined beliefs. How can Vilar possibly claim to know what motivates all women?

First Vilar asserts that the motivation of men and women toward work and education is radically different. She maintains that men view employment and higher education as serious tasks on which their future lives will depend, whereas women see work and study as games to be played while seeking a husband.

Furthermore, Vilar says that because of their different attitudes toward education, men and women develop different levels of intelligence. Women, she claims, merely have to memorize enough to get by while men have to understand the material on which their future careers depend. Vilar assumes that no men memorize their way through school, and no women understand what they study unless, as she claims, they are so unattractive that they can't find a man to support them and must become intelligent in order to survive. Innate intelligence exists and does not develop out of the blue at the age of nineteen because one cannot find a husband. Such simplistic reasoning is characteristic of Vilar's argument.

Vilar believes that women attend universities solely to find men. In her view, men achieve social status through their careers whereas women marry to better themselves. For this reason, she thinks women work to observe more closely the money-making potential of prospective husbands. Vilar uses the phrase "hunting ground" to express her thesis that women view the workplace and universities as "arenas" in which to "capture" their "prey." She describes men as having to struggle in a highly competitive work environment while women watch the battle, "cold-bloodedly" taking their pick. Vilar asserts that for a woman, sex-appeal is a commodity that can be translated into marriage and a life of ease. Vilar fails to cite even one case history that might support these claims.

Women at work, according to Vilar, will be less capable as employees since husband "hunting" and not work is their primary objective. She uses phrases like "odd bit of 'labor' done for the sake of appearances" and "for a time" to imply that women are not serious about their jobs. Vilar says that for women work means flirting and dates. What of those dedicated and skilled women who take their jobs seriously? How would Vilar account for these women?

Moreover, Vilar would have us believe that women choose low-paying jobs with little responsibility because they do not take work seriously. Her tactic of "blaming the victim" fails to acknowledge that very often women are excluded from executive positions and must take menial jobs in order to survive. Vilar often confuses cause and effect in this way.

Vilar's stereotyped view of women as sex objects doesn't take into account that beauty is in the "eye of the beholder," and more a matter of subjective choice than Vilar assumes. She also stereotypes men by portraying them as witless dupes who believe their wives have given up possible careers as famous surgeons, celebrated ballerinas, or brilliant journalists to marry them.

Vilar claims that "very successful men usually have abysmally stupid wives." She reaches this conclusion through a parody of reasoning that runs as follows: (1) "intelligence is developed only through competition," (2) "so-called 'beautiful' women . . . have had an easy life from their childhood days," (3) those who have had an easy life . . . have less reason . . . to develop their intellectual gifts," (4) "an attractive appearance" acts as "bait" for a "really successful man," therefore (5) "very successful men usually have abysmally stupid wives." Why must beauty and intelligence be mutually exclusive?

Vilar bases her argument on unexamined assumptions. For instance, she assumes that no woman wants to be single. She also assumes that no man wants to be married and therefore must be manipulated into a lifetime "obligation." Vilar ignores the many men who want to get married and the large number of women who want to remain single in order to pursue their education and careers.

Vilar claims that women obtain degrees in order to "raise their market value" or because they are so unattractive that they cannot find a man to support them. From this, she mistakenly concludes that only unattractive women go on to have successful careers. Vilar also fails to mention the large number of women who complete their degrees after getting married and overlooks the many women who return to work after marriage. In her view, only wives of unsuccessful husbands return to work after marriage.

Vilar discounts objections to her argument by using phrases like "might . . . get the impression," "appear" and "seem." In this way, she suggests that those who believe opposing arguments are being fooled and only she is telling the truth.

Instead of citing evidence, examples, statistics, testimony, quotations, and surveys, as support for her claims, Vilar uses imaginative metaphors such as "hunting ground," "prey," "victim," "arena," "capturing," "cold-bloodedly," and "slave." Her strategy is to use words to create images whose connotations imply foregone conclusions. For example, she states "the particular field chosen by any young woman as a hunting ground will depend to a large extent on the level of income of the man who has previously been her slave, in other words, her father." This statement appears to convey a conclusion, but is actually "begging the question." A closer look reveals Vilar's circular reasoning: Vilar asserts as a proven fact what the argument itself exists to prove—"all men are slaves of women."

Despite Vilar's catchy phrases and stylistic flair, the lack of any objective evidence to prove her assertions makes it impossible to perceive her as a reliable observer or take her views seriously. Vilar presents herself as a

> hard-working, truly emancipated woman surrounded by silly, conniving
> women who giggle, flirt, play games, and "design their spring wardrobes"
> while sizing up their "prey."
>
> Perhaps women do view the "business world as a hunting ground,"
> but they are "hunting" things other than husbands such as self-esteem
> and rewarding careers.

This student has done an excellent job in analyzing Esther Vilar's "The Business World as a Hunting Ground":

1. The title of the essay, "Are Men Really the Slaves of Women?" is effective in suggesting both the subject and the writer's skeptical attitude.

2. Santos identifies the subject, author, and title of the article early, and she announces the thesis of her essay in the first sentence.

3. She skillfully summarizes Vilar's chief claims in order to give her readers a necessary background against which to understand her analysis and evaluation.

4. She considers and evaluates all of Vilar's main points, identifying contradictions in Vilar's reasoning.

5. She does an exceptionally good job of locating and analyzing the implicit assumptions underlying Vilar's argument.

6. Santos adroitly incorporates a few brief quotations to let the reader hear Vilar's voice at crucial points in her analysis. This is especially effective when she turns her attention to questions of word choice and emotionally loaded language in Vilar's essay.

7. Her essay has a sensible, easy-to-recognize, consistent organization. She analyzes Vilar's essay without getting side-tracked.

8. Santos's conclusion ties up all the loose ends with some stylistic grace, using the metaphor of a "business world as a hunting ground" to challenge Vilar's main premise.

9. One area for improvement in Santos's essay is sentence structure. Several of the extremely long sentences might be divided into shorter, clearer sentences. Another fault that could be easily corrected is her unvaried use of "Vilar" to begin sentences. Simply varying the opening of sentences with "she," "the author," "the writer," or "Ms. Vilar" would solve the problem.

8 READING AND ANALYZING VISUAL TEXTS

OVERVIEW: In the discussions of critical reading and the strategies of argument, we looked at important rhetorical elements. We can also use these elements to analyze visual texts and understand design principles that govern Web sites, tables, graphs, and charts, as well as the images advertisers use to market their products. An application of these elements is explored in a case study of the Paper Clip Project.

Just as you can read written texts critically, you can also read visual texts. You encounter hundreds of them every day on television, in films, on the Internet, and in newspapers, magazines, and books. Some, like magazine ads, billboards, CD covers, store windows, and photographs, are purely visual images. Others, such as Web pages, films, and ads on TV, combine sound and movement with images. All of these visual texts have been artfully constructed to convey precise meanings and to influence your behavior. All of them can be analyzed by looking at how they use the elements of rhetoric and of design.

AUDIENCE For every visual image, the first question to ask is, who is the likely *audience*? The general public? Or some specialized segment of the general population, such as children, teenagers, senior citizens, parents, young professionals, baby boomers, men, women, or particular ethnic or racial groups? What might this intended audience be expected to know, believe, or feel about this particular image? For example, if you compare the ads on different kinds of television shows—soap operas, late-night talk shows, Monday night football, Saturday morning cartoons, cooking shows—you will observe different kinds of products being advertised and, correspondingly, different marketing appeals targeted for specific audiences.

PURPOSE The next thing to determine is the *purpose* for which the visual image was created. As with written texts, images may explain or inform, persuade, or entertain. Unlike the case in written texts, however, one of these usually predominates. For example, news photographs are primarily intended to inform an audience by showing events and persons. Ads obviously are intended to persuade while most films and television shows are intended to entertain.

TOPIC We can look at an image to see how it illustrates a *topic* or subject. Looked at in this way, the image serves the same function as clear-cut examples do in a written text. They clarify, illustrate, or support the main idea. For example, does a CD cover show a picture of the performer(s), or does it show an image that evokes a feeling or expresses a theme? Does an ad show a product in a literal way, or does it use images of celebrities, supermodels, or prominent athletes to promote the product's mystique? Or is the ad intended to offset criticism (as with oil or chemical companies) by highlighting the company's efforts to protect the environment?

OCCASION In general, visual texts are much more closely tied to specific *occasions* than are written texts. For example, does a cartoon strip reflect a current issue? Is a billboard or bumper sticker part of a political campaign? Does an ad introduce a new product or take advantage of a current trend? Is a public sculpture intended to commemorate a famous person or notable event?

ARTIST Last, what does the image suggest about the *artist* or *creator* who designed the image for a given audience, purpose, and occasion? This is analogous to analyzing a written text where the author is known, or at least is knowable.

ASSIGNMENT FOR READING AND ANALYZING VISUAL TEXTS Visit the Web site of the Pulitzer Prize winners for photography (http://www.pulitzer.org) and select and analyze one of the photos for the current year in terms of audience, purpose, topic, occasion, and artist.

Elements of Design

We analyze written texts in terms of rhetorical techniques. So, too, in understanding visual texts we can analyze the formal elements of design (balance, proportion, movement, contrast, and unity) according to basic principles that determine how we "read" an image in both a literal and figurative sense.

Our feeling that a design is *balanced* is determined by how symmetrical or asymmetrical the image is; if the top and bottom or right and left sides are of equal proportion or mirror each other, the effect is one of stability. For example, see the film still from the classic *Star Trek* episode "Let This Be Your Last Battlefield" (Figure 8.1); its right and left sides mirror each other. The effect is formal and static (and aptly communicates the perpetual and senseless

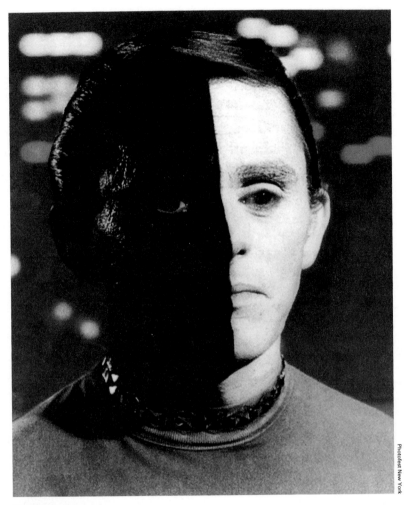

Photofest New York

FIGURE 8.1

battle between enemies). By contrast, an asymmetrical design will suggest informality and dynamic movement, as does the publicity photo for Beyoncé (Figure 8.2).

Next, the relative size of elements in a design will create a sense of *proportion* and determine what we notice first, second, and so on. By adjusting these elements, the designer can suggest an implicit agenda as to what is most important and least important.

We are accustomed to reading a page of text, and our sense of *movement* is created by the fact that we read from left to right and from top to bottom.

Albert Ferreira/Reuters/Corbis

FIGURE 8.2

However, the size and arrangement of elements in a visual text can make us scan differently. Horizontal and vertical lines in a two-dimensional image will suggest stability and lack of movement, whereas diagonal or angular lines imply movement and energy. For example, Beyoncé's photo appears to catch her in a dynamic gesture that emphasizes her energy as both singer and dancer, whereas a static pose would have simply shown her as a singer.

Visual images can also suggest an agenda through contrast of size, shape, and color and by placing the subject in sharp focus in the foreground.

Unity is the way all the elements (balance, proportion, movement, and contrast) work together to produce a feeling of completeness. Most ads are designed to function this way. In contrast are some commercial Web pages that carry ads and other elements to sidetrack you and persuade you to click on a link that will carry you somewhere you did not intend to go (for more on online design, see the Box "Analyzing a Web Site").

ANALYZING A WEB SITE

Aside from analyzing a Web site to evaluate its credibility as a potential source for an analysis (see the Box on p. 309-310 "Tips for Evaluating Electronic Sources"), you might choose or be assigned the task of analyzing a Web site as a class project. Or you might want to analyze your own Web site, whether it's one you've already created or one you're in the process of creating, to ensure the quality and effectiveness of its design and function. Today, more and more people can create their own Web sites—ones with a lot of bells and whistles—but the interactive nature of the medium requires some special design considerations, especially ease of use and a correspondence between form and content. Regardless of a site's intended purpose, if you're analyzing it, you'll need to keep the following design considerations in mind:

 ▪ Because the medium is primarily visual (rather than verbal), some designers are tempted to use more graphics and plug-ins than they need to simply because they want to use all the new technology they can. But too much can distract from the main message. The search engine Google at http://www.google.com gained quick popularity because of its simplicity. Its uncluttered home page promises a search engine and only that. It downloads quickly and provides search results quickly.

 ▪ Motion or animation should be used only when it enhances the content. A good example is Honda's Web site for the current model year at http://www.honda.com/, which lets potential buyers customize the color and other aspects of their model onscreen. Another good example is the Web site of the Fine Arts Museum of San Francisco at http://www.thinker.org, which lets users zoom in on parts of artworks in its extensive online collection.

▦ A Web site should not use such a complicated design that it will require a lot of memory and load time, unless its audience is only those with very powerful Internet access.

▦ Links to other Web sites should give credibility to the site; they should be reputable and useful links. The humanities Web site Voice of the Shuttle at http://vos.ucsb.edu is a good example of a site with useful links. And the links should be live. Dead links are a sign that the page is not being actively maintained and updated.

▦ A good Web site should have a consistent layout, with links to the home page and the top of the page on every page.

▦ A good Web site should have an organization that is not too complex. Ideally, users shouldn't have to click more than three times to find what they are looking for.

▦ Some designers use frames for complex sites, with a navigational index on the left side. This can be a solution for making navigation easier, but some Internet users dislike frames because they may increase download time, they decrease the size of the linked page, and they make going back to the previous Web site more difficult because it can't be accomplished by a simple click of the mouse.

▦ A professional Web site uses colors and font types and sizes consistently on all pages to give the site unity. Moreover, the font types and the colors are appropriate to the subject matter.

▦ A Web site should use plug-ins that are available to a large number of users. Users shouldn't have to take the time to download some obscure plug-in that is not on their computer, unless the intended audience is computer experts.

▦ Grammar and spelling errors are a signal to question the Web site creator's credibility.

ASSIGNMENT FOR ANALYZING A WEB SITE   Visit the Web Marketing Association's site for the best designed Web site awards at http://www.webaward.org/ and analyze one of the Web sites in terms of its elements of design and the criteria presented in "Analyzing a Web Site."

Using Tables, Graphs, and Charts to Present Information Through Visual Means

Tables offer an especially useful way to convey information (text and numbers in columns and rows) in a concise format (see Figure 8.3). They should be self-contained and labeled so that your audience can understand the information without reference to the text. Each table should include a title that communicates the subject covered. It should also specify the context in terms of the source of the data, where and when it was collected, and if relevant, the limiting factors that determined who was included in the data (for example, people in a certain age group, income level, or from a certain geographical area). Tables are numbered and titled; by contrast, graphs and charts are identified as figures.

Graphs and charts offer a convenient, engaging, and convincing way for the audience to visualize relationships, compare changes, and understand trends. The basic kinds are:

a. Line charts and graphs are used for direct comparisons and to demonstrate growth trends. These are among the most widely used (see Figure 8.4).

TABLE 1

LEADING CAUSES OF DALYs		
Rank	1990*	2020 Projection
1	Pneumonia and other respiratory infections	Heart disease
2	Diarrheal disease	Depression
3	Disorders of childbirth and newborns	Vehicular accidents
4	Depression	Stroke
5	Heart disease	Emphysema and bronchitis
6	Stroke	Pneumonia and other respiratory infections
7	Tuberculosis	Tuberculosis
8	Measles	War
9	Vehicular accidents	Diarrheal disease
10	Congenital defects	HIV

Source: Barry R. Bloom, "Public Health in Transition," *Scientific American,* September 2005, p. 95.

*Based on 1990 data later reanalyzed as DALYs

FIGURE 8.3
▦ Leading causes of disability-adjusted life years.

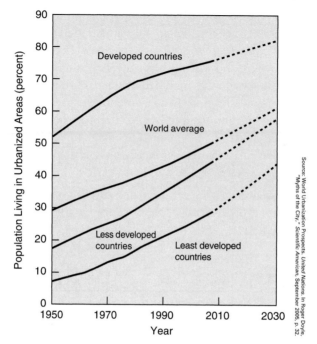

Source: World Urbanization Prospects, *United Nations*. In Roger Doyle, "Myths of the City," *Scientific American*, September 2005, p. 32.

FIGURE 8.4

▪ Current and projected population distribution patterns. *Solid lines are estimated; dotted lines are projections.*

b. Bar charts and graphs consist of an axis and a series of labeled horizontal or vertical bars that show different values for each bar. These are especially useful for showing comparisons. A double bar graph is similar to a regular bar graph but gives two pieces of information for each item on the vertical axis and allows the audience to compare values over time (see Figure 8.5).

c. Pie charts are among the easiest to grasp and consist of a circle graph divided into pieces with each displaying the size of some related piece of information. Pie charts are used for illustrating the relation of parts to the whole and for showing patterns of distribution in a clear-cut way. These are constructed and read clockwise with the largest portion occuring first (see Figure 8.6).

d. Flow charts are used to clarify stages or steps in a process or procedure or set of directions. They graphically show the sequence of events or the relationship of steps in a process. They are not used to show comparisons or trends (see Figure 8.7).

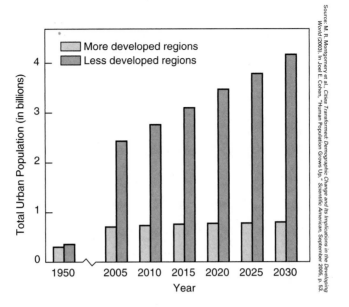

Source: M. R. Montgomery et al., *Cities Transformed: Demographic Change and Its Implications in the Developing World* (2003). In Joel E. Cohen, "Human Population Grows Up." *Scientific American*, September 2005, p. 53.

FIGURE 8.5

Comparison of urban population growth between rich and poor countries.

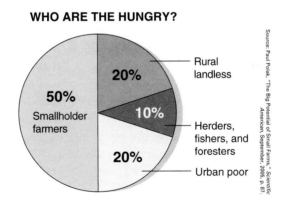

Source: Paul Polak, "The Big Potential of Small Farms," *Scientific American*, September, 2005, p. 87.

FIGURE 8.6

Distribution of hunger in the world.

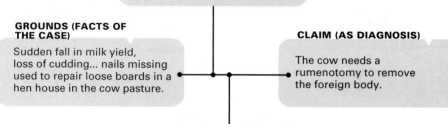

WARRANT DRAWN FROM EXPERIENCE

A cow that swallows a foreign body like a nail can be expected to show symptoms of sudden fall in milk yield.

GROUNDS (FACTS OF THE CASE)

Sudden fall in milk yield, loss of cudding... nails missing used to repair loose boards in a hen house in the cow pasture.

CLAIM (AS DIAGNOSIS)

The cow needs a rumenotomy to remove the foreign body.

QUALIFIER OR EXCEPTION

Unless it can be established that the cow definitely did not swallow one of the loose nails.

FIGURE 8.7

Flow chart of veterinary diagnosis according to Toulmin model.

Reading Images as Cultural Signs

Beyond the rhetorical elements (audience, purpose, topic, occasion, and designer or artist) and the principles of design that create moods and communicate messages, visual texts can also be *read* as signs for what they reveal about the surrounding culture. Cultural signs can include artifacts, objects, events, images, products, gestures, sounds, or indeed almost anything that when analyzed reveals something meaningful about a culture, its assumptions, values, beliefs, and struggles. The process of "decoding" these underlying meanings requires us to move from a literal analysis of the design principles in art reproductions, photographs, advertisements, and cartoons in order to discover the explicit and implicit messages conveyed and to think critically about the agendas of those who wish to influence our behavior.

The study of images for what they suggest about our culture puts us in a situation similar to that of anthropologists who discover and try to decipher the meaning of artifacts. Just as anthropologists have to form hypotheses about the context within which these objects and artifacts have meaning, so practitioners of semiotics (the study of signs) always try to recontextualize the meaning of any single sign or image by putting it in a broader cultural context. We do this by identifying the current themes, and issues of the moment that are reflected in the image (or visual text) and by becoming aware of the larger underlying framework in which the sign functions.

The key to interpreting ads and other cultural artifacts is to mentally link them to the associations, similarities, and differences that collectively make up that particular sign system (in the next image for example, the themes are religion, the Internet, and revelry).

ANALYZING AN ADVERTISEMENT

Just how this works can be seen by analyzing a rather interesting advertisement (see Figure 8.8) that appeared a few years ago for the service offered by an Internet portal, Yahoo! Since the ad is selling a service rather than a product, it uses an amusing photograph of nuns to promote its Web site. The design of the ad is highly effective: As we scan the page, we see the satisfied users of the service enclosed in a circle overlapping two successively smaller circles. The text suggests a stark contrast between daily meditation and nightly revelry ("We meditate all day and Yahoo like crazy all night"). The nuns' sense of buoyancy and elation is suggested by the large floating circle almost like bubbles in champagne. To underscore the contrast between self-contained tranquility and exhuberance, the radiating circles emanting from the Yahoo icon reinforce the sense of freedom the nuns seem to feel.

As a cultural sign, the ad makes us smile because it is congruous that (1) nuns would be as attached to the Internet as the rest of us and that (2) they would need such a secular outlet within the confines of their religious order. We also notice that the advertisers use the name of the service as a verb and reinforce the sense of euphoria implicit in the term (Yahoo!). The ad asks readers to compare themselves to the nuns in the image–as if to say–if even nuns are using Yahoo then why shouldn't you? As we can see from this ad, images are really another form of text that tell stories about ourselves, our culture, and our world.

ASSIGNMENT FOR READING IMAGES AS CULTURAL SIGNS   Visit the Web site at http://whc.unesco.org/criteria.htm for the criteria that determines whether a monument, group of buildings, or site should be nominated for inclusion in the World Heritage List. In your opinion does the Paper Clip Project at Whitwell Middle School in Tennessee (discussed next) qualify to be on this list? Why or why not? Make your case in a short essay drawing on the materials in both Web sites.

FIGURE 8.8

The Paper Clip Project

The Paper Clip Project was begun by eighth graders in the small (population 1,600) rural town of Whitwell, Tennessee. The children's goal was to collect 6 million paper clips—to commemorate the 6 million Jewish victims of the Holocaust—but they eventually received over 20 million paper clips, and letters of support from all over the world. They were inspired to choose the paper clip as a symbol because during World War II, Norwegians were forbidden from wearing buttons with the likenesses or initials of their king. In protest against the Nazi occupation, Norwegians began to wear paper clips (which were invented by Johan Vaaler, a Norwegian Jew).

The project began in 1998 when the faculty at Whitwell decided to teach the school's largely white and Protestant student population about the Holocaust and issues of hate and intolerance. Eventually, the entire school became involved and collected millions of paper clips and answered each letter and e-mail. The project was covered by two German journalists, Peter and Dagmer Schroeder, who helped the students obtain a railcar that was actually used to transport Jews to the concentration camps.

As a result, a World War II cattle car is located in front of the Whitwell Middle School and contains millions of paper clips—a testament to the millions who died under the Nazis and to the children's ability to reach across time and culture to create a living memorial.

This project is the subject of a documentary film titled *Paper Clips* (2004) and of a book, *Six Million Paper Clips: The Making of a Children's Holocaust Memorial*, by Peter and Dagmar Schroeder (2004).

Do some research on this project by renting the movie, reading the book, and visiting the home page at http://www.marionschools.org. Write a short essay on the indispensable function played by visual imagery and symbolism of the paper clip in this context.

What insight does the following image give you into this project?

Photofest New York

FIGURE 8.9

The Rhetoric of Advertising

Whether ads are presented as sources of information enabling the consumer to make educated choices between products or aim at offering memorable images, or witty, thoughtful, or poetic copy, the underlying intent of all advertising is to persuade specific audiences. Seen in this way, ads appear as mini-arguments whose strategies and techniques of persuasion can be analyzed just like a written argument. We can discover which elements are designed to appeal to the audience's emotions (*pathos* according to Aristotle), which elements make their appeal in terms of reasons, evidence, or logic (*logos*), and how the advertiser goes about winning credibility for itself or in terms of the spokesperson employed to speak on behalf of the product (the *ethos* dimension). Like arguments, ads can be effective if they appeal to the needs, values, and beliefs of the audience. Advertisers use a variety of visual and verbal means to encourage their audiences to identify with the people in the ads, the experiences the ads depict, and the values the ads promote. Although the verbal and visual elements within an ad are designed to work together, we can study these elements separately. We can look at how the composition of the elements within an ad is intended to function. We can look at the role of language and how it is used to persuade. We can study how objects and settings are used to promote the audience's identification with the products being sold. We can judge ads according to the skill with which they deploy all of these resources while at the same time being critically aware of their intended effects on us.

THE TECHNIQUES OF ADVERTISING

The claim the ad makes is designed to establish the superiority of the product in the minds of the audience and to create a distinctive image for the product, whether it is a brand of cigarettes, a financial service, or a type of gasoline. The single most important technique for creating this image depends on transferring ideas, attributes, or feelings from outside the product onto the product itself. In this way the product comes to represent an obtainable object or service that embodies, represents, or symbolizes a whole range of meanings. This transfer can be achieved in many ways. For example, when Nicole Kidman or Jennifer Lopez lends her glamour and beauty to the merchandising of a perfume, the consumer is meant to conclude that the perfume must be superior to other perfumes in the way that these celebrities embody beauty, glamour, and sex appeal. The attempt to transfer significance can operate in two ways. It can encourage the audience to discover meanings and to correlate feelings and attributes that the advertiser wishes the product to represent in ways that allow these needs and desires to become attached to specific products. It can also prevent the correlation of thoughts or feelings that might discourage the audience from purchasing a particular product. For example, the first most instinctive response to the thought of smoking a cigarette might be linked with the idea of inhaling hot and dry smoke from what are essentially burning tobacco leaves. Thus, any associations the audience might have with burning leaves, coughing, and dry hot smoke must be short-circuited by supplying them with a whole set of other associations to receive and occupy the perceptual "slot" that might have been triggered by their first reactions. Cigarette advertisers do this in a variety of ways:

> By showing active people in outdoorsy settings, they put the thought of emphysema, shortness of breath, or lung disease very far away indeed.

> By showing cigarette packs set against the background of grass glistening with morning dew or bubbling streams or cascading water falls, they subtly guide the audience's response away from what is dry, hot, congested, or burning toward what is open, airy, moist, cool, and clean.

In some brands, menthol flavoring and green and blue colors are intended to promote these associations.

Thus, ads act as do other kinds of persuasion to intensifying correlations that work to the advertiser's advantage and to suppress associations that would lessen the product's appeal.

The kinds of associations audiences are encouraged to perceive reflect a broad range of positive emotional appeals that encourage the audience to find self-esteem through the purchase of a product that by itself offers a way to meet personal and social needs. The particular approach taken in the composition of the ad, the way it is laid out, and the connotations of the advertising copy, vary according to the emotional appeal of the ad.

The most common manipulative techniques are designed to make consumers want to consume to satisfy deep-seated human drives. Of course, no one consciously believes that purchasing a particular kind of toothpaste, perfume, lipstick, or automobile will meet real psychological and social needs, but that is exactly how products are sold—through the promise of delivering unattainable satisfactions through tangible purchasable objects or services. In purchasing a certain product, we are offered the chance to create ourselves, our personality, and our relationships through consumption.

EMOTIONAL APPEALS USED IN ADVERTISING

The emotional appeals in ads function exactly the way value warrants do in written arguments. They supply the unstated major premise that supplies a rationale to persuade an audience that a particular product will meet one or another of several different kinds of needs. Some ads present the purchase of a product as a means by which consumers can find social acceptance.

These ads address the consumer as "you" ("wouldn't 'you' really rather have a Buick?"). The "you" here is plural but is perceived as being individual and personal by someone who has already formed the connection with the product. Ironically, the price of remaining in good standing with this "group" of fellow consumers requires the consumer to purchase an expensive automobile. In this sense, ads give consumers a chance to belong to social groups that have only one thing in common—the purchase of a particular product.

One variation on the emotional need to belong to a designated social group is the appeal to status or "snob appeal." Snob appeal is not new. In 1710, the *Spectator*, a popular newspaper of the time, carried an ad that read:

> An incomparable Powder for Cleaning Teeth, which has given great satisfaction
> to most of the Nobility Gentry in England.
> —*quoted in W. Duncan Reekie*, Advertising: Its Place in Political and Managerial Economics

Ads for scotch, expensive cars, boats, jewelry, and watches frequently place their products in upper-class settings or depict them in connection with the fine arts (sculpture, ballet, etc.). The *value warrant* in these ads encourages the consumer to imagine that the purchase of the item will confer qualities associated with the background or activities of this upper-class world onto the consumer.

In other ads, the need to belong takes a more subtle form by offering the product as a way to become part of a time in the past the audience might look back to with nostalgia. Grandmotherly figures wearing aprons and holding products that are advertised as being "like Grandma used to make" offer the consumer an imaginery past, a family tradition, or a simpler time looked back to with warmth and sentimentality. For many years, Smucker's preserves featured ads in which the product was an integral part of a scene emanating security and warmth, which the ad invited us to remember as if it were our own past. Ads of this kind are often photographed through filters that present misty sepia-tone images that carefully re-create old-fashioned kitchens with the accompanying appliances, dishes, clothes, and hairstyles. The ads thus supply us with false memories and invite us to insert ourselves into this imaginary past and to remember it as if it were our own. At the furthest extreme, ads employing the appeal to see ourselves as part of a group may try to evoke patriotic feelings so that the prospective consumer will derive the satisfactions of good citizenship and sense of participation in being part of the collective psyche of an entire nation. The point is that people really do have profound needs that advertisers can exploit, but it would be a rare product indeed that could really fulfill such profound needs.

Advertisers use highly sophisticated market research techniques to enable them to define and characterize precisely those people who are most likely to be receptive to ads of particular kinds. The science of demographics is aided and abetted by psychological research that enables advertisers to "target" a precisely designated segment of the general public. For example, manufacturers of various kinds of liquor can rely on studies that inform them that vodka drinkers are most likely to read *Psychology Today* and scotch drinkers *The New Yorker,* while readers of *Time* prefer rum and the audience for *Playboy* has a large number of readers who prefer gin. Once a market segment with defined psychological characteristics has been identified, an individual ad can be crafted for that particular segment and placed in the appropriate publication.

Ads, of course, can elicit responses by attempting to manipulate consumers through negative as well as positive emotional appeals. Helen Woodward, the head copywriter for an ad agency, once offered the following advice for ad writers trying to formulate a new ad for baby food: "Give 'em the figures about the baby death rate—but don't say it flatly . . . if we only had the nerve to put a hearse in the ad, you couldn't keep the women away from the food" (quoted in Stuart Ewen, *Captains of Consciousness: Advertising and the Social Roots of the Consumer Culture*). Ads of this kind must first arouse the consumer's anxieties and then offer the product as the solution to the problem that more often than not the ad has created.

For example, an advertisement for Polaroid evokes the fear of not having taken pictures of moments that cannot be re-created and then offers the product as a form of insurance that will prevent this calamity from occurring. Nikon does the same in claiming that "a moment is called a moment because it doesn't last forever. Think of sunsets. A child's surprise. A Labrador's licky kiss. This is precisely why the Nikon N50 has the simple 'Simple' switch on top of the camera."

Ads for products that promise to guarantee their purchasers sex appeal, youth, health, social acceptance, self-esteem, creativity, enlightenment, a happy family life, loving relationships, escape from boredom, vitality, and many other things, frequently employ scare tactics to frighten or worry the consumer into purchasing their product to ease his or her fears. These ads must first make the consumer dissatisfied with the self that exists. In this way, they function exactly as do *policy arguments* that recommend solutions to problems with measurably harmful consequences. The difference is that these kinds of ads actually are designed to arouse and then exploit the anxieties related to these problems.

Large industrial conglomerates, whether in oil, chemicals, pharmaceuticals, or agribusiness, frequently use advertising to accomplish different kinds of objectives than simply persuading the consumer to buy a particular product. These companies often seek to persuade the general public that they are not polluting the environment, poisoning the water, or causing environmental havoc in the process of manufacturing their products. The emotional appeal they use is to portray themselves as concerned "corporate citizens," vitally interested in the public good as a whole and especially in those communities where they conduct their operations. In some cases, the ads present products as if they were directly produced from nature without being subjected to intermediary processing, preservatives, and contaminants, thereby lessening concern that they produce harmful biproducts. For example, Mazola might depict a spigot producing corn oil directly inserted into an ear of corn. A jeep might appear to have materialized out of thin air on a seemingly inaccessible mountain peak. Companies sensitive to accusations that they are polluting the air and water can mount an advertising campaign designed to prove that they are not simply exploiting the local resources (whether timber, oil, fish, or coal) for profits but are genuinely interested in putting something back into the community. The folksy good-neighbor tone of these ads is designed to create a benign image of the company.

The Language of Advertising

We can see how the creation of a sense of the company's credibility as a concerned citizen corresponds to what Aristotle called the *ethos* dimension. For example, Chevron (in their classic "people do" ads) expressed concern (in "Racing to the Moon") that the light from their oil-drilling operations be shielded so that spawning sea turtles won't be unintentionally misdirected and lose their way! Another ad ("The Pipeline and the Dancing Bird") assured us that workers stopped construction on a pipeline in western Wyoming to allow chicks of the sage grouse to hatch, at which point they came back and completed the job.

The appeals to logic, statements of reasons, and presentations of evidence in ads correspond to the *logos* dimension of argument. The wording of the claims is particularly important since it determines whether companies are legally responsible for any claims they make.

Claims in advertising need to be evaluated to discover whether something is asserted that needs to be proved or is implied without actually being stated.

Claims may refer to authoritative-sounding results obtained by supposedly independent laboratories, teams of research scientists, or physicians, without ever saying how these surveys were conducted, what statistical methods were used, and who interpreted the results. Ads of this kind may make an impressive-sounding quasi-scientific claim; Ivory Soap used to present itself as "99 and 44/100% pure" without answering "pure" what. Some ads use technical talk and scientific terms to give the impression of a scientific breakthrough. For example, STP claims that it added "an anti-wear agent and viscosity improvers" to your oil. The copy for L. L. Bean claims of one of its jackets that "even in brutal ice winds gusting to 80 knots this remarkable anorak kept team members who wore it warm and comfortable." It would be important to know that the team members referred to are members of the "L. L. Bean test team."

Other claims cannot be substantiated, for example, "we're the Dexter Shoe Company. And for nearly four decades we put a lot of Dexter Maine into every pair of shoes we make."

In an ad for lipstick, Aveda makes the claim that "it's made of rich, earthy lip colours formulated with pure plant pigment from the Uruku tree. Organically grown by indigenous people in the rain forest."

Claims may be deceptive in other ways. Of all the techniques advertisers use to influence what people believe and how they spend their money, none is more basic than the use of so-called *weasel words*. This term was popularized by Theodore Roosevelt, in a speech he gave in St. Louis, May 31, 1916, when he commented that notes from the Department of State were filled with weasel words that retract the meaning of the words they are next to just as a weasel sucks the meat out of the egg.

In modern advertising parlance, a weasel word has come to mean any qualifier or comparative that is used to imply a positive quality that cannot be stated as a fact because it cannot be substantiated. For example, if an ad claims a toothpaste will "help" stop cavities, it does not obligate the manufacturer to substantiate this claim. So, too, if a product is advertised as "fighting" germs, the equivocal claim hides the fact that the product may fight and lose.

The words *virtually* (as in "virtually spotless") and *up to* or *for as long as* (as in "stops coughs up to 8 hours") also remove any legal obligation on the part of the manufacturer to justify the claim.

Other favorite words in the copywriter's repertoire, such as *free* and *new*, are useful in selling everything from cat food to political candidates.

Questions for Discussion and Writing

1. How are each of the following ads designed to create a distinctive image for the company, product, or service being promoted? In each case, what function does the picture serve? What psychological needs or values do the advertisers appeal to? How is the ad copy or language designed to manipulate the emotions of the readers in ways that are positive for the advertisers? In your opinion, is the approach taken by each advertiser in the following ads successful? Why or why not?

    Get Real: How is this ad structured as a conversation in which the speaker is rebuked? How does this ad attempt to link having sex without the use of a condom to skydiving without a parachute? How does the use of the term *genius* present it as sarcastic advice to a young person by a well-meaning adult? How does the use of the word *helps* seem to guarantee protection while removing the manufacturer of Trojans (Carter-Wallace) from responsibility? What connotations and associations does the name *Trojan* evoke and how is this effective in defining the product.

FIGURE 8.10

There Will Always Be Those Who Refuse to Ski Mammoth: Is equating the reluctant skier, who for one reason or another, has not skied Mammoth mountain in California to a giant chicken, an effective tactic? How does the fine print offer a way out for those skiers who are not daredevils? How does the oversized nature of the chicken and the pattern of its feathers suggest the enormous skiing resort?

THERE WILL ALWAYS BE THOSE WHO REFUSE TO SKI MAMMOTH.

Admittedly, with an elevation of 11,053 feet and 3,100 foot vertical, there are those of you who just flat out won't pay us a visit. Guess you probably don't realize we have 150 trails – spread out over 3,500 skiable acres – so there's lots of prime terrain, no matter what your ability. But hey, if you don't want to call 1-800-832-7320 and get the complete story in our free travel planner, far be it for us to insist. We certainly wouldn't want to ruffle anyone's feathers.

MAMMOTH
No other mountain lives up to its name.

FIGURE 8.11

FIGURE 8.12

2. How does this Web site (for the Office of Community Service Learning) use the principles of design (balance, proportion, movement, contrast, and unity) to reach its audience? Who is the likely audience, what is the purpose for which this site was created, how does it illustrate the topic it addresses, and what occasion does it reflect. How effective do you find the approach taken by the designer of this site?

WRITING AN ARGUMENT FROM SOURCES

OVERVIEW: Each of the previous chapters has introduced you to ways of analyzing arguments. In the process, you have explored several controversies through essays written by a wide range of professionals including journalists and academic researchers in different fields of study. Doubtless, some of these controversies have sparked your curiosity and made you want to delve into the ideas, opinions, facts, and arguments involved in that issue to a much greater degree. This chapter will introduce you to the methods by which you can pursue your inquiry.

Finding a Question to Answer

Preparing a research paper requires you to select a subject and formulate a question on it that you would like to answer in a certain number of pages, given the resources of your library and the time available to you. The research process begins with careful consideration of a wide range of thought-provoking questions connected with your subject. If, for example, you were assigned the broad subject of "drug use and drug addiction in contemporary society," each question you thought of would limit this wide-ranging subject to a more manageable topic. Some interesting questions that might be asked on this subject are these:

1. What has caused such a massive upswing of drug use in our society?

2. Are "legal" drugs less addictive or less dangerous than illegal drugs?

3. Should marijuana use be decriminalized?

4. How dependent are the economies of other countries on the billions of dollars generated by producing cocaine that is sold in the United States?

5. Does mandatory drug testing provide reliable results? Does it violate the Fourth Amendment guarantee against "illegal search and seizure" and constitute an invasion of privacy?

6. What level of success has been achieved by the voluntary "just say no" program?

7. Are athletes coerced into using performance-enhancing drugs, such as steroids, in order to remain competitive?

8. What part do drugs play in highly competitive areas such as professional sports, the entertainment industry, and the financial world?

9. How do drugs affect the central nervous system?

10. What part have hallucinogenic substances played in religions down through the ages?

Some topics, such as the one in question 10, are still too wide-ranging to be researched within the time available. Other topics, such as that in question 9, might be too difficult since they would require you to possess a high level of technical information. Still other topics, such as that in question 6, might be subjects on which sufficient information is not readily available or might be too narrow to be the subject of a research paper. Since the process of writing a research paper often discloses unsuspected relationships, you may discover that different questions focus on different but related aspects of the same topic.

For example, questions 1, 7, and 8 might be combined as a question that asked, "What part does the idea of competition and winning at all costs play in the massive upswing in drug use in professional sports, the entertainment industry and in the world of finance?" Or, the research process might create the possibility for an interesting comparative analysis (combining questions 4, 5, and 6) expressed in the question "Are attempts to curtail the demand side of drug use through 'just say no' programs and mandatory drug testing more effective than governmental efforts to limit the supply side of drug trafficking by encouraging other countries to grow crops other than coca?"

From all the questions you have generated on a subject, choose several that seem especially interesting. The next step is to determine whether adequate material exists in the library to enable you to produce a well-researched paper drawn from a variety of relevant sources. Avoid topics that are either so new or so old that sources may not be readily available. Some questions such as the more factual ones will have already been answered. You might discover that a certain percentage of the cocaine coming to the United States is grown in Peru, Bolivia, and Colombia, or that the government spends a certain amount on drug-treatment programs. These and any other questions that have already been answered must be eliminated from contention. Only those questions for which satisfactory answers have not been found should be considered as possible topics for your research paper.

Using the Library

Libraries contain a range of resources that can help you investigate your topic. These include encyclopedias, dictionaries, and handbooks, which provide broad coverage of your topic.

General Encyclopedias

General encyclopedias provide brief overviews and analyses of topics written by experts that are useful in giving you a framework to begin your study. Any of the following should prove helpful:

Chambers Encyclopedia

Collier's Encyclopedia (as of 1998, *Encarta*)

Encyclopædia Americana

Encyclopædia Britannica

Merriam Webster's Collegiate Encyclopedia

Encyclopedias include an index that lists all the relevant discussions and cross-references to your topic. The articles written by specialists also include bibliographies that you can use for further research.

There are also specialized encyclopedias that provide more narrowly focused discussions of specific subjects.

Dictionaries

As you investigate your topic, you may need to discover the meaning of an unfamiliar term. For this purpose, a general dictionary such as *Webster's Collegiate Dictionary* may be sufficient. If you need to follow the changes in the meaning of a word, you can consult the twenty-volume *Oxford English Dictionary*, also available in a one-volume reduced-type edition.

If these general dictionaries do not provide the information you need, you might wish to consult more specialized dictionaries within the particular field of study you are investigating.

Finding Information on People

To locate information on people who are living consult *Who's Who in America* or *Current Biography*. Two valuable resources on prominent people are *Dictionary of National Biography* (DNB) and the *Dictionary of American Biography* (DAB). If the subject of your inquiry is no longer alive, you might try *Who Was Who in America*. In addition, more specialized resources are available in a variety of disciplines. For example, *Contemporary Authors* covers more than 120,000 writers who are alive or who have died since 1960.

The Library of Congress System

Libraries mainly use the Library of Congress System to categorize their holdings, which include books, newspapers and periodicals, dissertations, some government documents, and various multimedia items. This system classifies books according to the alphabet and uses numbers for further subdivisions.

The *Library of Congress Subject Headings* is a book that lists the phrases used for cataloging materials. These headings are the same as those used in citations and thus provide an ideal way to begin your inquiry.

For example, if you were pursuing an inquiry on the causal relationship between drug use and the effect on adolescence, you would see the following entry:

Drugs and Youth	(*Indirect*)
sa	Alcohol and youth
	Narcotics and youth
	Smoking and youth
x	Counter culture
	Youth and drugs
xx	Drug abuse

The bold-faced heading is an entry you would look for to search for sources. Headings listed as sa (see also) and xx indicate other headings under which material would be listed. The x indicates an unused heading. You can use these headings to widen or limit your search for sources.

USING THE ONLINE CATALOG

Your library's online catalog lists all the available materials including titles, as well as subjects and authors, location of materials, publication information, and availability there or at other libraries.

Most systems will allow you to enter keywords and the computer will look for a match anywhere in the records in the library. Keyword searches are fine if you are doing a preliminary search and need ideas for additional search terms, but they retrieve a volume of records that may prove unmanagable.

The terms that you use to search (along with the titles of works and the names of authors) have been obtained from your previous research using general and specialized encyclopedias, biographical dictionaries, and handbooks in specific subject areas. Here, too, the Library of Congress list of subject headings will prove invaluable in providing you with a list of search terms.

When you find a title that offers a promising lead, record its call number on a note card along with all the information you will later need to cite in your bibliography, including the author, editor, title and subtitle, publisher's name and location, year of publication, translator if any, and edition. Search for the book on the shelves. Be sure to look carefully at the books placed on the shelf on either side in case there are other books similar in subject matter that may be useful to you. Books that include bibliographies may provide further leads.

USING PERIODICAL INDEXES

Periodicals include both general works such as newspapers and magazines as well as specialized journals in which recent research results are published. These indexes alphabetically list the subjects and authors of the articles in periodicals.

A particularly useful index (which itself is a periodical) is *The Reader's Guide to Periodical Literature* (which covers more than 200 general magazines and journals).

Sometimes your topic will require you to consult specialized indexes such as *The Social Sciences Index* and/or *The Humanities Index*. Figure 9.1 shows some of the listings in the part of *The Social Sciences Index* that provides information on studies produced in one year on drugs and athletes, children, crime, employment, police, the handicapped, women, and youth.

Keep accurate records by noting the author, title of the article, journal title, volume number, page numbers, and publication date.

USING BOOK REVIEWS

There are a number of sources you can use to investigate whether a book whose title interests you is worth pursuing. *The Book Review Digest* contains selected reviews of both fiction and nonfiction with over 100,000 full-text reviews. *The Book Review Index* is an index to reviews in more than 600 English-language journals in the humanities and social sciences.

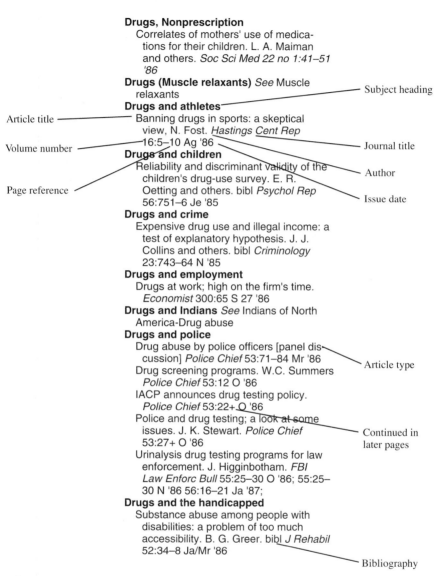

Drugs, Nonprescription
Correlates of mothers' use of medications for their children. L. A. Maiman
and others. *Soc Sci Med 22 no 1:41–51*
'86

Drugs (Muscle relaxants) *See* Muscle
relaxants — Subject heading

Drugs and athletes

Article title — Banning drugs in sports: a skeptical
view, N. Fost. *Hastings Cent Rep*

Volume number — 16:5–10 Ag '86 — Journal title

Drugs and children

Reliability and discriminant validity of the — Author
children's drug-use survey. E. R.

Page reference — Oetting and others. bibl *Psychol Rep*
56:751–6 Je '85 — Issue date

Drugs and crime
Expensive drug use and illegal income: a
test of explanatory hypothesis. J. J.
Collins and others. bibl *Criminology*
23:743–64 N '85

Drugs and employment
Drugs at work; high on the firm's time.
Economist 300:65 S 27 '86

Drugs and Indians *See* Indians of North
America-Drug abuse

Drugs and police
Drug abuse by police officers [panel dis-
cussion] *Police Chief* 53:71–84 Mr '86 — Article type
Drug screening programs. W.C. Summers
Police Chief 53:12 O '86
IACP announces drug testing policy.
Police Chief 53:22+ O '86
Police and drug testing; a look at some
issues. J. K. Stewart. *Police Chief* — Continued in
53:27+ O '86 later pages
Urinalysis drug testing programs for law
enforcement. J. Higginbotham. *FBI
Law Enforc Bull* 55:25–30 O '86; 55:25–
30 N '86 56:16–21 Ja '87;

Drugs and the handicapped
Substance abuse among people with
disabilities: a problem of too much
accessibility. B. G. Greer. bibl *J Rehabil* — Bibliography
52:34–8 Ja/Mr '86

FIGURE 9.1
▪ Sample entries from the *Social Sciences Index.*

Other valuable resources are *The Library Journal Book Review* and *The Social
Sciences and Humanities Index.*

A compilation of all *The New York Times Book Review* issues published since
1896 appears in *The New York Times Book Review.* You can use the *New York*

Times Index (under the heading "Book Reviews") to locate the date, issue, and location in the *New York Times* where the review first appeared.

USING NEWSPAPER INDEXES

The *New York Times Index* provides summaries of news stories arranged alphabetically under specific subject headings. Entries conclude with information on the issue, date, and location of where the story originally appeared. You can then obtain a microfilm edition and view the story as it was originally printed.

Indexes are also available for the *Wall Street Journal* and the *Christian Science Monitor*. *The Newspaper Index* is another resource you may wish to consult, which gives information on articles in the *Chicago Tribune*, the *Los Angeles Times*, and the *Washington Post*, among other papers.

USING ABSTRACTS

An abstract is like an index but also includes short summaries of the articles it lists. Abstracts exist for major subject areas such as *Psychological Abstracts* and *Women's Studies Abstracts*. For example, *Psychological Abstracts* contains listings of books, journal articles, and dissertations with signed short summaries or abstracts. There are indexes (*Cumulated Author Index* and *Cumulated Subject Index*) as well that enable you to locate articles by particular authors or subjects.

Figure 9.2 shows a sample entry from *Psychological Abstracts* along with annotations to demonstrate how abbreviations and headings are used.

USING FIELD RESEARCH—INTERVIEWS

For some papers you may wish to go beyond the sources available to you in the library to conduct interviews or surveys. Faculty members probably will be glad to share their expertise. Or you may want to interview someone whose experiences provide valuable insights into the subject of your study. Plan your interview ahead of time by first finding out from your instructor whether information gained from interviews would be considered acceptable and appropriate for the particular assignment. You should have the questions you want to ask already formulated. Check them to see whether you have unintentionally worded them in such a way as to elicit certain answers. If you would like to use a recorder, first clear this with the person you plan to interview. Plan to take accurate notes during the interview, including keywords and phrases, to make it easier to recall the substance of the interview later. After the interview, review your notes as soon as you can and put down a few sentences that summarize the most important points.

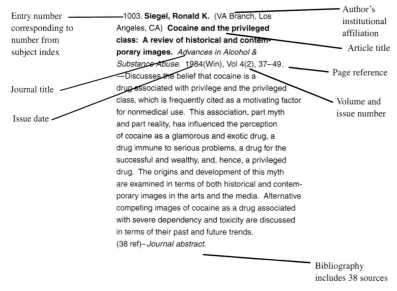

FIGURE 9.2
■ Sample summary from *Psychological Abstracts.*

Don't forget to record the date, time, full name, and title, if any, of the person you have interviewed.

USING DATABASES

College libraries also allow users to gain access to various databases including indexes, abstracts, and, in some cases, the complete text of the source.

Frequently used services include BRS (Bibliographical Retrieval Service), DIALOG (which provides access to more than 400 databases), COMPSERVE (for business information), LEXIS (for legal information), THE SOURCE (for business information), NEXIS (for news and public affairs), RLIN (research libraries information network), OCLC (online computer library center), and DOW JONES.

When you search use exact terms or keywords (descriptors) and avoid those that are too general. The Library of Congress list of subject headings supplies key terms that refer to important concepts. By combining general search terms with more specific ones (for example, the broad term *genetic* with the more narrow term *screening*) you can quickly narrow down your search to produce a small number of pertinent sources.

In addition to these online services (which have the advantage of being up-dated daily), libraries provide CD-ROMs (Compact Disc, Read Only Memory) that are usually already installed in computers ready to use. You use these as you would an online service, by entering search terms and retrieving lists of refer-ences that you can print out. It is usually best to start with general-coverage databases such as:

CIS/Masterfile I and II (index and abstracts for congressional proceedings)

ERIC (Education Resources Information Center)

InfoTrac (general-interest publications)

ProQuest (business and trade journals)

Silver Platter (includes PAIS, sociological abstracts, psychological ab-stracts, corporate and industry research reports, and much more)

EBSCOhost (journals in business, academic, and general circulation)

CQ Researcher (formerly Editorial Research Reports, Current and Controversial Issues)

Wilson Disc (comprehensive)

Some databases contain a list of cross-referenced terms set up in the same way as the Library of Congress list of subject headings. You can use these terms to search the database for exactly what you need. For example, a student doing research on "genetic engineering" who used this phrase to search the **ERIC** database would discover 135 citations. When the term *screening* was typed in along with *genetic engineering* (a process of cross-referencing called Boolean logic), the resulting search disclosed four hits in which both concepts appeared. The student can then print out abstracts for each of the four references and decide which, if any, would warrant retrieving the full text. In addition, there are specialized databases that are useful for pursuing inquiries within specific academic disciplines. Some of these are

American and English Literature Internet Resources

Anthropology Resources on the Internet

Biography Master Index

GDCS (Government Documents Catalog Service; includes GPO Index)

JSTOR (humanities)

National Science Digital Library

PaperChase (four databases: MEDLINE, HEALTH, AIDSLINE, CANCERLIT)

PsycheINFO (psychology)

SOSIG: Social Science Information Gateway (social sciences)

Ulrich's International Periodicals Directory

WWW VirtualLibrary: History Central Catalogue

Evaluating Source Material

Research for an argument-based paper begins with questions about a topic in which you are interested. Becoming familiar with the resources offered in your library makes it easier for you to enter existing debates on the subject. By investigating a topic from many angles, you will see how this topic is viewed from many different perspectives and develop a more complete picture. By discovering how researchers have answered questions in different ways, you will be better able to decide which position merits support. **Research should not involve looking for support for a predetermined position but rather should be a process in which you become well enough informed on a topic to express and support an opinion.** Your paper will reflect both your search and what you discovered along the way.

DRAWING UP A WORKING BIBLIOGRAPHY

A recommended way of keeping track of the results of your library search to discover which source materials are useful is to draw up a working bibliography. This preliminary or tentative bibliography will contain all the information on books, periodicals, abstracts, newspapers, online services, and other source materials held by the library that you consider useful. You can add new source materials or discard those you discover to be irrelevant.

When you have finished your paper you will be ready to make up a final bibliography listing only those works actually cited. A separate 3-by-5-inch or 4-by-6-inch bibliography card needs to be created for each source. This card should record the library call number, the complete title of the work, the author's full name, and the place, date, and publisher of the work. A bibliography card for an article in a journal, periodical, or magazine should record the complete name of the author, the title of the article, the name of the journal or magazine, the volume number, the day, month, and year of publication (if given), and the complete run of page numbers of the article.

On the same card, jot down your impression of how the source might be used in your paper, or where it might fit into the overall investigation. You can begin to evaluate the quality of the source materials by answering the following questions:

1. Does the information presented in the source material bear directly on the question you are interested in exploring?

2. Does the author have appropriate credentials, experience, or expertise in the field?

3. Is the author's research timely, or has it been superseded by more recent research?

4. Are the conclusions presented by the author clearly drawn from well-documented and reliable evidence?

5. Does the book, chapter in a book, article from a magazine or journal, or other source contain a sufficient amount of discussion to warrant its use as a source from which notes will be taken? (Frequently, the best way to determine this for a book is by checking the page numbers on the subject listed in the index. An index entry on "crop substitution programs in Peru" on pp. 17–28 would be a more useful source than the same entry followed by pages 17, 28. The first entry covers a discussion of twelve pages, whereas the second indicates that the entire book touches on the subject on only two separate pages.)

TIPS FOR EVALUATING ELECTRONIC SOURCES

As we have emphasized, the library is the first and in many ways the best place to begin your research. Many students only go to the Web for information. The Web is useful for finding current information (on well-known events or individuals) and for learning about companies and nonprofit organizations, colleges, museums, auctions, travel services, and government (federal and local). Although you can locate a range of expert and popular opinions, and catch up on the news here and abroad, most information on the Web is not reviewed, permanent, nor by any means comprehensive. Moreover, some commercial sites charge a fee to access their information. Most people are familiar with directory services that do not charge the user a fee and are relatively easy to use such as Yahoo! (http://www.yahoo.com) and Google (http://www.google.com).

The ease with which anyone can create a Web page and post information on it requires you to carefully evaluate the pages you intend to use as
sources. When you look at a Web page's address—its uniform resource location, or URL—check to see whether it contains a tilde (̃), which indicates
that the site is a personal page. Without knowing the purpose of the Web
page (to entertain, to sell a product or service, to provide information, to
promote a cause), you might find it difficult to gauge the objectivity and reliability of the information it contains. Therefore, you must evaluate the extent to which your source is:

- Authoritative (what are the author's credentials?),

- Unbiased (is the purpose to get you to buy or believe something?),

- Timely (when was the content posted?), and

- Reliable (can the information be verified by other sites or by comparison to printed information?).

The domain name (the letters between the double slash and the first
single slash) can provide a clue about the nature of the source. Common
abbreviations include .com for commercial, .edu for educational, .gov for
governmental, .mil for the military, .net for some Internet service providers,
and .org for organizational. You can often find the sponsor or creator of the
Web page by going to the home page of the Web site; if there is not a link
to the home page, try deleting the last part of the URL (for example, if the
URL is http://www.mundanebehavior.org/issues/vlinl/caesar.htm, you
would go to http://www.mundanebehavior.org/). In addition, most reliable
Web pages have links that provide information about the creator or the
document or at least give the e-mail address of the creator or Webmaster.

The Dangers of Undocumented Sources

A research paper requires you to document all information taken from sources,
whether in the form of quotations, paraphrases, summaries, or factual references.
This is important even if you are not using the exact language used by the author.
You must provide an in-text reference specifying the author, title of the work,
and location within the work where the reference can be found. It is important
that you accurately note down the source, including specific page numbers on
each note card. Not to do this may later lead you to believe that these were your
own ideas, and you may fail to acknowledge that this information derives from
an external source. Be especially careful in making sure you have included quotation marks so that you do not, however unintentionally, mistake someone else's
words for you own and not give proper credit.

Note-Taking Procedures

Notes should be legible, written on one side of a 4-by-6-inch index card and contain information from only one source per card. On each card, write the title of the work from which the note was taken, along with exact page numbers, in the upper right-hand corner. In the upper left-hand corner, write a short phrase identifying the particular aspect of the research question to which the note relates.

Your comments can refer to your evaluation of the source's qualifications; the author's purpose in writing the essay, article, or book in question; the audience being addressed; the methods used; and the conclusions reached. You may wish to comment on how persuasive the evidence is or whether the author agrees or disagrees with others studying the same issue. Most important, even at this early stage, consider how this piece of information could be used as evidence in your argument. The actual note should be clearly written, preferably in ink, in the center of the card.

Only information on the source and the exact page number need appear on the card, since you have already made up a card with complete bibliographical information. If you are using more than one work by the same author however, put an abbreviation of the title along with the author's last name and page number to avoid confusing this note with others drawn from a different work by the same author. Notes can take the form of (1) paraphrases, (2) summaries, (3) quotations, or (4) factual references. (We covered summarizing in Chapter 1 and paraphrases and quotations in Chapter 7.)

Note cards are also used to keep track of significant facts you will use to document assertions in your paper. Such hard statistical data serve an important function in substantiating your claims. Keep in mind that only one piece of information, whether it is a summary, a quotation, a combined note (your summary plus a short quotation), a fact or an observation, should be recorded on each note card.

Using Your Notes to Create an Outline

Once you are satisfied with the results of your initial investigation, you will need to sort your notes to discover the arrangement that will best allow you to develop a coherent structure for the entire paper. To do this, group together index cards with the same or similar headings (indicated in the upper left-hand corner).

These groups represent sections of your paper that should be placed in a logical and coherent order. Since there are so many ways you can arrange the sections, it is imperative that you let the question you wish to explore suggest the direction you should take in developing your argument.

Once the note cards have been organized in groups that define the individual sections of the paper and cards within groups have been arranged in a sequence that defines the order in which information will be developed within sections, the key phrases on each of the note cards can be used to create a working outline. You may decide to use a general heading or a key phrase that appears frequently in each group as a main heading in your outline. Once the cards with similar content have been grouped together, a working outline created from the headings would begin to give you a more accurate picture of the order, arrangement, and divisions of the sections of your paper.

Test the ideas expressed in the headings. Material that does not illuminate, support, develop, or explain the main idea should be omitted. Are there approximately the same number of note cards for each major section? Use your outline to check whether individual sections provide equal levels of support to develop the entire paper. If any sections are insufficiently developed, you may need to return to the library to gather more material.

The Preliminary Thesis Statement

The question around which your paper is organized should be stated in the form of a tentative thesis, as a declarative sentence. The thesis statement represents your view on the subject and is stated in such a way that it is apparent to your readers that your paper will make a case for this point of view. Don't feel that you are locked into specific formulation of your thesis. At this point it is just a means to guide your reading and note taking. What you discover may require you to substantially alter the scope or direction of your paper. If this occurs, you will need to revise your thesis accordingly.

Revising your thesis in the light of new information will require you to consider the views of others fairly and to offer an opinion that accommodates and takes into account opposing views or differences in perspective on the issue.

Discovering Your Own Position

Writing a research paper involves more than finding and evaluating sources. You must define your own viewpoint on the issue in relationship to the different viewpoints expressed by your sources. Then you must formulate a response that stakes out a distinct defensible claim. In essence, you are trying to formulate your own unique response to the issue in relationship to the map of possible responses that are represented by your print and electronic sources.

To help you see your own position more clearly you might construct a chart with each source's position on a particular point listed in columns placed side by side. Thus, you will have an array that visually represents the various positions held by each source on a number of points. This chart will enable you to quickly evaluate each of your source's views on a particular point and to identify authors with whom you agree or disagree. Your range of responses to each of these positions can be from total agreement to total disagreement. Even for those authors with whom you agree, you may wish to qualify your agreement or to suggest more effective ways of proving their point.

Creating the Rough Draft

In writing a rough draft, many students find it helpful to compose the introduction first, informing the reader in a straightforward way what issue, topic, or idea the paper will cover. Asking a provocative question catches the audience's attention and challenges them to reexamine their unquestioned assumptions and beliefs on the subject. Another effective way of introducing the reader to the issue is with a brief review of the controversy that gives the reader a historical context in which to understand the discussion. The introduction not only states the question at issue, but also should tell the reader how you plan to demonstrate the validity of your hypothesis. If you wish, you may include some general comments on the kinds of sources you intend to use, and give an overview as to the approach you intend to follow in developing your argument.

Before beginning to write the main portion of your paper, be sure to have your outline and note cards in front of you. Detach each group of note cards and spread them out in front of you so you can clearly see the contents of each card. In the rough draft, you are concerned only with writing or typing the information from your note cards in a coherent order, using the information on each card to illustrate, explain, or substantiate headings from your outline. Don't be concerned about questions of style or grammar. Your primary goal should be to get down the ideas in your outline and support them with the specific quotations, summaries, facts, and observations written on your cards. As you write, be sure to leave extra space between lines and a wide margin on both sides that will give you room to add corrections or make changes in the original text.

Frequently compare what you are writing against the note cards and outline to check that you have not omitted any important points or supporting evidence. Check the wording of any quotations you have copied from your note cards to make sure you have not unintentionally omitted any of the original wording.

For a full discussion of quoting see Chapter 7 ("Writing and Refuting Arguments").

Revising the Rough Draft into a Final Draft

While writing the rough draft, look at what you have put down from the reader's perspective. Would a change in the order of the presentation make your ideas clearer? To help the reader understand the main idea of your paper, use clear transitional words, phrases, and sentences to signal how parts of the paper are connected to each other. Even though the ideas are presented in an order that is clear to you, you need to help your reader understand the organization of your paper and perceive the relationships between the sections. Short transitional phrases (or even short paragraphs) are invaluable in informing the reader how paragraphs are related to each other and signal the relationship between paragraphs and sections.

Transitions can serve different purposes. Some signal your reader that you are following a chronological order with words such as *now, when, before, after, during, while, next, finally, later, meanwhile,* and *soon.* Other linking words express causal relationships such as *as a result, since, consequently, because, therefore,* and *thus.* Still other guide words express intensification, such as *furthermore, really, in addition, ultimately,* and *moreover.* Some express limitation, restriction or concession such as *although, yet, however, even though, still, despite, but,* and *granted.*

As with the introduction, there are many choices available when deciding how to end your paper. If your paper has investigated a problem, and considered alternative solutions offered by others, your conclusion might present your own solution to the problem along with evidence and reasons required to ensure its acceptance. Some writers prefer to end their papers, especially those that deal with complex issues, with a thought-provoking question intended to keep readers thinking about the implications of the issue. Other writers prefer to use the conclusion to suggest how the issue relates to a wider context. Most frequently, however, writers briefly enumerate the most important points turned up by their research and emphasize how these points prove the validity of the idea expressed by the thesis statement in the introduction.

Transforming a rough draft into a final draft entails testing everything that you have put down—every sentence, every paragraph, every section—to see whether it relates to the central idea expressed in your thesis.

What passages, words, or sentences, would the reader see as unnecessary or confusing? At what points would your reader require additional examples or evidence to emphasize an idea or more effective transitions to signal the relationship between different parts of your paper? You can revise best by going through your paper several times, looking for different kinds of things to improve each time. For a full discussion of this procedure and for revising your paper to improve style, see Chapter 7.

Last, reread your paper, this time double-checking to see whether you have accurately transcribed the information from your note cards. If you have combined direct quotations from one source with supporting interpretations from other sources, make sure that you have not omitted any necessary documentation. Is every source that you have cited also included in the list of works cited or bibliography that will be turned in along with your paper?

REVISING AND EDITING WITH A COMPUTER

Revising with a computer offers several advantages. You can create multiple drafts and try out different configurations. You can easily move sentences and paragraphs by cutting and pasting. Some computer programs also provide outline tools and spell checkers that can help you edit and proofread your paper. But there are several cautions to remember when you revise with a computer:

■ Although useful, spell-checking programs cannot detect an error if the unintended word is a correctly spelled word (for example, *to* for *too* or *two, these* for *there,* or *peace* for *piece*).

■ Print out a version of each draft before you revise it just in case you accidentally delete some material (and be sure to create a backup file at the end of each session at the computer).

■ When you move text within a file, make sure that you have moved everything in the passage to its new location.

■ Work done on a computer looks far more polished than its handwritten equivalent and can therefore delude you into thinking it is a final draft when it is still a work in progress.

Using the MLA, APA, and CSE Styles to Document the Manuscript

The MLA Style of In-Text Citation

The primary method of formatting and documentation for the liberal arts is the MLA (Modern Language Association) style discussed in the *MLA Handbook for Writers of Research Papers* (6th ed., New York: MLA, 2003). It consists of an in-text parenthetical citation and a list of works cited at the end of the paper. It has the advantage of providing the reader with documentation when a source is quoted, paraphrased, or summarized directly within the text. The parenthetical citations identify sources briefly; provide page references, including the author's name, and a shortened version of the title if necessary; and must follow each occurrence of a source that needs to be documented. A complete description of each source appears in a final alphabetical listing of works cited at the end of the paper.

The paper that appears at the end of this chapter ("Prelude to the Internet") uses this system. For example, notice the following sentence taken from the sample student research paper:

> Using electricity, an American named Joseph Henry used Sturgeons's device to ring a bell at the end of a one-mile wire (Bellis "History").

The parenthetical reference indicates that this citation refers to material taken from a work by Mary Bellis. A complete reference on the page listing works cited at the end of the paper gives all necessary information:

> Bellis, Mary. "The History of the Telegraph and Telegraphy." Inventors 15 Oct. 2004. <http://inventors.about.com/library/inventors/bltelegraph.htm>

A citation should follow the mention of the source and precede your own punctuation. The form the reference will take depends on the nature of the source and the amount of information already provided in your paper.

AUTHOR NOT NAMED IN THE TEXT: AUTHOR AND PAGE NUMBER IN PARENTHESES

> One archaeologist concludes that "Noah's Flood was not a universal deluge; it was a vast flood in the Valley of the Rivers Tigres and Euphrates" (Woolley 242).

AUTHOR NAMED IN THE TEXT: PAGE REFERENCE IN PARENTHESES

> One archaeologist, Sir Leonard Woolley, concludes that "Noah's Flood was not a universal deluge; it was a vast flood in the Valley of the Rivers Tigres and Euphrates" (242).

BLOCK QUOTATIONS

Quotations over four lines in length are separated from the text, indented one inch from the left margin, double-spaced like the rest of the manuscript, and reproduced without quotation marks. These block quotations are introduced with a colon (:) following a grammatically complete lead-in. Parenthetical citation of page numbers follows the quotation's final punctuation. For example: In "The Praying Mantis," the entomologist Jean Henri Fabre dramatically observes the habits of the praying mantis:

The Mantis naturally wants to devour the victuals in peace, without being troubled by the plunges of a victim who absolutely refuses to be devoured. A meal liable to interruptions lacks savour (4).

WORK WITH TWO OR THREE AUTHORS OR EDITORS

One study investigated the question, "How do salmon remember their birth place and how do they find their way back, sometimes from 800 or 900 miles away" (Hasler and Larsen 317).

WORK WITH MORE THAN THREE AUTHORS

The concept of *fail-safe* refers to components which, if they fail, do not jeopardize the entire system (Williams, *et al.* 53).

A MULTIVOLUME WORK

Speaking on the rise and decline of civilizations, a historian observes that "in primitive societies, as we know them, Mimesis is directed towards the older generation and towards dead ancestors who stand, unseen, but not unfelt, at the back of living elders, reinforcing their prestige" (Toynbee 7: 114).

NEWSPAPER

According to a *Newark Star-Ledger* editorial, peace in the Middle East is still elusive because "Hamas, an Islamic fundamentalist group, continues to fight for the destruction of Israel and refuses to accept the PLO's authority" ("Building Mideast Peace" A26).

REFERENCE WORK

According to *The Concise Columbia Encyclopedia*, not withstanding the fact that Einstein was a pacifist, "he urged Pres. Franklin Roosevelt to investigate the possible use of atomic energy in bombs" ("Einstein, Albert").

REVIEW

Of demonstrative audiences, the acerbic New York theater critic says, "They erupt into promiscuous roars of *bravo* and even *bravi* and *brava* to display either their knowledge of Italian or their deafness in distinguishing the number and sex of the performers" (Simon 17).

SELECTION IN AN ANTHOLOGY

"You walk among clattering four-foot marine iguanas heaped on the shore lava, and on each other, like slag" (Dillard 181).

A WORK BY AN AUTHOR WITH TWO OR MORE WORKS

In his later years, his cautionary fables concentrate on hypocrisy and greed (Twain, *Hadleyburg* 377–85).

TWO OR MORE SOURCES IN A CITATION

There is intense debate over such basic definitional questions as whether the most serious manifestations of alcohol disorders should be treated as "diseases" (Keller 1976; Robinson 1972; Room 1972).

A GOVERNMENT DOCUMENT

According to the Congressional Committee on Labor and Human Resources, broader legal definitions of sexual harassment are necessary to combat instances of employment discrimination (*Fair Employment Practices* 13–15).

A WORK WITH A CORPORATE AUTHOR

The use of euphemistic labels to describe nursing homes and retirement villages eases the public's guilt and remorse over accepting the isolation of elders (*Understanding Aging, Inc.* 35–36).

AN INDIRECT SOURCE—QUOTING SOMEONE ELSE

Lykken asserts that "more of these unique characteristics than we previously thought may be determined by a particular combination of genes" (qtd. in Holden 35).

Literary Works

NOVELS

At the beginning of Anne Tyler's novel *Saint Maybe,* the main character, Ian, is introduced: "now Ian was seventeen, and, like the rest of his family, large-boned and handsome and easy-going, quick to make friends, fond of a good time" (2; ch. 1).

PLAYS

Later in *The Lion and the Jewel* Soyinka has the chief Baroka proclaim, "I change my wrestlers when I have learnt to throw them" (34; act 2).

POEMS

Diane Wakowski explores the speaker's sensation of freedom: "Driving through the desert at night in summer/can be/like peeling an orange" ("The Orange" 1–3).

THE BIBLE

St. Paul makes the meaning of the term resonate with spiritual depth: "in a word, there are three things that last forever: faith, hope, and love; but the greatest of them all is love" (*I Corinthians 13 . 13*).

NONPRINT SOURCES (INCLUDING INTERVIEWS, RADIO AND TELEVISION PROGRAMS, MOVIES)

A recent documentary explores ancient knowledge of star positions (*Egypt: Quest for Eternity*).

Documenting Sources in the MLA "Works Cited" Format

In the following list of examples, the most commonly encountered forms of citation are listed for a wide variety of references.

AN ARTICLE IN A JOURNAL WITH CONTINUOUS PAGINATION OF THE VOLUME FOR THAT PARTICULAR YEAR

Rockas, Leo. "A Dialogue on Dialogue." *College English* 41 (1980):570–80.

The issue number is not mentioned because the volume is continuously paginated throughout the year; hence, only the volume number (41) is necessary.

AN ARTICLE FROM A MAGAZINE ISSUED WEEKLY

Sanders, Sol W. "The Vietnam Shadow Over Policy for El Salvador." *Business Week* 16 Mar. 1981:52.

Note that all months except May, June, and July are abbreviated in MLA style.

A BOOK BY A SINGLE AUTHOR

Shiska, Bob. *An Introduction to Broadcasting*. Chicago: Wade, 1980.

A BOOK BY TWO OR THREE AUTHORS

Murphy, Mark, and Rhea White. *Psychic Side of Sports*. Reading: Addison-Wesley, 1979.

A BOOK BY MORE THAN THREE AUTHORS

Allen, David Yale, et al. *Classic Cars*. London: Macmillan, 1978.

Only the first author's name, as it is given on the title page, appears—last name first.

MORE THAN ONE BOOK BY THE SAME AUTHOR

Hellman, Leo. *Children Today*. Miami, FL: U of Miami P, 1995.

_ _ _. *Children Yesterday*. Chicago: U of Chicago P, 2004.

AUTHOR UNKNOWN

How to Raise a Wheaton Terrier for Show and Profit. Cherry Hill: Solo
International, 2003.

Do not use "anonymous" or "anon."

A BOOK BY A CORPORATE AUTHOR

Modern Language Association. *MLA Handbook for Writers of Research Papers*,
6th ed. New York: Modern Language Association, 2003.

EDITED BOOK IN A NEW EDITION

Adler, Freda, ed. *Women and Crime*. 4th ed. Cambridge, MA: Harvard UP, 1976.

A COLLECTION OF ESSAYS BY DIFFERENT AUTHORS COMPILED
BY AN EDITOR

Sebeok, Ted, ed. *How Animals Communicate*. Bloomington: Indiana UP, 1977.

A WORK IN AN ANTHOLOGY

Arnold, Charles. "How Monkeys Use Sign Language." *How Animals
Communicate*. Ed. Ted Sebeok. Bloomington: Indiana UP, 1977. 40–50.

A BOOK THAT IS TRANSLATED WITH BOTH THE AUTHOR AND
TRANSLATOR NAME

Fernandez, Ruth. *The Architectural Heritage of the Moors*. Trans. Wanda Garcia.
London: Routledge, 1980.

A BOOK BY TWO OR THREE AUTHORS; A REVISED OR LATER EDITION

Reichman, Stuart, and Marsha Deez. *The Washington Lobbyist*, 10th ed. New
York: Random House, 2004.

A BOOK PUBLISHED IN MORE THAN ONE VOLUME

Thorndike, Lynn. *A History of Magic and Experimental Science*. 3 vols. New
York: Columbia UP, 1941.

A REPUBLISHED OR REPRINTED BOOK

Nilsson, Martin P. *Greek Folk Religion*. 1940. Philadelphia: U of Pennsylvania
P, 1972.

A NEWSPAPER ARTICLE

Petzinger, Thomas J., Gary Putka, and Stephen J. Sansweet. "High Fliers."
Wall Street Journal 12 Sept. 1983, sec. 1:1+.

A BOOK REVIEW

Katz, Bill. Rev. of *Norman Rockwell: My Adventures as an Illustrator,* by Norman Rockwell. *Library Journal* 85 (1960): 648.

AN ENCYCLOPEDIA

Academic American Encyclopedia. 21 vols. Danbury: Grolier, 1987.

A DICTIONARY

The Agriculture Dictionary. Albany: Delmar, 1991.

AN UNSIGNED ARTICLE IN A NEWSPAPER

"Executive Changes." *New York Times* 8 Aug. 1991, natl. ed.: C3.

AN EDITORIAL IN A NEWSPAPER

"Breakthrough for Peace." Editorial. *Miami Herald* 2 Dec. 1994, final ed.: 20A.

A LETTER TO AN EDITOR

Mirski, Roberto. "Property Taxes Are Too High." Letter. *The Newark Star Ledger* 3 Nov. 1991: A16.

Guidelines for Citing Electronic Media

CD-ROMS AND OTHER PORTABLE DATABASES: PERIODICALLY PUBLISHED DATABASES

Hellman, Leo. "Nutritionists find new growth enzyme in roses." *New York Times* 12 June 1992, late ed.: B1. *New York Times Ondisc.* CD-ROM. UMI-Proquest. Nov. 1992.

Reeves, Tony. "The Illegal Parrot Trade." *The Consumer's Advocate* Mar./Apr. 1993: 22–24. *Sociofile.* CD-ROM. Silver Platter. Sept. 1993.

Stewart, Terri. "Islamic Influences in the Mevlana Monastary." *DAI* June 1993. Missouri State University 1993. *Dissertation Abstracts Ondisc.* CD-ROM. UM-Proquest. June 1993.

Citations in this form should consist of the following items: Author. "Title" of article and publication data. *Title* of the database. Publication medium (CD-ROM). Vendor (distributor). Date of publication (release data, as shown on the title screen or above the menu of the database).

CD-ROMS AND OTHER PORTABLE DATABASES: NONPERIODICALLY PUBLISHED DATABASES

The Oxford English Dictionary. 2nd ed. CD-ROM, Oxford: Oxford UP, 1992.

CD-ROM publications in this form are not continually revised but are issued a single time. The work is cited as you would a book, but add a description of the medium of publication.

A PUBLICATION ON MAGNETIC TAPE OR DISKETTE

"Missouri State University." *Peterson's College Database*. Magnetic tape. Princeton: Peterson's, 1994.

"Sorrentino, Fernando." Vers. 1. 1 *Disclit: World Authors*. Diskette. Dublin: Hall and OCLC, 1994.

A magnetic-tape publication or a diskette is also cited as you would a book and includes the following items: Author. "Title" of a portion of the work (if appropriate). Title of product. Edition, release, or version (if relevant). Publication medium (magnetic tape or diskette). City: Publisher, Year.

CITING ONLINE DATABASES

McLean, David. "The King of Pop Strikes Again." *Longevity*. Jan. 1995: 62–4. *Magazine Index*. Dialog. 5 May 1995.

Reed, Janice. "Can Alzheimer's Be Cured?" *New York Times* 21 Apr. 1993, late ed.: C1. *New York Times Online*. Online. Nexis. 7 Feb. 1994.

An entry for an online information service would include these items: Author. "Title" of article and publication data for printed source. *Title* of the database. Publication medium (Online). Name of computer service date of access (when you access the file).

MATERIAL ACCESSED THROUGH A COMPUTER NETWORK: INTERNET

Lund, Diana. "New Therapies for Autism." *Journal of Clinical Psychology*. 4 (1994): 8 pp. Online. Internet. 17 May 1994.

Patrick, Deborah. "Third World Population Trends." *World Scope*. 1.1 (1995): 12 pp. Online. U. of Vermont. Internet. 7 Feb. 1995. <gopher://gopher.vt.edu>.

Citations should contain these items: Author. "Title" of article. *Title* of journal or other source. Volume number. (year or issue data of publication): Number of pages (if given). Publication medium (Online). Name of computer network.

Date of access (when you accessed the source). As in the second example, you may also include the electronic address, in angle brackets, you used to access the document.

CITING AN ELECTRONIC TEXT

James, Henry. *The Aspern Papers*. New York: Scribner's, 1908. Online. Project Gutenberg, Illinois Benedictine Coll. Internet. 15 Jan. 1995. <http://www.w3.org>.

An entry citing an electronic text contains these items: Author. *Title* of text. Year of original publication (if appropriate). Publication data. Publication medium (Online). Repository of text. Computer network. Date of access. Electronic address (if required).

E-MAIL

Pepin, Jacques. "Lemon Cake." E-mail to the author. 2 Dec. 2004.

ARTICLE IN AN ONLINE REFERENCE BOOK

"Barthes, Roland." *Encyclopaedia Britanica Online*. Vers. 99.1. 1994–2000. Encyclopaedia Britanica. 19 June 2000 <http://search.eb.com/bol/topic?eu=13685&sctn=1&pm=1>.

ARTICLE IN AN ONLINE JOURNAL

Caesar, Terry. "In and Out of Elevators in Japan." *Journal of Mundane Behavior* 1.1 (2000): 6 pars. 12 Mar. 2000 <http://www.mundanebehavior.org/issues/v1n1/caesar.htm>.

If the pages or paragraphs are numbered, include that information. The abbreviation for *pages* is *pp.*, and the abbreviation for *paragraphs* is *pars.*

ARTICLE IN AN ONLINE MAGAZINE

Ollivier, Debra S. "Mothers Who Think: Les birds et les bees." *Salon* 12 May 1998. 19 June 2000 <http://www.salon.com/mwt/feature/1998/05/12feature2.html>.

WEB SITE

Eyewire Studios. Home page. Apr. 1999. 19 Aug. 1999 <http://www.eyewire.com>.

Sample Annotated Student Research Paper in MLA Style

Miles 1

Tara Miles

Professor Guffey

Economics 20

19 October 2004

Prelude to the Internet

"Ever since the beginnings of time, people have been trying to communicate over distances greater than the human voice could reach" (Perera). Methods for doing so have included smoke signals, mirrors, fires, and flags. On May 24, 1844, a new method was demonstrated. Samuel Morse sent a message from the Supreme Court room in the Capitol to a railroad depot in Baltimore. This message was "What hath God wrought" (Numbers 23:23). What makes this event so momentous in our history is the speed with which this message was carried. It didn't go by boat, horse or wagon, but by an invention called the electric telegraph. Though Morse was not the first to invent the idea, he was the man with the desire and dedication to see it brought to life. Within nine years of this first transmission, Florida was the only state east of the Mississippi that was not connected. Seventeen years later the entire American Continent was linked, and after only twenty-two years, continents spanning the Atlantic Ocean were able to communicate with each other almost simultaneously. We can see the economic impact of the telegraph if we examine its influence on the infrastructure, the military, and businesses.

First, it will be helpful to discuss the invention of the telegraph, which was a long process combining the ideas of many

Miles 2

different individuals. In 1825, a British inventor named William

Sturgeon designed the electromagnet. Using electricity, an

American named Joseph Henry used Sturgeons's device to ring a

bell at the end of a one-mile wire (Bellis "History"). In 1832, Dr.

Charles T. Jackson of Boston started Samuel Morse's mind on the

path of designing a telegraph. While returning from overseas,

Jackson shared with Morse the experiments with electromagnetism

that were occurring in Europe (Bellis "Timeline"). The following

years included many changes to Morse's original ideas for the

telegraph. Through collaboration and trial and error, Morse continued

to design a working model. He also worked diligently on creating a

universal code to be used with the telegraph. This code also

underwent many changes, but the final result is still known as

Morse code. Morse acquired several partners for his project, but

the actual contributions of each partner are still debated today.

His most notable partners included Leonard Gale, a science

professor; Alfred Vail, a steelworks heir; and Francis O.J. Smith, a

politician ("Inventor"). Though Morse was eager to share his

discoveries with America, it wasn't until 1843 that he finally

received support from society in the form of a grant from the

federal government. The grant was passed through the House of

Representatives by a vote of 89 to 83 and barely passed the

Senate on the last day of its session ("Collection"). This grant was

used to construct a forty-mile long wire stretching between

Baltimore and Washington that became the carrier of the famous

first message, "What hath God wrought." Although there were

many improvements and additions to the telegraph from that

Omits page numbers for electronic (Bellis) sources

Synthesizes various sources

Miles 3

point forward, the telegraph had been invented and the growth of the economy was quickened in response.

With the invention of the telegraph, the infrastructures of the United States underwent massive expansion. Morse was already aware of the advantages for the railroad companies long before the unveiling of his telegraph in 1844. According to Library of Congress records, "In 1838 . . . Morse was in Europe attempting to obtain a patent for a telegraph system that would indicate by sound the presence of a railroad train at any chosen point on the track" ("Samuel" 1). Although he wasn't successful at the time, it didn't take long for the railroad companies to understand the benefits of such a system of communication along their tracks. They already had a system of timetables to deal with the sharing of the tracks, but the telegraph allowed the railroad companies to deal efficiently with extra trains, late trains, and disabled trains. The first telegraph train order was sent in 1851 on the Erie Railroad. "The new technology was quickly implemented by the railroads, which sharply decreased the number of accidents, collisions, and derailments" (Hempell). The telegraph was directly responsible for the expansion of the railroads. Within a couple of years, the number of telegraph stations, employees, and miles of wire expanded greatly. This not only created a more efficient and safer railroad service, but it also added many jobs to the economy. "The telegrapher was as much a part of the railroad as the ties that supported its rails. Without his services trains could not have moved safely any faster than horse-drawn coaches" (Grumbine). With the rise in usage of the telegraph by the railroad, many improvements were designed to

Repeats and develops key ideas while indicating method of causal analysis

Supplies supporting analysis as self-sustaining cycle of causes and effects

Miles 4

further its viability across the states. Because of this improved value, more lines were put up, enlarging their significance to the economy. The expansion of the railroads was tied directly to the growth of the telegraph and vice versa. Increased development furthered the use of railroads to transport goods and people, adding to the growth of the country. It also offered reasonable transportation and increased movement among the citizens of the United States.

Along with the railroads, other common infrastructures also grew because of the telegraph. Concepts from the telegraph were adapted to meet the needs of the growing economy and were modified into communication lines for fires and emergencies, allowing for a quicker response time. Criminals on the run were caught when the speed of the telegraph message allowed the police to be waiting for them at the other end. Services provided by these infrastructures were improved and the costs were lessened, making them more efficient. With early notification of a fire, the response was quicker, reducing the damage. The reduction of damage helped lower the cost to the economy as a whole.

Provides vivid examples that warrant a conclusion

What started as a government-funded project was quickly enlarged by businesses with an eye for profit. "By 1846 private companies, using Morse's patent, had built telegraph lines from Washington reaching to Boston and Buffalo, and were pushing further" (Mabee). Telegraph companies began opening up left and right trying to make revenue from this new invention. The expansion of the telegraph across the country was mainly funded through the entrepreneurship of individual businessmen. Not only did they earn money from its expansion, but they also gained more opportunities

Miles 5

to further their business. Within a matter of years, the Pony Express was superseded by the electric telegraph, which was quicker and cheaper. Businesses benefited from readily available communication with each other. "Industry found the telegraph indispensable for the transmission of business related communication including information on stocks and commodities" (Raven). The stock market became easier to participate in from greater distances. Business could create a stable market by comparing the costs of items around the United States. Newspapers also realized the benefits of such a quick sending of information. "The proprietors of these newspapers saw that this new instrument was bound to affect all newspaperdom profoundly" (Thompson). With the ability to share news quickly across large areas of land, the newspapers companies found the need to improve their printing services. By encouraging the inventions of new things, the telegraph promoted an increase in the market.

Supplies supporting detail

As the market grew, the correlation between the telegraph and the growth was obvious. By October 24, 1861, the first transcontinental telegraph system was completed, providing new business opportunities. By 1866, a telegraph cable had been successfully laid across the Atlantic Ocean, a feat that enabled the growth of the nation through foreign contact and trade.

Summarizes previous discussion

While the resources of the United States grew, the social climate underwent turmoil. The Civil War had a negative bearing on the financial system of the time, but that influence was minimized by the telegraph. "The American Civil War was one of the first demonstrations of the military value of the telegraph in the control of troop deployment and intelligence" (Raven). The leaders of the

Broadens discussion to argue for positive effect of the telegraph in a time of social turmoil

Miles 6

troops were able to communicate with each other to coordinate their actions. Telegraphs were also used to coordinate the transfer of soldiers, weapons, and supplies. When the military wanted to use a train for such transportation, it was essential to have communication along the way to avoid an ambush. Often the lines were tapped by the opposite side in order to glean information. Oftentimes false messages were sent with the knowledge that the enemy was listening. Encryption was also used to safeguard the messages being sent. "The exigencies and experiences of the Civil War demonstrated, among other theorems, the vast utility and indispensable importance of the electric telegraph both as an administrative agent and as a tactical factor in military operations" (Greely). The telegraph is acknowledged as a deciding factor in the early end of the Civil War, allowing the economy to begin recovering quickly. Without the use of the telegraph, the outcome of the Civil War would have been very different, creating lasting effects on the economy.

Before the completion of the telegraph, communication was no faster than the fastest horse available. If people in New York wanted to speak to someone in California, they had no choice but to send a message by Pony Express. It would take at least 20 days before they heard a response. The concept of instant communication opened up the economy in the United States. Railroads flourished, wars were won, business grew, papers expanded, and people connected. Without this discovery, the growth of the United States would have been seriously hampered by the size of the country. Not only did the government take advantage, but businesses and civilians did too. The rapid expansion of the economy can be attributed to

Returns to ideas stated in opening paras, then summarizes key points

Miles 7

the determination and drive of one man to see the electric telegraph become a reality. "It may be difficult to visualize, but if it had not been for the era of telegraphy we might still be looking over the horizon today for arrival of the Pony Express to bring us the latest news, and be watching for the cow to jump over the moon instead of already having placed our flag upon it. Telegraphy was the basic forerunner of all modern communication" (Grumbine). The Internet is nothing more than a complex telegraph. Also originally government sponsored, it now allows worldwide communication with the touch of a button. The modern day miracles that support our economy would not have been discovered without the initial impetus of the electric telegraph.

Reaches conclusion that links to title

**1-inch from
top of page**

Miles 8

**1/2 inch
from top**

**Page numbers
continue**

Works Cited

**Heading
centered**

**Sources listed
alphabetically**

Beavon, Rod. "Samuel Morse." 7 October 2004.

<http://www.rod.beavon.clara.netisamuel.htm>

Bellis, Mary. "The History of the Telegraph and Telegraphy." Inventors

15 Oct. 2004. <http://inventors.about.com/library/inventors/

bltelegraph.htm>

_ _ _. "Timeline: Biography of Samuel Morse." *Inventors* 15 Oct. 2004.

<http://inventors.about.com/library/inventors/bl_morse_timeline

.htm>

"Collection Highlights." *Samuel F.B. Morse Papers.* Library of Congress.

**All lines double-
spaced**

13 Oct. 2004. <http://memory.loc.gov/ammem/sfbmhtml/

sfbmhighlights01.html>

**First line of
each entry not
indented**

Greely, A. W. "The Military-Telegraph Service." 17 Sept. 2004.

<http://www.civilwarhome.com/telegraph.htm>

Grumbine, Arthur. "The Era of Morse Telegraphy." 15 Sept. 2004.

**Additional
lines indented
5 spaces**

<http://www.faradic.netl-gsraven/telegraph_tales/grumbine/

grumbine_1.html>

Hempell, Anthony. "A History of Modern Telecommunications: Part 1:

The Telegraph." 25 Sept. 2004. <http://www.peak.sfu.ca/cmass/

issue1/telegraph.html>

"Inventor of the Week." *Massachusetts Institute of Technology lact.*

2004. <http://web.mit.edu/inventJiow/morse.html>

Mabee, Carleton. "Samuel F. B. Morse." 22 Sept. 2004.

<http://www.morsehistoricsite.orgihistory/morse.html>

Perera, Tom. "History, Theory & Construction of the "Electric Telegraph."

WI TP Telegraph & Scientific Instrument Museums 2 October 2004.

<http://www.chss.montclair.edu/pereratipertel.htm>

Miles 9

Raven, G.S. "A Brief History of the Morse Telegraph." 3 Sept. 2004.

<http://www.faradic.net!~gsraven/history.html>

"Samuel F. Morse Preview." Library of Congress: 1–6

<http://lcweb2.loc.gov/ammern/atthtml/morsel.html>

Thompson, Holland. "Agents of Communication -Newspaper Printing."

16 Sept. 2004. <http://inventors.about.com!cs/

inventorsalphabetla/media_2.htm>

The APA Style of In-Text Citation

Although most humanities courses require you to follow the style described by the *MLA Handbook*, most scientific and technical courses require quite different procedures of documentation. Publications in the social sciences (anthropology, education, law, psychology, sociology, etc.) often use the APA style of documentation outlined in the *Publication Manual of the American Psychological Association*, 5th ed. (Washington: APA, 2001). Sources used are listed alphabetically on a separate page titled "References" following the final page of the text.

In-text citations of sources present the *author* and *date* in parenthetical references throughout the paper. Most often the citation consists of the author's name and the year of publication:

A study of interactions between doctors and nurses (Stewart, 1992) explains . . .

If the author has already been named in the text, only the year is cited:

Stewart (1992) analyzes the interactions between doctors and nurses.

Specific page references to a source can follow a quotation or be part of the parenthetical citation:

The interactions between doctors and nurses, according to Stewart (1992) fit "the non zero sum game model" (p. 77).

The interactions between doctors and nurses fit "the non zero sum game model" (Stewart, 1992, p. 77).

Other possibilities for the APA in-text citations might include the following:

WORK BY TWO AUTHORS

The summary of prior research on genetic factors in crime (Rubenstein & Horowitz, 1992, pp. 35–42) challenges the economic models.

PUBLICATIONS BY THE SAME AUTHOR IN DIFFERENT YEARS OR WITHIN THE SAME YEAR

Carlson has studied the community policing model in several contexts (1983, 1991a, 1991b).

WORK BY THREE TO FIVE AUTHORS

Names of all authors appear in the first reference. Subsequent references give only the first author's name followed by et al. Use et al. for six or more authors.

Peterson, Thomas, and Zimbardo (1976) sought correlations between television violence and real-life violence. Like other approaches to the study of violence in the 1970s, the researchers (Peterson et al.) found that portrayals of violence have little impact on inner city residents.

TWO OR MORE SOURCES IN A SINGLE REFERENCE

List authors alphabetically and separate multiple sources by a semicolon.

The question which crimes are victimless and which victims merit concern has been viewed from many perspectives (Adler, 1975; Lambert, 1987; Wilson, 1990).

PERSONAL COMMUNICATION (LETTER, MEMO, TELEPHONE CONVERSATION, FAX, E-MAIL, INTERVIEW)

Donald Singletary (telephone conversation, Oct. 11, 2004) stated that . . .

Preparing a List of References in the APA Format

The APA style of documentation provides much of the same bibliographical information as the MLA style but differs from it in some important ways. Note that the author and date sequence begins each entry. Capitals, quotation marks, and parentheses appear differently in the APA style than they do in the MLA style.

The following examples are keyed to the previously shown examples of the MLA style.

AN ARTICLE IN A JOURNAL WITH CONTINUOUS PAGINATION OF THE VOLUME FOR THAT PARTICULAR YEAR

Rockas, L. (1980). A dialogue on dialogue. *College English, 41,* 570–580.

AN ARTICLE FROM A MAGAZINE ISSUED WEEKLY

Sanders, S. W. (1981, March 16) The Vietnam shadow over policy for El

Salvador. *Business Week,* 52.

A BOOK BY A SINGLE AUTHOR

Shiska, B. (1980). *An introduction to broadcasting.* Chicago: Wade Press.

A BOOK BY TWO OR MORE AUTHORS

Murphy, M., & White, R. (1979). *Psychic side of sports.* Reading,

MA: Addison-Wesley.

A BOOK BY A CORPORATE AUTHOR

Modern Language Association. (2003). *MLA handbook for writers of research

papers* (6th ed.). New York: Author.

APA substitutes *Author* for the publisher's name when a book is published by its author.

MORE THAN ONE BOOK BY THE SAME AUTHOR

Unlike the MLA style, APA style repeats the author's name and puts works in chronological order.

Hellman, L. (1995). *Children today.* Miami, FL: University of Miami Press.

Hellman, L. (2004). *Children yesterday.* Chicago: University of Chicago Press.

A COLLECTION OF ESSAYS BY DIFFERENT AUTHORS COMPILED BY AN EDITOR

Sebeok, T. (Ed.). (1977). *How animals communicate.* Bloomington: Indiana

University Press.

A WORK IN AN ANTHOLOGY

Arnold, C. (1977). How monkeys use sign language. In T. Sebeok (Ed.), *How animals communicate* (pp. 40–50). Bloomington: Indiana University Press.

A BOOK THAT IS TRANSLATED WITH BOTH THE AUTHOR AND TRANSLATOR NAMED

Fernandez, R. (1980). *The architectural heritage of the moors* (W. Garcia, Trans.). London: Routledge.

A BOOK BY TWO OR MORE AUTHORS; A REVISED OR LATER EDITION

Reichman, S., & Deez, M. (2004). *The Washington lobbyist* (10th ed.). New York: Random House.

A NEW EDITION OF AN EDITED BOOK

Adler, F. (Ed.). (1976). *Women and crime* (4th ed.). Cambridge, MA: Harvard University Press.

A BOOK PUBLISHED IN MORE THAN ONE VOLUME

Thorndike, L. (1941). *A history of magic and experimental science.* (Vols. 1–3). New York: Columbia University Press.

A REPUBLISHED OR REPRINTED BOOK

Nilsson, M. P. (1972). *Greek folk religion*. Philadelphia: University of Pennsylvania Press. (Original work published 1940)

A NEWSPAPER ARTICLE

Petzinger, T. J., Putka, G., & Sansweet, S. J. (1983, September 12). High fliers. *Wall Street Journal,* sec. 1, pp. 1, 7.

AN UNSIGNED ARTICLE IN A NEWSPAPER

Executive Changes. (1991, August 8). *New York Times,* p. C3.

A BOOK REVIEW

Katz, B. (1960). [Review of the book *Norman Rockwell: My adventures as an illustrator*]. *Library Journal, 85,* 648.

ARTICLE FROM ENCYCLOPEDIA OR REFERENCE WORK

Albert Einstein. In *The concise Columbia encyclopedia* (2nd ed.). New York:
Columbia University Press.

ONLINE JOURNAL ARTICLE

Caesar, Terry. (2000). In and out of elevators in Japan [Electronic version].
Journal of Mundane Behavior, 1, 1. Retrieved March 12, 2000, from
http://www.mundanebehavior.org/issues/v1n1/caesar.htm

Sample Annotated Student Research Paper in APA Style

Supply abbreviated title for heading

1 inch margin on each side

Indent paras 1/2 inch

Problem for current research

Number title page (not shown) and all others using short title

Supply name and institution

Déjà vu Experience 2

Ken Takenaka

University of Central Florida

The Déjà vu Experience: Seeing Things for the First Time . . . Again

Déjà vu has often been misunderstood. It is fairly uncommon to hear someone see an event and say, "Wow, I had a dream that this exact same thing happened," and label it as déjà vu. This, however, is a completely erroneous analysis. Knowing that one has dreamed about this event means that this person had knowledge of this event happening before it came to pass. This is a different phenomenon altogether, known as precognition.

Precognition is oftentimes mistaken for déjà vu because of the relatively similar sensation of having experienced an event more than once. The difference is that in precognition, the event has actually been experienced before in a subconscious or conscious state, whereas in the case of déjà vu, the event never transpired. They do have something in common, however, both are very difficult to document because they exist only as a feeling or dream

**1-inch from top
of new page**

Déjà vu Experience 3

without any actual physical proof. In today's society, déjà vu has

become a term that is thrown about without much thought. If

people knew just how rare this occurrence was, it would be held

in a much higher regard.

New theories have arisen as a result of work in areas once thought

unrelated. Studies pertaining to the neurophysiology of attention,

**Overview of
prior research**
memory, illusion, and sight have all served to explain parts of the

puzzle. Theories included the idea that déjà vu is a disorder associated

with the amygdala and the hippocampus resulting in a lapse of

attention, temporary loss of short-term memory, and the idea that

déjà vu has to do with an abnormality in the transmission of the data

from the eyes to the brain (Carey, 2004, p. F1).

Prior to speaking about the theories of déjà vu, however, it is

necessary to outline the roles played by the thalamus, hippocampus,

and the brain stem in the processing of information. The thalamus

is a structure in the brain that is responsible for relaying information

to the cortex. Its primary function is to handle incoming and

outgoing signals. It is responsible for taking in the information

that is absorbed by the eyes and transmitting it to the visual

cortex located in the back of the brain where information about

what is seen is processed. The information from each eye is handled

separately by the thalamus. Information from the right eye will

ultimately be processed by the left hemisphere and information

from the left eye by the right hemisphere. The hippocampus is

thought to play a very important role in learning and memory,

especially long term. It is one of the first parts of the brain that

is damaged in the course of Alzheimer's disease. The brainstem is

Déjà vu Experience 4

another key component of the brain. It is connected to the spinal cord and is deep within the brain itself. It controls breathing and heart rate, and damage to the brainstem can cause impaired or double vision. The amygdala, part of the limbic system, is involved in controlling autonomic responses to stimuli from a sensory organ. In the case of déjà vu, the visual received from the eyes is processed and an autonomic response signal is sent to the brain. Each of these parts of the brain has a significant role in déjà vu (Kleiner-Fisman, 2001; Limbic System, n.d. Weiten, 2005, pp. 69, 97–99, 211).

Multiple sources in one citation

One theory is based on the human sense of sight. It is thought that déjà vu applies to the sense of sight exclusively. This is based on the premise that each eye interprets data separately and not necessarily at the same time. The lapse in time between the recognition of a visual stimuli in the eyes is so small, however, that the brain perceives it to be one instant. According to research, the human brain can only perceive two visual stimuli at one instant if they are less than 25 milliseconds apart. Since the human brain is capable of interpreting both signals well within this time, when events are perceived normally, they are seen and recognized by the brain as one event. Occasionally, however, the neurological impulses that carry the data from each eye to the brain are delayed. One signal may reach the brain in under 25 milliseconds, while the other signal is slowed and reaches the brain later. This causes the brain to interpret the stimuli as two separate events rather than one event, causing the person to have the sensation of having seen the event before because the brain has recognized it as a memory. The brain

Review of earlier studies identifies key assumptions

Déjà vu Experience 5

is incapable of storing data with respect to time and is only able to show things in relation to others.

For example, the brain does not know that an event had transpired on Thursday at 6:15 P.M., but rather looks at it chronologically and in relation to other memories in conjunction with the learned information of dates, times, night, and day. In this theory, the thalamus is responsible for the abnormality that causes déjà vu. When information is received by the thalamus and is transcribed into data that can be used by the brain, one-half of the information is processed more slowly than the other, therefore sending signals in a delayed interval, causing the sensation of two separate events rather than one event, leading to a sense of déjà vu (Johnson, 2001).

Presents alternative theory

Vilayanur Ramachandran proposes another theory based on his finding that there are actually two different pathways in the human brain associated with the sense of sight. One pathway is linked to the brainstem while the other, the one aforementioned, is linked to the thalamus. The thalamus-centered pathway is the one we use today, but the more primitive pathway, the brainstem pathway, was used before the thalamus-centered pathway became more efficient, that is, faster. In some people, if both pathways are active, this may be the cause of déjà vu. If the thalamus pathway were active in one eye or one part of the brain and the slower brainstem pathway was active in the other part of the brain, the brain would interpret the stimuli differently, therefore causing the sensation of two different events. In people who have an active brainstem pathway, this would mean that déjà vu might occur regularly. In most other people, it would mean that the more efficient

Déjà vu Experience 6

thalamus-centered pathway would be used and the less often used brainstem pathway would begin to degrade after having not been used at all, thereby allowing that person to have sensations of déjà vu only occasionally or perhaps not at all. However, this could only occur in very young children because if both pathways were indeed active since birth and continual déjà vu was experienced, the brain would adapt and interpret the two signals as one (Johnson, 2001).

In 1878, researchers had speculated that déjà vu was brought on by fatigue. Just 11 years later, it was thought that déjà vu was, conversely, brought on by an over-rested brain. The idea behind this strange theory is that when the brain is introduced to a new image or event, the brain in a normal state will interpret the signal at a normal speed and store it as memory. In an overactive brain, however, the brain will interpret the incoming signal even faster than normal. The fact that the new signal took less time than usual convinces the brain that it has indeed seen the image before. In a metaphoric sense, this can be likened to a cookie that is downloaded by a computer. When a computer accesses new information via the Internet, part of the Web page is saved onto the hard drive and stored so that the next time the same page is accessed, the computer will not have to interpret new information, but instead will bring up prior information, thereby allowing the user to access and view the information faster. In this analogy, the computer is accessing information at a faster rate, and therefore we recognize it as a website that we have previously visited. In the same sense, when our brains process a visual stimulus faster than normal, our brains may cause us to think that we have seen the

Uses an analogy to explain theory

Déjà vu Experience 7

image before and that we are actually remembering it rather than seeing it for the first time. On the flip side, the theory that déjà vu is a result of fatigue is actually supported by the newly interpreted information aforementioned in this paper. When the brain is fatigued and working more slowly than usual, the messages relayed from our eyes to our brains may be altered, causing the abnormal behavior of the thalamus (Glenn, 2004, p. A12).

In the late twentieth century, a researcher by the name of Brown proposed several theories about déjà vu. One is that déjà vu is actually akin to the epileptic seizure, supported by claims of epileptic patients saying they experience déjà vu just prior to having an attack. Seizures are brought on by an improper firing of neural impulses in the brain that result in strange sensations, behaviors, and emotions. This misfiring of neurons may be what the brain is experiencing when feeling déjà vu (Glenn, 2004, p. A12).

A theory related to Ramachandran's idea of a thalamus-centered visual pathway proposes that because there are two visual pathways to the brain, one being slightly slower than the other, an imbalance in these two pathways causes déjà vu. The first visual pathway goes directly into the visual cortex in the occipital lobe. The second pathway is slightly slower, going into other parts of the brain such as the parietal cortex before reaching the occipital lobe. This pathway, while being slightly slower, is not slow enough for the brain to identify visual stimuli as two separate events. However, if this second pathway were just slightly slower than normal, the amount of time that it takes for both signals to reach the occipital lobe would most likely differ by more than the allotted 25 milliseconds,

Discuss recent theories in detail

Déjà vu Experience 8

therefore signaling the brain to interpret the stimuli as two separate events (Glenn, 2004, p.A12).

Another part of the brain, the amygdala, which is responsible for involuntary physical responses to physical stimuli called the fight or flight response, may be involved in déjà vu. When the amygdala functions abnormally, the thought process that will succeed a visual stimulus is altered. The amygdala receives the visual stimulus and processes it incorrectly, a response to the brain that is abnormal. A hypothetical response in the case of déjà vu is that the brain receives information and the amygdala gives the physical response of having had the same experiences once before. The amygdala, however, is not directly associated with parts of the brain that pertain to memory. Therefore the subject does not have a recollection of the memory, but the initial feeling of familiarity brought on when the amygdala's interpretation lingers (Limbic System, n.d.).

While all of these theories attempt to explain the phenomenon that we have come to know as déjà vu, there are many instances in which, as mentioned before, déjà vu is mistaken for precognition or

Déjà vu defined more accurately

some other illusion of the brain that has been identified as an abnormality. Included in this category is the déjà vu experience as opposed to actual déjà vu. The déjà vu experience occurs when a person has no recollection of the details of the event, nor do they know beyond a doubt that the event actually happened. A part of this déjà vu experience can be inattentional blindness, people experience something for the first time without concentrating on it. Their attention may be elsewhere. When the event happens again,

Déjà vu Experience 9

this time with their full attention, they recognize the situation or event as something that has happened before, but are unsure of whether or not the event actually transpired. They experience a déjà vu-like sensation (Glenn, 2004, p. A12).

As you can see from all of these theories, nearly all imply the same thing. They see the cause of déjà vu as a delay in neurological impulses that produce feelings of familiarity. Each theory, however, uses different reasoning to support the claim. At this point in

Presents conclusion

research, it can be assumed that déjà vu is most likely associated with the abnormal sending of information from receptors to other parts of the brain.

The fact of the matter is, déjà vu has no physical explanation nor is it able to be documented scientifically or accurately due to the fact that its entire existence is based in a realm to which the researcher cannot gain access: the subjects' thoughts. Researchers can only speculate about the causes of the phenomenon based on other physical or psychological evidence and personal testimony. It is clear, however, that déjà vu is an out of the ordinary experience involving

Possibilities for further research

the brain and thought process. Once perceived to be a physical phenomenon, it is now clear that it is indeed encompassed in the psychological territory. Will research and study ever prove for certain what causes déjà vu? Perhaps with the furthering of study in the area of psychology, it may be possible. The human mind is complex in its working, which is what makes it so difficult to study. That is also why there are so many abnormalities that can occur and why it may be so difficult to solve problems associated with brain functions.

Déjà vu Experience 10

Begin on new page

References

Brown, A. (2004). The déjà vu illusion. *Current Directions in Psychological Science. 13*(6), 256.

Carey, B. (2004, September 14). Déjà vu: If it all seems familiar, there may be a reason. *New York Times*, p. F1.

Glenn, D. (2004, July 23). The tease of memory. *Chronicle of Higher Education, 50*(46), A12.

Johnson, C. (2001, December 8). *A theory on the déjà vu phenomenon*. Retrieved December 6, 2004, from http://mb-soft.com/public/dejavu.html

Kleiner-Fisman, G. (2001, April 15). *Brainstem function*. Retrieved December 3, 2004, from http://www.nlm.nih.gov/medlineplus/ency/imagepages/18007.htm

Lerner, R. M. (1993). Déjà vu, dialects, and the constancies of controversies involving the nature-nurture issue. *International Journal of Comparative Psychology, 6*(3), 163.

Limbic System. (n.d.). Retrieved December 7, 2004, from http://thalamus.wustl.edu/course/limbic.html

Thompson, R., Moulin, C., Conway, M., & Jones R. (2004, September). Persistent déjà vu: A disorder of memory. *International Journal of Geriatric Psychiatry, 19*, 906.

Weiten, W. (2005). *Psychology themes and variations*. Belmont, CA: Wadsworth.

The CSE Style of In-Text Citation

For courses in the sciences, and the engineering or technical fields, the primary formatting and documentation used is that of the Council of Science Editors (CSE), as of 2000, previously CBE (Council of Biology Editors). In-text references may take one of two forms: (1) the number method in which numbers are in parentheses or are superscript figures that refer to numbered items in a reference list at the end of the paper or (2) the name and date method in which the name of the author(s) appears in the text along with the date of publication, usually but not always in parentheses. The first method saves space but requires the reader to turn to the reference list to identify the source whereas as the second method takes more space but allows the reader to identify the source without stopping.

The differences between the CSE style and those of the MLA and APA can be seen in the sample student research paper ("Louis Pasteur: Father of Microbiology") and in the following examples of in-text citations and in the end-of-text reference list.

Notice the following sentence taken from the sample student research paper:

> In fact, Pasteur stated that he would "never introduce an instrument in the human body without having passed it through boiling water" (Meadows 1987, p 178).

Using the name-and-date method, the student includes the name of the author(s) along with the publication date of the text. A complete reference on the page at the end of the text called "Cited References" gives all the necessary information:

> Meadows, AJ. 1987. The great scientist. New York: Oxford University Press, Inc. 248 p.

Documenting Sources in the CSE Style

A BOOK BY A SINGLE AUTHOR

> Shishka B. 1980. An introduction to broadcasting. Chicago: Wade, 320 p.

Give the author's name in inverted order, beginning with the last name and followed by the initials. Next give the year of publication and the title of the work followed by a period and a space. Do not underline the title and capitalize only the first word and proper names or adjectives. For more than one author follow the same pattern for each author and separate the names with a comma. Indicate the city, publisher and total number of pages in the work.

ARTICLE IN A JOURNAL PAGINATED BY VOLUME

Rockas L. 1980. A dialogue on dialogue. College English 41: 570–80.

ONLINE ARTICLE

[Anonymous]. Louis Pasteur. Ambafrance: Embassy of France in Canada [online]. Available from: http://www.ambafrance-ca.org/HYPERLAB/ PEOPLE/_pasteur.html. Accessed 2000 Oct 10.

Sample Annotated Student Research Paper in CSE Style

1

Stefanie Milne

NorthWest Arkansas Community College

2005 April 22

Supply name, institution and date

Louis Pasteur: Father of Microbiology

"Let me tell you the secret that has led me to my goal. My strength relies solely on my tenacity."--Louis Pasteur

Paper takes the form of a profile biography

This quote is posted to the office door of Carey Chaney, an anatomy and physiology instructor at NorthWest Arkansas Community College. According to Chaney (2000, p 10), persistence and hard work led Pasteur to many discoveries and advancements in medicine. A biographer of Pasteur, Rene Dubos, states Pasteur was "enthusiastic about whatever he was working on . . . He had patience. He also possessed a fighting spirit and the capacity to work untiringly." Tenacity was the characteristic that led Louis Pasteur to become one of the greatest men of the history of science.

Uses CSE name-year citations

Introduces thesis as defining characteristic

The birth of Louis Pasteur on December 27, 1822, was surrounded by many important events including the death of Napoleon, the reign of Louis XVIII, and the birth of the "father of genetics," Gregor Mendel. Greece was fighting for its freedom, and Brazil, Argentina, and Peru had gained their independence.

2

Beethoven's <u>Ninth Symphony</u> and Schubert's <u>Unfinished Symphony</u>
were composed. Pasteur, according to Chaney, "was born into
humble circumstances," his father a tanner by trade. He was
extremely close to his family; in fact, he was so close that when he
began attending the preparatory school of M. Barber, he became so
homesick that his father came to retrieve him. Throughout his
education, Pasteur's family kept in close contact with him and
followed his studies with interest. Chaney states that his "successes
in school were a great source of pride to his family."

According to Chaney, Pasteur's tenacity began at a young age.
Pasteur started down the road to success with his talent for art. His
attention to every detail in his painting led family and neighbors to
request portraits. According to Rene Dubos (1998, p 9), the Finnish
artist Albert Edelfelt stated, "Outside of science, painting is one of
the few things that interest him . . . I am certain that had
M. Pasteur selected art instead of science, France would count today
one more able painter." Despite his great promise as an artist,
Pasteur elected to work in the field of science and research.

Pasteur's tenacity again led him to success in his scholastic
life. He returned to the preparatory school of M. Barber. Pasteur
took his studies very seriously and could have been considered an
"over-achiever" (Chaney 2000). He went on for further study at
Besancon, but his desire was to attend the famed Ecole Normale
Superieure in Paris. In 1842, at the age of twenty, he took the exam
that was necessary for admission into Ecole Normale. He ranked
fifteenth out of twenty-two and was admitted. Most would have
been satisfied with this, but Pasteur was not happy with his results

3

and returned to Besancon for further study. After one year, he again tried the exam and ranked fourth. This time, Pasteur accepted admission. This "urge for perfection" (Dubos 1998, p 11) was prevalent throughout Pasteur's entire life.

Ecole Normale was France's leading institution for preparing students for the examination of <u>agregation</u>, a teaching qualification that allowed its students the highest rate of salary as professors in the French secondary schools. At Ecole Normale, Pasteur chose to study physics and chemistry. In 1847, at the age of 26, he tackled the problem of why the solutions of the two different kinds of organic compounds of tartaric acid in crystal shapes appear to be identical, but have different effects on polarized light. This began his studies in crystallography for his agregation doctorate. From his studies, he "formulated a fundamental law: asymmetry differentiates the organic world from the mineral world" (Ambafrance 2000, p 1). These studies were a basis for a new field of science known as stereochemistry. According to Chaney, Pasteur's involvement with crystallography and molecular asymmetry was a learning tool that furthered his interest in the research process.

Strikes a balance between telling the story and providing clear scientific information

After he attained his doctorate in 1849, he began teaching in the secondary schools in Dijon. Within a matter of three months, he became the professor of chemistry at the University of Strasbourg, where he met and married Marie Laurent. From this time on, Pasteur would focus his studies on the world of microorganisms.

In 1854, Pasteur moved to Lille, a French industrial center, and became the dean of science for a school for higher education. Here, Pasteur began studying fermentation. Pasteur's biological view of

4

fermentation depended on the presence of microorganisms. In the "predominant view of alcohol fermentation" during this time, fermentation was a "purely chemical process in which sugar is transformed into alcohol" (Meadows 1987, p. 173). Pasteur concluded that fermentation depended on microorganisms. Pasteur's study of bacteria became known as the science of bacteriology.

In 1857, Pasteur moved to Paris to begin work at his former school, Ecole Normale, as the "director of scientific studies" (Meadows 1987, p 173). Unfortunately, there was no lab in which Pasteur could perform his experiments, so he personally funded the construction of a lab for his work. He was then able to conduct more studies on bacteria.

Pasteur, through his development of culturing bacteria using growth mediums, discovered that certain bacteria could not function in the presence of oxygen. These bacteria he called "anaerobic." Conversely, some bacteria could only function with oxygen present. These he called "aerobic" bacteria. Pasteur found that without anaerobic bacteria, there could be no decomposition of dead matter. Through even further studies of these different types of bacteria, Pasteur again noted that fermentation could only occur in the presence of microorganisms. These experiments led Pasteur into the debate on spontaneous generation, "the theory . . . that life could arise spontaneously in organic materials" (Ambafrance 2000, p 2).

We again see Pasteur's tenacity when he began to argue his findings against spontaneous generation. During this time, a German microscopist named Theodor Schwann had proven that yeast cells

Provides a context for understanding scientific discoveries

5

could reproduce and grow during fermentation. A chemist named Justus von Liebig disputed this idea by stating that living yeast cells do not ferment; instead, sugar is transformed into alcohol. Pasteur, using his experiments with anaerobic bacteria, had stated that fermentation would only occur with microbes present. Finally, in 1864, Felix-Archimede Pouchet, one of the stronger advocates of spontaneous generation, wanted this debate to be settled by a "special committee of the French Academy of Sciences" (Meadows 1987, p 177). Pasteur had opposed the idea of spontaneous generation due to his strong Roman Catholic background because it "reduced life to chemical reactions" (Meadows 1987, p 176). This was the fuel that helped fire his experimentation to disprove the theory. The members of the committee were primarily Roman Catholic and were thus biased towards Pasteur. They tended to view only Pasteur's case. According to Meadows, although Pasteur was correct in his findings, this caused his case "embarrassment" and it "delayed the understanding of bacterial life by a decade." All of these intense arguments and Pasteur's thorough study of anaerobic life further "paved the way for the study of germs" (Ambafrance 2000, p 2).

Explains competing theories

Pasteur's studies on bacteria helped two major industries survive during this period. In 1864, Pasteur was asked by Napoleon III to study the bacterial diseases causing the "considerable loss to the wine industry" (Ambafrance 2000, p 2). Pasteur concluded that heating the wine to 55 degrees Celsius for a period of time would kill the microorganisms that caused the diseases in the wine. This process was found to be effective on milk and beer also, and came to be known as "pasteurization" in honor of Pasteur's work.

Provides examples of the effects of research discoveries

6

The next year, Pasteur was asked to investigate the diseases in silkworms that were causing yet another industry to suffer economic loss. He examined the eggs of the silkworm for infection. Pasteur found two entirely different diseases, one caused primarily by nutrition, and the other caused by a "parasitic protozoan" (Dubos 1998, p 94). He formulated a way to breed silkworms without the diseases and instructed the silkworm industry on his findings. It would seem at this point that there would be no stopping Pasteur in his discoveries. The more he researched, the more he became involved in utilizing his findings to improve everyday life.

Through Pasteur's tenacious study of bacteria, the "germ theory" was formulated. In the mid-1800s, disease was believed to be spread by poisonous fumes given off from dung heaps and decaying matter blown by the wind from one place to another. However, according to Pasteur's research, breakdown or decay of matter was associated with microorganisms. Pasteur believed these same microbes could further infect humans and interfere with the normal functions of the body. In fact, Pasteur stated that he would "never introduce an instrument in the human body without having passed it through boiling water" (Meadows 1987, p 178). Thus he would tackle the involvement between microorganisms and humans, and introduce the need for aseptic procedures.

"Pasteur was a key figure in understanding the link between microorganisms and the aseptic procedures used in fighting them" (Chaney 2000). Women of Pasteur's time were dying of fever following childbirth. Unknown to the medical community, a tiny organism caused this tragedy. Pasteur directed the doctors and

Shows how changing views of this aspect of science evolved

Describes both the context and consequence of research discoveries

7

midwives attending these births to wash their hands and instruments after each delivery to kill the microbes causing the fever and ultimately the deaths of the mothers. Unfortunately, it took some time for the doctors to believe Pasteur regardless of his findings because he was not an actual doctor. This did not stop Pasteur from further study leading him to vaccine therapy.

With the knowledge of the smallpox vaccine, Pasteur, who had already noted the bacteria from different types of animal diseases, was ready to experiment with vaccine therapy. Chickens were wiped away by cholera, and whole herds of sheep and cattle were destroyed by anthrax, causing trouble to farmers and ranchers. Pasteur cultivated the bacteria that caused both diseases and exposed the cultures to air that remained at an even temperature for a long period of time, producing an "attenuated form" (Meadows 1987, p 184) of the disease. The animals injected with these attenuated forms later known as vaccines, developed a resistance to the actual disease. Pasteur's tenacity was again shown through this hard work in developing these vaccines to save livestock, leading to his greatest endeavor: the rabies vaccine.

Rabies was a lethal disease passed from animals, primarily dogs, to humans. Pasteur believed through his work with the cholera and anthrax vaccines that he could develop a vaccine to benefit humans and save lives from this dreadful disease. According to Chaney, Pasteur "could not find the causative agent of rabies," but he was able to grow cultures in the brain tissue of dogs and rabbits. After left to open air for a period of time, the vaccine was developed. Pasteur tried the vaccine therapy on a young boy named Joseph

Shows relationship of biography and scientific discovery

8

Meister, who had been attacked by a rabid dog. The disease never attacked the boy's body. A wonderful vaccine had been developed that could not only prevent rabies in animals, but also cure the disease in humans.

The rabies vaccine influenced many people to donate money to erect a center and laboratory for rabies vaccination therapy in 1888. This center was appropriately named the Pasteur Institute, where Pasteur spent the remaining seven years of his life dedicating himself to further research of infectious diseases. After suffering a second stroke on September 22, 1895, at the age of seventy-two, Louis Pasteur passed away and was given a "state funeral and buried in a magnificent tomb within the Pasteur Institute" (Meadows 1987, p 188).

"'Do not put forth anything that you cannot prove by experimentation,' Pasteur would teach his disciples" (Ambafrance 2000, p 3). The thought behind this statement, along with his tenacious personality, is what later led him to be referred to as the "Father of Microbiology." Tenacity had its price, though.

During my interview with Chaney, I learned that Pasteur's tenacity led him to have strong friends as well as strong enemies. Chaney states, "Pasteur could be defined as a polarized person." His close friends respected him. He believed in hard work and would often drive himself and his fellow workers to the point of exhaustion. This may have contributed to his poor health in the end. Along with his perseverance in finding treatments to benefit humanity, he withstood the deaths of his father, his sister, and three daughters during the period of seven years. His human body could only handle

9

so much before he suffered his first stroke. But, he was a humanitarian, and he would have endured anything for the sake of improving conditions for mankind. Pasteur expressed his feelings toward humanity by stating, "I beseech you to take interest in these sacred domains so expressively called laboratories. Ask that there be more and that they be adorned for these are the temples of the future, wealth, and well-being. It is here that humanity will grow, strengthen, and improve. Here, humanity will learn to read progress and individual harmony in the works of nature, while humanity's own works are all too often those of barbarism, fanaticism, and destruction" (quoted in Ambafrance 2000, p 3).

Several writers have also concluded that Pasteur was pompous. According to Reynolds, Pasteur "illustrated his pride and egotism" when he sent letters to his sister, Josephine, while he was in school. His letter "advised her in a paternalistic tone, that if resolve is firm, a given task will be accomplished" (Reynolds 1994, p 5). Although Pasteur has been referred to as pompous, Chaney states "he was only blunt, having to defend himself and his work." He believed in what he accomplished. He was introducing new things to the medical profession. Maybe he stepped on a few toes in the process since he was not a medical professional. According to Dubos (1998, p 4), "Pasteur . . . had many occasions to capitalize on [his] fame and to acquire wealth from the practical applications of [his] discoveries, yet [he] resisted the temptations for the sake of higher values."

Whether or not Pasteur was pompous, egotistical, or just proud of what he had accomplished in his great life, the trait of Pasteur

Summarizes interaction between biography and scientific discoveries

10

that we should be thankful for was his tenacity in studying the effects the microorganism could have on humanity. Pasteur was "probably the most dedicated servant that science ever had" (Dubos 1998, p 11). Chaney states that through the opposition, Pasteur "remained tough and unafraid to go against the system." Throughout his life, Pasteur was recognized for his contributions to science, but I believe we are more thankful today for his accomplishments for we have seen the actual results of his tenacity.

11

Cited References

Chaney C. 2000 Oct 26. Personal interview.

Dubos, RJ. 1998. Pasteur and modern science. Ed. TD Brock. Washington, D.C.: ASM Press. 168 p.

[Anonymous]. Louis Pasteur. Ambafrance: Embassy of France in Canada [online]. Available from: http://www.ambafrance-ca.org/ HYPERLAB/PEOPLE/_pasteur.html. Accessed 2000 Oct 10.

Meadows, AJ. 1987. The great scientists. New York: Oxford University Press, Inc. 248 p.

Reynolds, MD. 1994. How Pasteur changed history: The story of Louis Pasteur and the Pasteur Institute. Bradenton, Florida: McGuinn & McGuire Publishing, Inc. 151 p.

Double-space entries and use hanging indentation

Alphabetical list for CSE name-year citations

PART :: 2

LIBERAL ARTS

Art and Architecture

Richard Keller Simon

The Shopping Mall and the Formal Garden

Richard Keller Simon is professor of English at California Polytechnic State University–San Luis Obispo and director of the Humanities Program. He is the author of The Labyrinth of the Comic *(1986) and* Trash Culture: Popular Culture and the Great Tradition *(1999), in which the following selection first appeared. In addition to being a vital feature of modern culture, the contemporary shopping mall updates and incorporates garden designs of the past to create a self-enclosed world devoted to consumption.*

The contemporary shopping mall is a great formal garden of American culture, a commercial space that shares fundamental characteristics with many of the great garden styles of Western history. Set apart from the rest of the world as a place of earthly delight like the medieval walled garden; filled with fountains, statuary, and ingeniously devised machinery like the Italian Renaissance garden; designed on grandiose and symmetrical principles like this seventeenth-century French garden; made up of the fragments of cultural and architectural history like the eighteenth-century irregular English garden; and set aside for the public like the nineteenth-century American park, the mall is the next phase of this garden history, a synthesis of all these styles that have come before. But it is now joined with the shopping street, or at least a sanitized and standardized version of one, something never before allowed within the garden. In this latest version of the earthly paradise, people live on the goods of the consumer economy peacefully, pleasurably, and even with sophisticated complexity, for although their pleasure comes from buying and everything is set up to facilitate that pleasure, the garden itself is no simple place. Nordstrom has come to Eden. There were dangers and temptations in the very first garden, of course, and the delights dangled before us have been equally powerful. We have moved from the knowledge of good and evil to the joys of shopping.

Visitors learn the meanings of consumer society at the mall, not only in the choices they make in their purchases but also in the symbol systems they walk through, just as visitors to those earlier gardens were invited to learn about the meanings of their own times from the pastoral adventures presented to them. Like the formal garden, the shopping mall is a construct of promenades, walls, vistas, mounts, labyrinths, fountains, statues, archways, trees, grottoes, theaters, flowering plants and shrubs, trellises, and assorted reproductions from architectural history, all artfully arranged. Some of these features, such as the mount, have undergone technological or economic modification. The mount—the manmade earthworks designed to present a vista of the garden to the visitor and typically reached by path or staircase—was a standard part of garden design from the Middle Ages to the eighteenth century. This has been replaced by the escalator, which rises at key points in the enclosed central parts of the mall, where it presents a similar vista of the space to the visitor, who is now lifted dramatically from the floor below by unseen forces without any effort on his or her part. And this, in its turn, is only the modification of a standard feature from Italian Renaissance gardens, the elaborate hydraulic machinery or automata that engineers had devised to move statues about in striking dramatic tableaux. Now in the mall it is the visitors who are moved about by the escalators, becoming themselves the actors in a tableau we might title "modern shopping." Combining the mount with the automata, the mall then encloses this machinery in two or three stories of space, topped with skylights. The result is something like Houston's Galleria Mall, a massive, three-story, enclosed mall topped with skylights. This, in turn, is an updated version of Henry VIII's great garden at Hampton Court, where a mount was topped by a three-story glass arbor surrounded by figures of the king's beasts and royal crown. We have dispensed with the beasts and crown; joggers now run on the roof of the Galleria. But the mount in the king's garden allowed the visitor to look both inside and outside of his garden; the escalator within the enclosed mall of the Galleria, by contrast, only allows the visitor to look at the inside space.

Similarly, the labyrinth—the maze of pathways or hedges that confounded the visitor's attempts to find an easy way out and was a favorite device of Renaissance gardens—is now the cleverly laid out pattern of aisles with department stores, which can be designed to discourage the visitor's easy exit. Shoppers simply cannot find a way out. A decade ago Bloomingdale's in the Willow Grove Mall in suburban Philadelphia received so many complaints from irate shoppers lost in its mazes that finally small, discreet exit signs were posted. What might have originated in the mazes of the early Christian Church, which penitents traveled on their knees while praying at particular points, was first moved outside into the garden, where it was secularized, and has now become thoroughly commodified, a journey in which purchases have replaced prayers. Buy enough and we will let you out.

Played against the maze and labyrinth in the Renaissance garden were the axial and radial avenues that began as extensions of hallways of the palace and ended in suitably grand natural vistas. Played against the department store maze in the mall are the axial and radial avenues that begin as extensions of hallways of one anchor department store and end in the grand vistas of the entrances to other anchor department stores.

5   The kitchen garden, that area of the formal garden closest to the house and set aside for the production of food, has become the food court, that area of the mall set aside for the consumption of food. The statues—the assorted imitations of Greek and Roman models, portraits of contemporary royalty, or stylized representations of the ancient virtues—have become mannequins decked out in fashionable clothing, the generalized imitations of consumers in their most beautiful, heroic, and changeable poses, portraits of contemporary anonymous life that we should see as stylized representations of the modern virtues: pose, flexibility, nubility, interchangeability, emotional absence. The generalized faces on the statues are now the empty faces of the mannequins. And the various architectural antiquities that became a feature of eighteenth-century English irregular gardens—the miscellaneous copies of Greek temples, Gothic ruins, Japanese pagodas, Roman triumphal arches, and Italian grottoes—are now represented not so much by the miscellaneous architectural reproductions that appear seasonally in the mall, as in the Easter Bunny's cottage or Santa's Workshop, but much more profoundly by many of the stores themselves, which present idealized versions of architectural and cultural history to the consumer: the Victorian lingerie shop, the high modernist fur salon, the nineteenth-century Western goods store, the Mexican restaurant, the country store designed as a red barn, the dark bar designed as a grotto. Also present in smaller details—in the grand staircase, the wall of mirrors, the plush carpeting, the man playing the white grand piano—are echoes of the 1930s movie set; in the merry-go-round, the popcorn cart, and the clown with balloons, the echoes of funland. The eighteenth-century garden included such historical reproductions in an effort to make sense of its past and to accommodate its cultural inheritances to new situations. One can say the same about the mall's inclusion of historical recollections. If we judge this to be playful and parodic, then we can also call the space postmodern, but if it is only a nostalgic recovery of history, we cannot. This can be a tricky thing. The mall's appropriation of history into

idealized spaces of consumption can be a nostalgia or parody, or both at the same time.

The Stanford Shopping Center near Palo Alto presents such a parodic and nostalgic bricolage of cultural and architectural history: Crabtree and Evelyn with its images of eighteenth-century life; Laura Ashley with its images of Romantic and early Victorian life; Victoria's Secret, the late Victorian whore-house with overtones of French fashion; Banana Republic, the late Victorian colonial outfitter; the Disney Store with its images of 1940s art; and The Nature Company, closest to the sixteenth century and the rise of science in its stock of simple instruments and decor of simple observations of nature. One walks through the images of history just as one did in the formal garden, but now they can be appropriated through the act of consuming. One buys images but learns "history." It is a clean, neat, middle-class version of history without the homeless of a downtown big city, and thus a retreat from the frenzy of urban life and of contemporary history, which is exactly what the formal garden was designed to be. To one side is an alley devoted to food: a lavishly idealized greengrocer, a pseudo-Italian coffee bar, and Max's Opera Café, a reproduction of a grand nineteenth-century cafe in Vienna—but what one finds when one wanders inside is not real or ersatz Vienna, but a glorified Jewish deli. Here the history of central Europe is rewritten as it might have been.

In one Renaissance garden a grotto dedicated to Venus and voluptuous pleasure was juxtaposed with one dedicated to Diana and virtuous pleasure. In another a Temple of Ancient Virtue was contrasted with one representing Modern Virtue. In a similar manner the visitor to the modern garden at Stanford is presented with choices between Victoria's Secret, the shop of voluptuous pleasure, and Westminster Lace, the shop of virtuous pleasure and chastity, but he or she does not have to choose between the Temple of Modern Virtue, the modern shopping center itself, or the Temple of Ancient Virtue, the remnants of the gardens of the past, because the mall artfully combines both.

We are almost at an end of our catalogue of garden elements. In fact, the only standard feature of garden design not present in the modern mall, either in original or in modified form, is the hermitage ruin, a favorite eighteenth-century architectural device designed to allow the visitor to pretend to be a hermit, to be alone and to meditate. There are only two places where a visitor can be alone in the mall: in the lavatories and in the clothing store changing room, but even there one can find surveillance cameras. Meditation and isolation are not virtues encouraged by the modern garden because, interestingly enough, given the opportunity, too many consumers will not meditate there at all, but try to steal whenever they can.

The shopping mall is, of course, quite an imperfect paradise, but the fault does not lie so much with the garden as with the shopping street it has come to assimilate. It is true that there are very few trees in these postmodern gardens, and those that do appear are typically confined in antipastoral concrete planters, but such subordination of nature has occurred before in garden history. Plants were incidental to the Renaissance garden, where visitors instead were expected to direct their attention to the grottoes, fountains, and various mechanical automata.

10   By bringing the mundane world of commerce into the garden, along with its attendant ills, the mall appears to be inverting the fundamental purposes of many of those earlier gardens as places of repose and contemplation, of escape from the mundane world. Conspicuous consumption has replaced quiet repose. But many of the great styles of garden history have been practical, if not precisely in this way, for example, the *ferme ornée* or eighteenth-century ornamented working farm with its fields, kitchen gardens, orchards, and pastures placed beside the more decorative and formal elements of the garden. These were gardens that had their practical commercial aspects. But although the mall is a far more commercial place than the practical garden, the shift has not so much destroyed the garden—for most of history a space set aside for the rich—as adapted it to new social and economic realities, and it thus can be seen as the appropriate garden for a consumer-oriented culture. In the formal gardens of the past, where nature was rearranged to fit the aesthetic taste of the period, one walked through the landscape contemplating the vistas and approaching the beautiful. In the shopping mall, where nature is similarly rearranged to fit the commercial needs of the period, one walks through the landscape, now contemplating not the vistas of nature, which have been completely blocked out, but rather the vistas presented by the entrances to the anchor department stores, and now approaching not the beautiful but rather the commodities by means of which one can become beautiful. These are practical times. The aristocrat who walked down the path of the garden admired the flowers and smelled their scents; the consumer who walks down the path of the shopping mall buys the flower scents in bottles and then smells like the flower or the musk ox. The focus has shifted from the individual in reverie facing an artificial version of nature to the individual in excitement facing a garden of consumer products. In the eighteenth century the visitor to the garden was expected to feel the elevation of his or her soul. It is unlikely that the visitor to the modern mall has a comparable experience.

ENGAGING the Text

1. What are some of the features found in the modern shopping mall and what function do they serve?

2. How does the modern shopping mall incorporate features of gardens from the past to promote consumerism?

EVALUATING the Argument

1. Why is it significant that, of all past garden features, only the hermitage (where one meditated) is not found in shopping malls?

2. In what ways have past historical eras been re-presented in commercialized forms in particular stores? What are some of the "worlds" one can enter in these stores?

EXPLORING the Issue

1. How is the fantasy dimension designed to stimulate consumer purchases? Aside from shopping, what other activities do shopping malls encourage?

2. Analyze the design of a mall that you frequent to discover the unique features that encourage you to spend time and money there.

CONNECTING Different Perspectives

1. Compare the function advertising serves, for children, (as discussed by Eric Schlosser in "Kid Kustomers" in Chapter 1) with the function malls serve for teenagers and adults as analyzed by Simon.

Ethics and Bioethics

Hans Ruesch

Slaughter of the Innocent

Hans Ruesch (b. 1913) is a modern-day Renaissance man who not only is a scholar of the history of medicine but also has written best-selling novels, including Savage Innocents *(1960) and* Back to the Top *(1973), and many short stories that have appeared in* The Saturday Evening Post *and* Esquire. *He is best known for his brilliant exposés of the animal experimentation industry, cataloged in such books as* Naked Empress: The Great Medical Fraud *(1982) and* Slaughter of the Innocent *(1983), from which the following chapter is drawn. He is the founder and director of* Civis: The International Foundation Report Dedicated to the Abolition of Vivisection.

What Is Vivisection?

The term vivisection "is now used to apply to all types of experiments on living animals, whether or not cutting is done." So states the *Encyclopedia Americana* (International Edition, 1974). And the large *Merriam-Webster* (1963): ". . . broadly, any form of animal experimentation, especially if considered to cause distress to the subject. "Thus the term also applies to experiments done with the administration of noxious substances, burns, electric or traumatic shocks, drawn-out deprivations of food and drink, psychological tortures leading to mental imbalance, and so forth. The term was employed in that sense by the physiologists of the last century who started this kind of "medical research," and so it will be used by me. By "vivisectionist" is usually meant every upholder of this method; by "vivisector" someone who performs such experiments or participates in them.

The "scientific" euphemism for vivisection is "basic research" or "research on models"—"model" being the euphemism for laboratory animal.

Though the majority of practicing physicians defend vivisection, most of them don't know what they are defending, having never set foot in a vivisection laboratory. Conversely, the great majority of vivisectors have never spent five minutes at a sick man's bedside, for the good reason that most of them decide to dedicate themselves to laboratory animals when they fail that most important medical examination, the one that would allow them to practice medicine. And many more take up "research" because that requires no formal studying. Any dunce can cut up live animals and report what he sees.

The number of animals dying of tortures through the practice of vivisection is estimated at around 400,000 a day worldwide at the time of this writing, and is growing at an annual rate of about 5 percent. Those experiments are performed in tens of thousands of clinical, industrial and university laboratories. All of them, without exception, deny access to channels of independent information. Occasionally, they take a journalist, guaranteed "tame," on a guided tour of a laboratory as carefully groomed as one of Potemkin's villages.

5   Today we no longer torture in the name of the Lord, but in the name of a new, despotic divinity—a so-called Medical Science which, although amply demonstrated to be false, successfully uses through its priests and ministers the tactics of terrorism: "If you don't give us plenty of money and a free hand with animals, you and your children will die of cancer"—well knowing that modern man does not fear God, but fears Cancer, and has never been told that most cancers, and maybe all, are fabricated through incompetence in the vivisection laboratories.

In the past, humanity was trained to tolerate cruelty to human beings on the grounds of a widespread superstition. Today humanity has been trained to tolerate cruelty to animals on the grounds of another superstition, equally wide-spread. There is a chilling analogy between the Holy Inquisitors[1] who extracted confessions by torture from those suspected of witchcraft, and the priests of modern science who employ torture trying to force information and answers from animals. Meanwhile, the indifferent majority prefers to ignore what is going on around them, so long as they are left alone.

Vivisectors indignantly reject charges that their driving motive is avarice, ambition, or sadism disguised as scientific curiosity. On the contrary, they present themselves as altruists, entirely dedicated to the welfare of mankind. But intelligent people of great humanity—from Leonardo da Vinci to Voltaire to Goethe to Schweitzer[2]—have passionately declared that a species willing to be "saved" through such means would not be worth saving. And furthermore there exists by now a crushing documentation that vivisection is not only an inhuman and dehumanizing practice, but a continuing source of errors that have grievously damaged true science and the health of humanity at large.

If such a sordid approach to medical knowledge were as useful as advertised, the nation with the highest life expectancy should be the United States, where expenditures for vivisection are a multiple of those in any other country, where more "life-saving" operations are performed, and whose medical profession considers itself to be the world's finest, besides being the most expensive. In fact, "Among the nations that measure average life expectancy, America ranks a relatively low 17th—behind most of Western Europe, Japan, Greece, and even Bulgaria," reported *Time* Magazine, July 21, 1975, after having reported on December 17, 1973, that "The U.S. has twice as many surgeons in proportion to population as Great Britain—and Americans undergo twice as many operations as Britons. Yet, on the average, they die younger."

All this in spite of Medicare and Medicaid and the formidable therapeutic arsenal at the disposal of American doctors and patients.

Man and Animals

10 Many of the medical men who have denounced the practice of vivisection as inhuman, fallacious and dangerous have been among the most distinguished in

---

[1]Refers to the Inquisition in Spain during the fifteenth century, in which a special tribunal was established to combat and punish heresy in the Roman Catholic Church.

[2]*Leonardo da Vinci (1452–1519):* Italian painter, sculptor, architect, and mathematician; *Voltaire (1694–1778):* pen name of Francois Marie Arouet, French philosopher, historian, dramatist, and essayist; *Johann Wolfgang von Goethe (1749–1832)* German poet, dramatist, and novelist; *Albert Schweitzer (1875–1965):* Alsatian missionary, doctor, and musician in Africa who received the Nobel Peace Prize in 1952.

their profession. Rather than a minority, they ought to be called an élite. And in fact, opinions should not only be counted—they should also be weighed.

The first great medical man who indicated that vivisection is not just inhuman and unscientific, but that it is unscientific *because* it is inhuman was Sir Charles Bell (1774–1824), the Scottish physician, surgeon, anatomist and physiologist to whom medical science owes "Bell's law" on motor and sensory nerves. At the time the aberration of vivisection began to take root in its modern form, he declared that it could only be practiced by callous individuals, who couldn't be expected to penetrate the mysteries of life. Such individuals, he maintained, lack real intelligence—sensibility being a component, and certainly not the least, of human intelligence.

Those who hope to find remedies for human ills by inflicting deliberate sufferings on animals commit two fundamental errors in understanding. The first is the assumption that results obtained on animals are appropriate to man. The second, which concerns the inevitable fallacy of experimental science in respect to the field of organic life, will be analyzed in the next chapter. Let us examine the first error now. Already the Pharaohs knew that to find out whether their food was poisoned they had to try it on the cook, not on the cat.

Since animals react differently from man, every new product or method tried out on animals must be tried out again on man, through careful clinical tests, before it can be considered safe. *This rule knows no exceptions.* Therefore, tests on animals are not only dangerous because they may lead to wrong conclusions, but they also retard clinical investigation, which is the only valid kind.

René Dubos, Pulitzer Prize-winner and professor of microbiology at the Rockefeller Institute of New York, wrote in *Man, Medicine and Environment* (Praeger, New York, 1968, p. 107): "Experimentation on man is usually an indispensable step in the discovery of new therapeutic procedures or drugs . . . The first surgeons who operated on the lungs, the heart, the brain were by necessity experimenting on man, since knowledge deriving from animal experimentation is never entirely applicable to the human species."

15   In spite of this universally recognized fact, not only, the vivisectors, but also health authorities everywhere, having been trained in the vivisectionist mentality, which is a throwback to the last century, allow or prescribe animal tests, thus washing their hands of any responsibility if something goes wrong, as it usually does.

This explains the long list of products developed in laboratories, *and* presumed safe after extensive animal tests, which eventually prove deleterious for man:

Due to a "safe" painkiller named Paracetamol, 1,500 people had to be hospitalized in Great Britain in 1971. In the United States, Orabilex caused kidney damages with fatal outcome, MEL/29 caused cataracts, Metaqualone caused psychic disturbances leading to at least 366 deaths. Worldwide Thalidomide caused more than 10,000 deformed children. Chloramphenicol (Chloromycetin) caused leukemia; Stilbestrol cancer in young women. In the sixties a mysterious epidemic killed so many thousands of asthma sufferers in various countries that Dr. Paul D. Stolley of Johns Hopkins Hospital—who in July 1972 finally found the killer in Isoproterenol, packaged in England as an aerosol spray—spoke of the "worst therapeutic drug disaster on record." In the fall of 1975, Italy's health authorities seized the anti-allergic Trilergan, responsible for viral hepatitis. In early 1976 the laboratories Salvoxyl-Wander, belonging to Switzerland's gigantic Sandoz enterprise, withdrew their Flamanil, created to fight rheumatisms, but capable of causing loss of consciousness in its consumers—certainly one effective way to free them of all pains. A few months later, Great Britain's chemical giant, ICI (Imperial Chemical Industries), announced that it had started paying compensations to the victims (or their survivors) of its cardiotonic Eraldin, introduced on the market after 7 years of "very intensive" tests; but hundreds of consumers had then suffered serious damages to the eyesight or the digestive tract, and 18 had died.

The Great Drug Deception by Dr. Ralph Adam Fine (Stein and Day, New York, 1972) is just one of the many books published in the last decade on the subject of dangerous and often lethal drugs, but it achieved no practical results. Health authorities, as well as the public stubbornly refused to take cognizance of the fact that all those drugs had been okayed and marketed after having been proved safe for animals. Actually it is unfair to single out just a few dangerous drugs, since there are thousands of them.

Of course the fallacy works both ways, precluding the acceptance of useful drugs. There is the great example of penicillin—if we want to consider this a useful drug. Its discoverers said they were fortunate. No guinea pigs were available for the toxicity tests, so they used mice instead. Penicillin kills guinea pigs. But the same guinea pigs can safely eat strychnine, one of the deadliest poisons for humans—but not for monkeys.

20 Certain wild berries are deadly for human beings, but birds thrive on them. A dose of belladonna that would kill a man is harmless for rabbits and goats. Calomelan doesn't influence the secretion of bile in dogs, but can treble it in man. The use of digitalis—the main remedy for cardiac patients and the savior of countless lives the world over—was retarded for a long time because it was first tested on dogs, in which it dangerously raises blood pressure. And chloroform is so toxic to dogs that for many years this valuable anesthetic was not employed on patients. On the other hand a dose of opium that would kill a man is harmless to dogs and chickens.

Datura and henbane are poison for man, but food for the snail. The mushroom *amanita phalloides*, a small dose of which can wipe out a whole human family is consumed without ill effects by the rabbit, one of the most common laboratory animals. A porcupine can *eat* in one lump without discomfort as much opium as a human addict *smokes* in two weeks, and wash it down with enough prussic acid to poison a regiment of soldiers.

The sheep can swallow enormous quantities of arsenic, once the murderers' favorite poison.

Potassium cyanide, deadly for us, is harmless for the owl, but one of our common field pumpkins can put a horse into a serious state of agitation. Morphine, which calms and anesthetizes man, causes maniacal excitement in cats and mice, but dogs can stand doses up to twenty times higher than man. On the other hand, our sweet almonds can kill foxes and chickens, and our common parsley is poison to parrots.

Robert Koch's Tuberkulin, once hailed as a vaccine against tuberculosis because it cured TB in guinea pigs, was found later on to *cause* TB in man[3].

25   There are enough such instances to fill a book—all proving that it would be difficult to find a more absurd and less scientific method of medical research.

Moreover, the anguish and sufferings of the animals, deprived of their natural habitat or habitual surroundings, terrorized by what they see in the laboratories and the brutalities they are subjected to, alter their mental balance and organic reactions to such an extent that *any* result is a priori valueless. The laboratory animal is a monster, made so by the experimenters. Physically and mentally it has very little in common with normal animal and much less with man.

As even Claude Bernard (1813–1878), founder of the modern vivisectionist method, wrote in his *Physiologie opératoire* (p. 152): "The experimental animal is never in a normal state. The normal state is merely a supposition, an assumption." (*Une pure conception de l'esprit.*)

Not only do all animals react differently—even kindred species like rat and mouse, or like the white rat and brown rat—not even two animals of the identical strain react identically; furthermore, they may be suffering from different diseases.

To counter this disadvantage, somebody launched the idea of breeding strains of bacteriologically sterile laboratory animals—mass-born by Caesarean section in sterile operating rooms, raised in sterile surroundings and fed with sterile foods—to provide what the researchers called a "uniform biological material," free of diseases.

30   One delusion spawned another. Consistent failures made certain of those misguided scientists realize—some haven't realized it yet—that organic "material" raised under such abnormal conditions differs more than ever from normal

---

[3]*Robert Koch (1843–1910):* German bacteriologist and physician who won the Nobel Prize in 1905.

organisms. Animals so raised never develop the natural defense mechanism, the so-called immunological reaction, which is a salient characteristic of every living organism. So it would be difficult to devise a less reliable experimental material. Besides, animals are by nature immune to most human infections—diphtheria, typhus, scarlet fever, German measles, smallpox, cholera, yellow fever, leprosy, and bubonic plague, while other infections, such as TB and various septicemias, take up different forms in animals. So the claim that through animals we can learn to control human diseases could seem a sign of madness if we didn't know that it is just a pretext for carrying on "experiments" which, however dangerously misleading for medical science, are either intimately satisfying for those who execute them, or highly lucrative.

The Solid Gold Source

The cancer bogy has become the vivisectionists' most powerful weapon. Dr. Howard M. Temin, a well-known scientist, said in a recent address at the University of Wisconsin that scientists are also interested in money, power, publicity and prestige, and that "some promise quick cures for human diseases, provided they are given more power and more money." He added that there is a tremendous advantage in the assertion that "If I am given 500 million dollars for the next five years, I can cure cancer," pointing out that if a rainmaker puts the time far enough in the future, no one can prove him wrong.

But so far as cancer is concerned, the rain may not come in our lifetime. It is obvious to anybody who has not been brainwashed in the western hemisphere's medical schools that an experimental cancer, one caused by grafting cancerous cells into an animal, or in other arbitrary ways, is entirely different from cancer that develops on its own and, furthermore, in a human being. A spontaneous cancer has an intimate relationship to the organism that developed it, and probably to the mind of that organism as well, whereas cancerous cells implanted into another organism have no "natural" relationship whatsoever to that organism, which merely acts as a soil for the culture of those cells.

However, the ably exploited fear of this dread disease has become an inexhaustible source of income for the researchers. In the course of our century, experimental cancer has become a source of solid gold without precedent.

ENGAGING the Text

1. What moral objections does Ruesch raise to the practice of vivisection?

2. What features of his analysis are designed to show that animal experimentation in medical research is not only sadistic, but unreliable, misleading, and even dangerous when the results are used as models for humans?

EVALUATING the Argument

1. The assumptions on which animal research is based are so commonly accepted that Ruesch's counterargument may strike some readers as unwarranted. What means does he take to forestall criticism and better support his argument?

2. In what respects does the search for a "cure" for cancer illustrate Ruesch's thesis?

EXPLORING the Issue

1. What guidelines and controls operate at your college or university to prevent the kind of abuses Ruesch describes? You might interview a faculty member who does research and write a report on your findings.

2. What insights does Ruesch offer into the motives of the researchers and the pharmaceutical companies and government agencies that explain the relationship between them?

CONNECTING Different Perspectives

1. In what way does Mark Twain's satire "The Lowest Animal" (Chapter 6) turn the tables on animal experimentation that Ruesch condemns?

Philip Wheelwright

The Meaning of Ethics

> *For you see, Callicles, our discussion is concerned with a matter in which even a man of slight intelligence must take the profoundest interest—namely, what course of life is best.* —SOCRATES, *in Plato's* Gorgias

Philip Wheelwright (1901–1970) was born in New Jersey and earned a Ph.D. from Princeton University in 1924. He was professor of philosophy at Princeton, Dartmouth, and the University of California–Riverside. His many influential studies of philosophy and ethics include Philosophy as the Art of Living *(1956),* Heraclitus *(1959), and* A Critical Introduction to Ethics *(1959), in which the following essay originally appeared.*

Man is the animal who can reflect. Like other animals, no doubt, he spends much of his time in merely reacting to the pressures and urgencies of his environment. But being a man he has moments also of conscious stock-taking, when he becomes aware not only of his world but of himself confronting his world, evaluating it, and making choices with regard to it. It is this ability to know himself and on the basis of self-knowledge to make evaluations and reflective choices that differentiates man from his subhuman cousins.

There are, as Aristotle has pointed out, two main ways in which man's power of reflection becomes active. They are called, in Aristotle's language, *theoretikos* and *praktikos* respectively; which is to say, thinking about what is actually the case and thinking about what had better be done. In English translation the words *contemplative* and *operative* probably come closest to Aristotle's intent. To think contemplatively is to ask oneself what *is;* to think operatively is to ask oneself what to *do.* These are the two modes of serious, one might even say of genuine thought—as distinguished from daydreams, emotional vaporizings, laryngeal chatter, and the repetition of clichés. To think seriously is to think either for the sake of knowing things as they are or for the sake of acting upon, and producing or helping to produce, things as they might be.

Although in practice the two types of thinking are much interrelated, it is operative thinking with which our present study is primarily concerned. Ethics, although it must be guided, limited, and qualified constantly by considerations of what is actually the case, is focused upon questions of what should be done. The converse, however, does not follow. Not all questions about what should be done are ethical questions. Much of our operative thinking is given to more immediate needs—to means whereby some given end can be achieved. A person who deliberates as to the most effective way of making money, or of passing a course, or of winning a battle, or of achieving popularity, is thinking operatively, but if that is as far as his planning goes it cannot be called ethical. Such deliberations about adapting means to an end would acquire an ethical character only if some thought were given to the nature and value of the end itself. Ethics cannot dispense with questions of means, but neither can it stop there.

Accordingly, ethics may be defined as that branch of philosophy which is the systematic study of reflective choice, of the standards of right and wrong by which it is to be guided, and of the goods toward which it may ultimately be directed. The relation between the parts of this definition, particularly between standards of right and wrong on the one hand and ultimately desirable goods on the other, will be an important part of the forthcoming study.

The Nature of Moral Deliberation

5 The soundest approach to ethical method is through reflection on our experience of moral situations which from time to time we have had occasion to face, or through an imagined confrontation of situations which others have faced and which we can thus make sympathetically real to ourselves. For instance:

> Arthur Ames is a rising young district attorney engaged on his most important case. A prominent political boss has been murdered. Suspicion points at a certain ex-convict, known to have borne the politician a grudge. Aided by the

newspapers, which have reported the murder in such a way as to persuade the public of the suspect's guilt, Ames feels certain that he can secure a conviction on the circumstantial evidence in his possession. If he succeeds in sending the man to the chair he will become a strong candidate for governor at the next election.

During the course of the trial, however, he accidentally stumbles on some fresh evidence, known only to himself and capable of being destroyed if he chooses, which appears to establish the ex-convict's innocence. If this new evidence were to be introduced at the trial an acquittal would be practically certain. What ought the District Attorney to do? Surrender the evidence to the defence, in order that, as a matter of fair play, the accused might be given every legitimate chance of establishing his innocence? But to do that will mean the loss of a case that has received enormous publicity; the District Attorney will lose the backing of the press; he will appear to have failed, and his political career may be blocked. In that event not only will he himself suffer disappointment, but his ample plans for bestowing comforts on his family and for giving his children the benefits of a superior education may have to be curtailed. On the other hand, ought he to be instrumental in sending a man to the chair for a crime that in all probability he did not commit? And yet the ex-convict is a bad lot; even if innocent in the present case he has doubtless committed many other crimes in which he has escaped detection. Is a fellow like that worth the sacrifice of one's career? Still, there is no proof that he has ever committed a crime punishable by death. Until a man had been proved guilty he must be regarded, by a sound principle of American legal theory, as innocent. To conceal and destroy the new evidence, then, is not that tantamount to railroading an innocent man to the chair?

So District Attorney Ames reasons back and forth. He knows that it is a widespread custom for a district attorney to conceal evidence prejudicial to his side of a case. But is the custom, particularly when a human life is at stake, morally right? A district attorney is an agent of the government, and his chief aim in that capacity should be to present his accusations in such a way as to ensure for the accused not condemnation but justice. The question, then, cannot be answered by appealing simply to law or to legal practice. It is a moral one: *What is Arthur Ames's duty? What ought he to do?*

Benjamin Bates has a friend who lies in a hospital, slowly dying of a painful and incurable disease. Although there is no hope of recovery, the disease sometimes permits its victim to linger on for many months, in ever greater torment and with threatened loss of sanity. The dying man, apprised of the outcome and knowing that the hospital expenses are a severe drain on his family's limited financial resources, decides that death had better come at once. His physician, he knows, will not run the risk of providing him with the necessary drug. There is only his friend Bates to appeal to.

How shall Bates decide? Dare he be instrumental in hastening another's death? Has he a moral right to be an accessory to the taking of a human life? Besides, suspicion would point his way, and his honorable motives would not avert a charge of murder. On the other hand, can he morally refuse to alleviate a friend's suffering and the financial distress of a family when the means of doing so are in his hands? And has he not an obligation to respect a friend's declared will in the matter? To acquiesce and to refuse seem both somehow in different ways wrong, yet one course or the other must be chosen. *What ought Bates to do? Which way does his duty lie?*

In the city occupied by Crampton College a strike is declared by the employees of all the public-transit lines. Their wages have not been increased to meet the rising cost of living, and the justice of their grievance is rather widely admitted by neutral observers. The strike ties up business and causes much general inconvenience; except for the people who have cars of their own or can afford taxi fare, there is no way of getting from one part of the city to another. Labor being at this period scarce, an appeal is made by the mayor to college students to serve the community by acting in their spare time as motormen and drivers. The appeal is backed by a promise of lucrative wages and by the college administration's agreement to cooperate by permitting necessary absences from classes.

What ought the students of Crampton College to do? If they act as strikebreakers, they aid in forcing the employees back to work on the corporation's own terms. Have they any right to interfere so drastically and one-sidedly in the lives and happiness of others? On the other hand, if they turn down the mayor's request the community will continue to suffer grave inconveniences until the fight is somehow settled. *What is the students' duty in the matter? What is the right course for them to follow?*

These three situations, although perhaps unusual in the severity of their challenge, offer examples of problems distinctively moral. When the act of moral deliberation implicit in each of them is fully carried out, certain characteristic phases can be discerned.

(I) EXAMINATION AND CLARIFICATION OF THE ALTERNATIVES What are the relevant possibilities of action in the situation confronting me? Am I clear about the nature of each? Have I clearly distinguished them from one another? And are they mutually exhaustive, or would a more attentive search reveal others? In the case of District Attorney Ames, for example, a third alternative might have been to make a private deal with the ex-convict by which, in exchange for his acquittal, the District Attorney would receive the profits from some lucrative racket of which the ex-convict had control. No doubt to a reputable public servant this line of conduct would be too repugnant for consideration; it exemplifies, nevertheless, the ever-present logical possibility of going "between the horns"[1] of the original dilemma.

(II) RATIONAL ELABORATION OF CONSEQUENCES   The next step is to think out the probable consequences of each of the alternatives in question. As this step involves predictions about a hypothetical future, the conclusions can have, at most, a high degree of probability, never certainty. The degree of probability is heightened accordingly as there is found some precedent in past experience for each of the proposed choices. Even if the present situation seems wholly new, analysis will always reveal *some* particulars for which analogies in past experience can be found or to which known laws of causal sequence are applicable. Such particulars will be dealt with partly by analogy (an act similar to the one now being deliberated about had on a previous occasion such and such consequences) and partly by the inductive-deductive method: appealing to general laws (deduction) which in turn have been built up as generalizations from observed particulars (induction). Mr. Ames, we may suppose, found the materials for this step in his professional knowledge of law and legal precedent, as well as in his more general knowledge of the policies of the press, the gullibility of its readers, and the high cost of domestic luxuries.

(III) IMAGINATIVE PROJECTION OF THE SELF INTO THE PREDICTED SITUATION   It is not enough to reason out the probable consequences of a choice. In a moral deliberation the chief interests involved are not scientific but human and practical. The only way to judge the comparative desirability of two possible futures is to live through them both in imagination. The third step, then, is to project oneself imaginatively into the future; i.e., establish a dramatic identification of the present self with that future self to which the now merely imagined experiences may become real. Few persons, unfortunately, are capable of an imaginative identification forceful enough to give the claims of the future self an even break. Present goods loom larger than future goods, and goods in the immediate future than goods that are remote. The trained ethical thinker must have a sound *temporal perspective*, the acquisition of which is to be sought by a frequent, orderly, and detailed exercise of the imagination with respect to not yet actual situations.

---

[1] *"between the horns"*: In essence, finding a viable third alternative.

10 **(IV) IMAGINATIVE IDENTIFICATION OF THE SELF WITH THE POINTS OF VIEW OF THOSE PERSONS WHOM THE PROPOSED ACT WILL MOST SERIOUSLY AFFECT**   What decision I make here and now, if of any importance, is likely to have consequences, in varying degrees, for persons other than myself. An important part of a moral inquiry is to envisage the results of a proposed act as they will appear to those other persons affected by them. I must undertake, then, a dramatic identification of my own self with the selves of other persons. The possibility of doing this is evident from a consideration of how anyone's dramatic imagination works in the reading of a novel or the witnessing of a play. If the persons in the novel or play are dramatically convincing it is not because their characters and actions have been established by logical proof, but because they are presented so as to provoke in the reader an impulse to project himself into the world of the novel or play, to identify himself with this and that character in it, to share their feelings and moods, to get their slant on things.

In most persons, even very benevolent ones, the social consciousness works by fits and starts. To examine fairly the needs and claims of other selves is no less hard and is often harder than to perform a similar task with regard to one's future self. Accordingly the ethical thinker must develop *social perspective*—that balanced appreciation of others' needs and claims which is the basis of justice.

In this fourth, as in the third step, the imaginative projection is to be carried out for each of the alternatives, according as their consequences shall have been predicted by Step ii.

(V) ESTIMATION AND COMPARISON OF THE VALUES INVOLVED   Implicit in the third and fourth steps is a recognition that certain values both positive and negative are latent in each of the hypothetical situations to which moral choice may lead. The values must be made explicit in order that they may be justly compared, for it is as a result of their comparison that a choice is to be made. To make values explicit is to give them a relatively abstract formulation; they still, however, derive concrete significance from their imagined exemplifications. District Attorney Ames, for example, might have envisaged his dilemma as a choice between family happiness and worldly success on the one hand as against professional honor on the other. Each of these is undoubtedly good, that is to say a value, but the values cannot be reduced to a common denominator. Family happiness enters as a factor into Benjamin Bates's dilemma no less than into that of Arthur Ames, but it stands to be affected in a different way and therefore, in spite of the identical words by which our linguistic poverty forces us to describe it, it does not mean the same thing. Family happiness may mean any number of things; so may success, and honor—although these different meanings have, of course, an intelligible bond of unity. Arthur Ames's task is to compare not just any family happiness with any professional honor but the particular exemplifications of each that enter into his problem. The comparison is not a simple calculation but an imaginative deliberation, in which the abstract values that serve as the logical ground of the comparison are continuous with, and interactive with, the concrete particulars that serve as its starting-point.

(VI) DECISION   Comparison of the alternative future situations and the values embodied in each must terminate in a decision. Which of the possible situations do I deem it better to bring into existence? There are no rules for the making of this decision. I must simply decide as wisely and as fairly and as relevantly to the total comparison as I can. Every moral decision is a risk, for the way in which a person decides is a factor in determining the kind of self he is going to become.

15 **(VII) ACTION**   The probable means of carrying out the decision have been established by Step ii. The wished-for object or situation is an end, certain specific means toward the fulfillment of which lie here and now within my power. These conditions supply the premises for an ethical syllogism. When a certain end, x, is recognized as the best of the available alternatives, and when the achievement of it is seen to be possible through a set of means $a, b, c \ldots$ which lie within my power, then whichever of the means $a, b, c \ldots$ is an action that can here and now be performed becomes at just this point my duty. If the deliberative process has been carried out forcefully and wisely it will have supplied a categorical answer to the question, What ought I to do?—even though the answer in some cases may be, Do nothing.

Naturally, not all experiences of moral deliberation and choice reveal these seven phases in a distinct, clear-cut way. Nor is the order here given always the actual order. Sometimes we may begin by deliberating about the relative merits of two ends, seeking the means simultaneously with this abstract inquiry, or after its completion. The foregoing analysis does, however, throw some light on the nature of a moral problem, and may be tested by applying it to the three cases described at the beginning of the chapter.

ENGAGING the Text

1. Why does solving an ethical problem always involve an examination of alternatives and a consideration of consequences?

2. How is Wheelwright's emphasis on fair consideration of the effect of proposed actions on others an essential component of ethical inquiry?

EVALUATING the Argument

1. What kinds of ethical dilemmas do Wheelwright's three hypothetical situations illustrate? Why is the ability to create hypothetical situations so important in the process of ethical inquiry?

2. Evaluate the effectiveness of Wheelwright's use of examples to define different contexts in which moral problems can occur.

EXPLORING the Issue

1. Choose one of Wheelwright's three hypothetical cases and, using his outline of stages in the process of ethical inquiry, describe what you would do in each situation and why.

2. Read and analyze the ethical dilemmas inherent in any of the arguments presented in this text or in any current issue. For example, you might choose to explore ethical issues addressed by Hans Ruesch ("Slaughter of the Innocent"), Stanley Milgram ("The Perils of Obedience"), Philip G. Zimbardo ("The Stanford Prison Experiment"), or Garrett Hardin ("Lifeboat Ethics).

CONNECTING Different Perspectives

1. According to the process of ethical inquiry described by Wheelwright, is deception ever justified in the conduct of social science experiments (for example, in John M. Darley and Bibb Latané in "Why People Don't Help in a Crisis")?

....

History

Fred Kaplan

The End of History

Fred Kaplan holds a Ph.D. from MIT and was one of the original donors of documents to the National Security Archive. He is a columnist who writes the "War Stories" Column for Slate, *the Microsoft online magazine. His work has also appeared in such magazines and newspapers as the* New Yorker, Atlantic Monthly, Harper's, New York Times, *and* Boston Globe. *He is the author of* The Wizards of Armageddon *(1991). This selection was first posted in the June 4, 2003, issue of* Slate. *Kaplan points out a basic change in the way people generate and retrieve information: we rely on e-mail but don't take any measures to preserve them. Thus, historians of the future will be deprived of the documentation that would have been traditionally available as part of the historical record.*

When tomorrow's historians go to write the chronicles of decision-making that led to Gulf War II [2003], they may be startled to find there's not much history to be written. The same is true of Clinton's war over Kosovo, Bush Sr.'s Desert Storm, and a host of other major episodes of U.S. national security policy. Many of the kinds of documents that historians of prior wars, and of the Cold War, have taken for granted—memoranda, minutes, and the routine back-and-forth among assistant secretaries of state and defense or among colonels and generals in the Joint Chiefs of Staff—simply no longer exist.

The problem is not some deliberate plot to conceal or destroy evidence. The problem—and it may seem churlish to say so in an online publication—is the advent of e-mail.

In the old days, before the mid-to-late 1980s, Cabinet officials and their assistants and deputy assistants wrote memos on paper, then handed them to a secretary in a typing pool. The secretary would type it on a sheet of paper backed by two or three carbon sheets, then file the carbons. Periodically, someone from the national archive would stop by with a cart and haul away the carbons for posterity.

Nobody does this today. There are no typing pools to speak of. There are few written memos.

5   Eduard Mark, a Cold War historian who has worked for 15 years in the U.S. Air Force historian's office, has launched a one-man crusade to highlight, and repair, this situation. He remembers an incident from the early '90s, when he was researching the official Air Force history of the Panama invasion, which had taken place only a few years earlier. "I went to the Air Force operations center," Mark says. "They had a little Mac computer on which they'd saved all the briefings. They were getting ready to dump the computer. I stopped them just in time, and printed out all the briefings. Those printouts I made are the only copies in existence."

That was a decade ago, when computers were not yet pervasive in the Pentagon and many offices still printed important documents on paper. The situation now, Mark says, is much worse.

Almost all Air Force documents today, for example, are presented as Power-Point briefings.* They are almost never printed and rarely stored. When they are saved, they are often unaccompanied by any text. As a result, in many cases, the briefings are incomprehensible.

The new, paperless world has encouraged a general carelessness in official record-keeping. Mark says that J5, the planning department of the Joint Chiefs

---

*PowerPoint is a software program used to prepare presentations. it allows for the creation and display—generally projected—of textual and graphic information.

of Staff, does not, as a rule, save anything. When I talked with Mark on the phone Tuesday, he said he had before him an unclassified document, signed by the Air Force chief of staff and the secretary of the Air Force, ordering the creation of a senior steering group on "transformation" (the new buzzword for making military operations more agile and more inter-service in nature). The document was not dated.

Mark has personal knowledge of the situation with the Air Force. However, officials and historians in other branches of the national-security bureaucracy say, on background, that the pattern is pretty much the same across the board.

10   Certain high-level documents are usually (but, even then, not always) saved—memos that cross the desks of the president, Cabinet secretaries, and military chiefs (the Air Force and Army chiefs of staff, and the chief of naval operations). But beneath that level, it's hit and miss, more often miss.

An enterprising historian writing about World Wars I or II can draw on the vast military records at the National Archive, as well as letters from Churchill, Roosevelt, de Gaulle, and others. (Who writes letters anymore?) Those chronicling the Cold War or the Vietnam War can plumb the presidential libraries of Truman, Eisenhower, Kennedy, Johnson, and Ford (less so of Nixon because it's a privately funded library), and find plenty of illuminating memos written to and from not just Cabinet officers, such as John Foster Dulles, Robert McNamara, and Dean Rusk, but the crucial sub-Cabinet officials and security advisers, such as Andrew Goodpaster, Walt Rostow, John McNaughton, McGeorge Bundy, and George Ball.

Twenty years from now, if someone went looking for similar memos by Paul Wolfowitz, Richard Perle, Richard Armitage, and Elliott Abrams on, say, the Bush administration's Middle East policies, not many memos would be found because they don't exist. Officials today e-mail their thoughts and proposals. Perhaps some individuals have been fastidious about printing and saving their e-mails, but there is no system in place for automatically doing so.

Robert Caro, author of the revealingly massive and detailed biographies of Lyndon Johnson and Robert Moses, often advises aspiring historians, "Turn every page." What to do, though, if there aren't any pages to turn?

ENGAGING the Text

1. According to Kaplan, in what way has e-mail eroded the preservation of historical records?

2. How will the loss of a permanent written record make it difficult for future historians to reconstruct the time line of important military and political decisions?

EVALUATING the Argument

1. How does Kaplan use the testimony of Eduard Mark to illustrate his thesis? Why is Mark an effective source on this question?

2. How does Kaplan's title focus on the essential problem that his essay highlights? From what field does Kaplan draw most of his examples? To what extent is Kaplan's analysis effective because he alternates between a then-and-now scenario?

EXPLORING the Issue

1. If you were a history major, what problems in doing research projects on a chosen subject could arise if your source documents were in a fragmentary or ephemeral electronic form?

2. How has the manipulation of the historical record of the kind described by George Orwell in *1984* (1949) become possible because of what Kaplan describes?

CONNECTING Different Perspectives

1. In what way has email resulted in an inability to extrapolate the past into the future in ways that correspond to Gloria Steinem's analysis in "The Time Factor"?

Journalism

Lance Morrow

Imprisoning Time in a Rectangle

Lance Morrow was born in Philadelphia in 1939, received a his B. A. from Harvard in 1963, and joined the staff of Time *magazine shortly after graduation. As one of the magazine's regular contributors, he has written articles on a broad range of topics. Among his published works are* The Best Years of Their Lives: Kennedy, Johnson, and Nixon in 1948; Learning the Secrets of Power *(2005) and, most recently,* Second Drafts of History: Essays *(2006). The following essay first appeared in a special issue of* Time *(Fall 1989) devoted to photojournalism.*

Balzac[1] had a "vague dread" of being photographed. Like some primitive peoples, he thought the camera steals something of the soul—that, as he told a

---

[1] *Honoré de Balzac (born Honoré Balssa, 1799–1850):* French writer, best known for the novels and short stories of *La Comédie Humaine (The Human Comedy).*

friend "every body in its natural state is made up of a series of ghostly images superimposed in layers to infinity, wrapped in infinitesimal films." Each time a photograph was made, he believed, another thin layer of the subject's being would be stripped off to become not life as before but a membrane of memory in a sort of translucent antiworld.

If that is what photography is up to, then the onion of the world is being peeled away, layer by layer—lenses like black holes gobbling up life's emanations. Mere images proliferate, while history pares down to a phosphorescence of itself.

The idea catches something of the superstition (sometimes justified, if you think about it) and the spooky metaphysics that go ghosting around photography. Taking pictures is a transaction that snatches instants away from time and imprisons them in rectangles. These rectangles become a collective public memory and an image-world that is located usually on the verge of tears, often on the edge of a moral mess.

It is possible to be entranced by photography and at the same time disquieted by its powerful capacity to bypass thought. Photography, as the critic Susan Sontag has pointed out, is an elegiac, nostalgic phenomenon. No one photographs the future. The instants that the photographer freezes are ever the past, ever receding. They have about them the brilliance or instancy of their moment but also the cello sound of loss that life makes when going irrecoverably away and lodging at last in the dreamworks.

5   The pictures made by photojournalists have the legitimacy of being news, fresh information. They slice along the hard edge of the present. Photojournalism is not self-conscious, since it first enters the room (the brain) as a battle report from the far-flung Now. It is only later that the artifacts of photojournalism sink into the textures of the civilization and tincture its memory: Jack Ruby shooting Lee Harvey Oswald,[2] an image so raw and shocking, subsides at last into the ecology of memory where we also find thousands of other oddments from the time—John John saluting at the funeral, Jack and Jackie on Cape Cod, who knows?—bright shards that stimulate old feelings (ghost pangs, ghost tendernesses, wistfulness) but not thought really. The shocks turn into dreams. The memory of such pictures, flipped through like a disordered Rolodex, makes at last a cultural tapestry, an inventory of the kind that brothers and sisters and distant cousins may rummage through at family reunions, except that the greatest photojournalism has given certain memories the emotional prestige of icons.

---

[2]*Jack L. Ruby (1911–1967):* shot and killed Lee Harvey Oswald (1939–1963), the accused assassin of President John F. Kennedy, on November 24, 1963, two days after Kennedy was shot, in the Dallas County Jail, where Oswald was being held under arrest. A national television audience witnessed the event.

If journalism—the kind done with words—is the first draft of history, what is photojournalism? Is it the first impression of history, the first graphic flash? Yes, but it is also (and this is the disturbing thing) history's lasting visual impression. The service that the pictures perform is splendid, and so powerful as to seem preternatural. But sometimes the power they possess is more than they deserve.

Call up Eddie Adams's 1968 photo of General Nguyen Ngoc Loan, the police chief of Saigon, firing his snub-nosed revolver into the temple of a Viet Cong officer. Bright sunlight, Saigon: the scrawny police chief's arm, outstretched, goes by extension through the trigger finger into the V.C.'s brain. That photograph, and another in 1972 showing a naked young Vietnamese girl running in arms outstretched terror up a road away from American napalm, outmanned the force of three U.S. Presidents and the most powerful Army in the world. The photographs were considered, quite ridiculously, to be a portrait of America's moral disgrace. Freudians spend years trying to call up the primal image-memories, turned to trauma, that distort a neurotic patient's psyche. Photographs sometimes have a way of installing the image and legitimizing the trauma: the very vividness of the image, the greatness of the photograph as journalism or even as art, forestalls examination.

Adams has always felt uncomfortable about his picture of Loan executing the Viet Cong officer. What the picture does not show is that a few moments earlier the Viet Cong had slaughtered the family of Loan's best friend in a house just up the road. All this occurred during the Tet offensive, a state of general mayhem all over South Vietnam. The Communists in similar circumstances would not have had qualms about summary execution.

But Loan shot the man; Adams took the picture. The image went firing around the world and lodged in the conscience. Photography is the very dream of the Heisenberg[3] uncertainty principle, which holds that the act of observing a physical event inevitably changes it. War is merciless, bloody, and by definition it occurs outside the orbit of due process. Loan's Viet Cong did not have a trial. He did have a photographer. The photographer's picture took on a life of its own and changed history.

10   All great photographs have lives of their own, but they can be as false as dreams. Somehow the mind knows that and sorts out the matter, and permits itself to enjoy the pictures without getting sunk in the really mysterious business that they involve.

---

[3]*Werner Heisenberg (1901–1976):* German physicist famous for formulating the quantum theory, which converted the laws of physics into statements about relative, instead of absolute, certainties. He received the 1932 Nobel Prize in physics.

Still, a puritan conscience recoils a little from the sheer power of photo-graphs. They have lingering about them the ghost of the golden calf—the bright object too much admired, without God's abstract difficulties. Great photographs bring the mind alive. Photographs are magic things that traffic in mystery. They float on the surface, and they have a strange life in the depths of the mind. They bear watching.

ENGAGING the Text

1. In Morrow's view, how does photojournalism go beyond merely recording events to actually help create history?

2. What insight does Morrow offer into the process by which particular photos can become iconic and come to represent the era in which they were taken?

EVALUATING the Argument

1. How does Morrow use the photos of Jack Ruby shooting Lee Harvey Oswald and a police chief in Saigon shooting a Viet Cong prisoner to illustrate the power of photojournalism to affect history?

2. Where does Morrow express reservations about the power of "great photographs"? How does Morrow's ambivalence toward the hypnotic and numbing power of striking images add to the credibility of his overall argument?

EXPLORING the Issue

1. In your opinion, will the images of the Iraqi prisoners in Abu Ghraib (hooded, standing on a box, with attached electrodes, or on a dog leash, or naked in a pyramid) come to represent the war in Iraq as the photo by Eddie Adams did for the war in Vietnam? Why or why not?

2. What photographs would you nominate as being iconic in the sense that Morrow describes? Write a few paragraphs along with a copy of this image.

CONNECTING Different Perspectives

1. In what sense can pictures be an unreliable source for future historians since they create their own world and are not mediated and explained within their context (see Fred Kaplan's "The End of History")?

Language and Linguistics

Helen Keller

The Day Language Came into My Life

Helen Keller (1880–1968) was born, without handicaps, in Alabama; she contracted a disease at the age of nineteen months that left her both deaf and blind. Because of the extraordinary efforts of Annie Sullivan, Keller overcame her isolation and learned what words meant. She graduated with honors from Radcliffe College and devoted herself for most of her life to helping the blind and deaf through the American Foundation for the Blind. She was awarded the Presidential Medal of Freedom by Lyndon Johnson in 1964. "The Day Language Came into My Life" is taken from her autobiography, The Story of My Life *(1902). This work served as the basis for a film,* The Unconquered *(1954), and the acclaimed play by William Gibson,* The Miracle Worker *(1959), which was subsequently made into a movie with Anne Bancroft and Patty Duke.*

The most important day I remember in all my life is the one on which my teacher, Anne Mansfield Sullivan, came to me. I am filled with wonder when I consider the immeasurable contrast between the two lives which it connects. It was the third of March 1887, three months before I was seven years old.

On the afternoon of that eventful day, I stood on the porch, dumb, expectant. I guessed vaguely from my mother's signs and from the hurrying to and fro in the house that something unusual was about to happen, so I went to the door and waited on the steps. The afternoon sun penetrated the mass of honeysuckle that covered the porch and fell on my upturned face. My fingers lingered almost unconsciously on the familiar leaves and blossoms which had just come forth to greet the sweet southern spring. I did not know what the future held of marvel or surprise for me. Anger and bitterness had preyed upon me continually for weeks and a deep languor had succeeded this passionate struggle.

Have you ever been at sea in a dense fog, when it seemed as if a tangible white darkness shut you in, and the great ship, tense and anxious, groped her way toward the shore with plummet and sounding-line, and you waited with beating heart for something to happen? I was like that ship before my education began, only I was without compass or sounding-line and had no way of knowing how near the harbor was. "Light! give me light!" was the wordless cry of my soul, and the light of love shone on me in that very hour.

I felt approaching footsteps. I stretched out my hand as I supposed to my mother. Someone took it, and I was caught up and held close in the arms of her who had come to reveal all things to me, and, more than all things else, to love me.

5   The morning after my teacher came she led me into her room and gave me a doll. The little blind children at the Perkins Institution had sent it and Laura Bridgman had dressed it; but I did not know this until afterward. When I had played with it a little while, Miss Sullivan slowly spelled into my hand the word "d-o-l-l." I was at once interested in this finger play and tried to imitate it. When I finally succeeded in making the letters correctly I was flushed with childish pleasure and pride. Running downstairs to my mother I held up my hand and made the letters for doll. I did not know that I was spelling a word or even that words existed; I was simply making my fingers go in monkeylike imitation. In the days that followed I learned to spell in this uncomprehending way

a great many words, among them *pin, hat, cup* and a few verbs like *sit, stand* and *walk*. But my teacher had been with me several weeks before I understood that everything has a name.

One day, while I was playing with my new doll, Miss Sullivan put my big rag doll into my lap also, spelled "d-o-l-l" and tried to make me understand that "d-o-l-l" applied to both. Earlier in the day we had had a tussle over the words "m-u-g" and "w-a-t-e-r." Miss Sullivan had tried to impress it upon me that "m-u-g" is *mug* and that "w-a-t-e-r" is *water*, but I persisted in confounding the two. In despair she had dropped the subject for the time, only to renew it at the first opportunity. I became impatient at her repeated attempts and, seizing the new doll, I dashed it upon the floor. I was keenly delighted when I felt the fragments of the broken doll at my feet. Neither sorrow nor regret followed my passionate outburst. I had not loved the doll. In the still, dark world in which I lived there was no strong sentiment or tenderness. I felt my teacher sweep the fragments to one side of the hearth, and I had a sense of satisfaction that the cause of my discomfort was removed. She brought me my hat, and I knew I was going out into the warm sunshine. This thought, if a wordless sensation may be called a thought, made me hop and skip with pleasure.

We walked down the path to the well-house, attracted by the fragrance of the honeysuckle with which it was covered. Some one was drawing water and my teacher placed my hand under the spout. As the cool stream gushed over one hand she spelled into the other the word *water*, first slowly, then rapidly. I stood still, my whole attention fixed upon the motions of her fingers. Suddenly I felt a misty consciousness as of something forgotten—a thrill of returning thought; and somehow the mystery of language was revealed to me. I knew then that "w-a-t-e-r" meant the wonderful cool something that was flowing over my hand. The living word awakened my soul, gave it light, hope, joy, set it free! There were barriers still, it is true, but barriers that could in time be swept away.

I left the well-house eager to learn. Everything had a name, and each name gave birth to a new thought. As we returned to the house every object which I touched seemed to quiver with life. That was because I saw everything with the strange, new sight that had come to me. On entering the door I remembered the doll I had broken. I felt my way to the hearth and picked up the pieces. I tried vainly to put them together. Then my eyes filled with tears; for I realized what I had done, and for the first time I felt repentance and sorrow.

I learned a great many new words that day. I do not remember what they all were; but I do know that *mother, father, sister, teacher* were among them—words that were to make the world blossom for me, "like Aaron's rod, with flowers." It would have been difficult to find a happier child than I was as I lay in my crib at the close of that eventful day and lived over the joys it had brought me, and for the first time longed for a new day to come.

ENGAGING the Text

1. Why is it important for the reader to understand Keller's state of mind in the days preceding the events she describes?

2. How did Keller's understanding of language when she became conscious of the meaning of words differ from her previous experience of spelling them by rote?

EVALUATING the Argument

1. How does the simile Keller uses in para. 3 ("in a dense fog . . . as if a tangible white darkness shut you in . . . I was like that ship") communicate her condition in ways that a literal description would not? Can you think of other similes or metaphors that would express her predicament?

2. How does the episode of the broken doll reveal how much Keller was transformed by the experience she describes?

EXPLORING the Issue

1. If you have ever been temporarily physically incapacitated or have a disability, write a short essay that will help your readers understand your plight.

2. To become aware of the formidable difficulties Keller experienced, think of how you would describe music to someone who is deaf, or colors to someone who is blind.

CONNECTING Different Perspectives

1. How did the accounts by Keller and Eric Scigliano in "Through the Eye of an Octopus" reveal unsuspected qualities of intelligence?

Literature

Ursula Le Guin

American SF and The Other

Ursula Le Guin was born in 1929 in Berkeley, California, and earned a B.A. from Radcliffe in 1951 and an M.A. from Columbia University in 1952. She is the author of many acclaimed science fiction novels including The Lathe of Heaven *(1971), which was made into a PBS television movie. Her most recent works include* Gifts *(2004) and* Voices *(2006). Among other distinctions, Le Guin has won a National Book Award and five Science Fiction of America Nebula Awards. Her work envisions utopian and magical worlds (such as* Orsinia *and* The Imagined Archipelago of Earthsea*) that offer alternatives to the male-dominated technological societies of traditional American science fiction. In "American SF and the Other" (1975) Le Guin points out the regressive, sexist nature of much supposedly progressive science fiction.*

One of the great early socialists said that the status of women in a society is a pretty reliable index of the degree of civilization of that society. If this is true, then the very low status of women in SF should make us ponder about whether SF is civilized at all.

The women's movement has made most of us conscious of the fact that SF has either totally ignored women, or presented them as squeaking dolls subject to instant rape by monsters—or old-maid scientists desexed by hypertrophy of the intellectual organs—or, at best, loyal little wives or mistresses of accomplished heroes. Male elitism has run rampant in SF. But is it only male elitism? Isn't the "subjection of women" in SF merely a symptom of a whole which is authoritarian, power-worshiping, and intensely parochial?

The question involved here is the question of The Other—the being who is different from yourself. This being can be different from you in its sex; or in its annual income; or in its way of speaking and dressing and doing things; or in the color of its skin, or the number of its legs and heads. In other words, there is the sexual Alien, and the social Alien, and the cultural Alien, and finally the racial Alien.

Well, how about the social Alien in SF? How about, in Marxist terms, "the proletariat"? Where are they in SF? Where are the poor, the people who work hard and go to bed hungry? Are they ever *persons,* in SF? No. They appear as vast anonymous masses fleeing from giant slime-globules from the Chicago sewers, or dying off by the billion from pollution or radiation, or as faceless armies being led to battle by generals and statesmen. In sword and sorcery they behave like the walk-on parts in a high-school performance of *The Chocolate Prince.* Now and then there's a busty lass amongst them who is honored by the attentions of the Captain of the Supreme Terran Command, or in a spaceship crew there's a quaint old cook, with a Scots or Swedish accent, representing the Wisdom of the Common Folk.

5   The people, in SF, are not people. They are masses, existing for one purpose: to be led by their superiors.

From a social point of view most SF has been incredibly regressive and unimaginative. All those Galactic Empires, taken straight from the British Empire of 1880. All those planets—with 80 trillion miles between them!—conceived of as warring nation-states, or as colonies to be exploited, or to be nudged by the benevolent Imperium of Earth toward self-development—the White Man's Burden all over again. The Rotary Club on Alpha Centauri, that's the size of it.

What about the cultural and the racial Other? This is the Alien everybody recognizes as alien, supposed to be the special concern of SF. Well, in the old pulp SF, it's very simple. The only good alien is a dead alien—whether he is an Aldebaranian Mantis-Man, or a German dentist. And this tradition still flourishes: witness Larry Niven's story "Innocent Moon" (in *All the Myriad Ways*, 1971) which has a happy ending—consisting of the fact that America, including Los Angeles, was not hurt by a solar flare. Of course a few million Europeans and Asians were fried, but that doesn't matter, it just makes the world a little safer for democracy, in fact. (It is interesting that the female character in the same story is quite brainless; her only function is to say Oh? and Ooooh! to the clever and resourceful hero.)

Then there's the other side of the same coin. If you hold a thing to be totally different from yourself, your fear of it may come out as hatred, or as awe—reverence. So we get all those wise and kindly beings who deign to rescue Earth from her sins and perils. The Alien ends up on a pedestal in a white nightgown and a virtuous smirk—exactly as the "good woman" did in the Victorian Age.

In America, it seems to have been Stanley Weinbaum who invented the sympathetic alien, in *A Martian Odyssey*. From then on, via people like Cyril Kornbluth, Ted Sturgeon, and Cordwainer Smith, SF began to inch its way out of simple racism. Robots—the alien intelligence—begin to behave nicely. With Smith, interestingly enough, the racial alien is combined with the social alien, in the "Underpeople," and they are allowed to have a revolution. As the aliens got more sympathetic, so did the heroes. They began to have emotions, as well as rayguns. Indeed they began to become almost human.

10 If you deny any affinity with another person or kind of person, if you declare it to be wholly different from yourself—as men have done to women, and class has done to class, and nation has done to nation—you may hate it, or deify it; but in either case you have denied its spiritual equality, and its human reality. You have made it into a thing, to which the only possible relationship is a power relationship. And thus you have fatally impoverished your own reality. You have, in fact, alienated yourself.

This tendency has been remarkably strong in American SF. The only social change presented by most SF has been toward authoritarianism, the domination of ignorant masses by a powerful elite—sometimes presented as a warning, but often quite complacently. Socialism is never considered as an alternative, and democracy is quite forgotten. Military virtues are taken as ethical ones. Wealth is assumed to be a righteous goal and a personal virtue. Competitive free-enterprise capitalism is the economic destiny of the entire Galaxy. In general, American SF has assumed a permanent hierarchy of superiors and inferiors, with rich, ambitious, aggressive males at the top, then a great gap, and then at the bottom the poor, the uneducated, the faceless masses, and all the women. The whole picture is, if I may say so, curiously "un-American." It is a perfect baboon patriarchy, with the Alpha Male on top, being respectfully groomed, from time to time, by his inferiors.

Is this speculation? Is this imagination? Is this extrapolation? I call it brainless regressivism.

I think it's time SF writers—and their readers—stopped daydreaming about a return to the age of Queen Victoria, and started thinking about the future. I would like to see the Baboon Ideal replaced by a little human idealism, and some serious consideration of such deeply radical, futuristic concepts as Liberty, Equality, and Fraternity. And remember that about 53 percent, of the Brotherhood of Man is the Sisterhood of Woman.

ENGAGING the Text

1. What is the significance of the "other" and in what forms can it appear?

2. What contrast does Le Guin discover between the advances women have made and the ways in which they are depicted in much of science fiction?

EVALUATING the Argument

1. How does Le Guin structure her argument to remind her readers of the standard by which to measure the portrayal of women and to evaluate how far below this standard much of science fiction falls?

2. Why is it ironic that a genre supposedly so progressive is in fact so parochial and backward in its depiction of women?

EXPLORING the Issue

1. How is the "other" depicted in genres other than science fiction, for example, the western, horror films, detective stories? Do these portrayals reflect the same stereotypes Le Guin finds in science fiction?

2. What science fiction films have you seen that reverse the stereotypes Le Guin criticizes? Alternatively, read any of Le Guin's novels to discover how she corrects the deficiency she identifies in science fiction.

CONNECTING Different Perspectives

1. In what respects do both Le Guin and Martin Luther King Jr. in "I Have a Dream" make the case for a less stereotyped view of the racial "other"?

....

Music

Aaron Copland

Film Music

Aaron Copland (1900–1990), one of the most influential American composers of the twentieth century, was born in Brooklyn, New York. He developed a distinctly American sound and style, incorporating not only Stravinsky's influence but jazz, folk songs, cowboy tunes, and Shaker hymns in works such as Billy the Kid *(1941),* Rodeo *(1942),* Fanfare for the Common Man *(1943), and the Pulitzer Prize–winning ballet* Appalachian Spring *(1944). He continued to compose music for orchestra, ballet, stage, films, chamber groups, and voice and to conduct, lecture, and write books, including* Music and Imagination *(1952). He won an Academy Award in 1950 for the musical score he wrote for the film* The Heiress. *In the following selection (from* What to Listen for in Music, *1957) we can appreciate Copland's engaging explanation of the qualities of effective music scored for films.*

Film music constitutes a new musical medium that exerts a fascination of its own. Actually, it is a new form of dramatic music—related to opera, ballet, incidental theater music—in contradistinction to concert music of the symphonic or chamber-music kind. As a new form it opens up unexplored possibilities for composers and poses some interesting questions for the musical film patron.

Millions of movie-goers take the musical accompaniment to a dramatic film entirely too much for granted. Five minutes after the termination of a picture they couldn't tell you whether they had heard music or not. To ask whether they thought the score exciting or merely adequate or downright awful would be to give them a musical inferiority complex. But, on second thought, and possibly in self-protection, comes the query: "Isn't it true that one isn't supposed to be listening to the music? Isn't it supposed to work on you unconsciously without being listened to directly as you would listen at a concert?"

No discussion of movie music ever gets very far without having to face this problem: Should one hear a movie score? If you are a musician there is no problem because the chances are you can't help but listen. More than once a good picture has been ruined for me by an inferior score. Have you had the same experience? Yes? Then you may congratulate yourself: you are definitely musical.

But it's the average spectator, so absorbed in the dramatic action that he fails to take in the background music, who wants to know whether he is missing anything. The answer is bound up with the degree of your general musical perception. It is the degree to which you are aurally minded that will determine how much pleasure you may derive by absorbing the background musical accompaniment as an integral part of the combined impression made by the film.

5   Knowing more of what goes into the scoring of a picture may help the movie listener to get more out of it. Fortunately, the process is not so complex that it cannot be briefly outlined.

In preparation for composing the music, the first thing the composer must do, of course, is to see the picture. Almost all musical scores are written *after* the film itself is completed. The only exception to this is when the script calls for realistic music—that is, music which is visually sung or played or danced to on the screen. In that case the music must be composed before the scene is photographed. It will then be recorded and the scene in question shot to a playback of the recording. Thus, when you see an actor singing or playing or dancing, he is only making believe as far as the sound goes, for the music had previously been put down in recorded form.

The first run-through of the film for the composer is usually a solemn moment. After all, he must live with it for several weeks. The solemnity of the occasion is emphasized by the exclusive audience that views it with him: the producer, the director, the music head of the studio, the picture editor, the music cutter, the conductor, the orchestrater—in fact, anyone involved with the scoring of the picture.

The purpose of the run-through is to decide how much music is needed and where it should be. (In technical jargon this is called "to spot" the picture.) Since no background score is continuous throughout the full length of a film (that would constitute a motion-picture opera, an almost unexploited cinema form), the score will normally consist of separate sequences, each lasting from a few seconds to several minutes in duration. A sequence as long as seven minutes would be exceptional. The entire score, made up of perhaps thirty or more such sequences, may add up to from forty to ninety minutes of music.

Much discussion, much give-and-take may be necessary before final decisions are reached regarding the "spotting" of the picture. It is wise to make use of music's power sparingly, saving it for absolutely essential points. A composer knows how to play with silences—knows that to take music out can at times be more effective than any use of it on the sound track might be.

10   The producer-director, on the other hand, is more prone to think of music in terms of its immediate functional usage. Sometimes he has ulterior motives: anything wrong with a scene—a poor bit of acting, a badly read line, an

embarrassing pause—he secretly hopes will be covered up by a clever composer. Producers have been known to hope that an entire picture would be saved by a good score. But the composer is not a magician; he can hardly be expected to do more than to make potent through music the film's dramatic and emotional values.

When well-contrived, there is no question but, that a musical score can be of enormous help to a picture. One can prove that point, laboratory-fashion, by showing an audience a climactic scene with the sound turned off and then once again with the sound track turned on. Here briefly are listed a number of ways in which music serves the screen:

CREATING A MORE CONVINCING ATMOSPHERE OF TIME AND PLACE   Not all Hollywood composers bother about this nicety. Too often, their scores are interchangeable: a thirteenth-century Gothic drama and a hardboiled modern battle of the sexes get similar treatment. The lush symphonic texture of late nineteenth-century music remains the dominating influence. But there are exceptions. Recently, the higher-grade horse opera has begun to have its own musical flavor, mostly a folksong derivative.

UNDERLINING PSYCHOLOGICAL REFINEMENTS—THE UNSPOKEN THOUGHTS OF A CHARACTER OR THE UNSEEN IMPLICATIONS OF A SITUATION   Music can play upon the emotions of the spectator, sometimes counterpointing the thing seen with an aural image that implies the contrary of the thing seen. This is not as subtle as it sounds. A well-placed dissonant chord can stop an audience cold in the middle of a sentimental scene, or a calculated woodwind passage can turn what appears to be a solemn moment into a belly laugh.

SERVING AS A KIND OF NEUTRAL BACKGROUND FILLER   This is really the music one isn't supposed to hear, the sort that helps to fill the empty spots, such as pauses in a conversation. It's the movie composer's most ungrateful task. But at times, though no one else may notice, he will get private satisfaction from the thought that music of little intrinsic value, through professional manipulation, has enlivened and made more human the deathly pallor of a screen shadow. This is hardest to do, as any film composer will attest, when the neutral filler type of music must weave its way underneath dialogue.

15 **BUILDING A SENSE OF CONTINUITY**   The picture editor knows better than anyone how serviceable music can be in tying together a visual medium which is, by its very nature, continually in danger of falling apart. One sees this most obviously in montage scenes where the use of a unifying musical idea may save the quick flashes of disconnected scenes from seeming merely chaotic.

UNDERPINNING THE THEATRICAL BUILD-UP OF A SCENE, AND ROUNDING IT OFF WITH A SENSE OF FINALITY The first instance that comes to mind is the music that blares out at the end of a film. Certain producers have boasted their picture's lack of a musical score, but I never saw or heard of a picture that ended in silence.

We have merely skimmed the surface, without mentioning the innumerable examples of utilitarian music—offstage street bands, the barn dance, merry-go-rounds, circus music, café music, the neighbor's girl practicing her piano, and the like. All these, and many others, introduced with apparent naturalistic intent, serve to vary subtly the aural interest of the sound track.

But now let us return to our hypothetical composer. Having determined where the separate musical sequences will begin and end, he turns the film over to the music cutter, who prepares a so-called cue sheet. The cue sheet provides the composer with a detailed description of the physical action in each se-quence, plus the exact timings in thirds of seconds of that action, thereby mak-ing it possible for a practiced composer to write an entire score without ever again referring to the picture.

The layman usually imagines that the most difficult part of the job in composing for the films has to do with the precise "fitting" of the music to the action. Doesn't that kind of timing strait-jacket the composer? The an-swer is no, for two reasons: First, having to compose music to accompany specific action is a help rather than a hindrance, since the action itself induces music in a composer of theatrical imagination, whereas he has no such visual stimulus in writing absolute music. Secondly, the timing is mostly a matter of minor adjustments, since the over-all musical fabric will have already been determined.

20   For the composer of concert music, changing to the medium of celluloid does bring certain special pitfalls. For example, melodic invention, highly prized in the concert hall, may at times be distracting in certain film situations. Even phrasing in the concert manner, which would normally emphasize the indepen-dence of separate contrapuntal lines, may be distracting when applied to screen accompaniments. In orchestration there are many subtleties of timbre—distinc-tions meant to be listened to for their own expressive quality in an auditorium—which are completely wasted on sound track.

As compensation for these losses, the composer has other possibilities, some of them tricks, which are unobtainable in Carnegie Hall. In scoring one section of *The Heiress*, for example, I was able to superimpose two orchestras, one upon another. Both recorded the same music at different times, one orchestra consist-ing of strings alone, the other constituted normally. Later these were combined by simultaneously rerecording the original tracks, thereby producing a highly expressive orchestral texture. Bernard Herrmann,[1] one of the most ingenious of screen composers, called for (and got) eight celestas—an unheard-of combination on 57th Street—to suggest a winter's sleigh ride. Miklos Rozsa's[2] use of the "echo chamber"—a device to give normal tone a ghostlike aura—was widely remarked, and subsequently done to death.

Unusual effects are obtainable through overlapping incoming and outgoing music tracks. Like two trains passing one another, it is possible to bring in and take out at the same time two different musics. *The Red Pony*[3] gave me an opportunity to use this cinema specialty. When the daydreaming imagination of a little boy turns white chickens into white circus horses the visual image is mirrored in an aural image by having the chicken music transform itself into circus music, a device only obtainable by means of the overlap.

Let us now assume that the musical score has been completed and is ready for recording. The scoring stage is a happy-making place for the composer. Hollywood has gathered to itself some of America's finest performers; the music will be beautifully played and recorded with a technical perfection not to be matched anywhere else.

Most composers like to invite their friends to be present at the recording session of important sequences. The reason is that neither the composer nor his friends are ever again likely to hear the music sound out in concert style. For when it is combined with the picture most of the dynamic levels will be changed. Otherwise the finished product might sound like a concert with pictures. In lowering dynamic levels niceties of shading, some inner voices and bass parts may be lost. Erich Korngold[4] put it well when he said: "A movie composer's immortality lasts from the recording stage to the dubbing room."

25   The dubbing room is where all the tracks involving sound of any kind, including dialogue, are put through the machines to obtain one master sound track. This is a delicate process as far as the music is concerned, for it is only a hairbreadth that separates the "too loud" from the "too soft." Sound engineers, working the dials that control volume, are not always as musically sensitive as composers would like them to be. What is called for is a new species, a sound mixer who is half musician and half engineer; and even then, the mixing of dialogue, music, and realistic sounds of all kinds must always remain problematical.

---

[1] *Bernard Herrmann (1911–1975):* composed the music for *Citizen Kane* (1941) and many Alfred Hitchcock films, including *Psycho* (1960).
[2] *Miklos Rozsa (1907–1995):* Hungarian composer who wrote the film score for *Ben Hur* (1959).
[3] *The Red Pony:* 1948 film for which Copland wrote the music.
[4] *Erich Korngold (1897–1957):* Austrian composer who wrote the film score for *The Adventures of Robin Hood* (1938).

In view of these drawbacks to the full sounding out of his music, it is only natural that the composer often hopes to be able to extract a viable concert suite from his film score. There is a current tendency to believe that movie scores are not proper material for concert music. The argument is that, separated from its visual justification, the music falls flat.

Personally, I doubt very much that any hard and fast rule can be made that will cover all cases. Each score will have to be judged on its merits, and, no doubt, stories that require a more continuous type of musical development in a unified atmosphere will lend themselves better than others to reworking for concert purposes. Rarely is it conceivable that the music of a film might be extracted without much reworking. But I fail to see why, if successful suites like Grieg's[5] *Peer Gynt*[6] can be made from nineteenth-century incidental stage music, a twentieth-century composer can't be expected to do as well with a film score.

As for the picture score, it is only in the motion-picture theater that the composer for the first time gets the full impact of what he has accomplished, tests the dramatic punch of his favorite spot, appreciates the curious importance and unimportance of detail, wishes that he had done certain things differently, and is surprised that others came off better than he had hoped. For when all is said and done, the art of combining moving pictures with musical tones is still a mysterious art. Not the least mysterious element is the theatergoers' reaction: Millions will be listening but one never knows how many will be really hearing. The next time you go to the movies, remember to be on the composer's side.

ENGAGING the Text

1. According to Copland, in what ways can a musical score enhance a film?

2. What qualities in film music that would be applauded in a concert would prove distracting for a movie audience?

EVALUATING the Argument

1. What examples best illustrate that the role of film music must be subordinated to the images on the screen?

2. How does Copland's personal experience enhance the credibility of his analysis?

---

[5]*Edvard Grieg (1843–1907):* Norway's greatest composer.
[6]*Peer Gynt:* incidental music composed by Grieg for Henrik Ibsen's 1875 play.

EXPLORING the Issue

1. Analyze one of your favorite films by paying particular attention to the ways in which music achieves some of the objectives Copland describes.

2. Is there any movie score that you would consider owning for its intrinsic musical value? Explain why you liked it.

CONNECTING Different Perspectives

1. How does Copland's analysis apply to any of the movie scores for the films mentioned by Roger Ebert in "Great Movies" in Chapter 1?

Philosophy and Religion

Jean-Paul Sartre

Existentialism

Jean-Paul Sartre (1905–1980), the French philosopher and author, was born in Paris. In 1929 he met the writer and feminist Simone de Beauvoir with whom he had a lifelong relationship. He taught for many years in secondary schools and briefly served in the army. Sartre studied in Berlin where he developed his ideas on existentialism, a philosophy that views the individual as a responsible but lonely being. His works include Being and Nothingness *(1943), written while he was a prisoner of war. After Paris was liberated in 1945, Sartre delivered a lecture that was later published as a book,* Existentialism and Humanism *(1946), from which the following selection is drawn. His other works include* The Age of Reason *(1945) and* The Critique of Dialectical Reason *(1960). He declined the 1964 Nobel Prize in Literature.*

Atheistic existentialism, which I represent, . . . states that if God does not exist, there is at least one being in whom existence precedes essence, a being who exists before he can be defined by any concept, and that this being is man, or, as Heidegger says, human reality. What is meant here by saying that existence precedes essence? It means that, first of all, man exists, turns up, appears on the scene, and, only afterwards, defines himself. If man, as the existentialist conceives him, is indefinable, it is because at first he is nothing. Only afterward will he be something, and he himself will have made what he will be. Thus, there is no human nature, since there is no God to conceive it. Not only is man what he conceives himself to be, but he is also only what he wills himself to be after this thrust toward existence.

Man is nothing else but what he makes of himself. Such is the first principle of existentialism. It is also what is called subjectivity. But what do we mean by this, if not that man has a greater dignity than a stone or table? For we mean that man first exists, that is, that man first of all is the being who hurls himself toward a future and who is conscious of imagining himself as being in the future. Man is at the start a plan which is aware of itself, rather than a patch of moss, a piece of garbage, or a cauliflower; nothing exists prior to this plan; there is nothing in heaven; man will be what he will have planned to be. Not what he will want to be. Because by the word "will" we generally mean a conscious decision, which is subsequent to what we have already made of ourselves. I may want to belong to a political party, write a book, get married; but all that is only a manifestation of an earlier, more spontaneous choice that is called "will." But if existence really does precede essence, man is responsible for what he is. Thus, existentialism's first move is to make every man aware of what he is and to make the full responsibility of his existence rest on him. And when we say that a man is responsible for himself, we do not only mean that he is responsible for his own individuality, but that he is responsible for all men.

The word "subjectivism" has two meanings. Subjectivism means, on the one hand, that an individual chooses and makes himself; and, on the other, that it is impossible for man to transcend human subjectivity. The second of these is the essential meaning of existentialism. When we say that man chooses his own self, we mean that every one of us does likewise; but we also mean by that that in making this choice he also chooses all men. In fact, in creating the man that we want to be, there is not a single one of our acts which does not at the same time create an image of man as we think he ought to be. To choose to be this or that is to affirm at the same time the value of what we choose, because we can never choose evil. We always choose the good, and nothing can be good for us without being good for all.

If, on the other hand, existence precedes essence, and if we grant that we exist and fashion our image at one and the same time, the image is valid for everybody and for our whole age. Thus, our responsibility is much greater than we might have supposed, because it involves all mankind. If I am a workingman and choose to join a Christian trade union rather than be a Communist, and if by being a member, I want to show that the best thing for a man is resignation, that the kingdom of man is not of this world, I am not only involving my own case—I want to be resigned for everyone. As a result, my action has involved all humanity. To take a more individual matter, if I want to marry, to have children, even if this marriage depends solely on my own circumstances or passion or wish, I am involving all humanity in monogamy and not merely myself. Therefore, I am responsible for myself and for everyone else. I am creating a certain image of man of my own choosing. In choosing myself, I choose man.

5   The existentialist thinks it very distressing that God does not exist, because all possibility of finding values in a heaven of ideas disappears along with Him; there can no longer be an a priori Good, since there is no infinite and perfect consciousness to think it. Nowhere is it written that the good exists, that we must be honest, that we must not lie; because the fact is we are on a plane where there are only men. Dostoievsky said, "If God didn't exist, everything would be possible." That is the very starting point of existentialism. Indeed, everything is permissible if God does not exist, and as a result man is forlorn, because neither within him or without does he find anything to cling to. He can't start making excuses for himself.

If existence really does precede essence, there is no explaining things away by reference to a fixed and given nature. In other words, there is no determinism, man is free, man is freedom. On the other hand, if God does not exist, we find no values or commands to turn to which legitimize our conduct. So, in the bright realm of values, we have no excuse behind us, nor justification before us. We are alone, with no excuses.

That is the idea I shall try to convey when I say that man is condemned to be free. Condemned, because he did not create himself, yet, in other respects is free; because, once thrown into the world, he is responsible for everything he does.

To give you an example which will enable you to understand forlornness better, I shall cite the case of one of my students who came to see me under the following circumstances: his father was on bad terms with his mother, and, moreover, was inclined to be a collaborationist, his older brother had been killed in the German offensive of 1940, and the young man, with somewhat immature but generous feelings, wanted to avenge him. His mother lived alone with him, very much upset by the half-treason of her husband and the death of her older son; the boy was her only consolation.

The boy was faced with the choice of leaving for England joining the Free French forces—that is, leaving his mother behind—or remaining with his mother and helping her to carry on. He was fully aware that the woman lived only for him and that his going off—and perhaps his death—would plunge her into despair. He was also aware that every act that he did for his mother's sake was a sure thing, in the sense that it was helping her to carry on, whereas every effort he made toward going off and fighting was an uncertain move which might run aground and prove completely useless; for example, on his way to England he might, while passing through Spain, be detained indefinitely in a Spanish camp; he might reach England or Algiers and be stuck in an office at a desk job. As a result, he was faced with two very different kinds of action: one, concrete, immediate, but concerning only one individual; the other concerned an incomparably vaster group, a national collectivity, but for that very reason was dubious, and might be interrupted en route. And, at the same time, he was wavering between two kinds of ethics. On the one hand, an ethics of sympathy, of personal devotion; on the other, a broader ethics, but one whose efficacy was more dubious. He had to choose between the two.

10   Who could help him choose? Christian doctrine? No. Christian doctrine says, "Be charitable, love your neighbor, take the more rugged path, etc., etc." But which is the more rugged path? Whom should he love as a brother? The fighting man or his mother? Which does the greater good, the vague act of fighting in a group, or the concrete one of helping a particular human being to go on living? Who can decide a priori? Nobody. No book of ethics can tell him. The Kantian ethics says, "Never treat any person as a means, but as an end." Very well, if I stay with my mother, I'll treat her as an end and not as a means; but by virtue of this very fact, I'm running the risk of treating the people around me who are fighting, as means; and conversely, if I go to join those who are fighting, I'll be treating them as an end, and, by doing that, I run the risk of treating my mother as a means.

If values are vague, and if they are always too broad for the concrete and specific case that we are considering, the only thing left for us is to trust our instincts. That's what this young man tried to do; and when I saw him, he said, "In the end, feeling is what counts. I ought to choose whichever pushes me in one direction. If I feel that I love my mother enough to sacrifice everything else for her—my desire for vengeance, for action, for adventure—then I'll stay with her. If, on the contrary, I feel that my love for my mother isn't enough, I'll leave."

But how is the value of a feeling determined? What gives his feeling for his mother value? Precisely the fact that he remained with her. I may say that I like so-and-so well enough to sacrifice a certain amount of money for him, but I may say so only if I've done it. I may say "I love my mother well enough to remain with her" if I have remained with her. The only way to determine the value of this affection is, precisely, to perform an act which confirms and defines it. But, since I require this affection to justify my act, I find myself caught in a vicious circle.

Given that men are free and that tomorrow they will freely decide what man will be, I cannot be sure that, after my death, fellow-fighters will carry on my work to bring it to its maximum perfection. Tomorrow, after my death, some men may decide to set up Fascism, and the others may be cowardly and muddled enough to let them do it. Fascism will then be the human reality, so much the worse for us.

Actually, things will be as man will have decided they are to be. Does that mean that I should abandon myself to quietism? No. First, I should involve myself; then, act on the old saw, "Nothing ventured, nothing gained." Nor does it mean that I shouldn't belong to a party, but rather that I shall have no illusions and shall do what I can. For example, suppose I ask myself, "Will socialization, as such, ever come about?" I know nothing about it. All I know is that I'm going to do everything in my power to bring it about. Beyond that, I can't count on anything. Quietism is the attitude of people who say, "Let others do what I can't do." The doctrine I am presenting is the very opposite of quietism, since it declares, "There is no reality except in action." Moreover, it goes further, since it adds, "Man is nothing else than his plan; he exists only to the extent that he fulfills himself; he is therefore nothing else than the ensemble of his acts, nothing else than his life."

15   Now, for the existentialist there is really no love other than one which manifests itself in a person's being in love. There is no genius other than one which is expressed in works of art; the genius of Proust is the sum of Proust's works; the genius of Racine is his series of tragedies. Outside of that, there is nothing. Why say that Racine could have written another tragedy, when he didn't write it? A man is involved in life, leaves his impress on it, and outside of that there is nothing. To be sure, this may seem a harsh thought to someone whose life hasn't been a success. But, on the other hand, it prompts people to understand that reality alone is what counts, that dreams, expectations, and hopes warrant no more than to define a man as a disappointed dream, as miscarried hopes, as vain expectations. In other words, to define him negatively and not positively. However, when we say, "You are nothing else than your life," that does not imply that the artist will be judged solely on the basis of his works of art; a thousand other things will contribute toward summing him up. What we mean is that a man is nothing else than a series of undertakings, that he is the sum, the organization, the ensemble of the relationships which make up these undertakings.

When all is said and done, what we are accused of, at bottom, is not our pessimism, but an optimistic toughness. If people throw up to us our works of fiction in which we write about people who are soft, weak, cowardly, and sometimes even downright bad, it's not because these people are soft, weak, cowardly, or bad; because if we were to say, as Zola did, that they are that way because of heredity, the workings of environment, society, because of biological or psychological determinism, people would be reassured. They would say, "Well, that's what we're like, no one can do anything about it." But when the existentialist writes about a coward, he says that this coward is responsible for his cowardice. He's not like that because he has a cowardly heart or lung or brain; he's not like that on account of his physiological make-up; but he's like that because he has made himself a coward by his acts. There's no such thing as a cowardly constitution; there are nervous constitutions; there is poor blood, as the common people say, or strong constitutions. But the man whose blood is poor is not a coward on that account, for what makes cowardice is the act of renouncing or yielding. A constitution is not an act; the coward is defined on the basis of the acts he performs. People feel, in a vague sort of way, that this coward we're talking about is guilty of being a coward, and the thought frightens them. What people would like is that a coward or a hero be born that way.

Existentialism is nothing else than an attempt to draw all the consequences of a coherent atheistic position. It isn't trying to plunge man into despair at all. But if one calls every attitude of unbelief despair, like the Christians, then the word is not being used in its original sense. Existentialism isn't so atheistic that it wears itself out showing that God doesn't exist. Rather, it declares that even if God did exist, that would change nothing. There you've got our point of view. Not that we believe that God exists, but we think that the problem of His existence is not the issue. In this sense existentialism is optimistic, a doctrine of action, and it is plain dishonesty for Christians to make no distinction between their own despair and ours and then to call us despairing.

ENGAGING the Text

1. Sartre assumes as an existentialist that there is no creator or indeed any plan for human existence. What kind of burden does this impose on us, and correspondingly, what freedoms does it permit?

2. In what way does existentialism emphasize the uselessness of preexisting value systems? How in making important decisions do you literally create your identity?

EVALUATING the Argument

1. Who is this essay designed to persuade and where in it does Sartre take into account the views of his opponents?

2. How does Sartre use the case of one of his students who faced a dilemma to illustrate existentialism?

EXPLORING the Issue

1. Have you ever faced a choice comparable to that confronting the young man in Sartre's example or an instance of indecision or temptation? How did this dilemma illustrate both the burden and freedom of existentialism?

2. Much of psychology asserts that our behavior is determined by unconscious motivations or genetics. How would Sartre and followers of existentialism refute these theories?

CONNECTING Different Perspectives

1. How did the analyses by Sartre and Philip Wheelwright in "The Meaning of Ethics" reveal the importance of an ethical framework in life-altering decisions?

....

American Studies

Philip Slater

Want-Creation Fuels Americans' Addictiveness

Philip Slater (b. 1927) was professor of sociology at Harvard and is the author of The Pursuit of Loneliness *(1970) and* Wealth Addiction *(1980). His latest book is* The Temporary Society *with Warren Bennis (1998). The following essay first appeared in the* St. Paul Pioneer Press Dispatch *(September 6, 1984).*

Imagine what life in America would be like today if the surgeon general convinced Congress that cigarettes, as America's most lethal drug, should be made illegal.

The cost of tobacco would increase 5,000 percent. Law enforcement budgets would quadruple but still be hopelessly inadequate to the task. The tobacco industry would become mob-controlled, and large quantities of Turkish tobacco would be smuggled into the country through New York and Miami.

Politicians would get themselves elected by inveighing against tobacco abuse. Some would argue shrewdly that the best enforcement strategy was to go after the growers and advertisers—making it a capital offense to raise or sell tobacco. And a great many Americans would try smoking for the first time.

Americans are individualists. We like to express our opinions much more than we like to work together. Passing laws is one of the most popular pastimes, and enforcing them one of the least. We make laws like we make New Year's resolutions—the impulse often exhausted by giving voice to it. Who but Americans would have their food grown and harvested by people who were legally forbidden to be in the country?

5   We are a restless, inventive, dissatisfied people. We like novelty. We like to try new things. We may not want to change in any basic sense, any more than other people, but we like the illusion of movement.

We like anything that looks like a quick fix—a new law, a new road, a new pill. We like immediate solutions. We want the pain to stop, the dull mood to pass, the problem to go away. The quicker the action, the better we like it. We like confrontation better than negotiation, antibiotics better than slow healing, majority rule better than community consensus, demolition better than renovation.

When we want something we want it fast and we want it cheap. Obstacles and complications annoy us. We don't want to stop to think about side effects, the Big Picture, or how it's going to make things worse in the long run. We aren't too interested in the long run, as long as something brings more money, a promotion or a new status symbol in the short.

Our model for problem-solving is the 30-second TV commercial, in which change is produced instantaneously and there is always a happy ending. The side effects, the pollution, the wasting diseases, the slow poisoning—all these unhappy complications fall into the great void outside that 30-second frame.

Nothing fits this scenario better than drugs—legal and illegal. The same impatience that sees an environmental impact report as an annoying bit of red tape makes us highly susceptible to any substance that can make us feel better within minutes after ingesting it—whose immediate effects are more or less predictable and whose negative aspects are generally much slower to appear.

10   People take drugs everywhere, of course, and there is no sure way of knowing if the United States has more drug abusers than other countries. The term "abuse" itself is socially defined.

The typical suburban alcoholic of the '40s and '50s the wealthy drunks glamorized in Hollywood movies of that period were not considered "drug abusers." Nor is the ex-heroin addict who has been weaned to a lifetime addiction to Methadone.

In the 19th century, morphine addicts (who were largely middle-aged, middle-class women) maintained their genteel but often heavy addictions quite legally, with the aid of the family doctor and local druggist. Morphine only became illegal when its use spread to young, poor, black males. (This transition created some embarrassment for political and medical commentators, who argued that a distinction had to be made between "drug addicts" and "dope fiends.")

Yet addiction can be defined in a way that overrides these biases. Anyone who cannot or will not let a day pass without ingesting a substance should be considered addicted to it, and by this definition Americans are certainly addiction-prone.

It would be hard to find a society in which so great a variety of different substances have been "abused" by so many different kinds of people. There are drugs for every group, philosophy and social class: marijuana and psychedelics for the '60s counterculture, heroin for the hopeless of all periods, PCP for the angry and desperate, and cocaine for modern Yuppies and Yumpies.[1]

15   Drugs do, after all; have different effects, and people select the effects they want. At the lower end of the social scale people want a peaceful escape from a hopeless and depressing existence, and for this heroin is the drug of choice. Cocaine, on the other hand, with its energized euphoria and illusion of competence is particularly appealing to affluent achievers—those both obsessed and acquainted with success.

Addiction among the affluent seems paradoxical to outsiders. From the view-point of most people in the world an American man or woman making over $50,000 a year has everything a human being could dream of. Yet very few such people—even those with hundreds of millions of dollars—feel this way themselves. While they may not suffer the despair of the very poor, there seems to be a kind of frustration and hopelessness that seeps into all social strata in our society. The affluent may have acquired a great deal, but they seem not to have acquired what they wanted.

Most drugs—heroin, alcohol, cocaine, speed, tranquilizers, barbiturates—virtually all of them except the psychedelics and to some extent marijuana—have a numbing effect. We might then ask: Why do so many Americans need to numb themselves?

Life in modern society is admittedly harsh and confusing considering the pace for which our bodies were designed. Noise pollution alone might justify turning down our sensory volume: It's hard today even in a quiet suburb or rural setting to find respite from the harsh sound of "labor-saving" machines.

But it would be absurd to blame noise pollution for drug addiction. This rasping clamor that grates daily on our ears is only a symptom—one tangible consequence of our peculiar lifestyle. For each of us wants to be able to exert his or her will and control without having to negotiate with anyone else.

20   I have a right to run my machine and do my work" even if it makes your rest impossible. "I have a right to hear my music" even if this makes it impossible to hear your music, or better yet, enjoy that most rare and precious of modern commodities: silence. "I have a right to make a profit" even if it means poisoning you, your children and your children's children. "I have a right to have a drink when I want to and drive my car when I want to" even if it means totaling your car and crippling your life.

---

[1]*Yumpies:* young, upper-middle-class professionals.

This intolerance of any constraint or obstacle makes our lives rich in conflict and aggravation. Each day we encounter the noise, distress and lethal fallout of the dilemmas we brushed aside so impatiently the day before. Each day the postponed problems multiply, proliferate, metastasize—but this only makes us more aggravated and impatient than we were before. And since we're unwilling to change our ways it becomes more and more necessary to anesthetize ourselves to the havoc we've wrought.

We don't like the thought of attuning ourselves to nature or to a group or community. We like to fantasize having control over our lives, and drugs seem to make this possible. With drugs you are not only master of your fate and captain of your soul, you are dictator of your body as well.

Unwilling to respond to its own needs and wants, you goad it into activity with caffeine in the morning and slow it down with alcohol at night. If the day goes poorly, a little cocaine will set it right, and if quiet relaxation and sensual enjoyment is called for, marijuana.

Cocaine or alcohol makes a party or a performance go well. Nothing is left to chance. The quality of experience is measured by how many drugs or drinks were consumed rather than by the experience itself. Most of us are unwilling to accept the fact that life has good days and bad days. We attempt—unsuccessfully but valiantly—to postpone all the bad days until that fateful moment when the body presents us with all our IOUs, tied up in a neat bundle called cancer, heart disease, cirrhosis or whatever.

25 Every great sage and spiritual leader throughout history has emphasized that happiness comes not from getting more but from learning to want less. Clearly this is a hard lesson for humans, since so few have learned it.

But in our society we spend billions each year creating want. Covetousness, discontent and greed are taught to our children, drummed into them—they are bombarded with it. Not only through advertising, but in the feverish emphasis on success, on winning at all costs, on being the center of attention through one kind of performance or another, on being the first at something—no matter how silly or stupid (*The Guinness Book of Records*). We are an addictive society.

Addiction is a state of wanting. It is a condition in which the individual feels he or she is incomplete, inadequate, lacking, not whole, and can only be made whole by the addition of something external.

This need not be a drug. It can be money, food, fame, sex, responsibility, power, good deeds, possessions, cleaning—the addictive impulse can attach itself to anything, real or symbolic. You're addicted to something whenever you feel it completes you—that you wouldn't be a whole person without it. When you try to make sure it's always there, that there's always a good supply on hand.

Most of us are a little proud of the supposed personality defects that make addiction "necessary"—the "I can't . . .," "I have to . . .," "I always . . .," "I never . . ." But such "lacks" are all delusional. It's fun to brag about not being able to live without something but it's just pomposity. We are all human, and given water, a little food, and a little warmth, we'll survive.

30   But it's very hard to hang onto this humanity when we're told every day that we're ignorant, misguided, inadequate, incompetent and undesirable and that we will emerge from this terrible condition only if we eat or drink or buy something, at which point we'll magically and instantly feel better.

We may be smart enough not to believe the silly claims of the individual ad, but can we escape the underlying message on which all of them agree? That you can only be made whole and healthy by buying or ingesting something? Can we reasonably complain about the amount of addiction in our society when we teach it every day?

A Caribbean worker once said, apropos of the increasing role of Western products in the economy of his country: "Your corporations are like mosquitoes. I don't so much mind their taking a little of my blood, but why do they have to leave that nasty itch in its place?"

It seems futile to spend hundreds of billions of dollars trying to intercept the flow of drugs—arresting and imprisoning those who meet the demand for them, when we activate and nourish that demand every day. Until we get tired of encouraging the pursuit of illusory fixes and begin to celebrate and refine what we already are and have, addictive substances will always proliferate faster than we can control them.

ENGAGING the Text

1. In Slater's view, how is the "quick fix" mentality responsible for rampant drug use and addiction in the United States?

2. What relationship does Slater discover between financial and social status and drug use?

EVALUATING the Argument

1. How does Slater use the analogy between noise pollution and drug addiction to develop his argument?

2. How does Slater's argument depend on the assumption that corporations exploit the ever-increasing pace of life of Americans, through advertising?

EXPLORING the Issue

1. What current ads set up hypothetically stressful situations and push products as a quick and easy way to alleviate them? Analyze one of these ads.

2. Do you agree or disagree with Slater's definition of addiction and the way he frames the debate? Explain your answer.

CONNECTING Different Perspectives

1. In what way do the analyses by Slater and by Hans Ruesch (see "Slaughter of the Innocent") explore and condemn the supply and demand sides of the drug problem in America?

Business and Marketing

Robert F. Hartley

The Edsel: Marketing, Planning and Research Gone Awry

Robert F. Hartley (b. 1927) has been professor of marketing at Cleveland State University. His research emphasizes the need for businesses to be responsive to the needs of consumers. His many works include Marketing Fundamentals for Responsive Management *(1976) and* Marketing Mistakes and Successes, *7th ed. (2003), in which the following essay first appeared.*

Perhaps the classic marketing mistake of the modern business era, the one most widely publicized and commented upon, is the Edsel. Interestingly enough, the same firm, the Ford Motor Company, also was responsible for another monumental marketing blunder, this one before the era of modern business with its emphasis on marketing.

An Earlier Blunder

Henry Ford introduced the Model T in 1909. It sold initially for 850 dollars and was available only in one color, black. The Model T quickly became a way of life. Ford conducted mass production on a scale never before seen, introducing and perfecting the moving assembly line so that the work moved to the worker. Ford sold half the new cars made in this country up to 1926 and had more than double the output of his nearest competitor, General Motors. Prices by 1926 had fallen to as low as 263 dollars. For seventeen years the Model T had neither model changes nor significant improvements, except for a lowering selling price as more production economies were realized.

But by the mid-1920s, millions of Americans wanted something fancier, and General Motors brought out Chevrolet featuring color, comfort, styling, safety, modernity—and most of all—a showy appearance. And the Model T was doomed.

In desperation, Henry Ford had the Model T painted attractive colors, fenders were rounded, the body lengthened and lowered, the windshield slanted. But still sales declined. Finally in May 1927, Ford stopped production altogether for nearly a year while 60,000 workers in Detroit were laid off, and a new car, the Model A, slowly took shape with a changeover estimated to have cost Ford 100 million dollars. While the Model A was successful, the lead lost to General Motors was never to be regained.

In the 1920s a failure in market assessment was devastating. To some extent the failure of the Edsel was also due to bad market assessment, but this time not for want of trying.

The Edsel

The Edsel, Ford's entry into the medium-price field, was introduced for the 1958 model year in early September 1957. This gave it a jump on competitors who traditionally introduce new models in October and November of the previous year. Ernest Breech, the board chairman of the Ford Motor Company set the 1958 goal for the Edsel Division at 3.3 to 3.5 percent of the total auto market. In a six-million car year, this would be about 200,000 cars. However, the company executives considered this a very conservative estimate and expected to do much better. Ten years of planning, preparation and research had gone into the Edsel. The need for such a car in the Ford product line appeared conclusive. Approximately 50 million dollars was spent for advertising and promotion in the preintroduction and introduction of the car. And in late summer of 1957 the success of the massive venture seemed assured. The company did not expect to recover the 250 million dollars of development costs until the third year, but the car was expected to be operationally profitable in 1958.

Rationale

The rationale for the Edsel seemed inescapable. For some years there had been a growing trend toward medium-price cars. Such cars as Pontiac, Oldsmobile, Buick, Dodge, DeSoto, and Mercury were accounting for one-third of all car sales by the middle 1950s, whereas they had formerly contributed only one-fifth.

5   Economic projections confirmed this shift in emphasis from low-priced cars and suggested a continuing demand for higher-priced models in the decade of the 1960s. Disposable personal income (expressed in 1956 dollars) had increased from about 138 billion dollars in 1939 to 287 billion dollars in 1956, with forecasts of 400 billion dollars by 1965. Furthermore, the percent of this income spent for automobiles had increased from around 3.5 percent in 1939 to 5.5 or 6.0 percent in the middle 1950s. Clearly the economic climate seemed to favor a medium-price car such as the Edsel.

The Ford Motor Company had been weakest in this very sector where all economic forecasts indicated was the greatest opportunity. General Motors had three makes, Pontiac, Oldsmobile, and Buick, in the medium-price class; Chrysler had Dodge and DeSoto appealing to this market; but Ford had only Mercury to compete for this business, and Mercury accounted for a puny twenty percent of the company's business.

Studies had revealed that every year one out of five people who buy a new car traded up to a medium-price model from a low-price car. As Chevrolet owners traded up, 87 percent stayed with General Motors and one of its three makes of medium-priced cars. As Plymouth owners traded up, 47 percent bought a Dodge or DeSoto. But as Ford owners traded up, only 26 percent stayed with the Ford Motor Company and the Mercury, its one entry in this price line. Ford executives were describing this phenomenon as "one of the greatest philanthropies of modern business," the fact that Ford uptraders contributed almost as much to GM's medium-price penetration as Chevrolet had been able to generate for GM.

So the entry of the Edsel seemed necessary if not overdue.

Research Efforts

Marketing research studies on the Edsel automobile covered a period of almost ten years. Some studies dealt with owner likes and dislikes, other studies with market and sales analyses. Earlier research had determined that cars have definite personalities to the general public, and a person buys a car best thought to exemplify his or her own personality. Consequently, "imagery" studies were considered important to find the best "personality" for the car and to find the best name. The personality sought was one that would make the greatest number of people want the car. Ford researchers thought they had a major advantage over the other manufacturers of medium-priced cars because they did not have to change an existing personality; rather, they could create what they wanted from scratch.

10   Columbia University was engaged to interview eight hundred recent car buyers in Peoria, Illinois, and another eight hundred in San Bernardino, California

(considered to be rather typical cities) as to what images they had of the various makes. Thereby a personality portrait of each make was developed. For example, the image of a Ford was that of a fast, masculine car of no particular social pretension. On the other hand, Chevrolet's image was of a car for an older, wiser, slower person. Mercury had the image of a hot-rod, best suited to a young racing driver, this despite its higher-price tag.

The conclusions were that the personality of the new car (called the "E-car" initially before the Edsel name had been selected) should be one that would be regarded as the smart car for the younger executive or professional family on its way up. Advertising and promotion accordingly would stress this theme. And the appointments of the car would offer status to the owner.

The name for the E-car should also fit the car's image and personality. Accordingly, some two thousand different names were gathered and several research firms sent interviewers with the list to canvass sidewalk crowds in New York City, Chicago, Willow Run and Ann Arbor, Michigan. The interviewers asked what free associations each name brought to mind; they also asked what words were considered the opposite of each name since opposite associations might also be important. But the results were inconclusive.

Edsel, the name of Henry Ford's only son, had been suggested for the E-car. However, the three Ford brothers in active management of the company, Henry II, Benson, and William Clay, were lukewarm to this idea of their father's name spinning "on a million hubcaps." And the free associations with the name Edsel were on the negative side, being "pretzel," "diesel," and "hard sell."

At last ten names were sent to the executive committee. None of the ten aroused any enthusiasm, and the name Edsel was finally selected, although not one of the recommended names. Four of the ten names submitted were selected for the different series of Edsel: Corsair, Citation, Pacer, and Ranger.

Search for a Distinctive Style

15 Styling of the Edsel began in 1954. Stylists were asked to be both distinctive and discreet, in itself a rather tall order. The stylists studied existing cars and even scanned the tops of cars from the roof of a ten-story building to determine any distinguishing characteristics that might be used for the Edsel. The consumer research could provide some information as to image and personality desired, but furnished little guidance for the actual features and shape of the car. Groups of stylists considered various "themes" and boiled down hundreds of sketches to two dozen to show top management. Clay and plaster mock-ups were prepared so that three-dimensional highlights and flair could be observed. The final concept was satisfying to all eight hundred stylists.

The result was a unique vertical front grill—a horse-collar shape, set vertically in the center of a conventionally low, wide front end—pushbutton transmission, and luxury appointments. The vertical grille of the Edsel was compared by some executives to the classic cars of the 1930s, the LaSalle and Pierce Arrow. Push buttons were stressed as the epitome of engineering advancement and convenience. The hood and trunk lid were push button; the parking brake lever was push button; the transmission was push button. Edsel salesmen could demonstrate the ease of operation by depressing the transmission buttons with a tooth pick.

The Edsel was not a small car. The two largest series, the Corsair and the Citation, were two inches longer than the biggest Oldsmobile. It was a powerful car, one of the most powerful made, with a 345 horsepower engine. The high performance possible from such horsepower was thought to be a key element in the sporty, youthful image that was to be projected.

A Separate Division for Edsel

Instead of distributing the new Edsel through established Ford, Mercury, and Lincoln dealers, a separate dealer organization was decided upon to be controlled by a separate headquarters division. These new dealers were carefully selected from over 4,600 inquiries for dealer franchises in every part of the United States. Most of the 1,200 dealers chosen were to handle only Edsel, with dual dealerships restricted to small towns. Consequently, there were now five separate divisions for the Ford Motor Company: Ford, Mercury, Lincoln, Continental, and Edsel.

While establishing Edsel as a separate division added to the fixed costs of operation, this was thought to be desirable in the long run. An independent division could stand alone as a profit center, and this should encourage more aggressive performance than if Edsel were merely a second entry to some other division.

20   The dealer appointments were made after intensive market research to learn where to place each dealer in the nation's sixty major metropolitan areas. Population shifts and trends were carefully considered, and the planned dealer points were matched with the 4,600 inquiries for franchises. The Edsel was to have the best located dealer body in the automobile industry. Applicants for dealerships were carefully screened, of course. Guides used in selection included: reputation, adequate finances, adequate facilities, demonstrated management ability, the ability to attract and direct good people, sales ability, proper attitude toward ethical and competitive matters, and type of person to give proper consideration to customers in sales and service. The average dealer had at least a hundred thousand dollars committed to his agency. Edsel Division was

prepared to supply skilled assistance to dealers so that each could operate as effectively and profitably as possible and also provide good service to customers.

Promotional Efforts

July 22, 1957, was the kickoff for the first consumer advertising. It was a two-page spread in *Life* magazine in plain black and white, and showed a car whooshing down a country highway at such high speed it was a blur. The copy read: "Lately some mysterious automobiles have been seen on the roads." It went on to say that the blur was an Edsel and was on its way. Other "pre-announcement" ads showed only photographs of covered cars. Not until late August were pictures of the actual cars released.

The company looked beyond their regular advertising agencies to find a separate one for the Edsel. Foote, Cone and Belding was selected, this being one of the two in the top ten who did not have any other automobile clients. The campaign designed was a quiet, self-assured one which avoided as much as possible the use of the adjective "new," since this was seen as commonplace and not distinctive enough. The advertising was intended to be calm, not to overshadow the car.

The General Sales and Marketing Manager, J. C. Doyle, insisted on keeping Edsel's appearance one of the best kept secrets of the auto industry. Never before had an auto manufacturer gone to so much trouble to keep the appearance hidden. Advertising commercials were filmed behind closed doors, the cars were shipped with covers, and no press people were given any photographs of the car before its introduction. The intent was to build up an overwhelming public interest in the Edsel, causing its arrival to be anticipated and the car itself to be the object of great curiosity.

Some fifty million dollars were allocated for the introductory period. Traditional automobile advertising media were used. Newspaper advertising was allocated forty percent of all expenditures; magazines were budgeted at twenty percent (trade publication advertising started on April 29 with a two-color spread in *Automotive News* as part of a dealer recruitment campaign); TV and radio were budgeted at twenty percent; outdoor billboards were given ten percent of the budget, with a final ten percent for miscellaneous media.

25   The advertising agency and the marketing executives at Edsel recognized that they faced a challenge in most effectively promoting the car. Because of the determined need for secrecy, traditional advertising research had to be eliminated. For example, copy tests could not be made without disclosing the features of the car. Furthermore, the introduction of the car and the promotion to accompany it had to be done at one time all over the country; there was no possibility of testing various alternatives and approaches.

The Results

Introduction Day was September 4, 1957, and 1,200 Edsel dealers eagerly opened their doors. And most found potential customers streaming in, out of curiosity if nothing else. On the first day more than 6,500 orders were taken. This was considered reasonably satisfying. But there were isolated signs of resistance. One dealer selling Edsels in one showroom and Buicks in an adjacent showroom reported that some prospects walked into the Edsel showroom, looked at the Edsel, and placed orders for Buicks on the spot.

In the next few days, sales dropped sharply. For the first ten days of October there were only 2,751 sales, an average of just over 300 cars a day. In order to sell the 200,000 cars per year (the minimum expectation), between six and seven hundred would need to be sold each day.

On Sunday night, October 13th, the Ford Motor Company put on a mammoth television spectacular for Edsel. The show cost $400,000 and starred Bing Crosby and Frank Sinatra, two of the hottest names in show business at that time. Even this failed to cause any sharp spurt in sales. Things were not going well.

For all of 1958 only 34,481 Edsels were sold and registered with motor-vehicle bureaus, less than one-fifth the target sales. The picture looked a little brighter in November 1958 with the introduction of the second year models. These Edsels were shorter, lighter, less powerful, and had a price range from five hundred to eight hundred dollars less than their predecessors.

30   Eventually the Edsel Division was merged into a Lincoln-Mercury-Edsel Division. In mid-October 1959 a third series of annual models of Edsels were brought out. These aroused no particular excitement either, and on November 19, 1959 production was discontinued. The Edsel was dead.

Between 1957 and 1960, 109,466 Edsels were sold. Ford was able to recover 150 million dollars of its investment by using Edsel plants and tools in other Ford divisions, leaving a nonrecoverable loss of more than a hundred million dollars on the original investment plus an estimated hundred million dollars in operating losses.

What Went Wrong?

So carefully planned. Such a major commitment of manpower and financial resources, supported by decades of experience in producing and marketing automobiles. How could this have happened? Where were the mistakes? Could they have been prevented? As with most problems there is no one simple answer. The marketplace is complex. Many things contributed to the demise of the Edsel: among them, poor judgment by people who should have known better (except that they were so confident because of the abundance of planning) and economic conditions outside the company's control. We will examine some of the factors that have been blamed for Edsel's failure. None of these alone would have been sufficient to destroy the Edsel; in combination, the car didn't have a chance.

Exogenous Factors

One article in discussing the failure of the Edsel, said, "In addition to mistakes, real and alleged, the Edsel encountered incredibly bad luck. Unfortunately it was introduced at the beginning of the 1958 recession. Few cars sold well in 1958; few middle-price cars sold, even fewer Edsels." A dealer in San Francisco summed it up this way: "The medium-priced market is extremely healthy in good times, but it is also the first market to be hurt when we tighten our belts during depression . . . when they dreamed up the Edsel, medium-priced cars were a big market, but by the time the baby was born, that market had gone 'helter-skelter'."

The stock market collapsed in 1957, marking the beginning of the recession of 1958. By early August of 1957, sales of medium-priced cars of all makes were declining. Dealers were ending their season with the second largest number of unsold new cars in history up to that time. Table [1] shows total U.S. car sales from 1948 (as the country was beginning production after World War II) until 1960. You can see from this table that 1958 sales were the lowest since 1948.

TABLE [1]   U.S. Motor Vehicle Sales, 1948–1960

Year	Units Sold
1948	3,909,270
1949	5,119,466
1950	6,665,863
1951	5,338,436
1952	4,320,794
1953	6,116,948
1954	5,558,897
1955	7,920,186
1956	5,816,109
1957	6,113,344
1958	4,257,812
1959	5,591,243
1960	6,674,796

Source: *1973 Ward's Automotive Yearbook* (Detroit: Ward's Communications), p. 86.

TABLE [2]   U.S. Medium-price Car Production, 1955–1959 (units)

	1955	1956	1957	1958	1959
Mercury	434,911	246,629	274,820	128,428	156,765
Edsel			54,607	26,563	29,677
Pontiac	581,860	332,268	343,298	219,823	388,856
Oldsmobile	643,460	432,903	390,091	310,795	366,305
Buick	781,296	535,364	407,283	257,124	232,579
Dodge	313,038	205,727	292,386	114,206	192,798
DeSoto	129,767	104,090	117,747	36,556	41,423

Source: 1973 *Ward's*, pp. 112, 113.

35   Table [2] shows the production of the major makes of medium-price cars from 1955 to 1960. Note the drastic dropoff of all makes of cars in 1958, but the trend had been downward since 1955.

The trend was changing from bigger cars to economy cars. American Motors had been pushing the compact Rambler, and in the year when the Edsel came on the market sales of small foreign cars more than doubled. This change in consumer preferences was not alone a product of the 1958 recession, which would indicate that it would not reverse once the economy improved. Sales of small foreign cars continued very strong in the following years, reflecting public disillusionment with big cars and desire for more economy and less showy transportation. Table [3] shows the phenomenal increase in import car sales during this period, a trend which should have alerted the Edsel planners.

Other exogenous factors were also coming into play at the time of Edsel's introduction. The National Safety Council had become increasingly concerned with the "horsepower race" and the way speed and power were translating into highway accidents. In 1957, the Automobile Manufacturing Association, in deference to the criticisms of the National Safety Council, signed an agreement against advertising power and performance. But the Edsel had been designed with these very two features uppermost: a big engine with 345 horsepower to support a high performance, powerful car on the highways. Designed to handle well at high speeds, its speed, horsepower, and high performance equipment could not even be advertised.

Consumer Reports was not overly thrilled about the Edsel. Its 800,000 subscribers found this as the first sentence in the magazine's evaluation of the Edsel: "The Edsel has no important basic advantage over the other brands." Negative articles and books regarding the "power merchants" of Detroit were also appearing about this time. John Keats published his *Insolent Chariots*, and the poet, Robert Lowell, condemned our "tailfin culture."

TABLE [3]   U.S. Sales of Import Cars, 1948–1960

	Units
1948	28,047
1949	7,543
1950	21,287
1951	23,701
1952	33,312
1953	29,505
1954	34,555
1955	57,115
1956	107,675
1957	259,343
1958	430,808
1959	668,070
1960	444,474

Source: *Automobile Facts and Figures, 1961 Edition* (Detroit: Automobile Manufacturers Association), p. 5, compiled from U.S. Department of Commerce statistics.

Marketing Research

The failure of the Edsel cannot be attributed to a lack of marketing research. Indeed, considerable expenditures were devoted to this. However, these efforts can be faulted in three respects.

40   First, the motivation research efforts directed to establishing a desirable image for the new car were not all that helpful. While they were of some value in determining how consumers viewed the owners of Chevrolets, Fords, Mercurys, and other brands and led the Edsel executives into selecting the particular image for their car, in reality there was an inability to translate this desired image into tangible product features. For example, while upwardly mobile young executives and professionals seemed a desirable segment of consumers for Edsel to appeal to, was this best done through heavy horsepower and high speed performance features, or might other characteristics have been more attractive to these consumers? (Many of these consumers were shifting their sentiments to the European compacts about this time, repudiating the "horsepower race" and the chrome-bedecked theme of bigness.)

Second, much of the research was conducted several years before the introduction of the Edsel in 1957. While demand for medium-priced cars seemed strong at that time, the assumption that such attitudes would be static and unchanging was unwise. A strong shift in consumer preferences was undetected— and should have been noticed. The increasing demand for imported cars should have warranted further investigation and even a reexamination of plans in light of changing market conditions.

The last area where the marketing research efforts can be criticized is in the name itself, Edsel. Here the blame lies not so much with the marketing research, which never recommended the name in the first place, as with a Ford management which disregarded marketing research conclusions and opted for the name regardless.

Now much has been written about the negative impact of the name. Most of this may be unjustified. Many successful cars on the market today do not have what we would call winning names. For example, Buick, Oldsmobile, Chrysler, even Ford itself are hardly exciting names. A better name could have been chosen—and was a few years later with the Mustang, and also the Maverick—but it is doubtful that the Edsel's demise can justifiably be laid to the name.

The Product

Changing consumer preferences for smaller cars came about the time of the introduction of the Edsel. Disillusionment was setting in regarding large size, powerful cars. However, other characteristics of the car also hurt. The styling, especially the vertical grille, aroused both positive and negative impressions. Some liked its distinctiveness, seeing it as a restrained classic look without extremes. But the horse-collar shaped grille turned other people off.

45   The biggest product error had to do with quality control. There was a failure to adhere to quality standards; cars were released that should not have been. Production was rushed to get the Edsel to market on schedule and also to get as many Edsels as possible on the road so that people could see the car. But many bugs had not been cleared up. The array of models increased the production difficulties, with eighteen models in the four series of Ranger, Pacer, Corsair, and Citation.

As a result, the first Edsels had brakes that failed, leaked oil, were beseiged with rattles, and sometimes the dealers could not even start them. Before these problems could be cleared up, the car had gained the reputation of being a lemon, and this was a tough image to overcome. The car quickly became the butt of jokes.

The Separate Edsel Organization

Another mistake that can be singled out in retrospect was the decision to go with a separate division and separate dealerships for Edsel. While this separation was supposed to lead to greater dealer motivation and consequently stronger selling push than where such efforts are diluted among several makes of cars, the cost factors of such separation were disregarded. Having a separate division was expensive and raised breakeven points very high due to the additional personnel and facilities needed. Furthermore, Ford did not have ample management personnel to staff all its divisions adequately.

Despite the care used in selecting the new Edsel dealers, some of these were underfinanced, and many were underskilled in running automobile dealerships compared to the existing dealers selling the regular Ford products. Other Edsel dealers were "dropouts" or the less successful dealers of other car makers.

An additional source of difficulty for the viability of the Edsel dealers was they had nothing else to offer but Edsel sales and service. Dealers usually rely on the shop and maintenance sections of their businesses to cover some expenses. Edsel dealers not only did not have any other cars besides the Edsel to work on, but the work on the Edsel was usually a result of factory deficiencies so the dealers could not charge for this work. The dealers quickly faced financial difficulties with sales not up to expectations and service business yielding little revenue.

Promotional Efforts

50 Contrary to what could be reasonably expected, the heavy promotional efforts before the Edsel was finally unveiled may have produced a negative effect. The general public had been built up to expect the Edsel to be a major step forward, a significant innovation. And many were disillusioned. They saw instead a new styled luxury Ford, uselessly overpowered, gadget and chrome bedecked, but nothing really so very different, this car was not worth the build-up.

Another problem was that the Edsel came out too early in the new-car model year—in early September—and had to suffer the consequences of competing with 1957 cars that were going through clearance sales. Not only did people shy away from the price of the Edsel, but in many instances they did not know if it was a 1957 or 1958 model. *Business Week* reported dealer complaints: "We've been selling against the clean-up of 1957 models. We were too far ahead of the 1958 market. Our big job is getting the original lookers back in the showrooms."

While some dealers had complained about over-advertising too early, now they were complaining of lack of promotion and advertising in October and November when the other cars were being introduced. At the time when the Edsel was competing against other new models, advertising was cut back as the Edsel executives saw little point in trying to steal attention normally focused on new models.

Finally, one of the more interesting explanations for the failure of the Edsel was:

> oral symbolism . . . responsible for the failure of the Edsel. The physical appearance was displeasing from a psychological and emotional point of view because

the front grille looked like a huge open mouth . . . Men do not want to associate oral qualities with their cars, for it does not fit their self-image of being strong and virile.

ENGAGING the Text

1. What errors in marketing doomed Ford's entry into the medium-price field with its 1958 Edsel? What part did underfinanaced dealerships, poor workmanship, the switch from big cars to smaller, economy cars, and the onset of a recession play in the failure of the Edsel?

2. What made Ford think that the Edsel was a sure thing? Explain how the ad agency's lack of familiarity with the automotive field and vague ad copy contribute to the poor reception of the Edsel.

EVALUATING the Argument

1. How does Hartley use statistical tables and interviews to effectively pinpoint specific problems responsible for the Edsel's demise?

2. How is Hartley's analysis organized to segment the overall question of the Edsel's failure into smaller, easier-to-analyze questions of (a) market research, (b) sales techniques, (c) quality control, and (d) the state of the economy in 1958?

EXPLORING the Issue

1. Identify and analyze strategies that you believe are responsible for the marketing success of a product (such as the iPod).

2. Analyze the causes responsible for a major marketing miscalculation, such as Classic Coke, the Susan B. Anthony dollar, and advertising for the perfume Opium.

3. How have some of the marketing miscalculations responsible for the Edsel's demise also played a part in the decline of General Motors in 2005 when its stock lost over half its value?

CONNECTING Different Perspectives

1. Are the hybrid species envisioned by corporations as described by Carol Grunewald in "Monsters of the Brave New World" the Edsels of biotechnology?

How does the image above suggest the reason why potential buyers were turned off by the Edsel's appearance?

Communication

Neil Postman and Steve Powers

The Bias of Language, The Bias of Pictures

Neil Postman (1931–2003) was a University Professor, Paulette Goddard Chair of Media Ecology, and Chair of the Department of Culture and Communication at New York University. He investigated the effects of the media in books such as Amusing Ourselves to Death *(1985) and* Conscientious Objections *(1992). His last work was* Building a Bridge to the 18th Century: How the Past Can Improve Our Future *(1999). Together with Steve Powers, an award-winning journalist, he wrote* How to Watch TV News *(1992), from which the following essay is drawn.*

When a television news show distorts the truth by altering or manufacturing facts (through re-creations), a television viewer is defenseless even if a recreation is properly labeled. Viewers are still vulnerable to misinformation since they will not know (at least in the case of docudramas) what parts are fiction and what parts are not. But the problems of verisimilitude posed by recreations pale to insignificance when compared to the problems viewers face when encountering a straight (no-monkey-business) show. All news shows, in a sense, are recreations in that what we hear and see on them are attempts to represent actual events, and are not the events themselves. Perhaps, to avoid ambiguity, we might call all news shows "re-presentations" instead of "re-creations." These representations come to us in two forms: language and pictures. The question then arises: what do viewers have to know about language and pictures in order to be properly armed to defend themselves against the seductions of eloquence (to use Bertrand Russell's apt phrase)? . . .

[Let us look at] the problem of pictures. It is often said that a picture is worth a thousand words. Maybe so. But it is probably equally true that one word is worth a thousand pictures, at least sometimes—for example, when it comes to understanding the world we live in. Indeed, the whole problem with news on television comes down to this: all the words uttered in an hour of news coverage could be printed on one page of a newspaper. And the world cannot be understood in one page. Of course, there is a compensation: television offers pictures, and the pictures move. Moving pictures are a kind of language in themselves, but the language of pictures differs radically from oral and written language, and the differences are crucial for understanding television news.

To begin with, pictures, especially single pictures, speak only in particularities. Their vocabulary is limited to concrete representation. Unlike words and sentences, a picture does not present to us an idea or concept about the world, except as we use language itself to convert the image to idea. By itself, a picture cannot deal with the unseen, the remote, the internal, the abstract. It does not speak of "man," only of *a* man; not of "tree," only of *a* tree. You cannot produce an image of "nature," any more than an image of "the sea." You can only show a particular fragment of the here-and-now—a cliff of a certain terrain, in a certain condition of light; a wave at a moment in time, from a particular point of view. And just as "nature" and "the sea" cannot be photographed, such larger abstractions as truth, honor, love, and falsehood cannot be talked about in the lexicon of individual pictures. For "showing of" and "talking about" are two very different kinds of processes: individual pictures give us the world as object; language, the world as idea. There is no such thing in nature as "man" or "tree." The universe offers no such categories or simplifications; only flux and infinite variety. The picture documents and celebrates the particularities of the universe's infinite variety. Language makes them comprehensible.

Of course, moving pictures, video with sound, may bridge the gap by juxtaposing images, symbols, sound, and music. Such images can present emotions and rudimentary ideas. They can suggest the panorama of nature and the joys and miseries of humankind.

5   Picture—smoke pouring from the window, cut to people coughing, an ambulance racing to a hospital, a tombstone in a cemetery.

Picture—jet planes firing rockets, explosions, lines of foreign soldiers surrendering, the American flag waving in the wind.

Nonetheless, keep in mind that when terrorists want to prove to the world that their kidnap victims are still alive, they photograph them holding a copy of a recent newspaper. The dateline on the newspaper provides the proof that the photograph was taken on or after that date. Without the help of the written word, film and videotape cannot portray temporal dimensions with any precision. Consider a film clip showing an aircraft carrier at sea. One might be able to identify the ship as Soviet or American, but there would be no way of telling where in the world the carrier was, where it was headed, or when the pictures were taken. It is only through language—words spoken over the pictures or reproduced in them—that the image of the aircraft carrier takes on specific meaning.

Still, it is possible to enjoy the image of the carrier for its own sake. One might find the hugeness of the vessel interesting; it signifies military power on the move. There is a certain drama in watching the planes come in at high speeds and skid to a stop on the deck. Suppose the ship were burning: that would be even more interesting. This leads to an important point about the language of pictures. Moving pictures favor images that change. That is why violence and dynamic destruction find their way onto television so often. When something is destroyed violently it is altered in a highly visible way; hence the entrancing power of fire. Fire gives visual form to the ideas of consumption, disappearance, death—the thing that burned is actually taken away by fire. It is at this very basic level that fires make a good subject for television news. Something was here, now it's gone, and the change is recorded on film.

Earthquakes and typhoons have the same power. Before the viewer's eyes the world is taken apart. If a television viewer has relatives in Mexico City and an earthquake occurs there, then he or she may take a special interest in the images of destruction as a report from a specific place and time; that is, one may look at television pictures for information about an important event. But film of an earthquake can be interesting even if the viewer cares nothing about the event itself. Which is only to say, as we noted earlier, that there is another way of participating in the news—as a spectator who desires to be entertained. Actually to see buildings topple is exciting, no matter where the buildings are. The world turns to dust before our eyes.

10   Those who produce television news in America know that their medium favors images that move. That is why they are wary of "talking heads," people

who simply appear in front of a camera and speak. When talking heads appear on television, there is nothing to record or document, no change in process. In the cinema the situation is somewhat different. On a movie screen, closeups of a good actor speaking dramatically can sometimes be interesting to watch. When Clint Eastwood narrows his eyes and challenges his rival to shoot first, the spectator sees the cool rage of the Eastwood character take visual form, and the narrowing of the eyes is dramatic. But much of the effect of this small movement depends on the size of the movie screen and the darkness of the theater, which make Eastwood and his every action "larger than life."

The television screen is smaller than life. It occupies about 15 percent of the viewer's visual field (compared to about 70 percent for the movie screen). It is not set in a darkened theater closed off from the world but in the viewer's ordinary living space. This means that visual changes must be more extreme and more dramatic to be interesting on television. A narrowing of the eyes will not do. A car crash, an earthquake, a burning factory are much better.

With these principles in mind, let us examine more closely the structure of a typical newscast, and here we will include in the discussion not only the pictures but all the nonlinguistic symbols that make up a television news show. For example, in America, almost all news shows begin with music, the tone of which suggests important events about to unfold. The music is very important, for it equates the news with various forms of drama and ritual—the opera, for example, or a wedding procession—in which musical themes underscore the meaning of the event. Music takes us immediately into the realm of the symbolic, a world that is not to be taken literally. After all, when events unfold in the real world, they do so without musical accompaniment. More symbolism follows. The sound of teletype machines can be heard in the studio, not because it is impossible to screen this noise out, but because the sound is a kind of music in itself. It tells us that data are pouring in from all corners of the globe, a sensation reinforced by the world map in the background (or clocks noting the time on different continents). The fact is that teletype machines are rarely used in TV news rooms, having been replaced by silent computer terminals. When seen, they have only a symbolic function.

Already, then, before a single news item is introduced, a great deal has been communicated. We know that we are in the presence of a symbolic event, a form of theater in which the day's events are to be dramatized. This theater takes the entire globe as its subject, although it may look at the world from the perspective of a single nation. A certain tension is present, like the atmosphere in a theater just before the curtain goes up. The tension is represented by the music, the staccato beat of the teletype machines, and often the sight of news workers scurrying around typing reports and answering phones. As a technical matter, it would be no problem to build a set in which the newsroom staff remained off camera, invisible to the viewer, but an important theatrical effect would be lost. By being busy on camera, the workers help communicate urgency about the events at hand, which suggests that situations are changing so rapidly that constant revision of the news is necessary.

The staff in the background also helps signal the importance of the person in the center, the anchor, "in command" of both the staff and the news. The anchor plays the role of host. He or she welcomes us to the newscast and welcomes us back from the different locations we visit during the filmed reports.

15   Many features of the newscast help the anchor to establish the impression of control. These are usually equated with production values in broadcasting. They include such things as graphics that tell the viewer what is being shown, or maps and charts that suddenly appear on the screen and disappear on cue, or the orderly progression from story to story. They also include the absence of gaps, or "dead time," during the broadcast, even the simple fact that the news starts and ends at a certain hour. These common features are thought of as purely technical matters, which a professional crew handles as a matter of course. But they are also symbols of a dominant theme of television news: the imposition of an orderly world—called "the news"—upon the disorderly flow of events.

While the form of a news broadcast emphasizes tidiness and control, its content can best be described as fragmented. Because time is so precious on television, because the nature of the medium favors dynamic visual images, and because the pressures of a commercial structure require the news to hold its audience above all else, there is rarely any attempt to explain issues in depth or place events in their proper context. The news moves nervously from a warehouse fire to a court decision, from a guerrilla war to a World Cup match, the quality of the film most often determining the length of the story. Certain stories show up only because they offer dramatic pictures. Bleachers collapse in South America: hundreds of people are crushed—a perfect television news story, for the cameras can record the face of disaster in all its anguish. Back in Washington, a new budget is approved by Congress. Here there is nothing to photograph because a budget is not a physical event; it is a document full of language and numbers. So the producers of the news will show a photo of the document itself, focusing on the cover where it says "Budget of the United States of America." Or sometimes they will send a camera crew to the government printing plant where copies of the budget are produced. That evening, while the contents of the budget are summarized by a voice-over, the viewer sees stacks of documents being loaded into boxes at the government printing plant. Then a few of the budget's more important provisions will be flashed on the screen in written form, but this is such a time-consuming process—using television as a printed page—that the producers keep it to a minimum. In short, the budget is not televisable, and for that reason its time on the news must be brief. The bleacher collapse will get more time that evening.

While appearing somewhat chaotic, these disparate stories are not just dropped in the news program helter-skelter. The appearance of a scattershot story order is really orchestrated to draw the audience from one story to the next—from one section to the next—through the commercial breaks to the end of the show. The story order is constructed to hold and build the viewership rather than place events in context or explain issues in depth.

Of course, it is a tendency of journalism in general to concentrate on the surface of events rather than underlying conditions; this is as true for the newspaper as it is for the newscast. But several features of television undermine whatever efforts journalists may make to give sense to the world. One is that a television broadcast is a series of events that occur in sequence, and the sequence is the same for all viewers. This is not true for a newspaper page, which displays many items simultaneously, allowing readers to choose the order in which they read them. If newspaper readers want only a summary of the latest tax bill, they can read the headline and the first paragraph of an article, and if they want more, they can keep reading. In a sense, then, everyone reads a different newspaper, for no two readers will read (or ignore) the same items.

But all television viewers see the same broadcast. They have no choices. A report is either in the broadcast or out, which means that anything which is of narrow interest is unlikely to be included. As NBC News executive Reuven Frank once explained:

> A newspaper, for example, can easily afford to print an item of conceivable interest to only a fraction of its readers. A television news program must be put together with the assumption that each item will be of some interest to everyone that watches. Every time a newspaper includes a feature which will attract a specialized group it can assume it is adding at least a little bit to its circulation. To the degree a television news program includes an item of this sort . . . it must assume that its audience will diminish.

20   The need to "include everyone," an identifying feature of commercial television in all its forms, prevents journalists from offering lengthy or complex explanations, or from tracing the sequence of events leading up to today's headlines. One of the ironies of political life in modern democracies is that many problems which concern the "general welfare" are of interest only to specialized groups. Arms control, for example, is an issue that literally concerns everyone in the world, and yet the language of arms control and the complexity of the subject are so daunting that only a minority of people can actually follow the

issue from week to week and month to month. If it wants to act responsibly, a newspaper can at least make available more information about arms control than most people want. Commercial television cannot afford to do so.

But even if commercial television could afford to do so, it wouldn't. The fact that television news is principally made up of moving pictures prevents it from offering lengthy, coherent explanations of events. A television news show reveals the world as a series of unrelated, fragmentary moments. It does not—and cannot be expected to—offer a sense of coherence or meaning. What does this suggest to a TV viewer? That the viewer must come with a prepared mind—information, opinions, a sense of proportion, an articulate value system. To the TV viewer lacking such mental equipment, a news program is only a kind of rousing light show. Here a falling building, there a five-alarm fire, everywhere the world as an object, much without meaning, connections, or continuity.

ENGAGING the Text

1. Why have TV news programs become a form of theater according to Postman and Powers? How is this transformation related to the nature of television?

2. What factors determine what is and is not reported? What agendas determine the composition and sequencing of news stories?

EVALUATING the Argument

1. How do the examples of how television mishandles a new U.S. budget or arms control illustrate Postman and Powers's thesis?

2. What means do Postman and Powers use to communicate the fragmentary nature of television news broadcasts and their limitations?

EXPLORING the Issue

1. Compare the coverage of an important story on the nightly news and in a daily newspaper. What different emphases and depth of coverage did you discover?

2. Choose a story that has been reported on the news for weeks or even months and analyze how it has been made to appear more like a soap opera than a news report.

CONNECTING Different Perspectives

1. Postman and Powers stress the ephemeral nature of the nightly news while Lance Morrow in "Imprisoning Time in a Rectangle" emphasizes

the potential permanence of images shown on television. Write a synthesis essay that takes both views into account, draws on outside sources, and expresses your opinion on the issue.

Cultural Anthropology

Harold Miner

Body Ritual Among the Nacirema

Horace Mitchell (Harold) Miner (1912–1993) studied at the University of Chicago and taught at the University of Michigan (1946–1985). An early work is St. Denis: A French Canadian Parish *(1936). This classic essay (written as a spoof) was originally published in the* American Anthropologist *(June 1956) and has become a defining work in an ever-expanding field devoted to research on this little-known North American tribe.*

The anthropologist has become so familiar with the diversity of ways in which different peoples behave in similar situations that he is not apt to be surprised by even the most exotic customs. In fact, if all of the logically possible combinations of behavior have not been found somewhere in the world, he is apt to suspect that they must be present in some yet undescribed tribe. This point has, in fact, been expressed with respect to clan organization by Murdock (1949: 71). In this light, the magical beliefs and practices of the Nacirema present such unusual aspects that it seems desirable to describe them as an example of the extremes to which human behavior can go.

Professor Linton first brought the ritual of the Nacirema to the attention of anthropologists twenty years ago (1936: 326), but the culture of this people is still very poorly understood. They are a North American group living in the territory between the Canadian Cree, the Yaqui and Tarahumare of Mexico, and the Carib and Arawak of the Antilles. Little is known of their origin, though tradition states that they came from the east. According to Nacirema mythology, their nation was originated by a culture hero, Notgnishaw, who is otherwise known for two great feats of strength—the throwing of a piece of wampum across the river Pa-To-Mac and the chopping down of a cherry tree in which the Spirit of Truth resided.

Nacirema culture is characterized by a highly developed market economy which has evolved in a rich natural habitat. While much of the people's time is devoted to economic pursuits, a large part of the fruits of these labors and a considerable portion of the day are spent in ritual activity. The focus of this activity is the human body, the appearance and health of which loom as a dominant concern in the ethos of the people. While such a concern is certainly not unusual, its ceremonial aspects and associated philosophy are unique.

The fundamental belief underlying the whole system appears to be that the human body is ugly and that its natural tendency is to debility and disease. Incarcerated in such a body, man's only hope is to avert these characteristics through the use of the powerful influences of ritual and ceremony. Every household has one or more shrines devoted to this purpose. The more powerful individuals in the society have several shrines in their houses and, in fact, the opulence of a house is often referred to in terms of the number of such ritual centers it possesses. Most houses are of wattle and daub construction, but the shrine rooms of the more wealthy are walled with stone. Poorer families imitate the rich by applying pottery plaques to their shrine walls.

5   While each family has at least one such shrine, the rituals associated with it are not family ceremonies but are private and secret. The rites are normally only discussed with children, and then only during the period when they are being initiated into these mysteries. I was able, however, to establish sufficient rapport with the natives to examine these shrines and to have the rituals described to me.

The focal point of the shrine is a box or chest which is built into the wall. In this chest are kept the many charms and magical potions without which no native believes he could live. These preparations are secured from a variety of specialized practitioners. The most powerful of these are the medicine men, whose assistance must be rewarded with substantial gifts. However, the medicine men do not provide the curative potions for their clients, but decide what the ingredients should be and then write them down in an ancient and secret language. This writing is understood only by the medicine men and by the herbalists who, for another gift, provide the required charm.

The charm is not disposed of after it has served its purpose, but is placed in the charm-box of the household shrine. As these magical materials are specific for certain ills, and the real or imagined maladies of the people are many, the charm-box is usually full to overflowing. The magical packets are so numerous that people forget what their purposes were and fear to use them again. While the natives are very vague on this point, we can only assume that the idea in retaining all the old magical materials is that their presence in the charm-box, before which the body rituals are conducted, will in some way protect the worshipper.

Beneath the charm-box is a small font. Each day every member of the family, in succession, enters the shrine room, bows his head before the charm-box, mingles different sorts of holy water in the font, and proceeds with a brief rite of ablution. The holy waters are secured from the Water Temple of the community, where the priests conduct elaborate ceremonies to make the liquid ritually pure.

In the hierarchy of magical practitioners, and below the medicine men in prestige, are specialists whose designation is best translated "holy-mouth-men." The Nacirema have an almost pathological horror and fascination with the mouth, the condition of which is believed to have a supernatural influence on all social relationships. Were it not for the rituals of the mouth, they believe that their teeth would fall out, their gums bleed, their jaws shrink, their friends desert them, and their lovers reject them. (They also believe that a strong relationship exists between oral and moral characteristics. For example, there is a ritual ablution of the mouth for children which is supposed to improve their moral fiber.)

10 The daily body ritual performed by everyone includes a mouth-rite. Despite the fact that these people are so punctilious about care of the mouth, this rite involves a practice which strikes the uninitiated stranger as revolting. It was reported to me that the ritual consists of inserting a small bundle of hog hairs into the mouth, along with certain magical powders, and then moving the bundle in a highly formalized series of gestures.

In addition to the private mouth-rite, the people seek out a holy-mouth-man once or twice a year. These practitioners have an impressive set of paraphernalia, consisting of a variety of augers, awls, probes, and prods. The use of these objects in the exorcism of the evils of the mouth involves almost unbelievable ritual torture of the client. The holy-mouth-man opens the client's mouth and, using the above mentioned tools, enlarges any holes which decay may have created in the teeth. Magical materials are put into these holes. If there are no naturally occurring holes in the teeth, large sections of one or more teeth are gouged out so that the supernatural substance can be applied. In the client's view, the purpose of these ministrations is to arrest decay and to draw friends. The extremely sacred and traditional character of the rite is evident in the fact that the natives return to the holy-mouth-men year after year, despite the fact that their teeth continue to decay.

It is to be hoped that, when a thorough study of the Nacirema is made, there will be a careful inquiry into the personality structure of these people. One has but to watch the gleam in the eye of a holy-mouth-man, as he jabs an awl into an exposed nerve, to suspect that a certain amount of sadism is involved. If this can be established, a very interesting pattern emerges, for most of the population shows definite masochistic tendencies. It was to these that Professor Linton referred in discussing a distinctive part of the daily body ritual which is performed only by men. This part of the rite involves scraping and lacerating the surface of the face with a sharp instrument. Special women's rites are performed only four times during each lunar month, but what they lack in frequency is made up in bar barity. As part of this ceremony, women bake their heads in small ovens for about an hour. The theoretically interesting point is that what seems to be a preponderantly masochistic people have developed sadistic specialists.

The medicine men have an imposing temple, or *latipso*, in every community of any size. The more elaborate ceremonies required to treat very sick patients can only be performed at this temple. These ceremonies involve not only the thaumaturge but a permanent group of vestal maidens who move sedately about the temple chambers in distinctive costume and headdress.

The *latipso* ceremonies are so harsh that it is phenomenal that a fair proportion of the really sick natives who enter the temple ever recover. Small children whose indoctrination is still incomplete have been known to resist attempts to take them to the temple because "that is where you go to die." Despite this fact, sick adults are not only willing but eager to undergo the protracted ritual purification, if they can afford to do so. No matter how ill the supplicant or how grave the emergency, the guardians of many temples will not admit a client if he cannot give a rich gift to the custodian. Even after one has gained admission and survived the ceremonies, the guardians will not permit the neophyte to leave until he makes still another gift.

15 The supplicant entering the temple is first stripped of all his or her clothes. In every-day life the Nacirema avoids exposure of his body and its natural functions. Bathing and excretory acts are performed only in the secrecy of the household shrine, where they are ritualized as part of the body-rites. Psychological shock results from the fact that body secrecy is suddenly lost upon entry into the *latipso*. A man, whose own wife has never seen him in an excretory act, suddenly finds himself naked and assisted by a vestal maiden while he performs his natural functions into a sacred vessel. This sort of ceremonial treatment is necessitated by the fact that the excreta are used by a diviner to ascertain the course and nature of the client's sickness. Female clients, on the other hand, find their naked bodies are subjected to the scrutiny, manipulation, and prodding of the medicine men.

Few supplicants in the temple are well enough to do anything but lie on their hard beds. The daily ceremonies, like the rites of the holy-mouth-men, involve discomfort and torture. With ritual precision, the vestals awaken their miserable charges each dawn and roll them about on their beds of pain while performing ablutions, in the formal movements of which the maidens are highly trained. At other times they insert magic wands in the supplicant's mouth or force him to eat substances which are supposed to be healing. From time to time the medicine men come to their clients and jab magically treated needles into their flesh. The fact that these temple ceremonies may not cure, and may even kill the neophyte, in no way decreases the people's faith in the medicine men.

There remains one other kind of practitioner, known as a "listener." This witch-doctor has the power to exorcise the devils that lodge in the heads of people who have been bewitched. The Nacirema believe that parents bewitch their own children. Mothers are particularly suspected of putting a curse on children while teaching them the secret body rituals. The counter-magic of the witch-doctor is unusual in its lack of ritual. The patient simply tells the "listener" all his troubles and fears, beginning with the earliest difficulties he can remember. The memory displayed by the Nacirema in these exorcism sessions is truly remarkable. It is not uncommon for the patient to bemoan the rejection he felt upon being weaned as a babe, and a few individuals even see their troubles going back to the traumatic effects of their own birth.

In conclusion, mention must be made of certain practices which have their base in native esthetics but which depend upon the pervasive aversion to the natural body and its functions. There are ritual fasts to make fat people thin and ceremonial feasts to make thin people fat. Still other rites are used to make women's breasts large if they are small, and smaller if they are large. General dissatisfaction with breast shape is symbolized in the fact that the ideal form is virtually outside the range of human variation. A few women afflicted with almost inhuman hyper mammary development are so idolized that they make a handsome living by simply going from village to village and permitting the natives to stare at them for a fee.

Reference has already been made to the fact that excretory functions are ritualized, routinized, and relegated to secrecy. Natural reproductive functions are similarly distorted. Intercourse is taboo as a topic and scheduled as an act. Efforts are made to avoid pregnancy by the use of magical materials or by limiting intercourse to certain phases of the moon. Conception is actually very infrequent. When pregnant, women dress so as to hide their condition. Parturition takes place in secret, without friends or relatives to assist, and the majority of women do not nurse their infants.

20   Our review of the ritual life of the Nacirema has certainly shown them to be a magic-ridden people. It is hard to understand how they have managed to exist so long under the burdens which they have imposed upon themselves. But even such exotic customs as these take on real meaning when they are viewed with the insight provided by Malinowski when he wrote (1948: 70):

> Looking from far and above, from our high places of safety in the developed civilization, it is easy to see all the crudity and irrelevance of magic. But without

its power and guidance early man could not have mastered his practical difficulties as he has done, nor could man have advanced to the higher stages of
civilization.

References

Linton, Ralph. 1936. *The Study of Man.* New York, D. Appleton-Century Co.
Malinowski, Bronislaw. 1948. *Magic, Science, and Religion.* Glencoe, The Free
Press.
Murdock, George P. 1949. *Social Structure.* New York, The Macmillan Co.

ENGAGING the Text

1. What bizarre attitudes do the Nacirema have toward the human body?

2. What different kinds of body rituals, shrines, and practitioners do the
Nacirema make use of as part of their obsession?

EVALUATING the Argument

1. How do assumptions about what a normal society would look like form
the basis for Miner's argument?

2. How does Miner approach this issue as an anthropologist and what
function do citations from others in the field serve in enhancing the
credibility of his analysis?

EXPLORING the Issue

1. At what point did the Nacirema, their rituals, and their culture hero,
Notgnishaw, become familiar to you? Why do you think Miner took
this approach as opposed to writing a straightforward descriptive
analysis?

2. Write an essay modeled on Miner's in which you describe rituals (fitness clubs, teeth whitening, carrying cell phones and bottled water) in
our culture that might be seen as strange and fascinating to an outside
observer.

CONNECTING Different Perspectives

1. How do the analyses by Miner and Edward T. Hall ("Hidden Culture"
in Chapter 1) illustrate the way anthropologists try to understand the
culture "scripts" that govern behavior in different societies?

Economics

Thomas Robert Malthus

The Principle of Population

Thomas Robert Malthus (1766–1834), considered the founder of social demography, was born in Surrey, England, and was trained as a mathematician, graduating in 1788 from Cambridge University. His first essay "The Crisis," written in response to Pitt's Poor Law Bill (1796), showed his concern about society's ability to cope with drastic increases in population. In 1799 Malthus and William Otter traveled through Scandinavia and Russia and his later arguments were based on evidence from the diaries he kept. His major work, An Essay on the Principle of Population *(1798; revised edition 1803), from which the following excerpt is taken, asserted that geometrical growth of population would always outstrip the arithmetically increasing food supply. Darwin declared that because of this essay, he began to think in terms of a "struggle for existence."*

The great and unlooked for discoveries that have taken place of late years in natural philosophy, the increasing diffusion of general knowledge from the extension of the art of printing, the ardent and unshackled spirit of inquiry that prevails throughout the lettered and even unlettered world, the new and extraordinary lights that have been thrown on political subjects which dazzle and astonish the understanding, and particularly that tremendous phenomenon in the political horizon, the French revolution, which, like a blazing comet, seems destined either to inspire with fresh life and vigour, or to scorch up and destroy the shrinking inhabitants of the earth, have all concurred to lead able men into the opinion that we were touching on a period big with the most important changes, changes that would in some measure be decisive of the future fate of mankind.

It has been said that the great question is now at issue, whether man shall henceforth start forwards with accelerated velocity towards illimitable, and hitherto unconceived improvement, or be condemned to a perpetual oscillation between happiness and misery, and after every effort remain still at an immeasurable distance from the wished-for goal. . . .

I have read some of the speculations of the perfectibility of man and society with great pleasure. I have been warmed and delighted with the enchanting picture which they hold forth. I ardently wish for such happy improvements. But I see great, and, to my understanding, unconquerable difficulties in the way to them. These difficulties it is my present purpose to state, declaring, at the same time, that so far from exulting in them, as a cause of triumph over the friends of innovation, nothing would give me greater pleasure than to see them completely removed.

The most important argument that I shall adduce is certainly not new. The principles on which it depends have been explained in part by Hume, and more at large by Dr. Adam Smith. It has been advanced and applied to the present subject, though not with its proper weight, or in the most forcible point of view, by Mr. Wallace, and it may probably have been stated by many writers that I have never met with. I should certainly therefore not think of advancing it again, though I mean to place it in a point of view in some degree different from any that I have hitherto seen, if it had ever been fairly and satisfactorily answered.

5   The cause of this neglect on the part of the advocates for the perfectibility of mankind is not easily accounted for. I cannot doubt the talents of such men as Godwin and Condorcet. I am unwilling to doubt their candour. To my understanding, and probably to that of most others, the difficulty appears insurmountable. Yet these men of acknowledged ability and penetration, scarcely deign to notice it, and hold on their course in such speculations, with unabated ardour and undiminished confidence. I have certainly no right to say that they purposely shut their eyes to such arguments. I ought rather to doubt the validity of them, when neglected by such men, however forcibly their truth may strike my own mind. Yet in this respect it must be acknowledged that we are all of us too prone to err. If I saw a glass of wine repeatedly presented to a man, and he took no notice of it, I should be apt to think that he was blind or uncivil. A juster philosophy might teach me rather to think that my eyes deceived me and that the offer was not really what I conceived it to be.

In entering upon the argument I must premise that I put out of the question, at present, all mere conjectures, that is, all suppositions, the probable realization of which cannot be inferred upon any just philosophical grounds. A writer may tell me that he thinks man will ultimately become an ostrich. I cannot properly contradict him. But before he can expect to bring any reasonable person over to his opinion, he ought to shew, that the necks of mankind have been gradually elongating, that the lips have grown harder and more prominent, that the legs and feet are daily altering their shape, and that the hair is beginning to change into stubs of feathers. And till the probability of so wonderful a conversion can be shewn, it is surely lost time and lost eloquence to expatiate on the happiness of man in such a state; to describe his powers, both of running and flying, to paint him in a condition where all narrow luxuries would be contemned, where he would be employed only in collecting the necessaries of life, and where, consequently, each man's share of labour would be light, and his portion of leisure ample.

I think I may fairly make two postulata.

First, That food is necessary to the existence of man.

Secondly, That the passion between the sexes is necessary and will remain nearly in its present state.

10 These two laws, ever since we have had any knowledge of mankind, appear to have been fixed laws of our nature, and, as we have not hitherto seen any alteration in them, we have no right to conclude that they will ever cease to be what they now are, without an immediate act of power in that Being who first arranged the system of the universe, and for the advantage of his creatures, still executes, according to fixed laws, all its various operations.

I do not know that any writer has supposed that on this earth man will ultimately be able to live without food. But Mr. Godwin has conjectured that the passion between the sexes may in time be extinguished. As, however, he calls this part of his work a deviation into the land of conjecture, I will not dwell longer upon it at present than to say that the best arguments for the perfectibility of man are drawn from a contemplation of the great progress that [man] has already made from the savage state and the difficulty of saying where he is to stop. But towards the extinction of the passion between the sexes, no progress whatever has hitherto been made. It appears to exist in as much force at present as it did two thousand or four thousand years ago. There are individual exceptions now as there always have been. But, as these exceptions do not appear to increase in number, it would surely be a very unphilosophical mode of arguing, to infer merely from the existence of an exception, that the exception would, in time, become the rule, and the rule the exception.

Assuming then, my postulata as granted, I say, that the power of population is indefinitely greater than the power in the earth to produce subsistence for man.

Population, when unchecked, increases in a geometrical ratio. Subsistence increases only in an arithmetical ratio. A slight acquaintance with numbers will shew the immensity of the first power in comparison of the second.

By that law of our nature which makes food necessary to the life of man, the effects of these two unequal powers must be kept equal.

15 This implies a strong and constantly operating check on population from the difficulty of subsistence. This difficulty must fall some where and must necessarily be severely felt by a large portion of mankind.

Through the animal and vegetable kingdoms, nature has scattered the seeds of life abroad with the most profuse and liberal hand. She has been comparatively sparing in the room and the nourishment necessary to rear them. The germs of existence contained in this spot of earth, with ample food, and ample room to expand in, would fill millions of worlds in the course of a few thousand years. Necessity, that imperious all pervading law of nature, restrains them within the prescribed bounds. The race of plants, and the race of animals shrink under this great restrictive law. And the race of man cannot, by any efforts of reason, escape from it. Among plants and animals its effects are waste of seed, sickness, and premature death. Among mankind, misery and vice. The former, misery, is an absolutely necessary consequence of it. Vice is a highly probable consequence, and we therefore see it abundantly prevail, but it ought not, perhaps, to be called an absolutely necessary consequence. The ordeal of virtue is to resist all temptation to evil.

This natural inequality of the two powers of population and of production in the earth and that great law of our nature which must constantly keep their effects equal form the great difficulty that to me appears insurmountable in the way to the perfectibility of society. All other arguments are of slight and subordinate consideration in comparison of this. I see no way by which man can escape from the weight of this law which pervades all animated nature. No fancied equality, no agrarian regulations in their utmost extent, could remove the pressure of it even for a single century. And it appears, therefore, to be decisive against the possible existence of a society, all the members of which should live in ease, happiness, and comparative leisure; and feel no anxiety about providing the means of subsistence for themselves and families.

Consequently, if the premises are just, the argument is conclusive against the perfectibility of the mass of mankind. . . .

ENGAGING the Text

1. Explain Malthus's theory of the "geometrical" increase in population as compared with the "arithmetical" increase in the food supply. Why will this disproportion always defeat plans for social perfectability?

2. What additional factors other than the food supply does Malthus discuss that also act to limit population growth?

EVALUATING the Argument

1. Where does Malthus use parallelism to emphasize relationships between his ideas?

2. How does Malthus use an analogy of an ostrich to satirize those who propose a vision of societal perfectability? How effective do you find his use of irony and humor to communicate his ideas?

EXPLORING the Issue

1. Implicit in Malthus's argument is a critique of population overload. What relevance does his message have for today?

2. How do different societies cope with the dual problem of over-population and scarcity of food (for example, China's mandatory one-child policy)? To what extent have advances in genetic engineering made Malthus's argument more or less relevant? For example, you might research the bioengineering of seed that self-destructs after the first crop in traditional societies like India where it was customary for farmers to stockpile seed from one season to the next. Do a research paper on this issue and include a discussion of the political turmoil that has resulted and the resolutions that have been reached.

CONNECTING Different Perspectives

1. What elements in Malthus's classic 1798 essay influenced Charles Darwin's concept of a struggle for existence, as a key concept in "On the Origin of Species"?

Education

Nat Hentoff

"Speech Codes" on the Campus and Problems of Free Speech

Nat Hentoff was born in 1925 in Boston, graduated from Northeastern University in 1945, and did postgraduate work at Harvard and the Sorbonne. He is a regular contributor to the Washington Post, *the* New Yorker, *and the* Village Voice. *His most recent works are* War on the Bill of Rights and the Gathering Resistance *(2003) and* American Music Is *(2004). The following article first appeared in the Fall 1991 issue of* Dissent.

During three years of reporting on anti-free-speech tendencies in higher education, I've been at more than twenty colleges and universities—from Washington and Lee and Columbia to Mesa State in Colorado and Stanford.

On this voyage of initially reverse expectations—with liberals fiercely advocating censorship of "offensive" speech and conservatives merrily taking the moral high ground as champions of free expression—the most dismaying moment of revelation took place at Stanford.

An Ecumenical Call for a Harsh Code

In the course of a two-year debate on whether Stanford, like many other universities, should have a speech code punishing language that might wound minorities, women, and gays, a letter appeared in the *Stanford Daily*. Signed by the African-American Law Students Association, the Asian-American Law Students Association, the Jewish Law Students Association, and the letter called for a harsh code. It reflected the letter and the spirit of an earlier declaration by Canetta Ivy, a black leader of student government at Stanford during the period of the great debate. "We don't put as many restrictions on freedom of speech," she said, "as we should."

Reading the letter by this rare ecumenical body of law students (so pressing was the situation that even Jews were allowed in), I thought of twenty, thirty years from now. From so bright a cadre of graduates, from so prestigious a law school would come some of the law professors, civic leaders, college presidents, and even maybe a Supreme Court justice of the future. And many of them would have learned—like so many other university students in the land—that censorship is okay provided your motives are okay.

5   The debate at Stanford ended when the president, Donald Kennedy, following the prevailing winds, surrendered his previous position that once you start telling people what they can't say, you will end up telling them what they can't think. Stanford now has a speech code.

This is not to say that these gags on speech—every one of them so overboard and vague that a student can violate a code without knowing he or she has done so—are invariably imposed by student demand. At most colleges, it is the administration that sets up the code. Because there have been racist or sexist or homophobic taunts, anonymous notes or graffiti, the administration feels it must *do something*. The cheapest, quickest way to demonstrate that it cares is to appear to suppress racist, sexist, homophobic speech.

"The Pall of Orthodoxy"

Usually, the leading opposition among the faculty consists of conservatives—when there is opposition. An exception at Stanford was law professor Gerald Gunther, arguably the nation's leading authority on constitutional law. But Gunther did not have much support among other faculty members, conservative or liberal.

At the University of Buffalo Law School, which has a code restricting speech, I could find just one faculty member who was against it. A liberal, he spoke only on condition that I not use his name. He did not want to be categorized as a racist.

On another campus, a political science professor, for whom I had great respect after meeting and talking with him years ago, has been silent—students told me—on what Justice William Brennan once called "the pall of orthodoxy" that has fallen on his campus.

10   When I talked to him, the professor said, "It doesn't happen in my class. There's no 'politically correct' orthodoxy here. It may happen in other places at this university, but I don't know about that." He said no more.

One of the myths about the rise of P.C. (politically correct) is that, coming from the left, it is primarily intimidating conservatives on campus. Quite the contrary. At almost every college I've been, conservative students have their own newspaper, usually quite lively and fired by a muckraking glee at exposing "politically correct" follies on campus.

By and large, those most intimidated—not so much by the speech codes themselves but by the Madame Defarge-like spirit behind them—are liberal students and those who can be called politically moderate.

I've talked to many of them, and they no longer get involved in class discussions when their views would go against the grain of P.C. righteousness. Many, for instance, have questions about certain kinds of affirmative action. They are not partisans of Jesse Helms or David Duke, but they wonder whether progeny of middle-class black families should get scholarship preference. Others have a question about abortion. Most are not prolife, but they believe that fathers should have a say in whether the fetus should be sent off into eternity.

Self-Censorship

Jeff Shesol, a recent graduate of Brown and now a Rhodes scholar at Oxford, became nationally known while at Brown because of his comic strip, "Thatch," which, not too kindly, parodied P.C. students. At a forum on free speech at Brown before he left, Shesol said he wished he could tell the new students at Brown to have no fear of speaking freely. But he couldn't tell them that, he said, advising the new students to stay clear of talking critically about affirmative action or abortion, among other things, in public.

15   At that forum, Shesol told me, he said that those members of the left who regard dissent from their views as racist and sexist should realize that they are discrediting their goals. "They're honorable goals," said Sheshol, "and I agree with them. I'm against racism and sexism. But these people's tactics are obscuring

the goals. And they've resulted in Brown's no longer being an open-minded place." There were hisses from the audience.

Students at New York University Law School have also told me that they censor themselves in class. The kind of chilling atmosphere they describe was exemplified as a case assigned for a moot court competition became subject to denunciation when a sizable number of law students said it was too "offensive" and would hurt the feelings of gay and lesbian students. The case concerned a divorced father's attempt to gain custody of his children on the grounds that their mother had become a lesbian. It was against P.C. to represent the father.

Although some of the faculty responded by insisting that you learn to be a lawyer by dealing with all kinds of cases, including those you personally find offensive, other faculty members supported the rebellious students, praising them for their sensitivity. There was little public opposition from the other students to the attempt to suppress the case. A leading dissenter was a member of the conservative Federalist Society.

What is P.C. to white students is not necessarily P.C. to black students. Most of the latter did not get involved in the N.Y.U. protest, but throughout the country many black students do support speech codes. A vigorous exception was a black Harvard law school student during a debate on whether the law school should start punishing speech. A white student got up and said that the codes are necessary because without them, black students would be driven away from colleges and thereby deprived of the equal opportunity to get an education.

A black student rose and said that the white student had a hell of a nerve to assume that he—in the face of racist speech—would pack up his books and go home. He's been familiar with that kind of speech all his life, and he had never felt the need to run away from it. He'd handled it before and he could again.

20 The black student then looked at his white colleague and said that it was condescending to say that blacks have to be "protected" from racist speech. "It is more racist and insulting," he emphasized, "to say that to me than to call me a nigger."

But that would appear to be a minority view among black students. Most are convinced they do need to be protected from wounding language. On the other hand, a good many black student organizations on campus do not feel that Jews have to be protected from wounding language.

Presence of Anti-Semitism

Though it's not much written about in reports of the language wars on campus, there is a strong strain of anti-Semitism among some—not all, by any means—black students. They invite such speakers as Louis Farrakhan, the former Stokely Carmichael (now Kwame Touré), and such lesser but still burning bushes as Steve Cokely, the Chicago commentator who has declared that Jewish doctors inject the AIDS virus into black babies. That distinguished leader was invited to speak at the University of Michigan.

The black student organization at Columbia University brought to the campus Dr. Khallid Abdul Muhammad. He began his address by saying: "My leader, my teacher, my guide is the honorable Louis Farrakhan. I thought that should be said at Columbia Jewniversity."

Many Jewish students have not censored themselves in reacting to this form of political correctness among some blacks. A Columbia student, Rachel Stoll, wrote a letter to the *Columbia Spectator.* "I have an idea. As a white Jewish American, I'll just stand in the middle of a circle comprising . . . Khallid Abdul Muhammad and assorted members of the Black Students Organization and let them all hurl large stones at me. From recent events and statements made on this campus, I gather this will be a good cheap method of making these people feel good."

25   At UCLA, a black student magazine printed an article indicating there is considerable truth to the *Protocols of the Elders of Zion* [a document forged c. 1897 alleging that an international Jewish conspiracy was plotting the overthrow of Christian civilization]. For months, the black faculty, when asked their reactions, preferred not to comment. One of them did say that the black students already considered the black faculty to be insufficiently militant, and the professors didn't want to make the gap any wider. Like white liberal faculty members on other campuses, they want to be liked—or at least not too disliked.

Along with quiet white liberal faculty members, most black professors have not opposed the speech codes. But unlike the white liberals many honestly do believe that minority students have to be insulated from barbed language. They do not believe—as I have found out in a number of conversations—that an essential part of an education is to learn to demystify language, to strip it of its ability to demonize and stigmatize you. They do not believe that the way to deal with bigoted language is to answer it with more and better language of your own. This seems very elementary to me, but not to the defenders, black and white, of the speech codes.

"Fighting Words"

Consider University of California president David Gardner. He has imposed a speech code on all the campuses in his university system. Students are to be punished—and this is characteristic of the other codes around the country—if they use "fighting words"—derogatory references to "race, sex, sexual orientation, or disability."

The term "fighting words" comes from a 1942 Supreme Court decision, *Chaplinsky v. New Hampshire*, which ruled that "fighting words" are not protected by the First Amendment. That decision, however, has been in disuse at the High Court for many years. But it is thriving on college campuses.

In the California code, a word becomes "fighting" if it is directly addressed to "any ordinary person" (presumably, extraordinary people are above all this). These are the kinds of words that are "inherently likely to provoke a violent action, *whether or not they actually do.*" (Emphasis added.)

30 Moreover, he or she who fires a fighting word at any ordinary person can be reprimanded or dismissed from the university because the perpetrator should "reasonably know" that what he or she has said will interfere with the "victim's ability to pursue effectively his or her education or otherwise participate fully in university programs and activities."

Asked Gary Murikami, chairman of the Gay and Lesbian Association at the University of California, Berkeley: "What does it mean?"

Among those—faculty, law professors, college administrators—who insist such codes are essential to the university's purpose of making *all* students feel at home and thereby able to concentrate on their work, there has been a celebratory resort to the Fourteenth Amendment.

That amendment guarantees "equal protection of the laws" to all, and that means to all students on campus. Accordingly, when the First Amendment rights of those engaging in offensive speech clash with the equality rights of their targets under the Fourteenth Amendment, the First Amendment must give way.

This is the thesis, by the way, of John Powell, legal director of the American Civil Liberties Union, even though that organization has now formally opposed all college speech codes—after a considerable civil war among and within its affiliates.

35 The battle of the amendments continues, and when harsher codes are called for at some campuses, you can expect the Fourteenth Amendment—which was not intended to censor *speech*—will rise again.

A precedent has been set at, of all places, colleges and universities, that the principle of free speech is merely situational. As college administrators change, so will the extent of free speech on campus. And invariably, permissible speech will become more and more narrowly defined. Once speech can be limited in such subjective ways, more and more expression will be included in what is forbidden.

Freedom of Thought

One of the exceedingly few college presidents who speaks out on the consequences of the anti-free-speech movement is Yale University's Benno Schmidt:

> Freedom of thought must be Yale's central commitment. It is not easy to embrace. It is, indeed, the effort of a lifetime. . . . Much expression that is free may deserve our contempt. We may well be moved to exercise our own freedom to counter it or to ignore it. But universities cannot censor or suppress speech, no matter how obnoxious in content, without violating their justification for existence. . . .
>
> On some other campuses in this country, values of civility and community have been offered by some as paramount values of the university, even to the extent of superseding freedom of expression.
>
> Such a view is wrong in principle and, if extended, is disastrous to freedom of thought. . . . The chilling effects on speech of the vagueness and open-ended nature of many universities' prohibitions. . . . are compounded by the fact that these codes are typically enforced by faculty and students who commonly assert that vague notions of community are more important to the academy than freedom of thought and expression. . . .
>
> This is a flabby and uncertain time for freedom in the United States.

On the Public Broadcasting System in June 1991, I was part of a Fred Friendly panel at Stanford University in a debate on speech codes versus freedom of expression. The three black panelists strongly supported the codes. So did the one Asian-American on the panel. But then so did Stanford law professor Thomas Grey, who wrote the Stanford code, and Stanford president Donald Kennedy, who first opposed and then embraced the code. We have a new ecumenicism of those who would control speech for the greater good. It is hardly a new idea, but the mix of advocates is rather new.

But there are other voices. In the national board debate at the ACLU on college speech codes, the first speaker—and I think she had a lot to do with making the final vote against codes unanimous—was Gwen Thomas.

40   A black community college administrator from Colorado, she is a fiercely persistent exposer of racial discrimination.

She started by saying, "I have always felt as a minority person that we have to protect the rights of all because if we infringe on the rights of any persons, we'll be next.

"As for providing a nonintimidating educational environment, our young people have to learn to grow up on college campuses. We have to teach them how to deal with adversarial situations. They have to learn how to survive offensive speech they find wounding and hurtful." Gwen Thomas is an educator—an endangered species in higher education.

ENGAGING the Text

1. With which of the assumptions underlying the imposition of speech codes does Hentoff disagree? How do Hentoff's own experiences or the examples he cites from campuses around the country challenge the presumed benefits of speech codes?

2. Why does Hentoff find it ironic that a double standard seems to exist in regard to anti-Semitic speech?

EVALUATING the Argument

1. How does Hentoff frame the debate as to whether the First or the Fourteenth Amendment ought to take precedence?

2. Why does Hentoff focus on the reactions of students with moderate views who feel inhibited from discussing controversial issues? Is this an effective tactic? Why or why not?

EXPLORING the Issue

1. Does your experience in classrooms confirm or disprove Hentoff's contention that students with moderate views feel inhibited in discussing issues because they may be accused of being politically incorrect?

2. In your opinion, is the First Amendment's guarantee of free speech or the Fourteenth Amendment's guarantee of equal protection under the law most relevant to speech codes on campus?

CONNECTING Different Perspectives

1. How do the issues of political correctness and stereotyping overlap in Hentoff's article and in Ursula Le Guin's argument "American SF and The Other"?

Political Science

Daniela Deane

The Little Emperors

Daniela Deane is a staff writer for the Washington Post. *The following article first appeared in the* Los Angeles Times Magazine *(July 26, 1992) and describes the consequences of China's one-child policy intended to cope with China's burgeoning population. The progam encourages couples to marry late and have only one child. It is strictly enforced in urban areas, but in rural areas, couples are often allowed to have two children.*

Xu Ming sits on the worn sofa with his short, chubby arms and legs splayed, forced open by fat and the layers of padded clothing worn in northern China to ward off the relentless chill. To reach the floor, the tubby 8-year-old rocks back and forth on his big bottom, inching forward slowly, eventually ending upright. Xu Ming finds it hard to move.

"He got fat when he was about 3," says his father, Xu Jianguo, holding the boy's bloated, dimpled hand. "We were living with my parents and they were very good to him. He's the only grandson. It's a tradition in China that boys are very loved. They love him very much, and so they feed him a lot. They give him everything he wants."

Xu Ming weighs 135 pounds, about twice what he should at his age. He's one of hundreds of children who have sought help in the past few years at the Beijing Children's Hospital, which recently began the first American-style fat farm for obese children in what was once the land of skin and bones.

"We used to get a lot of cases of malnutrition," says Dr. Ni Guichen, director of endocrinology at the hospital and founder of the weight reduction classes. "But in the last 10 years, the problem has become obese children. The number of fat children in China is growing very fast. The main reason is the one-child policy," she says, speaking in a drab waiting room. "Because parents can only have one child, the families take extra good care of that one child, which means feeding him too much."

5   Bulging waistlines are one result of China's tough campaign to curb its population. The one-child campaign, a strict national directive that seeks to limit each Chinese couple to a single son or daughter, has other dramatic consequences: millions of abortions, fewer girls and a generation of spoiled children.

The 10-day weight-reduction sessions—a combination of exercise, nutritional guidance and psychological counseling—are very popular. Hundreds of children—some so fat they can hardly walk—are turned away for each class.

According to Ni, about 5% of children in China's cities are obese, with two obese boys for every overweight girl, the traditional preference toward boys being reflected in the amount of attention lavished on the child. "Part of the course is also centered on the parents. We try to teach them how to bring their children up properly, not just by spoiling them," Ni says.

Ming's father is proud that his son, after two sessions at the fat farm, has managed to halve his intake of *jiaozi*, the stodgy meat-filled dumplings that are

Ming's particular weakness, from 30 to 15 at a sitting. "Even if he's not full, that's all he gets," he says. "In the beginning, it was very difficult. He would put his arms around our necks and beg us for more food. We couldn't bear it, so we'd give him a little more."

Ming lost a few pounds but hasn't been able to keep the weight off. He's a bit slimmer now, but only because he's taller. "I want to lose weight," says Ming, who spends his afternoons snacking at his grandparents' house and his evenings plopped in front of the television set at home. "The kids make fun of me, they call me a fat pig. I hate the nicknames. In sports class, I can't do what the teacher says. I can run a little bit, but after a while I have to sit down. The teacher puts me at the front of the class where all the other kids can see me. They all laugh and make fun of me."

10   The many fat children visible on China's city streets are just the most obvious example of 13 years of the country's one-child policy. In the vast countryside, the policy has meant shadowy lives as second-class citizens for thousands of girls, or, worse, death. It has made abortion a way of life and a couple's sexual intimacy the government's concern. Even women's menstrual cycles are monitored. Under the directive, couples literally have to line up for permission to procreate. Second children are sometimes possible, but only on payment of a heavy fine.

The policy is an unparalleled intrusion into the private lives of a nation's citizens, an experiment on a scale never attempted elsewhere in the world. But no expert will argue that China—by far the world's most populous country with 1.16 billion people—could continue without strict curbs on its population.

China's communist government adopted the one-child policy in 1979 in response to the staggering doubling of the country's population during Mao Tse-tung's rule. Mao, who died in 1976, was convinced that the country's masses were a strategic asset and vigorously encouraged the Chinese to produce even-larger families.

But large families are now out for the Chinese—20% of the world's population living on just 7% of the arable land. "China has to have a population policy," says Huang Baoshan, deputy director of the State Family Planning Commission. With the numbers ever growing, "how can we feed them, house them?"

Dinner time for one 5-year-old girl consists of granddad chasing her through the house, bowl and spoon in hand, barking like a dog or mewing like a cat. If he performs authentically enough, she rewards him by accepting a mouthful of food. No problem, insists granddad, "it's good exercise for her."

15   An 11-year-old boy never gets up to go to the toilet during the night. That's because his mother, summoned by a shout, gets up instead and positions a bottle

under the covers for him. "We wouldn't want him to have to get up in the night," his mother says.

Another mother wanted her 16-year-old to eat some fruit, but the teenager was engrossed in a video game. Not wanting him to get his fingers sticky or daring to interrupt, she peeled several grapes and popped one after another into his mouth. "Not so fast," he snapped. "Can't you see I have to spit out the seeds?"

Stories like these are routinely published in China's newspapers, evidence that the government-imposed birth-control policy has produced an emerging generation of spoiled, lazy, selfish, self-centered and overweight children. There are about 40 million only children in China. Dubbed the country's "Little Emperors," their behavior toward their elders is likened to that of the young emperor Pu Yi, who heaped indignities on his eunuch servants while making them cater to his whims, as chronicled in Bernardo Bertolucci's film *The Last Emperor.*

Many studies on China's only children have been done. One such study confirmed that only children generally are not well liked. The study, conducted by a team of Chinese psychologists, asked a group of 360 Chinese children, half who have siblings and half who don't, to rate each other's behavior. The only children were, without fail, the least popular, regardless of age or social background. Peers rated them more uncooperative and selfish than children with brothers and sisters. They bragged more, were less helpful in group activities and more apt to follow their own selfish interests. And they wouldn't share their toys.

The Chinese lay a lot of blame on what they call the "4-2-1" syndrome—four doting grandparents, two overindulgent parents, all pinning their hopes and ambitions on one child.

20   Besides stuffing them with food, Chinese parents have very high expectations of their one *bao bei*, or treasured object. Some have their still-in-strollers babies tested for IQ levels. Others try to teach toddlers Tang Dynasty poetry. Many shell out months of their hard-earned salaries for music lessons and instruments for children who have no talent or interest in playing. They fill their kids' lives with lessons in piano, English, gymnastics and typing.

The one-child parents, most of them from traditionally large Chinese families, grew up during the chaotic, 10-year Cultural Revolution, when many of the country's cultural treasures were destroyed and schools were closed for long periods of time. Because many of that generation spent years toiling in the fields rather than studying, they demand—and put all their hopes into—academic achievement for their children.

"We've already invested a lot of money in his intellectual development," Wang Zhouzhi told me in her Spartan home in a tiny village of Changping country outside Beijing, discussing her son, Chenqian, an only child. "I don't care how much money we spend on him. We've bought him an organ and we push him hard. Unfortunately, he's only a mediocre student," she says, looking toward the 10-year-old boy. Chenqian, dressed in a child-sized Chinese army uniform, ate 10 pieces of candy during the half-hour interview and repeatedly fired off his toy pistol, all without a word of reproach from his mother.

Would Chenqian have liked a sibling to play with? "No," he answers loudly, firing a rapid, jarring succession of shots. His mother breaks in: "If he had a little brother or sister, he wouldn't get everything he wants. Of course he doesn't want one. With only one child, I give my full care and concern to him."

But how will these children, now entering their teen-age years and moving quickly toward adulthood, become the collectivist-minded citizens China's hard-line communist leadership demands? Some think they never will. Ironically, it may be just these overindulged children who will change Chinese society. After growing up doing as they wished, ruling their immediate families, they're not likely to obey a central government that tells them to fall in line. This new generation of egotists, who haven't been taught to take even their parents into consideration, simply may not be able to think of the society as a whole—the basic principle of communism.

25   The need for family planning is obvious in the cities, where living space is limited and the one-child policy is strictly enforced and largely successful. City dwellers are slowly beginning to accept the notion that smaller families are better for the country, although most would certainly want two children if they could have them. However, in the countryside, where three of every four Chinese live—nearly 900 million people—the goal of limiting each couple to only one child has proved largely elusive.

In the hinterlands, the policy has become a confusing patchwork of special cases and exceptions. Provincial authorities can decide which couples can have a second child. In the southern province of Guangdong, China's richest, two children are allowed and many couples can afford to pay the fine to have even a third or fourth child. The amounts of the fines vary across the country, the highest in populous Sichuan province, where the fine for a second child can be as much as 25% of a family's income over four years. Special treatment has been given to China's cultural minorities such as the Mongolians and the Tibetans because of their low numbers. Many of them are permitted three or four children without penalty, although some Chinese social scientists have begun to question the privilege.

"It's really become a two-child policy in the countryside," says a Western diplomat. "Because of the traditional views on labor supply, the traditional bias toward the male child, it's been impossible for them to enforce a one-child policy outside the cities. In the countryside, they're really trying to stop that third child."

Thirteen years of strict family planning have created one of the great mysteries of the vast and remote Chinese countryside: Where have all the little girls gone? A Swedish study of sex ratios in China, published in 1990, and based on China's own census data, concluded that several million little girls are "missing"—up to half a million a year in the years 1985 to 1987—since the policy was introduced in late 1979.

In the study, and in demographic research worldwide, sex ratio at birth in humans is shown to be very stable, between 105 and 106 boys for every 100 girls. The imbalance is thought to be nature's way of compensating for the higher rates of miscarriage, stillbirth and infant mortality among boys.

30   In China, the ratio climbed consistently during the 1980s, and it now rests at more than 110 boys to 100 girls. "The imbalance is evident in some areas of the country," says Stirling Scruggs, director of the United Nations Population Fund in China. "I don't think the reason is widespread infanticide. They're adopting out girls to try for a boy, they're hiding their girls, they're not registering them. Throughout Chinese history, in times of famine, and now as well, people have been forced to make choices between boys and girls, and for many reasons, boys always win out."

With the dismantling of collectives, families must, once again, farm their own small plots and sons are considered necessary to do the work. Additionally, girls traditionally "marry out" of their families, transferring their filial responsibilities to their in-laws. Boys carry on the family name and are entrusted with the care of their parents as they age. In the absence of a social security system, having a son is the difference between starving and eating when one is old. To combat the problem, some innovative villages have begun issuing so-called girl insurance, an old-age insurance policy for couples who have given birth to a daughter and are prepared to stop at that.

"People are scared to death to be childless and penniless in their old age," says William Hinton, an American author of seven books chronicling modern China. "So if they don't have a son, they immediately try for another. When the woman is pregnant, they'll have a sex test to see if it's a boy or a girl. They'll abort a girl, or go in hiding with the girl, or pay the fine, or bribe the official or leave home. Anything. It's a game of wits."

Shen Shufen, a sturdy, round-faced peasant woman of 33, has two children—an 8-year-old girl and a 3-year-old boy—and lives in Sihe, a dusty, one-road, mud-brick village in the countryside outside Beijing. Her husband is a truck driver. "When we had our girl, we knew we had to have another child somehow. We saved for years to pay the fine. It was hard giving them that money, 3,000 yuan ($550 in U.S. dollars), in one night. That's what my husband makes in three years. I was so happy when our second child was a boy."

The government seems aware of the pressure its policies put on expectant parents, and the painful results, but has not shown any flexibility. For instance, Beijing in 1990 passed a law forbidding doctors to tell a couple the results of ultrasound tests that disclose the sex of their unborn child. The reason: Too many female embryos were being aborted.

35 And meanwhile, several hundred thousand women—called "guerrilla moms"—go into hiding every year to have their babies. They become part of China's 40-million-strong floating population that wanders the country, mostly in search of work, sleeping under bridges and in front of railway stations. Tens of thousands of female children are simply abandoned in rural hospitals.

And although most experts say female infanticide is not widespread, it does exist. "I found a dead baby girl," says Hinton. "We stopped for lunch at this mountain ravine in Shaanxi province. We saw her lying there, at the bottom of the creek bed. She was all bundled up, with one arm sticking out. She had been there a while, you could tell, because she had a little line of mold growing across her mouth and nostrils."

Death comes in another form, too: neglect. "It's female neglect, more than female infanticide, neglect to the point of death for little girls," says Scruggs of the U.N. Population Fund. "If you have a sick child, and it's a girl," he says, "you might buy only half the dose of medicine she needs to get better."

Hundreds of thousands of unregistered little girls—called "black children"—live on the edge of the law, unable to get food rations, immunizations or places in school. Many reports are grim. The government-run China News Service reported last year that the drowning of baby girls had revived to such an extent in Guangxi province that at least 1 million boys will be unable to find wives in 20 years. And partly because of the gender imbalance, the feudalistic practice of selling women has been revived.

The alarming growth of the flesh trade prompted authorities to enact a law in January that imposes jail sentences of up to 10 years and heavy fines for people caught trafficking. The government also recently began broadcasting a television dramatization to warn women against the practice. The public-service message shows two women, told that they would be given high-paying jobs, being lured to a suburban home. Instead, they are locked in a small, dark room, and soon realize that they have been sold.

40 Li Wangping is nervous. She keeps looking at the air vents at the bottom of the office door, to see if anyone is walking by or, worse still, standing there listening. She rubs her hands together over and over. She speaks in a whisper. "I'm afraid to get into trouble talking to you," Li confides. She says nothing for a few minutes.

"After my son was born, I desperately wanted another baby," the 42-year-old woman finally begins. "I just wanted to have more children, you understand? Anyway, I got pregnant three times, because I wasn't using any birth control. I didn't want to use any. So, I had to have three abortions, one right after the other. I didn't want to at all. It was terrible killing the babies I wanted so much. But I had to."

By Chinese standards, Li (not her real name) has a lot to lose if she chooses to follow her maternal yearnings. As an office worker at government-owned CITIC, a successful and dynamic conglomerate, she has one of the best jobs in Beijing. Just being a city dweller already puts her ahead of most of the population.

"One of my colleagues had just gotten fired for having a second child. I couldn't afford to be fired," continues Li, speaking in a meeting room at CITIC headquarters. "I had to keep everything secret from the family-planning official at CITIC, from everyone at the office. Of course, I'm supposed to be using birth control. I had to lie. It was hard lying, because I felt so bad about everything."

She rubs her hands furiously and moves toward the door, staring continuously at the air slats. "I have to go now. There's more to say, but I'm afraid to tell you. They could find me."

45 China's family-planning officials wield awesome powers, enforcing the policy through a combination of incentives and deterrents. For those who comply, there are job promotions and small cash awards. For those who resist, they suffer stiff fines and loss of job and status within the country's tightly knit and heavily regulated communities. The State Family Planning Commission is the government ministry entrusted with the tough task of curbing the growth of the world's most populous country, where 28 children are born every minute. It employs about 200,000 full-time officials and uses more than a million volunteers to check the fertility of hundreds of millions of Chinese women.

"Every village or enterprise has at least one family-planning official," says Zhang Xizhi, a birth-control official in Changping county outside Beijing. "Our main job is propaganda work to raise people's consciousness. We educate people and tell them their options for birth control. We go down to every household to talk to people. We encourage them to have only one child, to marry late, to have their child later."

China's population police frequently keep records of the menstrual cycles of women of childbearing age, on the type of birth control they use and the pending applications to have children. If they slip up, street committees—half-governmental, half-civilian organizations that have sprung up since the 1949 communist takeover—take up the slack. The street committees, made up mostly of retired volunteers, act as the central government's ear to the ground, snooping, spying and reporting on citizens to the authorities.

When a couple wants to have a child—even their first, allotted one—they must apply to the family-planning office in their township or workplace, literally lining up to procreate. "If a woman gets pregnant without permission, she and her husband will get fined, even if it's their first," Zhang says. "It is fair to fine her, because she creates a burden on the whole society by jumping her place in line."

If a woman in Nanshao township, where Zhang works, becomes pregnant with a second child, she must terminate her pregnancy unless she or her husband or their first child is disabled or if both parents are only children. Her local family-planning official will repeatedly visit her at home to pressure her to comply. "Sometimes I have to go to people's homes five or six times to explain everything to them over and over to get them to have an abortion," says Zhang Cuiqing, the family-planning official for Sihe village, where there are 2,900 married women of childbearing age, of which 2,700 use some sort of birth control. Of those, 570 are sterilized and 1,100 have IUDs. Zhang recites the figures proudly, adding, "If they refuse, they will be fined between 20,000 and 50,000 yuan (U.S. $3,700 to $9,500)." The average yearly wage in Sihe is 1,500 yuan ($285).

50   The lack of early sexual education and unreliable IUDs are combining to make abortion—which is free, as are condoms and IUDs—a cornerstone of the one-child policy. Local officials are told not to use force, but rather education and persuasion, to meet their targets. However, the desire to fulfill their quotas, coupled with pressure from their bosses in Beijing, can lead to abuses by overzealous officials.

"Some local family-planning officials are running amok, because of the targets they have to reach," a Western health specialist says, "and there are a bunch of people willing to turn a blind eye to abuses because the target is so important."

The official *Shanghai Legal Daily* last year reported on a family-planning committee in central Sichuan province that ordered the flogging of the husbands of 10 pregnant women who refused to have abortions. According to the newspaper, the family-planning workers marched the husbands one by one into an empty room, ordered them to strip and lie on the floor and then beat them with a stick, once for every day their wives were pregnant.

"In some places, yes, things do happen," concedes Huang of the State Family Planning Commission. "Sometimes, family-planning officials do carry it too far."

The young woman lies still on the narrow table with her eyes shut and her legs spread while the doctor quickly performs a suction abortion. A few moments, and the fetus is removed. The woman lets out a short, sharp yell. "OK, next," the doctor says.

55 She gets off the table and, holding a piece of cloth between her legs to catch the blood and clutching her swollen womb, hobbles over to a bed and collapses. The next patient gets up and walks toward the abortion table. No one notices a visitor watching. "It's very quick, it only takes about five minutes per abortion," says Dr. Huang Xiaomiao, chief physician at Beijing's Maternity Hospital. "No anesthetic. We don't use anesthetic for abortions or births here. Only for Cesarean sections, we use acupuncture."

Down the hall, 32-year-old Wu Guobin waits to be taken into the operating room to have her Fallopian tubes untied—a reversal of an earlier sterilization. "After my son was killed in an accident last year, the authorities in my province said I could try for another." In the bed next to Wu's, a dour-faced woman looks ready to cry. "She's getting sterilized," the nurse explains. "Her husband doesn't want her to, but her first child has mental problems."

Although it's a maternity hospital, the Family Planning Unit—where abortions, sterilizations, IUD insertions and the like are carried out—is the busiest department. "We do more abortions than births," says Dr. Fan Huimin, head of the unit. "Between 10 and 20 a day."

Abortions are a way of life in China, where about 10.5 million pregnancies are terminated each year. (In the United States, 1.6 million abortions are performed a year, but China's population is four to five times greater than the United States'.) One fetus is aborted for about every two children born and Chinese women often have several abortions. Usually, abortions are performed during the first trimester. But because some women resist, only to cave in under mental bullying further into their terms, abortions are also done in the later months of pregnancy, sometimes up till the eighth month.

Because of their population problem, the Chinese have become pioneers in contraceptive research. China will soon launch its own version of the controversial French abortion pill RU-486, which induces a miscarriage. They have perfected a non-scalpel procedure for male sterilization, with no suture required, allowing the man to "ride his bicycle home within five minutes." This year, the government plans to spend more than the $34 million it spent last year on contraception. The state will also buy some 961 million condoms to be distributed throughout the country, 11% more than in 1991.

60   But even with a family-planning policy that sends a chill down a Westerner's spine and touches every Chinese citizen's life, 64,000 babies are born every day in China and overpopulation continues to be a paramount national problem. Officials have warned that 24 million children will be born in 1992—a number just slightly less than the population of Canada. "The numbers are staggering," says Scruggs, the U.N. Population Fund official, noting that "170 million people will be added in the 1990s, which is the current population of England, France and Italy combined. There are places in China where the land can't feed that many more people as it is."

China estimates that it has prevented 200 million births since the one-child policy was introduced. Women now are having an average of 2.4 children as compared to six in the late '60s. But the individual sacrifice demanded from every Chinese is immense.

Large billboards bombard the population with images of happy families with only one child. The government is desperately trying to convince the masses that producing only one child leads to a wealthier, healthier and happier life. But foreigners in China tell a different story, that the people aren't convinced. They tell of being routinely approached—on the markets, on the streets, on the railway and asked about the contraceptive policies of their countries. Expatriate women in Beijing all tell stories of Chinese women enviously asking them how many sons they have and how many children they plan to have. They explain that they only have one child because the government allows them only one.

"When I'm out with my three children on the weekend," says a young American father who lives in Beijing, "people are always asking me why am I allowed to have three children. You can feel when they ask you that there is envy there. There's a natural disappointment among the people. They just want to have more children. But there's a resigned understanding, an acceptance that they just can't."

ENGAGING the Text

1. How has China's one-child policy affected the ratio of the sexes of children?

2. What cultural values and economic forces are responsible for the preference for boys and correspondingly, what has been the fate of newborn girls?

EVALUATING the Argument

1. How do the examples Deane uses help explain the expectations and hopes that parents have projected onto their "little emperors"?

2. How does Deane use statistics to emphasize the reality of the one-child policy and its impact on the life of the average citizen in China?

EXPLORING the Issue

1. How does the way the "little emperors" have been raised create a potential conflict with the Maoist collective value system that was an essential part of the Cultural Revolution?

2. If you are an only child, to what extent have you been treated similarly to the "little emperors"? If not, do you wish you were? Why or why not?

CONNECTING Different Perspectives

1. In what respects is China's one-child policy similar to Thomas Robert Malthus's argument in "The Principle of Population"?

Martin Luther King Jr.

I Have a Dream

Martin Luther King Jr. (1929–1968), an influential figure in the civil rights movement, was ordained a Baptist minister and founded the Southern Christian Leadership Conference. He received the Nobel Prize for Peace in 1964. His writings include "Letter from Birmingham Jail" (1968). The following selection is the speech King delivered in 1963 to the 250,000 people who had assembled in Washington, D.C., to commemorate the centennial of Lincoln's Emancipation Proclamation.

I am happy to join with you today in what will go down in history as the greatest demonstration for freedom in the history of our nation.

Five score years ago, a great American, in whose symbolic shadow we stand today, signed the Emancipation Proclamation.[1] This momentous decree came as a great beacon light of hope to millions of Negro slaves who had been seared in the flames of withering injustice. It came as a joyous daybreak to end the long night of their captivity. But one hundred years later, the Negro is still not free. One hundred years later, the life of the Negro is still sadly crippled by the manacles of segregation and the chains of discrimination. One hundred years later, the Negro lives on a lonely island of poverty in the

---

[1]The Emancipation Proclamation: the executive order abolishing slavery in the confederacy that President Abraham Lincoln signed on January 1, 1863.

midst of a vast ocean of material prosperity. One hundred years later, the Negro is still anguished in the corners of American society and finds himself in exile in his own land. And so we have come here today to dramatize a shameful condition.

In a sense we have come to our nation's capital to cash a check. When the architects of our republic wrote the magnificent words of the Constitution and the Declaration of Independence, they were signing a promissory note to which every American was to fall heir. This note was the promise that all men—yes, Black men as well as white men—would be guaranteed the inalienable rights of life, liberty, and the pursuit of happiness.

It is obvious today that America has defaulted on this promissory note insofar as her citizens of color are concerned. Instead of honoring this sacred obligation, America has given the Negro people a bad check, a check which has come back marked "insufficient funds." But we refuse to believe that the bank of justice is bankrupt. We refuse to believe that there are insufficient funds in the great vaults of opportunity of this nation; and so we have come to cash this check, a check that will give us upon demand the riches of freedom and the security of justice.

5   We have also come to this hallowed spot to remind America of the fierce urgency of *now*. This is no time to engage in the luxury of cooling off or to take the tranquilizing drug of gradualism. *Now* is the time to make real the promises of democracy. *Now* is the time to rise from the dark and desolate valley of segregation to the sunlit patch of racial justice. *Now* is the time to lift our nation from the quicksands of racial injustice to the solid rock of brotherhood. *Now* is the time to make justice a reality for all of God's children.

It would be fatal for the nation to overlook the urgency of the moment. This sweltering summer of the Negro's legitimate discontent will not pass until there is an invigorating autumn of freedom and equality. Nineteen Sixty-three is not an end, but a beginning. And those who hope that the Negro needed to blow off steam and will now be content will have a rude awakening if the nation returns to business as usual. There will be neither rest nor tranquility in America until the Negro is granted his citizenship rights. The whirlwinds of revolt will continue to shake the foundations of our nation until the bright day of justice emerges.

But there is something that I must say to my people who stand on the warm threshold which leads into the palace of justice. In the process of gaining our rightful place, we must not be guilty of wrongful deeds. Let us not seek to satisfy our thirst for freedom by drinking from the cup of bitterness and hatred. We must forever conduct our struggle on the high plane of dignity and discipline. We must not allow our creative protest to degenerate into physical violence.

Again and again we must rise to the majestic heights of meeting physical force with soul force. And the marvelous new militancy which has engulfed the Negro community must not lead us to a distrust of all white people; for many of our white brothers, as evidenced by their presence here today, have come to realize that their destiny is tied up with our destiny, and they have come to realize that their freedom is inextricably bound to our freedom.

We cannot walk alone. And as we walk we must make the pledge that we shall always march ahead. We cannot turn back. There are those who are asking the devotees of civil rights, "When will you be satisfied?" We can never be satisfied as long as the Negro is the victim of the unspeakable horrors of police brutality. We can never be satisfied as long as our bodies, heavy with the fatigue of travel, cannot gain lodging in the motels of the highways and the hotels of the cities. We cannot be satisfied as long as the Negro's basic mobility is from a smaller ghetto to a larger one. We can never be satisfied as long as our children are stripped of their selfhood and robbed of their dignity by signs stating "For Whites Only." We cannot be satisfied as long as the Negro in Mississippi cannot vote and a Negro in New York believes he has nothing for which to vote. No, no, we are not satisfied, and we will not be satisfied until justice rolls down like waters and righteousness like a mighty stream.

I am not unmindful that some of you have come here out of great trials and tribulations. Some of you have come fresh from narrow jail cells. Some of you have come from areas where your quest for freedom left you battered by the storms of persecution and staggered by the winds of police brutality. You have been the veterans of creative suffering. Continue to work with the faith that unearned suffering is redemptive.

10 Go back to Mississippi, and go back to Alabama. Go back to South Carolina. Go back to Georgia. Go back to Louisiana. Go back to the slums and ghettos of our Northern cities, knowing that somehow this situation can and will be changed. Let us not wallow in the valley of despair.

I say to you today, my friends, even though we face the difficulties of today and tomorrow, I still have a dream. It is a dream deeply rooted in the American dream. I have a dream that one day this nation will rise up and live out the true meaning of its creed: "We hold these truths to be self-evident, that all men are created equal." I have a dream that one day, on the red hills of Georgia, sons of former slaves and the sons of former slave owners will be able to sit down together at the table of brotherhood. I have a dream that one day even the state of Mississippi, a state sweltering with the heat of injustice, sweltering with the heat of oppression, will be transformed into an oasis of freedom and justice. I have a dream that my four little children will one day live in a nation where they will not be judged by the color of their skin, but by the content of their character.

I have a dream today. I have a dream that one day down in Alabama—with its vicious racists, with its governor's lips dripping with the words of interposition and nullification—one day right there in Alabama, little Black boys and Black girls will be able to join hands with little white boys and white girls as sisters and brothers.

I have a dream today. I have a dream that one day every valley shall be exalted and every hill and mountain shall be made low, the rough places will be made plain and the crooked places will be made straight, and the glory of the Lord shall be revealed, and all flesh shall see it together.

This is our hope. This is the faith that I go back to the South with. And with this faith we will be able to hew out of the mountain of despair a stone of hope. With this faith we will be able to transform the jangling discords of our nation into a beautiful symphony of brotherhood. With this faith we will be able to work together, to play together, to struggle together, to go to jail together, to stand up for freedom together, knowing that we will be free one day.

15   And this will be the day—this will be the day when all of God's children will be able to sing with new meaning.

> My country, 'tis of thee,
> Sweet land of liberty,
>   Of thee I sing;
> Land where my fathers died,
> Land of the Pilgrims' pride,
> From every mountainside
>   Let freedom ring.

And if America is to be a great nation, this must become true.

And so let freedom ring from the prodigious hilltops of New Hampshire. Let freedom ring from the mighty mountains of New York. Let freedom ring from the heightening Alleghenies of Pennsylvania. Let freedom ring from the snow-capped Rockies of Colorado. Let freedom ring from the curvaceous slopes of California.

But not only that. Let freedom ring from Stone Mountain of Georgia. Let freedom ring from Lookout Mountain of Tennessee. Let freedom ring from every hill and molehill of Mississippi. "From every mountainside let freedom ring."

And when this happens—when we allow freedom to ring, when we let it ring from every village and every hamlet, from every state and every city—we will be able to speed up that day when all of God's children, Black men and white men, Jews and Gentiles, Protestants and Catholics, will be able to join hands and sing in the words of the old Negro spiritual: "Free at last! Free at last! Thank God Almighty. We are free at last!"

ENGAGING the Text

1. What importance does King place on the idea of nonviolent protest? What injustices have been overcome to reach this historic moment?

2. How do King's references to the Bible and the Emancipation Proclamation enhance the effectiveness of his speech?

EVALUATING the Argument

1. What sustained analogy does King use to make the abstract concepts of freedom and equality more tangible?

2. How does King use parallelism and figurative language to enhance the effectiveness of his speech?

EXPLORING the Issue

1. In a short essay, discuss how the civil rights movement expressed ideas of equality and freedom that are deeply rooted in the Constitution.

2. As a research project, trace the rationale for nonviolent protest back to its roots in the works of Thoreau and Gandhi. How did King adapt this principle to meet the challenges faced by the civil rights movement in the 1960s?

CONNECTING Different Perspectives

1. How does Kenneth M. Stampp's analysis in "To Make Them Stand in Fear" (in Chapter 4) deepen your understanding of the underlying racial crisis from its earliest days until King's speech in 1963?

Psychology

Stanley Milgram

The Perils of Obedience

Stanley Milgram (1933–1984) was born in New York, holds a Ph.D. from Harvard, and taught at Yale, Harvard, and the City University of New York. His research into human conformity and aggression, the results of which were published in 1974 in Obedience to Authority *(from which the following selection was drawn), began a national debate. His thesis cast new light on the Holocaust. He has also written* Psychology in Today's World *(1975) and* The Individual in a Social World: Essays and Experiments *(1977).*

Obedience is as basic an element in the structure of social life as one can point to. Some system of authority is a requirement of all communal living, and it is only the person dwelling in isolation who is not forced to respond, with defiance or submission, to the commands of others. For many people, obedience is a deeply ingrained behavior tendency, indeed a potent impulse overriding training in ethics, sympathy, and moral conduct.

The dilemma inherent in submission to authority is ancient, as old as the story of Abraham, and the question of whether one should obey when commands conflict with conscience has been argued by Plato, dramatized in *Antigone,* and treated to philosophic analysis in almost every historical epoch.[1] Conservative philosophers argue that the very fabric of society is threatened by disobedience, while humanists stress the primacy of the individual conscience.

The legal and philosophic aspects of obedience are of enormous import, but they say very little about how most people behave in concrete situations. I set up a simple experiment at Yale University to test how much pain an ordinary citizen would inflict on another person simply because he was ordered to by an experimental scientist. Stark authority was pitted against the subjects' strongest moral imperatives against hurting others, and, with the subjects' ears ringing with the screams of the victims, authority won more often than not. The extreme willingness of adults to go to almost any lengths on the command of an authority constitutes the chief finding of the study and the fact most urgently demanding explanation.

In the basic experimental design, two people come to a psychology laboratory to take part in a study of memory and learning. One of them is designated as a "teacher" and the other a "learner." The experimenter explains that the study is concerned with the effects of punishment on learning. The learner is conducted into a room, seated in a kind of miniature electric chair; his arms are strapped to prevent excessive movement, and an electrode is attached to his wrist. He is told that he will be read lists of simple word pairs, and that he will then be tested on his ability to remember the second word of a pair when he hears the first one again. Whenever he makes an error, he will receive electric shocks of increasing intensity.

---

[1]*Antigone:* a play by Sophocles that depicts the confrontation between an individual and the state in the person of Creon.

5   The real focus of the experiment is the teacher. After watching the learner being strapped into place, he is seated before an impressive shock generator. The instrument panel consists of thirty lever switches set in a horizontal line. Each switch is clearly labeled with a voltage designation ranging from 15 to 450 volts. The following designations are clearly indicated for groups of four switches, going from left to right: Slight Shock, Moderate Shock, Strong Shock, Very Strong Shock, Intense Shock, Extreme Intensity Shock, Danger: Severe Shock. (Two switches after this last designation are simply marked XXX.)

When a switch is depressed, a pilot light corresponding to each switch is illuminated in bright red; an electric buzzing is heard; a blue light, labeled "voltage energizer," flashes; the dial on the voltage meter swings to the right; and various relay clicks sound off.

The upper left-hand corner of the generator is labeled SHOCK GENER-ATOR, TYPE ZLB, DYSON INSTRUMENT COMPANY, WALTHAM, MASS. OUTPUT 15 VOLTS–450 VOLTS.

Each subject is given a sample 45-volt shock from the generator before his run as teacher, and the jolt strengthens his belief in the authenticity of the machine.

The teacher is a genuinely naïve subject who has come to the laboratory for the experiment. The learner, or victim, is actually an actor who receives no shock at all. The point of the experiment is to see how far a person will proceed in a concrete and measurable situation in which he is ordered to inflict increasing pain on a protesting victim.

10   Conflict arises when the man receiving the shock begins to show that he is experiencing discomfort. At 75 volts, he grunts; at 120 volts, he complains loudly; at 150, he demands to be released from the experiment. As the voltage increases, his protests become more vehement and emotional. At 285 volts, his response can be described only as an agonized scream. Soon thereafter, he makes no sound at all.

For the teacher, the situation quickly becomes one of gripping tension. It is not a game for him; conflict is intense and obvious. The manifest suffering of the learner presses him to quit; but each time he hesitates to administer a shock, the experimenter orders him to continue. To extricate himself from this plight, the subject must make a clear break with authority.

The subject, Gretchen Brandt, is an attractive thirty-one-year-old medical technician who works at the Yale Medical School. She had emigrated from Germany five years before.[2]

---

[2]Names of subjects described in this piece have been changed.

On several occasions when the learner complains, she [Gretchen] turns to the experimenter coolly and inquires, "Shall I continue?" She promptly returns to her task when the experimenter asks her to do so. At the administration of 210 volts, she turns to the experimenter, remarking firmly, "Well, I'm sorry, I don't think we should continue."

EXPERIMENTER: The experiment requires that you go on until he has learned all the word pairs correctly.

BRANDT: He has a heart condition, I'm sorry. He told you that before.

EXPERIMENTER: The shocks may be painful but they are not dangerous.

BRANDT: Well, I'm sorry, I think when shocks continue like this, they *are* dangerous. You ask him if he wants to get out. It's his free will.

EXPERIMENTER: It is absolutely essential that we continue. . . .

BRANDT: I'd like you to ask him. We came here of our free will. If he wants to continue I'll go ahead. He told you he had a heart condition. I'm sorry. I don't want to be responsible for anything happening to him. I wouldn't like it for me either.

EXPERIMENTER: You have no other choice.

BRANDT: I think we are here on our own free will. I don't want to be responsible if anything happens to him. Please understand that.

She refuses to go further and the experiment is terminated.

15   The woman is firm and resolute throughout. She indicates in the interview that she was in no way tense or nervous, and this corresponds to her controlled appearance during the experiment. She feels that the last shock she administered to the learner was extremely painful and reiterates that she "did not want to be responsible for any harm to him."

The woman's straightforward, courteous behavior in the experiment, lack of tension, and total control of her own action seem to make disobedience a simple and rational deed. Her behavior is the very embodiment of what I envisioned would be true for almost all subjects.

An Unexpected Outcome

Before the experiments, I sought predictions about the outcome from various kinds of people—psychiatrists, college sophomores, middle-class adults, graduate students and faculty in the behavioral sciences. With remarkable similarity, they predicted that virtually all subjects would refuse to obey the experimenter. The psychiatrists, specifically, predicted that most subjects would not go beyond 150 volts, when the victim makes his first explicit demand to be freed. They expected that only 4 percent would reach 300 volts, and that only a pathological fringe of about one in a thousand would administer the highest shock on the board.

These predictions were unequivocally wrong. Of the forty subjects in the first experiment, twenty-five obeyed the orders of the experimenter to the end, punishing the victim until they reached the most potent shock available on the generator. After 450 volts were administered three times, the experimenter called a halt to the session. Many obedient subjects then heaved sighs of relief, mopped their brows, rubbed their fingers over their eyes, or nervously fumbled cigarettes. Others displayed only minimal signs of tension from beginning to end.

When the very first experiments were carried out, Yale undergraduates were used as subjects, and about 60 percent of them were fully obedient. A colleague of mine immediately dismissed these findings as having no relevance to "ordinary" people, asserting that Yale undergraduates are a highly aggressive, competitive bunch who step on each other's necks on the slightest provocation. He assured me that when "ordinary" people were tested, the results would be quite different. As we moved from the pilot studies to the regular experimental series, people drawn from every stratum of New Haven life came to be employed in the experiment: professionals, white-collar workers, unemployed persons, and industrial workers. *The experiment's total outcome was the same as we had observed among the students.*

20   Moreover, when the experiments were repeated in Princeton, Munich, Rome, South Africa, and Australia, the level of obedience was invariably somewhat *higher* than found in the investigation reported in this article. Thus one scientist in Munich found 85 percent of his subjects obedient.

Fred Prozi's reactions, if more dramatic than most, illuminate the conflicts experienced by others in less visible form. About fifty years old and unemployed at the time of the experiment, he has a good-natured, if slightly dissolute, appearance, and he strikes people as a rather ordinary fellow. He begins the session calmly but becomes tense as it proceeds. After delivering the 180-volt shock, he pivots around in his chair and, shaking his head, addresses the experimenter in agitated tones:

PROZI: I can't stand it. I'm not going to kill that man in there. You hear him hollering?

EXPERIMENTER: As I told you before, the shocks may be painful, but . . .

PROZI: But he's hollering. He can't stand it. What's going to happen to him?

EXPERIMENTER (his voice is patient, matter-of-fact): The experiment requires that you continue, Teacher.

PROZI: Aaah, but, unh, I'm not going to get that man sick in there—know what I mean?

EXPERIMENTER: Whether the learner likes it or not, we must go on, through all the word pairs.

PROZI: I refuse to take the responsibility. He's in there hollering!

EXPERIMENTER: It's absolutely essential that you continue, Prozi.

PROZI: (indicating the unused questions): There's too many left here, I mean, Jeez, if he gets them wrong, there's too many of them left. I mean, who's going to take the responsibility if anything happens to that gentleman?

EXPERIMENTER: I'm responsible for anything that happens to him. Continue, please.

PROZI: All right. (Consults list of words.) The next one's "Slow—walk, truck, dance, music." Answer, please. (A buzzing sound indicates the learner has signaled his answer.) Wrong. A hundred and ninety-five volts. "Dance." (Zzumph!)

LEARNER (yelling): Let me out of here! My heart's bothering me! (Teacher looks at experimenter.)

EXPERIMENTER: Continue, please.

LEARNER (screaming): Let me out of here! You have no right to keep me here! Let me out of here, my heart's bothering me, let me out!

PROZI (shakes head, pats the table nervously): You see, he's hollering. Hear that? Gee, I don't know.

EXPERIMENTER: The experiment requires . . .

PROZI (interrupting): I know it does, sir, but I mean—hunh! He don't know what he's getting in for. He's up to 195 volts! (Experiment continues, through 210 volts, 225 volts, 240 volts, 255 volts, 270 volts, at which point Prozi, with evident relief, runs out of word-pair questions.)

EXPERIMENTER: You'll have to go back to the beginning of that page and go through them again until he's learned them all correctly.

PROZI: Aw, no. I'm not going to kill that man. You mean I've got to keep going up with the scale? No sir. He's hollering in there. I'm not going to give him 450 volts.

EXPERIMENTER: The experiment requires that you go on.

LEARNER: Ohhh. I absolutely refuse to answer anymore. (Shouting urgently now.) Let me out of here! You can't hold me here! Get me out. Get-me-out-of-here!

EXPERIMENTER: Continue. The next word is "Green," please.

PROZI: "Green—grass, hat, ink, apple." (Nothing happens. No answering buzz. Just gloomy silence.)

PROZI: I don't think he is going to answer.

EXPERIMENTER: If the learner doesn't answer in a reasonable time, about four or five seconds, consider the answer wrong. And follow the same procedures you have been doing for wrong answers. Say, "Wrong," tell him the number of volts, give him the punishment, read him the correct answer. Continue, please.

PROZI: "Green—grass, hat, ink, apple." Answer, please. (More silence. Subject just sits there.)

EXPERIMENTER: Go on with the procedure, please.

PROZI: Three hundred and fifteen volts. The answer is "ink." (Zzumph!)

LEARNER: Ohh. Ooohh.

PROZI (relieved to hear response): Next one . . .

LEARNER: I absolutely refuse to answer.

PROZI: You got to. You get a shock if you don't answer. (Experiment continues with learner refusing to answer, and, finally, failing even to grunt or groan. At 375 volts, the subject stands up.)

PROZI: I think something's happened to that fellow in there. I don't get no answer. He was hollering at less voltage. Can't you check in and see if he's all right, please?

EXPERIMENTER (with same detached calm): Not once we've started. Please continue, Teacher.

PROZI (sits down, sighs deeply): "Cool—day, shade, water, paint." Answer, please. Are you all right in there? Are you all right?

EXPERIMENTER: Please continue, Teacher. Continue, please. (Subject pushes lever. Zzumph!)

PROZI (swiveling around in his chair): Something's happened to that man in there. (Swiveling back.) Next one. "Low—dollar, necklace, moon, paint." (Turning around again.) Something's happened to that man in there. You better check in on him, sir. He won't answer or nothing.

EXPERIMENTER: Continue. Go on, please.

PROZI: You accept all responsibility?

EXPERIMENTER: The responsibility is mine. Correct. Please go on. (Subject returns to his list, starts running through words as rapidly as he can read them, works through to 450 volts.)

PROZI: That's that.

EXPERIMENTER: Continue using the 450 switch for each wrong answer. Continue, please.

PROZI: But I don't get anything!

EXPERIMENTER: Please continue. The next word is "white."

PROZI: Don't you think you should look in on him, please?

EXPERIMENTER: Not once we've started the experiment.

PROZI: What if he's dead in there? (Gestures toward the room with the electric chair.) I mean, he told me he can't stand the shock, sir. I don't mean to be rude, but I think you should look in on him. All you have to do is look in on him. All you have to do is look in the door. I don't get no answer, no noise. Something might have happened to the gentleman in there, sir.

EXPERIMENTER: We must continue. Go on, please.

PROZI: You mean keep giving him what? Four-hundred-fifty volts, what he's got now?

EXPERIMENTER: That's correct. Continue. The next word is "white."

PROZI (now at a furious pace): "White—cloud, horse, rock, house." Answer, please. The answer is "horse." Four hundred and fifty volts. (Zzumph!) Next word, "Bag—paint, music, clown, girl." The answer is "paint." Four hundred and fifty volts. (Zzumph!) Next word is "Short—sentence, movie . . ."

EXPERIMENTER: Excuse me, Teacher. We'll have to discontinue the experiment.

Peculiar Reactions

Morris Braverman, another subject, is a thirty-nine-year-old social worker. He looks older than his years because of his bald head and serious demeanor. His brow is furrowed, as if all the world's burdens were carried on his face. He appears intelligent and concerned.

When the learner refuses to answer and the experimenter instructs Braverman to treat the absence of an answer as equivalent to a wrong answer, he takes his instruction to heart. Before administering 300 volts he asserts officiously to the victim, "Mr. Wallace, your silence has to be considered as a wrong answer." Then he administers the shock. He offers half-heartedly to change places with the learner, then asks the experimenter. "Do I have to follow these instructions literally?" He is satisfied with the experimenter's answer that he does. His very refined and authoritative manner of speaking is increasingly broken up by wheezing laughter.

The experimenter's notes on Mr. Braverman at the last few shocks are:

- Almost breaking up now each time gives shock. Rubbing face to hide laughter.

- Squinting, trying to hide face with hand, still laughing.

- Cannot control his laughter at this point no matter what he does.

- Clenching fist, pushing it onto table.

25   In an interview after the session, Mr. Braverman summarizes the experiment with impressive fluency and intelligence. He feels the experiment may have been designed also to "test the effects on the teacher of being in an essentially sadistic role, as well as the reactions of a student to a learning situation that was authoritative and punitive." When asked how painful the last few shocks administered to the learner were, he indicates that the most extreme category on the scale is

not adequate (it read EXTREMELY PAINFUL) and places his mark at the edge of the scale with an arrow carrying it beyond the scale.

It is almost impossible to convey the greatly relaxed, sedate quality of his conversation in the interview. In the most relaxed terms, he speaks about his severe inner tension.

EXPERIMENTER: At what point were you most tense or nervous?

MR. BRAVERMAN: Well, when he first began to cry out in pain, and I realized this was hurting him. This got worse when he just blocked and refused to answer. There was I. I'm a nice person, I think, hurting somebody, and caught up in what seemed a mad situation . . . and in the interest of science, one goes through with it.

When the interviewer pursues the general question of tension, Mr. Braverman spontaneously mentions his laughter.

"My reactions were awfully peculiar. I don't know if you were watching me, but my reactions were giggly, and trying to stifle laughter. This isn't the way I usually am. This was a sheer reaction to a totally impossible situation. And my reaction was to the situation of having to hurt somebody. And being totally helpless and caught up in a set of circumstances where I just couldn't deviate and I couldn't try to help. This is what got me."

Mr. Braverman, like all subjects, was told the actual nature and purpose of the experiment, and a year later he affirmed in a questionnaire that he had learned something of personal importance: "What appalled me was that I could possess this capacity for obedience and compliance to a central idea, i.e., the value of a memory experiment, even after it became clear that continued adherence to this value was at the expense of violation of another value, i.e., don't hurt someone who is helpless and not hurting you. As my wife said, 'You can call yourself Eichmann.' I hope I deal more effectively with any future conflicts of values I encounter."

The Etiquette of Submission

30 One theoretical interpretation of this behavior holds that all people harbor deeply aggressive instincts continually pressing for expression, and that the experiment provides institutional justification for the release of these impulses. According to this view, if a person is placed in a situation in which he has complete power over another individual, whom he may punish as much as he likes, all that is sadistic and bestial in man comes to the fore. The impulse to shock the victim is seen to flow from the potent aggressive tendencies, which are part of the motivational life of the individual, and the experiment, because it provides social legitimacy, simply opens the door to their expression.

It becomes vital, therefore, to compare the subject's performance when he is under orders and when he is allowed to choose the shock level.

The procedure was identical to our standard experiment, except that the teacher was told that he was free to select any shock level on any of the trials. (The experimenter took pains to point out that the teacher could use the highest levels on the generator, the lowest, any in between, or any combination of levels.) Each subject proceeded for thirty critical trials. The learner's protests were coordinated to standard shock levels, his first grunt coming at 75 volts, his first vehement protest at 150 volts.

The average shock used during the thirty critical trials was less than 60 volts—lower than the point at which the victim showed the first signs of discomfort. Three of the forty subjects did not go beyond the very lowest level on the board, twenty-eight went no higher than 75 volts, and thirty-eight did not go beyond the first loud protest at 150 volts. Two subjects provided the exception, administering up to 325 and 450 volts, but the overall result was that the great majority of people delivered very low, usually painless, shocks when the choice was explicitly up to them.

This condition of the experiment undermines another commonly offered explanation of the subjects' behavior—that those who shocked the victim at the most severe levels came only from the sadistic fringe of society. If one considers that almost two-thirds of the participants fall into the category of "obedient" subjects, and that they represented ordinary people drawn from working, managerial, and professional classes, the argument becomes very shaky. Indeed, it is highly reminiscent of the issue that arose in connection with Hannah Arendt's 1963 book, *Eichmann in Jerusalem*. Arendt contended that the prosecution's effort to depict Eichmann as a sadistic monster was fundamentally wrong, that he came closer to being an uninspired bureaucrat who simply sat at his desk and did his job. For asserting her views, Arendt became the object of considerable scorn, even calumny. Somehow, it was felt that the monstrous deeds carried out by Eichmann required a brutal, twisted personality, evil incarnate. After witnessing hundreds of ordinary persons submit to the authority in our own experiments, I must conclude that Arendt's conception of the banality of evil comes closer to the truth than one might dare imagine. The ordinary person who shocked the victim did so out of a sense of obligation—an impression of his duties as a subject—and not from any peculiarly aggressive tendencies.

35   This is, perhaps, the most fundamental lesson of our study: ordinary people, simply doing their jobs, and without any particular hostility on their part, can become agents in a terrible destructive process. Moreover, even when the destructive effects of their work become patently clear, and they are asked to

carry out actions incompatible with fundamental standards of morality, relatively few people have the resources needed to resist authority.

Many of the people were in some sense against what they did to the learner, and many protested even while they obeyed. Some were totally convinced of the wrongness of their actions but could not bring themselves to make an open break with authority. They often derived satisfaction from their thoughts and felt that—within themselves, at least—they had been on the side of the angels. They tried to reduce strain by obeying the experimenter but "only slightly," encouraging the learner, touching the generator switches gingerly. When interviewed, such a subject would stress that he had "asserted my humanity" by administering the briefest shock possible. Handling the conflict in this manner was easier than defiance.

The situation is constructed so that there is no way the subject can stop shocking the learner without violating the experimenter's definitions of his own competence. The subject fears that he will appear arrogant, untoward, and rude if he breaks off. Although these inhibiting emotions appear small in scope alongside the violence being done to the learner, they suffuse the mind and feelings of the subject, who is miserable at the prospect of having to repudiate the authority to his face. (When the experiment was altered so that the experimenter gave his instructions by telephone instead of in person, only a third as many people were fully obedient through 450 volts.) It is a curious thing that a measure of compassion on the part of the subject—an unwillingness to "hurt" the experimenter's feelings—is part of those binding forces inhibiting his disobedience. The withdrawal of such deference may be as painful to the subject as to the authority he defies.

Duty Without Conflict

The subjects do not derive satisfaction from inflicting pain, but they often like the feeling they get from pleasing the experimenter. They are proud of doing a good job, obeying the experimenter under difficult circumstances. While the subjects administered only mild shocks on their own initiative, one experimental variation showed that, under orders, 30 percent of them were willing to deliver 450 volts even when they had to forcibly push the learner's hand down on the electrode.

Bruno Batta is a thirty-seven-year-old welder who took part in the variation requiring the use of force. He was born in New Haven, his parents in Italy. He has a rough-hewn face that conveys a conspicuous lack of alertness. He has some difficulty in mastering the experimental procedure and needs to be corrected by the experimenter several times. He shows appreciation for the help and willingness to do what is required. After the 150-volt level, Batta has to force the learner's hand down on the shock plate, since the learner himself refuses to touch it.

40   When the learner first complains, Mr. Batta pays no attention to him. His face remains impassive, as if to dissociate himself from the learner's disruptive behavior. When the experimenter instructs him to force the learner's hand down, he adopts a rigid, mechanical procedure. He tests the generator switch. When it fails to function, he immediately forces the learner's hand onto the shock plate. All the while he maintains the same rigid mask. The learner, seated alongside him, begs him to stop, but with robotic impassivity he continues the procedure.

What is extraordinary is his apparent total indifference to the learner; he hardly takes cognizance of him as a human being. Meanwhile, he relates to the experimenter in a submissive and courteous fashion.

At the 330-volt level, the learner refuses not only to touch the shock plate but also to provide any answers. Annoyed, Batta turns to him, and chastises him: "You better answer and get it over with. We can't stay here all night." These are the only words he directs to the learner in the course of an hour. Never again does he speak to him. The scene is brutal and depressing, his hard, impassive face showing total indifference as he subdues the screaming learner and gives him shocks. He seems to derive no pleasure from the act itself, only quiet satisfaction at doing his job properly.

When he administers 450 volts, he turns to the experimenter and asks, "Where do we go from here, Professor?" His tone is deferential and expresses his willingness to be a cooperative subject, in contrast to the learner's obstinacy.

At the end of the session he tells the experimenter how honored he has been to help him, and in a moment of contrition, remarks, "Sir, sorry it couldn't have been a full experiment."

45   He has done his honest best. It is only the deficient behavior of the learner that has denied the experimenter full satisfaction.

The essence of obedience is that a person comes to view himself as the instrument for carrying out another person's wishes, and he therefore no longer regards himself as responsible for his actions. Once this critical shift of viewpoint has occurred, all of the essential features of obedience follow. The most far-reaching consequence is that the person feels responsible *to* the authority directing him but feels no responsibility *for* the content of the actions that the authority prescribes. Morality does not disappear—it acquires a radically different focus: the subordinate person feels shame or pride depending on how adequately he has performed the actions called for by authority.

Language provides numerous terms to pinpoint this type of morality: *loyalty, duty, discipline* all are terms heavily saturated with moral meaning and refer to the degree to which a person fulfills his obligations to authority. They refer not to the "goodness" of the person per se but to the adequacy with which a subordinate fulfills his socially defined role. The most frequent defense of the individual who has performed a heinous act under command of authority is that he has simply done his duty. In asserting this defense, the individual is not introducing an alibi concocted for the moment but is reporting honestly on the psychological attitude induced by submission to authority.

For a person to feel responsible for his actions, he must sense that the behavior has flowed from "the self." In the situation we have studied, subjects have precisely the opposite view of their actions—namely, they see them as originating in the motives of some other person. Subjects in the experiment frequently said, "If it were up to me, I would not have administered shocks to the learner."

Once authority has been isolated as the cause of the subject's behavior, it is legitimate to inquire into the necessary elements of authority and how it must be perceived in order to gain his compliance. We conducted some investigations into the kinds of changes that would cause the experimenter to lose his power and to be disobeyed by the subject. Some of the variations revealed that:

- *The experimenter's physical presence has a marked impact on his authority.* As cited earlier, obedience dropped off sharply when orders were given by telephone. The experimenter could often induce a disobedient subject to go on by returning to the laboratory.

- *Conflicting authority severely paralyzes action.* When two experimenters of equal status, both seated at the command desk, gave incompatible orders, no shocks were delivered past the point of their disagreement.

- *The rebellious action of others severely undermines authority.* In one variation, three teachers (two actors and a real subject) administered a test and shocks. When the two actors disobeyed the experimenter and refused to go beyond a certain shock level, thirty-six of forty subjects joined their disobedient peers and refused as well.

50   Although the experimenter's authority was fragile in some respects, it is also true that he had almost none of the tools used in ordinary command structures. For example, the experimenter did not threaten the subjects with punishment— such as loss of income, community ostracism, or jail—for failure to obey. Neither could he offer incentives. Indeed, we should expect the experimenter's authority to be much less than that of someone like a general, since the experimenter has no power to enforce his imperatives, and since participation in a psychological experiment scarcely evokes the sense of urgency and dedication found in warfare. Despite these limitations, he still managed to command a dismaying degree of obedience.

I will cite one final variation of the experiment that depicts a dilemma that is more common in everyday life. The subject was not ordered to pull the lever that shocked the victim, but merely to perform a subsidiary task (administering the word-pair test) while another person administered the shock. In this situation, thirty-seven of forty adults continued to the highest level on the shock generator. Predictably, they excused their behavior by saying that the responsibility belonged to the man who actually pulled the switch. This may illustrate a dangerously typical arrangement in a complex society: it is easy to ignore responsibility when one is only an intermediate link in a chain of action.

The problem of obedience is not wholly psychological. The form and shape of society and the way it is developing have much to do with it. There was a time, perhaps, when people were able to give a fully human response to any situation because they were fully absorbed in it as human beings. But as soon as there was a division of labor things changed. Beyond a certain point, the breaking up of society into people carrying out narrow and very special jobs takes away from the human quality of work and life. A person does not get to see the whole situation but only a small part of it, and is thus unable to act without some kind of overall direction. He yields to authority but in doing so is alienated from his own actions.

Even Eichmann was sickened when he toured the concentration camps, but he had only to sit at a desk and shuffle papers. At the same time the man in the camp who actually dropped Cyclon-b into the gas chambers was able to justify *his* behavior on the ground that he was only following orders from above. Thus there is a fragmentation of the total human act; no one is confronted with the consequences of his decision to carry out the evil act. The person who assumes responsibility has evaporated. Perhaps this is the most common characteristic of socially organized evil in modern society.

ENGAGING the Text

1. How is Milgram's experiment designed to test whether obedience to authority would override a presumed sense of right and wrong and the basic quality of compassion toward others?

2. How does the meaning of terms like loyalty, duty, and discipline come to be defined by how well the subjects perform the assigned task rather than their asking whether the task itself is good or bad?

EVALUATING the Argument

1. How does Milgram's inclusion of the full transcript rather than a summary of Mr. Prozi's experience enable the reader to have a better understanding of why the subjects acted as they did?

2. How does the last paragraph make it clear that Milgram has created this experiment in part to answer the question as to how the Holocaust could have happened?

EXPLORING the Issue

1. Did you ever have an experience where you were required by an authority figure to perform an action that you felt was wrong, but in a situation where it would have been very hard to refuse? How did you react? What insight did Milgram's study give you into what transpired?

2. This classic experiment has never been duplicated because Milgram was criticized for conducting a study that deceived the subjects. Try to design your own experiment that would measure the same phenomenon, but would not deceive the subjects.

CONNECTING Different Perspectives

1. Compare the design of Milgram's experiment with that of Philip G. Zimbardo's in "The Stanford Prison Experiment." In what respects are they similar and different? In your opinion, whose results seem more persuasive in determining under what conditions people will obey authority figures?

Philip G. Zimbardo

The Stanford Prison Experiment

Philip G. Zimbardo is a professor of psychology at Stanford University and is the author or editor of many definitive works, including Psychology and Life, *with Richard J. Gerrig (17th ed., 2005) and* Psychology: Core Concepts, *with Robert L. Johnson and Ann L. Weber (5th ed., 2006). The following essay originally appeared under the title "The Mind Is a Formidable Jailor" in the* New York Times Magazine *(April 8, 1973). In it, Zimbardo describes an experiment he created to test how much individuals would identify with their roles as either prisoner or guard.*

> *In prison, those things withheld from and denied to the prisoner become precisely what he wants most of all.*
>
> —Eldridge Cleaver, "Soul on Ice"

> *Our sense of power is more vivid when we break a man's spirit than when we win his heart.*
>
> —Eric Hoffer, "The Passionate State of Mind"

Every prison that men build / Is built with bricks of shame, / And bound with bars lest Christ should see / How men their brothers maim.
> —Oscar Wilde, "The Ballad of Reading Gaol"

Wherever anyone is against his will that is to him a prison.
> —Epictetus, "Discourses"

The quiet of a summer morning in Palo Alto, Calif., was shattered by a screeching squad car siren as police swept through the city picking up college students in a surprise mass arrest. Each suspect was charged with a felony, warned of his constitutional rights, spread-eagled against the car, searched, handcuffed, and carted off in the back seat of the squad car to the police station for booking.

After fingerprinting and the preparation of identification forms for his "jacket" (central information file), each prisoner was left isolated in a detention cell to wonder what he had done to get himself into this mess. After a while, he was blindfolded and transported to the "Stanford County Prison." Here he began the process of becoming a prisoner—stripped naked, skin-searched, deloused, and issued a uniform, bedding, soup, and towel.

The warden offered an impromptu welcome:

As you probably know, I'm your warden. All of you have shown that you are unable to function outside in the real world for one reason or another— that somehow you lack the responsibility of good citizens of this great country. We of this prison, your correctional staff, are going to help you learn what your responsibilities as citizens of this country are. Here are the rules. Sometime in the near future there will be a copy of the rules posted in each of the cells. We expect you to know them and to be able to recite them by number. If you follow all of these rules and keep your hands clean, repent for your misdeeds, and show a proper attitude of penitence, you and I will get along just fine."

5   There followed a reading of the 16 basic rules of prisoner conduct, "Rule Number One: Prisoners must remain silent during rest periods, after lights are out, during meals, and whenever they are outside the prison yard. Two: Prisoners must eat at mealtimes and only at mealtimes. Three: Prisoners must not move, tamper, deface, or damage walls, ceilings, windows, doors, or other prison property. . . . Seven: Prisoners must address each other by their ID number only. Eight: Prisoners must address the guards as 'Mr. Correctional Officer.'. . . Sixteen: Failure to obey any of the above rules may result in punishment."

By late afternoon these youthful "first offenders" sat in dazed silence on the cots in their barren cells trying to make sense of the events that had transformed their lives so dramatically.

If the police arrests and processing were executed with customary detachment, however, there were some things that didn't fit. For these men were now part of a very unusual kind of prison, an experimental mock prison, created by social psychologists to study the effects of imprisonment upon volunteer research subjects. When we planned our two-week-long simulation of prison life, we sought to understand more about the process by which people called "prisoners" lose their liberty, civil rights, independence, and privacy, while those called "guards" gain social power by accepting the responsibility for controlling and managing the lives of their dependent charges.

Why didn't we pursue this research in a real prison? First, prison systems are fortresses of secrecy, closed to impartial observation, and thereby immune to critical analysis from anyone not already part of the correctional authority. Second, in any real prison, it is impossible to separate what each individual brings into the prison from what the prison brings out in each person.

We populated our mock prison with a homogeneous group of people who could be considered "normal-average" on the basis of clinical interviews and personality tests. Our participants (10 prisoners and 11 guards) were selected from more than 75 volunteers recruited through ads in the city and campus newspapers. The applicants were mostly college students from all over the United States and Canada who happened to be in the Stanford area during the summer and were attracted by the lure of earning $15 a day for participating in a study of prison life. We selected only those judged to be emotionally stable, physically healthy, mature, law-abiding citizens.

10   The sample of average, middle-class, Caucasian, college-age males (plus one Oriental student) was arbitrarily divided by the flip of a coin. Half were randomly assigned to play the role of guards, the others of prisoners. There were no measurable differences between the guards and the prisoners at the start of the experiment. Although initially warned that as prisoners their privacy and other civil rights would be violated and that they might be subjected to harassment, every subject was completely confident of his ability to endure whatever the prison had to offer for the full two-week experimental period. Each subject unhesitatingly agreed to give his "informed consent" to participate.

The prison was constructed in the basement of Stanford University's psychology building, which was deserted after the end of the summer-school session. A long corridor was converted into the prison "yard" by partitioning off both ends. Three small laboratory rooms opening onto this corridor were made into cells by installing metal barred doors and replacing existing furniture with cots, three to a cell. Adjacent offices were refurnished as guards' quarters, interview-testing rooms, and bedrooms for the "warden" (Jaffe) and the "superintendent" (Zimbardo). A concealed video camera and hidden microphones recorded much of the activity and conversation of guards and prisoners. The physical environment was one in which prisoners could always be observed by the staff, the only exception being when they were secluded in solitary confinement (a small, dark storage closet, labeled "The Hole").

Our mock prison represented an attempt to simulate the psychological state of imprisonment in certain ways. We based our experiment on an in-depth analysis of the prison situation, developed after hundreds of hours of discussion with Carlo Prescott (our ex-con consultant), parole officers, and correctional personnel, and after reviewing much of the existing literature on prisons and concentration camps.

"Real" prisoners typically report feeling powerless, arbitrarily controlled, dependent, frustrated, hopeless, anonymous, dehumanized, and emasculated. It was not possible, pragmatically or ethically, to create such chronic states in volunteer subjects who realize that they are in an experiment for only a short time. Racism, physical brutality, indefinite confinement, and enforced homosexuality were not features of our mock prison. But we did try to reproduce those elements of the prison experience that seemed most fundamental.

We promoted anonymity by seeking to minimize each prisoner's sense of uniqueness and prior identity. The prisoners wore smocks and nylon stocking caps; they had to use their ID numbers; their personal effects were removed and they were housed in barren cells. All of this made them appear similar to each other and indistinguishable to observers. Their smocks, which were like dresses, were worn without undergarments, causing the prisoners to be restrained in their physical actions and to move in ways that were more feminine than masculine. The prisoners were forced to obtain permission from the guard for routine and simple activities such as writing letters, smoking a cigarette, or even going to the toilet; this elicited from them a childlike dependency.

15 Their quarters, though clean and neat, were small, stark, and without esthetic appeal. The lack of windows resulted in poor air circulation, and persistent odors arose from the unwashed bodies of the prisoners. After 10 p.m. lockup, toilet privileges were denied, so prisoners who had to relieve themselves would have to urinate and defecate in buckets provided by the guards. Sometimes the guards refused permission to have them cleaned out, and this made the prison smell.

Above all, "real" prisons are machines for playing tricks with the human conception of time. In our windowless prison, the prisoners often did not even know whether it was day or night. A few hours after falling asleep, they were roused by shrill whistles for their "count." The ostensible purpose of the count was to provide a public test of the prisoners' knowledge of the rules and of their ID numbers. But more important, the count, which occurred at least once on each of the three different guard shifts, provided a regular occasion for the guards to relate to the prisoners. Over the course of the study, the duration of the counts was spontaneously increased by the guards from their initial perfunctory 10 minutes to a seemingly interminable several hours. During these confrontations, guards who were bored could find ways to amuse themselves, ridiculing recalcitrant prisoners, enforcing arbitrary rules, and openly exaggerating any dissension among the prisoners.

The guards were also "deindividualized": They wore identical khaki uniforms and silver reflector sunglasses that made eye contact with them impossible. Their symbols of power were billy clubs, whistles, handcuffs, and the keys to the cells and the "main gate." Although our guards received no formal training from us in how to be guards, for the most part they moved with apparent ease into their roles. The media had already provided them with ample models of prison guards to emulate.

Because we were as interested in the guards' behavior as in the prisoners', they were given considerable latitude to improvise and to develop strategies and tactics of prisoner management. Our guards were told that they must maintain "law and order" in this prison, that they were responsible for handling any trouble that might break out, and they were cautioned about the seriousness and potential dangers of the situation they were about to enter. Surprisingly, in most prison systems, "real" guards are not given much more psychological preparation or adequate training than this for what is one of the most complex, demanding, and dangerous jobs our society has to offer. They are expected to learn how to adjust to their new employment mostly from on-the-job experience, and from contacts with the "old bulls" during a survival-of-the-fittest orientation period. According to an orientation manual for correctional officers at San Quentin, "the only way you really get to know San Quentin is through experience and time. Some of us take more time and must go through more experiences than others to accomplish this; some really never do get there."

You cannot be a prisoner if no one will be your guard, and you cannot be a prison guard if no one takes you or your prison seriously. Therefore, over time a perverted symbiotic relationship developed. As the guards became more aggressive, prisoners became more passive; assertion by the guards led to dependency in the prisoners; self-aggrandizement was met with self-deprecation, authority with helplessness, and the counterpart of the guards' sense of mastery and control was the depression and hopelessness witnessed in the prisoners. As these differences in behavior, mood, and perception became more evident to all, the need for the now "righteously" powerful guards to rule the obviously inferior and powerless inmates became a sufficient reason to support almost any further indignity of man against man:

20   Guard K: "During the inspection, I went to cell 2 to mess up a bed which the prisoner had made and he grabbed me, screaming that he had just made it, and he wasn't going to let me mess it up. He grabbed my throat, and although he was laughing I was pretty scared. . . . I lashed out with my stick and hit him in the chin (although not very hard), and when I freed myself I became angry. I wanted to get back in the cell and have a go with him, since he attacked me when I was not ready."

Guard M: "I was surprised at myself . . . I made them call each other names and clean the toilets out with their bare hands. I practically considered the prisoners cattle, and I kept thinking: 'I have to watch out for them in case they try something.' "

Guard A: "I was tired of seeing the prisoners in their rags and smelling the strong odors of their bodies that filled the cells. I watched them tear at each other on orders given by us. They didn't see it as an experiment. It was real and they were fighting to keep their identity. But we were always there to show them who was boss."

Because the first day passed without incident, we were surprised and totally unprepared for the rebellion that broke out on the morning of the second day. The prisoners removed their stocking caps, ripped off their numbers, and barricaded themselves inside the cells by putting their beds against the doors. What should we do? The guards were very much upset because the prisoners also began to taunt and curse them to their faces. When the morning shift of guards came on, they were upset at the night shift who, they felt, must have been too permissive and too lenient. The guards had to handle the rebellion themselves, and what they did was startling to behold.

At first they insisted that reinforcements be called in. The two guards who were waiting on stand-by call at home came in, and the night shift of guards voluntarily remained on duty (without extra pay) to bolster the morning shift. The guards met and decided to treat force with force. They got a fire extinguisher that shot a stream of skin-chilling carbon dioxide and forced the prisoners away from the doors; they broke into each cell, stripped the prisoners naked, took the beds out, forced the prisoners who were the ringleaders into solitary confinement, and generally began to harass and intimidate the prisoners.

25   After crushing the riot, the guards decided to head off further unrest by creating a privileged cell for those who were "good prisoners" and then, without explanation, switching some of the troublemakers into it and some of the good prisoners out into the other cells. The prisoner ringleaders could not trust these new cellmates because they had not joined in the riot and might even be "snitches." The prisoners never again acted in unity against the system. One of the leaders of the prisoner revolt later confided:

"If we had gotten together then, I think we could have taken over the place. But when I saw the revolt wasn't working, I decided to toe the line. Everyone settled into the same pattern. From then on, we were really controlled by the guards."

It was after this episode that the guards really began to demonstrate their inventiveness in the application of arbitrary power. They made the prisoners obey petty, meaningless, and often inconsistent rules, forced them to engage in tedious, useless work, such as moving cartons back and forth between closets and picking thorns out of their blankets for hours on end. (The guards had previously dragged the blankets through thorny bushes to create this disagreeable task.) Not only did the prisoners have to sing songs or laugh or refrain from smiling on command; they were also encouraged to curse and vilify each other publicly during some of the counts. They sounded off their numbers endlessly and were repeatedly made to do pushups, on occasion with a guard stepping on them or a prisoner sitting on them.

Slowly the prisoners became resigned to their fate and even behaved in ways that actually helped to justify their dehumanizing treatment at the hands of the guards. Analysis of the tape-recorded private conversations between prisoners and of remarks made by them to interviewers revealed that fully half could be classified as nonsupportive of other prisoners. More dramatic, 85 percent of the evaluative statements by prisoners about their fellow prisoners were uncomplimentary and deprecating.

This should be taken in the context of an even more surprising result. What do you imagine the prisoners talked about when they were alone in their cells with each other, given a temporary respite from the continual harassment and surveillance by the guards? Girl friends, career plans, hobbies or politics?

30 No, their concerns were almost exclusively riveted to prison topics. Their monitored conversations revealed that only 10 percent of the time was devoted to "outside" topics, while 90 percent of the time they discussed escape plans, the awful food, grievances or ingratiating tactics to use with specific guards in order to get a cigarette, permission to go to the toilet, or some other favor. Their obsession with these immediate survival concerns made talk about the past and future an idle luxury.

And this was not a minor point. So long as the prisoners did not get to know each other as people, they only extended the oppressiveness and reality of their life as prisoners. For the most part, each prisoner observed his fellow prisoners allowing the guards to humiliate them, acting like compliant sheep, carrying out mindless orders with total obedience, and even being cursed by fellow prisoners (at a guard's command). Under such circumstances, how could a prisoner have respect for his fellows, or any self-respect for what *he* obviously was becoming in the eyes of all those evaluating him?

The combination of realism and symbolism in this experiment had fused to create a vivid illusion of imprisonment. The illusion merged inextricably with reality for at least some of the time for every individual in the situation. It was remarkable how readily we all slipped into our roles, temporarily gave up our identities, and allowed these assigned roles and the social forces in the situation to guide, shape, and eventually to control our freedom of thought and action.

But precisely where does one's "identity" end and one's "role" begin? When the private self and the public role behavior clash, what direction will attempts to impose consistency take? Consider the reactions of the parents, relatives, and friends of the prisoners who visited their forlorn sons, brothers, and lovers during two scheduled visitors' hours. They were taught in short order that they were our guests, allowed the privilege of visiting only by complying with the regulations of the institution. They had to register, were made to wait half an hour, were told that only two visitors could see any one prisoner; the total visiting time was cut from an hour to only 10 minutes, they had to be under the surveillance of a guard, and before any parents could enter the visiting area, they had to discuss their son's case with the warden. Of course they complained about these arbitrary rules, but their conditioned, middle-class reaction was to work within the system to appeal privately to the superintendent to make conditions better for their prisoners.

In less than 36 hours, we were forced to release prisoner 8612 because of extreme depression, disorganized thinking, uncontrollable crying, and fits of rage. We did so reluctantly because we believed he was trying to "con" us—it was unimaginable that a volunteer prisoner in a mock prison could legitimately be suffering and disturbed to that extent. But then on each of the next three days another prisoner reacted with similar anxiety symptoms, and we were forced to terminate them, too. In a fifth case, a prisoner was released after developing a psychosomatic rash over his entire body (triggered by rejection of his parole appeal by the mock parole board). These men were simply unable to make an adequate adjustment to prison life. Those who endured the prison experience to the end could be distinguished from those who broke down and were released early in only one dimension—authoritarianism. On a psychological test designed to reveal a person's authoritarianism, those prisoners who had the highest scores were best able to function in this authoritarian prison environment.

35   If the authoritarian situation became a serious matter for the prisoners, it became even more serious—and sinister—for the guards. Typically, the guards insulted the prisoners, threatened them, were physically aggressive, used instruments (night sticks, fire extinguishers, etc.) to keep the prisoners in line, and referred to them in impersonal, anonymous, deprecating ways: "Hey, you," or "You [obscenity], 5401, come here." From the first to the last day, there was

a significant increase in the guards' use of most of these domineering, abusive tactics.

Everyone and everything in the prison was defined by power. To be a guard who did not take advantage of this institutionally sanctioned use of power was to appear "weak," "out of it," "wired up by the prisoners," or simply a deviant from the established norms of appropriate guard behavior. Using Erich Fromm's definition of sadism, as "the wish for absolute control over another living being," all of the mock guards at one time or another during this study behaved sadistically toward the prisoners. Many of them reported—in their diaries, on critical-incident report forms, and during post-experimental interviews—being delighted in the new-found power and control they exercised and sorry to see it relinquished at the end of the study.

Some of the guards reacted to the situation in the extreme and behaved with great hostility and cruelty in the forms of degradation they invented for the prisoners. But others were kinder; they occasionally did little favors for the prisoners, were reluctant to punish them, and avoided situations where prisoners were being harassed. The torment experienced by one of these good guards is obvious in his perceptive analysis of what if felt like to be responded to as a "guard":

"What made the experience most depressing for me was the fact that we were continually called upon to act in a way that just was contrary to what I really feel inside. I don't feel like I'm the type of person that would be a guard, just constantly giving out [orders] . . . and forcing people to do things, and pushing and lying—it just didn't seem like me, and to continually keep up and put on a face like that is just really one of the most oppressive things you can do. It's almost like a prison that you create yourself—you get into it, and it becomes almost the definition you make of yourself, it almost becomes like walls, and you want to break out and you want just to be able to tell everyone that 'this isn't really me at all, and I'm not the person that's confined in there—I'm a person who wants to get out and show you that I am free, and I do have my own will, and I'm not the sadistic type of person that enjoys this kind of thing.' "

Still, the behavior of these good guards seemed more motivated by a desire to be liked by everyone in the system than by a concern for the inmates' welfare. No guard ever intervened in any direct way on behalf of the prisoners, ever interfered with the orders of the cruelest guards, or ever openly complained about the subhuman quality of life that characterized this prison.

40   Perhaps the most devastating impact of the more hostile guards was their creation of a capricious, arbitrary environment. Over time the prisoners began to react passively. When our mock prisoners asked questions, they got answers about half the time, but the rest of the time they were insulted and punished—and it

was not possible for them to predict which would be the outcome. As they began to "toe the line," they stopped resisting, questioning and, indeed, almost ceased responding altogether. There was a general decrease in all categories of response as they learned the safest strategy to use in an unpredictable, threatening environment from which there is no physical escape—do nothing, except what is required. Act not, want not, feel not, and you will not get into trouble in prisonlike situations.

Can it really be, you wonder, that intelligent, educated volunteers could have lost sight of the reality that they were merely acting a part in an elaborate game that would eventually end? There are many indications not only that they did, but that, in addition, so did we and so did other apparently sensible, responsible adults.

Prisoner 819, who had gone into an uncontrollable crying fit, was about to be prematurely released from the prison when a guard lined up the prisoners and had them chant in unison, "819 is a bad prisoner. Because of what 819 did to prison property we all must suffer. 819 is a bad prisoner." Over and over again. When we realized 819 might be overhearing this, we rushed into the room where 819 was supposed to be resting, only to find him in tears, prepared to go back into the prison because he could not leave as long as the others thought he was a "bad prisoner." Sick as he felt, he had to prove to them he was not a "bad" prisoner. He had to be persuaded that he was not a prisoner at all, that the others were also just students, that this was just an experiment and not a prison and the prison staff were only research psychologists. A report from the warden notes, "While I believe that it was necessary for *staff* [me] to enact the warden role, at least some of the time, I am startled by the ease with which I could turn off my sensitivity and concern for others for 'a good cause.'"

Consider our overreaction to the rumor of a mass escape plot that one of the guards claimed to have overheard. It went as follows: Prisoner 8612, previously released for emotional disturbance, was only faking. He was going to round up a bunch of his friends, and they would storm the prison right after visiting hours. Instead of collecting data on the pattern of rumor transmission, we made plans to maintain the security of our institution. After putting a confederate informer into the cell 8612 had occupied to get specific information about the escape plans, the superintendent went back to the Palo Alto Police Department to request transfer of our prisoners to the old city jail. His impassioned plea was only turned down at the last minute when the problem of insurance and city liability for our prisoners was raised by a city official. Angered at this lack of cooperation, the staff formulated another plan. Our jail was dismantled, the prisoners, chained and blindfolded, were carted off to a remote storage room. When the conspirators arrived, they would be told the study was over, their friends had been sent home, there was nothing left to liberate. After they left, we would redouble the security features of our prison making any future escape attempts futile. We even planned to lure ex-prisoner 8612 back on some pretext and imprison him again, because he had been released on false pretenses! The rumor turned out to be just that—a full day had passed in which we collected little or no data, worked incredibly hard to tear down and then rebuild our prison. Our reaction, however, was as much one of relief and joy as of exhaustion and frustration.

When a former prison chaplain was invited to talk with the prisoners (the grievance committee had requested church services), he puzzled everyone by disparaging each inmate for not having taken any constructive action in order to get released. "Don't you know you must have a lawyer in order to get bail, or to appeal the charges against you?" Several of them accepted his invitation to contact their parents in order to secure the services of an attorney. The next night one of the parents stopped at the superintendent's office before visiting time and handed him the name and phone number of her cousin who was a public defender. She said that a priest had called her and suggested the need for a lawyer's services! We called the lawyer. He came, interviewed the prisoners, discussed sources of bail money, and promised to return again after the weekend.

45   But perhaps the most telling account of the insidious development of this new reality, of the gradual Kafkaesque metamorphosis of good into evil, appears in excerpts from the diary of one of the guards, Guard A:

Prior to start of experiment: "As I am a pacifist and nonaggressive individual. I cannot see a time when I might guard and/or maltreat other living things."

After an orientation meeting: "Buying uniforms at the end of the meeting confirms the gamelike atmosphere of this thing. I doubt whether many of us share the expectations of 'seriousness' that the experimenters seem to have."

First Day: "Feel sure that the prisoners will make fun of my appearance and I evolve my first basic strategy—mainly not to smile at anything they say or do which would be admitting it's all only a game. . . . At cell 3 I stop and setting my voice hard and low say to 5486, 'What are you smiling at?' 'Nothing, Mr. Correctional Officer.' 'Well, see that you don't.' (As I walk off I feel stupid.)"

Second Day: "5704 asked for a cigarette and I ignored him—because I am a non-smoker and could not empathize. . . . Meanwhile since I was feeling empathetic towards 1037, I determined not to talk with him. . . . After we had count and lights out [Guard D] and I held a loud conversation about going home to our girl friends and what we were going to do to them."

50   *Third Day (preparing for the first visitors' night):* "After warning the prisoners not to make any complaints unless they wanted the visit terminated fast, we finally

brought in the first parents. I made sure I was one of the guards on the yard, because this was my first chance for the type of manipulative power that I really like—being a very noticed figure with almost complete control over what is said or not. While the parents and prisoners sat in chairs, I sat on the end of the table dangling my feet and contradicting anything I felt like. This was the first part of the experiment I was really enjoying. . . . 817 is being obnoxious and bears watching."

Fourth Day: ". . . The psychologist rebukes me for handcuffing and blind-folding a prisoner before leaving the [counseling] office, and I resentfully reply that it is both necessary security and my business anyway."

Fifth Day: "I harass 'Sarge' who continues to stubbornly overrespond to all commands. I have singled him out for the special abuse both because he begs for it and because I simply don't like him. The real trouble starts at dinner. The new prisoner (416) refuses to eat his sausage . . . we throw him into the Hole ordering him to hold sausages in each hand. We have a crisis of authority; this rebellious conduct potentially undermines the complete control we have over the others. We decide to play upon prisoner solidarity and tell the new one that all the others will be deprived of visitors if he does not eat his dinner. . . . I walk by and slam my stick into the Hole door. . . . I am very angry at this prisoner for causing discomfort and trouble for the others. I decided to force-feed him, but he wouldn't eat. I let the food slide down his face. I didn't believe it was me doing it. I hated myself for making him eat but I hated him more for not eating."

Sixth Day: "The experiment is over. I feel elated but am shocked to find some other guards disappointed somewhat because of the loss of money and some because they are enjoying themselves."

We were no longer dealing with an intellectual exercise in which a hypothesis was being evaluated in the dispassionate manner dictated by the canons of the scientific method. We were caught up in the passion of the present, the suffering, the need to control people, not variables, the escalation of power, and all the unexpected things that were erupting around and within us. We had to end this experiment: So our planned two-week simulation was aborted after only six (was it only six?) days and nights.

55   Was it worth all the suffering just to prove what everybody knows—that some people are sadistic, others weak, and prisons are not beds of roses? If that is all we demonstrated in this research, then it was certainly not worth the anguish. We believe there are many significant implications to be derived from this experience, only a few of which can be suggested here.

The potential social value of this study derives precisely from the fact that normal, healthy, educated young men could be so radically transformed under the institutional pressures of a "prison environment." If this could happen in so short a time, without the excesses that are possible in real prisons, and if it could happen to the "cream-of-the-crop of American youth," then one can only shudder to imagine what society is doing both to the actual guards and prisoners who are at this very moment participating in that unnatural "social experiment."

The pathology observed in this study cannot be reasonably attributed in pre-existing personality differences of the subjects, that option being eliminated by our selection procedures and random assignment. Rather, the subjects' abnormal social and personal reactions are best seen as a product of their transaction with an environment that supported the behavior that would be pathological in other settings, but was "appropriate" in this prison. Had we observed comparable reactions in a real prison, the psychiatrist undoubtedly would have been able to attribute any prisoner's behavior to character defects or personality maladjustment, while critics of the prison system would have been quick to label the guards as "psychopathic." This tendency to locate the source of behavior disorders inside a particular person or group underestimates the power of situational forces.

Our colleague, David Rosenhan, has very convincingly shown that once a sane person (pretending to be insane) gets labeled as insane and committed to a mental hospital, it is the label that is the reality which is treated and not the person. This dehumanizing tendency to respond to other people according to socially determined labels and often arbitrarily assigned roles is also apparent in a recent "mock hospital" study designed by Norma Jean Orlando to extend the ideas in our research.

Personnel from the staff of Elgin State Hospital in Illinois role-played either mental patients or staff in a weekend simulation on a ward in the hospital. The mock mental patients soon displayed behavior indistinguishable from that we usually associate with the chronic pathological syndromes of acute mental patients: Incessant pacing, uncontrollable weeping, depression, hostility, fights, stealing from each other, complaining. Many of the "mock staff" took advantage of their power to act in ways comparable to our mock guards by dehumanizing their powerless victims.

60   During a series of encounter debriefing sessions immediately after our experiment, we all had an opportunity to vent our strong feelings and to reflect upon the moral and ethical issues each of us faced, and we considered how we might react more morally in future "real-life" analogues to this situation. Year-long follow-ups with our subjects via questionnaires, personal interviews, and group reunions indicate that their mental anguish was transient and situationally specific, but the self-knowledge gained has persisted.

By far the most disturbing implication of our research comes from the parallels between what occurred in that basement mock prison and daily experiences in our own lives—and we presume yours. The physical institution of prison is but a concrete and steel metaphor for the existence of more pervasive, albeit less obvious, prisons of the mind that all of us daily create, populate, and perpetuate. We speak here of the prisons of racism, sexism, despair, shyness, "neurotic hang-ups," and the like. The social convention of marriage, as one example, becomes for many couples a state of imprisonment in which one partner agrees to be prisoner or guard, forcing or allowing the other to play the reciprocal role—invariable without making the contract explicit.

To what extent do we allow ourselves to become imprisoned by docilely accepting the roles others assign us or, indeed, choose to remain prisoners because being passive and dependent frees us from the need to act and be responsible for our actions? The prison of fear constructed in the delusions of the paranoid is no less confining or less real than the cell that every shy person to limit his own freedom in anxious anticipation of being ridiculed and rejected by his guards—often guards of his own making.

ENGAGING the Text

1. What objective motivated Zimbardo to design this prison experiment with his students at Stanford as subjects? Why didn't he pursue his research in a real prison setting?

2. After only a few days into the experiment, what perverse psychological relationship developed between the guards and prisoners who were randomly assigned to play either role?

EVALUATING the Argument

1. What relevance do the quotations at the beginning of Zimbardo's report have on the nature of his experiment?

2. In what respects do the quoted remarks from Guard A's journal illustrate the unwholesome transformation of a normal college student into a sadistic prison guard in only five days?

EXPLORING the Issue

1. Zimbardo originally had planned to conduct a two-week experiment and his subjects felt confident in being able to carry it out. Instead, Zimbardo had to cut it short after six days. Should he have allowed the experiment to continue for the planned two weeks? Why or why not?

2. A good deal of what Zimbardo learned surprised him. What insights did he gain into the psychological processes that can make anyone's mind into a prison of their own making? In a short essay, address the question of how racism, sexism, despair, or shyness can become a prison.

CONNECTING Different Perspectives

1. How does Zimbardo's experiment demostrate the process by which the "other" as analyzed by Ursula Le Guin is created in "American SF and The Other"?

Sociology

Gloria Steinem

The Time Factor

Gloria Steinem (b. 1934) is perhaps best known as the founder of Ms. *magazine. She has played a crucial role as a writer, speaker, and political activist in promoting women's rights. Her books include* Revolution from Within *(1991) and* Moving Beyond Words *(1993). "The Time Factor," which originally appeared in* Ms. *in 1980, analyzes how the lack of social power, whether due to economic deprivation, gender, or race, impairs the ability to plan for the future.*

Planning ahead is a measure of class. The rich and even the middle class plan for future generations, but the poor can plan ahead only a few weeks or days.

I remember finding this calm insight in some sociological text and feeling instant recognition. Yes, of course, our sense of time was partly a function of power, or the lack of it. It rang true even in the entirely economic sense the writer had in mind. "The guys who own the factories hand them down to their sons and great-grandsons," I remember a boy in my high school saying bitterly. "On this side of town, we just plan for Saturday night."

But it also seemed equally true of most of the women I knew—including myself—regardless of the class we supposedly belonged to. Though I had left my factory-working neighborhood, gone to college, become a journalist, and thus was middle class, I still felt that I couldn't plan ahead. I had to be flexible—first, so that I could be ready to get on a plane for any writing assignment (even though the male writers I knew launched into books and other long-term projects on their own), and then so that I could adapt to the career and priorities of an eventual husband and children (even though I was leading a rewarding life without either). Among the results of this uncertainty were a stunning lack of career planning and such smaller penalties as no savings, no insurance, and an apartment that lacked basic pieces of furniture.

On the other hand, I had friends who were married to men whose longer-term career plans were compatible with their own, yet they still lived their lives in day-to-day response to any possible needs of their husbands and children. Moreover, the one male colleague who shared or even understood this sense of powerlessness was a successful black journalist and literary critic who admitted that even after twenty years he planned only one assignment at a time. He couldn't forget his dependence on the approval of white editors.

5   Clearly there is more to this fear of the future than a conventional definition of class could explain. There is also caste: the unchangeable marks of sex and race that bring a whole constellation of cultural injunctions against power, even the limited power of controlling one's own life.

We haven't yet examined time-sense and future planning as functions of discrimination, but we have begun to struggle with them, consciously or not. As a movement, women have become painfully conscious of too much reaction and living from one emergency to the next, with too little initiative and planned action of our own; hence many of our losses to a much smaller but more entrenched and consistent right wing.

Though the cultural habit of living in the present and glazing over the future goes deep, we've begun to challenge the cultural punishment awaiting the "pushy" and "selfish" women (and the "uppity" minority men) who try to break through it and control their own lives.

Even so, feminist writers and theorists tend to avoid the future by lavishing all our analytical abilities on what's wrong with the present, or on revisions of history and critiques of the influential male thinkers of the past. The big, original, and certainly courageous books of this wave of feminism have been more diagnostic than prescriptive. We need pragmatic planners and visionary futurists, but can we think of even one feminist five-year-plan? Perhaps the closest we have come is visionary architecture or feminist science fiction, but they generally avoid the practical steps of how to get from here to there.

Obviously, many of us need to extend our time-sense—to have the courage to plan for the future, even while most of us are struggling to keep our heads above water in the present. But this does not mean a flat-out imitation of the culturally masculine habit of planning ahead, living in the future, and thus living a deferred life. It doesn't mean the traditional sacrifice of spontaneous action, or a sensitive awareness of the present, that comes from long years of career education with little intrusion of reality, from corporate pressure to work now for the sake of a reward after retirement, or, least logical of all, from patriarchal religions that expect obedience now in return for a reward after death.

10   In fact, the ability to live in the present, to tolerate uncertainty, and to remain open, spontaneous, and flexible are all culturally female qualities that many men need and have been denied. As usual, both halves of the polarized masculine-feminine division need to learn from each other's experiences. If men spent more time raising small children, for instance, they would be forced to develop more patience and flexibility. If women had more power in the planning of natural resources and other long-term processes—or even in the planning of our own careers and reproductive lives—we would have to develop more sense of the future and of cause and effect.

An obsession with reacting to the present, feminine-style, or on controlling and living in the future, masculine-style, are both wasteful of time.

And time is all there is.

ENGAGING the Text

1. What does Steinem mean when she claims that "our sense of time [is] partly a function of power, or the lack of it"?

2. Why, in Steinem's view, are those who are poor, female, or a member of a minority group at a disadvantage in planning for the future?

EVALUATING the Argument

1. Of the examples that Steinem presents to support her claim that lack of power, whether due to economic deprivation, gender, or race, impairs the ability to plan ahead, which do you find the most persuasive? Do the conclusions she draws from them seem to be warranted? Why or why not?

2. How does the kind of planning Steinem advocates borrow equally from the opposite ways in which men and women react to the present and plan for the future?

EXPLORING the Issue

1. Compare the quality of your decision making when you had to make a choice under the pressure of immediate circumstances with decisions you made when you were not under pressure.

2. From what you have read written by feminist writers, evaluate Steinem's critique.

CONNECTING Different Perspectives

1. Compare Steinem's argument to the kind of feminist science fiction Ursula Le Guin advocates in "American SF and The Other."

Biology

Charles Darwin

from The Origin of Species[1]

Charles Darwin (1809–1882), the British naturalist and geologist, initially studied medicine but left medical school to study for the ministry at Cambridge. His interest in natural history was encouraged by John Stevens Henslow, who was responsible for Darwin's being invited to join the Admiralty Surveyship H.M.S. Beagle. Its five-year voyage to South America and the Galapagos Islands provided Darwin with a wealth of observations and many unanswered questions. Darwin's answer took the form of a theory that in the competitive struggle for existence, species possessing advantageous mutations would thrive, whereas less adapted species would become extinct. His principle works include On the Origin of Species by Means of Natural Selection *(1859), from which the following selection is drawn, and* The Descent of Man *(1871).*

Natural Selection; or The Survival of The Fittest

Summary of Chapter

If under changing conditions of life organic beings present individual differences in almost every part of their structure, and this cannot be disputed; if there be, owing to their geometrical rate of increase, a severe struggle for life at some age, season, or year, and this certainly cannot be disputed; then, considering the infinite complexity of the relations of all organic beings to each other and to their conditions of life, causing an infinite diversity in structure, constitution, and habits, to be advantageous to them, it would be a most extraordinary fact if no variations had ever occurred useful to each being's own welfare, in the same manner as so many variations have occurred useful to man. But if variations useful to

[1]This selection is excerpted from the sixth edition of Darwin's 1872 book, the last edition published during his lifetime.

any organic being ever do occur, assuredly individuals thus characterised will have the best chance of being preserved in the struggle for life; and from the strong principle of inheritance, these will tend to produce offspring similarly characterised. This principle of preservation, or the survival of the fittest, I have called Natural Selection. It leads to the improvement of each creature in relation to its organic and inorganic conditions of life; and consequently, in most cases, to what must be regarded as an advance in organisation. Nevertheless, low and simple forms will long endure if well fitted for their simple conditions of life.

Natural selection, on the principle of qualities being inherited at corresponding ages, can modify the egg, seed, or young, as easily as the adult. Amongst many animals, sexual selection[2] will have given its aid to ordinary selection, by assuring to the most vigorous and best adapted makes the greatest number of offspring. Sexual selection will also give characters useful to the males alone, in their struggles or rivalry with other males; and these characters will be transmitted to one sex or to both sexes, according to the form of inheritance which prevails.

Whether natural selection has really thus acted in adapting the various forms of life to their several conditions and stations, must be judged by the general tenor and balance of evidence given in the following chapters. But we have already seen how it entails extinction; and how largely extinction has acted in the world's history, geology plainly declares. Natural selection, also leads to divergence of character; for the more organic beings diverge in structure, habits, and constitution, by so much the more can a large number be supported on the area,—of which we see proof by looking to the inhabitants of any small spot, and to the productions naturalised in foreign lands. Therefore, during the modification of the descendants of any one species, and during the incessant struggle of all species to increase in numbers, the more diversified the descendants become, the better will be their chance of success in the battle for life. Thus the small differences distinguishing varieties of the same species, steadily tend to increase, till they equal the greater differences between species of the same genus, or even of distinct genera. . . .

Natural selection, as has just been remarked, leads to divergence of character and to much extinction of the less improved and intermediate forms of life. On these principles, the nature of the affinities, and the generally well-defined distinctions between the innumerable organic beings in each class throughout the world, may be explained. It is a truly wonderful fact—the wonder of which we are apt to overlook from familiarity—that all animals and all plants throughout all time and space should be related to each other in groups, subordinate to groups, in the manner which we everywhere behold—namely,

---

[2]Sexual selection refers to the mating preferences within a species that ensure the most vigorous and best adapted offspring.

varieties of the same species most closely related, species of the same genus less closely and unequally related, forming sections and sub-genera, species of distinct genera much less closely related, and genera related in different degrees, forming sub-families, families, orders, sub-classes and classes. The several subordinate groups in any class cannot be ranked in a single file, but seem clustered round points, and these round other points, and so on in almost endless cycles. If species had been independently created, no explanation would have been possible of this kind of classification; but it is explained through inheritance and the complex action of natural selection, entailing extinction and divergence of character. . . .

5   The affinities of all the beings of the same class have sometimes been represented by a great tree. I believe this simile largely speaks the truth. The green and budding twigs may represent existing species; and those produced during former years may represent the long succession of extinct species. At each period of growth all the growing twigs have tried to branch out on all sides, and to overtop and kill the surrounding twigs and branches, in the same manner as species and groups of species have at all times overmastered other species in the great battle for life. The limbs divided into great branches, and these into lesser and lesser branches, were themselves once, when the tree was young, budding twigs, and this connection of the former and present buds by ramifying branches may well represent the classification of all extinct and living species in groups subordinate to groups. Of the many twigs which flourished when the tree was a mere bush, only two or three, now grown into great branches, yet survive and bear the other branches; so with the species which lived during long-past geological periods, very few have left living and modified descendants. From the first growth of the tree, many a limb and branch has decayed and dropped off; and these fallen branches of various sizes may represent those whole orders, families, and genera which have now no living representatives, and which are known to us only in a fossil state. As we here and there see a thin straggling branch springing from a fork low down in a tree, and which by some chance has been favoured and is still alive on its summit, so we occasionally see an animal like the Ornithorhynchus or Lepidosiren,[3] which in some small

---

[3]Ornithorhynchus anatinus refers to the duck-billed platypus, a semi-aquatic, egg-laying mammal of Tasmania and East Australia. It has a rubbery duck-bill-shaped muzzle; no teeth; no external ears; head, body, and tail are broad, flat, and covered with dark brown fur; its feet are webbed; and the adult male is about two feet long. Lepidosiren refers to a lung-bearing fish often resembling an eel that is found in rivers in South America, Africa, and Australia and ancestrally is related to four-footed land animals. They indicate a point of bifurcation in evolution since some species breathe through gills in water and other species will drown if held under water.

degree connects by its affinities two large branches of life, and which has apparently been saved from fatal competition by having inhabited a protected station. As buds give rise by growth to fresh buds, and these, if vigorous, branch out and overtop on all sides many a feebler branch, so by generation I believe it has been with the great Tree of Life, which fills with its dead and broken branches the crust of the earth, and covers the surface with its ever-branching and beautiful ramifications. . . .

On the Imperfection of the Geological Record

In the sixth chapter I enumerated the chief objections which might be justly urged against the views maintained in this volume. Most of them have now been discussed. One, namely the distinctness of specific forms, and their not being blended together by innumerable transitional links, is a very obvious difficulty. I assigned reasons why such links do not commonly occur at the present day under the circumstances apparently most favourable for their presence, namely, on an extensive and continuous area with graduated physical conditions. I endeavoured to show, that the life of each species depends in a more important manner on the presence of other already defined organic forms, than on climate, and, therefore, that the really governing conditions of life do not graduate away quite insensibly like heat or moisture. I endeavoured, also, to show that intermediate varieties, from existing in lesser numbers than the forms which they connect, will generally be beaten out and exterminated during the course of further modification and improvement. The main cause, however, of innumerable intermediate links not now occurring everywhere throughout nature, depends on the very process of natural selection, through which new varieties continually take the places of and supplant their parentforms. But just in proportion as this process of extermination has acted on an enormous scale, so must the number of intermediate varieties, which have formerly existed, be truly enormous. Why then is not every geological formation and every stratum full of such intermediate links? Geology assuredly does not reveal any such finely-graduated organic chain; and this, perhaps, is the most obvious and serious objection which can be urged against the theory. The explanation lies, as I believe, in the extreme imperfection of the geological record.

In the first place, it should always be borne in mind what sort of intermediate forms must, on the theory, have formerly existed. I have found it difficult, when looking at any two species, to avoid picturing to myself forms *directly* intermediate between them. But this is a wholly false view: we should always look for forms intermediate between each species and a common but unknown progenitor; and the progenitor will generally have differed in some respects from all its modified descendants. To give a simple illustration: the fantail and pouter pigeons are both descended from the rock-pigeon; if we possessed all the intermediate varieties which have ever existed, we should have an extremely close series between both and the rock-pigeon; but we should have no varieties directly intermediate between the fantail and pouter; none, for instance, combining a tail somewhat expanded with a crop somewhat enlarged, the characteristic features of these two breeds. These two breeds, moreover, have become so much modified, that, if we had no historical or indirect evidence regarding their origin, it would not have been possible to have determined, from a mere comparison of their structure with that of the rock-pigeon, C. livia, whether they had descended from this species or from some allied form, such as C. oenas.

So, with natural species, if we look to forms very distinct, for instance to the horse and tapir, we have no reason to suppose that links directly intermediate between them ever existed, but between each and an unknown common parent. The common parent will have had in its whole organisation much general re-semblance to the tapir and to the horse; but in some points of structure may have differed considerably from both, even perhaps more than they differ from each other. Hence, in all such cases, we should be unable to recognise the parent-form of any two or more species, even if we closely compared the struc-ture of the parent with that of its modified descendants, unless at the same time we had a nearly perfect chain of the intermediate links.

It is just possible by the theory, that one of two living forms might have de-scended from the other; for instance, a horse from a tapir; and in this case *direct* intermediate links will have existed between them. But such a case would imply that one form had remained for a very long period unaltered, whilst its descen-dants had undergone a vast amount of change; and the principle of competition between organism and organism, between child and parent, will render this a very rare event; for in all cases the new and improved forms of life tend to sup-plant the old and unimproved forms.

10   By the theory of natural selection all living species have been connected with the parent-species of each genus, by differences not greater than we see between the natural and domestic varieties of the same species at the present day; and these parent-species, now generally extinct, have in their turn been similarly connected with more ancient forms; and so on backwards, always coverging to the common ancestor of each great class. So that the number of intermediate and transitional links, between all living and extinct species, must have been inconceivably great. But assuredly, if this theory be true, such have lived upon the earth.

On the Lapse of Time, as Inferred from the Rate of Deposition and Extent of Denudation

Independently of our not finding fossil remains of such infinitely numerous connecting links, it may be objected that time cannot have sufficed for so great an amount of organic change, all changes having been effected slowly. It is hardly possible for me to recall to the reader who is not a practical geologist, the facts leading the mind feebly to comprehend the lapse of time. He who can read Sir Charles Lyell's[4] grand work on the Principles of Geology, which the future historian will recognise as having produced a revolution in natural science, and yet does not admit how vast have been the past periods of time, may at once close this volume. Not that it suffices to study the Principles of Geology, or to read special treatises by different observers on separate formations, and to mark how each author attempts to give an inadequate idea of duration of each formation, or even of each stratum. We can best gain some idea of past time by knowing the agencies at work, and learning how deeply the surface of the land has been denuded, and how much sediment has been deposited. As Lyell has well remarked, the extent and thickness of our sedimentary formations are the result and the measure of the denudation which the earth's crust has elsewhere undergone. Therefore a man should examine for himself the great piles of superimposed strata, and watch the rivulets bringing down mud, and the waves wearing away the sea-cliffs, in order to comprehend something about the duration of past time, the monuments of which we see all around us. . .

On the Poorness of Palaeontological Collections

Now let us turn to our richest geological museums, and what a paltry display we behold! That our collections are imperfect is admitted by every one. The remark of that admirable paleontologist, Edward Forbes, should never be forgotten, namely, that very many fossil species are known and named from single and often broken specimens, or from a few specimens collected on some one spot. Only a small portion of the surface of the earth has been geologically explored, and no part with sufficient care, as the important discoveries made every year in Europe prove. No organism wholly soft can be preserved. Shells and bones decay and disappear when left on the bottom of the sea, where sediment is not accumulating.

---

[4]Sir Charles Lyell (1797–1875) English geologist whose research helped win acceptance of Darwin's theory of evolution.

. . . Those who believe that the geological record is in any degree perfect, will undoubtedly at once reject the theory. For my part, following out Lyell's metaphor, I look at the geological record as a history of the world imperfectly kept, and written in a changing dialect; of this history we possess the last volume alone, relating only to two or three countries. Of this volume, only here and there a short chapter has been preserved; and of each page, only here and there a few lines. Each word of the slowly-changing language, more or less different in the successive chapters, may represent the forms of life, which are entombed in our consecutive formations, and which falsely appear to have been abruptly introduced. On this view, the difficulties above discussed are greatly diminished, or even disappear. . . .

Recapitulation and Conclusion

As this whole volume is one long argument, it may be convenient to the reader to have the leading facts and inferences briefly recapitulated.

15   That many and serious objections may be advanced against the theory of descent with modification through variation and natural selection, I do not deny. I have endeavored to give to them their full force. Nothing at first can appear more difficult to believe than that the more complex organs and instincts have been perfected, not by means superior to, though analogous with, human reason, but by the accumulation of innumerable slight variations, each good for the individual possessor. Nevertheless, this difficulty, though appearing to our imagination insuperably great, cannot be considered real if we admit the following propositions, namely, that all parts of the organisation and instincts offer, at least, individual differences—that there is a struggle for existence leading to the preservation of profitable deviations of structure or instinct—and, lastly, that gradations in the state of perfection of each organ may have existed, each good of its kind. The truth of these propositions cannot, I think, be disputed.

Now let us turn to the other side of the argument. Under domestication we see much variability, caused, or at least excited, by changed conditions of life; but often in so obscure a manner, that we are tempted to consider the variations as spontaneous. Variability is governed by many complex laws,—by correlated growth, compensation, the increased use and disuse of parts, and the definite action of the surrounding conditions. There is much difficulty in ascertaining how largely our domestic productions have been modified; but we may safely infer that the amount has been large, and that modifications can be inherited for long periods. As long as the conditions of life remain the same, we have reason to believe that a modification, which has already been inherited for many generations, may continue to be inherited for an almost infinite number of generations. On the other hand, we have evidence that variability when it has once come into play, does not cease under domestication for a very long period; nor do we know that it ever ceases, for new varieties are still occasionally produced by our oldest domesticated productions.

Variability is not actually caused by man; he only unintentionally exposes organic beings to new conditions of life, and then nature acts on the organisation and causes it to vary. But man can and does select the variations given to him by nature, and thus accumulates them in any desired manner. He thus adapts animals and plants for his own benefit or pleasure. He may do this methodically, or he may do it unconsciously by preserving the individuals most useful or pleasing to him without any intention of altering the breed. It is certain that he can largely influence the character of a breed by selecting, in each successive generation, individual differences so slight as to be inappreciable except by an educated eye. This unconscious process of selection has been the great agency in the formation of the most distinct and useful domestic breeds. That many breeds produced by man have to a large extent the character of natural species, is shown by the inextricable doubts whether many of them are varieties or aboriginally distinct species.

There is no reason why the principles which have acted so efficiently under domestication should not have acted under nature. In the survival of favoured individuals and races, during the constantly-recurrent Struggle for Existence, we see a powerful and ever-acting form of Selection. The struggle for existence inevitably follows from the high geometrical ratio of increase which is common to all organic beings. This high rate of increase is proved by calculation,—by the rapid increase of many animals and plants during a succession of peculiar seasons, and when naturalised in new countries. More individuals are born than can possibly survive. A grain in the balance may determine which individuals shall live and which shall die,—which variety or species shall increase in number, and which shall decrease, or finally become extinct. As the individuals of the same species come in all respects into the closest competition with each other, the struggle will generally be most severe between them; it will be almost equally severe between the varieties of the same species, and next in severity between the species of the same genus. On the other hand the struggle will often be severe between beings remote in the scale of nature. The slightest advantage in certain individuals, at any age of during any season, over those with which they come into competition, or better adaptation in however slight a degree to the surrounding physical conditions, will, in the long run, turn the balance.

With animals having separated sexes, there will be in most cases a struggle between the males for the possession of the females. The most vigorous males, or those which have most successfully struggled with their conditions of life, will generally leave most progeny. But success will often depend on the males having special weapons, or means of defense, or charms; and a slight advantage will lead to victory. . . .

20   If then, animals and plants do vary, let it be ever so slightly or slowly, why should not variations or individual differences, which are in any way beneficial, be preserved and accumulated through natural selection, or the survival of the fittest? If man can by patience select variations useful to him, why, under changing and complex conditions of life, should not variations useful to nature's living products often arise, and be preserved or selected? What limit can be put to this power, acting during long ages and rigidly scrutinising the whole constitution, structure, and habits of each creature,—favouring the good and rejecting the bad? I can see no limit to this power, in slowly and beautifully adapting each form to the most complex relations of life. The theory of natural selection, even if we look no farther than this, seems to be in the highest degree probable. I have already recapitulated, as fairly as I could, the opposed difficulties and objections: now let us turn to the special facts and arguments in favour of the theory. . . .

It can hardly be supposed that a false theory would explain, in so satisfactory a manner as does the theory of natural selection, the several large classes of facts above specified. It has recently been objected that this is an unsafe method of arguing; but it is a method used in judging of the common events of life, and has often been used by the greatest natural philosophers. The undulatory theory of light has thus been arrived at; and the belief in the revolution of the earth on its own axis was until lately supported by hardly any direct evidence. It is no valid objection that science as yet throws no light on the far higher problem of the essence or origin of life. Who can explain what is the essence of the attraction of gravity? No one now objects to following out the results consequent on this unknown element of attraction; notwithstanding that Leibnitz[5] formerly accused Newton of introducing "occult qualities and miracles into philosophy."

I see no good reason why the views given in this volume should shock the religious feelings of any one. It is satisfactory, as showing how transient such impressions are, to remember that the greatest discovery ever made by man, namely, the law of the attraction of gravity, was also attacked by Leibnitz, "as subversive of natural, and inferentially of revealed, religion." A celebrated author and divine has written to me that "he has gradually learnt to see that it is just as noble a conception of the Deity to believe that He created a few original forms capable of self-development into other and needful forms, as to believe

---

[5]Wilhelm Leibnitz (1646–1716) German philosopher and mathematician who invented calculus concurrently with, but independently of, Newton. His optimistic belief that a divine plan made this the best of all possible worlds was satirized by Voltaire in *Candide*.

that He required a fresh act of creation to supply the voids caused by the action of His laws.". . .

But the chief cause of our natural unwillingness to admit that one species has given birth to clear and distinct species, is that we are always slow in admitting great changes of which we do not see the steps. The difficulty is the same as that felt by so many geologists, when Lyell first insisted that long lines of inland cliffs had been formed, the great valleys excavated, by the agencies which we see still at work. The mind cannot possibly grasp the full meaning of the term of even a million years; it cannot add up and perceive the full effects of many slight variations, accumulated during an almost infinite number of generations.

Although I am fully convinced of the truth of the views given in this volume under the form of an abstract, I by no means expect to convince experienced naturalists whose minds are stocked with a multitude of facts all viewed, during a long course of years, from a point of view directly opposite to mine. It is so easy to hide our ignorance under such expressions as the "plan of creation," "unity of design," etc., and to think that we give an explanation when we only re-state a fact. Any one whose disposition leads him to attach more weight to unexplained difficulties than to the explanation of a certain number of facts will certainly reject the theory. A few naturalists, endowed with much flexibility of mind, and who have already begun to doubt the immutability of species, may be influenced by this volume; but I look with confidence to the future,—to young and rising naturalists, who will be able to view both sides of the question with impartiality. Whoever is led to believe that species are mutable will do good service by conscientiously expressing his conviction; for thus only can the load of prejudice by which this subject is overwhelmed be removed. . . .

25 Authors of the highest eminence seem to be fully satisfied with the view that each species has been independently created. To my mind it accords better with what we know of the laws impressed on matter by the Creator, that the production and extinction of the past and present inhabitants of the world should have been due to secondary causes, like those determining the birth and death of the individual. When I view all beings not as special creations, but as the lineal descendants of some few beings which lived long before the first bed of the Cambrian system was deposited, they seem to me to become ennobled. Judging from the past, we may safely infer that no one living species will transmit its unaltered likeness to a distant futurity. And of the species now living very few will transmit progeny of any kind to a far distant futurity; for the manner in which all organic beings are grouped, shows that the greater number of species in each genus, and all the species in many genera, have left no descendants, but have become utterly extinct. We can so far take a prophetic glance into futurity

as to foretell that it will be the common and widely-spread species, belonging to the larger and dominant groups within each class, which will ultimately prevail and procreate new and dominant species. As all the living forms of life are the lineal descendants of those which lived long before the Cambrian epoch, we may feel certain that the ordinary succession by generation has never once been broken, and that no cataclysm has desolated the whole world. Hence we may look with some confidence to a secure future of great length. And as natural selection works solely by and for the good of each being, all corporeal and mental endowments will tend to progress towards perfection.[6]

ENGAGING the Text

1. In Darwin's view, how do natural forces operate to select the best variations within a species to enable it to survive?

2. How does Darwin reply to objections that his theories are incompatible with existing religious beliefs?

EVALUATING the Argument

1. How does Darwin emphasize the merits of his own position by pointing out the disadvantages of his opponents' views?

2. On the point to which Darwin's theory is most vulnerable, how credible or persuasive do you find his explanation for the lack of adequate fossil records, which would be expected to show stages in adaptive evolution?

EXPLORING the Issue

1. How does Darwin's concept of natural selection challenge an anthropocentric view of nature, which assumes a master plan?

2. Do some research to discover the ways in which Darwin's theories of "survival of the fittest" have been applied in areas outside biology such as economics.

CONNECTING Different Perspectives

1. In what way does the adaptation of the rabies virus as discussed by Robert Sapolsky in "Bugs in the Brain" illustrate Darwin's theory that over time natural selection will produce forms better adapted to their particular environment?

---

[6]By progress towards perfection over time Darwin, means natural selection will produce forms better adapted to their particular environment.

Robert Sapolsky

Bugs in the Brain

Robert M. Sapolsky is a professor of biology and neurology at Stanford University whose research focuses on the effects of stress. He has received numerous awards including the prestigious MacArthur Fellowship. His latest work is Monkeyluv: And Other Essays on Our Lives as Animals *(2005). "Bugs in the Brain" first appeared in* Scientific American *(March 2003).*

Like most scientists, I attend professional meetings every now and then, one of them being the annual meeting of the Society for Neuroscience, an organization of most of the earth's brain researchers. This is one of the more intellectually assaulting experiences you can imagine. About 28,000 of us science nerds jam into a single convention center. After a while, this togetherness can make you feel pretty nutty: For an entire week, go into any restaurant, elevator, or bathroom, and the folks standing next to you will be having some animated discussion about squid axons. The process of finding out about the science itself is no easier. The meeting has 14,000 lectures and posters, a completely overwhelming amount of information. Of the subset of those posters that are essential for you to check, a bunch remain inaccessible because of the enthusiastic crowds in front of them, one turns out to be in a language you don't even recognize, and another inevitably reports every experiment you planned to do for the next five years. Amid it all lurks the shared realization that despite zillions of us slaving away at the subject, we still know squat about how the brain works.

My own low point at the conference came one afternoon as I sat on the steps of the convention center, bludgeoned by information and a general sense of ignorance. My eyes focused on a stagnant, murky puddle of water by the curb, and I realized that some microscopic bug festering in there probably knew more about the brain than all of us neuroscientists combined.

My demoralized insight stemmed from a recent extraordinary paper about how certain parasites control the brain of their host. Most of us know that bacteria, protozoa, and viruses have astonishingly sophisticated ways of using animal bodies for their own purposes. They hijack our cells, our energy, and our lifestyles so they can thrive. But in many ways, the most dazzling and fiendish thing that such parasites have evolved—and the subject that occupied my musings that day—is their ability to change a host's behavior for their own ends. Some textbook examples involve ectoparasites, organisms that colonize the surface of the body. For instance, certain mites of the genus *Antennophorus* ride on the backs of ants and, by stroking an ant's mouthparts, can trigger a reflex that culminates in the ant's disgorging food for the mite to feed on. A species of pinworm of the genus *Syphacia* lays eggs on a rodent's skin, the eggs secrete a substance that causes itchiness, the rodent grooms the itchy spot with its teeth, the eggs get ingested in the process, and once inside the rodent they happily hatch.

These behavioral changes are essentially brought about by annoying a host into acting in a way beneficial to the interlopers. But some parasites actually alter the function of the nervous system itself. Sometimes they achieve this change indirectly, by manipulating hormones that affect the nervous system. There are barnacles (*Sacculina granifera*), a form of crustacean, found in Australia that attach to male sand crabs and secrete a feminizing hormone that induces maternal behavior. The zombified crabs then migrate out to sea with brooding females and make depressions in the sand ideal for dispersing larvae. The males, naturally, won't be releasing any. But the barnacles will. And if a barnacle infects a female crab, it induces the same behavior—after atrophying the female's ovaries, a practice called parasitic castration.

5   Bizarre as these cases are, at least the organisms stay outside the brain. Yet a few do manage to get inside. These are microscopic ones, mostly viruses rather than relatively gargantuan creatures like mites, pinworms, and barnacles. Once one of these tiny parasites is inside the brain, it remains fairly sheltered from immune attack, and it can go to work diverting neural machinery to its own advantage.

The rabies virus is one such parasite. Although the actions of this virus have been recognized for centuries, no one I know of has framed them in the neurobiological manner I'm about to. There are lots of ways rabies could have evolved to move between hosts. The virus didn't have to go anywhere near the brain. It could have devised a trick similar to the one employed by the agents that cause nose colds—namely, to irritate nasal-passage nerve endings, causing the host to sneeze and spritz viral replicates all over, say, the person sitting in front of him or her at the movies. Or the virus could have induced an insatiable desire to lick someone or some animal, thereby passing on virus shed into the saliva. Instead, as we all know, rabies can cause its host to become aggressive so the virus can jump into another host via saliva that gets into the wounds.

Just think about this. Scads of neurobiologists study the neural basis of aggression: the pathways of the brain that are involved, the relevant neurotransmitters, the interactions between genes and environment, modulation by hormones, and so on. Aggression has spawned conferences, doctoral theses, petty academic squabbles, nasty tenure disputes, the works. Yet all along, the rabies virus has "known" just which neurons to infect to make a victim rabid. And as far as I am aware, no neuroscientist has studied rabies specifically to understand the neurobiology of aggression.

Despite how impressive these viral effects are, there is still room for improvement. That is because of the parasite's nonspecificity. If you are a rabid animal, you might bite one of the few creatures that rabies does not replicate well in, such as a rabbit. So although the behavioral effects of infecting the brain are quite dazzling, if the parasite's impact is too broad, it can wind up in a dead-end host.

Which brings us to a beautifully specific case of brain control and the paper I mentioned earlier, by Manuel Berdoy and his colleagues at the University of Oxford. Berdoy and his associates study a parasite called *Toxoplasma gondii*. In a toxoplasmic utopia, life consists of a two-host sequence involving rodents and cats. The protozoan gets ingested by a rodent, in which it forms cysts throughout the body, particularly in the brain. The rodent gets eaten by a cat, in which the toxoplasma organism reproduces. The cat sheds the parasite in its feces, which, in one of those circles of life, is nibbled by rodents. The whole scenario hinges on specificity: Cats are the only species in which toxoplasma can sexually reproduce and be shed. Thus, toxoplasma wouldn't want its carrier rodent to get picked off by a hawk or its cat feces ingested by a dung beetle. Mind you, the parasite can infect all sorts of other species; it simply has to wind up in a cat if it wants to spread to a new host.

10   This potential to infect other species is the reason all those "what to do during pregnancy" books recommend banning the cat and its litter box from the house and warn pregnant women against gardening if there are cats wandering about. If toxoplasma from cat feces gets into a pregnant woman, it can get into the fetus, potentially causing neurological damage. Well-informed pregnant women get skittish around cats. Toxoplasma-infected rodents, however, have the opposite reaction. The parasite's extraordinary trick has been to make rodents lose their skittishness.

All good rodents avoid cats—a behavior ethologists call a fixed action pattern, in that the rodent doesn't develop the aversion because of trial and error (since there aren't likely to be many opportunities to learn from one's errors around cats). Instead feline phobia is hard-wired. And it is accomplished through olfaction in the form of pheromones, the chemical odorant signals that animals release. Rodents instinctually shy away from the smell of a cat—even rodents that have never seen a cat in their lives, rodents that are the descendants of hundreds of generations of lab animals. Except for those infected with toxoplasma. As Berdoy and his group have shown, those rodents selectively lose their aversion to, and fear of, cat pheromones.

Now, this is not some generic case of a parasite messing with the head of the intermediate host and making it scatterbrained and vulnerable. Everything else seems pretty intact in the rodents. The social status of the animal doesn't change in its dominance hierarchy. It is still interested in mating and thus, de facto, in the pheromones of the opposite sex. The infected rodents can still distinguish other odors. They simply don't recoil from cat pheromones. This is flabbergasting. This is akin to someone getting infected with a brain parasite that has no effect whatsoever on the person's thoughts, emotions, SAT scores, or television preferences but, to complete its life cycle, generates an irresistible urge to go to the zoo, scale a fence, and try to French-kiss the pissiest-looking polar bear. A parasite-induced fatal attraction, as Berdoy's team noted in the title of its paper.

Obviously, more research is needed. I say this not only because it is obligatory at this point in any article about science, but because this finding is just so intrinsically cool that someone has to figure out how it works. And because— permit me a Stephen Jay Gould moment—it provides ever more evidence that evolution is amazing. Amazing in ways that are counterintuitive. Many of us hold the deeply entrenched idea that evolution is directional and progressive: Invertebrates are more primitive than vertebrates, mammals are the most evolved of vertebrates, primates are the genetically fanciest mammals, and so forth. Some of my best students consistently fall for that one, no matter how much I drone on in lectures. If you buy into that idea big-time, you're not just wrong, you're not all that many steps away from a philosophy that has humans directionally evolved as well, with the most evolved being northern Europeans with a taste for schnitzel and goose-stepping.

So remember, creatures are out there that can control brains. Microscopic and even larger organisms that have more power than Big Brother and, yes, even neuroscientists. My reflection on a curbside puddle brought me to the opposite conclusion that Narcissus reached in his watery reflection. We need phylogenetic humility. We are certainly not the most evolved species around, nor the least vulnerable. Nor the cleverest.

ENGAGING the Text

1. What conditions must exist if the rabies virus is to be spread to a new host?

2. By what unusual means does the rabies virus achieve this goal?

EVALUATING the Argument

1. How does Sapolsky's admiration of the ingenuity of the rabies virus put into perspective the cliché that humans are at the apex of evolution?

2. How effectively has Sapolsky explained the parasite-host scenario that has elicited his admiration?

EXPLORING the Issue

1. Do some research on the folklore and the reality of advice to pregnant women about staying away from cats and litter boxes.

2. Sapolsky rebukes those who believe that there is a progression in evolution and cites the case of the rabies virus as an example. To what extent did his essay change your thinking about the supposedly progressive and directional nature of evolution?

CONNECTING Different Perspectives

1. How do the analyses by Sapolsky and Loren Eiseley ("How Flowers Changed the World" in Chapter 1) illustrate adaptive mechanisms in nature?

Eric Scigliano

Through the Eye of an Octopus

Eric Scigliano's articles have appeared in Discover, Technology Review, *the* New Yorker, *and other publications. His books include* Love, War and Circuses: The Age-Old Relationship of Elephants and Humans *(2002) and most recently,* Michelangelo's Mountain: The Quest for Perfection in the Marble Quarries of Carrara *(2005). This article originally appeared in* Discover *(October 2003).*

When biologist Roland Anderson of the Seattle Aquarium pulled back the tank's lid, I wasn't sure whether it was to let me get a look at Steve or to let Steve get a look at me. Clearly, Steve was looking—his big hooded eye followed me, and a single five-foot-long arm reached out to the hand I held above the water's surface. The arm inched up past my wrist to my shoulder, its suckers momentarily attaching and releasing like cold kisses. I couldn't help feeling as if I was being tasted, and I was, by tens of thousands of chemoreceptors. And I couldn't help feeling as if I were being studied, that a measuring intelligence lay behind that intent eye and exploring arm.

Finally, when the arm's fingerlike tip reached my neck, it shot back like a snapped rubber band. Steve curled into a tight, defensive ball in the corner of the tank. His skin texture changed from glassy smooth to a fissured moonscape; his color changed from mottled brown to livid red—which seemed to signal anger—and he squinted at me. Had something alarmed or offended him? Perhaps we were both a great mystery to each other.

Octopuses and their cephalopod cousins the cuttlefish and the squid are evolutionary oxymorons: big-brained invertebrates that display many cognitive, behavioral, and affective traits once considered exclusive to the higher vertebrates. They challenge the deep-seated notion that intelligence advanced from fish and amphibians to reptiles, birds, mammals, early primates, and finally humans. These are mollusks, after all—cousins to brainless clams and oysters, passive filter feeders that get along just fine, thank you, with a few ganglia for central nervous systems. Genetic studies show that mollusk ancestors split from the vertebrates around 1.2 billion years ago, making humans at least as closely related to shrimps, starfish, and earthworms as to octopuses. And so questions loom: How could asocial invertebrates with short life spans develop signs of intelligence? And why?

Although biologists are just beginning to probe these questions, those who observe the creatures in their natural haunts have long extolled their intelligence. "Mischief and craft are plainly seen to be the characteristics of this creature," the Roman natural historian Claudius Aelianus wrote at the turn of the third century A.D. Today's divers marvel at the elaborate trails the eight-leggers follow along the seafloor, and at their irrepressible curiosity: Instead of fleeing, some octopuses examine divers the way Steve checked me out, tugging at their masks and air regulators. Researchers and aquarium attendants tell tales of octopuses that have tormented and outwitted them. Some captive octopuses lie in ambush and spit in their keepers' faces. Others dismantle pumps and block drains, causing costly floods, or flex their arms in order to pop locked lids. Some have been caught sneaking from their tanks at night into other exhibits, gobbling up fish, then sneaking back to their tanks, damp trails along walls and floors giving them away.

5 That Steve was named Steve was also revealing: Octopuses are the only animals, other than mammals like cuddly seals, that aquarium workers bother to name. So Anderson, Seattle's lead invertebrate biologist, began to wonder: If keepers recognize octopuses as individuals, how much difference is there among individual octopuses? Might these bizarre-looking mollusks have personalities? And if so, how else might their evolution have converged with ours across a billion-year chasm?

Meanwhile, in the waters off Bermuda, Canadian comparative psychologist Jennifer Mather was asking similar questions. Mather had observed an *Octopus vulgaris*, the common Atlantic octopus, catch several crabs and return to its rock den to eat them. Afterward it emerged, gathered four stones, propped these at the den entrance, and, thus shielded, took a safe siesta. The strategy suggested qualities that weren't supposed to occur in the lower orders: foresight, planning, perhaps even tool use.

When Mather and Anderson met at a conference, they discovered they had stumbled onto similar phenomena and began collaborating. Other scientists had already tested the ability of octopuses to solve mazes, learn cues, and remember solutions. They had found that octopuses solve readily, learn quickly, and, in the short term, remember what they have learned. Mather and Anderson delved deeper, documenting a range of qualities and activities closely associated with intelligence but previously known only in advanced vertebrates. Some of their work has been controversial, and some of their conclusions have been disputed. But other researchers are now confirming their key points and logging even more startling findings.

Anatomy confirms what behavior reveals: Octopuses and cuttlefish have larger brains, relative to body weight, than most fish and reptiles, larger on average than any animals save birds and mammals. Although an octopus brain differs from a typical vertebrate's brain—it wraps around the esophagus instead of resting in a cranium—it also shares key features such as folded lobes, a hallmark of complexity, and distinct visual and tactile memory centers. It even generates similar electrical patterns. Electroencephalograms of other invertebrates show spiky static—"like bacon frying," says neurophysiologist Ted Bullock of the University of California at San Diego, who nonetheless found vertebratelike slow waves in octopuses and cuttlefish. The pattern, he says, is "similar to but weaker than that of a dog, a dolphin, a human."

Researchers at the Konrad Lorenz Institute for Evolution and Cognition Research in Austria recently found one more telling indicator: Octopuses, which rely on monocular vision, favor one eye over the other. Such lateralization, corresponding to our right- and left-handedness, suggests specialization in the brain's hemispheres, which is believed to improve its efficiency and which was first considered an exclusively human, then an exclusively vertebrate, attribute.

10   The mystery deepens. According to the social theory of intelligence articulated by N. K. Humphrey and Jane Goodall, complex brains blossom in complex social settings; chimps and dolphins have to be smart to read the intentions of other chimps and dolphins. Moreover, such smarts arise in long-lived animals: Extended childhoods and parental instruction enable them to learn, and longevity justifies the investment in big brains. But many cephalopods live less than a year, and the giant Pacific octopus, which has one of the longest documented life spans, survives for only four years. Their social lives are simple to nonexistent: Squid form schools, but they don't seem to establish individual relationships. Cuttlefish gather while young and later on to mate, but they don't form social structures. Octopuses are solitary; they breed once, then waste away and die. Females tend their eggs, but the tiny hatchlings are on their own. As cephalopod-respiration expert Ron O'Dor of Dalhousie University in Nova Scotia wonders, "Why would you bother to get so smart when you're so short-lived?"

For Jennifer Mather, pursuing those questions marks a convergence of childhood and adult passions. Mather grew up in Victoria, British Columbia, along a biologically rich shoreline. "I got fascinated with intertidal life," she recalls. "I always thought I'd study mollusks." In college, she took an animal-behavior class and had an epiphany: "Most people in comparative psychology compare humans and other primates," she observes, which leaves the field wide open for studies of mollusk behavior and cognition. "And if you talk about mollusk behavior, you're talking about cephalopods."

Mather landed in an unlikely spot for marine research: at the University of Lethbridge in landlocked Alberta, which hasn't had any cephalopods since the Devonian Period. But in the 1980s academic jobs were scarce. Mather then found a lab with Anderson in Seattle and a field base near a secluded coral reef off Bonaire, an island in the Netherlands Antilles. There she leads an international investigation of communication and interactions among Caribbean reef squid—the first long-term study of a wild cephalopod population.

In Seattle, Mather and Anderson have pursued octopuses. Perhaps their most startling and controversial finding is that individuals show distinct personality traits, the first ever measured in an invertebrate. They found that octopuses confronted with the same threat alerts and food stimuli react in different ways. One might flee, but another might fight or show curiosity. That sets them apart from other invertebrates, says Shelley Adamo, a psychologist at Dalhousie who has studied both cephalopods and insects. For example, individual crickets may behave differently at different times—singing today and silent tomorrow. But they don't have consistent patterns that set one cricket apart from another.

Personality can be a controversial word. Some behavioralists call such labels anthropomorphic, while others contend that it's anthropocentric to presume other animals cannot have personalities. Some of Mather and Anderson's peers feel more comfortable with the findings than the terminology. "They do good work and ask interesting questions," says cephalopod researcher John Cigliano of Cedar Crest College in Allentown, Pennsylvania. "But I'm not entirely convinced. It's a tricky business just coming up with a definition of personality." David Sinn, a graduate student at Portland State University, followed up Mather and Anderson's personality work with a more extensive study that they coauthored. That study avoided the "p" word, charting the emergence of key "temperamental traits" in seventy-three lab-bred California octopuses. It found considerable temperamental variation and distinct developmental stages. Like mammals, Sinn's octopuses were more active and aggressive when young and grew more alert to danger as they matured—evidence that their behavior was learned.

15   Previous researchers tested octopuses in artificial mazes; Mather and Anderson found ways to observe learning and cognition in more natural circumstances. They charted the efficiency and flexibility with which giant Pacific octopuses switch strategies to open different shellfish—smashing thin mussels, prying open clams, drilling tougher-shelled clams with their rasplike radulae. When served clams sealed with steel wire, for example, octopuses deftly switched from prying to drilling.

Tool use was once commonly invoked as uniquely human. Scientists know better now, but they still cite it as evidence of distinguishing intelligence in chimpanzees, elephants, and crows. Mather describes several ways octopuses use their water jets as tools: to clean their dens, push away rocks and other debris, and drive off pesky scavenger fish.

In 1999 she and Anderson published an even more sensational claim: that octopuses engage in play, the deliberate, repeated, outwardly useless activity through which smarter animals explore their world and refine their skills. Amateur aquarists were the first to suspect that octopuses played. While still in high school, James Wood, now a marine biologist at the University of Texas's marine lab in Galveston, watched his pet octopus grab, submerge, and release her tank's floating hydrometer as if she were a toddler with a bath toy. She also spread her mantle and "bubble surfed" the tank's aerator jets.

Anderson tested for play by presenting eight giant Pacific octopuses with floating pill bottles in varying colors and textures twice a day for five days. Six octopuses examined the bottles and lost interest, but two blew them repeatedly into their tanks' jets. One propelled a bottle at an angle so it circled the tank; the other shot it so it rebounded quickly—and on three occasions shot it back at least twenty times, as if it were bouncing a ball.

One respected cephalopod expert isn't convinced. Jean Boal, an animal behaviorist at Millersville University in Pennsylvania, is acutely aware of the dangers of getting carried away when studying these charismatic megamollusks. She previously worked at the Zoological Station in Naples, a wellspring of cephalopod research. In 1992 Graziano Fiorito, a researcher at that lab, announced a bombshell: Octopuses could learn by watching other octopuses. Such observational learning, a hallmark of intelligent social animals, seemed impossible. And it probably was. Other researchers, including Boal, have been unable to reproduce Fiorito's results. Some questioned his methodology, and for a year or two the controversy cast a pall on research into octopus learning.

20   Boal subsequently withdrew her own initial findings of complex learning by octopuses. She has since carved herself a niche as the field's designated skeptic, often questioning conclusions and urging more rigor. "My bias is to build a case slowly, with careful science," Boal says quietly. "That's not the case with all

cephalopod biologists." She doesn't rule out the possibility that octopuses play, but she questions whether the bottle-jetters did: "It could reflect boredom, like a cat pacing."

One authority on play behavior, psychologist Gordon Burghardt at the University of Tennessee in Knoxville, says that as Anderson and Mather describe it, the bottle-jetting would qualify as play. Boredom, he says, can be "a trigger for play." And other confirmation is emerging. Doubting the Seattle findings, Ulrike Griebel of the Lorenz Institute recently conducted more extensive trials. She offered common octopuses varied objects, from Lego assemblies to floating bottles on strings (a favorite). Some octopuses took toys into their nests and toted them along while fetching food—acquisitive behavior that Griebel says "might be an early stage of object play."

Meanwhile, Anderson has been investigating another phenomenon little noted in invertebrates: sleep. Until recently, only vertebrates were believed to sleep in the full metabolic sense. But Anderson has observed that octopuses, ordinarily hypervigilant, may sleep deeply. Their eyes glaze over, their breathing turns slow and shallow, they don't respond to light taps, and a male will let his delicate ligula—the sex organ at the tip of one arm—dangle perilously.

Stephen Duntley, a sleep specialist at Washington University Medical School in St. Louis, has videotaped similar slumber in cuttlefish, with a twist: Sleeping cuttlefish lie still, their skin a dull brown, for ten- to fifteen-minute stretches, then flash bold colored patterns and twitch their tentacles for briefer intervals. After viewing Duntley's footage, Anderson suggests the cuttlefish might merely be waking to check for threats. But Duntley says the cycling resembles the rapid-eye-movement sleep of birds and mammals, when humans dream. If invertebrates undergo a similar cycle, Duntley argues, it would affirm "that REM sleep is very important to learning." Would it also suggest that cuttlefish and octopuses dream? "That's the ultimate question," Duntley responds.

The ultimate question, with octopuses as with other sentient creatures, may be how we should treat them. In 2001 Mather argued in *The Journal of Applied Welfare Science* that people should err on the humane side, since some octopuses "very likely have the capacity for pain and suffering and, perhaps, mental suffering." If captive cephalopods suffer mentally—or even get "bored," as Boal puts it—then they should benefit from enrichment: amenities and activities that replicate elements of their natural environment. Mather, Anderson, and Wood have urged enriched environments but have no experimental evidence that it makes a difference. Recently that evidence came from a French study that even the skeptical Boal calls "beautiful work." Ludovic Dickel, a neuroethologist at the University of Caen, found that cuttlefish raised in groups and in tanks with sand, rocks, and plastic seaweed grew faster, learned faster, and retained more of what they learned than those raised alone in bare tanks. Performance rose in animals transferred midway from impoverished to enriched conditions and declined in those transferred to solitary confinement.

25   Other evidence suggests that solitary octopuses, like solitary orangutans, may communicate more with others of their species than researchers previously realized. Cigliano found that California octopuses that were kept together quickly established hierarchies and avoided wasteful, dangerous confrontations; the weaker animals seemed to recognize and yield to the stronger ones, even when the latter were hidden in their dens. The flip side of communication is deception, another hallmark of intelligence. And some octopuses and cuttlefish practice it. Male cuttlefish adopt female coloring, patterns, and shape—to mate surreptitiously with females guarded by larger rivals. And the Indonesian mimic octopus fools predators by impersonating poisonous soles and venomous lionfish, sea snakes, and possibly jellyfish and sea anemones.

And so, piece by piece, Mather, Anderson, and other researchers fill in the puzzle. A picture emerges of convergent evolution across a billion-year gap. One after another, these precocious invertebrates display what were supposed to be special traits of advanced vertebrates. But one question nags: Why would short-lived, solitary creatures acquire so many of the cognitive and affective features of long-lived, social vertebrates?

Mather proposes "a foraging theory of intelligence." She says that animals like octopuses (or humans) that pursue varied food sources in changeable, perilous habitats must develop a wide range of hunting and defensive strategies. That takes brainpower. "If you find yourself foraging in a complex environment, where you have to deal with many kinds of prey and predators," she says, "it makes sense to invest more in cognition." Temperamental variation—call it personality—also helps a species survive in a volatile, super competitive milieu by ensuring that different individuals respond differently to changing conditions, so some will thrive. Even semelparity, the live-fast-die-young strategy of growing quickly and throwing everything into one breeding blast, may serve that end by assuring rapid turnover and regeneration.

Although cephalopods are an ancient order, shell-less cephalopods are relatively recent arrivals—about 200 million years old, like mammals and teleost, or bony, fishes. Before that, ammonites and other shelled cephalopods ruled the seas, but competition from the nimble, fast-swimming teleosts wiped out all but the relic nautilus. The cephalopods that survived were the zoological counterrevolutionaries that turned the vertebrates' weapons against them. They shed their shells and became speedy, like squid, or they became clever and elusive, like octopuses and cuttlefish. Octopuses, naked and vulnerable, took to dens, as early humans took to caves. Like humans, they became versatile foragers, using a wide repertoire of stalking and killing techniques. To avoid exposure, they developed spatial sense and learned to cover their hunting grounds methodically and efficiently. Mather and O'Dor found that the Bermudan *O. vulgaris* spends just 7 percent of its time hunting; Australian giant cuttlefish spend 3 percent.

In short, octopuses came to resemble us. Their hunting done, they huddle safely in their dens, a bit like early humans around campfires. "You have to wonder what they think about while they're tucked away," says O'Dor. Do they muse on the cruel turns of evolution, which have left them all dressed up with big brains but with no place to go and little time to use them?

ENGAGING the Text

1. Why did Scigliano come to believe that the octopus is capable of a broader range of behavior and possesses greater cognitive abilities than previously believed?

2. What theories had been advanced to explain this higher order of cognitive traits?

EVALUATING the Argument

1. Scigliano cites an extraordinarily broad range of testimony from experts as well as his own personal observations. How does this complex array of evidence enhance the persuasiveness of his thesis?

2. Why does Scigliano touch on areas such as play, tool use, and sleep that we normally think of only in connection with primates?

EXPLORING the Issue

1. To what extent does the evidence in this essay challenge the notion that intelligence increases on a progressive and directional scale from fish to reptiles to mammals to humans? Explain your answer in a short essay.

2. As a research project, look into the myths, legends, children's stories, and films that feature the octopus as intelligent and alien, from Jules Verne's *20,000 Leagues Under the Sea* to the character of Dr. Octavius in *Spider-Man 2*.

CONNECTING Different Perspectives

1. How do the analyses by Jean Henri Fabre and Scigliano ("The Praying Mantis") illustrate how scientists enter the realm of the creatures they study?

Ecology and Environmental Studies

Elizabeth Kolbert

Shishmaref, Alaska

Elizabeth Kolbert has been a staff writer for the New Yorker *since 1999. Her series on global warming, "The Climate of Man," which appeared in the* New Yorker *(Spring 2005), received the American Association for the Advancement of Sciences magazine-writing award. This series was the basis for her book* Field Notes from a Catastrophe: Man, Nature, and Climate Change *(2006), in which the following essay first appeared. From her travels to the Arctic and interviews with researchers and environmentalists, we gain an understanding of the truly cataclysmic effects of global warming and the melting of polar ice caps.*

The Alaskan village of Shishmaref sits on an island known as Sarichef, five miles off the coast of the Seward Peninsula. Sarichef is a small island—no more than a quarter of a mile across and two and a half miles long—and Shishmaref is basically the only thing on it. To the north is the Chukchi Sea, and in every other direction lies the Bering Land Bridge National Preserve, which probably ranks as one of the least visited national parks in the country. During the last ice age, the land bridge—exposed by a drop in sea levels of more than three hundred feet—grew to be nearly a thousand miles wide. The preserve occupies that part of it which, after more than ten thousand years of warmth, still remains above water.

Shishmaref (population 591) is an Inupiat village, and it has been inhabited, at least on a seasonal basis, for several centuries. As in many native villages in Alaska, life there combines—often disconcertingly—the very ancient and the totally modern. Almost everyone in Shishmaref still lives off subsistence hunting, primarily for bearded seals but also for walrus, moose, rabbits, and migrating birds. When I visited the village one day in April, the spring thaw was under way, and the seal-hunting season was about to begin. (Wandering around, I almost tripped over the remnants of the previous year's catch emerging from storage under the snow.) At noon, the village's transportation planner, Tony Weyiouanna, invited me to his house for lunch. In the living room, an enormous television set tuned to the local public-access station was playing a rock soundtrack. Messages like "Happy Birthday to the following elders . . ." kept scrolling across the screen.

Traditionally, the men in Shishmaref hunted for seals by driving out over the sea ice with dogsleds or, more recently, on snowmobiles. After they hauled the seals back to the village, the women would skin and cure them, a process that takes several weeks. In the early 1990s, the hunters began to notice that the sea ice was changing. (Although the claim that the Eskimos have hundreds of words for snow is an exaggeration, the Inupiat make distinctions among many different types of ice, including *sikuliaq*, "young ice," *sarri*, "pack ice," and *tuvaq*, "land-locked ice.") The ice was starting to form later in the fall, and also to break up earlier in the spring. Once, it had been possible to drive out twenty miles; now, by the time the seals arrived, the ice was mushy half that distance from shore. Weyiouanna described it as having the consistency of a "slush puppy." When you encounter it, he said, "your hair starts sticking up. Your eyes are wide open. You can't even blink." It became too dangerous to hunt using snowmobiles, and the men switched to boats.

Soon, the changes in the sea ice brought other problems. At its highest point, Shishmaref is only twenty-two feet above sea level, and the houses, most of which were built by the U.S. government, are small, boxy, and not particularly sturdy-looking. When the Chukchi Sea froze early, the layer of ice protected the village, the way a tarp prevents a swimming pool from getting roiled by the wind. When the sea started to freeze later. Shishmaref became more vulnerable to storm surges. A storm in October 1997 scoured away a hundred-and-twenty-five-foot-wide strip from the town's northern edge; several houses were destroyed, and more than a dozen had to be relocated. During another storm, in October 2001, the village was threatened by twelve-foot waves. In the summer of 2002, residents of Shishmaref voted, a hundred and sixty-one to twenty, to move the entire village to the main-land. In 2004, the U.S. Army Corps of Engineers completed a survey of possible sites. Most of the spots that are being considered for a new village are in areas nearly as remote as Sarichef, with no roads or nearby cities or even settlements. It is estimated that a full relocation would cost the U.S. government $180 million.

5   People I spoke to in Shishmaref expressed divided emotions about the pro-posed move. Some worried that, by leaving the tiny island, they would give up their connection to the sea and become lost. "It makes me feel lonely," one woman said. Others seemed excited by the prospect of gaining certain conve-niences, like running water, that Shishmaref lacks. Everyone seemed to agree, though, that the village's situation, already dire, was only going to get worse.

Morris Kiyutelluk, who is sixty-five, has lived in Shishmaref almost all his life. (His last name, he told me, means "without a wooden spoon.") I spoke to him while I was hanging around the basement of the village church, which also serves as the unofficial headquarters for a group called the Shishmaref Erosion and Relocation Coalition. "The first time I heard about global warming, I thought, I don't believe those Japanese," Kiyutelluk told me. "Well, they had some good scientists, and it's become true."

The National Academy of Sciences undertook its first major study of global warming in 1979. At that point, climate modeling was still in its infancy, and only a few groups, one led by Syukuro Manabe at the National Oceanic and Atmospheric Administration and another by James Hansen at NASA's Goddard Institute for Space Studies, had considered in any detail the effects of adding carbon dioxide to the atmosphere. Still, the results of their work were alarming enough that President Jimmy Carter called on the academy to investigate. A nine-member panel was appointed. It was led by the distinguished meteorologist Jule Charney, of MIT, who, in the 1940s, had been the first meteorologist to demonstrate that numerical weather forecasting was feasible.

The Ad Hoc Study Group on Carbon Dioxide and Climate, or the Charney panel, as it became known, met for five days at the National Academy of Sciences' summer study center, in Woods Hole, Massachusetts. Its conclusions were unequivocal. Panel members had looked for flaws in the modelers' work but had been unable to find any. "If carbon dioxide continues to increase, the study group finds no reason to doubt that climate changes will result and no reason to believe that these changes will be negligible," the scientists wrote. For a doubling of CO_2 from preindustrial levels, they put the likely global temperature rise at between two and a half and eight degrees Fahrenheit. The panel members weren't sure how long it would take for changes already set in motion to become manifest, mainly because the climate system has a built-in time delay. The effect of adding CO_2 to the atmosphere is to throw the earth out of "energy balance." In order for balance to be restored—as, according to the laws of physics, it eventually must be—the entire planet has to heat up, including the oceans, a process, the Charney panel noted, that could take "several decades." Thus, what might seem like the most conservative approach— waiting for evidence of warming to make sure the models were accurate—actually amounted to the riskiest possible strategy: "We may not be given a warning until the CO_2 loading is such that an appreciable climate change is inevitable."

It is now more than twenty-five years since the Charney panel issued its report, and, in that period, Americans have been alerted to the dangers of global warming so many times that reproducing even a small fraction of these warnings would fill several volumes; indeed, entire books have been written just on the history of efforts to draw attention to the problem. (Since the Charney report, the National Academy of Sciences alone has produced nearly two hundred more studies on the subject, including, to name just a few, "Radiative Forcing of Climate Change," "Understanding Climate Change Feedbacks," and "Policy Implications of Greenhouse Warming.") During this same period, worldwide carbon-dioxide emissions have continued to increase from five billion to seven billion metric tons a year, and the earth's temperature, much as predicted by Manabe's and Hansen's models, has steadily risen. The year 1990 was the warmest year on record until 1991, which was equally hot. Almost every subsequent year has been warmer still. As of this writing, 1998 ranks as the hottest year since the instrumental temperature record began, but it is closely followed by 2002 and 2003, which are tied for second; 2001, which is third; and 2004, which is fourth. Since climate is innately changeable, it's difficult to say when, exactly, in this sequence natural variation could be ruled out as the sole cause. The American Geophysical Union, one of the nation's largest and most respected scientific organizations, decided in 2003 that the matter had been settled. At the group's annual meeting that year, it issued a consensus statement declaring, "Natural influences cannot explain the rapid increase in global near-surface temperatures." As best as can be determined, the world is now warmer than it has been at any point in the last two millennia, and, if current trends continue, by the end of the century it will likely be hotter than at any point in the last two million years.

10   In the same way that global warming has gradually ceased to be merely a theory, so, too, its impacts are no longer just hypothetical. Nearly every major glacier in the world is shrinking; those in Glacier National Park are retreating so quickly it has been estimated that they will vanish entirely by 2030. The oceans are becoming not just warmer but more acidic; the difference between daytime and nighttime temperatures is diminishing; animals are shifting their ranges poleward; and plants are blooming days, and in some cases weeks, earlier than they used to. These are the warning signs that the Charney panel cautioned against waiting for, and while in many parts of the globe they are still subtle enough to be overlooked, in others they can no longer be ignored. As it happens, the most dramatic changes are occurring in those places, like Shishmaref, where the fewest people tend to live. This disproportionate effect of global warming in the far north was also predicted by early climate models, which forecast, in column after column of FORTRAN-generated figures, what today can be measured and observed directly: the Arctic is melting.

Most of the land in the Arctic, and nearly a quarter of all the land in the Northern Hemisphere—some five and a half billion acres—is underlaid by zones of permafrost. A few months after I visited Shishmaref, I went back to Alaska to take a trip through the interior of the state with Vladimir Romanovsky, a geophysicist and permafrost expert. I flew into Fairbanks—Romanovsky teaches at the University of Alaska, which has its main campus there—and when I arrived, the whole city was enveloped in a dense haze that looked like fog but smelled like burning rubber. People kept telling me that I was lucky I hadn't come a couple of weeks earlier, when it had been much worse. "Even the dogs were wearing masks," one woman I met said. I must have smiled. "I am not joking," she told me.

Fairbanks, Alaska's second-largest city, is surrounded on all sides by forest, and virtually every summer lightning sets off fires in these forests, which fill the air with smoke for a few days or, in bad years, weeks. In the summer of 2004, the fires started early, in June, and were still burning two and a half months later; by the time of my visit, in late August, a record 6.3 million acres—an area roughly the size of New Hampshire—had been incinerated. The severity of the fires was clearly linked to the weather, which had been exceptionally hot and dry; the average summertime temperature in Fairbanks was the highest on record, and the amount of rainfall was the third lowest.

On my second day in Fairbanks, Romanovsky picked me up at my hotel for an underground tour of the city. Like most permafrost experts, he is from Russia. (The Soviets more or less invented the study of permafrost when they decided to build their gulags in Siberia.) A broad man with shaggy brown hair and a square jaw, Romanovsky as a student had had to choose between playing professional hockey and becoming a geophysicist. He had opted for the latter, he told me, because "I was little bit better scientist than hockey player." He went on to earn two master's degrees and two Ph.D.s. Romanovsky came to get me at ten A.M.; owing to all the smoke, it looked like dawn.

Any piece of ground that has remained frozen for at least two years is, by definition, permafrost. In some places, like eastern Siberia, permafrost runs nearly a mile deep; in Alaska, it varies from a couple of hundred feet to a couple of thousand feet deep. Fairbanks, which is just below the Arctic Circle, is situated in a region of discontinuous permafrost, meaning that the city is pocked with regions of frozen ground. One of the first stops on Romanovsky's tour was a hole that had opened up in a patch of permafrost not far from his house. It was about six feet wide and five feet deep. Nearby were the outlines of other, even bigger holes, which, Romanovsky told me, had been filled with gravel by the local public-works department. The holes, known as thermokarsts, had appeared suddenly when the permafrost gave way, like a rotting floorboard. (The technical term for thawed permafrost is "talik," from a Russian word meaning "not frozen.") Across the road, Romanovsky pointed out a long trench running into the woods. The trench, he explained, had been formed when a wedge of underground ice had melted. The spruce trees that had been growing next to it, or perhaps on top of it, were now listing at odd angles, as if in a gale. Locally, such trees are called "drunken." A few of the spruces had fallen over. "These are very drunk," Romanovsky said.

15   In Alaska, the ground is riddled with ice wedges that were created during the last glaciation, when the cold earth cracked and the cracks filled with water. The wedges, which can be dozens or even hundreds of feet deep, tended to form

in networks, so when they melt, they leave behind connecting diamond-or hexagon-shaped depressions. A few blocks beyond the drunken forest, we came to a house where the front yard showed clear signs of ice-wedge melt-off. The owner, trying to make the best of things, had turned the yard into a miniature-golf course. Around the corner, Romanovsky pointed out a house—no longer occupied—that basically had split in two; the main part was leaning to the right and the garage toward the left. The house had been built in the sixties or early seventies; it had survived until almost a decade ago, when the permafrost under it started to degrade. Romanovsky's mother-in-law used to own two houses on the same block. He had urged her to sell them both. He pointed out one, now under new ownership; its roof had developed an ominous-looking ripple. (When Romanovsky went to buy his own house, he looked only in permafrost-free areas.)

"Ten years ago, nobody cared about permafrost," he told me. "Now every-body wants to know." Measurements that Romanovsky and his colleagues at the University of Alaska have made around Fairbanks show that the temperature of the permafrost in many places has risen to the point where it is now less than one degree below freezing. In places where the permafrost has been disturbed, by roads or houses or lawns, much of it is already thawing. Romanovsky has also been monitoring the permafrost on the North Slope and has found that there, too, are regions where the permafrost is very nearly thirty-two degrees Fahren-heit. While thermokarsts in the roadbeds and talik under the basement are the sort of problems that really only affect the people right near—or above—them, warning permafrost is significant in ways that go far beyond local real estate losses. For one thing, permafrost represents a unique record of long-term tem-perature trends. For another, it acts, in effect, as a repository for greenhouse gases. As the climate warms, there is a good chance that these gases will be released into the atmosphere, further contributing to global warming. Although the age of permafrost is difficult to determine, Romanovsky estimates that most of it in Alaska probably dates back to the beginning of the last glacial cycle. This means that if it thaws, it will be doing so for the first time in more than a hundred and twenty thousand years. "It's really a very interesting time," Romanovsky told me.

ENGAGING the Text

1. How have changes in the ice pack threatened the traditional way of life in this native community in Alaska?

2. Why have long-range projections in climate change focused on the amount of CO_2 being released into the atmosphere?

EVALUATING the Argument

1. How does Kolbert use the trend line of yearly temperatures and changes in the permafrost to substantiate her analysis?

2. How does Kolbert use allusions to a vast time scale to underscore the unique nature of the events in climate change that are now becoming noticeable?

EXPLORING the Issue

1. Contrast the skeptical attitude of public officials with the implications of Kolbert's analysis and the opinions of researchers.

2. In what way is Kolbert's technique of visiting precisely the people in remote regions whose lives are being changed because of global warming an effective one in drawing attention to the issue?

CONNECTING Different Perspectives

1. In a short essay, explore the bio-environmental effects analyzed by Kolbert and by Joseph K. Skinner in "Big Mac and the Tropical Forests."

Joseph K. Skinner

Big Mac and the Tropical Forests

Joseph K. Skinner graduated in 1979 from the University of California–Davis. This essay first appeared in the Monthly Review *of December 1985. His still-pertinent analysis explores the connection between the destruction of tropical forests in Central and Latin America to raise cattle for cheap beef for fast-food chains and the possible effects on the atmosphere in accelerating global warming.*

Hello, fast-food chains.

Goodbye, tropical forests.

Sound like an odd connection? The "free-market" economy has led to results even stranger than this, but perhaps none have been as environmentally devastating.

These are the harsh facts: the tropical forests are being leveled for commercial purposes at the rate of 150,000 square kilometers a year, an area the size of England and Wales combined.[1]

---

[1]Jean-Paul Landley, "Tropical Forest Resources," *FAO Forestry Paper* 30 (Rome: FAO, 1982). This UN statistic is the most accurate to date. For further extrapolations from it, see Nicholas Guppy, "Tropical Deforestation: A Global View," *Foreign Affairs* 62, no. 4 (Spring 1984).

5   At this rate, the world's tropical forests could be entirely destroyed within seventy-three years. Already as much as a fifth or a quarter of the huge Amazon forest, which constitutes a third of the world's total rain forest, has been cut, and the rate of destruction is accelerating. And nearly two thirds of the Central American forests have been cleared or severely degraded since 1950.

Tropical forests, which cover only 7 percent of the Earth's land surface (it used to be 12 percent), support half the species of the world's living things. Due to their destruction, "We are surely losing one or more species a day right now out of the five million (minimum figure) on Earth," says Norman Myers, author of numerous books and articles on the subject and consultant to the World Bank and the World Wildlife Fund. "By the time ecological equilibrium is restored, at least one-quarter of all species will have disappeared, probably a third, and conceivably even more. . . . If this pattern continues, it could mean the demise of two million species by the middle of next century." Myers calls the destruction of the tropical forests "one of the greatest biological debacles to occur on the face of the Earth." Looking at the effects it will have on the course of biological evolution, Myers says:

> The impending upheaval in evolution's course could rank as one of the greatest biological revolutions of paleontological time. It will equal in scale and significance the development of aerobic respiration, the emergence of flowering plants, and the arrival of limbed animals. But of course the prospective degradation of many evolutionary capacities will be an impoverishing, not a creative, phenomenon.[2]

In other words, such rapid destruction will vacate so many niches so suddenly that a "pest and weed" ecology, consisting of a relatively few opportunistic species (rats, roaches, and the like) will be created.

Beyond this—as if it weren't enough—such destruction could well have cataclysmic effects on the Earth's weather patterns, causing, for example, an irreversible desertification of the North American grain belt. Although the scope of the so-called greenhouse effect—in which rising levels of carbon dioxide in the atmosphere heat the planet by preventing infrared radiation from escaping into space—is still being debated within the scientific community, it is not at all extreme to suppose that the fires set to clear tropical forests will

---

[2]There are amazingly few scientists in the world with broad enough expertise to accurately assess the widest implications of tropical deforestation; Norman Myers is one of them. His books include *The Sinking Ark* (Oxford: Pergamon Press, 1979). See also *Conversion of Moist Tropical Forests* (Washington, D.C.: National Academy of Sciences, 1980), "The End of the Line." *Natural History* 94, no. 2 (February 1985), and "The Hamburger Connection," *Ambio* 10, no. 1 (1981). I have used Myers extensively in the preparation of this article. The quotes in this paragraph are from "The Hamburger Connection," pp. 3, 4, 5.

contribute greatly to this increase in atmospheric CO_2 and thereby to untold and possibly devastating changes in the world's weather systems.

Big Mac Attack

So what does beef, that staple of the fast-food chains and of the North American diet in general, have to do with it?

10   It used to be, back in 1960, that the United States imported practically no beef. That was a time when North Americans were consuming a "mere" 85 pounds of beef per person per year. By 1980 this was up to 134 pounds per person per year. Concomitant with this increase in consumption, the United States began to import beef, so that by 1981 some 800,000 tons were coming in from abroad, 17 percent of it from tropical Latin America and three fourths of that from Central America. Since fastfood chains have been steadily expanding and now are a $5-billion-a-year business, accounting for 25 percent of all the beef consumed in the United States, the connections between the fast-food empire and tropical beef are clear.

Cattle ranching is "by far the major factor in forest destruction in tropical Latin America," says Myers. "Large fast-food outlets in the U.S. and Europe foster the clearance of forests to produce cheap beef."[3]

And cheap it is, compared to North American beef: by 1978 the average price of beef imported from Central America was $1.47/kg, while similar North American beef cost $3.30/kg.

Cheap, that is, for North Americans, but not for Central Americans. Central Americans cannot afford their own beef. Whereas beef production in Costa Rica increased twofold between 1959 and 1972, per capita consumption of beef in that country went down from 30 lbs. a year to 19. In Honduras, beef production increased by 300 percent between 1965 and 1975, but consumption decreased from 12 lbs. per capita per year to 10. So, although two thirds of Central America's arable land is in cattle, local consumption of beef is decreasing; the average domestic cat in the United States now consumes more beef than the average Central American.[4]

Brazilian government figures show that 38 percent of all deforestation in the Brazilian Amazon between 1966 and 1975 was attributable to large-scale cattle ranching. Although the presence of hoof-and-mouth disease among Brazilian cattle has forced U.S. lawmakers to prohibit the importation of chilled

[3]Myers, "End of the Line," p. 2.
[4]See James Nations and Daniel I. Komer "Rainforests and the Hamburger Society," *Environment* 25, no. 3 (April 1983).

or frozen Brazilian beef, the United States imports $46 million per year of cooked Brazilian beef, which goes into canned products. Over 80 percent of Brazilian beef is still exported, most of it to Western Europe, where no such prohibition exists.

15   At present rates, all remaining Central American forests will have been eliminated by 1990. The cattle ranching largely responsible for this is in itself highly inefficient: as erosion and nutrient leaching eat away the soil production drops from an average one head per hectare—measly in any case—to a pitiful one head per five to seven hectares within five to ten years. A typical tropical cattle ranch employs only one person per 2,000 head, and meat production barely reaches 50 lbs./acre/year. In Northern Europe, in farms that do not use imported feed, it is over 500 lbs./acre/year.

This real-term inefficiency does not translate into bad business, however, for although there are some absentee landowners who engage in ranching for the prestige of it and are not particularly interested in turning large profits, others find bank loans for growing beef for export readily forthcoming, and get much help and encouragement from such organizations as the Pan American Health Organization, the Organization of American States, the U.S. Department of Agriculture, and U.S. AID, without whose technical assistance "cattle production in the American tropics would be unprofitable, if not impossible."[5] The ultimate big winner appears to be the United States, where increased imports of Central American beef are said to have done more to stem inflation than any other single government initiative.

"On the good land, which could support a large population, you have the rich cattle owners, and on the steep slopes, which should be left in forest, you have the poor farmers," says Gerardo Budowski, director of the Tropical Agricultural Research and Training Center in Turrialba, Costa Rica. "It is still good business to clear virgin forest in order to fatten cattle for, say, five to eight years and then abandon it."[6]

(Ironically, on a trip I made in 1981 to Morazán, a Salvadoran province largely under control of FMLN guerrillas, I inquired into the guerilla diet and discovered that beef, expropriated from the cattle ranches, was a popular staple.)

Swift-Armour's Swift Armor

The rain forest ecosystem, the oldest on Earth, is extremely complex and delicate. In spite of all the greenery one sees there, it is a myth that rain forest soil

---

[5]Nations and Komer, "Rainforests and the Hamburger Society," p. 17.
[6]Catherine Caufield, "The Rain Forests," *New Yorker* (January 14, 1985), p. 42. This excellent article was later incorporated in a book, *In the Rainforest* (New York: Knopf, 1985).

is rich. It is actually quite poor, leached of all nutrients save the most insoluble (such as iron oxides, which give lateritic soil—the most common soil type found there—its red color). Rather, the ecosystem of the rain forest is a "closed" one, in which the nutrients are to be found in the biomass, that is, in the living canopy of plants and in the thin layer of humus on the ground that is formed from the matter shed by the canopy. Hence the shallow-rootedness of most tropical forest plant species. Since the soil itself cannot replenish nutrients, nutrient recycling is what keeps the system going.

20   Now, what happens when the big cattle ranchers, under the auspices of the Swift-Armour Meat Packing Co., or United Brands, or the King Ranch sling a huge chain between two enormous tractors, level a few tens of thousands of acres of tropical forest, burn the debris, fly a plane over to seed the ash with guinea grass, and then run their cattle on the newly created grasslands?[7]

For the first three years or so the grass grows like crazy, up to an inch a day, thriving on all that former biomass. After that, things go quickly downhill: the ash becomes eroded and leached, the soil becomes exposed and hardens to the consistency of brick, and the area becomes useless to agriculture. Nor does it ever regain anything near its former state. The Amazon is rising perceptibly as a result of the increased runoff due to deforestation.

Tractor-and-chain is only one way of clearing the land. Another common technique involves the use of herbicides such as Tordon, 2, 4-D, and 2,4,5-T (Agent Orange). The dioxin found in Agent Orange can be extremely toxic to animal life and is very persistent in the environment.

Tordon, since it leaves a residue deadly to all broad-leaved plants, renders the deforested area poisonous to all plants except grasses; consequently, even if they wanted to, ranchers could not plant soil-enriching legumes in the treated areas, a step which many agronomists recommend for keeping the land productive for at least a little longer.

The scale of such operations is a far cry from the traditional slash-and-burn practiced by native jungle groups, which is done on a scale small enough so that the forest can successfully reclaim the farmed areas. Such groups, incidentally, are also being decimated by cattle interests in Brazil and Paraguay—as missionaries, human rights groups, and cattlemen themselves will attest.

---

[7]Other multinationals with interests in meat packing and cattle ranching in tropical Latin America include Armour-Dial International, Goodyear Tire and Rubber Co., and Gulf and Western Industries, Inc. See Roger Burbach and Patricia Flynn, *Agribusiness in the Americas* (New York: Monthly Review Press, 1980).

25   Capital's "manifest destiny" has traditionally shown little concern for the lives of trees or birds or Indians, or anything else which interferes with immediate profitability, but the current carving of holes in the gene pool by big agribusiness seems particularly short-sighted. Since the tropical forests contain two thirds of the world's genetic resources, their destruction will leave an enormous void in pool of genes necessary for the creation of new agricultural hybrids. This is not to mention the many plants as yet undiscovered—there could be up to 15,000 unknown species in South America alone—which may in themselves contain remarkable properties. (In writing about alkaloids found in the Madagascar periwinkle which have recently revolutionized the treatment of leukemia and Hodgkin's disease, British biochemist John Humphreys said: "If this plant had not been analyzed, not even a chemist's wildest ravings would have hinted that such structures would be pharmacologically active."[8] Ninety percent of Madagascar's forests have been cut.)

But there is no small truth in Indonesian Minister for Environment and Development Emil Salim's complaint that the "South is asked to conserve genes while the other fellow, in the North, is consuming things that force us to destroy the genes in the South."[9]

Where's the Beef?

The marketing of beef imported into the United States is extremely complex, and the beef itself ends up in everything from hot dogs to canned soup. Fresh meat is exported in refrigerated container ships to points of entry, where it is inspected by the U.S. Department of Agriculture. Once inspected, it is no longer required to be labeled "imported."[10] From there it goes into the hands of customhouse brokers and meat packers, often changing hands many times; and from there it goes to the fast-food chains or the food processors. The financial structures behind this empire are even more complex, involving governments and quasipublic agencies, such as the Export-Import Bank and the Overseas Private Investment Corporation, as well as the World Bank and the Inter-American Development Bank, all of which encourage cattle raising in the forest lands. (Brazilian government incentives to cattle ranching in Amazonia include a 50 percent income-tax rebate on ranchers' investments elsewhere in Brazil, tax holidays of up to ten years, loans with negative interest rates in real terms, and

[8]Quoted in Caufield, "Rain Forests," p. 60.
[9]Caufield, "Rain Forests," p. 100.
[10]This is one way McDonald's, for example, can claim not to use foreign beef. For a full treatment of McDonald's, see M. Boas and S. Chain, *Big Mac: The Unauthorized Story of McDonald's* (New York: New American Library, 1976).

exemptions from sales taxes and import duties. Although these incentives were deemed excessive and since 1979 no longer apply to new ranches, they still continue for existing ones. This cost the Brazilian government $63,000 for each ranching job created.)

Beef production in the tropics may be profitable for the few, but it is taking place at enormous cost for the majority and for the planet as a whole. Apart from the environmental destruction, it is a poor converter of energy to protein and provides few benefits for the vast majority of tropical peoples in terms of employment or food. What they require are labor-intensive, multiple-cropping systems.

The world is obviously hostage to an ethic which puts short-term profitability above all else, and such catastrophes as the wholesale destruction of the tropical forests and the continued impoverishment of their peoples are bound to occur as long as this ethic rules.

ENGAGING the Text

1. What causal link does Skinner point out between hamburgers served in fast-food chains in America and the destruction of tropical rain forests in Central America?

2. What is the greenhouse effect and how is it related to the destruction of tropical forests? What other complex ecological effects are produced by deforestation?

EVALUATING the Argument

1. How effectively does Skinner use evidence in the form of facts, statistics, and the testimony of experts to support his thesis?

2. How does Skinner's discussion of the methods used by cattle ranchers to clear the land underscore his concern over a business ethic that "puts short-term profitability above all else"?

EXPLORING the Issue

1. About 40 percent of modern drugs have been derived from plants whose value was previously unrecognized. Discuss the implications of this fact in a short essay as it relates to Skinner's analysis.

2. To what extent has Skinner's article changed your attitude about fast food, especially hamburgers? An interesting research project might be to investigate the relationship between endangered species (animals and plants) and planned large public-works projects with their competing interests.

CONNECTING Different Perspectives

1. In what respects do both Skinner and Philip Slater (see "Want-Creation Fuels Americans' Addictiveness") agree that our culturally reinforced addictions ultimately destroy ourselves and the environment?

....

Engineering

Donald A. Norman ▰▰▰▰▰▰▰▰▰▰▰▰▰▰▰▰▰▰▰▰▰▰▰▰▰

Emotional Robots

Donald A. Norman is a professor of computer science and psychology at Northwestern University and cofounder of the Neilsen Norman Group, a consulting firm that promotes human-centered products and services. His books include The Design of Everyday Things *(1988),* Things That Make Us Smart *(1993), and* The Invisible Computer *(1998). The following selection is drawn from* Emotional Design: Why We Love (or Hate) Everyday Things *(2004).*

> The 1980s was the decade of the PC, the 90s of the Internet, but I believe the decade just starting will be the decade of the robot.
>
> —*Sony Corporation Executive*

Suppose we wish to build a robot capable of living in the home, wandering about, fitting comfortably into the family—what would it do? When asked this question, most people first think of handing over their daily chores. The robot should be a servant, cleaning the house, taking care of the chores. Everyone seems to want a robot that will do the dishes or the laundry. Actually, today's dishwashers and clothes washers and dryers could be considered to be very simple, special-purpose robots, but what people really have in mind is something that will go around the house and collect the dirty dishes and clothes, sort and wash them, and then put them back to their proper places—after, of course, pressing and folding the clean clothes. All of these tasks are quite difficult, beyond the capabilities of the first few generations of robots.

Today, robots are not yet household objects. They show up in science fairs and factory floors, search-and-rescue missions, and other specialized events. But this will change. Sony has announced this to be the decade of the robot, and even if Sony is too optimistic, I do predict that robots will blossom forth during the first half of the twenty-first century.

Robots will take many forms. I can imagine a family of robot appliances in the kitchen—refrigerator, pantry, coffeemaker, cooking, and dishwasher robots—all configured to communicate with one another and to transfer food, dishes, and utensils back and forth. The home servant robot wanders about, picking up dirty dishes, delivering them to the dishwasher robot. The dishwasher, in turn, delivers clean dishes and utensils to the robot pantry, which stores them until needed by person or robot. The pantry, refrigerator, and cooking robots work smoothly to prepare the day's menu and, finally, place the completed meal onto dishes provided by the pantry robot.

Some robots will take care of children by playing with them, reading to them, singing songs. Educational toys are already doing this, and the sophisticated robot could act as a powerful tutor, starting with the alphabet, reading, and arithmetic, but soon expanding to almost any topic. Neal Stephenson's science fiction novel, *The Diamond Age*, does a superb job of showing how an interactive book, *The Young Lady's Illustrated Primer,* can take over the entire education of young girls from age four through adulthood. The illustrated primer is still some time in the future, but more limited tutors are already in existence. In addition to education, some robots will do household chores: vacuuming, dusting, and cleaning up. Eventually their range of abilities will expand. Some may end up being built into homes or furniture. Some will be mobile, capable of wandering about on their own.

5   These developments will require a coevolutionary process of adaptation for both people and devices. This is common with our technologies: we reconfigure the way we live and work to make things possible for our machines to function. The most dramatic coevolution is the automobile system, for which we have altered our homes to include garages and driveways sized and equipped for the automobile, and built a massive worldwide highway system, traffic signaling systems, pedestrian passageways, and huge parking lots. Homes, too, have been transformed to accommodate the multiple wires and pipes of the ever-increasing infrastructure of modern life: hot and cold water, waste return, air vents to the roof, heating and cooling ducts, electricity, telephone, television, internet and home computer and entertainment networks. Doors have to be wide enough for our furniture, and many homes have to accommodate wheelchairs and people using walkers. Just as we have accommodated the home for all these changes, I expect modification to accommodate robots. Slow modification, to be sure, but as robots increase in usefulness, we will ensure their success by minimizing obstacles and, eventually, building charging stations, cleaning and maintenance places, and so on. After all, the vacuum cleaner robot will need a place to empty its dirt, and the garbage robot will need to be able to carry the garbage outside the home. I wouldn't be surprised to see robot quarters in homes, that is, specially built niches where the robots can reside, out of the way, when they are not active. We have closets and pantries for today's appliances, so why not ones especially equipped for robots, with doors that can be controlled by the robot,

electrical outlets, interior lights so robots can see to clean themselves (and plug themselves into the outlets), and waste receptacles where appropriate.

Robots, especially at first, will probably require smooth floors, without obstacles. Door thresholds might have to be eliminated or minimized. Some locations—especially stairways—might have to be especially marked, perhaps with lights, infrared transmitters, or simply special reflective tape. Barcodes or distinctive markers posted here and there in the home would enormously simplify the robot's ability to recognize its location.

Consider how a servant robot might bring a drink to its owner. Ask for a can of soda, and off goes the robot, obediently making its way to the kitchen and the refrigerator, which is where the soda is kept. Understanding the command and navigating to the refrigerator are relatively simple. Figuring out how to open the door, find the can, and extract it is not so simple. Giving the servant robot the dexterity, the strength, and the non-slip wheels that would allow it to pull open the refrigerator door is quite a feat. Providing the vision system that can find the soda, especially if it is completely hidden behind other food items, is difficult, and then figuring out how to extract the can without destroying objects in the way is beyond today's capabilities in robot arms.

How much simpler it would be if there were a drink dispenser robot tailored to the needs of the servant robot. Imagine a drink-dispensing robot appliance capable of holding six or twelve cans, refrigerated, with an automatic door and a push-arm. The servant robot could go to the drink robot, announce its presence and its request (probably by an infrared or radio signal), and place its tray in front of the dispenser. The drink robot would slide open its door, push out a can, and close the door again: no complex vision, no dexterous arm, no forceful opening of the door. The servant robot would receive the can on its tray, and then go back to its owner.

In a similar way, we might modify the dishwasher to make it easier for a home robot to load it with dirty dishes, perhaps give it special trays with designated slots for different dishes. But as long as we are doing that, why not make the pantry a specialized robot, one capable of removing the clean dishes from the dishwasher and storing them for later use? The special trays would help the pantry as well. Perhaps the pantry could automatically deliver cups to the coffeemaker and plates to the home cooking robot, which is, of course, connected to refrigerator, sink, and trash. Does this sound far-fetched? Perhaps, but, in fact, our household appliances are already complex, many of them with multiple connections to services. The refrigerator has connections to electric power and water. Some are already connected to the internet. The dishwasher and clothes washer have electricity, water and sewer connections. Integrating these units so that they can work smoothly with one another does not seem all that difficult.

10   I imagine that the home will contain a number of specialized robots: the servant is perhaps the most general purpose, but it would work together with a cleaning robot, the drink dispensing robot, perhaps some outside gardening robots, and a family of kitchen robots, such as dishwasher, coffee-making, and pantry robots. As these robots are developed, we will probably also design specialized objects in the home that simplify the tasks for the robots, coevolving robot and home to work smoothly together. Note that the end result will be better for people as well. Thus, the drink dispenser robot would allow anyone to walk up to it and ask for a can, except that you wouldn't use infrared or radio, you might push a button or perhaps just ask.

I am not alone in imagining this coevolution of robots and homes. Rodney Brooks, one of the world's leading roboticists, head of the MIT Artificial Intelligence Laboratory and founder of a company that builds home and commercial robots, imagines a rich ecology of environments and robots, with specialized ones living on devices, each responsible to keep its domain clean: one does the bathtub, another the toilet; one does windows, another manipulates mirrors. Brooks even contemplates a robot dining room table, with storage area and dishwasher built into its base so that "when we want to set the table, small robotic arms, not unlike the ones in a jukebox, will bring the required dishes and cutlery out onto the place settings. As each course is finished, the table and its little robot arms would grab the plates and devour them into the large internal volume underneath."

What should a robot look like? Robots in the movies often look like people, with two legs, two arms, and a head. But why? Form should follow function. The fact that we have legs allows us to navigate irregular terrain, something an animal on wheels could not do. The fact that we have two hands allows us to lift and manipulate, with one hand helping the other. The humanoid shape has evolved over eons of interaction with the world to cope efficiently and effectively with it. So, where the demands upon a robot are similar to those upon people, having a similar shape might be sensible.

If robots don't have to move—such as drink, dishwasher, or pantry robots—they need not have any means of locomotion, neither legs nor wheels. If the robot is a coffeemaker, it should look like a coffeemaker, modified to allow it to connect to the dishwasher and pantry. Robot vacuum cleaners and lawn mowers already exist, and their appearance is perfectly suited to their tasks: small, squat devices, with wheels. A robot car should look like a car. It is only the general-purpose home servant robots that are apt to look like animals or humans. The robot dining room table envisioned by Brooks would be especially bizarre, with a large central column to house the dishes and dishwashing equipment (complete with electric power, water and sewer connections). The top of the table would have places for the robot arms to manipulate the dishes and probably some stalk to hold the cameras that let the arms know where to place and retrieve the dishes and cutlery.

Should a robot have legs? Not if it only has to maneuver about on smooth surfaces—wheels will do for this; but if it has to navigate irregular terrain or stairs, legs would be useful. In this case, we can expect the first legged robots to have four or six legs: balancing is far simpler for four- and six-legged creatures than for those with only two legs.

15   If the robot is to wander about a home and pick up after the occupants, it probably will look something like an animal or a person: a body to hold the batteries and to support the legs, wheels, or tracks for locomotion; hands to pick up objects; and cameras (eyes) on top where they can better survey the environment. In other words, some robots will look like an animal or human, not because this is cute, but because it is the most effective configuration for the task. These robots will probably look something like R2D2: a cylindrical or rectangular body on top of some wheels, tracks, or legs; some form of manipulable arm or tray; and sensors all around to detect obstacles, stairs, people, pets, other robots, and, of course the objects they are supposed to interact with. Except for pure entertainment value, it is difficult to understand why we would ever want a robot that looked like C3PO.

In fact, making a robot humanlike might backfire, making it less acceptable. Masahiro Mori, a Japanese roboticist, has argued that we are least accepting of creatures that look very human, but that perform badly, a concept demonstrated in film and theater by the terrifying nature of zombies and monsters (think of Frankenstein's monster) that take on human form, but with inhuman movement and ghastly appearance. We are not nearly so dismayed—or frightened—by non-human shapes and forms. Even perfect replicas of humans might be problematic, for even if the robot could not be distinguished from humans, this very lack of distinction can lead to emotional angst (a theme explored in many a science fiction novel, especially Philip K. Dick's *Do Androids Dream of Electric Sheep?* and, in movie version, *Blade Runner*). According to this line of argument, C3PO gets away with its humanoid form because it is so clumsy, both in manner and behavior, that it appears more cute or even irritating than threatening.

Robots that serve human needs—for example, robots as pets—should probably look like living creatures, if only to tap into our visceral system, which is prewired to interpret human and animal body language and facial expressions. Thus, an animal or a childlike shape together with appropriate body actions, facial expressions, and sounds will be most effective if the robot is to interact successfully with people.

ENGAGING the Text

1. According to Norman, what different forms will home robots take in the near future? What tasks will they perform?

2. What adaptations or modifications will the home environment require to accommodate its new inhabitant?

EVALUATING the Argument

1. How do the examples, including the hypothetical ones, bring to life the premise on which Norman's essay is based?

2. How does Norman use the testimony of Rodney Brooks at MIT to strengthen his own case?

EXPLORING the Issue

1. To what extent does Norman establish a plausible scenario as to the integral function robots in the home will have and the role they will play?

2. You might wish to rent Woody Allen's 1973 movie *Sleeper* and compare Norman's vision of the future with Allen's spoof.

CONNECTING Different Perspectives

1. Draw on both Norman's essay and Richard Keller Simon's "The Shopping Mall and the Formal Garden" and describe the function that emotional robots will play in the shopping environment.

Epidemiology

Gina Kolata

An Incident in Hong Kong

Gina Kolata (b. 1948) is a science journalist who has been writing for the New York Times *since 1987. She studied molecular biology at the Massachusetts Institute of Technology and holds a master's degree in mathematics from the University of Maryland. Kolata is the author of* The Baby Doctors: Probing the Limits of Fetal Medicine *(1990),* Clone: The Road to Dolly and the Path Ahead *(1998), and* Ultimate Fitness: The Quest for Truth About Exercise and Health *(2003). The following selection is drawn from her book* Flu: The Story of the Great Influenza Pandemic of 1918 and the Search for the Virus That Caused It *(1999).*

As you read, consider how this diagram complements Kolata's account.

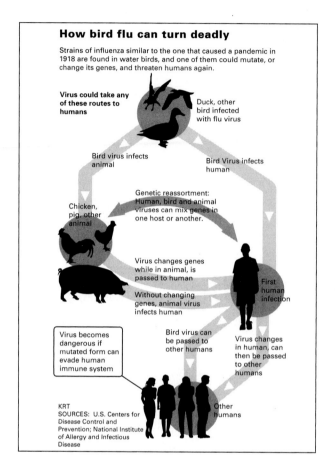

How bird flu can turn deadly

Strains of influenza similar to the one that caused a pandemic in 1918 are found in water birds, and one of them could mutate, or change its genes, and threaten humans again.

Virus could take any of these routes to humans

Duck, other bird infected with flu virus

Bird virus infects animal

Bird Virus infects human

Genetic reassortment: Human, bird and animal viruses can mix genes in one host or another.

Chicken, pig, other animal

Virus changes genes while in animal, is passed to human

Without changing genes, animal virus infects human

First human infection

Virus becomes dangerous if mutated form can evade human immune system

Bird virus can be passed to other humans

Virus changes in human, can then be passed to other humans

KRT
SOURCES: U.S. Centers for Disease Control and Prevention; National Institute of Allergy and Infectious Disease

Other humans

Dr. Nancy Cox was on vacation in Wyoming when she got the call from her lab in Atlanta. Virologists there had done what they thought would be a routine test to determine the strain of an influenza virus isolated from a patient that past May. The sample had been stored at the lab for about a month and taken up in its turn for analysis. But when Cox, who directs the influenza lab at the Centers for Disease Control and Prevention, heard the result, her heart started to pound and she felt adrenaline rush through her body. The virus was of type H5N1. It was a flu strain that should never have infected a human being. Even worse, Cox was told, the person it infected was a child, a three-year-old boy in Hong Kong. And he had died.

It was August 1997. Jeffery Taubenberger had just published his initial analysis of the 1918 flu virus genes that he had extracted from Private Vaughan's lung tissue. But it was too soon to say what had made the 1918 flu virus so lethal. The flu virologists in Cox's group had no way of knowing whether the virus that had killed the Hong Kong boy shared deadly features with the 1918 flu and whether, like the 1918 virus, the Hong Kong virus would sweep the world, spreading a swath of devastation in its wake. The question leaped to Cox's mind: Was this the first sounding of a fatal pandemic? On the other hand, she realized, it might instead be a repeat of the sort of false alarm raised by the soldier who died of a swine flu virus in 1976.

Cox spent long afternoons in conference calls with her staff and other scientists discussing what to do. She tossed in bed through several long, sleepless nights worrying. The flu virologists of the world could not afford to make a mistake.

Until that moment, there was little reason to panic over the viral infection. Yes, the boy's illness had been frightening, but his doctors were not even convinced that a virus had killed him.

5   The boy had died on May 9, in a hospital, tethered to a respirator. He had been healthy and entirely normal, striding into his preschool class, playing with his friends, with no illnesses other than the usual runny noses and earaches that plague young children. Then, one day in early May, he got a respiratory infection that quickly turned into viral pneumonia. Soon he was hospitalized, unable to breathe on his own. His doctors diagnosed viral pneumonia complicated by Reye's syndrome, a disorder that sometimes follows viral infections like influenza or chicken pox. It is a rare disease that strikes children and teenagers and it can be fatal. The patient's brain fills with fluid, creating so much pressure inside the skull that the brain starts to compress the delicate nerves at its base, the brain stem, that control breathing and heart rate. When the brain stem is damaged, Reye's victims die.

So even though the child died within days of becoming ill, it was not clear what had killed him—a viral illness or Reye's syndrome. Nonetheless, the hospital staff was frightened and saddened and sought answers. What kind of virus had precipitated this death? How could a vibrant and robust child have become so sick and died so quickly? The child's doctors sent washings from his throat to a government virology lab for analysis. The samples, tests revealed, contained just one kind of virus, an influenza virus. Then the difficulty occurred. Try as they might, the lab scientists could not identify the strain of influenza.

Labs, like the one in Hong Kong that analyzed the throat washings from the three-year-old boy, keep a set of antibodies that recognize the most common types of the viral surface proteins—hemagglutinin and neuraminidase—that define flu strains. Scientists mark the antibodies with chemicals that will glow if the antibodies latch on to a flu virus. Then they swish a solution of these antibodies onto a petri dish where the flu virus is growing. If the antibodies hook up with a flu virus, the petri dish's contents will glisten red.

The boy's virus never elicited such an effect. Even though the lab workers tested the boy's flu virus with every antibody they had, they came up empty-handed. Nothing matched.

The lab workers in Hong Kong were not alarmed. After all, their set of antibodies would attach to the most likely strains of flu viruses, but they by no means had a complete set of antibodies. They passed the sample on to a specialty lab in Rotterdam for further testing.

10   Since the Hong Kong scientists did not convey a sense of urgency, the Rotterdam scientists simply put the specimen on their list of things to do. In July, they sent some of the sample to Cox's group at the Centers for Disease Control and Prevention.

"They didn't send us any paperwork indicating that it was anything unusual," Cox said. "As far as they knew, it was just another influenza virus." And so her group put the specimen in its queue. "It was processed along with other viruses," Cox notes.

That meant that it was a month before Cox's group got around to looking at it. The Atlanta lab, one of four in the world that keep a lookout for emerging flu strains, is awash in flu samples, receiving several thousand specimens each year. It's part of the global flu surveillance network that allows virologists to discern the first signs of the next year's predominant flu strain—in time to start making vaccines—and that lets them keep an ever-vigilant watch for new strains of flu.

The surveillance network evolved over the years so that now, in the United States, about 110 local influenza centers collect flu viruses in their own regions and determine their type. About eighty-four countries are linked in an international network. The group from the Centers for Disease Control and Prevention looks at flu viruses submitted from all of them. Some places send in just a subset of their viruses, a representative sample. Others send in everything they come across.

We ask for viruses isolated early and late in the flu season—that sometimes gives us a clue to what is going to happen in the season that is coming or the next season. We ask for isolates from the peak of flu activity and we ask for typical strains and unusual strains," Cox said.

15   The Hong Kong virus came through that surveillance network.

As a reference lab for influenza, Cox's lab—and the one in Rotterdam—had sets of antibodies to flu strains that no one ever expected to see in humans. These were strains of flu viruses that infect birds. While very occasionally a bird flu mutates and kills birds, for the most part bird flus are entirely benign. Instead of infecting cells of the lung and causing sickness, the virus lives peacefully in cells of the birds' intestines, causing no symptoms. In theory, a bird flu could not infect a human because the virus should require cellular enzymes found in bird intestinal cells but not in human lung cells. Yet if, against all odds, a bird flu virus was infecting people, it would have hemagglutinin and neuraminidase proteins that had never been seen before by a human being. No human would be immune to such a virus. The whole world was at risk.

Worse yet, if a bird flu did jump to humans, and if the event happened in Asia, the scenario fit all too well into a chilling story developed by two leading flu virologists, Dr. Robert Webster of St. Jude Children's Research Hospital in Memphis and Dr. Kennedy Shortridge of the University of Hong Kong.

Webster proposed that the worst flu pandemics, the one in 1918 being at the far end of bad, start with a bird flu. But before it can infect a person, it has to be humanized—that is, to change in a way that would allow it to keep the birdlike features that make it so infectious and yet acquire human flu-like properties that would allow it to grow in the lung cells of a human being. That crucial step, Webster said, typically takes place in pigs. Pigs bridge the gap between birds and humans—both bird flu strains and human flu strains can grow in pigs' bodies.

An unfortunate pig that happens to be infected with both a bird and human virus at the same time can become a mixing bowl, with the genes from the two types of flu viruses recombining in its cells to form a new hybrid virus that can infect humans but has some genes from the bird flu, genes that make the newly emerging virus more dangerous than any that had been around before. Thus the stage can be set for a worldwide pandemic.

20 As evidence for his hypothesis, Webster posited that the 1918 virus probably started out in a bird, moved to a pig, and then infected people, which is why those who lived through the epidemic had antibodies to swine flu. Moreover, the only two pandemics in which flu viruses had been isolated, the "Asian" flu of 1957 and the "Hong Kong" flu of 1968, involved virus strains that seem to have come, indirectly, from birds. (Earlier pandemics took place before virologists knew how to test flu strains and there were no subsequent pandemics.)

Kennedy Shortridge elaborated from there. Asia, he said, is the influenza epicenter. The virus thrives in ducks, in particular, that are omnipresent in southern China. Those birds have served as a reservoir for dangerous viral strains that have become converted into human flus because of an ingenious system devised by Chinese rice farmers that inadvertently ensures that the flu strains have plenty of opportunity to jump from ducks to pigs to people.

As early as the seventeenth century, these farmers discovered a way to keep their rice crops free of weeds and insects and, at the same time, keep a flock of plump ducks around for food. While the rice is growing, they put ducks on the flooded fields. The ducks eat insects and even weeds, but do not touch the rice. When the rice starts to blossom, the farmers remove the ducks from the rice fields and put them on waterways and ponds. After the rice is harvested, the farmers put the ducks back on the dry rice fields, where they eat the grains of rice that have fallen to the ground. Now the ducks are ready for slaughter.

The problem, however, is that the farmers also keep pigs that live alongside the ducks. And so, Shortridge said, "when you domesticate the duck, you unwittingly bring the flu virus to humans."

Shortridge notes that influenza epidemics always seem to start in Asia—in southern China in particular, exactly the place where the rice-duck-pig system is in place. "Historical records always refer to this part of the world," he said.

25   Now, as Cox looked at the lab records from the little boy who died in Hong Kong, she knew she was seeing an unprecedented and possibly horrifying event. Here was a flu virus. It came from Hong Kong. It was a bird virus, but unlike any other bird flu virus ever known, it seemed to have skipped the pig step altogether since it had hemagglutinin and neuraminidase proteins that are characteristic of bird, but not pig, flus. It infected a three-year-old boy. And it killed him.

ENGAGING the Text

1. Why was it vitally important for scientists to determine the mechanism by which the boy who died was infected?

2. How is understanding the connection between swine flu, bird flu, and human influenza necessary to appreciate why the recurrence of a 1918-style outbreak is a real possibility?

EVALUATING the Argument

1. How does Kolata write in a way designed to make technical procedures and facts understandable, and even fascinating, for her general readers?

2. Why is the case-history method Kolata adopts following a doctor on her quest to discover why a 3-year-old boy has died in Hong Kong communicate the abstract notion of the flu epidemic in specific and human terms?

EXPLORING the Issue

1. For a research project, investigate current measures that are being taken to forestall a 1918-type pandemic that killed a hundred million people worldwide.

2. The 1918 pandemic was forgotten and virtually ignored for 80 years until the 1997 outbreak of bird flu in Asia. What does this reveal about the
short-sighted nature of epidemiology? What other "conquered" diseases
such as polio, smallpox, and tuberculosis have recently reappeared?

CONNECTING Different Perspectives

1. In what respects has the flu virus discussed by Kolata showed itself as
capable of adapting and finding new hosts as the rabies virus has done
in animals as described by Robert Sapolsky in "Bugs in the Brain"?

Genetics and Bioengineering

Carol Grunewald

Monsters of the Brave New World

Carol Grunewald is a Times Mirror *newspaper reporter and former editor of the magazine the*
Animal Rights Agenda. *She currently works for the National Humane Society, Washington,*
D.C. This essay originally appeared in the January 1991 issue of the New Internationalist.

It's probably no accident that some of the most fearsome monsters invented by
the human mind have been composed of body parts of various animal—including human—species.

Ancient and mediaeval mythology teem with "transgenic" creatures who
have served through the ages as powerful symbols and movers of the human
subconscious. In Greek mythology the Chimera—a hideous fire-breathing she-
monster with the head of a lion, the body of a goat and a dragon's tail—was
darkness incarnate and a symbol of the underworld.

At the beginning of the industrial or technological age, the collective consciousness conjured monsters from a new but related fear—the consequences of
human interference with nature. Fears of science and technology gone out of
control created the stories of *Dr. Jekyll and Mr. Hyde*[1] and *Dr. Frankenstein*[2].

---

[1]*Dr. Jekyll and Mr. Hyde:* a person marked by a dual personality, one aspect of which is good and the
other evil, after the protagonist of Robert Louis Stevenson's novel, *The Strange Case of Dr. Jekyll and*
Mr. Hyde (1886).
[2]*Dr. Frankenstein:* a person who creates a destructive agency that cannot be controlled or brings
about the ruin of the creator. A character from the 1818 novel by Mary Shelley.

The contemporary monster is apt to be a real human being, but an amoral, sociopathic one—a Mengele[3] or an Eichmann[4] who imposes his evil will not in the heat of passion, but in cold detachment.

Deepest Human Fears

5 Our nightmares, our mythologies, our movies, our real-life monsters reveal many of our deepest human fears: of the unknown, of the unnatural, of science gone berserk and of the dark side of the human psyche. With such an intense subliminal heritage, no wonder many people are instinctively wary of the new and revolutionary science of genetic engineering—a science born just 15 years ago but which is already creating its own monsters. They have good reason to be afraid.

The goal of genetic engineering is to break the code of life and to reform and "improve" the biological world according to human specifications. It is the science of manipulating genes either within or between organisms. Genes are the fundamental and functional units of heredity; they are what make each of us similar to our species but individually different.

There are two astonishing aspects to this new science. For the first time, humankind has the capacity to effect changes in the genetic code of individual organisms which will be passed down to future generations.

Equally startling, humankind now has the ability to join not only various animal species that could never mate in nature but also to cross the fundamental biological barriers between plants and animals that have always existed.

Experiments have already produced a few animal monstrosities. "Geeps," part goat, part sheep, have been engineered through the process of cell-fusion— mixing cells of goat and sheep embryos. A pig has been produced whose genetic structure was altered by the insertion of a human gene responsible for producing a growth hormone. The unfortunate animal (nicknamed "super-pig") is so riddled with arthritis she can barely stand, is nearly blind, and prone to developing ulcers and pneumonia. No doubt researchers will create many such debilitated and pain-racked animals until they get it right.

Custom-Designed Creatures

10 Meanwhile, the world's knowledge of genetic engineering is growing apace. Much of what is now only theoretically possible will almost certainly be realized.

[3]*Josef Mengele (1911–1979):* nicknamed "the angel of death" because of his role in deciding who would live and die at the Auschwitz concentration camp.
[4]*Adolf Eichmann (1906–1962):* German Nazi official responsible for the killing of millions of Jews during the Holocaust. In 1960, he was hanged for crimes against humanity by the government of Israel.

With the world's genetic pool at a scientist's disposal, the possibilities are endless. It's just a matter of time.

But two historic events spurred the growth in what is now referred to as the "biotech industry." In 1980 the U.S. Supreme Court ruled, in a highly controversial 5–4 vote, that "man-made" micro-organisms can be patented. Then in April 1987, without any public debate, the U.S. Patent Officer suddenly announced that all forms of life—including animals but excluding human beings—may be considered "human inventions." These could qualify as "patentable subject matter," provided they had been genetically engineered with characteristics not attainable through classical breeding techniques.

The economic incentives were impossible for researchers and corporations to resist. The genetic engineering of animals was a biological gold mine waiting to be exploited. In hope of getting rich off the "inventions," scientists have so far "created" thousands of animals nature could never have made. Now more than 90 patents are pending for transgenic animals, and some 7,000 are pending for genetically engineered plant and animal micro-organisms.

Until now animal rights activists have been the foremost opponents of genetic engineering. The reason: animals are already the worse for it. Because they are powerless, animals have always suffered at the hands of humankind. When a new technology comes along, new ways are devised to exploit them. But genetic engineering represents the most extreme and blatant form of animal exploitation yet.

Genetic engineers do not see animals as they are: inherently valuable, sentient creatures with sensibilities very similar to ours and lives of their own to live. To them, animals are mere biological resources, bits of genetic code that can be manipulated at will and "improved" to serve human purposes. They can then be patented like a new toaster or tennis ball.

15   In a recent article, the U.S. Department of Agriculture crows that "the face of animal production in the twenty-first century could be . . . broilers blooming to market size 40 percent quicker, miniature hens cranking out eggs in double time, a computer 'cookbook' of recipes for custom-designed creatures."

The trade journal of the American beef industry boasts that in the year 2014 farmers will be able to order "from a Sears-type catalog, specific breeds or mixtures of breeds of (genetically engineered) cattle identified by a model number and name. Just like the 2014's new model pick-up truck, new model animals can be ordered for specific purposes."

A university scientist says, "I believe it's completely feasible to specifically design an animal for a hamburger."

A Canadian researcher speaking at a farmers' convention eagerly tells the group that "at the Animal Research Institute we are trying to breed animals without legs and chickens without feathers."

Huge profits are to be made from new cows, pigs, chickens and other farm animals whose genetic scripts will be written and "improved" to grow faster and leaner on less food and on new foods such as sawdust, cardboard and industrial and human waste.

20   Researchers have been straining at the bit to design and patent new animal "models" of human disease—living, breathing "tools" who will be experimented to death in the laboratory. Scientists have also created "medicine factories" out of mice by implanting in them human genes for producing human enzymes, proteins and drugs that can be harvested. Cows, sheep and other milk-producing animals have been targeted for further experimentation in this area.

Animals already suffer abominably in intensive-confinement factory farms and laboratories. Genetic manipulations will result in further subjugation of animals and increase and intensify their stress, pain, and mental suffering.

But genetic engineering also imposes risks on wildlife and the environment. Many questions need to be asked. For example, what will happen when genetically-altered animals and plants are released into the environment? Once they're out there we can't get them back. What if they run amok? Carp and salmon are currently engineered to grow twice as large as they do in nature. But will they also consume twice as much food? Will they upset the ecological balance and drive other animal or plant species to extinction?

Indeed, the genetic engineering of animals will almost certainly endanger species and reduce biological diversity. Once researchers develop what is considered to be the "perfect carp" or "perfect chicken" these will be the ones that are reproduced in large numbers. All other "less desirable" species would fall by the wayside and decrease in number. The "perfect" animals might even be cloned—reproduced as exact copies—reducing even further the pool of available genes on the planet.

Such fundamental human control over all nature would force us to view it differently. Which leads us to the most important examination of all: our values.

How Human?

25 We need to ask ourselves what are the long term consequences for civilization of reducing all of life to engineering values." These are the words of Foundation on Economic Trends President Jeremy Rifkin, the leading opponent

of genetic engineering in the U.S. Rifkin warns that the effects of new technologies are pervasive. They reach far beyond the physical, deep into the human psyche and affect the well-being of all life on earth.

In the brave new world of genetic engineering will life be precious? If we could create living beings at will—and even replace a being with an exact clone if it died—would life be valued? The patenting of new forms of life has already destroyed the distinction between living things and inanimate objects. Will nature be just another form of private property?

The intermingling of genes from various species, including the human species, will challenge our view of what it means to be human. If we inject human genes into animals, for example, will they become part human? If animal genes are injected into humans will we become more animal? Will the distinctions be lost? And if so, what will the repercussions be for all life?

And will humans be able to create, patent, and thus own a being that is, by virtue of its genes, part human? In other words, how human would a creature have to be in order to be included in the system of rights and protections that are accorded to "full humans" today?

We may already know the answer to that question. Chimpanzees share 99 per cent of our human genetic inheritance, yet nowhere in the world is there a law that prevents these nearly 100-percent human beings from being captured, placed in leg-irons, owned, locked in laboratory and zoo cages and dissected in experiments.

30   The blurring of the lines between humans and animals could have many interesting consequences. All of us (humans and animals) are really made of the same "stuff" and our genes will be used interchangeably. Since we are already "improving" animals to serve our needs, why not try and improve ourselves as well? With one small step, we could move from animal eugenics to human eugenics and, by means of genetic engineering, make the plans of the Nazis seem bumbling and inefficient.

Life as Property

Finally, who will control life? Genetic technology is already shoring up the mega-multinational corporations and consolidating and centralizing agribusiness. Corporate giants like General Electric, Du Pont, Upjohn, Ciba-Geigy, Monsanto, and Dow Chemical have multibillion-dollar investments in genetic engineering technology. It is becoming increasingly clear that we are placing the well-being of the planet and all its inhabitants in the hands of a technological elite. Our scientists, corporations and military are playing with, and may eventually own, our genes.

The arrogance and foolishness of humankind! With everything on the planet existing just to be used and exploited—with nothing existing without a "reason" and a "use"—where is the joy of life? What is the reason for living?

People and animals are inseparable; our fates are inextricably linked. People are animals. What is good for animals is good for the environment is good for people. What is bad for them is bad for us.

The first line of resistance should be to scrap the patenting of animals. And the release of any genetically altered organisms into the environment should be prohibited.

35   Finally, we must remember that the mind that views animals as pieces of coded genetic information to be manipulated and exploited at will is the mind that would view human beings in a similar way. People who care about people should listen carefully to what Animals Rights activists and environmentalists have to say about obtaining justice for, and preserving the integrity of, *all* life.

ENGAGING the Text

1. How do new capabilities of genetic engineering raise concerns about a new type of abuse of the animals that are used in this research?

2. What concerns does Grunewald have about cross-breeding between laboratory-produced animals and species that exist in nature?

EVALUATING the Argument

1. What kinds of evidence does Grunewald use to dramatize how changes in the patent law raise questions about whether corporations should be able to invent, control, and own new life forms?

2. Evaluate Grunewald's strategy of equating the dangers posed by creating new species with unforeseen characteristics and eugenics.

EXPLORING the Issue

1. With which of Grunewald's assumptions are you in sympathy? Would you necessarily draw the same conclusions that she does? Why or why not?

2. Were it possible to genetically engineer your children to suppress undesirable traits and to add desirable ones, would you do so? What would these characteristics be?

CONNECTING Different Perspectives

1. In what way do ethical concerns overlap in Grunewald's essay and in Hans Ruesch's "Slaughter of the Innocent"?

Medicine

George E. Vaillant

We Should Retain the Disease Concept of Alcoholism

George E. Vaillant was born in 1934 in New York City. He is the Director of Adult Develop-
ment at Harvard University from which he received an M.D. in 1965. Vaillant is the author
of The Natural History of Alcoholism *(1983) and* The Wisdom of the Ego *(1993) and*
received the Jellinck Prize for alcoholism research. This article first appeared in the August 1990
Harvard Medical School Mental Health Letter.

When I read expert discussions of why alcoholism is not a disease, I am reminded of the equally learned discussions by "the best and the brightest" of why the Viet Nam War was a good idea. These discussants had intelligence, advanced degrees, scholarship, prestige, literacy—every qualification but one. They lacked experience. None had spent much time in Viet Nam. Just so, the philosopher Herbert Fingarette, the psychoanalyst Thomas Szasz, the sociologist and theoretician Robin Room, and provocative, thoughtful psychologists like Stanton Peele and Nicholas Heather have every qualification but one for explaining why alcoholism is not a disease—they have never worked in an alcohol clinic. Why, I wonder, do experienced alcohol workers and recovering alcoholics, the thousands of competent common folk in the trenches, accept the view that alcoholism is a disease? Why is it mainly less competent people, the active alcoholics, who agree with Professor Fingarette that they are just "heavy drinkers"?

Let me summarize the evidence provided by the learned academics who have pointed out the folly of the medical model of alcoholism. First, alcohol abuse—unlike coughing from pneumonia, for example—is a habit under considerable volitional control. Second, there is compelling evidence that variations in alcohol consumption are distributed along a smooth continuum, although a medical model would suggest that in any individual, alcoholism is either present or absent. Third, when alcoholism is treated as a disease it can be used both by individuals and by society to explain away major underlying problems—poverty, mental deficiency, crime, and the like—which require our attention if efforts at prevention, treatment and understanding are to succeed. Fourth, to diagnose people as alcoholic is to label them in a way that can damage both self-esteem and public acceptance. Fifth, alcoholism should not be considered a disease if it is regarded as merely a symptom of underlying personality or depression.

Refutation of Objections

Let me try to refute these objections one by one. First, it may be true that there is no known underlying biological defect in alcoholism. Rather, alcohol abuse is a multidetermined continuum of drinking behaviors whose causes are differently weighted for different people and include culture, habits, and genes. But the same can be said of high blood pressure and coronary heart disease. The incidence of hypertension varies with measurement procedures and psychological circumstances. It lies on a physiological continuum which defies precise definition. It has no known specific cause. It is powerfully affected by social factors; for example, it has become epidemic among young urban black males. The point of using the term 'disease' for alcoholism is simply to underscore that once a person has lost the capacity to control consistently how much and how often he or she drinks, continued use of alcohol can be both a necessary and a sufficient cause of a syndrome that produces millions of invalids and causes millions of deaths.

The second objection to the medical model of alcoholism is that only opinion separates the alcoholic from the heavy drinker. Supposedly one either has a disease or does not have it; diagnosis should depend on signs and symptoms, not value judgments. But consider the example of coronary heart disease. We regard it as a medical illness, although its causes are diverse and often poorly understood and there is no fixed point at which we can decide that coronary arteries become abnormal. So it is with alcoholism. Normal drinking merges imperceptibly with pathological drinking. Culture and idiosyncratic viewpoints will always determine where the line is drawn.

5   The third objection is that alcoholism is affected by so many situational and psychological factors that the drinking must often be viewed as reactive. Some people drink uncontrollably only after a serious loss or in certain specific situations, and some alcoholics return to normal drinking by an act of will. But these observations are equally true of hypertension, which often has an extremely important psychological component. Nevertheless, prospective studies show that alcohol dependence causes depression, anxiety, and poverty far more often than the other way around. In citing psychological problems as a cause of alcoholism, Fingarette reverses the position of cart and horse.

The fourth objection to calling alcoholism a disease is that it involves both labeling and a disparagement of free will. But in this case both labeling and the denial of free will are therapeutic. Some people believe that the label 'alcoholic' transforms a person into an outcast, akin to a leper. Well, should a doctor who knows that a person has leprosy keep the fact secret lest the patient be labeled a leper? Some people believe that if alcoholics are taught to regard alcoholism as a disease they will use this label as an excuse to drink or a reason why they should not be held responsible for their own recovery. It does not work out that way. Like people with high blood pressure, alcoholics who understand that they have a disease become more rather than less willing to take responsibility for self-care. That is why the self-help group, Alcoholics Anonymous, places such single-minded emphasis on the idea that alcoholism is a disease.

Diagnosis Helps

Once patients accept the diagnosis, they can be shown how to assume responsibility for their own care. Physicians stress the value of diagnosing hypertension early because it can provide a rational explanation for headaches and other symptoms that were hitherto regarded as neurotic or irrational. For years alcoholics themselves have labeled themselves 'wicked,' 'weak,' and 'reprehensible.' The offer of a medical explanation does not lead to irresponsibility, only to hope and improved morale.

The fifth argument against calling alcoholism a disease is the most compelling; it is said that uncontrolled maladaptive ingestion of alcohol is not a biological disorder but a disorder of behavior. Like compulsive fingernail biting, gambling, or child molesting, this form of deviant behavior can often be better classified by sociologists than by physiologists, and better treated by psychologists skilled in behavior therapy than by physicians with their medical armamentarium.

But unlike giving up gambling or fingernail biting, giving up alcohol abuse often requires skilled medical attention during acute withdrawal. Unlike gamblers and fingernail biters, most alcoholics develop secondary symptoms that do require medical care. Unlike child molesters, but like people with high blood pressure, alcoholics have a mortality rate two to four times as high as the average. In order to receive the medical treatment they require, alcoholics need a label that will allow them unprejudiced access to emergency rooms, detoxification clinics, and medical insurance.

10   The final argument for regarding alcoholism as a disease rather than a behavior disorder is that it often causes alcoholics to mistreat persons they love. Very few sustained human experiences involve as much abuse as the average close family member of an alcoholic must tolerate. Fingarette's "heavy drinking" model (which conveys a concept of misbehavior) only generates more denial in the already profoundly guilt-ridden alcoholic. Calling alcoholism a disease rather than a behavior disorder is a useful device both to persuade the alcoholic to acknowledge the problem and to provide a ticket for admission to the health care system. In short, in our attempts to understand and study alcoholism, we should employ the models of the social scientist and the learning theorist. But in order to treat alcoholics effectively we need to invoke the medical model.

Let me close with an anecdote. My research associate, reviewing the lives of 100 patients who had been hospitalized eight years previously for detoxification from alcohol, wrote to me that she mistrusted the diagnosis of alcoholism. To illustrate, she described one man who drank heavily for seven years after his initial detoxification. Although the alcohol clinic's staff agreed that his drinking was alcoholic, neither he nor his wife acknowledged that it was a problem. Finally he required a second detoxification, and the clinic staff claimed that they had been right.

"How can you call such behavior a disease," my associate wrote, "when you cannot decide if it represents a social problem [that is, requires a value judgment] or alcohol-dependent drinking?" Then she shifted her attention to the ninety-nine other tortured lives she had been reviewing. Oblivious of the contradiction, she concluded: "I don't think I ever fully realized before I did this follow-up what an absolutely devastating disease alcoholism is." I respectfully submit that if Professor Fingarette were to work in an alcohol clinic for two years, he would agree with the last half of my research associate's letter rather than the first half.

ENGAGING the Text

1. What defining criteria does Vaillant propose by which to evaluate whether alcoholism is or is not a disease? Do they make sense to you?

2. According to Vaillant, what would be the disadvantages of failing to view alcoholism as a disease?

EVALUATING the Argument

1. How does Vaillant draw correspondences to hypertension in order to develop his case?

2. Of the various kinds of evidence Vaillant presents to support his thesis or claim, which, in your opinion, seems the strongest and which the weakest? Is there one phase of his argument you feel he should have developed more fully in order to make his case more persuasive?

EXPLORING the Issue

1. On the basis of personal experience or based on the observation of others, would you agree that alcoholism is more of an inherited tendency rather than a result of psychological and social factors?

2. Using Vaillant's essay as a model, write a short essay in which you make a case for the distinctive nature of some phenomenon as a form of "addictive behavior." You should develop criteria, specify attributes and offer examples that would lead your readers to have a clear idea of (a) food related disorders such as anorexia, (b) compulsive behaviors such as gambling or shopping, (c) addictions to exercise, sports, drugs, pornography.

CONNECTING Different Perspectives

1. Would Philip Slater (see "Want-Creation Fuels Americans' Addictive-ness") be inclined to view alcoholism as a medical problem as does Vaillant or a behavioral disorder with its roots in contemporary culture?

Oceanography

Thor Heyerdahl

How to Kill an Ocean

Thor Heyerdahl (1914–2002), the Norwegian explorer and anthropologist, was educated at the University of Oslo. His seafaring odysseys sought evidence that ancient cultures could have been spread by transoceanic travelers. Heyerdahl sailed across the Pacific (1947), the Atlantic (1970), and the Persian Gulf (1977) in replicas of primitive crafts made out of balsa, papyrus, and reeds. The results are recounted in The Kon Tiki Expedition *(1948),* Aku-Aku *(1958), and* The Maldive Mystery *(1986). His last work was* In the Footsteps of Adam *(2000). The following essay originally appeared in* Saturday Review *(1975). Heyerdahl disputes the concept of a "boundless ocean" and identifies threats to the oceans of the world in ways that are more relevant now than ever.*

Since the ancient Greeks maintained that the earth was round and great naviga-tors like Columbus and Magellan demonstrated that this assertion was true, no geographical discovery has been more important than what we all are beginning to understand today: that our planet has exceedingly restricted dimensions. There is a limit to all resources. Even the height of the atmosphere and the depth of soil and water represent layers so thin that they would disappear entirely if reduced to scale on the surface of a commonsized globe.

The correct concept of our very remarkable planet, rotating as a small and fertile oasis, two-thirds covered by life-giving water, and teeming with life in a solar system otherwise unfit for man, becomes clearer for us with the progress of moon travel and modern astronomy. Our concern about the limits to human expansion increases as science produces ever more exact data on the measurable resources that mankind has in stock for all the years to come.

Because of the population explosion, land of any nature has long been in such demand that nations have intruded upon each other's territory with armed forces in order to conquer more space for overcrowded communities. During the last few years, the United Nations has convened special meetings in Stockholm, Caracas, and Geneva in a dramatic attempt to create a "Law of the Sea" designed to divide vast sections of the global ocean space into national waters. The fact that no agreement has been reached illustrates that in our ever-shriveling world there is not even ocean space enough to satisfy everybody. And only one generation ago, the ocean was considered so vast that no one nation would bother to lay claim to more of it than the three-mile limit which represented the length of a gun shot from the shore.

It will probably take still another generation before mankind as a whole begins to realize fully that the ocean is but another big lake, landlocked on all sides. Indeed, it is essential to understand this concept for the survival of coming generations. For we of the 20th century still treat the ocean as the endless, bottomless pit it was considered to be in medieval times. Expressions like "the bottomless sea" and "the boundless ocean" are still in common use, and although we all know better, they reflect the mental image we still have of this, the largest body of water on earth. Perhaps one of the reasons why we subconsciously consider the ocean a sort of bottomless abyss is the fact that all the rain and all the rivers of the world keep pouring constantly into it and yet its water level always remains unchanged. Nothing affects the ocean, not even the Amazon, the Nile, or the Ganges. We know, of course, that this imperviousness is no indicator of size, because the sum total of all the rivers is nothing but the return to its own source of the water evaporated from the sea and carried ashore by drilling clouds.

5   What is it really then that distinguishes the ocean from the other more restricted bodies of water? Surely it is not its salt content. The Old and the New World have lakes with a higher salt percentage than the ocean has. The Aral Sea, the Dead Sea, and the Great Salt Lake in Utah are good examples. Nor is it the fact that the ocean lacks any outlet. Other great bodies of water have abundant input and yet no outlet. The Caspian Sea and Lake Chad in Central Africa are valid examples. Big rivers, among them the Volga, enter the Caspian Sea, but evaporation compensates for its lack of outlet, precisely as is the case with the ocean. Nor is it correct to claim that the ocean is open while inland seas and lakes are landlocked. The ocean is just as landlocked as any lake. It is flanked by land on all sides and in every direction. The fact that the earth is round makes the ocean curve around it just as does solid land, but a shoreline encloses the ocean on all sides and in every direction. The ocean is not even the lowest body of water on our planet. The surface of the Caspian Sea, for instance, is 85 feet below sea level, and the surface of the Dead Sea is more than 1,200 feet below sea level.

Only when we fully perceive that there is no fundamental difference between the various bodies of water on our planet, beyond the fact that the ocean is the largest of all lakes, can we begin to realize that the ocean has something else in common with all other bodies of water: it is vulnerable. In the long run the ocean can be affected by the continued discharge of all modern man's toxic waste. One generation ago no one would have thought that the giant lakes of America could be polluted. Today they are, like the largest lakes of Europe. A few years ago the public was amazed to learn that industrial and urban refuse had killed the fish in Lake Erie. The enormous lake was dead. It was polluted from shore to shore in spite of the fact that it has a constant outlet through Niagara Falls, which carries pollutants away into the ocean in a never-ending flow. The ocean receiving all this pollution has no outlet but represents a dead end, because only pure water evaporates to return into the clouds. The ocean is big: yet if 10 Lake Eries were taken and placed end to end, they would span the entire Atlantic from Africa to South America. And the St. Lawrence River is by no means the only conveyor of pollutants into the ocean. Today hardly a creek or a river in the world reaches the ocean without carrying a constant flow of nondegradable chemicals from industrial, urban, or agricultural areas. Directly by sewers or indirectly by way of streams and other waterways, almost every big city in the world, whether coastal or inland, makes use of the ocean as mankind's common sink. We treat the ocean as if we believed that it is not part of our own planet—as if the blue waters curved into space somewhere beyond the horizon where our pollutants would fall off the edge, as ships were believed to do before the days of Christopher Columbus. We build sewers so far into the sea that we pipe the harmful refuse away from public beaches. Beyond that is no man's concern. What we consider too dangerous to be stored under technical control ashore we dump forever out of sight at sea, whether toxic chemicals or nuclear waste. Our only excuse is the still-surviving image of the ocean as a bottomless pit.

It is time to ask: is the ocean vulnerable? And if so, can many survive on a planet with a dead ocean? Both questions can be answered, and they are worthy of our attention.

First, the degree of vulnerability of any body of water would of course depend on two factors: the volume of the water and the nature of the pollutants. We know the volume of the ocean, its surface measure, and its average depth. We know that it covers 71 percent of the surface of our planet, and we are impressed, with good reason, when all these measurements are given in almost astronomical figures. If we resort to a more visual image, however, the dimensions lose their magic. The average depth of all oceans is only 1,700 meters. The Empire State Building is 448 meters high. If stretched out horizontally instead of vertically, the average ocean depth would only slightly exceed the 1,500 meters than an Olympic runner can cover by foot in 3 minutes and 35 seconds. The average depth of the North Sea, however, is not 1,700 meters, but only 80 meters, and many of the buildings in downtown New York would emerge high above water level if they were built on the bottom of this sea. During the Stone Age most of the North Sea was dry land where roaming archers hunted deer and other game. In this shallow water, until only recently, all the industrial nations of Western Europe have conducted year-round routine dumping of hundreds of thousands of tons of their most toxic industrial refuse. All the world's sewers and most of its waste are dumped into waters as shallow as, or shallower than, the North Sea. An attempt was made at a recent ocean exhibition to illustrate graphically and in correct proportion the depths of the Atlantic, the Pacific, and the Indian oceans in relation to a cross section of the planet earth. The project had to be abandoned, for although the earth was painted with a diameter twice the height of a man, the depths of the world oceans painted in proportion became so insignificant that they could not be seen except as a very thin pencil line.

The ocean is in fact remarkably shallow for its size. Russia's Lake Baikal, for instance, less than 31 kilometers wide, is 1,500 meters deep, which compares well with the average depth of all oceans. It is the vast *extent* of ocean surface that has made man of all generations imagine a correspondingly unfathomable depth.

10   When viewed in full, from great heights, the ocean's surface is seen to have definite, confining limits. But at sea level, the ocean seems to extend outward indefinitely, to the horizon and on into blue space. The astronauts have come back from space literally disturbed upon seeing a full view of our planet. They have seen at first hand how cramped together the nations are in a limited space and how the "endless" oceans are tightly enclosed within cramped quarters by surrounding land masses. But one need not be an astronaut to lose the sensation of a boundless ocean. It is enough to embark on some floating logs tied together, as we did with the *Kon-Tiki* in the Pacific, or on some bundles of papyrus reeds, as we did with the *Ra* in the Atlantic. With no effort and no motor we were pushed by the winds and currents from one continent to another in a few weeks.

After we abandon the outworn image of infinite space in the ocean, we are still left with many wrong or useless notions about biological life and vulnerability. Marine life is concentrated in about 4 percent of the ocean's total body of water, whereas roughly 96 percent is just about as poor in life as is a desert ashore. We all know, and should bear in mind, that sunlight is needed to permit photosynthesis for the marine plankton on which all fishes and whales directly or indirectly base their subsistence. In the sunny tropics the upper layer of light used in photosynthesis extends down to a maximum depth of 80 to 100 meters. In the northern latitudes, even on a bright summer's day, this zone reaches no more than 15 to 20 meters below the surface. Because much of the most toxic pollutants are buoyant and stay on the surface (notably all the pesticides and other poisons based on chlorinated hydrocarbons), this concentration of both life and venom in the same restricted body of water is most unfortunate.

What is worse is the fact that life is not evenly distributed throughout this thin surface layer. Ninety percent of all marine species are concentrated above the continental shelves next to land. The water above these littoral shelves represents an area of only 8 percent of the total ocean surface, which itself represents only 4 percent of the total body of water, and means that much less than half a percent of the ocean space represents the home of 90 percent of all marine life. This concentration of marine life in shallow waters next to the coasts happens to coincide with the area of concentrated dumping and the outlet of all sewers and polluted river mouths, not to mention silt from chemically treated farm-land. The bulk of some 20,000 known species of fish, some 30,000 species of mollusks, and nearly all the main crustaceans lives in the most exposed waters around the littoral areas. As we know, the reason is that this is the most fertile breeding ground for marine plankton. The marine plant life, the phytoplankton, find here their mineral nutriments, which are brought down by rivers and silt and up from the ocean bottom through coastal upwellings that bring back to the surface the remains of decomposed organisms which have sunk to the bottom through the ages. When we speak of farmable land in any country, we do not include deserts or sterile rock in our calculations. Why then shall we deceive ourselves by the total size of the ocean when we know that not even 1 percent of its water volume is fertile for the fisherman?

Much has been written for or against the activities of some nations that have dumped vast quantities of nuclear waste and obsolete war gases in the sea and excused their actions on the grounds that it was all sealed in special containers. In such shallow waters as the Irish Sea, the English Channel, and the North Sea there are already enough examples of similar "foolproof" containers moving about with bottom currents until they are totally displaced and even crack open with the result that millions of fish are killed or mutilated. In the Baltic Sea, which is shallower than many lakes and which—except for the thin surface layer—has already been killed by pollution, 7,000 tons of arsenic were dumped in cement containers some 40 years ago. These containers have now started to leak. Their combined contents are three times more than is needed to kill the entire population of the earth today.

Fortunately, in certain regions modern laws have impeded the danger of dumpings; yet a major threat to marine life remains—the less spectacular but more effective ocean pollution through continuous discharge from sewers and seepage. Except in the Arctic, there is today hardly a creek or a river in the world from which it is safe to drink at the outlet. The more technically advanced the country, the more devastating the threat to the ocean. A few examples picked at random will illustrate the pollution input from the civilized world:

15   French rivers carry 18 billion cubic meters of liquid pollution annually into the sea. The city of Paris alone discharges almost 1.2 million cubic meters of untreated effluent into the Seine every day.

The volume of liquid waste from the Federal Republic of Germany is estimated at over 9 billion cubic meters per year, or 25.4 million cubic meters per day, not counting cooling water, which daily amounts to 33.6 million cubic meters. Into the Rhine alone 50,000 tons of waste are discharged daily, including 30,000 tons of sodium chloride from industrial plants.

A report from the U.N. Economic and Social Council, issued prior to the Stockholm Conference on the Law of the Sea four years ago, states that the world had then dumped an estimated billion pounds of DDT into our environment and was adding an estimated 100 million more pounds per year. The total world production of pesticides was estimated at more than 1.3 billion pounds annually, and the United States alone exports more than 400 million pounds per year. Most of this ultimately finds its way into the ocean with winds, rain, or silt from land. A certain type of DDT sprayed on crops in East Africa a few years ago was found and identified a few months later in the Bay of Bengal, a good 4,000 miles away.

The misconception of a boundless ocean makes the man in the street more concerned about city smog than about the risk of killing the ocean. Yet the tallest chimney in the world does not suffice to send the noxious smoke away into space; it gradually sinks down, and nearly all descends, mixed with rain, snow, and silt, into the ocean. Industrial and urban areas are expanding with the population explosion all over the world, and in the United States alone, waste products in the form of smoke and noxious fumes amount to a total of 390,000 tons of pollutants every day, or 142 million tons every year.

With this immense concentration of toxic matter, life on the continental shelves would in all likelihood have been exterminated or at least severely decimated long since if the ocean had been immobile. The cause for the delayed action, which may benefit man for a few decades but will aggravate the situation for coming generations, is the well-known fact that the ocean rotates like boiling water in a kettle. It churns from east to west, from north to south, from the bottom to the surface, and down again, in perpetual motion. At a U.N. meeting one of the developing countries proposed that if ocean dumping were prohibited by global or regional law, they would offer friendly nations the opportunity of dumping in their own national waters—for a fee, of course!

20   It cannot be stressed too often, however, that it is nothing but a complete illusion when we speak of national waters. We can map and lay claim to the ocean bottom, but not to the mobile sea above it. The water itself is in constant transit. What is considered to be the national waters of Morocco one day turns up as the national waters of Mexico soon after. Meanwhile Mexican national water is soon on its way across the North Atlantic to Norway. Ocean pollution abides by no law.

My own transoceanic drifts with the *Kon-Tiki* raft and the reed vessels *Ra I* and *II* were eye-openers to me and my companions as to the rapidity with which so-called national waters displace themselves. The distance from Peru to the Tuamotu Islands in Polynesia is 4,000 miles when it is measured on a map. Yet the *Kon-Tiki* raft had only crossed about 1,000 miles of ocean surface when we arrived. The other 3,000 miles had been granted us by the rapid flow of the current during the 101 days our crossing lasted. But the same raft voyages taught us another and less pleasant lesson: it is possible to pollute the oceans, and it is already being done. In 1947, when the balsa raft *Kon-Tiki* crossed the Pacific, we towed a plankton net behind. Yet we did not collect specimens or even see any sign of human activity in the crystal-clear water until we spotted the wreck of an old sailing ship on the reef where we landed. In 1969 it was therefore a blow to us on board the papyrus raft-ship *Ra* to observe, shortly after our departure from Morocco, that we had sailed into an area filled with ugly clumps of hard asphalt-like material, brownish to pitch black in color, which were floating at close intervals on or just below the water's surface. Later on, we sailed into other areas so heavily polluted with similar clumps that we were reluctant to dip up water with our buckets when we needed a good scrub-down at the end of the day. In between these areas the ocean was clean except for occasional floating oil lumps and other widely scattered refuse such as plastic containers, empty bottles, and cans. Because the ropes holding the papyrus reeds of *Ra I* together burst, the battered wreck was abandoned in polluted waters short of the island of Barbados, and a second crossing was effectuated all the way from Safi in Morocco to Barbados in the West Indies in 1970. This time a systematic day-by-day survey of ocean pollution was carried out, and samples of oil lumps collected were sent to the United Nations together with a detailed report on the observations. This was published by Secretary-General U Thant as an annex to his report to the Stockholm Conference on the Law of the Sea. It is enough here to repeat that sporadic oil clots drifted by within reach of our dip net during 43 out of the 57 days our transatlantic crossing lasted. The laboratory analysis of the various samples of oil clots collected showed a wide range in the level of nickel and vanadium content, revealing that they originated from different geographical localities. This again proves that they represent not the homogeneous spill from a leaking oil drill or from a wrecked super-tanker, but the steadily accumulating waste from the daily routine washing of sludge from the combined world fleet of tankers.

The world was upset when the *Torrey Canyon's* unintentionally spilled 100,000 tons of oil into the English Channel some years ago; yet this is only a small fraction of the intentional discharge of crude oil sludge through less spectacular, routine tank cleaning. Every year more than *Torrey Canyon's* spill of a 100,000 tons of oil is intentionally pumped into the Mediterranean alone, and a survey of the sea south of Italy yielded 500 liters of solidified oil for every square kilometer of surface. Both the Americans and the Russians were alarmed by our observations of Atlantic pollution in 1970 and sent out specially equipped oceanographic research vessels to the area. American scientists from Harvard University working with the Bermuda Biological Station for Research found more solidified oil than seaweed per surface unit in the Sargasso Sea and had to give up their plankton catch because their nets were completely plugged up by oil sludge. They estimated, however, a floating stock of 86,000 metric tons of tar in the Northwest Atlantic alone. The Russians, in a report read by the representative of the Soviet Academy of Sciences at a recent pollution conference in Prague, found that pollution in the coastal areas of the Atlantic had already surpassed their tentative limit for what had been considered tolerable, and that a new scale of tolerability would have to be postulated.

The problem of oil pollution is in itself a complex one. Various types of crude oil are toxic in different degrees. But they all have one property in common: they attract other chemicals and absorb them like blotting paper, notably the various kinds of pesticides. DDT and other chlorinated hydrocarbons do not dissolve in water, nor do they sink: just as they are absorbed by plankton and other surface organisms, so are they drawn into oil slicks and oil clots, where in some cases they have been rediscovered in stronger concentrations than when originally mixed with dissolvents in the spraying bottles. Oil clots, used as floating support for barnacles, marine worms, and pelagic crabs, were often seen by us from the *Ra*, and these riders are attractive bait for filter-feeding fish and whales, which cannot avoid getting gills and baleens cluttered up by the tarlike oil. Even sharks with their rows of teeth plastered with black oil clots are now reported from the Caribbean Sea. Yet the oil spills and dumping of waste from ships represent a very modest contribution compared with the urban and industrial refuse released from land.

That the ocean, given time, will cope with it all, is a common expression of wishful thinking. The ocean has always been a self-purifying filter that has taken care of all global pollution for millions of years. Man is not the first polluter.

Since the morning of time nature itself has been a giant workshop, experimenting, inventing, decomposing, and throwing away waste: the incalculable billions of tons of rotting forest products, decomposing flesh, mud, silt, and excrement. If this waste had not been recycled, the ocean would long since have become a compact soup after millions of years of death and decay, volcanic eruptions, and global erosion. Man is not the first large-scale producer, so why should he become the first disastrous polluter?

25   Man has imitated nature by manipulating atoms, taking them apart and grouping them together in different compositions. Nature turned fish into birds and beasts into man. It found a way to make fruits out of soil and sunshine. It invented radar for bats and whales, and shortwave transceivers for beetles and butterflies. Jet propulsion was installed on squids, and unsurpassed computers were made as brains, for mankind. Marine bacteria and plankton transformed the dead generations into new life. The life cycle of spaceship earth is the closest one can ever get to the greatest of all inventions, *perpetuum mobile*—the perpetual-motion machine. And the secret is that nothing was composed by nature that could not be recomposed, recycled, and brought back into service again in another form as another useful wheel in the smoothly running global machinery.

This is where man has sidetracked nature. We put atoms together into molecules of types nature had carefully avoided. We invent to our delight immediately useful materials like plastics, pesticides, detergents, and other chemical products hitherto unavailable on planet earth. We rejoice because we can get our laundry whiter than the snow we pollute and because we can exterminate every trace of insect life. We spray bugs and bees, worms and butterflies. We wash and flush the detergents down the drain out to the oysters and fish. Most of our new chemical products are not only toxic: they are in fact created to sterilize and kill. And they keep on displaying these same inherent abilities wherever they end up. Through sewers and seepage they all head for the ocean, where they remain to accumulate as undesired nuts and bolts in between the cog-wheels of a so far smoothly running machine. If it had not been for the present generation, man could have gone on polluting the ocean forever with the degradable waste he produced. But with ever-increasing speed and intensity we now produce and discharge into the sea hundreds of thousands of chemicals and other products. They do not evaporate nor do they recycle, but they grow in numbers and quantity and threaten all marine life.

We have long known that our modern pesticides have begun to enter the flesh of penguins in the Antarctic and the brains of polar bears and the blubber of whales in the Arctic, all subsisting on plankton and plankton-eating crustaceans and fish in areas far from cities and farmland. We all know that marine pollution has reached global extent in a few decades. We also know that very little or nothing is being done to stop it. Yet there are persons who tell us that there is no reason to worry, that the ocean is so big and surely science must have everything under control. City smog is being fought through intelligent legislation. Certain lakes and rivers have been improved by leading the sewers down to the sea. But where, may we ask, is the global problem of ocean pollution under control?

No breathing species could live on this planet until the surface layer of the ocean was filled with phytoplankton, as our planet in the beginning was only surrounded by sterile gases. These minute plant species manufactured so much oxygen that it rose above the surface to help form the atmosphere we have today. All life on earth depended upon this marine plankton for its evolution and continued subsistence. Today, more than ever before, mankind depends on the welfare of this marine plankton for his future survival as a species. With the population explosion we need to harvest even more protein from the sea. Without plankton there will be no fish. With our rapid expansion of urban and industrial areas and the continuous disappearance of jungle and forest, we shall be ever more dependent on the plankton for the very air we breathe. Neither man nor any other terrestrial beast could have bred had plankton not preceded them. Take away this indispensable life in the shallow surface areas of the sea, and life ashore will be unfit for coming generations. A dead ocean means a dead planet.

ENGAGING the Text

1. How have Heyerdahl's voyages changed his view of the "boundless" nature of the ocean?

2. To what types of pollution is the ocean most vulnerable? Why does one form of pollution often make another kind of pollution even worse?

EVALUATING the Argument

1. What dramatic examples of midocean pollution does Heyerdahl cite to help his readers understand the long-term nature of the problem?

2. What use does Heyerdahl make of statistics to support his claim about a fragile and vulnerable ocean environment?

EXPLORING the Issue

1. In a short essay, discuss the impact of disposable goods in a consumer culture on ocean pollution.

2. For a research project, read Heyerdahl's account of his pacific voyages in the *Kon-Tiki* and his Atlantic voyages in the *Ra* to assess the impact of ocean pollution that he discovered.

CONNECTING Different Perspectives

1. How do Heyerdahl and Joseph K. Skinner (see "Big Mac and the Tropical Forests") challenge our assumptions about the "boundless" ocean and the continued existence of the tropical forests?

Physics

Charles H. Townes

Harnessing Light

Charles H. Townes (b. 1915) has taught physics at Columbia University, M.I.T, and the University of California–Berkeley. He was awarded the Nobel Prize in Physics in 1964 for his research in lasers and quantum electronics. His published works include How the Laser Happened: Adventures of a Scientist *(1999). In the following essay, Townes describes the research that led to the discovery of the laser and the ways in which it has transformed our world.*

The laser was born early one beautiful spring morning on a park bench in Washington, D.C. As I sat in Franklin Square, musing and admiring the azaleas, an idea came to me for a practical way to obtain a very pure form of electromagnetic waves from molecules. I had been doggedly searching for new ways to produce radio waves at very high frequencies, too high for the vacuum tubes of the day to generate. This short-wavelength radiation, I felt, would permit extremely accurate measurement and analysis, giving new insights into physics and chemistry.

As it turned out, I was much too conservative; the field has developed far beyond my imagination and along paths I could not have foreseen at the time. Surveyors use the laser to guarantee straight lines; surgeons to weld new corneas into place and burn away blood clots; industry to drill tiny, precise holes; communications engineers to send information in vast quantities through glass fiber pipes. It is even built into the supermarket checkout scanner that reads prices by bouncing a beam of laser light off a pattern imprinted on the item.

But in the spring of 1951, as I sat on my park bench, it was all yet to come. In the quest for short-wavelength radio waves, I built on the knowledge of the time. In general terms, it was this. Atoms and molecules can absorb radiation as light, as radio waves, or as heat. The radiation is absorbed in the form of a quantum, or tiny packet of energy, that pushes the atom from one energy level to a higher one by exactly the amount of absorbed energy. The atom excited in this way may spontaneously fall to a lower energy level. As it does, it gives up a quantum of radiant energy and releases a burst of electromagnetic radiation, usually in the form of light. This happens in the sun, where atoms are excited by heat agitation or radiation and then drop to a lower level of energy, releasing light. But I was focusing on another way of producing radiation, understood in theory since Einstein discussed it in 1917: the stimulated emission of radiation.

In this case, radiation such as light passing by stimulates an atom to give up its energy to the radiation, at exactly the same frequency and radiated in exactly the same direction, and then drop to a lower state. If this process happened naturally, light striking one side of a black piece of paper would emerge from the other side stronger than it went in—and that's what happens in a laser. But such extraordinary behavior requires an unusual condition: More atoms must be in an excited energy state than in a lower energy one.

5   That morning in the park, I realized that if man was to obtain wavelengths shorter than those that could be produced by vacuum tubes, he must use the ready-made small devices known as atoms and molecules. And I saw that by creating this effect in a chamber with certain critical dimensions, the stimulated radiation could be reinforced, becoming steady and intense.

Later discussions with my students at Columbia University over lunch produced a new vocabulary. We chose the name "maser," for microwave amplification by stimulated emission of radiation, for a device based on the fundamental principle. We also proposed, somewhat facetiously, the "iraser" (infrared amplification by stimulated emission of radiation), "laser" (light amplification), and "xaser" (X-ray amplification). Maser and laser stuck.

The first device to use the new amplifying mechanism was a maser built around ammonia gas, since the ammonia molecule was known to interact more strongly than any other with microwaves. A three-year thesis project of graduate student James Gordon, with assistance from Herbert Zeiger, a young postdoctoral physicist, succeeded and immediately demonstrated the extreme purity of the frequency of radiation produced by the natural vibrations of ammonia molecules. A pure frequency can be translated into accurate timekeeping. Suppose we know that the power from a wall outlet has a frequency of exactly 60 cycles per second. It then takes exactly 1/60th of a second to complete one cycle, one second to complete 60 cycles, one minute for 3,600 of them, and so on. To build an accurate clock, we have only to count the cycles. In the mid-1950s, when the first ammonia maser was completed, the best clocks had a precision of about one part in a billion, about the same accuracy of the Earth's rotation about its axis. Today, a hydrogen maser is the heart of an atomic clock accurate to one part in 100 trillion, an improvement by a factor of at least 10,000. Such a clock, if kept running, would be off by no more than one second in every few million years.

The new process also immediately provided an amplifier for radio waves much more sensitive than the best then available. Later refinements provided very practical amplifiers, and masers now are typically used to communicate in space over long distances and to pick up radio waves from distant galaxies. Astrophysicists recently have discovered *natural* masers in interstellar space that generate enormous microwave intensity from excited molecules.

Although my main interest in stimulated emission of radiation had been to obtain wavelengths shorter than microwaves, the new possibilities for superaccurate clocks and supersensitive amplifiers, and their scientific uses, occupied everyone's attention for some time. By 1957 I felt it was time to get back on the track of shorter wavelengths. I decided that it would actually be easier to make a big step than a small one and jump immediately to light waves—wavelengths in the visible or short infrared, almost 10,000 times higher in frequency than microwaves. But there was a sticky problem: What kind of resonating chamber would function at a single and precisely correct frequency but could be built using ordinary engineering techniques? My friend Arthur Schawlow, then at the Bell Telephone Laboratories, helped provide the answer: an elongated chamber with a mirror at each end.

10   In December of 1958 we published a paper that discussed this and other aspects of a practical laser and set off an intense wave of efforts to build one. In 1960 Theodore H. Maiman, a physicist with Hughes Aircraft Company, demonstrated the first operating laser, while Ali Javan, William R. Bennett Jr., and Donald R. Herriott at Bell Labs built a second, completely different type. Rather than using gas, Maiman's laser used a small cylinder of synthetic ruby, its ends polished into mirrored surfaces. The firing of a helical flashbulb surrounding the rod triggered the ruby to send out a brief, intense pulse of laser light. Soon there were many variations on the laser theme, using different atoms or molecules and different methods of providing them with energy, but all used a mirrored chamber.

The laser quickly gained great notoriety with the public as a "death ray"; it is a popular science fiction motif and one with undeniable dramatic appeal. Lasers certainly have the power to injure. Even a weak laser shone into the eye will be focused by the lens of the eye onto the retina and damage it. But laser beams are not very advantageous as military weapons. Guns are cheaper, easier to build and use, and, in most cases, much more effective. Science fiction's death ray is still mostly science fiction, and it is likely to remain so.

The laser is, however, extremely powerful. The reason is that stimulated amplification adds energy "coherently"—that is, in exactly the same direction as the initial beam. This coherence conveys surprising properties. A laser emitting one watt of light has only a hundredth the power of a 100-watt light bulb. Yet the beam of a one-watt laser directed at the moon was seen by television equipment on the lunar surface when all the lights of our greatest cities were undetectable—simply because the beam is so directional. A simple lens can focus the beam of light from an ordinary one-watt laser into a spot so small that it produces 100 million watts per square centimeter, enormously greater than the intensity from any other type of source.

But a one-watt laser is not even a particularly powerful one. Pulsed lasers can produce a *trillion* watts of power by delivering energy over a very short period but at enormous levels. This power may last only one ten-billionth of a second, but during that time a lens can concentrate it to a level of 100 million million million watts per square centimeter. The trillion watts that such a laser delivers is approximately equal to the average amount of electric power being used over the entire Earth at any one time. Focused by a lens, this concentration or power is 100 trillion times greater than the light at the surface of the sun. It will melt or tear apart any substance, including atoms themselves. Drilling through diamonds is easy for a laser beam and produces no wear. Lasers have been developed that can compact small pellets of material and then heat them in a sudden flash to reproduce conditions similar to those in the sun's interior, where nuclear fusion occurs.

The laser's directed intensity quickly made it an effective industrial tool. Lasers cut or weld delicate electronic circuits or heavy metal parts. They can melt or harden the surface of a piece of steel so quickly that under a very thin skin, the metal is still cool and undamaged. Industrial interest was especially high. By the end of the 1960s, most new lasers were being designed in industrial laboratories, though many are important tools in university laboratories.

15   How useful lasers and quantum electronics have been to scientists is indicated by the fact that besides Nobel Prizes for work leading to the devices themselves, they have played an important role in other Nobel awards—for example, the one to Dennis Gabor of the University of London for the idea of holography (three-dimensional laser photography); the one to Schawlow of Stanford University for versatile new types of laser spectroscopy; to Nicolaas Bloembergen of Harvard University for discoveries in nonlinear optics made possible by high-intensity laser beams; and one to Arno Penzias and Robert W. Wilson of the Bell Telephone Laboratories for the discovery of microwave radiation from the Big Bang which initiated our universe. While the latter discovery might possibly have been made by other techniques, it was facilitated by very sensitive maser amplification.

Because of the unswerving directionality of laser beams, probably more lasers have been sold for producing the straight lines needed in surveying than for any other single purpose. The laser is now a common surveying instrument that helps to lay out roads.

Laser beams also can measure distance conveniently. By bouncing the beam from a reflector, a surveyor can measure distances to high precision. Beams sent from Earth have been bounced off reflectors placed on the moon by astronauts. By generating a short light pulse and measuring the elapsed time before it returns, the distance to the moon can be measured within one inch. Such measurements have revealed effects of general relativity and thus refined our knowledge of the theory of gravitation.

In scientific equipment or simply in machine shops, the laser's pure frequency allows the beam to be reflected and the peaks and troughs of its wave matched with those of the first part of the beam, thus providing distance measurements to within a small fraction of one wavelength—40 millionths of an inch. In scientific experiments, changes of length as small as one hundredth of the diameter of an atom have been measured in this way. There are efforts to use such supersensitive measurements to detect the gravity waves due to motions of distant stars.

Because lasers can be so finely focused and their intensity adjusted to make controlled cuts, they are used as a surgeon's scalpel. Not only can they be very precisely directed, but a particular color can be chosen to destroy certain types of tissue while leaving others relatively intact, an especially valuable effect for some cancers. In cutting, the laser also seals off blood vessels so that there is relatively little bleeding. For the eye, laser light has the interesting ability to go harmlessly through the pupil and perform operations within.

20 Of all the ways our lives are likely to be affected by lasers, perhaps none will be so unobtrusive and yet more important than cheaper and more effective communications. Within many metropolitan areas, the number of radio or television stations must be limited because the number of available frequencies is limited. For the same reason, large numbers of conversations cannot simultaneously be carried on a single telephone wire. But light is a superhighway of frequencies; a single light beam can, in principle, carry all the radio and TV stations and all telephone calls in the world without interfering with one another. These light beams can be transmitted on glass fibers onetenth the size of a human hair. In crowded cities where streets have been dug up for years and jammed beneath with all manner of pipes and wires, these tiny fibers can fit into the smallest spaces and provide enormous communication capacity. In long distance communication, they may replace most cables, and even satellites.

Even after the laser was invented and its importance recognized, it was by no means clear, even to those who worked on it, that it would see so many striking applications. And much undoubtedly lies ahead.

ENGAGING the Text

1. Why is it important to understand how the energy released in a laser beam is coherent; that is, it is composed of light waves of the exact same length? How does this differ from a normal beam of even very bright light?

2. How does the enormous range of applications of lasers directly depend on the specific qualities of the laser beam?

EVALUATING the Argument

1. How does Townes use an operational definition to give his readers insight into the laser by what it does?

2. How did the range of rhetorical strategies Townes uses — narratives about how the laser was invented, descriptions of how the laser works, or examples of the laser's uses—allow his readers to understand the research process and appreciate his contribution.

EXPLORING the Issue

1. What additional applications of the laser that Townes does not mention have permeated and transformed modern society (for example, bar codes)?

2. Write a short essay arguing that either lasers or computers have most significantly transformed modern society.

CONNECTING Different Perspectives

1. Draw on Townes's essay and Donald A. Norman's discussion in "Emotional Robots" to argue for the ways that technology transforms the way we live.

Zoology

Donald R. Griffin

Wordy Apes

Donald R. Griffin (1915–2003) was Professor of Animal Behavior at the Rockefeller University in New York. His original discoveries in the field of animal communication revealed the echolocation techniques of bats and the principles by which birds navigate. Listening in the Dark *(1958) won the Elliot Medal from the National Academy of Sciences in 1961. Griffin was awarded the Phi Beta Kappa Science Prize for* Bird Migration *(1964). His later research examines the linguistic abilities of chimpanzees and the possibility of human communication with whales and porpoises. The results of his research first appeared in* Animal Thinking *(1984), from which the following article is reprinted.*

Some of the most convincing recent evidence about animal thinking stems from the pioneering work of Alan and Beatrice Gardner of the University of Nevada (1969, 1979). The Gardners had noted that wild apes seem to communicate by observing each other's behavior, and they suspected that the extremely disappointing results of previous efforts to teach captive chimpanzees to use words reflected not so much a lack of mental ability as a difficulty in controlling the vocal tract. Captive chimpanzees had previously demonstrated the ability to solve complex problems and, like dogs and horses, they had learned to respond appropriately to many spoken words. The Gardners wanted to find out whether apes could also express themselves in ways that we could understand. In the late 1960s they made a concerted effort to teach a young chimpanzee named Washoe to communicate with people using manual gestures derived from American Sign Language. This language, one of many that have been developed in different countries for use by the deaf, consists of a series of gestures or signs, each of which serves the basic function of a single word in spoken or written language. To permit fluent conversation, these signs have evolved into clearly distinguishable hand motions and finger configurations that can be performed rapidly.

Washoe was reared in an environment similar to that in which an American baby would be raised. All the people who cared for Washoe "spoke" to her only in American Sign Language, and used it exclusively when conversing with each other in her presence. They signed to Washoe, much as parents talk to babies who have not yet learned to speak, but always in sign language rather than spoken English. Washoe was encouraged to use signs to ask for what she wanted, and she was helped to do this by a procedure called molding, in which the trainer gently held the chimpanzee's hand in the correct position and moved it to form a certain sign.

The Gardners were far more successful than most scientists would have predicted on the basis of what was previously known about the capabilities of chimpanzees or any other nonhuman species, although Robert Yerkes had anticipated such a possibility (Bourne, 1977). During four years of training Washoe learned to use more than 130 wordlike signs and to recognize these and other signs used by her human companions. She could make the appropriate sign when shown pictures of an object, and on a few occasions she seemed to improvise new signs or new two-sign combinations spontaneously. The best example of this was Washoe's signing "water bird" when she first saw a swan. She also signed to herself when no people were present.

Following the Gardners' lead, several other scientists have trained other great apes to use a quasilinguistic communication system. This work has been thoroughly and critically reviewed by Ristau and Robbins (1982) and widely discussed by many others, so I will give only a brief outline here. Most of the subjects have been female chimpanzees, but two gorillas (Patterson and Linden, 1981) and one orangutan (Miles, 1983) have also been taught gestures based on American Sign Language. Because gestures are variable and require the presence of a human signer, who may influence the ape in other ways that are difficult to evaluate, two groups of laboratory scientists have developed "languages" based on mechanical devices operated by the chimpanzees. David Premack of the University of Pennsylvania used colored plastic tokens arranged in patterns resembling strings of words. His star chimpanzee pupil, named Sarah, learned to select the appropriate plastic "words" to answer correctly when the experimenter presented her with similar chips arranged to form simple questions. Questions such as "What is the color of—?" were answered correctly about familiar objects when the objects were replaced by their plastic symbols, even if the colors were different from those of the objects they represented. Sarah thus learned to answer questions about *represented* objects (reviewed by Premack, 1976; and Premack and Premack, 1983). This type of communication has the property of displacement, as in the case of the honeybee dances.

5   In another ambitious project at the Yerkes Laboratory of Emory University, Duane Rumbaugh, Sue Savage-Rumbaugh, and their colleagues have used backlighted keys on a keyboard (Rumbaugh, 1977; Savage-Rumbaugh, Rumbaugh, and Boysen, 1980). Their chimpanzee subjects have learned to press the appropriate keys to communicate simple desires and answer simple questions. In some significant recent studies, two young male chimpanzees, Sherman and Austin, have not only learned to use simple tools to obtain food or toys but have learned to employ the keyboard to ask each other to hand over a certain type of tool. These investigations, as well as extensions of the Gardners' original studies using words derived from American Sign Language, have been extensively reviewed (Ristau and Robbins, 1982) and discussed by Patterson and Linden (1981) and Terrace (1979). Despite disagreement about many aspects of this work, almost everyone concerned agrees that the captive apes have learned, at the very least, to make simple requests and to answer simple questions through these word-like gestures or mechanical devices.

A heated debate has raged about the extent to which such learned communication resembles human language. Sebeok and Umiker-Sebeok (1980) and

Sebeok and Rosenthal (1981) have argued vehemently that the whole business is merely wishful and mistaken reading into the ape's behavior of much more than is really there. They stress that apes are very clever at learning to do what gets them food, praise, social companionship, or other things they want and enjoy. They believe that insufficiently critical scientists have overinterpreted the behavior of their charges and that the apes have really learned only something like: "If I do this she will give me candy," or "If I do that she will play with me," and so forth. They also believe that the apes may be reacting to unintentional signals from the experimenters and that the interpretations have involved what behavioral scientists call "Clever Hans errors." This term refers to a trained horse in the early 1900s that learned to count out answers to arithmetical questions by tapping with his foot. For instance if shown 4×4 written on a slate board, the horse would tap sixteen times. More careful studies showed that Hans could solve such problems only in the presence of a person who knew the answer. The person would inadvertently nod or make other small motions in time with Hans' tapping and would stop when the right number had been reached. Hans had learned to perceive this unintentional communication, not the arithmetic. The Sebeoks argue that Washoe and her successors have learned, not how to communicate with gestural words, but rather how to watch for signs of approval or disapproval from their human companions and to do what is expected.

Although students of animal behavior must constantly guard against such errors, many of the experiments described above included careful controls that seem to have ruled out this explanation of all the languagelike communication learned by Washoe and her successors. In many cases the ape's vocabulary was tested by having one person present a series of pictures that the animal was required to name, while a different person, who could not see the pictures, judged what sign Washoe used in response. Furthermore the sheer number of signs that the apes employed correctly would require a far more complex sort of Clever Hans error than an animal's simple noticing that a person has stopped making small-scale counting motions.

Another criticism of the ape language studies has been advanced by Terrace and colleagues (1979). Terrace, aided by numerous assistants, taught a young male chimpanzee named Nim Chimsky to use about 125 signs over a forty-five-month period. He agrees that Nim, like Washoe and several other language-trained apes, did indeed learn to use these gestures to request objects or actions he wanted and that Nim could use some of them to answer simple questions. But when Terrace analyzed videotapes of Nim exchanging signs with his trainers, he was disappointed to find that many of Nim's "utterances" were copies of what his human companion had just signed. This is scarcely surprising, inasmuch as his trainers had encouraged him to repeat signs throughout his training.

Terrace and his colleagues also concluded that Nim showed no ability to combine more than two signs into meaningful combinations and that his signing never employed even the simplest form of rule-guided sentences. It is not at all clear, however, whether Nim's training provided much encouragement to develop grammatical sentences. In any event, he did not do so, and Terrace doubts whether any of the other signing apes have displayed such a capability. But Miles (1983) reports that her orangutan Chantek's use of gestural signs resembled the speech of young children more closely than Nim's, and Patterson believes that her gorilla Koko follows some rudimentary rules in the sequence of her signs. Yet even on the most liberal interpretation there remains a large gap between the signing of these trained apes and the speech of children who have vocabularies of approximately the same size. The children tend to use longer strings of words, and the third or later words add important meaning to the first two. In contrast, Nim and other language-trained apes seem much more likely to repeat signs or add ones that do not seem, to us at least, to change the basic meaning of a two-sign utterance. For instance, the following is one of the longer utterances reported for the gorilla Koko: "Please milk please me like drink apple bottle"; and from Nim, "Give orange me give eat orange give me eat orange give me you." But grammatical or not, there is no doubt what Koko and Nim were asking for. To quote Descartes and Chomsky (1966), "*The word is the sole sign and certain mark of the presence of thought.*" Grammar adds economy, refinement, and scope to human language, but words are basic. Words without grammar are adequate though limited, but there is no grammar without words. And it is clear that Washoe and her successors use the equivalent of words to convey simple thoughts.

10   The enormous versatility of human language depends not only on large vocabularies of words known to both speakers and listeners but on mutually understood rules for combining them to convey additional meaning. George A. Miller (1967) has used the term "combinatorial productivity" for this extremely powerful attribute of human language. By combining words in particular ways we produce new messages logically and economically. If we had to invent a new word to convey the meaning of each phrase and sentence, the required vocabulary would soon exceed the capacity of even one of the most proficient human brains. But once a child learns a few words he can rapidly increase their effectiveness by combining them in new messages in accordance with the language's rules designating which word stands for actor or object, which are modifiers, and so forth.

Signing apes so far have made very little progress in combinatorial productivity, although some of their two-sign combinations seem to conform to simple rules. The natural communication systems of other animals make no use of combinatorial productivity, as far as we know. But the investigation of animal communication has barely begun, especially as a source of evidence about animal thoughts. What has emerged so far has greatly exceeded the prior expectations of scientists; we may be seeing only the tip of yet another iceberg. Extrapolation of scientific discovery is an uncertain business at best, but the momentum of discovery in this area does not seem to be slackening. The apparent lack of any significant combinatorial productivity in the signing of Washoe and her successors might turn out to be a temporary lull in a truly revolutionary development, which began only about fifteen years ago. Perhaps improved methods of investigation and training will lead to more convincing evidence of communicative versatility.

One relevant aspect of all the ape-language studies to date is that the native language of all the investigators has been English, and the signs taught to apes have been derived from American Sign Language. In English, word order is used to indicate actor or object, principal noun or modifying adjective, and many other rule-guided relationships. But this is very atypical; most other human languages rely much more on inflections or modifications of principal words to indicate grammatical relationships. No one seems to have inquired whether signing apes or naturally communicating animals might vary their signals in minor ways to communicate that a particular sign is meant to designate, for instance, the actor rather than the object. This would be a difficult inquiry, because the signals vary for many reasons, and only a laborious analysis of an extensive series of motion pictures or videotapes would disclose whether there were many consistent differences comparable to those conveyed by inflections of words in human speech.

Regardless of these controversies, there seems no doubt that through gestures or manipulation of token or keyboards apes can learn to communicate to their human companions a reasonable range of simple thoughts and desires. They also can convey emotional feelings, although an ape does not need elaborate gestures or other forms of symbolic communication to inform a sensitive human companion that it is afraid or hungry. What the artificial signals add to emotional signaling is the possibility of communicating about specific objects and events, even when these are not part of the immediate situation. Furthermore, when Washoe or any other trained ape signs that she wants a certain food, she must be thinking about that food or about its taste or odor. We cannot be certain just what the signing ape is thinking, but the content of her thought must include at least some feature of the object or event designated by the sign she has learned to use. For instance, the Gardners taught Washoe to use a sign that meant flower, to them. But Washoe used it not only for flowers but for pipe tobacco and kitchen fumes. To her it apparently meant smells. Washoe may have been thinking about smells when she used the sign, rather than about the visual properties of colored flowers, but she was certainly thinking about something that overlapped it with the properties conveyed by the word *flower* as we use it.

The major significance of the research begun by the Gardners is its confirmation that our closest animal relatives are quite capable of varied thoughts as well as emotions. Many highly significant questions flow from this simple fact. Do apes communicate naturally with the versatility they have demonstrated in the various sorts of languagelike behavior that people have taught them? One approach is to ask whether apes that have learned to use signs more or less as we use single words employ them to communicate with each other. This is being investigated by studying signing apes that have abundant opportunity to interact with each other. Few results have been reported so far, although some signing does seem to be directed to other apes as well as to human companions. When scientists have been looking for something, and when we hear little or nothing about the results, we conclude that nothing important has been discovered. But the lack of results may only mean that chimpanzees can communicate perfectly well without signs. The subject obviously requires further investigation, and we may soon hear about new and interesting developments.

References

Bourne, G. H., ed. *Progress in ape research.* New York: Academic Press. 1977.

Chomsky, N. *Cartesian linguistics.* New York: Harper and Row. 1966.

Gardner, R. A., and B. T. Gardner. Teaching sign language to a chimpanzee. *Science* 165:664–672. 1969.

Gardner, R. A., and B. T. Gardner. Two comparative psychologists look at language acquisition. In *Children's language,* ed. K. E. Nelson. New York: Halstead. 1979.

Miles, H. L. Apes and language: The search for communicative competence. In *Language in primates: Implications for linguistics, anthropology, psychology, and philosophy,* ed. J. de Luce and H. T. Wilder. New York: Springer. 1983.

Miller, G. A. *The psychology of communication.* New York: Basic Books. 1967.

Patterson, F. G., and E. Linden. *The education of Koko.* New York: Holt, Rinehart and Winston. 1981.

Premack, D. *Intelligence in ape and man.* Hillsdale, N. J.: Erlbaum. 1976.

Premack, D., and A. J. Premack. *The mind of an ape.* New York: Norton. 1983.

Ristau, C. A., and D. Robbins. Language in the great apes: A critical review. *Advances in Study of Behavior* 12:142–225. 1982.

Rumbaugh, D. M. *Language learning by a chimpanzee: The Lana Project.* New York: Academic Press. 1977.

Savage-Rumbaugh, E. S., D. M. Rumbaugh, and S. Boysen. Do apes use language? *Amer. Sci.* 68:49–61. 1980.

Sebeok, T. A., and R. Rosenthal. The Clever Hans phenomenon: Communication with horses, whales, apes, and people. *Ann. N. Y. Acad. Sci.* 364:1–311. 1981.

Sebeok, T. A., and J. Umiker-Sebeok, eds. *Speaking of apes, a critical anthology of two-way communication with man.* New York: Plenum. 1980.

Terrace, H. S. *Nim.* New York: Knopf. 1979.

Terrace, H. S., L. A. Petitto, and T. G. Bever. Can an ape create a sentence? *Science* 208:891–902. 1979.

ENGAGING the Text

1. How are the experiments discussed by Griffin designed to shed light on ways of assessing whether animals possess the capacity to use language to communicate with humans? Why was it important to eliminate the so-called "Clever Hans" fallacy?

2. Why is it significant that children can routinely combine longer strings of words than can apes with comparable-size signing vocabularies?

EVALUATING the Argument

1. To what extent does Griffin try to find a common ground on which all sides can agree despite differences on the question of whether primates can learn to communicate?

2. How does Griffin organize his summary of research around the question of what criteria should be used and what evidence should be accepted as proof of the ability of primates to communicate with humans?

EXPLORING the Issue

1. What single piece of evidence did you find the most persuasive of the ones presented by Griffin?

2. In a short essay, discuss how it might be possible to determine in a specific case whether a response was evidence of communication or merely imitative behavior that could be misinterpreted by researchers.

CONNECTING Different Perspectives

1. Compare and contrast the evidence for intelligence and the ability to communicate in the essay by Griffin and Eric Scigliano's "Through the Eye of an Octopus."

Gunjan Sinha

You Dirty Vole

Gunjan Sinha was born in Bihar, India, but grew up in Brooklyn, New York. She earned a graduate degree in molecular genetics from the University of Glasgow, Scotland (1993), and received a degree from New York University's Science and Environmental Reporting Program in 1996. She was life sciences editor for Popular Science *for five years and in 2000 was awarded the Ray Bruner Science Writing Award. In the following essay, written in 2002, Sinha explores the mating behavior of the common prairie vole (a mouselike rodent, about seven inches long with a two-inch tail) and what it reveals about the human pattern of monogamy.*

George is a typical Midwestern American male in the prime of his life, with an attractive spouse named Martha. George is a devoted husband, Martha an attentive wife. The couple has four young children, a typical home in a lovely valley full of corn and bean fields, and their future looks bright. But George is occasionally unfaithful. So, occasionally, is Martha. No big deal: That's just the way life is in this part of America.

This is a true story, though the names have been changed, and so, for that matter, has the species. George and Martha are prairie voles. They don't marry, of course, or think about being faithful. And a bright future for a vole is typically no more than 60 days of mating and pup-rearing that ends in a fatal encounter with a snake or some other prairie predator.

But if you want to understand more about the conflict in human relationships between faithfulness and philandering, have a peek inside the brain of this wee rodent. Researchers have been studying voles for more than 25 years, and they've learned that the mating behavior of these gregarious creatures uncannily resembles our own—including a familiar pattern of monogamous attachment: Male and female share a home and child care, the occasional dalliance notwithstanding. More important, researchers have discovered what drives the animals' monogamy: brain chemistry. And when it comes to the chemical soup that governs behavior associated with what we call love, prairie vole brains are a lot like ours.

Scientists are careful to refer to what voles engage in as "social monogamy," meaning that although voles prefer to nest and mate with a particular partner, when another vole comes courting, some will stray. And as many as 50 percent of male voles never find a permanent partner. Of course, there is no moral or religious significance to the vole's behavior—monogamous or not. Voles will be voles, because that's their nature.

5   Still, the parallels to humans are intriguing. "We're not an animal that finds it in our best interest to screw around," says Pepper Schwartz, a sociologist at the University of Washington, yet studies have shown that at least one-third of married people cheat. In many cases, married couples struggle with the simple fact that love and lust aren't always in sync, often tearing us in opposite directions. Vole physiology and behavior reinforce the idea that love and lust are biochemically separate systems, and that the emotional tug of war many of us feel between the two emotions is perfectly natural—a two-headed biological drive that's been hardwired into our brains through millions of years of evolution.

No one knew that voles were monogamous until Lowell Getz, a now-retired professor of ecology, ethology, and evolution at the University of Illinois, began studying them in 1972. At the time, Getz wanted to figure out why the vole population would boom during certain years and then slowly go bust. He set traps in the grassy plains of Illinois and checked them a few times a day, tagging the voles he caught. What surprised him was how often he'd find the same male and female sitting in a trap together.

Voles build soft nests about 8 inches below ground. A female comes of age when she is about 30 days old: Her need to mate is then switched on as soon as she encounters an unpartnered male and sniffs his urine. About 24 hours later, she's ready to breed—with the male she just met or another unattached one if he's gone. Then, hooked, the pair will stick together through thick and thin, mating and raising young.

Getz found vole mating behavior so curious that he wanted to bring the animals into the lab to study them more carefully. But he was a field biologist, not a lab scientist, so he called Sue Carter, a colleague and neuroendocrinologist. Carter had been studying how sex hormones influence behavior, and investigating monogamy in voles dovetailed nicely with her own research. The animals were small: They made the perfect lab rats.

The scientific literature was already rich with studies on a hormone called oxytocin that is made in mammalian brains and that in some species promotes bonding between males and females and between mothers and offspring. Might oxytocin, swirling around in tiny vole brains, be the catalyst for turning them into the lifelong partners that they are?

10   Sure enough, when Carter injected female voles with oxytocin, they were less finicky in choosing mates and practically glued themselves to their partners once they had paired. The oxytocin-dosed animals tended to lick and cuddle more than untreated animals, and they avoided strangers. What's more, when Carter injected females with oxytocin-blocking chemicals, the animals deserted their partners.

In people, not only is the hormone secreted by lactating women but studies have shown that oxytocin levels also increase during sexual arousal—and skyrocket during orgasm. In fact, the higher the level of oxytocin circulating in the blood during intercourse, the more intense the orgasm.

But there's more to vole mating than love; there's war too. Male voles are territorial. Once they bond with a female, they spend lots of time guarding her from other suitors, often sitting near the entrance of their burrow and aggressively baring their beaver-like teeth. Carter reasoned that other biochemicals must kick in after mating, chemicals that turn a once laid-back male into a territorial terror. Oxytocin, it turns out, is only part of the story. A related chemical, vasopressin, also occurs in both sexes. Males, however, have much more of it.

When Carter dosed male voles with a vasopressin-blocking chemical after mating, their feistiness disappeared. An extra jolt of vasopressin, on the other hand, boosted their territorial behavior and made them more protective of their mates.

Vasopressin is also present in humans. While scientists don't yet know the hormone's exact function in men, they speculate that it works similarly: It is secreted during sexual arousal and promotes bonding. It may even transform some men into jealous boyfriends and husbands. "The biochemistry [of attachment] is probably going to be similar in humans and in [monogamous] animals because it's quite a basic function," says Carter. Because oxytocin and vasopressin are secreted during sexual arousal and orgasm, she says, they are probably the key biochemical players that bond lovers to one another.

15   But monogamous animals aren't the only ones that have vasopressin and oxytocin in their brains. Philandering animals do too. So what separates faithful creatures from unfaithful ones? Conveniently for scientists, the generally monogamous prairie vole has a wandering counterpart: the montane vole. When Thomas Insel, a neuroscientist at Emory University, studied the two species' vasopressin receptors (appendages on a cell that catch specific biochemicals) he found them in different places. Prairie voles have receptors for the hormone in their brains' pleasure centers; montane voles have the receptors in other brain areas. In other words, male prairie voles stick with the same partner after mating because it feels good. For montane voles, mating is a listless but necessary affair, rather like scratching an itch.

Of course, human love is much more complicated. The biochemistry of attachment isn't yet fully understood, and there's clearly much more to it than oxytocin and vasopressin. Humans experience different kinds of love. There's "compassionate love," associated with feelings of calm, security, social comfort, and emotional union. This kind of love, say scientists, is probably similar to what voles feel toward their partners and involves oxytocin and vasopressin. Romantic love—that crazy obsessive euphoria that people feel when they are "in love"—is very different, as human studies are showing.

Scientists at University College London led by Andreas Bartels recently peered inside the heads of love-obsessed college students. They took 17 young people who claimed to be in love, stuck each of them in an MRI machine, and showed them pictures of their lovers. Blood flow increased to very specific areas of the brain's pleasure center—including some of the same areas that are stimulated when people engage in addictive behaviors. Some of these same areas are also active during sexual arousal, though romantic love and sexual arousal are clearly different: Sex has more to do with hormones like testosterone, which, when given to both men and women, increases sex drive and sexual fantasies. Testosterone, however, doesn't necessarily make people fall in love with, or become attached to, the object of their attraction.

Researchers weren't particularly surprised by the parts of the lovers' brains that were active. What astonished them was that two other brain areas were suppressed—the amygdala and the right prefrontal cortex. The amygdala is associated with negative emotions like fear and anger. The right prefrontal cortex appears to be overly active in people suffering from depression. The positive emotion of love, it seems, suppresses negative emotions. Might that be the scientific basis for why people who are madly in love fail to see the negative traits of their beloved? "Maybe," says Bartels cautiously. "But we haven't proven that yet."

The idea that romantic love activates parts of the brain associated with addiction got Donatella Marazziti at Pisa University in Tuscany wondering if it might be related to obsessive compulsive disorder (OCD). Anyone who has ever been in love knows how consuming the feeling can be. You can think of nothing but your lover every waking moment. Some people with OCD have low levels of the brain chemical serotonin. Might love-obsessed people also have low serotonin levels? Sure enough, when Marazziti and her colleagues tested the blood of 20 students who were madly in love and 20 people with OCD, she found that both groups had low levels of a protein that shuttles serotonin between brain cells.

20   And what happens when the euphoria of "mad love" wears off? Marazziti tested the blood of a few of the lovers 12 to 18 months later and found that their serotonin levels had returned to normal. That doesn't doom a couple, of

course, but it suggests a biological explanation for the evolution of relation-ships. In many cases, romantic love turns into compassionate love, thanks to oxytocin and vasopressin swirling inside the lovers' brains. This attachment is what keeps many couples together. But because attachment and romantic love involve different biochemical processes, attachment to one person does not suppress lust for another. "The problem is, they are not always well linked," says anthropologist Helen Fisher, who has written several books on love, sex and marriage.

In the wild, about half of male voles wander the fields, never settling down with one partner. These "traveling salesmen," as Lowell Getz calls them, are always "trying to get with other females." Most females prefer to mate with their partners. But if they get the chance, some will mate with other males too. And, according to Jerry Wolff, a biologist at the University of Memphis, female voles sometimes "divorce" their partners. In the lab, he re-stricts three males at a time in separate but connected chambers and gives a female free range. The female has already paired with one of the males and is pregnant with his pups. Wolff says about a third of the females pick up their nesting materials and move in with a different fellow. Another third actually solicit and successfully mate with one or both of the other males, and the last third remain faithful.

Why are some voles fickle, others faithful? Vole brains differ from one creature to the next. Larry Young, a neuroscientist at Emory University, has found that some animals have more receptors for oxytocin and vasopressin than others. In a recent experiment, he injected a gene into male prairie voles that permanently upped the number of vasopressin receptors in their brains. The animals paired with females even though the two hadn't mated. "Nor-mally they have to mate for at least 24 hours to establish a bond," he says. So the number of receptors can mean the difference between sticking around and skipping out after sex. Might these differences in brain wiring influence hu-man faithfulness? "It's too soon to tell," Young says. But it's "definitely got us very curious."

How does evolution account for the often-conflicting experiences of love and lust, which have caused no small amount of destruction in human history? Fisher speculates that the neural systems of romantic love and attachment evolved for different reasons. Romantic love, she says, evolved to allow people to distinguish between potential mating partners and "to pursue these part-ners until insemination has occurred." Attachment, she says, "evolved to make you tolerate this individual long enough to raise a child." Pepper Schwartz agrees: "We're biologically wired to be socially monogamous, but it's not a good evolutionary tactic to be sexually monogamous. There need to be ways to keep reproduction going if your mate dies."

Many of our marriage customs, say sociologists, derive from the need to reconcile this tension. "As much as people love passion and romantic love," Schwartz adds, "most people also want to have the bonding sense of loyalty and friendship love as well." Marriage vows are a declaration about romantic love and binding attachment, but also about the role of rational thought and the primacy of mind and mores over impulses.

25   Scientists hope to do more than simply decode the biochemistry of the emotions associated with love and attachment. Some, like Insel, are searching for treatments for attachment disorders such as autism, as well as pathological behaviors like stalking and violent jealousy. It is not inconceivable that someday there might be sold an attachment drug, a monogamy pill; the mind reels at the marketing possibilities.

Lowell Getz, the grandfather of all this research, couldn't be more thrilled. "I spent almost $1 million of taxpayer money trying to figure out stuff like why sisters don't make it with their brothers," he says. "I don't want to go to my grave feeling like it was a waste."

ENGAGING the Text

1. What insight does Sinha offer into the biochemical triggers that are responsible for the mating behavior of the prairie vole?

2. What parallel behaviors do humans display that suggest an underlying biochemical matrix similar to that of the vole?

EVALUATING the Argument

1. How does Sinha use the testimony of experts to support her thesis?

2. A good deal of Sinha's argument is based on extrapolating features of the vole's behavior onto humans. This argument by analogy may be effective up to a point. In what respects does the analogy fail to apply?

EXPLORING the Issue

1. In your opinion, are biology (hardwired primal drives) and psychology (learned social and cultural behaviors) ultimately irreconcilable explanations for the same observed effects in human beings?

2. As a research project, investigate the current findings on biochemical triggers involving the hormones discussed by Sinha.

CONNECTING Different Perspectives

1. In what way do social codes governing sexuality as discussed by Judith Ortiz Cofer ("The Myth of the Latin Woman" in Chapter 7) try to mimic the role played by hormones as analyzed by Sinha?

Glossary

ABSTRACT   designating qualities or characteristics apart from specific objects or events; opposite of **concrete**.

ANALOGY   a process of reasoning that assumes if two subjects share a number of specific observable qualities then they may be expected to share qualities that have not been observed; the process of drawing a comparison between two things based on a partial similarity of like features.

ARGUMENT   a process of reasoning and putting forth evidence on controversial issues; a statement or fact presented in support of a point.

ASSUMPTION   an idea or belief taken for granted; see **warrant**.

ATTITUDE   a writer's emotional stance toward a subject.

AUDIENCE   the people who read or hear an argument.

AUTHORITY   a person who is accepted as a source of reliable information because of his or her expertise in the field.

BACKING   authority providing the assurance that the body of experience relied on to establish the warrant is appropriate and justified.

CLAIM   the assertion that the arguer wishes the audience to discover as the logical outcome of the case being presented.

CLICHÉ   a timeworn expression that through overuse has lost its power to evoke concrete images.

CONCRETE   pertaining to actual things, instances, or experiences; opposite of **abstract**.

CONNOTATION   the secondary or associative meanings of a word as distinct from its explicit or primary meaning; the emotional overtones of a word or phrase; opposite of **denotation**.

DEDUCTION   a method of reasoning that infers the validity of a particular case from general statements or **premises** taken to be true.

DEFINITION   the method of identifying the distinguishing characteristics of an idea, term, or process to establish its meaning.

DENOTATION   the literal explicit meaning of a word or expression; opposite of **connotation**.

DOUBLESPEAK   intentionally deceptive or evasive language, often through a euphemism (for example, "friendly fire").

ENTHYMEME   an abbreviated syllogism expressed in ordinary language in which the major or minor **premise** is not explicitly stated.

ETHICAL ARGUMENT   one conducted in accordance with the rules of conduct or standards within a particular academic discipline.

EUPHEMISM   from the Greek word meaning *to speak well of*; the substitution of an inoffensive, indirect, or agreeable expression for a word or phrase perceived as socially unacceptable or unnecessarily harsh.

EVIDENCE   all material, including testimony of experts; statistics; cases whether real, hypothetical, or analogical; and reasons brought forward to support a claim.

EXCEPTION   an extraordinary instance or circumstance in which an otherwise valid claim would not hold true.

FALLACY   errors of pseudoreasoning caused by incorrect interpretations of evidence and incorrectly drawn inferences.

GROUNDS   specific facts relied on to support a given claim.

HYPERBOLE   a deliberate and obvious exaggeration to emphasize strong feeling (for example, "to wait an eternity").

HYPOTHESIS   a provisional thesis, subject to revision, accepted as a working **premise** in an argument.

INDUCTION   a process of reasoning that reaches a generalization by drawing inferences from particular cases.

INFERENCE   the process of reaching conclusions drawn from the interpretation of facts, circumstances, or statements.

IRONY   the use of words to convey a meaning different from—and usually opposite to—their actual meaning.

JARGON   the specialized language used by particular academic fields, trades, or professions (for example, medical jargon) that provides a shorthand method of quick communication that is not readily understood by the general public.

METAPHOR   a word or phrase applied to an object that it does not literally connote to suggest a comparison that evokes a vivid picture in the imagination of the audience.

PERSONA   literally, "actor's mask"; the way in which the writer chooses to project himself or herself.

PERSUASION   according to Aristotle, the act of winning acceptance of a claim achieved through the combined effects of the audience's confidence in the speaker's character (*ethos*), appeals to reason (*logos*), and the audience's emotional needs and values (*pathos*).

PICTURESQUE LANGUAGE words or phrases that evoke vivid images or pictures in the minds of the audience.

PLAGIARISM using someone's words or ideas without giving proper credit.

PREMISE statements or generalizations in deductive reasoning taken as self-evident that have been previously established through the process of inductive reasoning.

QUALIFIER a restriction that may have to be attached to a particular claim to indicate its relative strength or certainty.

REBUTTAL a special circumstance or extraordinary instance that challenges the claim being made.

REFUTATION showing a position to be false or erroneous in order to lessen its credibility.

RHETORIC according to Aristotle, the process of discovering all the available means of persuasion in any situation where the truth cannot be known for certain; includes seeking out the best arguments, arranging them in the most effective way, and presenting them in a manner calculated to win agreement from a particular audience.

RHETORICAL SITUATION the context in and for which a writer creates a piece; the author's purpose for writing in relation to the audience, the occasion, and the topic.

SATIRE a technique that uses parody, irony, and caricature to ridicule both people and social institutions, often in an effort to bring about social reform.

SIMILE a comparison of one object or experience to another using the words *like* or *as* to create a vivid picture.

SLANTING the presentation of information in such a way as to reflect a particular point of view.

STEREOTYPE labeling a person or a group in terms of a single character trait, usually pejorative.

SUPPORT all the evidence the writer brings forward to enhance the probability of a claim being accepted; can include evidence in the form of testimony of experts, statistics, examples from personal experience, hypothetical cases, appeals to the audience's emotions and values, and the speaker's own character or personality.

SYLLOGISM a classic form of deductive reasoning illustrating the relationship between a major and a minor **premise** and a conclusion in which the validity of a particular case is drawn from statements assumed to be true or self-evident.

THESIS   an expression of the claim, assertion, or position the writer wishes the audience to accept.

TONE   the voice the writer has chosen to project in order to adapt the argument for a specific occasion and a particular audience; produced by the combined effect of word choice, sentence structure, and the writer's attitude toward the subject.

UNDERSTATEMENT   a form of verbal irony, often used for humorous effect, in which an opinion is expressed less emphatically than the facts warrant.

VALUES   moral or ethical principles or beliefs that express standards or criteria by which actions may be considered right or wrong, good or bad, acceptable or unacceptable, appropriate or unseemly; value arguments supply ethical, moral, aesthetic, or utilitarian criteria against which proposed actions may be evaluated.

WARRANT   according to Stephen Toulmin, a general statement that expresses implicit or explicit assumptions about how the agreed-upon facts of a particular case are connected to the claim or conclusion being offered.

Credits

Index